IPv6 Fundamentals

This book explores the essential concepts and practical implementation of IPv6, the next-generation Internet Protocol designed to address the limitations of IPv4 and support the exponential growth of Internet-connected devices.

IPv6 Fundamentals: Packet and Data Structures, Addressing Architecture, Device Discovery, and Configuration Protocols delivers critical knowledge through detailed explanations of IPv6 header and extension formats, addressing architecture, neighbor discovery protocols, and DHCPv6 operations. Readers benefit from comprehensive coverage of mobility mechanisms that enable seamless roaming across networks, along with practical implementation guidance for transitioning from IPv4. This book uniquely bridges theoretical concepts with real-world applications, explaining not just how IPv6 functions work individually but also how they interconnect within the broader network ecosystem between hosts and routers. The author specifically focuses on the technical foundations of IPv6 packet structures and neighbor discovery protocols at a deeper level than existing titles. Finally, this book includes appendices covering Ethernet frame formats, IPv4 packet structures, and various ARP mechanisms, providing valuable context for understanding the evolution from IPv4 to IPv6.

This book is intended for network engineers, IT administrators, system architects, and telecommunications professionals responsible for planning, implementing, and managing network infrastructure. Academic readers, including advanced undergraduate and graduate students in computer networking courses, will appreciate the clear explanations of fundamental concepts.

IPv6 Fundamentals
Packet and Data Structures, Addressing Architecture, Device Discovery, and Configuration Protocols

James Aweya

CRC Press
Taylor & Francis Group
Boca Raton London New York

CRC Press is an imprint of the
Taylor & Francis Group, an **informa** business

Designed cover image: © Shutterstock

First edition published 2026
by CRC Press
2385 NW Executive Center Drive, Suite 320, Boca Raton FL 33431

and by CRC Press
4 Park Square, Milton Park, Abingdon, Oxon, OX14 4RN

CRC Press is an imprint of Taylor & Francis Group, LLC

© 2026 James Aweya

ISBN: 9781041192350 (hbk)
ISBN: 9781041192138 (pbk)
ISBN: 9781003710646 (ebk)

DOI: 10.1201/9781003710646

Typeset in Times
by codeMantra

Contents

Preface vi
About the Author xi

Chapter 1   Introduction to IPv6 1

Chapter 2   IPv6 Packet Format and Related Data Structures 26

Chapter 3   IPv6 Addressing Architecture 77

Chapter 4   IPv6 Neighbor Discovery, Address Configuration, and
                 IPv6 Routing Table 124

Chapter 5   Dynamic Host Configuration Protocol for IPv6 (DHCPv6) 244

Chapter 6   Mobile IP: Mobility Mechanisms for IPv4 and IPv6 319

Appendix A: Ethernet Frame Format 377

Appendix B: IPv4 Packet Format and Addressing 397

Appendix C: Address Resolution Protocol (ARP) for IPv4 425

Appendix D: Gratuitous ARP for IPv4 429

Appendix E: Proxy ARP for IPv4 432

Appendix F: Private VLANs and Port Isolation 436

Index 451

Preface

IPv6 Fundamentals: Packet and Data Structures, Addressing Architecture, Device Discovery, and Configuration Protocols

Internet Protocol version 6 (IPv6) was developed to address the limitations of Internet Protocol version 4 (IPv4) and to support the growth of the Internet and the increasing number of users well into the future. The features included in IPv6 allow it to support the rapidly growing Internet with a myriad of tethered and untethered devices, well beyond what IPv4 can handle. IPv6, which is designed to eventually replace IPv4, is more of a suite of protocols and features, not just longer IP addresses. A number of improvements over IPv4 were made in IPv6, including the following:

- **New IP Header Format**: Several non-essential fields in the IPv4 header were removed, making the IPv6 header processing more efficient for routing devices.
- **Extensibility**: IPv6 was designed to be easily extensible, allowing extension headers to be added after the fixed IPv6 header.
- **Large IP Address Space**: IPv6 was defined to have 128-bit address fields, allowing multiple levels of IP subnetting and enabling regional Internet providers to perform more efficient address allocation.
- **Better Security**: IPv6 was developed from the outset to use IP Security (IPSec) as its Network Layer security mechanism. IPv6 header extensions were defined for security purposes, allowing for the encryption and authentication of data at the Network Layer.
- **Stateless and Stateful Host Addressing**: IPv6 was designed to support both stateless and stateful assignment of IP addresses. Stateless addressing allows each host on a network segment to automatically configure a unique IPv6 address without any address server allocating and keeping track of the addresses assigned to each host, a process called Stateless Address Autoconfiguration (SLAAC). Hosts can use SLAAC to autoconfigure IP unicast addresses on their network interfaces and start communicating with other nodes on the network. In stateful addressing, a server assigns IPv6 addresses and other information to hosts on the network.
- **More Efficient Operations on Network Segments**: IPv6 was designed to support more efficient Layer 3 to Layer 2 address resolution mechanisms using multicast instead of broadcast as in IPv4. The broadcast-based IPv4 to Ethernet address resolution protocol, called ARP (Address Resolution Protocol), is replaced with the more secure and efficient IPv6 Neighbor Discovery protocol that uses multicast messages.
- **Multiple IPv6 Addresses per Device**: IPv6 was developed to allow host interfaces on the same network segment to support multiple IPv6 addresses. This feature enhances security, increases privacy, and enables IPv6 to support additional network features.
- **New Address Types**: IPv6 defined new Network Layer address types that are non-routable, such as IPv6 Link-Local addresses. These provide several advantages, including fewer routing table entries, better address management, and more secure network segments.

IPv4 addresses are 32 bits long, while IPv6 addresses are 128 bits long, providing a substantially larger number of possible IPv6 addresses. The 128-bit IPv6 address size theoretically allows for 2^{128} addresses, which is about 3.4×10^{38} addresses, that is, 340 trillion, trillion, trillion unique addresses (340 undecillion IPv6 addresses). By contrast, the 32-bit IPv4 address size allows for $2^{32} = 4.3$ billion addresses. In practice, the actual number of usable IPv6 addresses is slightly lower because IPv6 addresses in general are structured to have global scope (IPv6 Global Unicast addresses), site scope (IPv6 Unique-Local addresses), and link-local scope (IPv6 Link-Local addresses), with certain address ranges reserved for special use. Even with this structuring, the number of available IPv6 addresses is still extremely large and vastly exceeds the IPv4 address space. The 128-bit IPv6 address scheme allows for multiple levels of addressing and routing hierarchies to be created. IPv6 provides flexibility in designing hierarchical addressing and routing, features that IPv4 lacks.

There is currently a rapid and growing proliferation of distributed networked entities that require globally unique IP addresses. The following are examples of networked entities that can benefit significantly from using globally unique addresses from the larger IPv6 address space, without the need for Network Address Translation (NAT) techniques:

- Mobile devices (smartphones, tablets, laptops, wearables)
- Networked home appliances
- Smart metering devices
- Small cells (femtocells, picocells, microcells, metrocells)
- Disaggregated radio access network (RAN) components like the Radio Unit (RU), Distributed Unit (DU), and Centralized Unit (CU), which are often not co-located in the mobile network
- Internet of Things (IoT) devices
- Surveillance and security devices (cameras, sensors, alarms)
- Distributed control components (sensors, controllers, actuators)
- Robotic systems
- Mobile entities (vehicles, aircrafts, self-driving vehicles, unmanned aerial vehicles (UAVs))
- Networked green energy systems (solar energy systems, wind energy systems)
- Weather and environmental monitoring systems (temperature, humidity, pressure, wind speed)
- Seismic and earthquake monitoring systems
- Volcanic monitoring systems
- Ocean monitoring systems
- Artic and Antarctic monitoring systems
- AI-enabled and AI-driven entities, AI agents

The limited IPv4 address space simply cannot meet such high addressing demand. The IPv6 address space largely eliminates the need for NAT devices. The large IPv6 address space can accommodate all the addressing needs of networked entities for many years to come.

IP routing refers to the collection of methods and protocols that determine the paths across multiple internetworks that user data (in the form of packets) take in order to travel from its source to its destination. Packets are routed hop-by-hop through a series of routers and across multiple networks from their source to the destination. Each hop in this case represents a routing device (or router). IP routing protocols are used by routers to communicate with each other and exchange information about network reachability.

Each router uses this reachability information to build a network topology map and a local routing table that contains the network destination addresses, their associated next-hop addresses and outbound interfaces. A next-hop IP address is an entry in the router's routing table, which specifies the next best or closest router on the most optimal path to the packet's destination. The most common unicast routing protocols used in today's internetworks include RIP (Routing Information Protocol), EIGRP (Enhanced Interior Gateway Routing Protocol), OSPF (Open Shortest Path First), IS-IS (Intermediate System-to-Intermediate System), and BGP (Border Gateway Protocol).

Typically, a router uses an IP forwarding table for IP packet forwarding, which is a reduced/ optimized table containing only the most relevant information distilled from the routing table. The contents of the IP forwarding table are directly relevant to packet forwarding and mirror the main packet routing information in the routing table, such as destination IP addresses, outgoing interfaces, and next-hop IP addresses.

When a router receives an IP packet to be forwarded, it parses the destination IP address in the packet header, consults its forwarding table to determine the next-hop and outgoing interface for the packet's destination, and forwards the packet appropriately (after performing some required updates to the IP packet header fields). The next router (i.e., next-hop) receives the packet and repeats this process using its own IP forwarding table until the packet reaches its final destination. At each hop (router), the IP destination address in the packet header provides the basic routing instructions used to determine the next-hop and outgoing interface.

Typically, an Interior Gateway Protocol (IGP) determines the best or optimal routes within a single routing domain or Autonomous System. RIP, EIGRP, IS-IS, and OSPF are well-known examples of IGPs. The IGP enables routers on different networks within the same routing domain or Autonomous System to discover each other and send data to one another. Additionally, when an Autonomous System provides transit services, an IGP can be used to allow data to be forwarded across the transit Autonomous System from its ingress to egress. Routes are distributed between Autonomous Systems by an Exterior Gateway Protocol (EGP). BGP is currently the only EGP used in today's internetworks. The EGP enables routers within an Autonomous System to choose the best egress point when they have data for external destinations.

The IGPs and EGP running within each Autonomous System cooperate to route data across internetworks. The EGP determines the Autonomous Systems in the internetwork that data must traverse to get from its source to the destination, while the IGP determines the best or optimal path within each Autonomous System that data must take to get from the ingress point to the egress point.

The most common IPv6 routing protocols in use today are RIP next generation (RIPng), OSPF for IPv6 (OSPFv3), IS-IS for IPv6 (IS-ISv6), and Multiprotocol Extensions for BGP (MBGP or MP-BGP), also called Multiprotocol BGP. MBGP is an extension to BGP that was developed to enable BGP to carry routing information for multiple Network Layer protocols and address families (IPv4 unicast and multicast, IPv6 unicast and multicast, etc.).

This book discusses the fundamental concepts essential for understanding IPv6. The material covers the IPv6 header and extension header formats, related data structures, the IPv6 addressing architecture, neighbor discovery mechanisms, the Dynamic Host Configuration Protocol for IPv6 (DHCPv6), mobility mechanisms for IPv6, and the rationale behind each of these functions. This book explains the underlying concepts of each IPv6 function and describes how the function components and processes fit within and between IPv6 nodes (i.e., hosts and routers).

The goal of this book is to present the main concepts and applications, allowing readers to develop a better understanding of IPv6. It includes several appendices that discuss key background topics to help readers better understand the IPv6 discussions. The material is presented from a practicing engineer's perspective, linking theory and fundamental concepts to established industry practices and real-world examples. The straightforward presentation style adopted in this book makes it appealing to undergraduate and graduate students, research and practicing engineers and scientists, IT personnel, and network engineers.

Chapter 1 discusses the limitations of IPv4, the changes made to IPv6 to address these limitations, and the various additional features of IPv6. This chapter also describes the different methods IP routers use to learn routing information in networks and internetworks. In this chapter, we introduce the main concepts of static and dynamic routing, including their benefits and limitations. We discuss the different sources from which IP routers obtain routing information, the classification of existing dynamic routing protocols, and the routing metrics that these protocols use to determine the best paths to network destinations.

Chapter 2 discusses the basic IPv6 header format and the different types of IPv6 extension headers and options that have been defined. The discussion includes IPv6 packet size issues and packet fragmentation, how IPv6 flow labels and traffic classes are created, and the effects of IPv6 on upper-layer protocols (such as IPv6 maximum transmission unit (MTU), upper-layer protocol checksums, and the IPv6 pseudo-header used for upper-layer protocol checksum computation), as well as basic IPv6 and IPv4 packet forwarding operations.

Chapter 3 discusses the IPv6 Addressing Architecture, representations of IPv6 addresses in textual form, definitions of the different types of IPv6 addresses (unicast, multicast, and anycast), and the types of addresses maintained by IPv6 hosts and routers. The discussion includes details of the basic formats of IPv6 addresses (unicast, anycast, and multicast) and how these addresses are used by nodes in an IPv6 internetwork. A good understanding of the IPv6 packet format (**Chapter 2**) and addressing structure (**Chapter 3**) helps to provide a proper context for understanding the IPv6 functions discussed in this book.

Chapter 4 discusses the Neighbor Discovery protocol for IPv6, which supports several functions that replace the IPv4 protocols: ARP, Internet Control Message Protocol for IPv4 (ICMPv4) Router Discovery, and ICMPv4 Redirect. The IPv6 Neighbor Discovery protocol also provides many enhancements over these IPv4-based protocols. Specifically, the IPv6 Neighbor Discovery protocol offers various capabilities that allow IPv6 nodes on the same network segment (IP subnet or Virtual LAN (VLAN)) to advertise their presence to neighboring nodes and learn about the presence of other active neighbors, including attached routers.

Chapter 5 describes the DHCPv6, a client/server protocol that enables IPv6 nodes to obtain IPv6 prefixes, addresses, and network configuration parameters for configuring their interfaces. This chapter discusses the various mechanisms that make up DHCPv6, as well as their applications. IPv6 hosts can obtain addresses and parameters using Stateless DHCPv6 or Stateful DHCPv6, which assigns one or more IPv6 prefixes and/or addresses in a stateful manner. IPv6 hosts can rely entirely on DHCPv6 for address assignment (i.e., via Stateful DHCPv6) or use it in conjunction with SLAAC, that is, via Stateless DHCPv6.

Chapter 6 describes Mobile IP, an IETF standard that specifies mobility mechanisms for IP nodes. Mobile IP allows a mobile IP node to move from its home network to another network (a foreign network) while keeping the original permanent IP address assigned by the home network and maintaining connectivity with it. Mobile IP provides location-independent routing of IP packets between the mobile node's home network and its current location (the foreign network) on the Internet.

Appendix A presents a brief discussion on Ethernet, a family of Link-Layer (equivalently, Layer 1 and Layer 2) networking technologies commonly used in Local Area Networks (LANs), Metropolitan Area Networks (MANs), and Wide Area Networks (WANs). The discussion includes a description of the Ethernet frame format, IEEE 802.1Q VLAN Tagging, and Ethernet byte and bit ordering.

Appendix B describes IPv4, which, along with IPv6, is one of the core internetworking (Network Layer) protocols used today on the Internet. IPv4, like IPv6, encompasses more than just addressing nodes in an internetwork; it consists of a family of internetworking protocols and functions. The discussion here includes the IPv4 packet format, IPv4 addressing and address depletion issues, the concepts of Variable-Length Subnet Masks (VLSMs) and Classless Inter-Domain Routing (CIDR), IPv4 packet fragmentation and reassembly, and IPv4 packet forwarding. **Chapter 1** discusses the limitations of IPv4 and outlines the reasons that spurred the development of IPv6. This **Appendix** provides the most important features of IPv4, allowing readers to better appreciate the improvements offered by IPv6.

Appendix C discusses the IPv4 ARP, a mechanism for discovering the Media Access Control (MAC) address associated with a specified IPv4 address. ARP enables an IPv4 host to obtain the MAC address linked to an IPv4 address within the local network, allowing the host to send IPv4 packets to the owner of that IPv4 address (i.e., the target node).

Appendix D describes IPv4 Gratuitous ARP, a mechanism for an IPv4 node on a network segment to announce or update its IPv4-to-MAC address mapping. IPv4 nodes also use Gratuitous ARP to detect duplicate IPv4 addresses on a network segment. ARP, as discussed in **Appendix C**, is a protocol that allows IPv4 nodes to map the IPv4 addresses of other nodes on the same network segment (IP subnet or VLAN) to their respective MAC addresses.

Appendix E discusses IPv4 Proxy ARP, the process by which an IPv4 node, usually a router, answers ARP queries (ARP Requests) received on a network segment (subnet/VLAN) on behalf of other nodes not on that segment. Using Proxy ARP, a router can respond to ARP queries for the

MAC address corresponding to a target IPv4 address that is not on that network. The Proxy ARP function on the router is aware of the actual location of the queried IPv4 address (i.e., target node) and offers its own MAC address in place of the target node's IPv4 address.

Appendix F describes Private VLANs and Port Isolation. Port Isolation is a method used to restrict specific ports on the same Layer 2 switch from communicating with each other. Devices connected to Layer 2 switch ports with Port Isolation enabled are unable to communicate with each other. These switch ports can still communicate with non-isolated switch ports. Isolated Ports can only communicate with each other through a special port called the Promiscuous Port. A Private VLAN (utilizing the concept of Port Isolation) is a method that allows certain switch ports in a VLAN to be restricted to communicate only with other switch ports on a given Uplink (called the Promiscuous Port).

IPv6 was designed such that many of its packet fields, header extensions, and addresses share similar goals or purposes as the data structures and addresses in IPv4. IPv6 has many functions equivalent to those in IPv4. However, despite many of the similarities in functions and goals, IPv6 can be seen as an entirely different design compared to IPv4. Additionally, other aspects of IPv6, such as the role of routers in host address and parameter configuration, IPv6-to-Link-Layer address resolution, router discovery on a network segment, SLAAC, Stateless and Stateful DHCPv6, IPv6 duplicate address detection, neighbor unreachability detection, and Mobile IPv6, use entirely different message types and internal procedures or mechanisms.

Particularly, the role of routers in host address and parameter configuration, SLAAC, Stateless DHCPv6, and neighbor unreachability detection are entirely new concepts not present in IPv4. The IPv6 equivalents of functions in IPv4 use entirely different messages and procedures. This means that even having a deep knowledge of only IPv4 does not necessarily translate into an automatic understanding of IPv6. IPv6, in many ways, is entirely different from IPv4 and must be studied on its own without assuming that prior knowledge of IPv4 will lead to an understanding of IPv6. Prior IPv4 knowledge surely helps greatly in understanding IPv6 since both IPv6 and IPv4 share many similar underlying concepts but use different message types and procedures.

From the above overview, it can be seen that IPv6 is more than just a longer IP address; it is a suite or collection of functions that provide significant improvements and extensibility over the IPv4 functions. Putting together all the often fragmented and dispersed pieces of information to have a better picture and understanding of how IPv6 works is daunting. Moreover, reading the numerous IPv6-related standards (referred to as Requests for Comments (RFCs)), which often appear cryptic in writing, as a way of understanding IPv6 does not help much, particularly for those who have limited knowledge of networking concepts and fundamentals.

This book attempts to compile the various pieces of information about IPv6 in a systematic and concise format to ensure that readers can easily grasp the foundational concepts of IPv6. It is hoped that after understanding the core concepts of IPv6, readers will be better positioned to comprehend more advanced IPv6-related functions, such as IPv6 routing protocols, as well as the applications and services that run over IPv6. The book's goal is to structure all the relevant information about IPv6 logically, using clear language to efficiently and effectively convey the information to readers.

Some networking books use configuration commands and routines (most of them vendor-specific) to explain how IP concepts work, often overwhelming newcomers to the field and leaving out many critical aspects or inadequately explaining them. This book, instead, takes the approach of concisely explaining the IP concepts, allowing readers to better understand the purpose of the IP configuration commands and routines and how they work (regardless of vendor product). The author sees this as a better approach to explaining IP concepts, especially IP network design, addressing, and routing concepts: a better understanding of IP concepts first, then configuration commands and routines next.

About the Author

James Aweya, PhD, was recently a Chief Research Scientist at the Etisalat British Telecom Innovation Center, Khalifa University, Etisalat British Telecom Innovation Center (EBTIC), Abu Dhabi, UAE. Before then, he was a technical lead and senior systems architect with Nortel, Ottawa, Canada, from 1996 to 2009. He was awarded the 2007 Nortel Technology Award of Excellence for his pioneering and innovative research on Timing and Synchronization across Packet and TDM Networks. He has been granted 70 US patents and has published over 54 journal papers, 40 conference papers, and 43 technical reports. He has extensive experience and expertise that cover many aspects of telecoms systems design and networking. He is the sole author of eight recent engineering books, including this book, on telecom systems and networks.

1 Introduction to IPv6

1.1 IPv4 TO IPv6: LOOKING AT THE CHANGES MADE

The initial design of IPv4 did not anticipate many of the problems discussed in this section. After decades of use, IPv4 was seen as having significant limitations and was not capable of supporting the continuous growth of the Internet and its increasing number of users well into the future. IPv4 is discussed in greater detail in **Appendix B** of this book.

1.1.1 LIMITATIONS OF IPv4

The limitations of IPv4 include the following:

- **Limited Address Space**: IPv4 addresses are 32 bits long, producing an address space that is insufficient for the growing number of Internet users, including millions of untethered devices such as sensors and those enabling the Internet of Things. IPv4 theoretically has $2^{32}=4,294,967,296$ addresses, equivalent to a 4.29×10^9 address space. In response, new IPv4 address allocation strategies and mechanisms such as variable-length subnet mask (VLSM) **[RFC1878]**, Classless Inter-Domain Routing (CIDR) **[RFC1517]** **[RFC1518]** **[RFC1519]**, Network Address Translation **[RFC2663]**, and Dynamic Host Configuration Protocol (DHCP) **[RFC2131]** were introduced to enable efficient use of the limited IPv4 address space. These approaches provide solutions for IPv4 address conservation and have extended the life of IPv4, but still do not expand the IPv4 address space for future needs.
- **Less Efficient Packet Forwarding**: The IPv4 header contains several fields (e.g., options and checksum) that often require more complex processing, which can slow down packet processing and forwarding.
- **Packet Fragmentation**: IPv4 was designed to allow routing devices to fragment packets larger than what an interface can handle, leading to inefficient processing on network nodes and increased chances of packets being corrupted or lost. In IPv4, packet fragmentation can be performed by the source and any intermediate routers along the routing path.
- **Broadcast Transmission Overhead**: IPv4 relies on broadcast when address resolution protocols such as Address Resolution Protocol (ARP) **[RFC826]** are used. For example, broadcast packets are used to communicate with multiple devices on a network when a local node wants to perform Layer 3 to Layer 2 address resolution, which can generate unnecessary traffic and reduce network performance.
- **Limited Support for Quality of Service (QoS)**: Before the introduction of the 6-bit DSCP and ECN fields, IPv4 had limited QoS capabilities. Even with these newer IPv4 header fields, IPv4 still lacks packet flow identification, meaning a mechanism for indicating that a packet belongs to a specific sequence (i.e., flow or stream) of IPv4 packets exchanged between a source and destination, which may require special handling by intermediate IPv4 processing nodes. Such capabilities are desirable for certain types of data, such as real-time streaming voice and video.
- **Complex Configuration**: IPv4 often requires network nodes to be manually configured with addresses, or assigned addresses automatically through the DHCP **[RFC2131]**. Manually configuring IP addresses can be time-consuming and prone to errors. IPv4 lacks more sophisticated mechanisms for automatic, stateless, and stateful assignment of IP addresses.

DOI: 10.1201/9781003710646-1

- **Security Issues**: IPv4 lacks built-in security features, meaning it must rely on a patchwork of other security mechanisms rather than on well-defined security mechanisms specifically targeting IPv4; the security mechanism used is most often dependent on the particular application in use. In IPv4, authentication and encryption facilities are application-dependent. IPv4 applications may use IP Security (IPSec) **[RFC4301]** to provide security for IPv4 packets, but the use of this standard is optional. Instead, in most cases, proprietary security solutions prevail.

1.1.2 CHANGES MADE TO IPv6 TO FIX IPv4 LIMITATIONS

IPv6 offers many improvements over IPv4 and was developed to address IPv4's limitations as well as provide additional features needed for the modern Internet. The changes made to IPv4 to obtain IPv6 can be summarized as follows:

- **Expanded IP Address Space**: In IPv6, the address size is increased to 128 bits (theoretically, $2^{128} = 3.4 \times 10^{38}$ address space) **[RFC4291]** **[RFC8200]**, and addressing is structured to support more levels of addressing hierarchies. The larger IPv6 address space allows for multiple levels of network hierarchies, as well as subnetting and address allocation, from the Internet backbone down to the individual subnets within an organization.

  Large enterprises and network operators may be assigned a /32 IPv6 address block (in CIDR notation), smaller enterprises a /48 IPv6 address block, and residential users a /56 IPv6 address block (when they would typically be allocated a single IPv4 address). This enables IPv6 addressing scalability and superior subnetting, as well as providing a virtually unlimited number of IPv6 addresses for subnetting.

  The IPv6 Global Unicast addresses used on the IPv6 Internet were designed to allow the creation of an efficient, hierarchical, and summarizable IPv6 routing infrastructure. IPv6 uses a hierarchical address structure that allows better route aggregation, reduces the size of IPv6 routing tables, and leads to faster routing table lookups. IPv6 supports a much greater number of addressable nodes and provides simpler autoconfiguration of addresses.

  With a much larger number of IPv6 addresses available, it is no longer necessary to deploy address-conservation techniques such as Network Address Translation **[RFC2663]**, which can also create security problems when connecting to organizations that use the IPv4 private address space. To provide more scalable and improved multicast routing, IPv6 adds a "Scope" field to multicast addresses. IPv6 also defines a new type of anycast address called the IPv6 Subnet-Router Anycast address that allows an IPv6 packet to be sent to any interface in a group of interfaces on an IPv6 subnet (see **Chapter 3**).
- **Simplification of Packet Header Format with a New Header Format**: The new IPv6 header format **[RFC8200]** was designed to minimize header overhead and simplify header processing. To achieve this optimization, IPv6 moved both non-essential header fields and optional fields to well-defined IPv6 extension headers placed after the IPv6 header. This allows routers to process the streamlined and simplified IPv6 header faster and more efficiently.

  IPv6 dropped or made optional some of the IPv4 header fields to reduce packet processing on routing devices and to limit the IPv6 header overhead. IPv6 has a fixed 40-byte header, followed by zero or more extension headers. The IPv4 header has a minimum length of 20 bytes (i.e., without option fields). This means the IPv6 header is only twice as large as the IPv4 header, even though the IPv6 address is four times as large as the IPv4 address. Note that the IPv6 and IPv4 headers do not interoperate, meaning that a router or host requiring both network functionalities must implement both IPv6 and IPv4 stacks to identify and process both header formats.

- **Support of Extensions and Options for Improved Performance**: IPv6 defined header extensions **[RFC8200]** to change the way IP header options are carried in packets, allowing for more efficient forwarding. The IPv6 header and extension headers were designed to replace the IPv4 header that contains option fields. These IPv6 extensions allow an IPv6 packet to carry more options and create greater flexibility for the introduction of new future IPv6 options when needed. The format of the IPv6 extension header allows for extensions to support future capabilities and needs.

  A node can extend IPv6 simply by adding extension headers after the IPv6 header. Unlike the IPv4 header, which can support only 40 bytes of options, the extension headers added to an IPv6 packet are constrained only by the maximum allowable size of the IPv6 packet. Unlike options in the IPv4 header, there is no maximum size on the IPv6 extension headers except for packet size limits. As far as the packet size allows, the IPv6 extension headers can be expanded to accommodate all the extension data needed for IPv6 communication.

  An IPv6 packet may contain zero or more extension headers of varying lengths. If a packet contains extension headers, a special field in the IPv6 header (called the Next Header field) indicates the first extension header. A typical IPv6 packet normally does not carry any extension headers. The IPv6 source adds one or more extension headers to an IPv6 packet only when it determines that the packet requires special handling at either an intermediate router or the destination.

  Each extension header contains a Next Header field that indicates the subsequent extension header. The last extension header of the IPv6 packet specifies the upper-layer protocol and data unit contained within the packet (such as Transmission Control Protocol (TCP), User Datagram Protocol (UDP), or Internet Control Message Protocol for IPv6 (ICMPv6)).
- **Elimination of Packet Header Checksum**: IPv6 removed the IPv4 Checksum field and instead relies on the checksums provided by the Link Layer and upper-layer protocols. Ethernet **[IEEE802.3.2022]** already supports a 32-bit Frame Check Sequence (FCS) field, and upper-layer protocols such as TCP and UDP also support 16-bit Checksum fields, thereby making the equivalent of the IPv4 Checksum field unnecessary in IPv6.
- **Elimination of Packet Fragmentation**: In IPv6, packet fragmentation is performed only by the source node. In IPv4, when a router receives a packet that is too large for the network interface on which it is to be forwarded, the router is allowed to perform fragmentation. In such cases, the router fragments the original IPv4 packet into smaller packets that fit on the outgoing network interface.

  In IPv6, only the source node performs fragmentation. If an IPv6 router cannot forward an IPv6 packet because it is too large for the outgoing interface, it sends an ICMPv6 "Packet Too Big" message to the packet's source and discards the packet. IPv6 defines the IPv6 Fragment extension header to facilitate fragmentation at the source node and packet reassembly at the destination node.
- **Flow Labeling and Identification Capability**: IPv6 introduces a new capability that enables the labeling of sequences of packets sent by a source, allowing network nodes to treat those packets as a single flow that may require special handling. A flow is simply a sequence of packets sent between a source and a destination. In IPv6, nodes perform packet flow labeling and identification using a 20-bit Flow Label field in the IPv6 header. By using the Flow Label in the IPv6 header, an intermediate router can identify the traffic and apply appropriate QoS even when the IPv6 packet payload is encrypted through IPSec.
- **Authentication and Privacy Capabilities**: IPv6 defines extensions that allow network nodes to support authentication, data integrity, and, optionally, data confidentiality. IPSec **[RFC4301]** is specified as the security mechanism for IPv6. All implementations of the

IPv6 protocol suite must support IPSec, providing a standards-based Network Layer security mechanism and promoting interoperability between different IPv6 implementations.

• **Elimination of Broadcast Addresses**: IPv6 defines special, well-known multicast addresses in place of the broadcast addresses used in IPv4. The IPv4 broadcast function is instead replaced by various types of special IPv6 multicast addresses.

The 128-bit IPv6 address is the most obvious and recognizable difference from IPv4 **[RFC4291]** **[RFC8200]**. The 32-bit IPv4 address is usually expressed in dotted-decimal notation, while the 128-bit IPv6 address is written in hexadecimal digits. A single hexadecimal digit can represent each 4-bit group in a 128-bit IPv6 address, giving a total of 32 hexadecimal values, from 0000 binary (or 0 in hexadecimal) to 1111 binary (or F in hexadecimal).

The preferred form of an IPv6 address is x:x:x:x:x:x:x:x, where each x is a 16-bit group (or segment) in the address that can be represented using up to four hexadecimal digits. The 16-bit groups are separated by colons (:). The resulting IPv6 address representation consists of eight 16-bit groups, or *hextets*, giving a total of 128 bits in the IPv6 address. The longest representation of an IPv6 address consists of a total of 32 hexadecimal digits. Colons (:) are used to separate the individual 4-hextet segments in the IPv6 address. **Chapter 3** discusses rules for reducing the number of hexadecimal digits required to represent an IPv6 address. The alphanumeric characters used in the hexadecimal representations of IPv6 addresses are not case sensitive; lowercase and uppercase characters are equivalent.

1.1.3   ADDITIONAL IPV6 FEATURES

The core protocols that make up the IPv6 protocol suite include IPv6 **[RFC4291]** **[RFC8200]**, Internet Control Message Protocol for IPv6 (ICMPv6) **[RFC4443]**, Neighbor Discovery **[RFC4861]**, and Multicast Listener Discovery (MLD) **[RFC2710][RFC3810]**. These core protocols replace those in the IPv4 protocol suite. The use of IPv6 requires that upper-layer protocols, such as TCP and UDP, be updated to perform checksum calculations that include the 128-bit IPv6 addresses. Additionally, dynamic routing protocols such as Routing Information Protocol (RIP) and Open Shortest Path First (OSPF) have been updated to send and receive IPv6 route prefixes. DHCPv4 was also extended (resulting in DHCPv6) to support the allocation of IPv6 addresses and prefixes, as well as other configuration information to IPv6 hosts **[RFC8415]**.

The following are additional IPv6 features, further demonstrating the improvements made from IPv4 to obtain IPv6:

• **Stateless and Stateful Address Configuration**: IPv6 defines several mechanisms that simplify the configuration of hosts in IPv6 networks. It supports both stateless address configuration **[RFC4862]** (in the absence of a DHCP server) and stateful address configuration **[RFC8415]** (when a DHCP server is present in the network).

   With stateless address configuration, a host on a link (or subnet) can automatically configure itself with an IPv6 address for the attached link (i.e., an IPv6 Link-Local address) as well as with an address derived from the IPv6 prefixes advertised by routers on the link. Even in the absence of local routers, each host on a link can configure itself with an IPv6 Link-Local address (without manual configuration) for communication with other nodes on the same link. Upon startup, a host must first auto-generate an IPv6 Link-Local address (with prefix FE80::/10) to be able to communicate with other hosts on the same link. Configuring a Link-Local address serves as a "bootstrap" address for communication on the local link (e.g., address resolution, router discovery, and neighbor discovery) since IPv6 does not support broadcast addresses. With stateful address auto-configuration, a host obtains an IPv6 address and other configuration information from a DHCPv6 server.

- **Neighbor Discovery**: IPv6 supports the Neighbor Discovery protocol [**RFC4861**], which consists of a series of ICMPv6 messages defined for managing the interaction of IPv6 nodes on the same link (i.e., neighboring nodes on the same link or subnet). It uses the Neighbor Discovery protocol to manage node-to-node communication on a link.

  The IPv6 Neighbor Discovery protocol includes various messages for Address Resolution, Duplicate Address Detection, Router Discovery, Router Redirects, Neighbor Unreachability Detection, and Proxy Neighbor Advertisements. The Neighbor Discovery protocol uses multicast and unicast Neighbor Discovery messages (providing more efficient operations) and replaces the IPv4 broadcast-based ARP [**RFC826**], ICMPv4 Router Discovery [**RFC1256**], and ICMPv4 Redirect messages [**RFC792**].

- **ICMPv6**: ICMPv6 [**RFC4443**] replaces ICMPv4 and is responsible for providing diagnostic and error reporting functions when IPv6 packets are unsuccessfully delivered. ICMPv6 is an updated version of ICMPv4; both support the functions needed for reporting packet forwarding and delivery errors, as well as providing a simple echo service for troubleshooting. ICMPv6 also provides the framework for the IPv6 Neighbor Discovery [**RFC4861**] and MLD protocols [**RFC2710**] [**RFC3810**]. ICMPv6 is required in every IPv6 implementation.

  Table 1.1 describes the key ICMPv6 messages that are defined for IPv6. Reference [**RFC4443**] also defines a number of ICMPv6 Destination Unreachable messages. ICMPv6 is used solely for reporting errors and providing feedback on specific conditions during packet delivery and does not make IPv6 a reliable protocol. ICMPv6 messages are carried in IPv6 packets that are never acknowledged, thereby making ICMPv6 messages themselves unreliable.

- **MLD**: MLD [**RFC2710**] [**RFC3810**] is a protocol for managing multicast group membership on a link or subnet. IPv6 multicast routers and hosts on a link (or subnet) exchange MLD messages (which are ICMPv6 messages defined for the MLD protocol) to enable routers to discover which multicast addresses have listening nodes on the link. MLD allows an IPv6 multicast router to discover only those IPv6 multicast addresses for which at least one IPv6 listener exists on the link, rather than the list of individual multicast listeners for each multicast group address. MLD currently has two versions, MLDv1 and MLDv2. MLDv1 [**RFC2710**] consists of three ICMPv6 messages that replace Internet Group Management Protocol version 2 (IGMPv2) for IPv4 [**RFC2236**]. MLDv2 [**RFC3810**] replaces IGMPv3 for IPv4 [**RFC3376**].

  The three types of MLDv1 messages are Multicast Listener Query (ICMPv6 Message Type 130), Multicast Listener Report (ICMPv6 Message Type 131), and Multicast Listener Done (ICMPv6 Message Type 132). Multicast routers send MLDv1 Multicast Listener Query messages (General Query or Multicast-Address-Specific Query) to determine if there are multicast listeners on a link. Routers send General Query messages to ascertain if there are multicast listeners for all multicast addresses on a link. Multicast routers send MLDv1 Multicast-Address-Specific Query messages to identify if there are multicast listeners for a specific multicast address on a link.

  Multicast listeners send MLDv1 Multicast Listener Report messages to multicast routers to either express interest in receiving multicast traffic for a specific multicast address or to respond to a MLDv1 Multicast Listener Query message [**RFC2710**]. Multicast listeners send MLDv1 Multicast Listener Done messages to multicast routers to indicate that they are no longer interested in receiving multicast traffic for a specific multicast address [**RFC2710**].

  MLDv2 defined the MLDv2 Multicast Listener Report message (ICMPv6 Message Type 143) [**RFC3810**]. IPv6 nodes send MLDv2 Multicast Listener Report messages to multicast routers to communicate their current multicast listening state or any changes in the multicast listening state of their interfaces. The MLDv2 Multicast Listener Report message allows an

IPv6 node to perform source filtering, which enables a node to express interest in receiving IPv6 packets only from specific source IPv6 addresses or from all source IPv6 addresses except certain specific source IPv6 addresses sent to a particular multicast address.

The discussion so far has presented the limitations of IPv4, the changes made to IPv4 to obtain IPv6, and the additional features that IPv6 supports. The features offered by IPv6 make it a more robust and capable protocol for the foreseeable future compared to IPv4. In particular, the IPv6 address space can meet the addressing needs of network entities for the foreseeable future. The key differences between IPv4 and IPv6 are highlighted in Table 1.2.

TABLE 1.1
Key ICMPv6 Messages

ICMPv6 Message	Message Type	Function
Destination Unreachable	1 [RFC4443]	Sent by a router or the destination host to inform the source host that an IPv6 packet or its payload cannot be delivered
Packet Too Big	2 [RFC4443]	Sent by a router to inform a source host that an IPv6 packet is too large to be forwarded
Time Exceeded	3 [RFC4443]	Sent by a router to inform a source host that the Hop Limit of an IPv6 packet has expired
Parameter Problem	4 [RFC4443]	Sent by a router to inform a source host that an error was encountered when processing an IPv6 header or an IPv6 extension header
Echo Request	128 [RFC4443]	Sent by a node to check IPv6 connectivity to a particular host for diagnostic purposes
Echo Reply	129 [RFC4443]	Sent by a node in response to an ICMPv6 Echo Request
Multicast Listener Query	130 [RFC2710]	Sent by a multicast router to determine if there are multicast listeners on a link
MLDv1 Multicast Listener Report	131 [RFC2710]	A multicast listener sends a MLDv1 Multicast Listener Report message to a multicast router to either express interest in receiving multicast traffic for a specific multicast address or as a response to a Multicast Listener Query message
Multicast Listener Done	132 [RFC2710]	Sent by a multicast listener to a multicast router to indicate that it is no longer interested in receiving multicast traffic for a specific multicast address
MLDv2 Multicast Listener Report	143 [RFC3810]	An IPv6 node sends an MLDv2 Multicast Listener Report message to a multicast router to communicate/report its current multicast listening state, or changes in the multicast listening state of its interfaces.
Router Solicitation	133 [RFC4861]	When an interface on an IPv6 host is enabled, it sends these messages to request IPv6 routers on the local network segment to send Router Advertisement messages immediately, rather than at their next scheduled time.
Router Advertisement	134 [RFC4861]	IPv6 routers send these messages on a network segment to advertise their presence, various link parameters, and Internet parameters. Routers send these messages either periodically or in response to a Router Solicitation message. Router Advertisement messages contain IPv6 prefixes (that are used for on-link determination or address configuration), recommended Hop Limit values, and other parameters.
Neighbor Solicitation	135 [RFC4861]	IPv6 nodes send these messages to determine the Link-Layer address of a neighboring node. These messages are also sent to verify that a neighbor is still reachable by a cached Link-Layer address. They are also used for IPv6 Duplicate Address Detection.
Neighbor Advertisement	136 [RFC4861]	An IPv6 node sends these messages in response to a Neighbor Solicitation message. A node can also send unsolicited Neighbor Advertisement messages to announce a Link-Layer address change.
Redirect Message	137 [RFC4861]	IPv6 routers send these messages to inform IPv6 hosts on a network segment of a better first-hop for a particular IPv6 destination or that the destination is on the same link/ segment.

TABLE 1.2
Key Differences between IPv4 and IPv6

IPv4	IPv6
32-bit (4-byte) source and destination addresses	128-bit (16-byte) source and destination addresses.
IPSec support is optional.	IPSec support is required.
IPv4 header does not support a field for packet flow identification for QoS processing in routers.	IPv6 header has a Flow Label field for packet flow identification for QoS processing in routers.
Both routers and the source host can fragment packets.	Only the source host can fragment packets; routers do not.
Header includes a checksum field.	Header does not include a checksum field.
Header includes options.	All optional data is moved to IPv6 extension headers.
Uses ARP and broadcast ARP Request frames to resolve an IPv4 address to a Link-Layer address (also called the Media Access Control (MAC) address).	Uses multicast Neighbor Solicitation and Neighbor Advertisement messages to resolve IPv6 addresses to Link-Layer addresses.
Uses IGMP for managing multicast group membership.	Uses MLD messages for managing multicast group membership locally.
Uses ICMP Router Discovery to determine the IPv4 address of the best default gateway, and this is optional.	Uses ICMPv6 Router Solicitation and Router Advertisement messages to determine the IPv6 address of the best default gateway, and these are required.
Uses broadcast addresses to send traffic to all nodes on a subnet.	Uses an IPv6 Link-Local scope All-Nodes multicast address (FF02::1).
Addresses must be configured either manually or through DHCPv4.	Address configuration can be through autoconfiguration, manual configuration, or DHCPv6.
Must support a 576-byte packet size (possibly, fragmented).	Must support a 1280-byte packet size (without fragmentation).

The rest of this chapter describes the different methods used by IP routers to learn network routing information. We introduce the main concepts of static and dynamic routing, including their benefits and limitations. We discuss the various sources from which routers obtain their routing information, the classification of different dynamic routing protocols, and the routing metrics or costs that routing protocols use to determine the best paths to network destinations.

1.2   IP ROUTING PROTOCOLS

To make IP networks more manageable, larger networks are typically divided into smaller network segments (also known in IPv6 as *links* or *subnets*). A network segment may also be a *virtual local area network (VLAN)*, which is a Link Layer broadcast domain based, for example, on Ethernet technologies. An IP subnet or VLAN is defined as a Layer 2 broadcast domain in which a transmitted packet can potentially reach all parts of that domain. These Layer 2 broadcast network segments, along with other autonomous networks (or systems) in the broader IP internetworking sense, are interconnected using *IP routers*. IP routers forward IP packets from one network segment (subnet or VLAN) to another, allowing a sender (source address) to send data across one or more network segments to one or more receivers (destination address).

Each IP packet sent has an IP header that contains a source IP address (i.e., address of the sending host) and a destination IP address (i.e., address of the receiving host). Unlike Link-Layer addresses (e.g., Ethernet Medium Access Control (MAC) addresses), the IP addresses in the IP header typically remain the same as the IP packet traverses an IP network. **Chapter 3** presents the conditions under which the IPv6 destination address in the IPv6 header may change as a packet travels to its final destination. Ethernet is discussed in greater detail in **Appendix A**. The process of forwarding IP packets across Layer 2 network segment boundaries from a sender to a receiver is known as *IP routing* **[AWE2BK21V1] [AWE2BK21V2]**. IP routers are placed at Layer 2 boundaries to interconnect the associated Layer 2 domains. In addition to the required routing functions, IP routers support several important features (e.g., broadcast traffic constraining, security, quality of service, unicast and multicast forwarding, tunneling) that make them the primary means for interconnecting two or more separate network segments.

IP routers are typically multihomed devices that have a network interface connected to each adjacent network segment. An IP router forwards an IP packet from a connected network segment to a directly connected host or to another network segment. All IP routers rely on a *routing table* to forward IP packets between network segments. To perform packet routing, IP routers use *routing protocols* to communicate and exchange information about paths/routes to network destinations. The routing information obtained through these protocols is populated in the IP router's routing table. The routing table may also contain *static routes*, which are manually installed routes that are not learned from the routing protocols.

Routing is the primary function of the *Internet Protocol (IP) Layer* of the *TCP/IP protocol suite* **[AWE2BK21V1] [AWE2BK21V2]**. IP hosts and routers exchange and process IP packets at the IP Layer. Services above the IP Layer on an IP node send data in the form of TCP segments or UDP messages to the IP Layer. The IP Layer encapsulates the TCP or UDP data in IP packets and creates the source and destination IP address information in the IP packet header for routing the data through the network to the destination node. The IP Layer then passes the IP packets down to the Link Layer, where they are placed in Link-Layer frames (e.g., Ethernet frames) for transmission over the Link Layer and Physical Layer-specific media to another IP node. The process of receiving data from the destination host occurs in the reverse order.

On issues related to routing, this book focuses mainly on the following IPv6 routing protocols:

- **Routing Information Protocol for IPv6**: RIP next generation (RIPng) **[RFC2080]**
- **OSPF for IPv6**: OSPF version 3 (OSPFv3) **[RFC5340]**
- Intermediate System-to-Intermediate System (IS-IS) Protocol for IPv6 (IS-ISv6) **[RFC5308]**
- Multiprotocol Extensions for BGP (MBGP) **[RFC4760]**

The companion books **[AWE2BK21V1]** and **[AWE2BK21V2]** focus on IPv4 routing protocols.

1.3   TYPES OF UNICAST DYNAMIC ROUTING PROTOCOLS

Dynamic routing protocols operate by distributing network topology information and routing updates between various routing functions in a network without manual intervention whenever network topology changes occur. After discovering or mapping out the network topology, each routing function attempts to select the best loop-free path in the network, on which each arriving packet should be forwarded to reach its destination.

IP routing protocols can be categorized into different groups according to where they operate (within an Autonomous System or between Autonomous Systems) or based on their design and operational characteristics (distance-vector, link-state, or path-vector routing). These classifications are discussed in this section. We consider only the most common IP routing protocols (see Figure 1.1).

1.3.1   INTERIOR VERSUS EXTERIOR ROUTING PROTOCOLS

A routing domain represents a collection of routers running a common routing protocol and under a single administrative control. The role of the Interior (or Internal) Gateway Protocol (IGP) within the routing domain is to provide routing information that allows connectivity between the routers. The routers running the common IGP also employ a common best path selection algorithm to determine the optimal paths to each network destination.

Within the Internet, an Autonomous System is a group of interconnected routers and network address prefixes that may be owned or controlled by one or more network operators

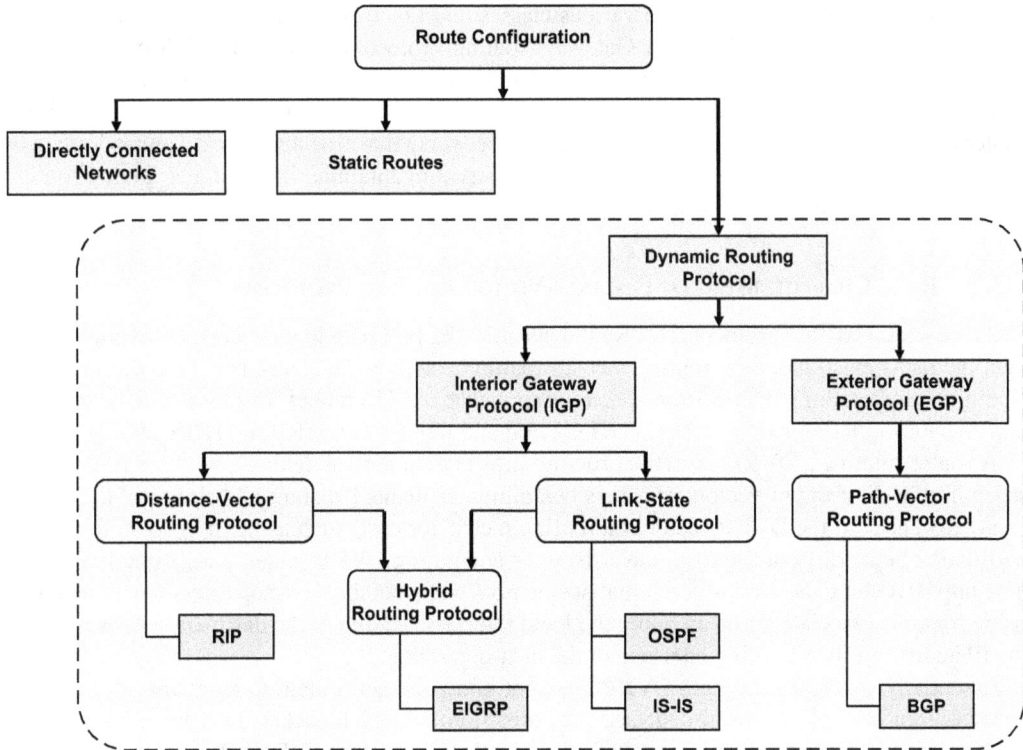

FIGURE 1.1 Types of unicast dynamic routing protocols.

(e.g., organizations) but are managed by a single administrative entity (e.g., an Internet service provider). Furthermore, these interconnected routers and network prefixes share a common routing policy or plan, and these prefixes are presented by the administrative entity to the Internet under this common, clearly defined routing policy. The entire Autonomous System is viewed by the outside world as a single entity.

A routing policy refers to how routing decisions are made within the administrative entity or domain. Using its routing policy, the Autonomous System presents a consistent and coherent view of the network destinations that can be reached through it to other Autonomous Systems. An Autonomous System requires an officially registered Autonomous System Number (ASN), assigned by the Internet Assigned Numbers Authority, to be visible to other Autonomous Systems on the Internet and to exchange routing information with them on the public Internet. Private ASNs are used if an Autonomous System only needs to communicate with a single provider or peer system via BGP without being visible on the public Internet. The routes exchanged along with their private ASNs will not be visible on the Internet.

An Exterior (or External) Gateway Protocol (EGP) refers to a routing protocol used to connect different Autonomous Systems on the Internet. BGP is currently the only EGP used for exchanging routing information between Autonomous Systems. When used between Autonomous Systems, BGP is referred to as external BGP. EGPs, such as BGP, are typically deployed to provide entry and exit points for communication between different Autonomous Systems. EGPs connect separate Autonomous Systems, providing transit paths between them and facilitating the forwarding of traffic across such internetworks. BGP can also be used for exchanging routing information between two peers within an Autonomous System; in this case, it is referred to as internal BGP.

The IGPs and EGPs shown in Figure 1.1 use different algorithms for route computation and best path selection. The standards-based dynamic routing protocols commonly used in today's networks are RIP, OSPF, IS-IS, and BGP. The various classes and types of routing protocols are presented in Figure 1.1. The Enhanced Interior Gateway Routing Protocol (EIGRP) **[RFC7868]** is a hybrid proprietary routing protocol developed by Cisco and mainly used by Cisco routers. RIP, OSPF, and IS-IS are IGPs designed for exchanging routing information within a routing domain or Autonomous System. IGPs allow a router to learn about routes to networks that are internal to a routing domain or Autonomous System. An IGP is responsible for constructing, maintaining, and distributing routing information within a single routing domain or Autonomous System.

1.3.2 Basic Characteristics of Distance-Vector Routing Protocols

Distance-vector routing protocols (DVRPs) determine the best path to a network destination (when multiple paths exist) based on routing metrics that indicate how far ("distance") the destination is from the router making the decision. The routing metric used to reflect "distance" can be a simple hop count (as in RIP for IPv4 (RIPv2) **[RFC2453]** and RIP for IPv6 (RIPng) **[RFC2080]**).

A router running a DVRP advertises routing information to its neighbors, with the information structured in the form of vectors or arrays containing elements ["distance," "direction"]. The element "distance" in the DVRP vector is a routing metric (or cost) such as the hop count to reach a destination network from the local advertising or computing DVRP router, and "direction" is the next-hop IP router to be used to reach that destination. Note that the next-hop router from the advertising router is associated with an outbound local interface leading to the destination network, plus the IP address of the receiving interface of the next-hop router.

Essentially, a router running a DVRP does not know the entire path to a network destination; instead, it knows only the local interface (i.e., direction) on which packets to a destination should be forwarded and the distance (i.e., how far it is) to that destination. A DVRP router is only aware of the IP addresses assigned to its local interfaces and the addresses of the remote networks it can reach through its neighbor DVRP routers. The local router does not possess any broader knowledge of the entire topology of the network in which it is operating. Essentially, the routers running the DVRP are not aware of the entire network topology.

The routing information that a DVRP router receives from its neighbors is stored ("as is") in a local routing database (i.e., a "route store") that the DVRP maintains. The DVRP router then uses a distance-vector algorithm (Bellman–Ford algorithm) to calculate the best (and possibly) loop-free paths/routes to each destination if multiple paths exist. The best paths are then installed in the DVRP router's IP routing table and also advertised as routing information to each neighboring DVRP router. Thus, once a router determines the best paths to all known destinations, it advertises its entire IP routing table containing these best paths to each directly connected adjacent router.

This behavior prevents a DVRP from having a complete map of the entire network for any given destination network. Instead, the routing table maintained by the protocol simply reflects how best a neighboring router knows how to reach a particular destination network based on how far that neighbor thinks it is from that destination network. The local router does not know how many hops (or how many other routers) are on the best path leading to any of those destination networks. This behavior led to distance-vector routing being sometimes nicknamed "routing by rumor." Each router learns from its neighbors how best to reach a particular destination, routing information that the neighbors, in turn, may have inferred from their neighbors, and so on.

The following are mechanisms for preventing routing loops and workarounds for enhancing the performance of DVRPs, particularly RIP:

- A RIP router initially sends a full routing table update to all neighboring routers and then performs periodic updates. The router also sends asynchronous routing updates when necessary.
- Performs route maintenance in the local routing database using various invalidation timers: Route Update Timer, Route Invalid Timer, Route Flush Timer, Holddown Timers.

- Sends Triggered Updates when necessary.
- Uses the Count-to-Infinity (maximum hop count) mechanism.
- Uses the Poison Reverse mechanism.
- Uses the Split Horizon mechanism.

All of these mechanisms are described in detail in **[AWE2BK21V1] [AWE2BK21V2]**.

1.3.3 BASIC CHARACTERISTICS OF LINK-STATE ROUTING PROTOCOLS

Unlike DVRPs, link-state routing protocols (LSRPs) determine the best path to a network destination using more complex methods and routing metrics that can take into account link variables such as bandwidth, delay, traffic load, and reliability. Both OSPF (OSPF for IPv4 (OSPFv2) **[RFC2328]**, OSPF for IPv6 (OSPFv3) **[RFC5340]**) and IS-IS (IS-IS **[ISO10589:2002]**, IS-IS for IPv4 **[RFC1195]**, IS-IS for IPv6 **[RFC5308]**) routers assign a cost to each of their interfaces, which is a routing metric that the router uses in its link-state calculations. Routes with lower total path costs to a network destination are preferred over those with higher path costs.

OSPF and IS-IS are the two most common LSRPs and IGPs used in today's enterprise and service provider networks. A router running an LSRP advertises the state (link state) and metric (link metric) for each of its connected links (including information about its directly connected networks and neighbors) to every other router in the network. OSPF sends advertisements in messages called link-state advertisements (LSAs), while IS-IS sends advertisements in link-state packets (LSPs). LSPs are also referred to as link-state Protocol Data Units **[ISO10589:2002]**. In our discussion, we use LSA to also represent LSP.

When a router receives an advertisement from a neighbor, it stores the link-state information in a local database called the *link-state database* (LSDB). The receiving router then advertises all the link-state information received to each of its neighbors exactly as it was received. The router essentially "floods" the received link-state information unmodified (just as advertised by the originating router) throughout the network from one router to another. This method allows all the LSRP routers in the network to have a consistent, identical, and always synchronized map of the overall network.

As part of the information exchange process, each router transmits to its neighbor routers information about itself and the links that are directly connected to it, including the state of these links. This information is propagated from the source router to the neighbors and from those routers to other routers in the network (router to router), with each router storing a copy of the information as received with no changes made to it. The flooding process results in each LSRP router having a complete picture of the entire network. When this process converges, every router will have identical information and a topology map of the entire network, which then allows each router to independently compute its own set of best routes to network destinations.

Each router in the network independently runs a shortest path first (SPF) algorithm (usually a variant of the Dijkstra algorithm) over the complete map of the network (stored in the local LSDB) to calculate the best shortest loop-free paths to network destinations. The router then uses the resulting best paths for all the reachable network destinations from the SPF calculations to populate the local routing table.

The requirement of flooding link-state information and maintaining a consistent, identical, and synchronized complete map of the network makes LSRPs more complex than DVRPs. LSRPs require more memory and are relatively more computationally intensive than DVRPs. The advantage, however, is that LSRPs make better path decisions that are less prone to routing loops.

Furthermore, LSRPs have future extensibility features and capabilities through the use of messages such as opaque LSAs for OSPF and TLVs for IS-IS. These features allow LSRPs to be extended for the transmission of arbitrary data that these protocols were not originally designed for. These extended capabilities allow LSRPs to add extra information to LSAs or LSPs. Routers can add extra information to OSPF LSAs or IS-IS LSPs to support, for example, services commonly required by service providers such as Multiprotocol Label Switching traffic engineering. Both OSPF and IS-IS support VLSM, which allows both protocols to support CIDR.

The main advantages of LSRPs are fast convergence and high scalability, making them more suitable for large networks. Their disadvantages, however, are relatively greater implementation complexity and high resource usage (CPU processing and memory resources). These drawbacks stem mainly from the higher CPU cycles and overhead involved in processing routing updates when network changes occur, and the higher memory resources required to store Neighbor Tables, LSDBs (containing the complete topology map), and routing tables.

Each LSRP router constructs and maintains three separate databases or tables: Neighbor Table (or Adjacency Database), LSDB (also known as the Topology Table), and routing table (see **[AWE2BK21V1] [AWE2BK21V2]**):

- **Neighbor Table**: This database maintains information about the LSRP neighbors of the local router.
- **LSDB**: This database stores the link-state routing information learned from all neighboring LSRP routers.
- **Routing Table**: This database stores the best routes computed from the LSDB (i.e., from the network topology information learned from neighbor routers).

Generally, the following processes take place before LSRP routers can forward traffic in the network:

- **Neighbor Discovery Process**: Determining the neighbors of each router, establishment, and maintenance of neighbor adjacencies.
- **LSA Flooding**: Each router floods its LSAs throughout the network, allowing the exchange of link-state information.
- **Construction and Maintenance of the LSDB**: Each router uses the flooded LSAs to create the complete network topology map or database (i.e., the LSDB).
- **Execution of the SPF Algorithm**: Each router uses the network-wide identical LSDB to compute the shortest path(s) to each network destination.
- **Construction and Maintenance of the IP Routing Table**: Each router then inserts the best paths to each network destination (derived from the SPF) into its IP routing table.

1.3.4 BASIC CHARACTERISTICS OF PATH-VECTOR ROUTING PROTOCOLS

Generally, a path-vector routing protocol (PVRP) is used for exchanging routing information between Autonomous Systems. BGP is currently the only PVRP used on the Internet (BGPv4 **[RFC4271]**, MGBP **[RFC4760]**). BGP carries as part of its routing information the ASNs that the routing information has passed through. The routing information passed to a BGP router consists of a set of network destination address prefixes that share the same path attributes and the ASNs that the information has traversed.

The BGP routers along the path to the network destination use the routing information (and the listed Autonomous Systems traversed) to prevent routing loops. References **[AWE2BK21V1]** and **[AWE2BK21V2]** discuss in detail the main features of BGP and how it is used to exchange routing information between Autonomous Systems.

BGP is designed with the following goals in mind:

- Prevent network changes in one routing domain/Autonomous System from propagating to other routing domains/Autonomous Systems.
- Hide information about a routing domain/Autonomous System and not make it visible to other routing domains/Autonomous Systems.
- Implement routing policies between routing domains/Autonomous Systems.

The following types of routing policies can be implemented with BGP:

- Prevent a network from accepting certain routing information from other routing domains/ Autonomous Systems.
- Prevent traffic from traversing certain routing domains/Autonomous Systems.
- Allow traffic to take the cheapest exit point.
- Specify the closest exit point for traffic to always take.
- Specify the closest exit point to the final destination for traffic to take.

The main functions of a BGP router are as follows:

- Prevention of routing loops
- Implementation of routing policy
- Determination of optimum loop-free paths

A PVRP like BGP determines the best loop-free path to a destination by checking and considering a number of BGP Path attributes. It also analyzes any given path to a destination to determine if the path is loop-free or not. BGP routers exchange network reachability information, called path-vectors, made up of path attributes. The path-vector information includes

- A list of the full path ASNs (listed hop-by-hop) necessary to reach a network destination.
- Other path attributes, including the interface IP address needed to reach the next Autonomous System (the BGP Next-Hop attribute), and how the network address prefixes at the end of the path were introduced into BGP (via the BGP Origin attribute).

A BGP router determines the best route from a source using a routing policy defined for the network without assigning costs to the links and routes, as done in DVRPs or LSRPs. The route from a source to all network destinations is determined by the best spanning tree that satisfies a pre-defined set of criteria based on a routing policy. A BGP router uses a best path selection algorithm based on a pre-defined set of criteria **[AWE2BK21V2]**.

BGP Path attributes contain the characteristics of a BGP route that a BGP router advertises to its BGP peers:

- BGP uses BGP Path attributes as pieces of information to describe the different network prefixes included in BGP UPDATE messages.
- BGP routers also use BGP Path attribute to communicate the routing information needed for implementing BGP routing policies.

1.4 ROUTING METRICS

When multiple paths exist to a network destination, a router needs a mechanism for determining the best or optimum path to that destination. Routing metrics are numeric values that routing protocols use to determine the best path to a network destination (see Figure 1.2). Each route to a destination is assigned a metric to provide the routing protocol a means of ranking the multiple routes to that destination, from best (or most preferred) to worst (or least preferred). Note that a routing metric is different from Administrative Distance or Route Preference.

Each dynamic routing protocol has its own routing metric that it uses to compare routes to given destinations when multiple routes exist. The routing metric represents the cost of sending traffic on a given route and is based on various criteria as discussed in **[AWE2BK21V1]** **[AWE2BK21V2]**: total/overall link conditions to a destination (bandwidth, delay, reliability); network operator's policies (monetary cost, autonomous systems that traffic must traverse). Each routing protocol (RIPng,

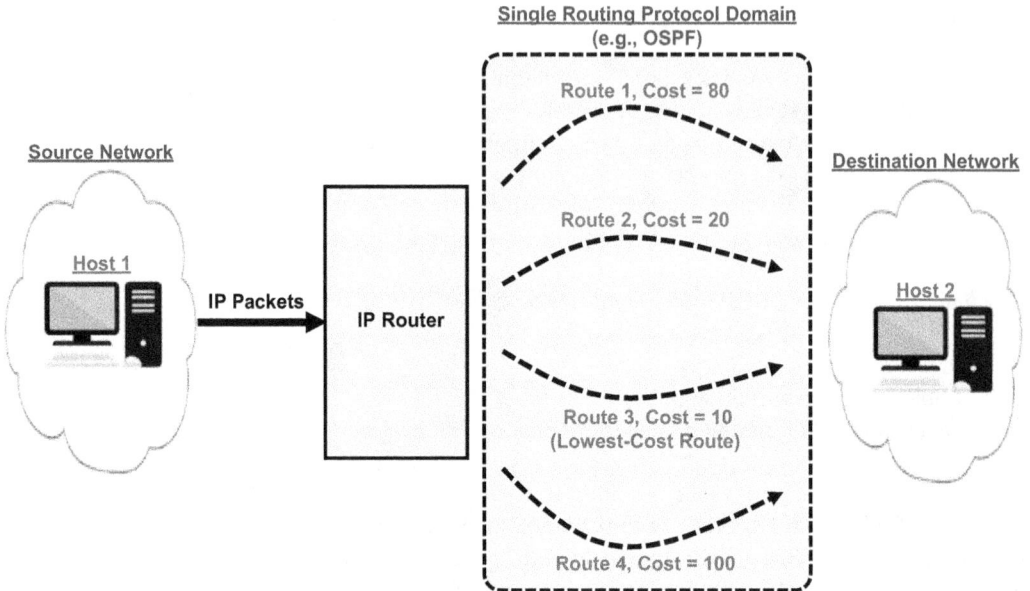

FIGURE 1.2 Multiple routes with different cost values to the same destination.

OSPFv3, IS-ISv6, MBGP) has its own method for computing the metric of a route. Typically, the default metric for static routes is "1" and may be configurable. Some routing protocols use a single metric only, while others use a combination of metrics (in EIGRP) or multiple metrics (IS-IS), as desired by the network operator.

1.4.1 EQUAL-COST MULTIPATH ROUTING

When multiple routes exist to the same destination, the route with the lowest costs is selected as the best route and installed in the IP routing table (Figure 1.2). When multiple equal lowest-cost routes exist to a given destination, the router may select all or a number of those routes for the IP routing table and perform load sharing of traffic over those routes, a process called equal-cost multipath (ECMP) routing. In this case, the ECMP routes installed in the IP routing table each have an outgoing interface and next-hop router associated with them. The ECMP routes collectively constitute one logical route to a single destination, even though they take different paths to that destination.

The criteria for performing load sharing on the ECMP routes may be based on several factors such as the source IP address, destination IP address, TCP/UDP port numbers, and others. Most often, the load sharing is based on factors that uniquely define a flow to avoid out-of-sequence packet transfer, for example, when per-packet load sharing is used. IPv6 has a 20-bit Flow Label field in the IPv6 header (see **Chapter 2**) that can be used to identify packets belonging to a particular flow. IPv4, on the other hand, has no such field for labeling flows. A router must support the necessary capabilities for ECMP and load sharing before multiple ECMP routes can be installed in its IP routing table.

Routing protocols such as RIP, OSPF, and IS-IS support ECMP routing **[AWE2BK21V2]**. A routing protocol like EIGRP supports both ECMP and unequal-cost multipath routing as discussed in **[AWE2BK21V1]**.

1.5 ROUTING PROTOCOL ADMINISTRATIVE DISTANCES OR ROUTE PREFERENCES

The IP routing table in a router typically contains a single manually configured or best dynamically learned route to each destination that the router has learned. Each routing protocol uses its own specific routing metric to select the best route when multiple routes exist to a destination. As noted above, some routing protocols support equal-cost (OSPF) and unequal-cost (EIGRP) multipath routing when multiple routes exist to a particular destination.

A router may have several routing information sources from which it can learn routes to a network destination (Figure 1.3). This means a router can learn (from these multiple sources) more than one route to a given destination. In this case, the router compares the Administrative Distances of these routes (i.e., routing information sources) to select the best route to add to its routing table. The rationale behind using the Administrative Distance mechanism is that different routing protocols use different metrics and algorithms for best path computations that are not similar or compatible with each other. In a router running multiple routing protocols, the situation sometimes arises where the routing function needs to select the best path for packet forwarding using routing information obtained across multiple protocols (via a process called *route redistribution*).

The *Administrative Distance* (also called the *Route Preference*) serves as an important parameter for comparing routes learned through different routing methods. It indicates how trustworthy, believable, or reliable the routing information source is when multiple sources provide routes to a given destination. The router considers the method through which it discovered the route when deciding which route to install in the IP routing table. A lower Administrative Distance value indicates a more trustworthy route (Figures 1.4 and 1.5). When multiple routing information sources provide routes to the same IP destination, the source (equivalently, route) with the lowest Administrative Distance is selected.

The Administrative Distance measure is not an important factor when using only static routes since one would most often consciously configure a static route for a good reason and would not typically configure multiple static routes to a given destination. However, if static routes are used in conjunction with one or more dynamic routing protocols such as OSPF to a given destination, the router selects the route with the lowest Administrative Distance. Typically, the default Administrative Distances are configured such that a static route supersedes dynamic routes to the same destination; static routes have the lowest default Administrative Distance.

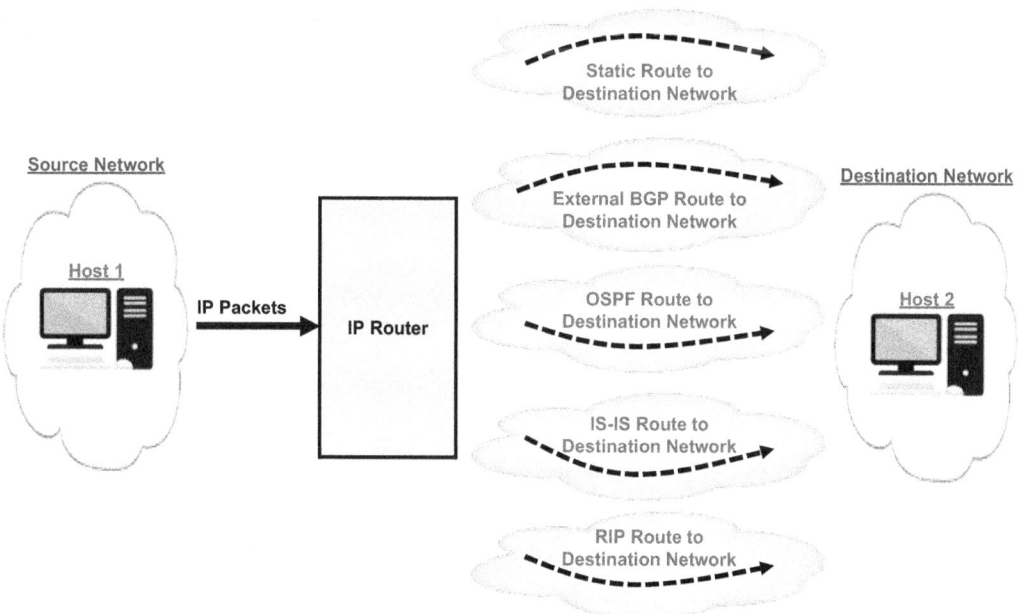

FIGURE 1.3   Routes from different routing information sources to the same destination.

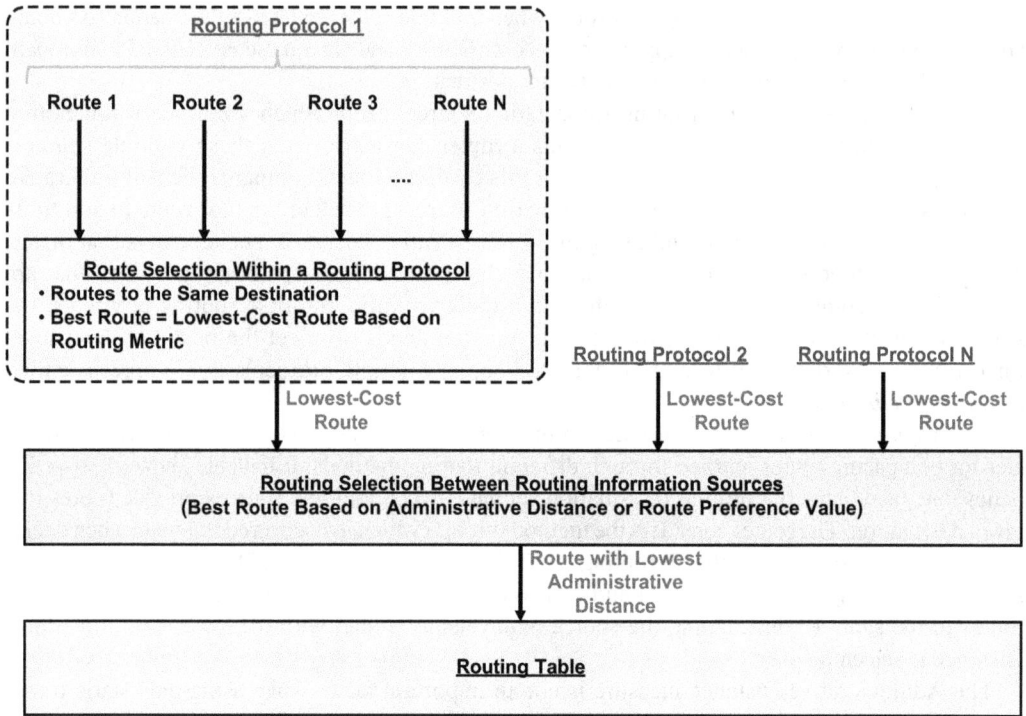

FIGURE 1.4   Route selection within a routing protocol.

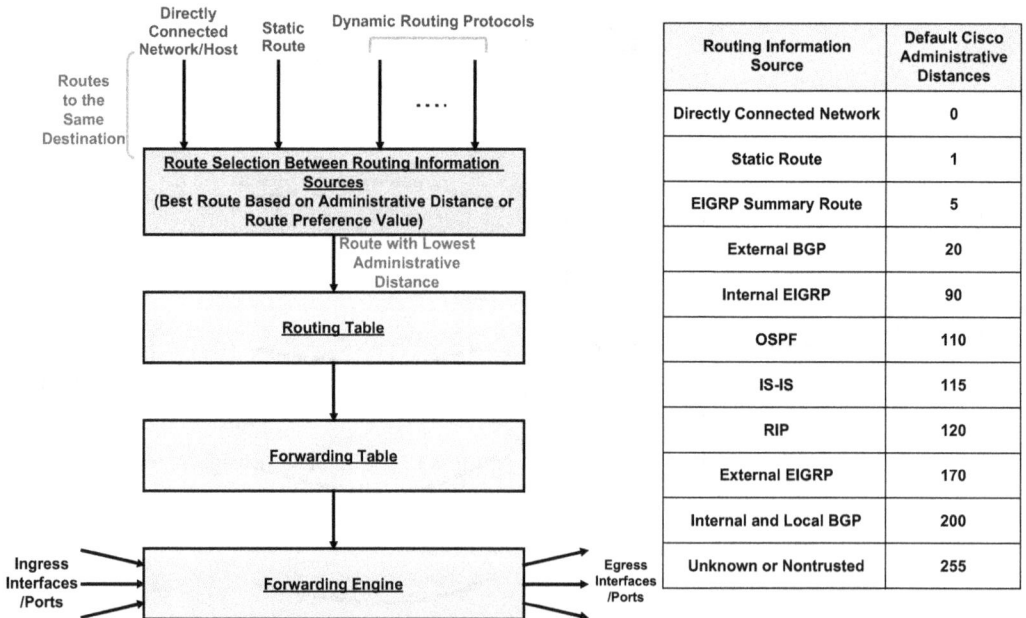

Routing Information Source	Default Cisco Administrative Distances
Directly Connected Network	0
Static Route	1
EIGRP Summary Route	5
External BGP	20
Internal EIGRP	90
OSPF	110
IS-IS	115
RIP	120
External EIGRP	170
Internal and Local BGP	200
Unknown or Nontrusted	255

FIGURE 1.5   Routing information sources and route selection.

1.6   THE IP ROUTING TABLE

IP routers run routing protocols to maintain the routing tables they use to route traffic to network destinations. The routing table (also called the routing information base (RIB)) is maintained to always contain the most current network reachability information. How this is done depends on the type of routing protocol used (DVRP, LSRP, or PVRP) and the specific mechanisms supported within the particular routing protocol (RIP, OSPF, IS-IS, BGP).

Typically, each IPv6 node has an IPv6 routing table, with IPv6 routers maintaining more comprehensive routing tables than IPv6 hosts. Similar to IPv4, IPv6 nodes use locally maintained routing tables to determine how to forward IPv6 packets to their destinations. An IPv6 node creates routing table entries by default when it initializes IPv6 and installs routing entries configured manually (by a system administrator) or automatically through communication with other routers in the IPv6 internetwork.

The IPv6 routing table stores information about IPv6 network prefixes and how these prefixes can be reached, either directly on an attached link or indirectly through other IPv6 routers. Typically, both IPv6 hosts and routers maintain IPv6 routing tables; they are not exclusive to IPv6 routers. In IPv6, hosts also maintain IPv6 routing tables. However, before an IPv6 host uses its routing table, it checks its locally maintained Destination Cache for an entry that matches the destination IPv6 address in the IPv6 packet to be forwarded. If the host determines that the Destination Cache does not contain an entry for the destination IPv6 address, it uses the IPv6 routing table to determine the routing information required to forward the packet (**Chapter 4** discusses how an IPv6 host determines on-link and off-link destinations).

The most basic pieces of information in the IPv6 routing table are the destination IPv6 address or prefix, the next-hop IPv6 address, and the next-hop interface:

- **Destination IPv6 Address or Prefix**: This is the IPv6 address of the intended receiver of the IPv6 packet. If an IPv6 routing header (see **Chapter 2**) is present in the IPv6 packet, then this may not be the ultimate receiver of the packet.
- **Next-hop Address**: For direct packet delivery (i.e., when the destination is on a link attached to the local node, also called an on-link destination), the next-hop address is the destination IPv6 address written in the IPv6 packet being forwarded. For an indirect packet delivery (i.e., when the destination is not on a local link, also called an off-link destination), the next-hop address is the IPv6 address of the interface of the next best router leading to that destination.
- **Next-hop Interface**: This is the interface that identifies the physical or logical interface on which the packet should be forwarded, either to its destination or to the next best router leading to the destination.

After an IPv6 node determines the next-hop address and interface, it updates its local Destination Cache (see **Chapter 4**). Subsequent IPv6 packets that are to be forwarded to the same cached destination will use the Destination Cache entry, rather than being forwarded through the more computationally extensive routing table lookups/searches.

1.6.1   TYPES OF IP ROUTES

An IP route can be viewed as a mapping of a particular destination IP address or prefix to a local interface and next-hop node (i.e., the next best router leading to the destination). The IPv6 routing table has entries that may store the following types of routes:

- **Directly Attached Network Routes**: These routes correspond to IPv6 network prefixes that are directly attached to the local node (on-link prefixes) and typically have 64-bit IPv6 prefixes.

- **Remote Network Routes**: These routes correspond to IPv6 network prefixes that are not directly attached to the local node (off-link prefixes) but can be reached through other routers. A remote network route may consist of IPv6 subnet network prefixes or IPv6 prefixes that cover address spaces using CIDR.
- **Host Routes**: These routes are for specific IPv6 node addresses (i.e., IPv6 hosts) that can be reached directly from the local node. The local node can send traffic directly to each host route corresponding to a 128-bit IPv6 address. The prefix length for host routes is a specific IPv6 address with a prefix length of 128 bits. The prefix lengths for network routes are shorter than 128 bits.
- **Default Route**: An IPv6 node uses a default route when a more specific IPv6 network route or host route is not found. The IPv6 prefix for a default route is ::/0.

1.6.2 IP ROUTE DETERMINATION PROCESS

When an IPv6 node uses the IPv6 routing table directly for packet forwarding (rather than the more optimized IPv6 forwarding table designed for efficient packet forwarding), the node can use the following process to determine which routing table entry to use for forwarding a received IPv6 packet. Note that, unlike the IPv6 forwarding table, which contains the relevant information needed for packet forwarding, the IPv6 routing table is generally bulky and contains information that is not needed for actual packet forwarding (e.g., routing metrics, Administrative Distances).

Because of the variable-length IP prefixes used in modern networks, IP nodes employ the longest prefix matching (LPM) search method to identify the best entry in the IP routing or forwarding table for forwarding a packet. The LPM method requires the IP node to find the entry in the routing or forwarding table that has the longest prefix matching the destination IP address of the received packet and forward the packet to the next-hop node corresponding to that matching entry. The entry with the longest prefix length is the most specific destination among all entries that may match the destination IP address of the received packet.

LPM is the process of determining which IP prefix (if any) in a set of IP prefixes covers a target IP address. A target IP address is covered by an IP prefix if all the bits in the IP prefix match the left-most bits of the target IP address. When multiple IP prefixes cover an IP address, the longest prefix is the one that matches and covers the most bits in the target IP address. Both IPv4 and IPv6 routing table searches use LPM since routing entries rely on VLSM and CIDR. IPv4 has not used classful addressing for several decades; only classless addressing based on VLSM and CIDR is in use.

LPM search works for both exact (full-length) IP address matches (32- or 128-bit addresses) and prefixes with variable lengths (less than 32 or 128 bits) in the routing or forwarding table. LPM treats all addresses as potentially having prefix lengths of up to 32 bits (in IPv4) or 128 bits (in IPv6) and makes no assumptions about the length of prefixes in the routing or forwarding table. Note that exact matching is a special case of LPM where the entry has a full prefix length of 32 or 128 bits.

- For exact matches, the IP node searches through each entry in the routing/forwarding table, comparing the bits in the entry's 32- or 128-bit network prefix to the corresponding bits in the destination IP address of the received IP packet. If all the bits in the entry's network prefix match all the bits in the destination IPv6 address, the entry is a match for the destination (a directly attached host). A host route is one that matches the entire destination IP address (a route with a 32- or 128-bit prefix length).
- For variable-length prefixes, the IP node chooses the route that has the longest prefix length (i.e., the route that matches the most high-order bits with the destination IPv6 address of the received packet). The longest matching entry provides the most specific route to the destination.

Note that an IP node may populate its routing table with multiple entries when multiple routes exist to a given destination. If the node finds multiple entries with the same network prefix but from different routing information sources (Figure 1.5), the node selects the route with the lowest Administrative Distance (also called *Route Preference*) as the best route. A node may perform *ECMP routing* to a destination if multiple equal-cost routes exist to that destination. An IP node may use ECMP routing when a routing protocol (e.g., RIP and OSPF) determines that there are multiple equal-cost routes to a given destination and the node decides to perform load sharing over those routes. In this case, the node installs all of these multiple routes in its routing table, each with its outgoing interface and next-hop, but all routes leading to that particular destination.

At the end of the route determination process for a received packet, the IP node selects a route and its corresponding outgoing interface and next-hop address for forwarding the packet. If the IPv6 route determination process on an IPv6 router fails to find a route for a packet's destination, the router sends an ICMPv6 Destination Unreachable (Type 1) message indicating "No Route To Destination" (Code 0) to the packet's source and discards the packet.

The IP route selection process for entering routes in the routing table can be summarized as follows:

- Each routing protocol uses its own routing metric to select the best route to a particular destination network, and that route is marked as a candidate for installation in the routing table by that specific routing protocol.
- When multiple routing protocols (i.e., routing information sources) present different best routes to a particular destination, the route with the lowest Administrative Distance value is selected for installation in the routing table. This means the routing table contains routes that have qualified as best routes within a routing protocol and have subsequently qualified as best routes based on the Administrative Distance values.
- Once the routing table entries are created on a router, the next step is to perform a LPM search to determine the best matching entry along with its outgoing interface and next-hop each time an IPv6 packet is received. For each packet, the router parses the packet's destination IPv6 address and searches the routing table for the best entry and its corresponding outgoing interface and next-hop to forward the packet. Note that the router has already imported the best routes into the routing table according to the best routing metric and Administrative Distance values. The routing table is continuously updated to reflect any changes in the network topology.

Chapter 2 discusses in detail the operations that a router performs on a packet before forwarding it on an interface to the next-hop.

1.7   THE IP FORWARDING TABLE

The IP forwarding table (also called the forwarding information base (FIB)) is generated from the IP routing table **[AWEYFCDM22]**. It contains the same routing information but is structured in a compact and optimized format to facilitate actual packet forwarding. Anytime there is a routing or network topology change, the routing protocol updates the routing table, and those changes are then reflected in the forwarding table. The router updates the forwarding table when one of the following occurs: the routing table entry for a network prefix changes or is removed; the routing table entry for the next hop changes or is removed; or the address resolution cache entry for the next hop times out, changes, or is removed.

The routing and forwarding tables contain essentially the same information needed for packet forwarding; the forwarding table merely removes information that is not directly relevant for packet forwarding (e.g., the routing metric associated with a route is not listed in the forwarding table). Due to the use of VLSM and CIDR, the address prefixes in the RIB and FIB can be of variable lengths (i.e., they can contain classless addresses). This means that address lookups in the RIB and FIB are based on LPM instead of exact matching. Note that the FIB does not contain recursive routes (and consequently does not require recursive lookups) because all recursive routes in the RIB are resolved before they are installed in the FIB.

1.8 MAPPING NETWORK DEVICE FUNCTIONS TO THE OSI AND TCP/IP REFERENCE MODELS

Network reference models (i.e., the Open Systems Interconnection (OSI) reference model **[ISO7498:1984]** and TCP/IP reference model **[DoDARCHM83]**) break down the tasks involved in exchanging information between communicating entities in a network into smaller, more manageable groups or modules called *layers*. A task or group of tasks is assigned to each layer. Each layer is designed to be reasonably self-contained so that the tasks (i.e., network functions) assigned to it can be implemented independently without being constrained by the other layers. This allows the services offered by any one layer in the model to be updated or modified without adversely affecting the other layers.

This section discusses various network devices (repeaters, also called hubs; Ethernet switches; routers; switch/routers; web, or content, switches; and IP hosts) according to the OSI and TCP/IP layers they support and operate at (see Figure 1.6). Hubs and repeaters are used interchangeably, similar to bridges and switches.

Traditionally, the networking industry has categorized network devices such as hubs (repeaters), bridges (or switches), and routers by the OSI or TCP/IP layer at which they operate and the role they play in a network.

1.8.1 REPEATERS OR HUBS

A repeater, commonly called a hub, allows multiple end-user devices to connect to the same physical LAN segment. It is a device for connecting multiple Ethernet devices together, making them act as a single physical LAN segment. The devices on that segment share the total available bandwidth among themselves. A hub is considered a Layer 1 (Physical Layer) device in reference to the OSI model (Figure 1.6).

A hub senses the electrical signal (on the wire attached to a port) on the LAN segment it is connected to and propagates this signal to the other ports. A hub has multiple input/output ports, such that a signal introduced at the input of any port appears at the output of every port except the original source port. Ethernet hubs also participate in Ethernet collision detection, allowing a hub to forward a jam signal to all other ports if it detects a media access collision.

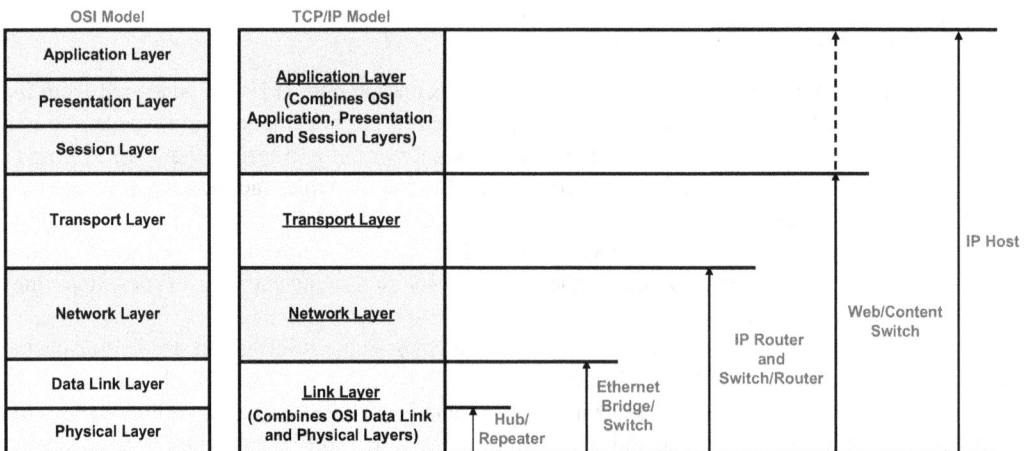

FIGURE 1.6 Layers covered by network devices in the OSI and TCP/IP reference models.

A multiport hub works by repeating bits received from one of its ports to all other ports. It can detect Physical Layer "packet" start (preamble) signals, idle line (interpacket gap) signals, and sense access collisions, which it also propagates to other ports by sending a jam signal. A hub cannot further examine or manage any of the traffic that comes through it – any packet entering any port is rebroadcast on all other ports. Essentially, a repeater provides signal regeneration by detecting a signal on an incoming port, cleaning up and restoring this signal to its original shape and amplitude, and then retransmitting (i.e., repeating) this restored signal on all ports except the port on which the signal was received.

The simple hub/repeater has no memory in which to store any data – a packet must be transmitted while it is received or is lost when a collision occurs (the sender should detect this and retry the transmission). Due to this property, hubs can only operate in half-duplex mode. Consequently, because of the larger collision domain they create, packet collisions are more frequent in networks connected using hubs than in networks connected using more sophisticated devices like bridges or switches. A network built using switches does not have these limitations. Hubs are now largely obsolete, having been replaced by network bridges (switches).

1.8.2 BRIDGES AND SWITCHES

Bridges and switches operate at the Link Layer and are used for forwarding traffic within LANs or virtual LANs (VLANs). Traditionally, they forward traffic based on Link Layer addresses. Bridges and switches, along with the LAN protocols they run, operate at the Physical and Data Link layers of the OSI model and provide communication over different LAN media (copper and fiber).

Bridges, developed to address the limitations of hubs, can physically replace hubs in a network. The terms "bridge" and "switch" are used interchangeably in many parts of this chapter and the rest of the book. A bridge allows multiple devices to connect to the same network, similar to a hub. However, a bridge enables each connected device to have dedicated bandwidth instead of shared bandwidth. The bandwidth between the bridge and each connected device is reserved for communication to and from that device alone.

An Ethernet LAN is traditionally implemented as a broadcast domain. This means all hosts connected to the LAN will receive all broadcast transmissions sent on the LAN. Each host uses the destination MAC address of the Ethernet frame to determine which frame it should receive and process. Hosts (i.e., end-systems) learn the MAC addresses on a LAN segment through the ARP [RFC826], while bridges learn and filter MAC addresses dynamically.

Unlike a hub, a bridge can greatly increase the available bandwidth in the network, leading to improved network performance. A hub simply passes electrical signals along to other ports, while a bridge assembles the signals (bits) into a Layer 2 frame and then decides how to forward the frame. After determining how to forward a received frame, the bridge forwards the frame out the appropriate port(s).

Bridging is the simplest and earliest form of packet forwarding in LANs. Bridges operate at the Data Link Layer of the OSI network model (see Figure 1.6) but also support the Physical Layer. They make address learning, filtering, and forwarding decisions based on the MAC address information carried in Ethernet frames. By reading the source MAC address for each packet received on a port, bridges learn where users are located on the network. The MAC address-to-port correlation is stored in a local address table for future reference. This *Layer 2 forwarding table* is also referred to as the *Filtering Database* or *MAC address table*.

1.8.3 ROUTERS

Routers operate at the Network (IP) Layer but also support the OSI Data Link and Physical Layers. They perform route calculations and packet forwarding based on Network Layer (IP) addresses. Routers are used for interconnecting separate IP subnets (or VLANs) and routing packets across internetworks in a hop-by-hop manner. Note that the layers in an IP router encompass the lower layers, but the Network Layer is the router's main operating layer. Similarly, an IP host encompasses all layers of the TCP/IP model, but the Transport and Application Layers are the host's main operating layers.

Routing was designed to remedy many of the earlier problems associated with bridges and switches. By operating at Layer 3 or the Network Layer of the OSI network model (Figure 1.6), routers can constrain the propagation of broadcast traffic and support advanced networking features, such as those for network security. The Network Layer uses a hierarchical and logical addressing scheme and routing protocols to divide a network into smaller broadcast domains (subnets or VLANs) that are interconnected by routers. Routers do not forward or propagate broadcast traffic from one broadcast domain to another, allowing network operators to create more manageable networks. As a result, the forwarding logic of a router is much more complex than that of a bridge.

The relatively more complex decision-making functions supported by routers provide increased network design flexibility compared to using only bridges. However, those superior capabilities tend to make a typical router much more expensive than a bridge of equal performance. Routers run routing protocols that specify how routers in a network communicate with each other to disseminate information about the network topology and conditions, as well as how packets are to be routed to their destinations. The routing protocols have built-in algorithms that allow routers to determine the best routes to network destinations. Using a routing protocol, a router shares routing information first with its immediate neighbors, and this information is then propagated to other routers in the network. Essentially, routing protocols allow routers to gain knowledge of the network's topology and prevailing conditions.

An IP router performs a lookup of the IP destination address of each incoming packet in its forwarding table (also called the FIB) to determine the IP address of the next-hop node and outbound interface, and then forwards the packet through that interface on its way to the final destination. This process is performed on the packet by every other router on the forwarding path from the source node to the destination. The two parameters of next-hop IP address and outbound interface at each router determine the path a packet takes through a network to its final destination.

The adoption of CIDR **[RFC4632]** means that a routing lookup must perform a longest prefix match (LPM) search in the forwarding table. A router maintains a set of IP destination address prefixes (of variable length) in its forwarding table, each associated with a next-hop IP address and outbound interface (along with possibly other important information). For each arriving packet, the LPM search involves finding the longest prefix in the forwarding table that matches the higher-order contiguous set of bits of the packet's IP destination address, as discussed above.

1.8.4 SWITCH/ROUTERS: INTEGRATED ROUTING AND SWITCHING DEVICES

A switch/router (also called a multilayer switch) is the integration of traditional Link-Layer switching of the bridge and the Network Layer routing and forwarding capabilities of the router into a single product, usually through a hardware implementation to enable high-speed packet forwarding. Switch/routers or multilayer switches implement both Layer 2 and Layer 3 functionalities; the functions of an Ethernet switch and a router are combined on a single platform (Figure 1.6).

The high-end, high-performance switch/router, for example, combines the functionality of a full-featured Layer 2 switch with that of an Internet core router. In addition to having switching and forwarding functionalities (including high packet processing capacity, port density, and redundancy features), the high-end switch/router typically supports comprehensive routing functionality required for Internet core routing.

By providing fully integrated switching and routing functionality on every port, switch/routers offer great network design flexibility and can be deployed in the access, aggregation, and core layers of any multi-tiered network architecture. Many switch/router vendors now offer a diverse range of platforms that meet the requirements of Layer 2/Layer 3 edge, aggregation, or small-network backbone connectivity. These devices typically support intelligent QoS and security features, provide predictable performance, and offer comprehensive management tools and integrated resiliency features. Integrating Layer 2 switching and routing in a single device simplifies the network topology by reducing the number of systems and network interfaces in multi-tiered network designs compared to a network designed with standalone bridges and routers.

1.8.5 WEB OR CONTENT SWITCHES

Today's data centers are expanding as demand for data and storage continues to grow exponentially. Moreover, requirements such as application hosting, non-stop operation, scalability, high availability, and power efficiency are placing even greater demands on the network infrastructure. To meet this challenge, today's data center network solutions provide a broad set of capabilities, including higher levels of performance, reliability, security, and QoS, as well as a low total cost of ownership.

A switch/router operates at both Layers 2 and 3, performing the functions of a LAN switch and router on one chassis. Web/content switches (also called Layer 4+ switches) refer to network devices that make various traffic handling decisions based on OSI Layer 4 (the Transport Layer) information and above in packets (Figure 1.6), where the end-station application is identified via the TCP or UDP port numbers. Layer 4 switching broadly refers to capabilities that augment the Layer 2 and 3 functions of a network device, rather than a new type of switching. Web/content switches use detailed "application-level" information beyond the traditional Layer 2 and 3 packet headers, directing client requests to the most available servers. They are sometimes referred to as content service switches or application switches.

More sophisticated (Layer 4–7) application switches support TCP- or UDP-based switching as well as specialized acceleration, content caching, firewall load balancing, network optimization, and host offload features for Web services. Web/content switches provide efficient traffic distribution among infrastructure devices such as firewalls, DNS servers, and cache servers. They also offer a reliable line of defense by securing servers and applications against various types of intrusion and attack without sacrificing performance. Most Web/content switches forward traffic flows based on Layer 4–7 definitions and provide high performance for higher-layer application switching functions. Sophisticated content switching capabilities include customizable rules based on Uniform Resource Locator (URL) and other HTTP headers, as well as cookies, Extensible Markup Language (XML), and application content.

Web/content switches may support many advanced features (integrated functionality) as stand-alone devices. For example, server load balancing, Secure Sockets Layer (SSL) termination/ acceleration, Virtual Private Network (VPN) termination, firewall, and packet filtering functionality may be integrated within a single device, reducing the number of devices while improving reliability and manageability in a data center.

Furthermore, Web/content switches may provide hardware-assisted, standards-based network monitoring for all application traffic flows, enhancing manageability and security for network and server resources. To enable real-time problem detection and troubleshooting, extensive and customizable service health check capabilities can monitor Layer 2–7 connectivity along with service availability and server response. If a problem arises, client requests can be automatically redistributed to other servers capable of delivering optimal service. This approach helps keep applications running smoothly.

To optimize application availability, Web/content switches may also support many high-availability options, using real-time session synchronization between two Web/content switches to protect against session loss during outages. As one device shuts down, the second device transparently resumes control of client traffic with no loss of existing sessions or connectivity. Organizations can use advanced synchronization capabilities to simplify managing two Web/content switches deployed in high-availability mode, minimizing network downtime caused by configuration errors.

REVIEW QUESTIONS

1.1. List four main limitations of IPv4.
1.2. List four main distinguishing features of IPv6.
1.3. What is an IP subnet or VLAN?
1.4. What is IP routing?
1.5. What is a dynamic routing protocol?
1.6. What is an IP routing table?
1.7. What is an IP forwarding table?
1.8. What is a directly connected network in IP routing?
1.9. What is a static route in IP routing?
1.10. What is the difference between an Interior Gateway Routing Protocol (IGP) and an Exterior Gateway Routing Protocol (EGP)?
1.11. What is a routing metric in IP routing?
1.12. What is equal-cost multipath (ECMP) routing in IP routing?
1.13. What is the purpose of the Administrative Distance (also called the Route Preference) in IP routing?
1.14. What are the basic characteristics of a distance-vector routing protocol?
1.15. What are the basic characteristics of a link-state routing protocol?
1.16. What are the basic characteristics of a path-vector routing protocol?
1.17. What is the purpose of the next-hop address in the IP routing table?
1.18. What is the purpose of the next-hop interface in the IP routing table?
1.19. What are directly attached network routes?
1.20. What are remote network routes?
1.21. What are host routes?
1.22. What is a default route?
1.23. What is a longest prefix matching (LPM) search in the IP routing table?
1.24. What is the main operating layer in the OSI model for a hub (or repeater)?
1.25. What is the main operating layer in the OSI model for a bridge (or switch)?
1.26. What are the characteristics of an IP router?
1.27. What are the characteristics of a switch/router?
1.28. What are the characteristics of a web/content switch?

REFERENCES

[AWE2BK21V1]. J. Aweya, *IP Routing Protocols: Fundamentals and Distance Vector Routing Protocols*, CRC Press, Taylor & Francis Group, ISBN 9780367710415, 2021.

[AWE2BK21V2]. J. Aweya, *IP Routing Protocols: Link-State and Path-Vector Routing Protocols*, CRC Press, Taylor & Francis Group, ISBN 9780367710361, 2021.

[AWEYFCDM22]. J. Aweya, *Designing Switch/Routers: Fundamental Concepts and Design Methods*, CRC Press, Taylor & Francis Group, ISBN 9781032317694, October 2022.

[DoDARCHM83]. V. G. Cerf and E. Cain, "The DoD Internet Architecture Model", *Computer Networks*, Vol. 7, pp. 307–318, 1983.

[IEEE802.3.2022]. IEEE 802.3–2022, IEEE Standard for Ethernet.

[ISO10589#: 2002]. ISO/IEC 10589:2002, "Information technology – Telecommunications and Information Exchange between Systems – Intermediate System to Intermediate System Intra-Domain Routing Information Exchange Protocol for use in Conjunction with the Protocol for Providing the Connectionless-Mode Network Service (ISO 8473)", International Organization for Standardization (ISO), November 2002.

[ISO7498#: 1984]. ISO 7498:1984, "Information Processing Systems – Open Systems Interconnection – Basic Reference Model", October 1984.

[RFC792]. J. Postel, "Internet Control Message Protocol", *IETF RFC 792*, September 1981.

[RFC826].   D. C. Plummer, "An Ethernet Address Resolution Protocol", *IETF RFC 826*, November 1982.

[RFC1195].   R. Callon, "Use of OSI IS-IS for Routing in TCP/IP and Dual Environments", *IETF RFC 1195*, December 1990.

[RFC1256].   S. Deering, Ed., "ICMP Router Discovery Messages", *IETF RFC 1256*, September 1991

[RFC1517].   R. Hinden, Ed., "Applicability Statement for the Implementation of Classless Inter-Domain Routing (CIDR)", *IETF RFC 1517*, September 1993.

[RFC1518].   Y. Rekhter and T. Li, "An Architecture for IP Address Allocation with CIDR", *IETF RFC 1518*, September 1993.

[RFC1519].   V. Fuller, T. Li, J. Yu, and K. Varadhan, "Classless Inter-Domain Routing (CIDR): An Address Assignment and Aggregation Strategy", *IETF RFC 1519*, September 1993.

[RFC1878].   T. Pummill and B. Manning, "Variable Length Subnet Table for IPv4", *IETF RFC 1878*, December 1995.

[RFC2080].   G. Malkin and R. Minnear, "RIPng for IPv6", *IETF RFC 2080*, January 1997.

[RFC2131].   R. Droms, "Dynamic Host Configuration Protocol", *IETF RFC 2131*, March 1997.

[RFC2236].   W. Fenner, "Internet Group Management Protocol, Version 2", *IETF RFC 2236*, November 1997.

[RFC2328].   J. Moy, "OSPF Version 2", *IETF RFC 2328*, April 1998.

[RFC2453].   G. Malkin, "RIP Version 2", *IETF RFC 2453*, November 1998.

[RFC2663].   P. Srisuresh and M. Holdrege, "IP Network Address Translator (NAT) Terminology and Considerations", *IETF RFC 2663*, August 1999.

[RFC2710].   S. Deering, W. Fenner, and B. Haberman, "Multicast Listener Discovery (MLD) for IPv6", *IETF RFC 2710*, October 1999.

[RFC3376].   B. Cain, S. Deering, I. Kouvelas, B. Fenner, and A. Thyagarajan, "Internet Group Management Protocol, Version 3", *IETF RFC 3376*, October 2002.

[RFC3810].   R. Vida and L. Costa, "Multicast Listener Discovery Version 2 (MLDv2) for IPv6", *IETF RFC 3810*, June 2004.

[RFC4271].   Y. Rekhter, T. Li, and S. Hares, Eds., "A Border Gateway Protocol 4 (BGP-4)", *IETF RFC 4271*, January 2006.

[RFC4291].   R. Hinden and S. Deering, "IP Version 6 Addressing Architecture", *IETF RFC 4291*, February 2006.

[RFC4301].   S. Kent and K. Seo, "Security Architecture for the Internet Protocol", *IETF RFC 4301*, December 2005.

[RFC4443].   A. Conta, S. Deering, and M. Gupta, Ed., "Internet Control Message Protocol (ICMPv6) for the Internet Protocol Version 6 (IPv6) Specification", *IETF RFC 4443*, March 2006.

[RFC4632].   V. Fuller and T. Li, "Classless Inter-Domain Routing (CIDR): The Internet Address Assignment and Aggregation Plan", *IETF RFC 4632*, August 2006.

[RFC4760].   T. Bates, R. Chandra, D. Katz, and Y. Rekhter, "Multiprotocol Extensions for BGP-4", *IETF RFC 4760*, January 2007.

[RFC4861].   T. Narten, E. Nordmark, W. Simpson, and H. Soliman, "Neighbor Discovery for IP version 6 (IPv6)", *IETF RFC 4861*, September 2007.

[RFC4862].   S. Thomson, T. Narten, and T. Jinmei, "IPv6 Stateless Address Autoconfiguration", *IETF RFC 4862*, September 2007.

[RFC5308].   C. Hopps, "Routing IPv6 with IS-IS", *IETF RFC 5308*, October 2008.

[RFC5340].   R. Coltun, D. Ferguson, J. Moy, and A. Lindem, Eds., "OSPF for IPv6", *IETF RFC 5340*, July 2008.

[RFC7868].   D. Savage, J. Ng, S. Moore, D. Slice, P. Paluch, and R. White, "Cisco's Enhanced Interior Gateway Routing Protocol (EIGRP)", *IETF RFC 7868*, May 2016.

[RFC8200].   S. Deering and R. Hinden, "Internet Protocol, Version 6 (IPv6) Specification", *IETF RFC 8200*, July 2017.

[RFC8415].   T. Mrugalski, M. Siodelski, B. Volz, A. Yourtchenko, M. Richardson, S. Jiang, T. Lemon, and T. Winters, "Dynamic Host Configuration Protocol for IPv6 (DHCPv6)", *IETF RFC 8415*, November 2018.

2 IPv6 Packet Format and Related Data Structures

2.1 INTRODUCTION

IPv6 was designed to support a 128-bit address length, four times larger than the 32-bit IPv4 address length [RFC4291] [RFC8200]. This change also meant that many protocols and network functions, such as routing protocols, had to undergo a number of changes to accommodate the 128-bit IPv6 address length. For example, routing protocols need to understand IP addresses and include them in routing updates and other messages that they exchange.

This chapter describes the IPv6 packet, the IPv6 header, the fields in the IPv4 header, a comparison between the fields in the IPv6 header and those in the IPv4 header, the IPv6 extension headers, the IPv6 Maximum Transmission Unit (MTU), and the IPv6 pseudo-header used for upper-layer checksum computation. A good understanding of the IPv6 packet format and addressing architecture (discussed in the next chapter) helps to provide a proper context for the IPv6 functions discussed in this book. We discuss IPv4 in greater detail in **Appendix B**.

2.2 IPv6 HEADER

Just like IPv4 packets, IPv6 packets are carried in Link-Layer packets (or frames) such as Ethernet, as shown in Figure 2.1. Ethernet has become the de facto Link-Layer protocol in today's networks. The Ethernet frame header has a 16-bit EtherType field that identifies the payload type and data carried in the Ethernet frame (see the **Ethernet Frame discussion in Appendix A**). The EtherType field identifies the protocol data in the Ethernet frame's payload portion. The EtherType value in the Ethernet frame header for IPv6 is 0x86DD (in hexadecimal), which indicates that the frame's payload is an IPv6 packet. The EtherType value for IPv4 is 0x0800, indicating that the frame carries an IPv4 packet. An EtherType value of 0x0806 indicates that the frame contains an Address Resolution Protocol (ARP) packet [RFC826].

An IPv6 packet consists of a fixed (basic) IPv6 header, zero or more IPv6 extension headers, and an upper-layer protocol data unit (PDU) [RFC8200]. Figure 2.1 also depicts the basic structure of an IPv6 packet. Note that the IPv6 extension headers and the upper-layer PDU combined constitute the payload of an IPv6 packet. Every IPv6 packet contains the fixed (basic) IPv6 header, which has a length of 40 bytes, as shown in Figure 2.2. The fixed IPv6 header has fewer fields compared to the IPv4 header, allowing routers to process and forward IPv6 packets more efficiently and quickly. Another significant advantage is that the fixed IPv6 header length of 40 bytes provides predictable header processing, compared to the variable-length IPv4 header that may contain IPv4 Options.

An IPv4 packet has an IPv4 header and possibly zero or more Options (Figure 2.3). The IPv6 header and extension headers were defined to replace some of the IPv4 header fields and all Options. The IPv6 extension headers allow IPv6 to support capabilities more flexibly, well beyond those supported in IPv4. Unlike the IPv4 header Options, the IPv6 extension headers have no maximum size limitations, allowing an IPv6 packet to extend in size to accommodate as much extension data as needed for IPv6 communication.

An IPv6 packet can carry zero or more IP extension headers, each of varying length. If a packet contains IPv6 extension headers, the Next Header field in the fixed (basic) IPv6 header indicates the type of IPv6 extension header immediately following it, specifically the first IPv6 extension header (Figure 2.2). Each subsequent extension header also contains a local Next Header field that

DOI: 10.1201/9781003710646-2

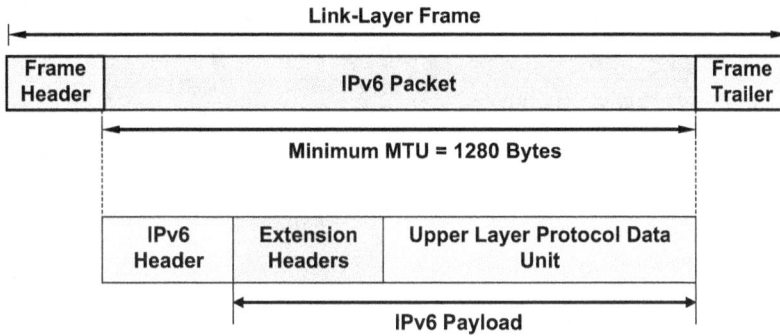

FIGURE 2.1 IPv6 packet carried by a Link-Layer frame.

points to the next IPv6 extension header. The Next Header field in the last IPv6 extension header of the IPv6 packet indicates the header of the upper-layer PDU (e.g., User Datagram Protocol (UDP), Transmission Control Protocol (TCP), Internet Control Message Protocol for version 6 (ICMPv6)). The code 59 (in decimal), when found in the Next Header field of the fixed IPv6 header or any extension header, signifies that there is no further data following that header (i.e., the node currently processing that IPv6 packet should disregard any additional information beyond that header).

An upper-layer PDU (e.g., TCP segment, UDP datagram, ICMPv6 message) typically consists of an upper-layer protocol header and its payload. As shown in Figure 2.1, the IPv6 extension headers and the upper-layer PDU combined make up the payload of the IPv6 packet **[RFC8200]**. In normal communication, the IPv6 payload can have a length of up to 65,535 bytes. However, in some cases, IPv6 packets known as *Jumbograms* can carry payloads larger than 65,535 bytes.

2.3 IPv4 HEADER

This section reviews the structure of the IPv4 header (Figure 2.3). This allows us to examine the changes made to the IPv4 header to obtain the IPv6 header and extension headers. By contrasting these two headers, we can better appreciate the rationale behind the design of the IPv6 header. Additional aspects of IPv4 are discussed in detail in **Appendix B**.

The value in the 4-bit Internet Header Length (IHL) field indicates the number of 4-byte (32-bit) blocks (not including padding bytes) that make up the IPv4 header. Given that the IPv4 header has a minimum length of 20 bytes, the smallest value that can be written in the IHL field is 5. The presence of IPv4 Options extends the minimum IPv4 header size in 4-byte block increments. If the IPv4 header carries an IPv4 Option with a length that is not an integral multiple of 4 bytes, the IPv4 header is padded with redundant bytes of all 0s (or padding bytes), making the entire IPv4 header an integral multiple of 4 bytes. With a maximum IHL field value of 1111 (binary), equivalent to 15 (decimal) or 0xF (hexadecimal), the maximum size of the IPv4 header, including all IPv4 Options, is 60 bytes (i.e., 15×4 bytes).

The DSCP and ECN fields combined (8 bits) were called the Type of Service (ToS) field **[RFC791]**. The ToS field was used to indicate the service (i.e., precedence, delay, throughput, reliability, and cost) expected by the IPv4 packet as it is forwarded across the IPv4 network to its destination. The DSCP and ECN fields combined are also referred to as the Differentiated Services (DS) field **[RFC2474] [RFC2475]**. The high-order 6-bit DS Code Point (DSCP) field is used to indicate to network devices on the packet forwarding path how to classify, queue, mark, and remark the current packet as it is being forwarded. Originally, only the first 3 bits of the IPv4 ToS field were used as a class-of-service field called IP Precedence, which was later superseded by the DSCP field.

The low-order 2-bit Explicit Congestion Notification (ECN) field **[RFC3168]** enables network devices to send notifications of network congestion to end devices, allowing them to react and send

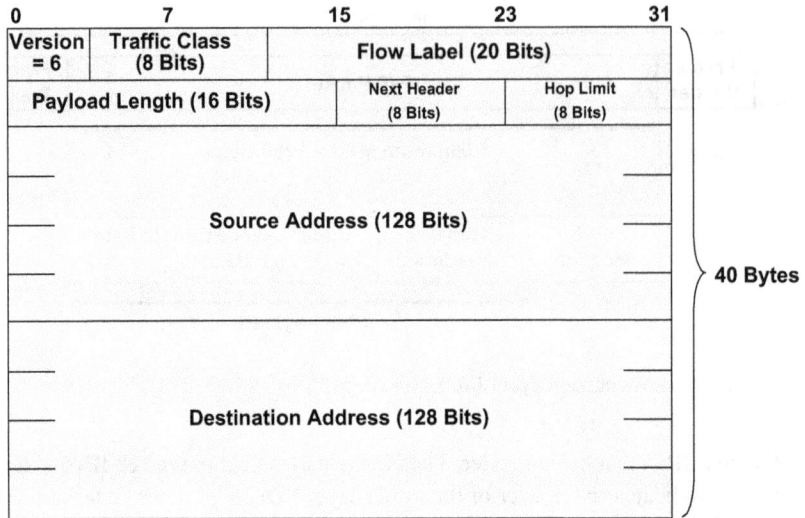

```
0              7              15             23             31
┌────────┬──────────────┬──────────────────────────────────┐ ╲
│Version │ Traffic Class│      Flow Label (20 Bits)         │  ╲
│  = 6   │   (8 Bits)   │                                   │   ╲
├────────┴──────────────┼───────────────┬──────────────────┤    ╲
│  Payload Length (16 Bits)│ Next Header │   Hop Limit      │     ╲
│                        │   (8 Bits)    │    (8 Bits)      │
├────────────────────────┴───────────────┴──────────────────┤
│                                                            │
│              Source Address (128 Bits)                     │  ┬ 40 Bytes
│                                                            │
│                                                            │
├────────────────────────────────────────────────────────────┤
│                                                            │
│           Destination Address (128 Bits)                   │
│                                                            │
│                                                            │
└────────────────────────────────────────────────────────────┘ ╱
```

- **Version (4 Bits)** : This indicates the version of IP which is 6. The version number for IPv4 is 4.

- **Traffic Class (8 Bits)** : This field is used in the network for traffic management purposes, for example, for Differentiated Services (DiffServ) and Explicit Congestion Notification (ECN).

- **Flow Label (20 Bits)** : This field is used by a source to label a sequence of packets so that they can be treated in the network as a single flow.

- **Payload Length (16 Bits)** : This field specifies the length of the IPv6 payload (in bytes), which is the length of the rest of the packet following the fixed IPv6 header. Note that any IPv6 extension headers that are present in the packet are considered part of the payload (i.e., they are included in the length count).

- **Next Header (8 Bits)** : This identifies either the first extension header type (if present) or the protocol in the upper-layer PDU (such as TCP, UDP, IGMP, OSPFv6 or ICMPv6) immediately following the fixed IPv6 header. The values/codes carried in this field are the same values as those used in the IPv4 packet Protocol field to indicate an upper-layer protocol.

- **Hop Limit (8 Bits)** : This indicates the maximum number of routing node over which the IPv6 packet can travel before being considered invalid and discarded. The value in this field is decremented by 1 by each routing node that forwards the packet. When a packet is to be forwarded by a node and the received Hop Limit value is already 0 or is decremented to 0, then the packet is discarded. A node that is the final destination of a packet should not discard a packet with Hop Limit value equal to 0; they node should process the packet normally.

- **Source Address (128 Bits)** : This field carries the Network Layer address of the originator of the IPv6 packet.

- **Destination Address (128 Bit)** : This field carries the Network Layer address of the intended recipient of the IPv6 packet. This recipient may not be the ultimate recipient of the packet, if a Routing header is present in the IPv6 header.

FIGURE 2.2   IPv6 header format – fixed header.

traffic without significant dropping of packets. ECN is an optional feature and is only used when the underlying network infrastructure (routers and switch/routers) supports it. It is normally used between two ECN-enabled endpoints communicating over an ECN-enabled network.

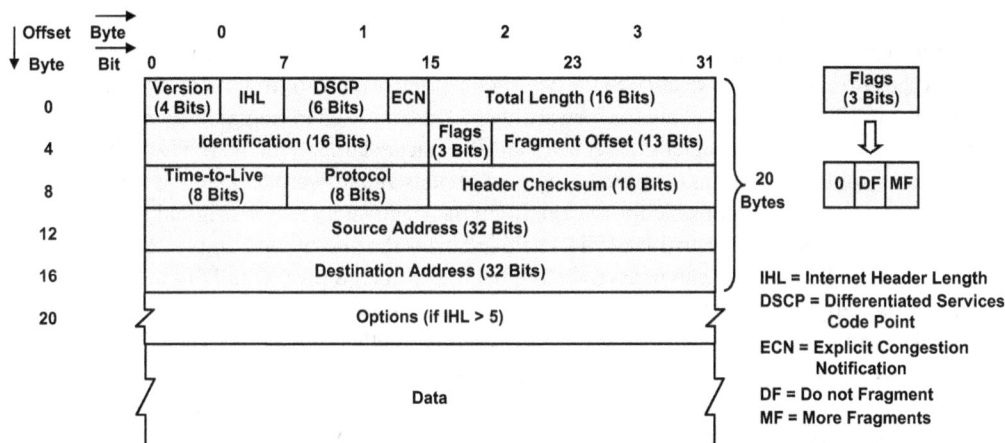

FIGURE 2.3 Changes made in the IPv4 header to obtain the IPv6 header.

The value in the 16-bit Total Length field indicates the total length (in bytes) of the entire IPv4 packet. This field specifies the total number of bytes that make up the IPv4 header plus the IPv4 payload, but it does not include the overhead of the Link-Layer frame (e.g., Ethernet header and trailer). This 16-bit field indicates that an IPv4 packet can be up to 65,535 bytes long. In reality, most IPv4 and IPv6 packets are limited to 1,500 bytes because network links/interfaces have an MTU that defines the maximum size of a packet that can be accepted and processed on a link/interface.

The value in the 16-bit Identification field identifies the specific IPv4 packet associated with that value. The sender of the IPv4 packet selects the value written in the Identification field when sending the packet. If the IPv4 packet undergoes fragmentation, each fragment carries the same Identification field value, allowing the destination node to reassemble the group of fragments belonging to the same IPv4 packet.

The 3-bit Flags field contains Flags that are used in the IPv4 packet fragmentation process (see Figure 2.3). Out of the two main Flags (DF and MF), the DF Flag indicates whether an IPv4 packet can be fragmented, while the MF Flag indicates whether more fragments of a particular packet follow the current fragment. The value in the 13-bit Fragment Offset field indicates the position (or offset) of the current fragment relative to the beginning of the original (unfragmented) IPv4 payload.

Note that in IPv4, all nodes along the forwarding path are allowed to fragment IPv4 packets if the DF bit is not set (i.e., is 0). A router that receives an IPv4 packet larger than the MTU of the outgoing interface may split the packet into multiple fragment packets and forward them to the next node. The final destination is then responsible for reassembling the fragments into the original IPv4 packet.

The value in the 8-bit Time-to-Live (TTL) field indicates the maximum number of routing nodes (or hops) that the IPv4 packet can traverse before being considered invalid and discarded. The TTL field was originally defined as a lifetime value that indicates the maximum number of seconds the IPv4 packet can exist on the network. Using the lifetime method, an IPv4 router determines the length of time the IPv4 packet has spent in the router (i.e., the residence time) and then decrements the TTL value accordingly.

Measuring the residence time of each packet as it traverses a router introduces additional complexity in the design of routers. Therefore, the TTL field was redefined as a hop count field; this approach has been in use for many years. Modern routers forward IPv4 packets much faster, in less than a second, and therefore decrement the TTL based on hop count, that is, by one at each routing node. The initial TTL field value, redefined as a maximum hop count value, is set by the sending node. Using this method, when the TTL reaches 0 at a routing node, that node sends an ICMPv4 "Time to Live Exceeded in Transit" message to the source of the IPv4 packet and then discards the packet. The default value of the TTL is 255.

The value in the 8-bit Protocol field identifies the type of upper-layer protocol and the data carried in the IPv4 packet. This field identifies the upper-layer protocol that is to receive the payload of the IPv4 packet at its final destination. For example, the upper-layer protocol TCP is identified by a decimal value of 6 in this field, while UDP is identified by a value of 17. A value of 1 identifies ICMPv4.

The 16-bit Header Checksum field carries a checksum that covers the IPv4 header only. The computation of the checksum does not include the IPv4 payload because the IPv4 packet payload, usually an upper-layer PDU, contains its own checksum. Each IPv4 node that receives an IPv4 packet performs a number of operations, including verifying the IPv4 header checksum. The IPv4 packet is silently discarded if checksum verification fails (i.e., if checksum errors occur). Before forwarding an IPv4 packet, a router must decrement the TTL field value. This means the router must also recompute the Header Checksum value after decrementing the TTL value. Each node along the forwarding path uses a 16-bit cyclic redundancy check (CRC) to recompute and validate each received IPv4 packet.

The variable-size IPv4 Options field carries one or more IPv4 Options. This variable-size field contains Options data that is a multiple of 4 bytes (32 bits). If an IPv4 Option does not fall on a 32-bit boundary, the router adds padding bytes so that the IPv4 header becomes an integral multiple of 4-byte blocks. The IHL field is then set to indicate the actual number of 4-byte blocks in the IPv4 header (not including padding bytes).

2.4   UNDERSTANDING THE IPv6 HEADER FORMAT

The IPv6 header was designed as a more efficient version of the IPv4 header. The new header removed IPv4 fields that are either rarely used or unnecessary. It also added a field (Traffic Class field) that allows IPv6 nodes to support the processing and forwarding of real-time traffic like voice and video more efficiently.

2.4.1   THE IPv6 HEADER FIELDS

The structure of the IPv6 header is shown in Figures 2.2 and 2.4 [RFC8200]. This section discusses the most important features of the IPv6 header fields.

2.4.1.1 The 8-Bit Traffic Class Field

The 8-bit Traffic Class (TC) field may contain a value that indicates the class or priority of the IPv6 packet. The IPv6 TC field provides functionality similar to the ToS or DS field in the IPv4 header. Similar to the ToS or DS field, the upper 6 bits of the TC field are designated as the DSCP field [RFC2474] [RFC2475], and the lower 2 bits are designated as the ECN field, as defined in [RFC3168]. An IPv6 network may use the TC field for traffic management. Note that an IPv6 node may receive an IPv6 packet or fragment with TC bits that differ from the value sent by the source of the packet (possibly due to remarking/remapping of the TC bits by an upstream node).

2.4.1.2 The 20-Bit Flow Label Field

The 20-bit Flow Label field carries a value indicating that the packet belongs to a specific sequence (i.e., flow or stream) of IPv6 packets between the source and destination and may require special handling by intermediate IPv6 processing nodes. An IPv6 source uses the Flow Label field to label a sequence of IPv6 packets so that they can be treated in the network as a single flow. Reference [RFC6437] discusses details of using the IPv6 Flow Label field and the minimum requirements for IPv6 nodes that perform labeling of flows, IPv6 nodes that forward labeled IPv6 packets, and the methods used for flow state establishment. The Flow Label field value allows IPv6 nodes on the forwarding path to prioritize packets of a particular flow, such as prioritizing and forwarding real-time voice and video. The default setting of the Flow Label is 0, meaning routers can forward the IPv6 packet without considering the Flow Label field; the IPv6 packet is not associated with any specific traffic flow.

In some cases, intermediate IPv6 routers can use the source address, destination address, and Flow Label of an IPv6 packet to distinguish a particular flow. This means multiple flows may exist between a source and destination, each flow distinguished by a different (unique) non-zero Flow Label. IPv6 routers use the values in the Flow Label field to distinguish between different traffic flows between the same source and destination. For example, the same source and destination

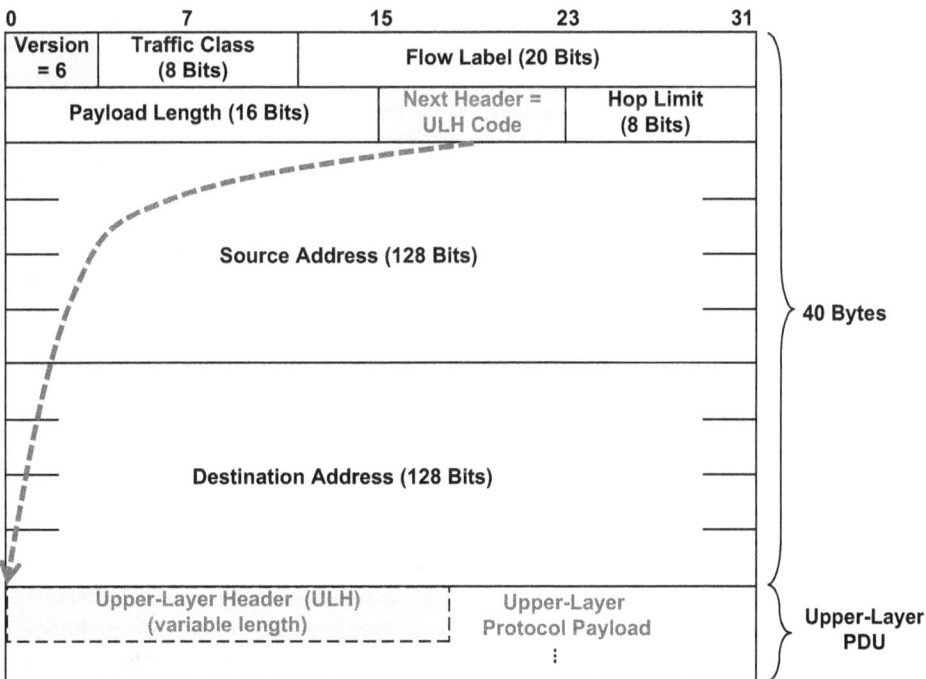

FIGURE 2.4 IPv6 packet without extension header.

may set up different TCP sessions between themselves, each having a different Flow Label value. Reference **[RFC6437]** provides details on how the Flow Label field is used in practice.

2.4.1.3 The 16-Bit Payload Length Field

The 16-bit Payload Length field contains a value indicating the length of the payload of the IPv6 packet (in bytes), which includes all IPv6 extension headers. The value in this field does not include the fixed IPv6 header. The Payload Length field value is computed to include all IPv6 extension headers and the upper-layer PDU carried in the packet. IPv6 considers any included extension headers as part of the payload portion. This 16-bit field allows the IPv6 packet to carry a payload of up to 65,535 bytes (similar to the IPv4 packet payload). When the IPv6 packet carries a payload greater than 65,535 bytes, then its Payload Length field is set to 0, and the IPv6 Jumbo Payload Option (with Option Type 194) is included in the IPv6 Hop-by-Hop Options extension header (extension header type 0).

2.4.1.4 The 8-Bit Next Header Field

The 8-bit Next Header field carries a value indicating either the type of the first IPv6 extension header (if present in the packet) or the upper-layer PDU type and data (such as UDP, TCP, or ICMPv6). When this field indicates an upper-layer PDU, the value in the IPv6 Next Header field uses protocol values that are the same as those used in the IPv4 Protocol field (see Figure 2.3). The Next Header field is similar to the IPv4 Protocol field in functionality but with additional capabilities.

2.4.1.5 The 8-Bit Hop Limit Field

The 8-bit Hop Limit field carries a value indicating the maximum number of router nodes (or hops) over which the IPv6 packet can traverse before being considered invalid and discarded. The Hop Limit field serves functions similar to the IPv4 TTL field. However, the Hop Limit field has no historical relation to the lifetime method originally defined for IPv4.

When an IPv6 router handles a packet with a Hop Limit field value equal to 0, it sends an ICMPv6 "Time Exceeded" message indicating "Hop Limit Exceeded in Transit" (Code = 0) to the packet's source and then discards the packet. The source node sets the Hop Limit when sending an IPv6 packet. The purpose of the Hop Limit is to prevent packets from circulating endlessly on the IPv6 internetwork. Each IP router decrements the Hop Limit value by one when forwarding an IPv6 packet.

2.4.1.6 The 128-Bit Source and Destination Address Fields

The value in the 128-bit Source Address field indicates the IPv6 address of the node that originated the IPv6 packet. In most cases, the value in the 128-bit Destination Address field indicates the IPv6 address of the packet's final destination node; the packet sender sets the Destination Address field to the final destination address. However, if the IPv6 packet carries an IPv6 Routing extension header (with extension header type 43), then the value in the packet's Destination Address field may be the IPv6 address of the next intermediate IPv6 routing node.

2.4.2 COMPARING THE IPv4 AND IPv6 HEADER FIELDS

The following observations can be made when comparing the IPv4 and IPv6 headers:

- The IPv4 header has 12 fields (including options), as shown in Figure 2.3. This number was reduced to 8 in the IPv6 header, as shown in Figure 2.2.
- The IPv4 header has 6 fields that must be processed by an intermediate router (IHL, TTL, Protocol, Header Checksum, Source Address, Destination Address). IPv6 reduced that number to 4 (Next Header, Hop Limit, Source Address, Destination Address), allowing more efficient forwarding of normal IPv6 packets.
- IPv4 header fields that are seldom used (such as Identification, Flags, Fragment Offset, Options) have been moved to well-defined IPv6 extension headers.

- The IPv4 header has a minimum size of 20 bytes, which was increased to 40 bytes for the IPv6 header. However, the source and destination addresses (128 bits) in the IPv6 header are four times larger than those in the IPv4 header (32 bits).

Table 2.1 summarizes the differences between the IPv4 and IPv6 header fields. The new Flow Label field in the IPv6 header is the only field not included in the IPv4 header. The streamlined IPv6 header results in a significant reduction in the number of instructions that a router must execute to forward an IPv6 packet.

TABLE 2.1

Comparing the IPv4 and IPv6 Header Fields

	IPv4 Header Field	IPv6 Header Field
Fields that are common to IPv4 and IPv6 and have the same functionality	4-bit Version field	IPv6 maintains the same 4-bit field but the version number is 6.
	32-bit Source Address	IPv6 keeps this field except that IPv6 addresses are 128 bits in length.
	32-bit Destination Address	IPv6 keeps this field except that IPv6 addresses are 128 bits in length.
Fields that have the same functionality in IPv4 and IPv6 but have different names	8-bit Type of Service was redefined as the DS field with 6-bit DSCP and 2-bit ECN subfields	IPv6 redefined the 8-bit DS field as the 8-bit Traffic Class (TC) field with the same subfields.
	16-bit Total Length: The IPv4 Total Length field indicates the length of the entire IPv4 packet, including the IPv4 header.	IPv6 replaced this field with the 16-bit Payload Length field, which indicates only the size of the IPv6 packet payload that includes any extension headers but excludes the main IP header.
	8-bit Time to Live (TTL)	IPv6 replaced this field with the 8-bit Hop Limit field.
	8-bit Protocol	IPv6 replaced this field with the 8-bit Next Header field. In IPv6, this indicates the protocol type and data in the payload portion but could also indicate the existence of an extension header.
Fields that exist in the IPv4 header and have been removed from the IPv6 header	4-bit Internet Header Length (IHL): IPv4 uses this field because packets can have variable-length IPv4 headers.	IPv6 removed this field because the IPv6 header always has a fixed length of 40 bytes. Each IPv6 extension header has either a fixed length or has a field that indicates its own length.
	16-bit Identification, 3-bit Flags, and 13-bit Fragment Offset: IPv4 uses these fields when packet fragmentation is being performed.	IPv6 removed these fields since fragmentation information is not included in the IPv6 header. IPv6 defined a Fragment extension header that contains this information. In IPv6, only the source of the packet performs fragmentation using the Fragment header.
	16-bit Header Checksum	IPv6 removed this field since the Link-Layer frame has a checksum (Ethernet Frame Check Sequence (FCS)) that allows the receiver to perform bit-level error detection for the entire Link-Layer frame and IPv6 packet.
	Variable-length Options	IPv6 removed this field and defined IPv6 extension headers as a replacement for IPv4 options. In IPv6, Options are handled using the IPv6 extension headers.
	Variable-length Padding	The IPv6 header is of fixed-sized and does not require padding.
Fields that are new in the IPv6 header but were not in the IPv4 header		The 20-bit Flow Label is a new field in IPv6 used for identifying a packet as belonging to a sequence of packets (a traffic flow) between a source and a destination and has to be handled as other packets in the flow.

IPv6 routers do not fragment packets when IPv6 packets larger than the MTU of the outgoing interface are received. In this case, an IPv6 router simply discards the IPv6 packet and transmits an ICMPv6 "Packet Too Big" message back to the packet's source. The ICMPv6 message includes the MTU value of the affected outgoing interface, allowing the source to adjust the packet size and make retransmissions. The process of discovering the MTU of the forwarding path is called Path MTU Discovery [RFC8201].

2.5   IPv6 EXTENSION HEADERS

When IPv4 Options are communicated to routers in the internetwork, those Options are included in the IPv4 header (subject to IPv4 packet size MTU limits). The IPv4 Options field in the IPv4 header is the only vehicle for sending IPv4 Options information to other routers. This requires each intermediate router on the forwarding path to check for the presence of IPv4 Options in the IPv4 packet and process them accordingly when needed. Examining each IPv4 header for Options and processing them can cause performance degradation when forwarding IPv4 packets. Some IPv4 packets may not contain Options relevant to the local processing node, but the node still has to examine all Options regardless of local relevance.

IPv6 eliminated the IPv4 Options field and introduced optional IPv6 extension headers, providing better scalability of the IPv6 header data and improved header processing efficiency. IPv6 moved Options to extension headers, allowing more efficient delivery and forwarding of IPv6 packets (see Table 2.2). This change allows for efficient and faster processing of the IPv6 header, thereby improving router performance and IPv6 packet forwarding. IPv6 nodes encode optional Internet-layer information in separate IPv6 extension headers that may be placed between the (main) IPv6 header and the upper-layer header in a packet. Each IPv6 extension header is identified by a distinct Next Header value.

A unique number is assigned to each IPv6 extension header type by the Internet Assigned Numbers Authority (IANA) IP Protocol Numbers; the same values are used by both IPv4 and IPv6. An IPv6 packet may carry zero or more extension headers, each header identified by the value in the Next Header field of the preceding header. When a node processes a sequence of IPv6 Next Header values in an IPv6 packet, the first value that does not correspond to an IPv6 extension header indicates that the next piece of data in the packet corresponds to an upper-layer header. The special "No Next Header" value of 59 is used if the IPv6 packet has no upper-layer header.

Several extension headers have been defined for IPv6. Table 2.2 lists some of the most common IPv6 extension headers and their decimal values. The IPv6 extension headers, including the Hop-by-Hop Options header, Destination Options header, Routing header, and Fragment header, are specified in [RFC8200]. The Authentication header (AH), Encapsulating Security Payload (ESP) header, and the remaining extension headers are specified in various standards as described in the corresponding sections below. The typical IPv6 packet does not contain extension headers. If the source of an IPv6 packet determines that the packet requires special handling by either intermediate routers or the destination, it adds one or more IPv6 extension headers as required.

An extension header value can be carried in the Next Header field of the fixed IPv6 header or in the Next Header field of an IPv6 extension header. Some of the IPv6 extension headers are discussed in this chapter. When no extension header (including any upper-layer header) follows the current header, the Next Header field of the current header is set to 59. The Hop-by-Hop Options header (with a value equal to 0) is the only extension header that must be processed by every intermediate router. This extension header is designed to carry a number of IPv6 options, as described in the Hop-by-Hop Options header section below.

Figures 2.5 and 2.6 show examples of protocols that work over IPv6 and IPv4, respectively. The IPv6 Next Header field and IPv4 Protocol Number field values are given in Table 2.2. Note that several protocols operate directly over IPv4 or IPv6, while others are higher-layer protocols that work over UDP, TCP, or SCTP. A protocol such as ARP for IPv4 operates directly over Ethernet with an EtherType of 0x0806. Figures 2.7–2.9 show details about the placement of the IPv6 extension headers in an IPv6 packet.

TABLE 2.2

Typical Values of the IPv6 Next Header Field

Value (Decimal)	Header
0	Hop-by-Hop Options header
2	IGMP
4	IPv4 (IPv4 encapsulation)
6	TCP
17	UDP
41	Encapsulated IPv6 header
43	Routing header
44	Fragment header
47	Generic Routing Encapsulation (GRE)
50	Encapsulating Security Payload header (ESP)
51	Authentication header (AH)
58	ICMPv6
59	No Next header
60	Destination Options header
89	OSPFv6 (OSPF for IPv6)
97	Ethernet-within-IP Encapsulation (ETHERIP)
103	Protocol Independent Multicast (PIM)
112	Virtual Router Redundancy Protocol (VRRP)
115	Layer Two Tunneling Protocol (L2TP)
132	Stream Control Transmission Protocol (SCTP)
135	Mobility Header
143	Ethernet

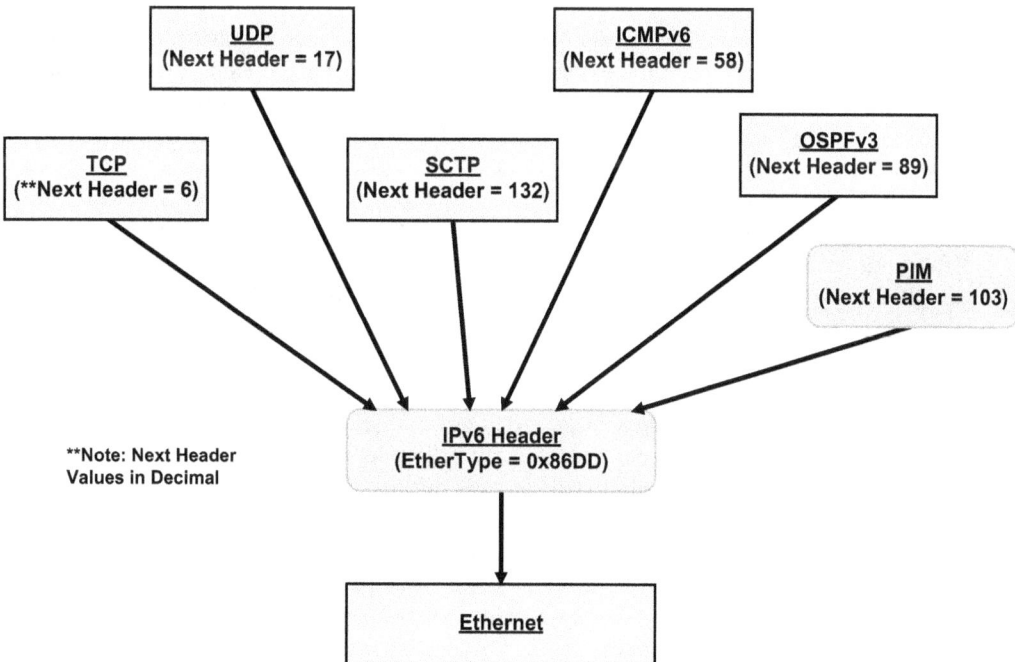

FIGURE 2.5 IPv6 and its related protocols.

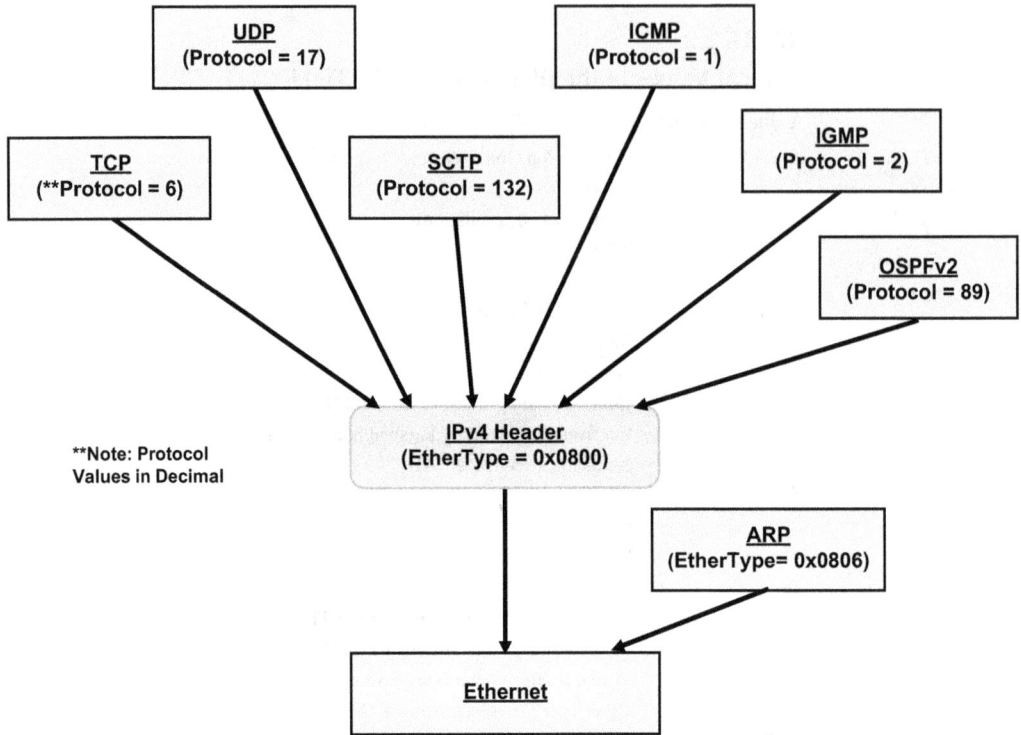

FIGURE 2.6 IPv4 and its related protocols.

2.5.1 PROCESSING IPV6 EXTENSION HEADERS

The following important observations apply to the processing of IPv6 extension headers:

- Any IP node that lies on the delivery path of an IPv6 packet with extension headers must not process, insert, or delete the extension headers (except for the Hop-by-Hop Options header) until the packet reaches the IPv6 node (or each of the set of IPv6 nodes, in the case of multicast packet delivery) identified in the Destination Address field of the packet's IPv6 header.
- Any IPv6 node along the delivery path of an IPv6 packet must not insert or delete the Hop-by-Hop Options header but may examine or process it until the packet reaches the IPv6 node (or each of the set of IPv6 nodes, in the case of multicast packet delivery) identified in the Destination Address field of the packet's IPv6 header. When an IPv6 packet carries the Hop-by-Hop Options header, the header must be placed immediately after the (main) IPv6 header. The Next Header field of the IPv6 header, with a value of zero, indicates the presence of this header in the packet.
  - While all IPv6 nodes along a packet's delivery path are required to examine and process the Hop-by-Hop Options header, it must be understood that only nodes explicitly configured to do so can examine and process this header.
- The destination node of an IPv6 packet performs normal demultiplexing on the Next Header field of the IPv6 header and processes the first IPv6 extension header or the upper-layer header if it finds no extension header in the packet. The contents and semantics of each IPv6 extension header carried in the packet determine whether or not the destination will continue to process the next header. Therefore, the destination node must process the IPv6 extension headers strictly in the order in which they appear in the packet.

A destination node must not, for example, inspect an IPv6 packet looking for a particular kind of extension header and process that header before processing all preceding headers.

- If a destination node, after processing a header, sees that it is required to proceed to the next header but the Next Header value in the current header is unrecognized, the node should discard the packet and send an ICMPv6 Type 4 Parameter Problem message indicating "unrecognized Next Header type encountered" (Code value of 1) to the source of the packet, with the ICMP Pointer field containing the offset of the unrecognized value within the original IPv6 packet. The node takes the same action if it encounters a Next Header field in any header other than the IPv6 header that has a value of zero.
- Each extension header in an IPv6 packet is an integer multiple of 8 bytes long, enabling subsequent headers to have 8-byte alignment. Multi-byte fields within each IPv6 extension header are aligned on their natural boundaries, meaning that fields that are n bytes long are placed at an integer multiple of n bytes from the beginning of the header, for $n=1, 2, 4,$ or 8.
- A node that supports a full implementation of IPv6 must also be capable of implementing the following IPv6 extension headers: Hop-by-Hop Options, Fragment, Destination Options, Routing, Authentication, and ESP.
- When an IPv6 packet carries an IPv4 packet, the Next Header in the fixed IPv6 header or in the IPv6 extension header just before the IPv4 packet is set to 4 (to indicate IPv4 encapsulation in the IPv6 packet). Note that zero or more IPv6 extension headers may precede the encapsulated IPv4 packet (e.g., Hop-by-Hop Options header, Destination Options header, Routing header, Fragment header, AH, and ESP header). In IPv4 encapsulation in IPv6, the IPv4 packet (plus any extension headers) constitutes the payload of the IPv6 packet.

2.5.2   IPv6 Extension Header Order

All IPv6 extension headers that are added to an IPv6 packet are processed in the order in which they are presented. Because the Hop-by-Hop Options header is the only IPv6 extension header that is processed by every IPv6 node on the forwarding path, it must be the first extension header immediately following the fixed IPv6 header. The recommended placement of IPv6 extension headers after the fixed IPv6 header must be in the following order **[RFC8200]**:

1. IPv6 header
2. Hop-by-Hop Options header, Header Code=0 (must always be the first when present in an IPv6 packet)
3. Destination Options header, Header Code=60 (for intermediate destinations when the Routing header is present)
    Note 1: This header contains IPv6 Options that are to be processed by the first destination in the packet's IPv6 Destination Address field and subsequent destinations listed in the IPv6 Routing header.
4. Routing header, Header Code=43
5. Fragment header, Header Code=44
6. AH, Header Code=51
    Note 2: Reference **[RFC4303]** provides additional recommendations regarding the relative order of the Authentication and ESP headers.
7. ESP header, Header Code=50 (see Note 2)
8. Destination Options header (for the final destination), Header Code=60
    Note 3: This header contains IPv6 Options that are to be processed only by the final destination of the IPv6 packet.

An IPv6 packet can carry only one IPv6 extension header, except for the Destination Options header, which can appear at most twice in the packet (i.e., once before an IPv6 Routing header and

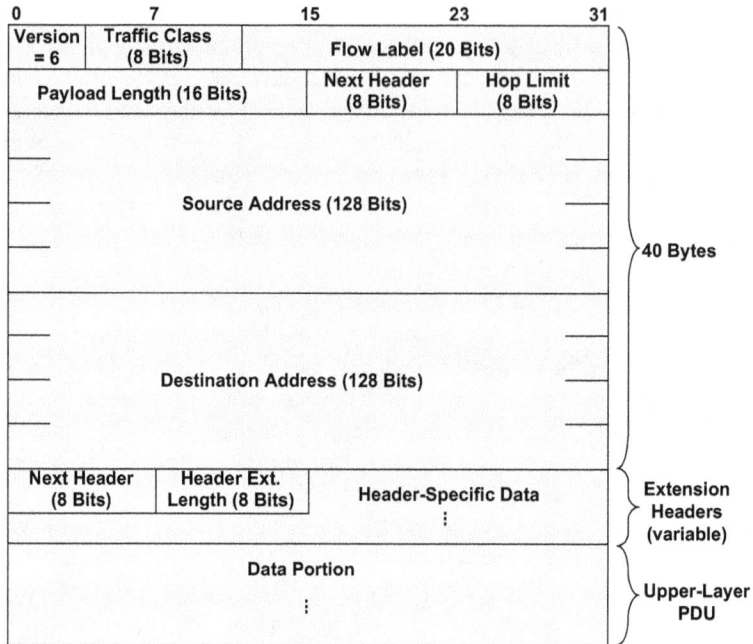

IPv6 extension headers are optional Network Layer information that is encoded in separate headers and placed between the fixed IPv6 header and the upper-layer header in an IPv6 packet.

- **Next Header (8 Bits)** : This field, in the IPv6 extension header, identifies the type of header immediately following the IPv6 extension header. Each extension header type including upper-layer protocols (e.g., TCP, UDP, ICMPv6, IGMP, OSPFv6), has a specific code.
  - Note that the 8-bit Next Header field in the fixed IPv6 header identifies the type of header immediately following the IPv6 header.

- **Header Ext. Length (8 Bits)** : This specifies the length of the IPv6 extension header in bytes, excluding the first 8 bytes.
  - Note that all IPv6 extension header types except the Fragment Header have the Next Header and Header Extension Length fields. The Fragment Header has no Header Ext. Length field.

- **Header-Specific Data**: This is a variable-length field that specifies information relevant to the IPv6 extension header. This field may contain sub-fields plus related information.

FIGURE 2.7   IPv6 header format – with extension header and data portion.

once before the upper-layer header). If the IPv6 packet contains an upper-layer protocol header that is another IPv6 header (e.g., when using IPv6 over IPv6 tunneling or IPv6 in IPv6 encapsulation), this header may be followed by its own IPv6 extension headers, which are also required to follow the same header ordering recommendations. Any future defined IPv6 extension headers must have their own ordering constraints relative to the headers already defined.

The values carried in the Next Header field of the IPv6 header and any IPv6 extension headers, when present in an IPv6 packet, form a chain of pointers that indicate the sequence of extension headers carried in the packet (see Figures 2.10 and 2.11). Each value in the current Next Header field (which functions as a pointer) indicates the type of IPv6 extension header or upper-layer protocol immediately following that header. The pointers (and corresponding extension headers) are

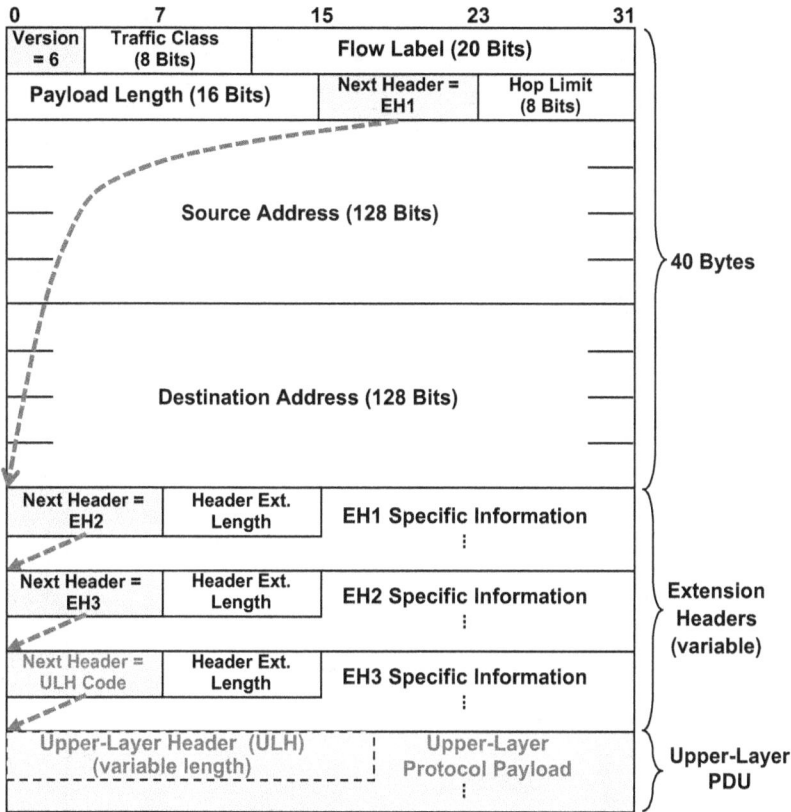

FIGURE 2.8 IPv6 packet extension header details.

followed in the IPv6 packet until the upper-layer protocol is ultimately identified. Figure 2.11 shows possible IPv6 packets with a chain of pointers formed by the values in the Next Header field.

If any IPv6 extension header in an IPv6 packet contains an unrecognized or incorrect Next Header field value, the node currently handling that IPv6 packet must discard it and transmit an ICMPv6 Type 4 "Parameter Problem" message indicating "Unrecognized Next Header Type Encountered" (Code = 1) to the source of the packet. For example, if a source sends an IPv6 packet with the Next Header field of the IPv6 header set to 0, pointing to a next IPv6 extension header that is not the Hop-by-Hop Options header, then this is an improper value that requires the IPv6 packet to be discarded, followed by the transmission of a corresponding ICMPv6 message. The Next Header field of the IPv6 header with a value of 0 is reserved solely for indicating that the next IPv6 extension header immediately following is the Hop-by-Hop Options header (see Table 2.2).

2.5.3 IPv6 Options

An IPv6 Option, encoded in the type–length–value (TLV) format, consists of three fields that either provide padding data for extension header alignment or contain data that describes a specific characteristic of the packet forwarding and delivery process **[RFC8200]**. The Hop-by-Hop Options

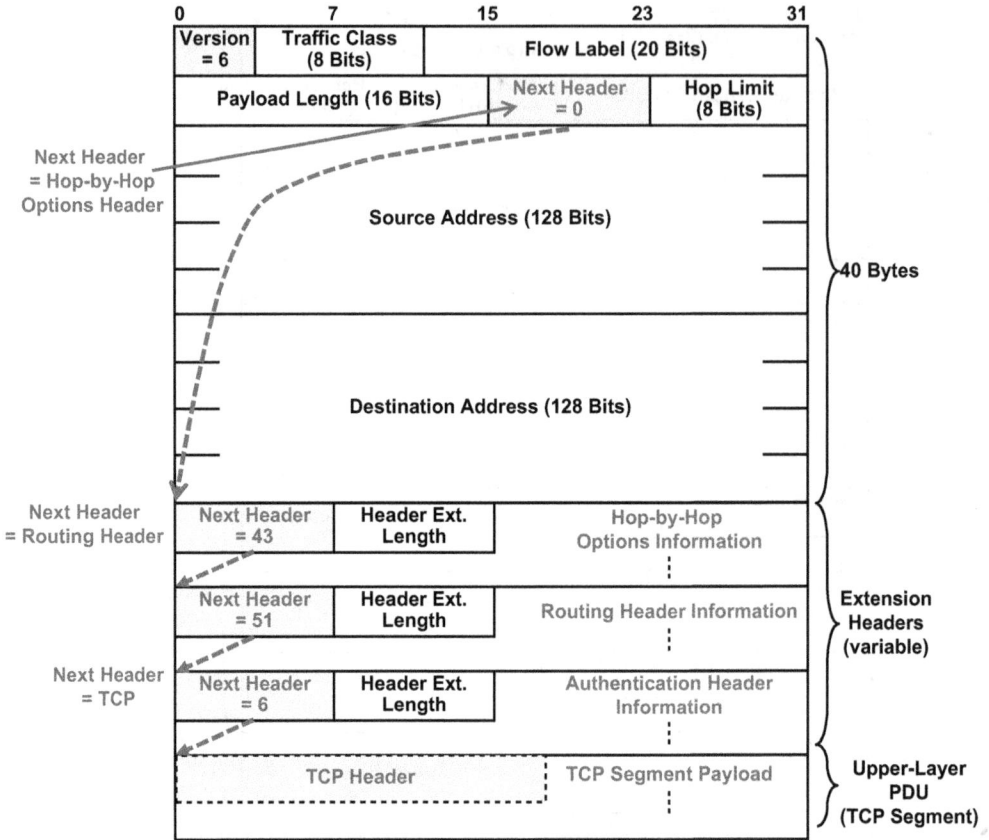

FIGURE 2.9 IPv6 packet extension header example.

header and Destination Options header contain a variable-length Options field that allows IPv6 Options to be sent. Figure 2.12 shows the format of an IPv6 Option. Both the Hop-by-Hop Options header and the Destination Options header share the same Option Type numbering space. However, the specification of a particular IPv6 Option (i.e., its specification according to the corresponding IETF standard) may restrict its use to only one of those two extension headers.

The receiver of an IPv6 packet with a sequence of Options within the IPv6 extension header must process them strictly in the order they appear in the header. The receiver must not, for example, search through the header looking for a particular kind of IPv6 Option and process that Option before processing all the Options placed before it.

The value in the Option Type field identifies a particular IPv6 Option and determines how the IPv6 processing node should handle that Option. The value in the Option Length field indicates the number of bytes in the Option, excluding the bytes in the Option Type and Option Length fields. The variable-length Option Data field contains the specific data associated with the specified IPv6 option. Table 2.3 lists some well-known IPv6 Option types.

The two high-order bits (xx) within the Option Type field (in Figure 2.12) indicate how the router processing the Option should handle it when the Option Type is not recognized. Figure 2.12 defines the settings of the xx values and their purpose. The third high-order bit (y) of the Option Type indicates whether a node on the IPv6 packet's forwarding path to the destination can change the Option Data ($y=1$) or not ($y=0$).

An IPv6 Option may require extra alignment padding data to ensure that the specified Option fields fall on the desired boundary. For example, IPv6 addresses are much easier to process if they align with an 8-byte boundary. The notation $xn+y$ is typically used to express the boundary alignment requirements for IPv6 extension headers and Option fields. This expression indicates that the

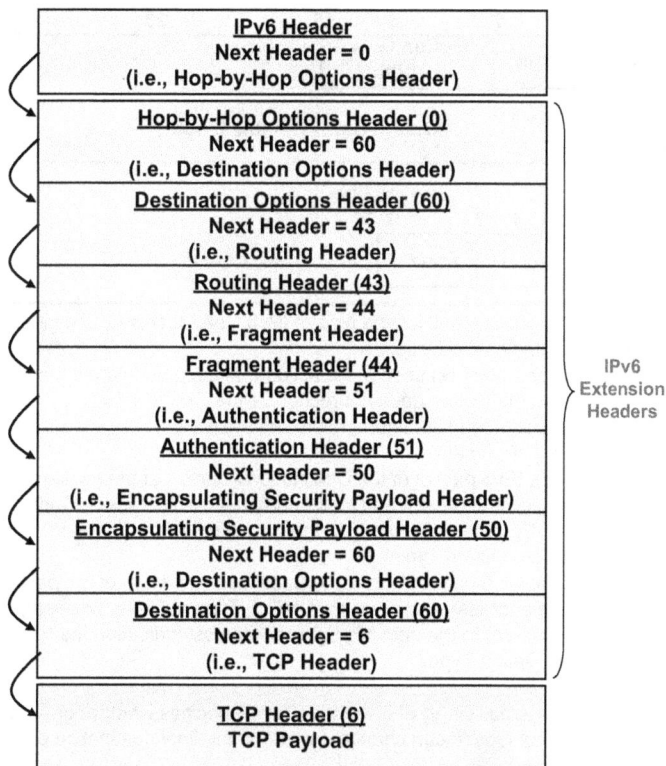

FIGURE 2.10 IPv6 extension header order.

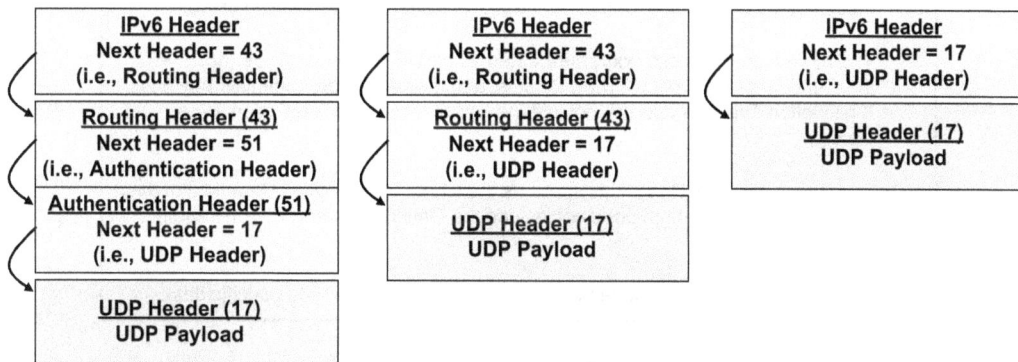

FIGURE 2.11 Examples of IPv6 packets with extension headers.

data placed in an IPv6 Option must start at a byte boundary that is an integral multiple of x bytes plus y bytes from the start of the carrying IPv6 extension header. Individual IPv6 Options have their own specific alignment requirements (see Table 2.3) to ensure that multi-byte values within the Option Data field align with the required byte boundaries.

For example, the notation $4n+2$ indicates an alignment requirement stating that the data in the IPv6 Option must start on a byte boundary that is an integral multiple of 4 bytes, plus 2 bytes from the start of the carrying IPv6 extension header. This means the IPv6 Option must start at byte boundaries of 6, 10, 14, and so on, relative to the start of the carrying IPv6 extension header, which can be either a Hop-by-Hop Options header or a Destination Options header. To implement

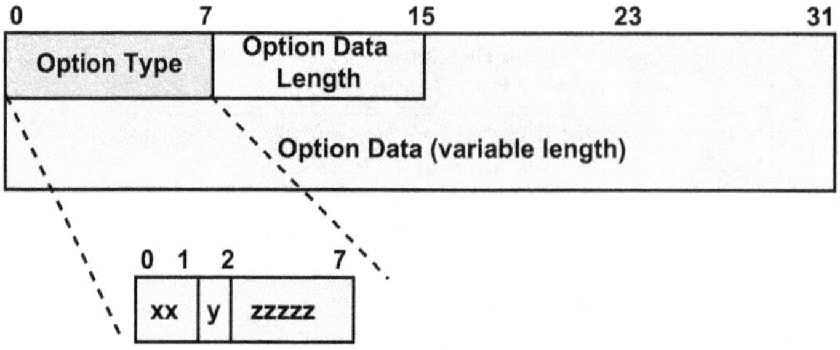

- **Option Type (8 Bit)** : This identifies the type of IPv6 Option. This determines how the processing nodes handles the Option.

  The highest-order 2 bits (**xx**) specify the action that must be taken if the IPv6 node that is processing the Option does not recognize the Option Type:
  - **00** - skip this Option and continue processing the header.
  - **01** - discard the IPv6 packet.
  - **10** - discard the IPv6 packet (if the Destination Address of the packet is a unicast or multicast address), and then send an ICMPv6 Type 4, Code 2 message (i.e., Parameter Problem) to the packet's Source Address, indicating the unrecognized Option Type.
  - **11** - discard the IPv6 packet (only if the Destination Address of the packet's is not a multicast address), and send an ICMPv6 Type 4, Code 2 message (i.e., Parameter Problem) to the packet's Source Address, indicating the unrecognized Option Type.

  The third-highest-order bit (**y**) of the Option Type specifies whether or not the Option Data of that Option can change enroute to the final destination of the packet.
  - **0** - Option Data does not change en route
  - **1** - Option Data may change en route

  When the packet carries an Authentication header, and has any Option whose data may change enroute, the entire Option Data field must be treated as zero-valued bytes when computing or verifying the packet's authenticating value.

  The three high-order bits (**xxy**) are treated as part of the Option Type (not independent of the Option Type). That is, a particular Option is identified by a full 8-bit Option Type (**xxyzzzzz**), not just the low-order 5 bits of an Option Type (**zzzzz**).

- **Option Data Length (8 Bits)**: This specifies the length of the Option Data field of this Option (in bytes). This length does not include the Option Type and Option Length fields.

- **Option Data**: This is a variable-length field that carries Option-Type-specific data.

FIGURE 2.12 IPv6 Type–Length–Value (TLV) Option format.

boundary alignment requirements, padding data is typically added before an IPv6 Option and between each IPv6 Option when the IPv6 extension header carries multiple IPv6 Options.

Reference **[RFC8200]** defines two IPv6 padding Options that IPv6 nodes can use when necessary to align IPv6 Options. A node can use these padding Options to pad out an IPv6 extension header containing Options so that it has a length that is a multiple of 8 bytes. All IPv6 implementations must be capable of recognizing these IPv6 padding Options.

2.5.3.1 Pad1 Option (Option Type 0)

Each IPv6 extension header added to an IPv6 packet after the fixed IPv6 header must fall on an 8-byte (64-bit) boundary. Fixed-size IPv6 extension headers must always be an integral multiple of

TABLE 2.3
IPv6 Option Types

Option Type		Option Name	IPv6 Extension Header in Which It Is Used	Alignment Requirement
Decimal	Hexadecimal			
0	0	Pad1 Option [RFC8200]	Hop-by-Hop and Destination Options headers	No
1	1	PadN Option [RFC8200]	Hop-by-Hop and Destination Options headers	No
5	5	Router Alert Option [RFC2711], [RFC6398]	Hop-by-Hop Options header	$2n+0$
194	0xC2	Jumbo Payload Option [RFC2675]	Hop-by-Hop Options header	$4n+2$
201	0xC9	Home Address Option [RFC6275]	Destination Options header	$8n+6$

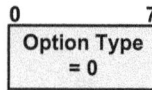

FIGURE 2.13 Pad1 Option (no alignment requirement).

8 bytes. However, variable-size IPv6 extension headers contain a Header Extension Length field, and the sending node must add padding (of all zeros) as needed to ensure that the size of each IPv6 extension header sent is an integral multiple of 8 bytes. The 1-byte Pad1 Option (with Option Type 0) [RFC8200], shown in Figure 2.13, is used to pad extension headers when necessary so that their size will be an integral multiple of 8 bytes.

The Pad1 Option is defined as a single byte with only an Option Type field set to 0. It has a special format with no Option Data Length and Option Data fields, as shown in Figure 2.13. An IPv6 node uses the Pad1 Option to insert 1 byte of padding data into the Options area of an IPv6 extension header. If the node determines that more than one byte of padding data is required, it uses the IPv6 PadN Option (described next) instead of using multiple Pad1 Options.

With the Option Type field of the Pad1 Option set to 0, an IPv6 processing node skips the Option if it is not recognized. Nodes are not allowed to change this Option while in transit. The source IPv6 node inserts a single byte of padding using the all-zeros Pad1 Option so that a Hop-by-Hop Options or Destination Options header being sent falls on an 8-byte boundary and satisfies the boundary alignment requirements of these Options. The 8-byte Pad1 Option itself has no boundary alignment requirements.

2.5.3.2 PadN Option (Option Type 1)

The PadN Option, defined in [RFC8200], is used by the source IPv6 node to insert multiple (two or more) bytes of padding data so that a Hop-by-Hop Options or Destination Options header being sent aligns with an 8-byte boundary and satisfies the boundary alignment requirements of these Options. Figure 2.14 shows the format of the PadN Option. The PadN Option itself, like the Pad1 Option, has no boundary alignment requirements.

The PadN Option consists of a 1-byte Option Type field set to 1, an Option Data Length field (which is set to the number of padding bytes added to the Option), and zero or more bytes of padding data. Even if the Option Type field is set to 1, the IPv6 processing node will still skip the Option if it is not recognized. Nodes are not allowed to change this Option while in transit.

An IPv6 node uses the PadN Option to insert two or more bytes of padding data into the Options area of an IPv6 extension header. For N bytes of padding data, the Option Data Length field will contain the value $N-2$, and the variable Option Data portion will contain $N-2$ zero-valued bytes.

2.5.3.3 Router Alert Option (Option Type 5)

The Router Alert Option (Option Type 5) **[RFC2711] [RFC6398]** is included in an IPv6 packet to indicate to intermediate IPv6 routers that the contents of the IPv6 packet require additional examination and possibly processing. The boundary alignment requirement of the Router Alert Option is $2n+0$, as shown in Table 2.3. Figures 2.15 and 2.16 show the format of the Router Alert Option.

The Router Alert Option may be used, for example, in Multicast Listener Discovery (MLD) (MLDv1 **[RFC2710]** and MLDv2 **[RFC3810]**), a protocol used by IPv6 routers for discovering multicast listeners, and in the Resource ReSerVation Protocol (RSVP) **[RFC2205]**, a protocol used for reserving resources in IP networks. If the Option Type field of the Router Alert Option is set to 5 and an IPv6 node does not recognize the Option, it simply skips it. This Option is not allowed to be changed in transit.

2.5.3.4 IPv6 Jumbo Payload Option (Option Type 194)

The Jumbo Payload Option (Option Type 194) is used in an IPv6 packet to indicate that its payload size is greater than 65,535 bytes **[RFC2675]**. The boundary alignment requirement of the Jumbo Payload Option is $4n+2$, as shown in Table 2.3. Figure 2.17 shows the structure of the Jumbo Payload Option.

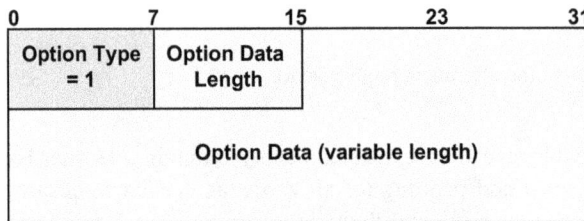

FIGURE 2.14 PadN Option (no alignment requirement).

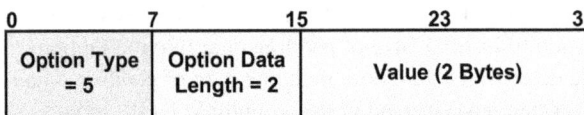

FIGURE 2.15 Router Alert Option (Option Type 5).

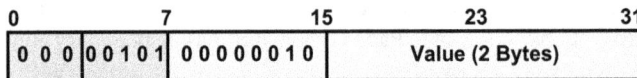

FIGURE 2.16 IPv6 Router Alert Option fields.

For an IPv6 packet that contains the Jumbo Payload Option, the Payload Length field of the IPv6 header is disregarded because it no longer indicates the actual size of the payload in the IPv6 packet. Instead, the actual size (in bytes) of the IPv6 packet payload is indicated by the Jumbo Payload Length field of the Jumbo Payload Option, as shown in Figure 2.17. Given that the Jumbo Payload Length field is 32 bits in length, an IPv6 packet with a Jumbo Payload Option can carry a payload of up to 4,294,967,295 bytes (i.e., $2^{32}-1$).

The 16-bit Payload Length field of a normal IPv6 packet means the normal payload size can be up to 65,535 bytes (i.e., $2^{32}-1$). An IPv6 packet with a payload greater than the normal size is known as a *Jumbogram*. If the Option Type field of the Jumbo Payload Option is set to 194 (binary 11000010 or 0xC2 hexadecimal) and an IPv6 node does not recognize the Option, and the destination address is not a multicast address, it discards the packet and sends an ICMPv6 Parameter Problem message to the packet's source. This Option is not allowed to be changed in transit. Note that the upper-layer protocol of the source/receiver of an IPv6 packet must be capable of sending/receiving *Jumbograms* before the Jumbo Payload Option can be used. With the Jumbo Payload Option, IPv6 packets can carry payloads (Jumbograms) between 65,536 and 4,294,967,295 bytes. These larger IPv6 packets are typically used within supercomputer centers and very high-speed data centers.

2.5.3.5 Home Address Option (Option Type 201)

The Home Address Option (Option Type 201) **[RFC6275]**, when included in an IPv6 packet, indicates the Home IPv6 Address of a particular Mobile Node (**see the "Mobile IP" discussion in Chapter 6**). The Mobile Node is assigned a permanent Home IPv6 Address when it is located on its Home Link. The Home IPv6 Address is the IPv6 address through which the Mobile Node is always reachable, regardless of its location on the IPv6 network **[RFC6275]**. The boundary alignment requirement of the Home Address Option is 8n+6, as indicated in Table 2.3. Figure 2.18 shows the format of the Home Address Option.

If the Option Type field of the Home Address Option is set to 201 (11001001 binary or 0xC9 hexadecimal), the current IPv6 processing discards the IPv6 packet and sends an ICMPv6 Parameter Problem message if it does not recognize the Option and the destination address is not a multicast address. This Option is not allowed to be changed in transit. The value in the Option Length field indicates the length of the Option (in bytes), excluding the 1-byte Option Type and 1-byte Option Length fields. The 128-bit Home Address field contains the Home IPv6 Address of the Mobile Node. Because the only field or data following the 1-byte Option Length field is the 128-bit IPv6 Home Address field (Figure 2.18), the Option Length field is set to 16.

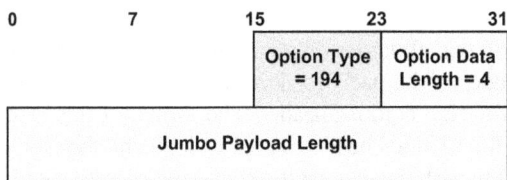

- **Option Type (8 Bits)**: The value in this field is equal to 194 (i.e., value 0xC2 in hexadecimal).

- **Option Data Length (8 Bits)**: The value in this field is equal to 4.

- **Jumbo Payload Length (32 Bits)**: This specifies the length of the IPv6 packet in bytes, excluding the IPv6 header but including the Hop-by-Hop Options header and any other extension headers present. The length must be greater than 65,535.

FIGURE 2.17 IPv6 Jumbo Payload Option (Option Type = 194).

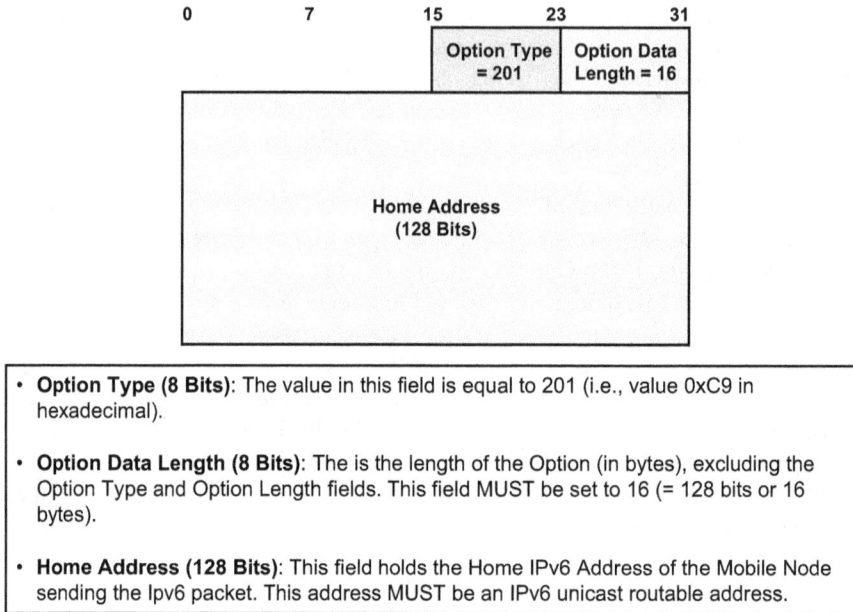

FIGURE 2.18   Home Address Option (Option Type 201).

2.5.4   NO NEXT HEADER (HEADER CODE 59)

When the IPv6 No Next Header **[RFC8200]** (which has an IPv6 extension header value of 59) is present in the Next Header field of the fixed IPv6 header or any extension header, it indicates that there is no further information following that header; any additional data must be disregarded. In other words, if the Payload Length field in the fixed IPv6 header indicates the presence of data (bytes) beyond the end of the IPv6 header or extension header whose Next Header field contains the header code 59, those bytes must be ignored and can be passed on to the next-hop unchanged when forwarding that IPv6 packet.

2.5.5   HOP-BY-HOP OPTIONS HEADER (HEADER CODE 0)

The Hop-by-Hop Options extension header is the only IPv6 extension header that must be processed at each intermediate router. The Hop-by-Hop Options header has one or more IPv6 Options fields that contain optional information that all nodes on a packet's forwarding path may examine and process **[RFC8200]**. The Next Header of the packet's IPv6 header is set to 0 to indicate that the next IPv6 extension header is a Hop-by-Hop Options header. The format of this extension header is shown in Figure 2.19. The Hop-by-Hop Options header serves as a mechanism for specifying and delivering parameters (or instructions) to each node along the packet's forwarding path to the destination.

The fields in the Hop-by-Hop Options header consist of a 1-byte Next Header field, a 1-byte Header Extension Length field, and a variable-length Options field that can carry one or more IPv6 Options. The value written in the Header Extension Length field represents the number of 8-byte blocks that make up the Hop-by-Hop Options header, excluding the first 8 bytes in the header. This means an 8-byte Hop-by-Hop Options header has a Header Extension Length field value of 0. The source node must add padding data to ensure that all IPv6 Options in the extension header align with 8-byte boundaries.

The Header Extension Length field in the Hop-by-Hop Options header allows intermediate routers on a packet's forwarding path to optimize the processing of IPv6 packets with this extension header. Upon receiving an IPv6 packet with a Hop-by-Hop Options header, a router first

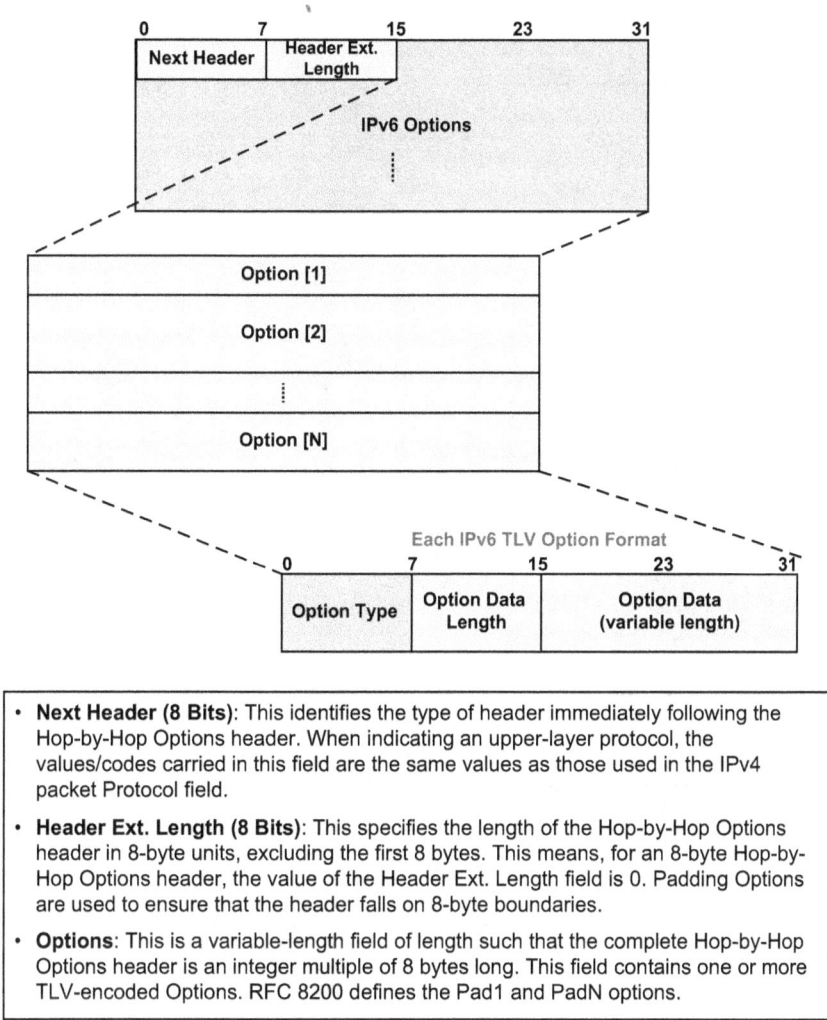

FIGURE 2.19   Hop-by-Hop Options header (Header Code=0).

determines the size of the extension header. The Hop-by-Hop Options header has a minimum size of 8 bytes (equal to a Header Extension Length field value of 0). Thus, an IPv6 node calculates the number of bytes in the Hop-by-Hop Options header as follows: (Header Extension Length + 1) × 8.

A Hop-by-Hop Options header in an IPv6 packet may contain the Router Alert Option (Option type 5) followed by the PadN option (Option type 1), which is used as padding in the Hop-by-Hop Options header to ensure it aligns with an 8-byte boundary. The Hop-by-Hop Options header in this case contains the following data: 1-byte Next Header field + 1-byte Header Extension Length field + 4-byte Router Alert Option + 2-byte PadN Option.

2.5.6   IPv6 Destination Options Header (Header Code 60)

The Destination Options header **[RFC8200]**, when included in an IPv6 packet, specifies optional information (or packet delivery parameters) that need to be examined only by intermediate destinations or the final destination of the IPv6 packet. This extension header is identified by the value of 60 in the Next Header field of the fixed IPv6 header or the extension header that immediately precedes it. The Destination Options header (shown in Figure 2.20) has the same format as the Hop-by-Hop Options header shown in Figure 2.19.

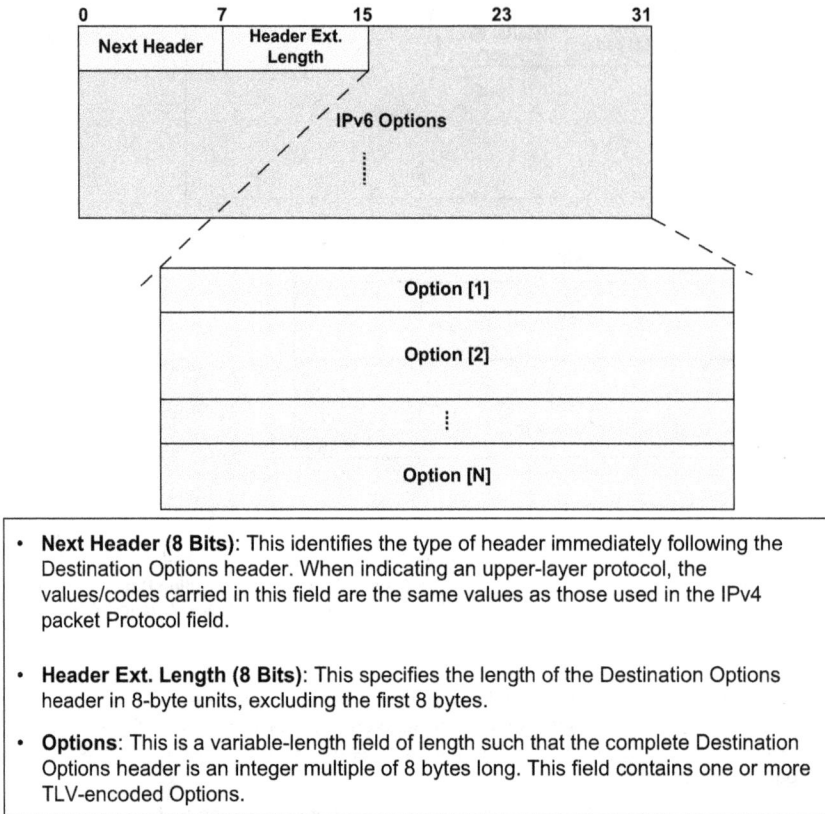

- **Next Header (8 Bits)**: This identifies the type of header immediately following the Destination Options header. When indicating an upper-layer protocol, the values/codes carried in this field are the same values as those used in the IPv4 packet Protocol field.

- **Header Ext. Length (8 Bits)**: This specifies the length of the Destination Options header in 8-byte units, excluding the first 8 bytes.

- **Options**: This is a variable-length field of length such that the complete Destination Options header is an integer multiple of 8 bytes long. This field contains one or more TLV-encoded Options.

FIGURE 2.20   IPv6 Destination Options header (Header Code = 60).

A source IPv6 node includes the Destination Options header in an IPv6 packet under the following two circumstances:

- If the IPv6 packet contains a Routing header, then the Destination Options header specifies delivery or processing parameters (optional information) for each intermediate destination. In this case, *the sending IPv6 node places the Destination Options header before the Routing header.*
- If the IPv6 packet contains no Routing header or if the Destination Options header occurs after the Routing header, *then the Destination Options header specifies delivery or processing parameters for the IPv6 packet's final destination.*

The Home Address Option (Option Type 201) for Mobile IPv6 described above (Figure 2.18) is an example of an Option that can be carried in the Destination Options header of an IPv6 packet.

2.5.6.1   Encoding Optional Destination Information in an IPv6 Packet

It is important to note that the two main approaches for encoding optional destination information in an IPv6 packet are: including that information as an option in the Destination Options header or placing it in a separate IPv6 extension header. Using the Fragment header and the AH in an IPv6 packet are examples of the latter approach. The approach an IPv6 node uses depends on the kind of action desired at an IPv6 destination node that does not understand the optional information sent:

- If discarding the IPv6 packet is the desired action at the destination node upon receiving the optional information (and only if the Destination Address of the packet is not a multicast address), the destination sends an ICMPv6 Type 4 "Parameter Problem" message indicating "Unrecognized Next Header Type Encountered by Intermediate Node" (Code 5) to the packet's source; **[RFC8883]** defines additional ICMPv6 errors that an IPv6 node sends when it discards IPv6 packets because it cannot process the IPv6 headers. The sending node may then encode the optional information either as a separate IPv6 extension header or as an IPv6 Option in the Destination Options header with the Option Type having the value 11 in its highest-order 2 bits. The approach taken by the sending node may depend on factors such as which approach requires fewer bytes or which yields better alignment or more efficient parsing.

- If any other action is desired at the IPv6 destination, the optional information must be encoded as an IPv6 Option in the Destination Options header with Option Type having the value 00, 01, or 10 in its highest-order 2 bits to specify the desired action to the destination.

2.5.7 ROUTING HEADER (HEADER CODE 43)

IPv4 defined two types of source routing: strict source routing and loose source routing. In strict source routing, the packet must visit all specified intermediate nodes between the packet's source and destination, with no deviation from this list of intermediate nodes allowed. In loose source routing, the packet must visit only certain specified intermediate nodes between the packet's source and destination, and it may take any optimal path to reach the next specified node, which can be multiple hops away from the current specified node.

IPv6 defines the Routing header to allow an IPv6 source to specify a source route that includes a list of intermediate nodes (destinations) through which the packet must pass to reach its final destination. The IPv6 Routing header provides functions very similar to the IPv4 Loose Source and Record Route Options. The Next Header field value of the fixed IPv6 header or an extension header is set to 43 to indicate that the next header following is the Routing header. Figure 2.21 shows the format of the IPv6 Routing header.

When an IPv6 packet contains a Routing header (Figure 2.21), the Next Header field of the fixed IPv6 header is set to 43 to indicate that the next IPv6 extension header is a Routing header. The Routing header itself also contains a Next Header field that indicates the IPv6 extension header that follows it. The IPv6 Routing (extension) header is defined in **[RFC8200]** as a generic header that can be formatted to define different routing types, depending on the value specified in the 8-bit Routing Type field (Figure 2.21).

The following are some examples of IPv6 routing types:

- **Routing Type = 2**: Type 2 Routing Header (for Mobile IPv6), defined in **[RFC6275]** (see "Mobile IP" in Chapter 6)
- **Routing Type = 3**: RPL Source Route Header, defined in **[RFC6554]**
- **Routing Type = 4**: Segment Routing Header (SRH), defined in **[RFC8754]**
- **Routing Type = 5**: CRH-16, defined in **[RFC9631]**
- **Routing Type = 6**: CRH-32, defined in **[RFC9631]**

IPv6 originally defined Routing Type 0 in **[RFC2460]**, which is used for loose source routing. However, because of security concerns, the Routing Type 0 header was deprecated in **[RFC5095]**. This section focuses only on the IPv6 SRH, which plays an important role in IPv6 routing.

Figures 2.21 and 2.22 show the various fields in the IPv6 Routing (extension) header (with an extension header value of 43). The Routing header consists of a 1-byte Next Header field, a 1-byte Header Extension Length field (defined the same way as in the Hop-by-Hop Options header), a 1-byte Routing Type field, a 1-byte Segments Left field that indicates the number of intermediate nodes (destinations) that the IPv6 packet is still to visit, and a variable-length Type-Specific Data field.

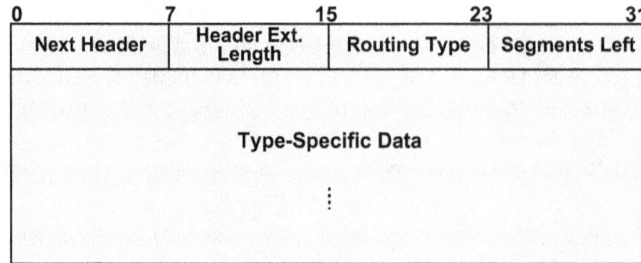

FIGURE 2.21   Routing header (Header Code=43).

The Next Header field in the IPv6 Routing header can be set to indicate IPv4, TCP, UDP, or any other appropriate protocol header. The IPv6 Routing (extension) header is ignored if the value in the Segments Left field is equal to 0 (see discussion below). The contents of the Type-Specific Data field depend on the value set in the Routing Type field (e.g., SRH-specific data). If an IPv6 packet has an incomplete Routing header, the current IPv6 processing node drops the packet and sends an ICMPv6 Type 4 "Parameter Problem" message indicating "Erroneous Header Field Encountered" (Code=0) to the packet's source.

2.5.7.1   Specific Notes on Processing the IPv6 Routing Header

If an IPv6 node encounters a Routing header with an unrecognized Routing Type value while processing a received IPv6 packet, the required behavior depends on the value in the Segments Left field of the Routing header:

- If the Segments Left value is 0, the Routing header must be ignored, and the node proceeds to process the next header in the IPv6 packet identified by the value in the Next Header field of the Routing header.
- If Segments Left is non-zero, the IPv6 packet must be discarded, and the node sends an ICMPv6 Type 4 "Parameter Problem" message (with Code 0) to the packet's source, pointing to the unrecognized Routing Type.

If an intermediate IPv6 node, after processing the Routing header of a received IPv6 packet, determines that the packet size exceeds the MTU of the link/interface over which it is to be forwarded, the node must discard the packet and send an ICMPv6 Type 2 "Packet Too Big" message (Code 0) to the packet's source.

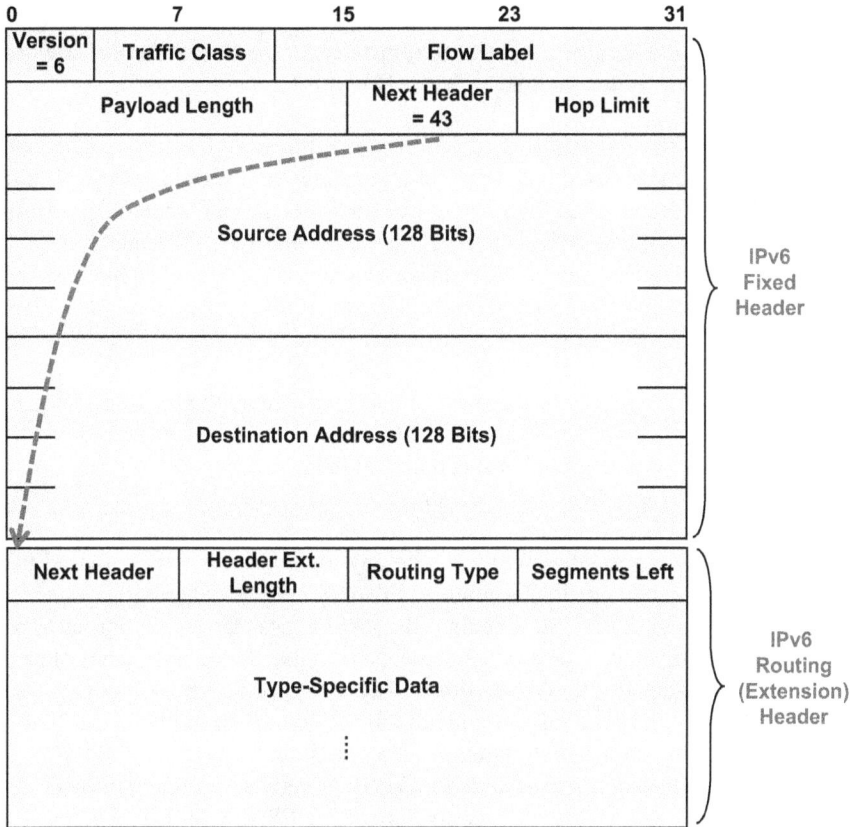

FIGURE 2.22 IPv6 header with Routing extension header.

2.5.7.2 Responding to IPv6 Packets Carrying Routing Headers

Let us consider the case where the upper-layer protocol on an IPv6 node sends one or more packets in response to receiving an IPv6 packet that included a Routing header. Sending a response here means the IPv6 node returns an IPv6 packet to the originator of the received IPv6 packet containing the Routing header. The IPv6 packet(s) that the node sends in response to this IPv6 packet must not include a Routing header that was automatically derived from the contents of the received Routing header UNLESS the node has verified the integrity and authenticity of the Source Address and Routing header in the received packet. The node may perform this verification using, for example, an AH in the received IPv6 packet. To elaborate, the IPv6 node is permitted to send only the following kinds of packets in response to a received IPv6 packet carrying a Routing header:

- Send IPv6 packets in response that do not include Routing headers.
- Send IPv6 packets in response that include Routing headers, but the IPv6 node did NOT derive these headers by reversing the Routing header of the received IPv6 packet (e.g., the node instead uses a Routing header that is provided through local configuration).
- Send IPv6 packets in response that include Routing headers, but the IPv6 node derived these headers by reversing the Routing header of the received packet. This is allowed IF AND ONLY IF the responding IPv6 node has verified the integrity and authenticity of the Source Address and Routing header of the received IPv6 packet.

2.5.7.3 IPv6 Segment Routing Header (Routing Type 4)

To help us better understand the IPv6 Segment Routing Header (SRH) and its uses, we first discuss what Segment Routing (SR) is and the role of the SRH in this type of routing.

2.5.7.3.1 What Is Segment Routing?

SR [**RFC8402**] [**RFC8754**] is based on an old concept called "source routing" [**SUNACMSIG77**] that was proposed many decades ago. In SR, a source node attaches an ordered list of instructions, called "Segments," to a packet, allowing a network to use the attached Segments to steer the packet to a destination node. A Segment can be viewed as a routing instruction that a node executes on an incoming packet to decide how the packet should be directed through the SR network to its destination. The node may forward the packet according to one of the following methods:

- Forward the packet according to the shortest path (determined by the underlying routing protocol) to the destination.
- Simply forward the packet through a specific local interface.
- Deliver the packet to a particular application or service instance.

A Segment has a broader representation and can be any topological or service-based instruction. Additionally, it can have a semantic that is confined to an SR node (local semantic) or global within an SR domain (global semantic). An SR domain is the set of nodes that are configured to participate in the source-based routing model. SR provides a mechanism that allows a sequence of packets with a common characteristic (called a flow) to be directed along a specific topological path to a destination node, while allowing only the ingress node to the SR domain to maintain per-flow state; the other nodes up to the destination do not maintain such state information.

SR can be implemented directly over an MPLS or IPv6 network architecture with no changes to their forwarding plane. On an MPLS network supporting SR (SR-MPLS), SR nodes encode a Segment as an MPLS label. SR-MPLS nodes encode an ordered list of Segments as a stack of labels (a label stack). At any given node in an MPLS network, the Segment to be processed is the one at the top of the label stack. Once a node has completed processing a Segment, it pops the corresponding label from the label stack.

A new type of IPv6 Routing header called the SRH, with Routing Type 4 [**RFC8754**] (see Figure 2.23), has been defined for SR over IPv6 infrastructure (SRv6). An SRv6 node encodes a Segment in the IPv6 SRH as an IPv6 address and represents an ordered list of Segments in the SRH as an ordered list of IPv6 addresses. SRv6 associates an instruction with a Segment and encodes it as an IPv6 address. The active Segment (i.e., the Segment to be immediately processed) in the IPv6 SRH is indicated by the Destination IPv6 Address of the IPv6 packet containing the SRH. The next active Segment is indicated by a pointer (in the Segment Left field) in the SRH (see Figure 2.24). When an SR node completes processing an SRv6 SID, it decrements the Segment Left field value and copies the next Segment into the Destination IPv6 Address field of the IPv6 packet. When the node directs an incoming IPv6 packet onto an SR Policy, it adds the related SRH to the packet.

A Segment in both SR-MPLS and SRv6 is often identified by its Segment Identifier (SID). An SR-MPLS SID is an MPLS label explicitly associated with a Segment, or an integer value that indexes into an MPLS label space associated with a Segment. An SRv6 SID is an IPv6 address that is configured and explicitly associated with a Segment. SRv6 instantiates an SR Policy on an SR node as an ordered list of SRv6 SIDs in the SRH. The headend (i.e., the ingress node of the SR domain) that supports an SR Policy binds a SID (called a Binding SID) to that policy. Upon receiving a packet with an active Segment matching the Binding SID of a local SR Policy, the headend uses that SR Policy to steer the packet into the SR domain.

The control plane in an SR-MPLS or SRv6 architecture may be distributed, centralized, or hybrid. In a distributed architecture, routing protocols such as IS-IS and OSPF (which are Interior Gateway

Routing Protocols (IGP)) or BGP are responsible for allocating and signaling the Segments. In this architecture, an SR-MPLS or SRv6 node computes an SR Policy individually and decides how to steer packets based on that SR Policy.

In a centralized architecture, an SR Controller is responsible for allocating and instantiating the Segments, as well as computing the source-routed policies to be used in the SR domain. The SR Controller decides which nodes will steer packets and the source-routed policies on which these packets are steered. This architecture does not restrict how the SR Controller programs SR policies on the SR network. The SR Controller can program SR policies on an SR node using the Network Configuration Protocol (NETCONF) **[RFC6241]**, Path Computation Element Communication Protocol (PCEP) **[RFC9168]**, or BGP **[RFC4271] [RFC4760]**.

The SR architecture also does not limit the number of SR controllers in an SR domain; a single SR domain can have multiple SR controllers performing the programming. This architecture allows one or more SR controllers to discover the SIDs that are to be instantiated at particular nodes, along with the sets of local (SR Local Block (SRLB)) and global (SR Global Block (SRGB)) labels to be used at each node.

A hybrid architecture adds a centralized SR Controller to the base distributed control plane. For example, when an ingress SR node receives a packet to be steered and its destination is outside the ingress node's IGP domain, the SR Controller may compute an SR Policy on behalf of the ingress SR node. This architecture does not impose restrictions on how the nodes belonging to the distributed control plane interact with the SR Controller. Possible protocols that can be used between the SR Controller and the SR nodes are PCEP and BGP.

2.5.7.3.2 *Understanding the IPv6 SRH*

Each entry (Segment) in the n Segment List fields of the SRH is an IPv6 address (128 bits), and the entries (Segments) are encoded in reverse order (Figures 2.23 and 2.24):

- The last entry (Segment) has an index of 0: Segment List [0].
- The first entry (Segment) has an index of n and is the First Segment: Segment List [n].
- The active entry (Segment) has an index equal to the value in the Segments Left field. The Active Segment is the next Segment to be visited from the current node.
- The Segments Left field indicates the number of route segments (IPv6 addresses) yet to be visited before reaching the final destination.
  - This is equal to the number of IPv6 addresses remaining, starting from the address in the main header's IPv6 Destination Address field (i.e., the Active Segment) up to the address before the final destination address (i.e., up to the penultimate IPv6 address).
- The current processing node copies the Active Segment (IPv6 address) to the Destination Address field of the IPv6 header, as shown in Figure 2.24.
- If there is any additional data that must be carried in the SRH, this information is entered as Optional TLV Objects in the SRH, as shown in Figures 2.23 and 2.24 (e.g., Security (Hash-Based Message Authentication Code (HMAC)), Network Functions Virtualization (NFV) metadata).

2.5.7.3.3 *Processing of SRH at a Segment Routing Capable Source Node*

The IPv6 node that originates an IPv6 packet with an SRH (i.e., the source node or the SRv6 head-end) must be an SR-capable node (Figure 2.25). The IPv6 processing at this SRv6 source node is described in this sub-section. The SRv6 node creates an SRH as follows:

- The Segment List of the IPv6 nodes to be visited is organized in reverse order.
- The IPv6 address in Segment List [0] is the LAST Segment to be visited.
- The IPv6 address in Segment List [n] is the FIRST (next) Segment to be visited after the SRv6 source node (i.e., the next SRv6 node immediately after the SRv6 source node).
- The value in the Segments Left field is set to n.

0	7	15	23	31
Next Header	Header Ext. Length	Routing Type = 4	Segments Left	
Last Entry	Flags	Tag		
Segment List [0] (128-bit IPv6 Address)				
⋮				
Segment List [n] (128-bit IPv6 Address)				
Optional Type Length Value (TLV) Objects (variable)				

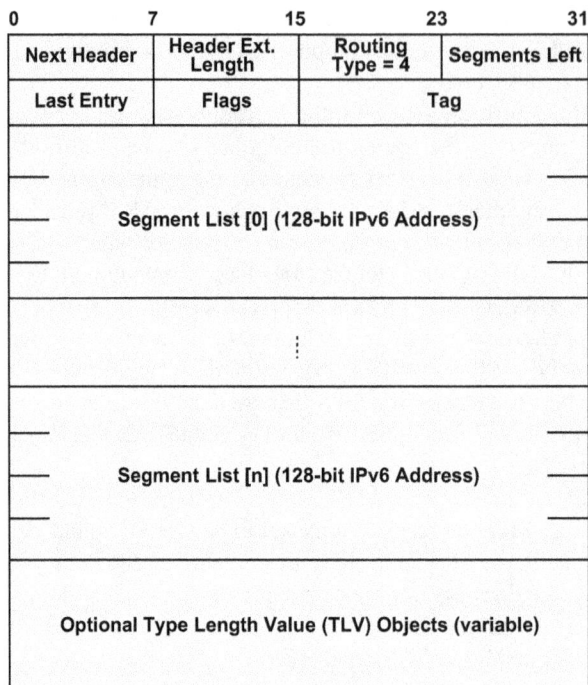

- **Next Header (8 Bits)**: This field, in the Segment Routing Header, identifies the type of header immediately following the Segment Routing Header. Each IPv6 extension header type including upper-layer protocols (e.g., TCP, UDP, ICMPv6, IGMP, OSPFv6) has a specific code.

- **Header Ext. Length (8 Bits)**: This specifies the length of the Segment Routing Header in bytes, excluding the first 8 bytes.

- **Segments Left (8 Bits)**: This specifies the number of route segments remaining (i.e., the number of explicitly listed intermediate nodes still to be visited before reaching the final destination).

- **Last Entry (8 Bits)**: This specifies the index (zero-based), in the Segment List, of the last element of the Segment List.

- **Flags (8 Bits)**: This contains 8 bits of flags.

- **Tag (16 Bits)**: This specifies a tag which is used to tag a packet as part of a class or group of packets (e.g., packets sharing the same set of properties).

- **Segment List [n]**: This is the 128-bit IPv6 address representing the nth segment in the Segment List. The Segment List is encoded starting from the last segment of the Segment Routing Policy. That is, the first element of the Segment List (Segment List [0]) contains the last segment of the Segment Routing Policy, the second element contains the penultimate segment of the Segment Routing Policy, and so on.

- **Optional TLV Objects**: This specifies a variable list of TLVs of the Segment Routing Header that provide metadata for segment processing.

FIGURE 2.23   IPv6 Segment Routing Header (Routing Type=4).

- The index of the First (next) Segment is set to n.
- The IPv6 Destination Address field in the fixed IPv6 header is set to the IPv6 address of the first segment, specifically the address in Segment List [n].
- The SRv6 source node sends the IPv6 packet containing the SRH to the next SRv6 node at the IPv6 address indicated in the IPv6 Destination Address field of the fixed IPv6 header.

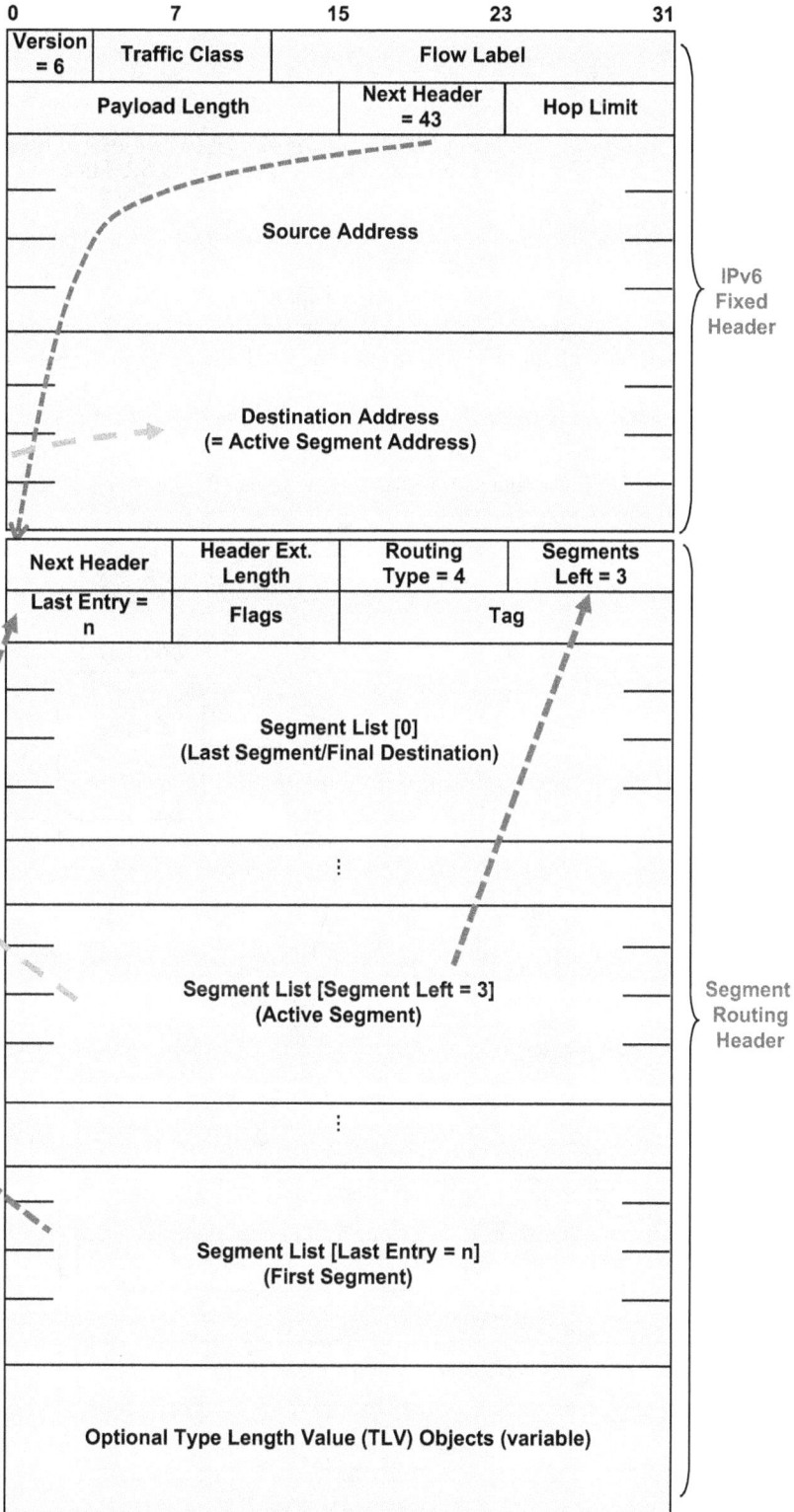

FIGURE 2.24 IPv6 header with Segment Routing Header.

- The IPv6 packet with SRH is sent to the next segment (Segment List [*n*]) using standard IPv6 routing.

The processing of an IPv6 packet with an SRH at a non-SR transit node (Node E in Figure 2.26) is simpler and involves only standard IPv6 forwarding based on the address in the IPv6 Destination Address field of the fixed IPv6 header. Node E does not perform any SRH inspection or update, only standard IPv6 forwarding.

2.5.7.3.4   Processing of SRH at an SR Endpoint

An SR endpoint is an SR-capable node whose IPv6 address is in the IPv6 Destination Address field of the IPv6 packet (i.e., Nodes B, C, and D, in Figures 2.25, 2.27, and 2.28). An SR endpoint that receives an IPv6 packet with an SRH will inspect the SRH and perform the following:

- IF the Segments Left field value > 0, THEN
  - Decrement the Segments Left field value by 1.
  - Update the IPv6 Destination Address in the fixed IPv6 header with the address in the Segment List [Segments Left].

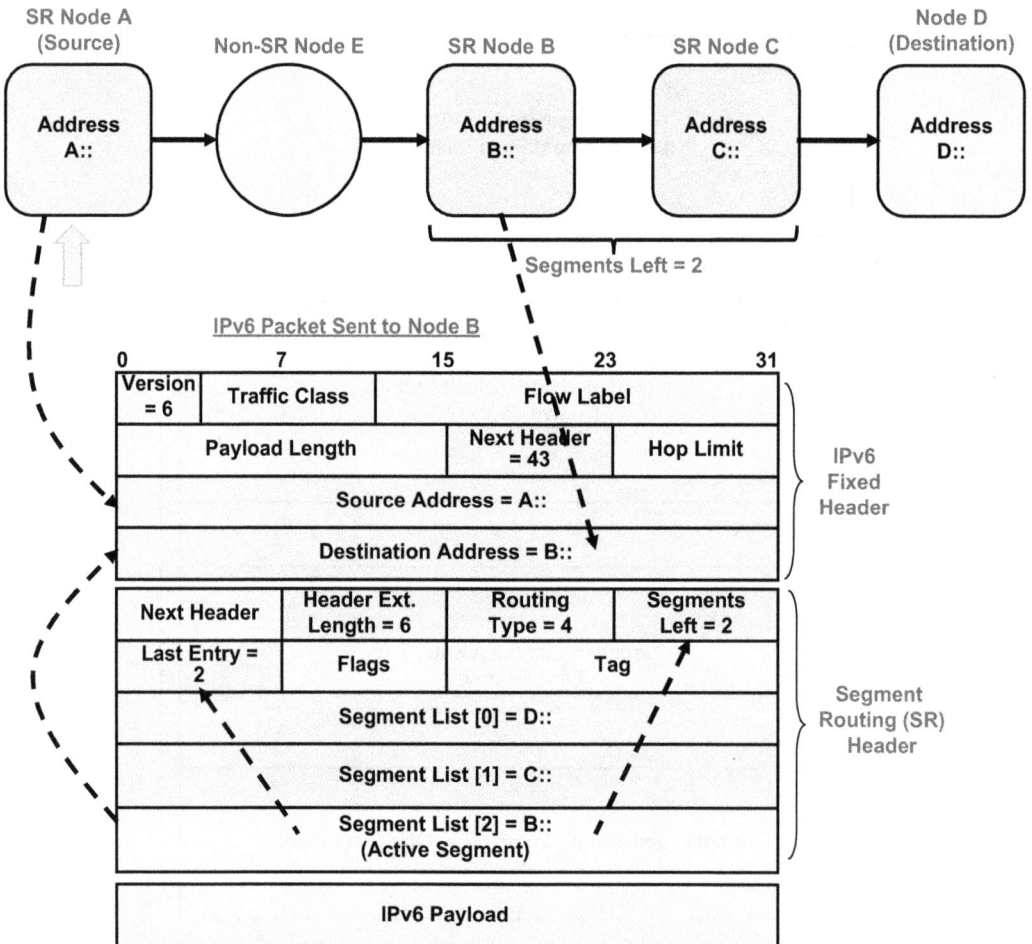

FIGURE 2.25   Processing of Segment Routing Header at a Segment Routing capable source node A.

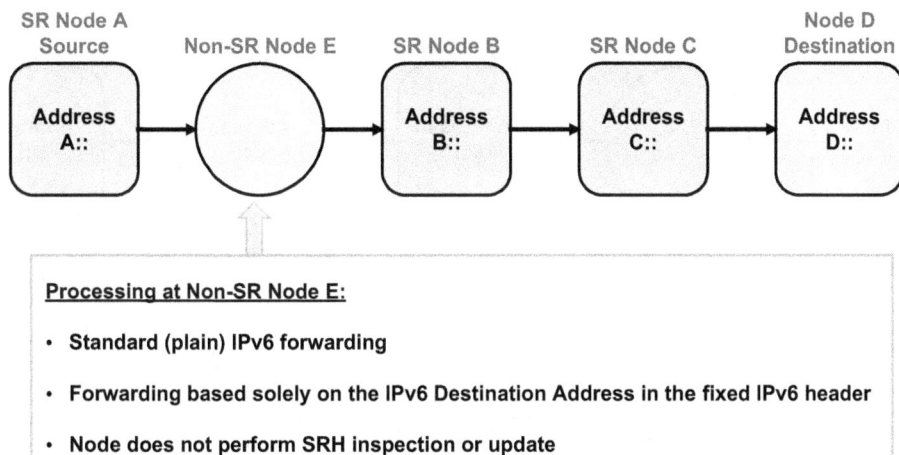

FIGURE 2.26 Processing of Segment Routing Header at a non-Segment Routing capable node E.

- Forward the resulting IPv6 packet with the updated SRH according to the new address in the IPv6 Destination Address field.
- (Note: The above actions are performed by Node B and Node C as shown in Figures 2.27 and 2.28).
- ELSE (i.e., Segments Left field value=0).
  - Remove the fixed IPv6 header and SRH.
  - Process the IPv6 packet payload.
  - If the IPv6 payload is an inner IPv4 or IPv6 packet, perform a lookup for the packet's Destination Address in the local IPv4/IPv6 routing/forwarding table, and then forward the IPv4/IPv6 packet accordingly.
  - If the IPv6 payload is a TCP, UDP, SCTP, ICMPv6, or any other upper-layer protocol PDU, forward the payload locally to the corresponding port/socket.
- (Note: The above actions are performed by Node D as shown in Figure 2.28. Node D, the final destination, performs standard IPv6 processing and does not need to be SR-capable.)

2.5.8 FRAGMENT HEADER (HEADER CODE 44)

The Fragment header is used by an IPv6 source to perform packet fragmentation and by a destination to perform packet reassembly [RFC8200]. The Next Header field of the fixed IPv6 header or an extension header is set to a value of 44 to indicate that the following extension header is a Fragment header. Figure 2.29 shows the format of the Fragment header. IPv6 is designed such that only a source node can fragment IPv6 packet payloads. An IPv6 source uses the Fragment header to send a packet that is larger than what would fit within the path MTU to the packet's destination. If the IPv6 source node determines that the data submitted by the upper-layer protocol entity to be placed in the IPv6 packet payload is larger than the link or path MTU, the source divides the submitted data into IPv6 fragment payloads and uses the Fragment header to specify information for fragment reassembly at the destination.

An IPv6 router must never fragment transit IPv6 packets that are being forwarded, but the router itself can originate IPv6 fragments from its internal upper-layer protocol entities. The nodes between the source and destination in the IPv6 internetwork do not fragment IPv6 packet payloads. This means that data sent from source applications that do not have knowledge of the path MTU to the destination but require fragmentation are discarded by IPv6 routers on the forwarding path.

The Fragment header (Figure 2.29) consists of a 1-byte Next Header field, a 13-bit Fragment Offset field, a More Fragments flag, and a 32-bit Identification field. The Fragment Offset, More

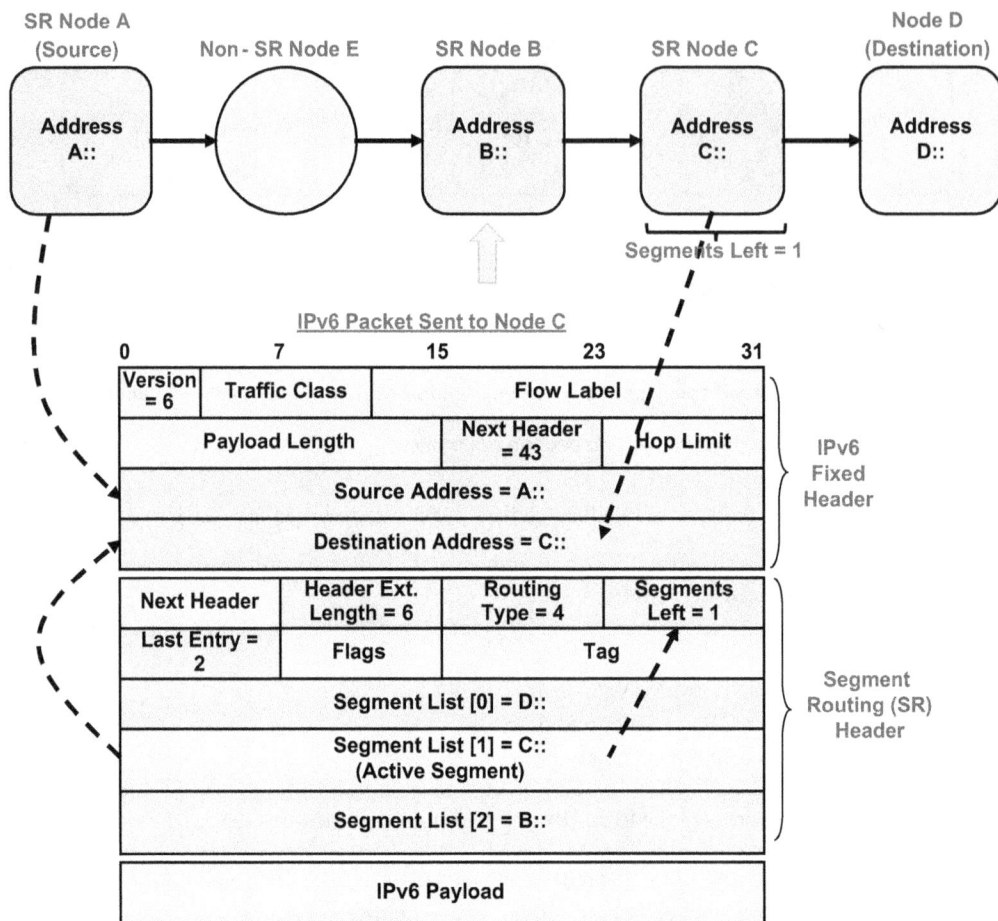

FIGURE 2.27 Processing of Segment Routing Header at a Segment Routing endpoint B.

Fragments flag, and Identification fields in Figure 2.29 have the same meaning and usage as the corresponding fields in the IPv4 header shown in Figure 2.3. The 1-byte Fragment Offset field is defined for IPv6 packets that carry 8-byte fragment blocks, *meaning the IPv6 Fragment header cannot be used for IPv6 packets that carry Jumbograms*. The 13-bit Fragment Offset field indicates that the maximum number of 8-byte blocks that can be expressed in this field is 8191. This also means that the Fragment Offset field can be used to indicate only a fragment data piece with a starting position of 1×8 bytes up to 8191×8 bytes, or 65,528 bytes.

A number of subtle distinctions exist between the IPv4 and IPv6 fragmentation fields:

- In IPv4, as shown in Figure 2.3, the flags related to fragmentation are the three high-order bits of the 16-bit block of the IPv4 header, which consists of the combination of the 3-bit Flags field and the 13-bit Fragment Offset field.
- In IPv6, the single flag used for fragmentation is the low-order bit of the 16-bit block that combines the 13-bit Fragment Offset field and the M flag bit, as shown in Figure 2.29.
- In IPv4, a 16-bit Identification field (Figure 2.3) is used, whereas IPv6 uses a 32-bit Identification field (Figure 2.29).
- IPv6 does not have a DF (Do not Fragment) flag because IPv6 routers never perform packet fragmentation. This means the DF Flag in IPv4 is always set to 1 for all IPv6 packets and is therefore not needed in IPv6.

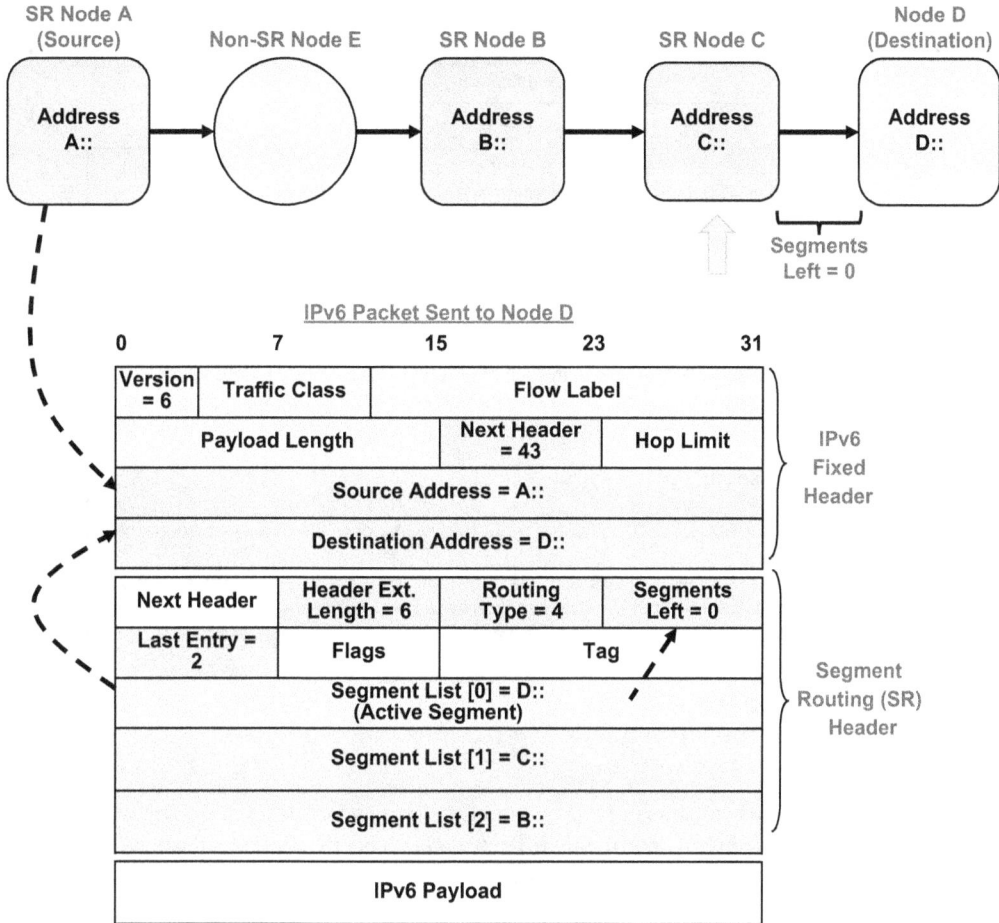

FIGURE 2.28 Processing of Segment Routing Header at a Segment Routing endpoint C.

When an IPv6 source sends a packet that is larger than the path MTU, it may divide the packet into fragments and send each fragment as a separate IPv6 packet. The receiver reassembles the received fragments into the original IPv6 packet. The source node generates an Identification value for each IPv6 packet that is to be fragmented. The source must ensure that the Identification value for a fragment packet is different from that of any other fragmented packet sent recently with the same Source Address and Destination Address. If a fragmented IPv6 packet contains a Routing header, the Destination Address of interest is the packet's final destination.

2.5.8.1 IPv6 Fragmentation Process
When a source is to forward an IPv6 packet that requires fragmentation, it first divides the packet into *unfragmentable* and *fragmentable* parts.

2.5.8.1.1 Original (Unfragmented) IPv6 Packet
The original, larger unfragmented IPv6 packet consists of three parts (see Figure 2.30): Per-Fragment headers, Extension and Upper-Layer headers, and Fragmentable Part:

- **Per-Fragment Headers**: This part of the original IPv6 packet must be processed by all intermediate IPv6 nodes between the source node performing the fragmentation and the packet's destination. This includes the fixed IPv6 header and the following optional

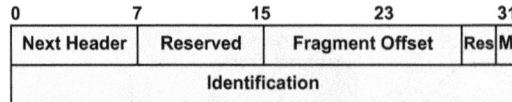

0	7	15	23	31
Next Header	Reserved	Fragment Offset	Res	M
Identification				

Res = Reserved; M = More Fragments

- **Next Header (8 Bits)**: This identifies the initial header type of the Fragmentable Part of the original IPv6 packet. When indicating an upper-layer protocol, the values/codes carried in this field are the same values as those used in the IPv4 packet Protocol field.

- **Reserved (8 Bits)**: This is a reserved field that is initialized to zero for transmission; and ignored on reception.

- **Fragment Offset (13 Bits)**: This is the offset (in 8-byte blocks) of the data following this header, relative to the start of the Fragmentable Part of the original IPv6 packet.

- **Res (2 Bits)**: This is a reserved field that is initialized to zero for transmission and ignored on reception.

- **M flag (1 Bit)**: When set to 1, indicates more fragments, or 0, indicates last fragment.

- **Identification (32 Bits)**: The source node generates an Identification value for every packet that is to be fragmented. The identification value is different for any other fragmented packet sent recently with the same Source Address and Destination Address.

FIGURE 2.29   Fragment header (Header Code=44).

extension headers when present: Hop-by-Hop Options header, Destination Options header intended for processing at intermediate IPv6 nodes, and the Routing header. This part includes all IPv6 headers up to and including the Routing header, if present.

- **Extension and Upper-Layer Headers**: The Extension headers consist of all other IPv6 extension headers that are not included in the Per-Fragment headers part of the IPv6 packet. For fragmentation purposes, the ESP header (Header Code 50) is not considered an IPv6 extension header. The Upper-Layer header consists of the first upper-layer protocol header that is not an IPv6 extension header (e.g., TCP, UDP, IPv4, IPv6, ICMPv6, including ESP for fragmentation purposes).
- **Fragmentable Part**: This part of the original IPv6 packet must be processed only at the final destination of the packet. It consists of the remainder of the IPv6 packet after the upper-layer protocol header or after any IPv6 header (i.e., the initial IPv6 header or extension header) that contains a value in the Next Header field equal to the No Next Header value (59).

The IPv6 source divides the Fragmentable Part of the original packet into fragments. The source chooses the length of each resulting fragment packet such that it fits within the MTU of the path to the packet's destination(s). The source must also ensure that each complete fragment, except possibly the last ("rightmost") fragment, has a length that is an integer multiple of 8 bytes. The source transmits the fragments in separate "fragment packets," as illustrated in Figure 2.30.

2.5.8.1.2   Composition of First IPv6 Fragment Packet

The source node forms IPv6 packets, each containing a fragment, as shown in Figure 2.30. Each IPv6 fragment packet is composed of the unfragmentable part (i.e., Per-Fragment headers), an IPv6 Fragment header, and a portion of the Fragmentable Part. Figure 2.30 illustrates an example fragmentation process for an IPv6 packet that is divided into three fragments.

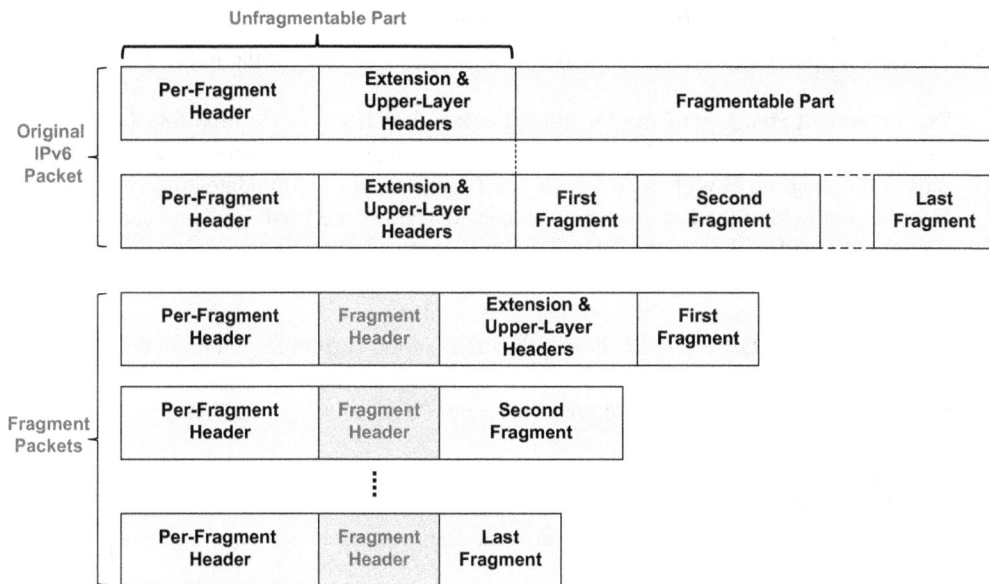

FIGURE 2.30 IPv6 packet fragmentation process.

The Next Header field value of the Fragment header for each fragment packet (Figures 2.29 and 2.30) indicates the first extension header or the upper-layer protocol in the original fragmentable part. The Fragment Offset field value in the Fragment header (Figure 2.29) indicates the offset (in 8-byte blocks, also known as fragment blocks) of the current IPv6 fragment relative to the beginning of the fragmentable part of the original IPv6 packet. The source IPv6 node sets the M (More Fragments) flag on all IPv6 fragment packets except the last fragment packet. The source node must also ensure that all fragment packets created from the same (original) IPv6 packet contain the same Identification field value.

The first fragment packet created by the IPv6 source consists of the following (see Figure 2.30):

1. **Per-Fragment Headers of the Original IPv6 Packet**: The IPv6 source updates the Payload Length field of the original IPv6 header to reflect the length of this (first) fragment packet only (excluding the length of the IPv6 header itself). The source also modifies the value in the Next Header field of the last extension header included in the Per-Fragment headers to 44.
2. **Fragment Header**: This part contains the following:
   a. The value in the Next Header field identifies the first header following the Per-Fragment headers of the original IPv6 packet.
   b. The Fragment Offset field indicates the offset of the fragment, in 8-byte units, relative to the start of the Fragmentable Part of the original IPv6 packet. The value in the Fragment Offset field of the first ("leftmost") fragment is 0.
   c. The M flag is set to 1 since this is the first fragment.
   d. The Identification field contains a value that the IPv6 source generated for the original IPv6 packet.
3. **IPv6 Extension Headers, If Any, and the Upper-Layer Protocol Header**: This part includes extension headers that must be placed in the first fragment, as illustrated in Figure 2.30. The size of the extension headers up to the Upper-Layer protocol header is limited to the path MTU to the packet's destination(s).
4. **First Fragment**: This part contains the first data piece (fragment) of the original IPv6 packet.

2.5.8.1.3   Composition of Subsequent IPv6 Fragment Packets
Each subsequent fragment packet created by the IPv6 source consists of the following:

1. **Per-Fragment Headers of the Original Packet**: The IPv6 source modifies the Payload
   Length field of the original IPv6 header to reflect the length of the current fragment packet
   only (excluding the IPv6 header length itself). The source also updates the value in the
   Next Header field of the last extension header included in the Per-Fragment headers to 44.
2. **Fragment Header**: This part contains the following:
   a. The value in the Next Header field identifies the first extension header following the
      Per-Fragment headers of the original IPv6 packet.
   b. The Fragment Offset field indicates the offset of the current fragment, in 8-byte units,
      relative to the start of the Fragmentable Part of the original IPv6 packet.
   c. The M flag is set to 0 if the fragment is the last ("rightmost") one; otherwise, the M flag
      is set to 1.
   d. The Identification field contains a value that the IPv6 source generated for the original
      IPv6 packet.
3. **Current Fragment**: This section contains the fragment itself.

While creating fragments, the IPv6 source must ensure that fragments do not overlap with any other
fragments created from the original IPv6 packet.

2.5.8.2   IPv6 Reassembly Process

After packet fragmentation, the intermediate IPv6 routers forward the fragment packets until they
reach the destination IPv6 address. Fragment packets belonging to the same original IPv6 packet
may take different paths to the destination and may arrive out of order. The IPv6 destination node
uses the Source Address and Destination Address fields in the fixed IPv6 header, along with the
Identification field in the Fragment header, to reassemble the fragment packets into the original IPv6
packet payload. Figure 2.31 illustrates the IPv6 reassembly process for the original IPv6 packet
fragmented in Figure 2.30.

After receiving all the fragments belonging to a packet, the destination node calculates the original payload length, and updates the Payload Length field in the IPv6 header of the reassembled
packet. Furthermore, the destination node sets the Next Header field of the last header of the unfragmentable part to the value in the Next Header field of the Fragment header of the first fragment.

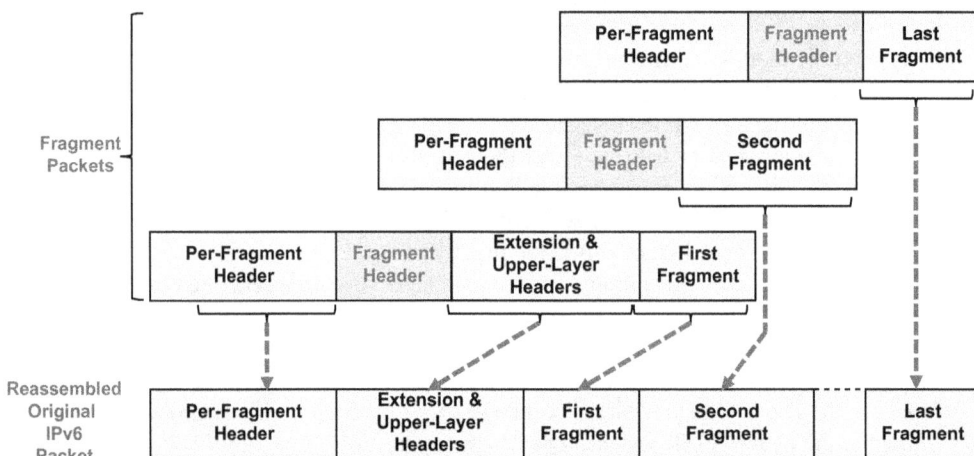

FIGURE 2.31   IPv6 packet reassembly process.

Reference **[RFC8200]** recommends that a destination node waits a reassembly time of 60 seconds before abandoning the reassembly process and discarding the partially reassembled IPv6 packet. If the destination determines that the first fragment has arrived but the reassembly of the original packet has not completed, it sends an ICMPv6 Type 3 "Time Exceeded" message indicating "Fragment Reassembly Time Exceeded" (Code = 1) to the source of the fragment.

2.5.8.2.1 Rules that Govern the Fragment Reassembly Process

The destination IPv6 node reassembles fragment packets into their original, unfragmented form, as illustrated in Figure 2.31. The following rules govern the fragment reassembly process:

- The IPv6 destination reassembles the original IPv6 packet only from fragment packets that have the same Source Address, Destination Address, and Fragment Identification.
- The Per-Fragment headers after fragment reassembly (i.e., of the reassembled original IPv6 packet) contain all headers up to, but excluding, the Fragment header of the first fragment packet created, with the following two changes (note that the Fragment Offset of the first fragment packet is 0):
  - The destination obtains the value in the Next Header field of the last header of the Per-Fragment headers from the Next Header field of the Fragment header of the first fragment.
  - The destination computes the value of the Payload Length field of the reassembled original IPv6 packet as the sum of the length of the Per-Fragment headers and the length and offset of the last fragment. For example, the destination can use the following formula for computing the Payload Length field value of the reassembled original IPv6 packet:

$$PayL.orig = PayL.first - FragL.first - 8 + (8 \times FragOff.last) + FragL.last$$

    where,
    $PayL.orig$ = Payload Length field value of the reassembled original IPv6 packet.
    $PayL.first$ = Payload Length field value of the first fragment packet.
    $FragL.first$ = Length of the fragment following the Fragment header of the first fragment packet.
    $FragOff.last$ = Fragment Offset field value of the Fragment header of the last fragment packet.
    $FragL.last$ = Length of the fragment following the Fragment header of the last fragment packet.
- The destination constructs the Fragmentable Part of the reassembled original IPv6 packet from the fragments that follow the Fragment headers in each fragment packet. The destination also computes the length of each fragment by subtracting the length of the headers occurring between the IPv6 header and the fragment itself from the value in the packet's Payload Length field; the destination calculates the fragment's relative position in the Fragmentable Part from its Fragment Offset field value. Note that the final reassembled IPv6 packet does not contain the Fragment header (see Figure 2.31).
- If the IPv6 destination node detects that a received fragment is a whole datagram (i.e., both the fragment's Fragment Offset field and the M flag are set to 0), then the fragment does not require any further reassembly, allowing the destination to process it as a fully reassembled IPv6 packet. In this case, the destination updates the Next Header field value, adjusts the value in the Payload Length field, removes the Fragment header, and so on. The destination should also independently process any other fragments that match this packet (i.e., fragments with the same IPv6 Source Address, IPv6 Destination Address, and Fragment Identification).

2.5.8.2.2   Error Conditions during Reassembly of Fragmented Packets

During the reassembly of fragmented packets at the IPv6 destination node, the following error conditions may arise:

- If the destination has received insufficient fragments to allow complete reassembly of the original IPv6 packet after 60 seconds have passed since receiving the first fragment of that packet, it must abandon reassembly of that packet and discard all the fragments received for it. If the destination has received the first fragment (i.e., the one with a zero in its Fragment Offset field), it should send an ICMPv6 Type 3 "Time Exceeded" message indicating "Fragment Reassembly Time Exceeded" (Code 1) to the source of that fragment.
- If the destination derives the length of a fragment (from the Payload Length field of the fragment packet) and finds that its length is not a multiple of 8 bytes, while the M flag of that fragment is set to 1, then the destination must discard that fragment and send an ICMPv6 Type 4 "Parameter Problem" message indicating "Erroneous Header Field Encountered" (Code 0) to the source of the fragment, pointing to the Payload Length field of the fragment packet.
- If the destination detects that the length and offset of a fragment would cause the Payload Length of the packet being reassembled to exceed 65,535 bytes, then it must discard that fragment and send an ICMPv6 Type 4 "Parameter Problem" message with Code 0 to the source of the fragment, pointing to the Fragment Offset field of the fragment packet.
- If the destination finds that the first fragment does not include all headers up to an Upper-Layer header (i.e., the entire IPv6 Header Chain **[RFC7112]**), then it should discard that fragment and send an ICMPv6 Type 4 "Parameter Problem" message indicating "IPv6 First Fragment has Incomplete IPv6 Header Chain" (Code 3) to the source of the fragment, with the Pointer field set to zero.
- If the destination finds that any of the fragments being reassembled overlap with any other fragments for the same IPv6 packet, then it must abandon the reassembly of that packet and discard all the fragments that have been received for it, but should not send ICMPv6 error messages to the fragment's source.
- It should be noted that there is a possibility that some fragments may be duplicated in the network. Instead of treating these exact duplicate fragments as overlapping fragments, the destination may support mechanisms that detect this condition and drop exact duplicates while retaining the other fragments belonging to the same original IPv6 packet.

2.5.8.2.3   Rare Events during Fragment Reassembly

There are some rare (infrequent) conditions that may occur at the destination node during fragment reassembly but are not considered errors:

- It may happen that the number and content of the headers placed before the IPv6 Fragment header of different fragments belonging to the same original packet may differ. In this case, the destination should process whatever headers are present before the Fragment header in each fragment packet, before queuing the fragments for reassembly. The destination retains only those headers in the Offset zero fragment packet in the reassembled packet.
- It is possible that the values in the Next Header field in the IPv6 Fragment headers of different fragments belonging to the same original IPv6 packet may differ. In this case, the destination uses only the value from the fragment packet with Offset zero for reassembly.
- It may happen that other fields in the IPv6 header vary across the fragments being reassembled. In this case, the IPv6 implementation has to consult the corresponding specifications that use those fields for additional instructions on how to handle this condition if the basic mechanism that uses the values from the Offset zero fragment packet is not sufficient.

2.5.9 AUTHENTICATION HEADER (HEADER CODE 51)

The AH, when included in an IPv6 packet, contains information that can be used for data authentication (verification of the IPv6 node that sent the packet), data integrity (verification that the contents of the packet were not modified in transit), and anti-replay protection (assurance that the packet, when captured or intercepted, cannot be retransmitted and its contents accepted as valid data). The authentication information also allows for the verification that the fields in the IPv6 header did not change while the packet was transiting the IPv6 internetwork. The AH, defined in **[RFC4302]**, is part of the security architecture for IPv6, as defined in **[RFC4301]**. To identify the next extension header as the AH, the source IPv6 node sets the Next Header field of the current header to the value of 51 **[RFC4302]**. Figure 2.32 shows the format of the AH.

The AH contains a 1-byte Next Header field, a 1-byte Payload Length field (which specifies the number of 4-byte blocks that exist in the AH, excluding the first two bytes), a 2-byte Reserved field, a 4-byte Security Parameters Index (SPI) field (used to identify a specific IP Security Association), a 4-byte Sequence Number field (used for anti-replay protection), and a variable-length Authentication Data field that contains an Integrity Value Check (ICV). The receiving IPv6 node uses the ICV for data authentication and data integrity checks.

The contents of the AH do not provide data confidentiality services for the IPv6 packet's upper-layer PDU. Data confidentiality involves encrypting the IPv6 packet's contents so that they cannot be viewed without the secret encryption key. To support data authentication and data integrity for the entire IPv6 packet as well as data confidentiality for the packet's upper-layer PDU, the sender of the IPv6 packet must include both the AH and the ESP header and trailer in the packet.

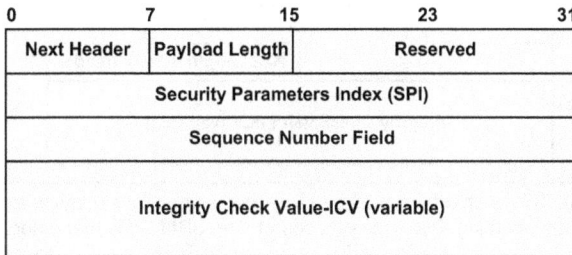

* **Next Header (8 Bits)**: This identifies the type of the next payload after the Authentication Header. The value of this field is chosen from the set of IP Protocol Numbers (e.g., a value of 4 indicates IPv4, a value of 41 indicates IPv6, and a value of 6 indicates TCP).

* **Payload Length (8 Bits)**: This specifies the length of Authentication Header in 32-bit words (4-byte units), minus "2".

* **Reserved (16 Bits)**: This field is reserved for future use. It must be set to "zero" by the sender, and it should be ignored by the recipient. Note that the value is included in the ICV calculation, but is otherwise ignored by the recipient.

* **SPI (32 Bits)**: This is an arbitrary 32-bit value that is used by a receiver to identify the Security Association (SA) to which an incoming IPv6 packet is bound.

* **Sequence Number (32 Bits)**: This field contains a counter value that increases by one for each IPv6 packet sent, i.e., a per-SA packet sequence number. The Sequence Number field provides anti-replay protection.

* **ICV**: This is a variable-length field that contains the ICV for this IPv6 packet. The field must be an integral multiple of 32 bits (IPv4 or IPv6) in length. The ICV provides data authentication and data integrity.

FIGURE 2.32 Authentication header (Header Code = 51).

2.5.10 Encapsulating Security Payload (ESP) Packet Format (Header Code 50)

The ESP header and trailer (defined in **[RFC4303]**) included in an IPv6 packet contains information used for data confidentiality, data authentication, data integrity, and replay protection services for the packet's payload. The information in the ESP header does not provide security services for the fixed IPv6 header or any extension headers placed before the ESP header. The Next Header field of the current header is set to 50 to indicate that the following extension header is the ESP header and trailer **[RFC4303]**. Figure 2.33 shows the format of the ESP header and trailer.

The ESP header contains a 4-byte SPI field used to identify the IPsec SA and a 4-byte Sequence Number field used for anti-replay protection. The ESP trailer contains a 0 to 255-byte Padding field, a 1-byte Padding Length, a 1-byte Next Header, and variable-length Authentication Data fields. The sending IPv6 node uses the Padding field to ensure that the ESP payload has a 4-byte boundary and that the encryption algorithms have appropriate data-block boundaries. The value in the Padding Length field indicates the number of bytes in the Padding field. The end of the ESP header is marked by the Authentication Data field, which contains the ICV.

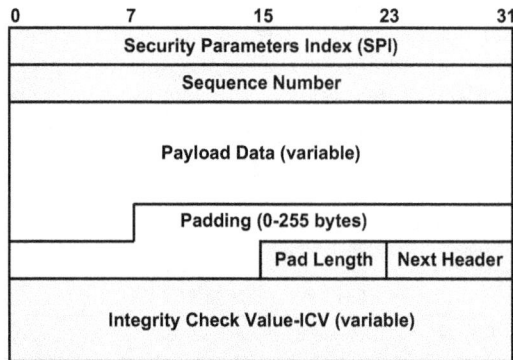

- **SPI (32 Bits)**: This is an arbitrary 32-bit value that is used by a receiver to identify the SA to which an incoming IPv6 packet is bound. The SPI field is mandatory.

- **Sequence Number (32 Bits)**: This field contains a counter value that increases by one for each packet sent, i.e., a per-SA packet sequence number.

- **Payload Data**: This is a variable-length field containing data (from the original IPv6 packet) described by the Next Header field. The Payload Data field is mandatory and is an integral number of bytes in length.

- **Padding (0-255 Bytes)**: This field is used to ensure 4-byte boundaries for the ESP payload and appropriate data-block boundaries for encryption algorithms.

- **Pad Length (8 Bits)**: This field indicates the number of pad bytes immediately preceding it in the Padding field. The range of valid values is 0 to 255, where a value of zero indicates that no Padding bytes are present. The Pad Length field is mandatory.

- **Next Header (8 Bits)**: This field is mandatory and identifies the type of data contained in the Payload Data field, for example, an IPv4 or IPv6 packet, or a next layer header and data. The value of this field is chosen from the set of IP Protocol Numbers (e.g., a value of 4 indicates IPv4, a value of 41 indicates IPv6, and a value of 6 indicates TCP).

- **ICV**: This is a variable-length field computed over the ESP header, Payload, and ESP trailer fields.

FIGURE 2.33 Encapsulating Security Payload packet format (Header Code = 50).

2.6   IPv6 PACKET SIZE ISSUES

IPv6 [**RFC8200**] requires that all interfaces in an IPv6 internetwork be capable of processing IPv6 packets with an MTU of at least 1,280 bytes. This MTU is referred to as the *IPv6 minimum link MTU*. Any interface that cannot forward a 1,280-byte IPv6 packet as a single block must provide link-specific fragmentation and reassembly at a processing entity below IPv6. Interfaces that support a configurable MTU must be set to an MTU of at least 1,280 bytes. In practice, it is recommended that IPv6 interfaces be configured with an MTU of 1,500 bytes or greater to accommodate possible overheads from packet encapsulation (i.e., tunneling) and to avoid performing IPv6-layer fragmentation. A receiving IPv6 interface must be able to accept IPv6 packets as large as the MTU of the upstream node to which it is directly attached.

The recommended best practice is for IPv6 nodes to implement Path MTU Discovery [**RFC8201**], which allows source nodes to discover and take advantage of MTUs of forwarding paths greater than 1,280 bytes. However, it is possible that a source node may have only a minimal IPv6 implementation (e.g., MTU configuration in its boot ROM) that omits the implementation of Path MTU Discovery, which may restrict it from sending IPv6 packets larger than 1,280 bytes.

When a source node sends an IPv6 packet larger than the MTU of a path, it usually includes the IPv6 Fragment header in fragment packets, allowing for packet reassembly at the destination(s). However, the use of packet fragmentation is not encouraged if an application can send packets that fit within the measured path MTU.

In practice, an IPv6 node must be able to accept a packet that, after fragment reassembly, is as large as 1,500 bytes. An IPv6 node is also permitted to accept fragmented packets that, after reassembly, exceed 1,500 bytes. It is recommended that an upper-layer protocol entity or application that relies on IPv6 fragmentation to send packets larger than a path's MTU should not send packets larger than 1,500 bytes (which is the untagged Ethernet frame payload size) unless it is certain that the destination can reassemble packets of that larger size.

The minimum frame size of Ethernet is 64 bytes, which comprises a 14-byte Ethernet frame header, 4-byte trailer (Frame Check Sequence (FCS)), and a 46-byte payload. The maximum untagged Ethernet frame size is 1,518 bytes, with a payload size of 1,500 bytes. If a source sends upper-layer data that results in an Ethernet frame size of less than the 64-byte minimum, it adds padding bytes to ensure that the frame meets the minimum Ethernet frame size.

The 7-byte Preamble, 1-byte Start of Frame Delimiter (SFD), and 12-byte Interframe Gap attached to every packet are not considered part of the Ethernet frame; however, when included with the 64-byte frame, they occupy $64+8+12=84$ bytes on the Ethernet link. Note that the TCP header is 20 bytes, with the option for additional header data (TCP Options and padding), while the UDP header is fixed at 8 bytes. If a source sends a TCP segment with no extra data bytes in an IPv6 packet (with no header extensions), this packet will contain 60 bytes (20-byte TCP header plus 40-byte IPv6 header). However, it is not possible to create a valid Ethernet frame smaller than this. Thus, this 40-byte packet will need to be padded to achieve a 46-byte packet before the 14-byte Ethernet frame header and FCS are attached.

If a source is to send a 1,500-byte IPv6 packet in a tagged Ethernet frame (i.e., IEEE 802.1Q tagged frame), the Ethernet frame maximum size needs to be 1,522 bytes due to the extra 4 bytes used in the tagged Ethernet frame. The untagged Ethernet frame size varies from 64 to 1,518 bytes, with a 46- to 1,500-byte payload. The minimum tagged Ethernet IEEE 802.1Q frame size remains 64 bytes, but an Ethernet bridge may extend the minimum frame size from 64 to 68 bytes when transmitting a frame, allowing other switches to remove the IEEE 802.1Q tag without having to add padding to a frame (if its size happens to fall below the minimum Ethernet frame size of 64 bytes). *In this case, when the Ethernet bridge receives a 64-byte frame with an IEEE 802.1Q tag, it will extend it to a 68-byte frame so that any other bridge that removes the tag will not have to add padding to the frame since it will still be a valid sized frame.* An Ethernet frame that is less than the minimum of 64 bytes is called a *runt frame*. A 1,280-byte IPv6 packet gives a 1,298-byte untagged Ethernet frame and a 1,302-byte tagged Ethernet frame.

2.6.1 Determining the Maximum Upper-Layer Payload Size for an IPv6 Packet

When an IPv6 node receives upper-layer data and wants to compute the maximum payload size for an IPv6 packet, it must take into account the size of the IPv6 header, which is larger than the IPv4 header. For example, an IPv4 node computes the TCP Maximum Segment Size (MSS) option as the maximum packet size (which can be a default value on the node or a value that the node has learned through the Path MTU Discovery mechanism **[RFC1191]**) minus 40 bytes (i.e., 20 bytes for the minimum-length IPv4 header and 20 bytes for the minimum-length TCP header).

For TCP over IPv6, the IPv6 node computes the MSS as the maximum packet size minus 60 bytes (i.e., 40 bytes for the fixed-length IPv6 header and 20 bytes for the minimum-length TCP header). This is because the IPv6 header has a minimum length of 40 bytes (i.e., an IPv6 header with no extension headers), which is 20 bytes larger than the minimum-length IPv4 header.

2.7 PATH MTU DISCOVERY

An IPv6 node that has a large amount of data to transmit to another node usually sends the data as a series of IPv6 packets, with each packet having a size smaller than or equal to the path MTU. Alternatively, the node can receive the data as larger packets, which it fragments into a series of fragments, each with a size smaller than or equal to the path MTU. *The path MTU is the minimum of all link MTUs on the path between an IPv6 packet's source and its* destination. Specifically, the path MTU is the largest packet size that can successfully traverse all the links from the source IPv6 node to the destination IPv6 node without requiring packet fragmentation. The link MTU is the maximum packet size (in bytes) that can be conveyed over a link in one piece.

The source node does not perform fragmentation on IPv6 packets that are smaller than the path MTU because they are small enough to be successfully forwarded by all routers on the path. Although not mandatory, it is recommended for IPv6 nodes to implement Path MTU Discovery **[RFC8201]** in order to discover paths with a path MTU greater than the IPv6 minimum link MTU **[RFC8200]**, and to send appropriately sized IPv6 packets over those paths. The source node uses the receipt of an ICMPv6 Type 2 "Packet Too Big" message (Code 0) to discover the path MTU **[RFC8201]**.

The following steps summarize the process through which a source node discovers the path MTU:

1. The source node assumes that the path MTU is the MTU of the interface on which the IPv6 packet is to be forwarded (i.e., the outgoing link MTU).
2. The source node sends IPv6 packets with a size equal to the assumed path MTU.
3. If an IPv6 router on the path is unable to forward the IPv6 packet over a link because the packet is larger than the outgoing link MTU, it transmits an ICMPv6 Packet Too Big message back to the source node and discards the packet. This ICMPv6 Packet Too Big message includes a 32-bit MTU field that contains the MTU of the link on which packet forwarding failed **[RFC8201]**.
4. The source node sets the path MTU to the value in the MTU field of the ICMPv6 Packet Too Big message, to be used for forwarding subsequent packets to the destination.
5. Upon receiving the ICMPv6 Packet Too Big message, the source node prepares an IPv6 packet for transmission and starts again at Step 2. It repeats Steps 2 through 4 as many times as necessary until it discovers the path MTU.
6. The source node discovers the path MTU when it receives either an acknowledgment from the packet's destination or no more ICMPv6 Packet Too Big messages.

It is recommended in **[RFC8201]** that IPv6 nodes support Path MTU Discovery. Recall from above that all IPv6 implementations are required to support the IPv6 minimum link MTU of 1,280 bytes. Thus, IPv6 nodes that do not support Path MTU Discovery must use the IPv6 minimum link MTU as the path MTU (i.e., as the maximum packet size). However, doing this may result in sending smaller IPv6 packets than necessary, because most links and paths in modern networks have a path MTU greater than the IPv6 minimum link MTU. Sending IPv6 packets much smaller than the path MTU leads to underutilization of network resources and wastage, and likely results in suboptimal data throughput.

The path between a packet's source and destination may change when there are alterations in the routing topology. If the path changes and the path MTU becomes smaller, the source node may receive ICMPv6 Packet Too Big messages, requiring it to repeat Steps 2 through 4 to discover the new path MTU. If the path MTU becomes larger, the source node can detect this change (as described in [RFC8201]) by attempting to transmit a larger IPv6 packet after a minimum delay of 5 minutes (the recommended time is 10 minutes) upon receiving an ICMPv6 Packet Too Big message.

2.8 UPPER-LAYER PROTOCOL ISSUES

The TCP/IP Transport Layer or other upper-layer protocols that include the IP addresses contained in the IP header in their checksum computation must be modified for use over IPv6. Such protocols must be adjusted to include the 128-bit IPv6 addresses instead of the 32-bit IPv4 addresses in the checksum computation. Figure 2.34 shows the TCP and UDP "pseudo-header" for IPv6 used in checksum computation.

With IPv6, both TCP and UDP must be updated to perform checksum calculations that include the 128-bit IPv6 addresses. For example, TCP stores various operational information in a special table known as the Transmission Control Block (TCB). Each entry in the TCB contains information

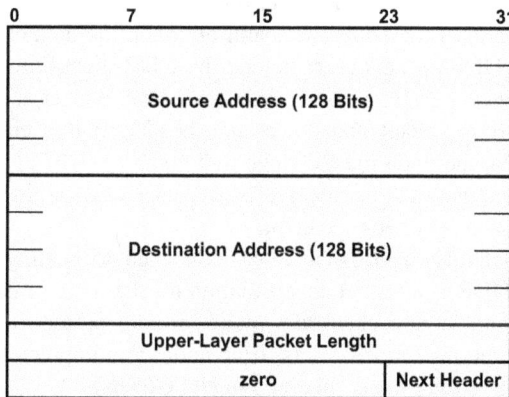

- **Destination Address (128 Bits)**: If the IPv6 packet contains a Routing header, the Destination Address used in the pseudo-header is that of the final destination. At the originating node, that address will be in the last element of the Routing header; at the recipient(s), that address will be in the Destination Address field of the IPv6 header.

- **Upper-Layer Packet Length (32 Bits)**: The Upper-Layer Packet Length in the pseudo-header is the length of the upper-layer header and data (e.g., TCP header plus TCP data). Some upper-layer protocols carry their own length information (e.g., the Length field in the UDP header); for such protocols, that is the length used in the pseudo-header. Other protocols (such as TCP) do not carry their own length information, in which case the length used in the pseudo-header is the Payload Length from the IPv6 header, minus the length of any extension headers present between the IPv6 header and the upper-layer header.

- **Next Header (8 Bits)**: The Next Header field value in the pseudo-header identifies the upper-layer protocol (e.g., 6 for TCP or 17 for UDP). It will differ from the Next Header value in the fixed IPv6 header if there are extension headers between the IPv6 header and the upper-layer header.

FIGURE 2.34 TCP and UDP "Pseudo-header" for IPv6.

about the TCP endpoints (IP addresses and TCP port), the status of the TCP connection, running data about the TCP segments being exchanged, and the buffers for sending and receiving TCP data.

Reference **[RFC8200]** makes the following important observations about the use of the IPv6 pseudo-header:

- If the IPv6 packet contains a Routing header, the final destination in this IPv6 extension header is used as the Destination Address in the IPv6 pseudo-header. At the IPv6 node that originates this packet, the final destination address is the last element/segment (i.e., Segment List [0]) of the Routing header. At the recipient(s), the final destination address will also be written in the Destination Address field of the packet's IPv6 header.
- The value in the Next Header field in the pseudo-header identifies the type of upper-layer protocol in the IPv6 packet (e.g., TCP=6, UDP=17). This value may differ from the value in the Next Header field in the IPv6 header if the IPv6 packet carries extension headers between the IPv6 header and the upper-layer header.
- The Packet Length of the upper-layer protocol data in the pseudo-header is the length of both the upper-layer header and its data (e.g., TCP header plus TCP data). Some upper-layer protocols have formats that allow them to carry their own length information (e.g., UDP datagrams have a Length field in the UDP header). For such protocols, the pseudo-header uses that length information. For PDUs (such as TCP segments) that do not contain their own length information, the length used in the pseudo-header is the value in the Payload Length field in the IPv6 header, minus the length of any IPv6 extension headers present between the IPv6 header and the upper-layer protocol header.
- Unlike IPv4, which makes the UDP checksum optional, the default behavior of an IPv6 node that originates UDP packets is to include the UDP checksum (this is not optional). This means that whenever an IPv6 node originates a UDP packet, it must compute a UDP checksum over the IPv6 packet and the pseudo-header. If that checksum computation yields a result of zero, the node must change that result to 0xFFFF for placement in the UDP header. IPv6 destinations that receive UDP packets containing a checksum of zero must discard those packets and log the error.
- An exception to the default behavior of an IPv6 node when originating a UDP packet occurs when protocols use UDP as a tunnel encapsulation mechanism. In this case, the originating IPv6 node may enable zero-checksum mode for a specific port (or a group of ports) for sending and/or receiving tunneled data. IPv6 nodes that implement the zero-checksum mode must follow the requirements specified in **[RFC6936]**.
- Unlike ICMP for IPv4 (ICMPv4) **[RFC792]**, which does not include a pseudo-header in its checksum, *ICMPv6 **[RFC4443]** includes the IPv6 pseudo-header in its checksum* computation. This change aims to prevent mis-delivery of ICMPv6 messages or protect the ICMPv6 functions in the event that the IPv6 header fields on which ICMPv6 depends are corrupted. Such protection does not exist in ICMPv4, which is not covered by an Internet-layer checksum. The value in the Next Header field in the IPv6 pseudo-header for ICMPv6 is 58.

2.8.1   TCP AND UDP CHECKSUMS

TCP, UDP, and ICMPv4 (ICMP for IPv4) messages all contain a Checksum field. Source nodes incorporate a *pseudo-header* that includes both the IPv4 Source Address and Destination Address fields when calculating the checksum for each of these messages. IPv6 modified the checksum calculation for TCP, UDP, and ICMPv6 to include IPv6 addresses when these messages are sent over IPv6. Figure 2.34 shows the structure of the IPv6 pseudo-header that an IPv6 source node uses when making checksum calculations for TCP, UDP, and ICMPv6 messages. *The Checksum field is optional in UDP, but since the IPv6 header has no Checksum field, it is mandatory when UDP is carried by IPv6.*

When calculating the checksum for TCP, UDP, and ICMPv6 messages carried in an IPv6 packet, the IPv6 pseudo-header (Figure 2.34) includes the packet's 128-bit Source Address field, the 128-bit Destination Address field, the 32-bit upper-layer Packet Length field (indicating the length of the upper-layer PDU), and the 8-bit Next Header field (indicating the type of upper-layer protocol).

IPv6 and IPv4 nodes both use the same algorithm for computing the TCP, UDP, and ICMPv6 message checksum value. The source uses a 16-bit cyclic redundancy check algorithm to compute a message checksum, and the receiver employs the same algorithm to recompute and validate the message. The pseudo-header is logically prefixed to the TCP, UDP, or ICMP message header when the source node computes the message checksum. The checksum is calculated over the entire TCP, UDP, or ICMP header and the payload, plus the prefixed pseudo-header (i.e., placed at the beginning) that mimics the real IPv4/v6 header.

The IPv4/v6 pseudo-header is used in TCP and UDP checksum calculations, for example, to maintain the end-to-end feature of a session and to avoid replication of data available in the IPv4/v6 header. *The purpose of including the pseudo-header in the TCP, UDP, and ICMP message checksum calculation is to allow the receiving node to confirm that the packet has reached the target destination and to mitigate IP spoofing attacks. The pseudo-header uses relevant fields of the IPv4/v6 header that are static (i.e., do not change when packets are* routed).

The pseudo-header (for TCP, UDP, and ICMPv6 messages) is not the real IPv4/v6 header used to send an IP packet, but rather one used solely for the upper-layer message checksum calculation. Note that the IPv6 header does not include a Checksum field because Link-Layer protocols (such as PPP and Ethernet) have checksums, and when combined with checksums in upper-layer protocols (such as TCP, UDP, and ICMP), they are sufficient for IPv6.

2.9 BASIC IPv4 PACKET FORWARDING OPERATIONS

The changes made to the IPv4 header to obtain the newer IPv6 header resulted in a reduction in the set of instructions an IPv6 router must execute to forward a packet. The forwarding path of an IPv4 router typically performs the following operations to forward a normal IPv4 packet (see also Figure 2.35):

1. Verify the Checksum field value in the IPv4 header by calculating a local checksum (using the same algorithm required by all IPv4 routers) and comparing this checksum with the value stored in the IPv4 header Checksum field. This step is required by **[RFC1812]**, however, most modern high-speed routers routinely skip this step because the Link-Layer frame carrying the IPv4 packet (e.g., Ethernet frame) already has an FCS that performs the same function.
2. Some IPv4 routers verify the value in the IPv4 header Version field to ensure that it is equal to 4. Although both **[RFC791]** and **[RFC1812]** do not require this step, enabling an IPv4 router to perform this check contributes to saving network bandwidth. This is because there is no benefit in forwarding an IPv4 packet with an invalid version number across the IPv4 network only to have it discarded by the IPv4 destination node.
3. Decrement the IPv4 header TTL field value by 1. If the resulting value is less than 1 (i.e., 0), transmit an ICMPv4 Type 11 Time Exceeded message indicating "Time to Live Exceeded in Transit" (Code=0) to the source of the IPv4 packet and then discard the packet. If not, write the resulting (updated) value in the packet's TTL field.
4. Examine the IPv4 header to see if it contains IPv4 Options (in the Options field). If the packet contains Options, proceed to process them.
5. Parse the address in the IPv4 header Destination Address field and perform a longest prefix matching (LPM) lookup of that address in the IPv4 local routing (or forwarding) table to determine the outgoing interface and the next-hop IPv4 address. If no matching entry (or route) is found, transmit an ICMPv4 Type 3 "Destination Unreachable" message indicating "Host Unreachable" (Code=1) to the source of the IPv4 packet and discard the packet.

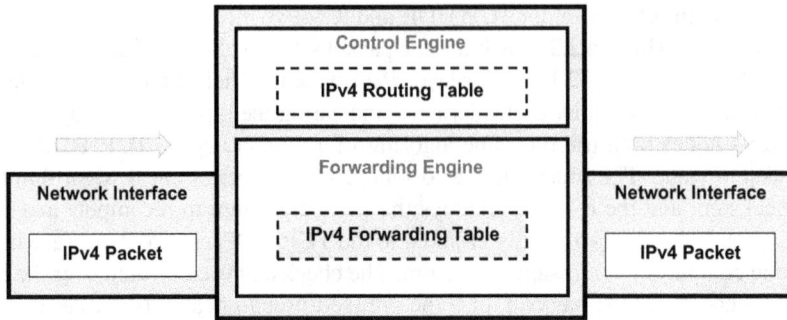

```
┌─────────────────────────────────────────┐
│          Control Engine                  │
│   ┌ ─ ─ ─ ─ ─ ─ ─ ─ ─ ─ ─ ─ ─ ─ ┐        │
│   │    IPv4 Routing Table         │       │
│   └ ─ ─ ─ ─ ─ ─ ─ ─ ─ ─ ─ ─ ─ ─ ┘        │
│                                           │
│          Forwarding Engine                │
│   ┌ ─ ─ ─ ─ ─ ─ ─ ─ ─ ─ ─ ─ ─ ─ ┐        │
│   │   IPv4 Forwarding Table        │      │
│   └ ─ ─ ─ ─ ─ ─ ─ ─ ─ ─ ─ ─ ─ ─ ┘        │
└─────────────────────────────────────────┘

Network Interface                 Network Interface

IPv4 Packet                       IPv4 Packet
```

1. **IPv4 Header Checksum verification**: The router calculates a checksum locally and compares the result with the value stored in the IPv4 header Checksum field. Most modern high-speed routers commonly skip this calculation although this step is required by RFC 1812,.
2. **Version verification**: The router checks if the value in the Version field is 4. Routers my choose to perform this step (although this step is not required by RFC 791 or 1812) to save network bandwidth because a packet carrying an invalid version number should not be propagated across the IPv4 network only to be discarded by the destination node. Given that we now have IPv6, performing this check is important.
3. **TTL update**: The router decrements the TTL value by 1 before deciding if to forward the packet. When a packet is to be forwarded by a node and the received TTL value is already zero or is decremented to zero, then the packet is discarded. A node that is the final destination of a packet should not discard a packet with TTL value equal to zero; they node should process the packet normally.
   - If the new TTL value is less than 1, the router sends an ICMPv4 Type 11, Code 0 message (i.e., Time Exceeded -Time to Live Exceeded in Transit) to the source of the packet and then discards the packet. If not, the router places the new value in the TTL field.
4. **Check for the presence of IPv4 header Options**: If Options are present, the router process them. To optimize operations, most modern routers ignore IPv4 Options when present.
5. **Destination Address lookup using the local IPv4 forwarding table**: The router performs a lookup to determine the correct outgoing interface and next-hop IPv4 address for the packet.
   - If a route is not found, the router sends an ICMPv4 Type 3, Code 1 message (i.e., Destination Unreachable -Host Unreachable) to the source of the packet and discards the packet.
6. **Perform Packet fragmentation if necessary**: If the router finds that the IPv4 MTU of the outgoing interface is less than the value of the Total Length field and the Don't Fragment (DF) flag is set to 0, it performs IPv4 fragmentation.
   - If the MTU of the outgoing interface is less than the value of the Total Length field and the DF flag is set to 1, it sends an ICMPv4 Type 3, Code 4 message (i.e., Destination Unreachable -Fragmentation Needed and DF Set) to the source of the packet and discards the packet.
7. **Header Checksum recalculation**: The router recalculates a new IPv4 Header Checksum value, and place this value in the Header Checksum field. A new value has to be calculated because fields such as the TTL field have been updated.
8. **Packet forwarding**: The router forwards the packet on the appropriate outgoing interface

FIGURE 2.35   Basic IPv4 packet forwarding operations.

6. Check if the MTU of the outgoing IPv4 forwarding interface is less than the value in the IPv4 header Total Length field. If true, set the Don't Fragment (DF) flag to 0, and perform IPv4 packet fragmentation. However, if the forwarding interface's MTU is less than the

Total Length field value and the DF flag is set to 1, send an ICMPv4 Type 3 "Destination Unreachable" message indicating "Fragmentation Needed and DF Set" (Code=4) to the source of the IPv4 packet and discard the packet.
7. Recalculate a new IPv4 header Checksum field value (because several fields such as the TTL have changed), and write this new value into the Checksum field.
8. Forward the updated IPv4 packet on the appropriate outgoing interface to the next-hop or final destination (i.e., directly attached network or host).

2.10   BASIC IPv6 PACKET FORWARDING OPERATIONS

By removing or simplifying certain IPv4 fields and Options, IPv6 streamlines the critical IPv4 router forwarding processing that must be performed by routers. The forwarding path of an IPv6 router typically performs the following operations to forward a normal IPv6 packet:

1. Check the value in the IPv6 header Version field to ensure it is equal to 6. This step is not required by **[RFC8200]**, however, performing this check contributes to saving network bandwidth as discussed above for IPv4.
2. Decrement the IPv6 header Hop Limit field value by 1. If the resulting value is less than 1, transmit an ICMPv6 Type 3 "Time Exceeded" message indicating "Hop Limit Exceeded

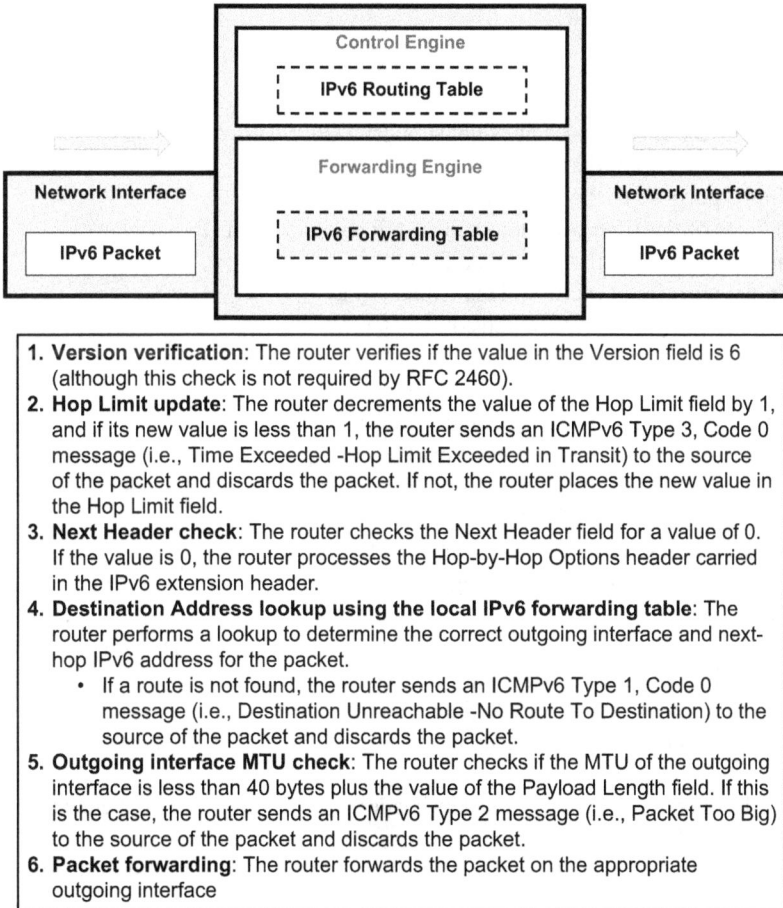

1. **Version verification**: The router verifies if the value in the Version field is 6 (although this check is not required by RFC 2460).
2. **Hop Limit update**: The router decrements the value of the Hop Limit field by 1, and if its new value is less than 1, the router sends an ICMPv6 Type 3, Code 0 message (i.e., Time Exceeded -Hop Limit Exceeded in Transit) to the source of the packet and discards the packet. If not, the router places the new value in the Hop Limit field.
3. **Next Header check**: The router checks the Next Header field for a value of 0. If the value is 0, the router processes the Hop-by-Hop Options header carried in the IPv6 extension header.
4. **Destination Address lookup using the local IPv6 forwarding table**: The router performs a lookup to determine the correct outgoing interface and next-hop IPv6 address for the packet.
   • If a route is not found, the router sends an ICMPv6 Type 1, Code 0 message (i.e., Destination Unreachable -No Route To Destination) to the source of the packet and discards the packet.
5. **Outgoing interface MTU check**: The router checks if the MTU of the outgoing interface is less than 40 bytes plus the value of the Payload Length field. If this is the case, the router sends an ICMPv6 Type 2 message (i.e., Packet Too Big) to the source of the packet and discards the packet.
6. **Packet forwarding**: The router forwards the packet on the appropriate outgoing interface

FIGURE 2.36   Basic IPv6 packet forwarding operations.

in Transit" (Code=0) to the source of the IPv6 packet and discard the packet. Otherwise, write the resulting value in the Hop Limit field.

3. Check the value in the Next Header field of the IPv6 header to see if it is equal to 0. If true, the IPv6 extension header following is the Hop-by-Hop Options header and must be processed.

4. Parse the address in the IPv6 header Destination Address field and perform a lookup in the local IPv6 routing/forwarding table to determine the outgoing forwarding interface and the next-hop IPv6 address. If no matching entry or route is found, transmit an ICMPv6 Type 1 "Destination Unreachable" message indicating "No Route To Destination" (Code=0) to the source of the IPv6 packet and then discard the packet.

5. If the MTU of the outgoing forwarding interface is less than the sum of 40 and the value in the IPv6 header Payload Length field, transmit an ICMPv6 Type 2 "Packet Too Big" message to the source of the IPv6 packet and discard the packet.

6. Forward the IPv6 packet on the appropriate outgoing interface to the next-hop or final destination.

The above IPv6 processing steps show that forwarding an IPv6 packet is much simpler than forwarding an IPv4 packet. This is because the IPv6 forwarding steps do not involve verifying and recalculating a header checksum, performing packet fragmentation (when the interface MTU is exceeded), or processing IP Options (when present) that are not intended for the local router (Figure 2.36).

REVIEW QUESTIONS

2.1. Explain why the IPv6 header does not support a Checksum field.

2.2. Explain the purpose of the IPv6 Traffic Class field.

2.3. Explain the purpose of the IPv6 Flow Label field.

2.4. Which fields of the IPv6 packet constitute the payload of an IPv6 packet?

2.5. Explain the purpose of the IPv6 Next Header field.

2.6. Explain the purpose of the IPv6 Hop Count field.

2.7. Why does IPv6 support IPv6 extension headers?

2.8. What is the purpose of the IPv6 Router Alert Option?

2.9. What is the purpose of the IPv6 Jumbo Payload Option?

2.10. What is the purpose of the IPv6 Home Address Option?

2.11. What is the purpose of the IPv6 No Next Header Option?

2.12. Explain the purpose of the IPv6 Hop-by-Hop Options extension header.

2.13. Explain the purpose of the IPv6 Destination Options header.

2.14. Explain the purpose of the IPv6 Routing header.

2.15. Explain briefly what Segment Routing is.

2.16. What is the purpose of the IPv6 Fragment header?

2.17. List which IPv6 extension headers are not fragmentable and explain why.

2.18. List which IPv6 extension headers are fragmentable and explain why.

2.19. What is the purpose of the IPv6 Authentication header?

2.20. What is the purpose of the Encapsulating Security Payload (ESP) header?

2.21. What is path MTU discovery?

2.22. Explain the purpose of the IPv6 pseudo-header in upper-layer protocol checksum calculation such as TCP and UDP.

2.23. Why do IPv4 routers have to recalculate a new IPv4 header Checksum field value when forwarding IPv4 packets?

2.24. Explain why it is beneficial to verify the version number of IPv4/v6 packets before processing and forwarding even it is not mandatory.

REFERENCES

[RFC791]. Information Sciences Institute, University of Southern California, "Internet Protocol", *IETF RFC 791*, September 1981.

[RFC792]. Internet Control Message Protocol, *IETF RFC 792*, September 1981.

[RFC826]. David C. Plummer, "An Ethernet Address Resolution Protocol", *IETF RFC 826*, November 1982.

[RFC1191]. J. Mogul and S. Deering, "Path MTU Discovery", *IETF RFC 1191*, November 1990.

[RFC1812]. F. Baker, Ed., "Requirements for IP Version 4 Routers", *IETF RFC 1812*, June 1995.

[RFC2205]. R. Braden, L. Zhang, S. Berson, S. Herzog, and S. Jamin, Eds., "Resource ReSerVation Protocol (RSVP) – Version 1 Functional Specification", *IETF RFC 2205*, September 1997.

[RFC2460]. S. Deering and R. Hinden, "Internet Protocol, Version 6 (IPv6) Specification", *IETF RFC 2460*, December 1998.

[RFC2474]. K. Nichols, S. Blake, F. Baker, and D. Black, "Definition of the Differentiated Services Field (DS Field) in the IPv4 and IPv6 Headers", *IETF RFC 2474*, December 1998.

[RFC2475]. S. Blake, D. Black, M. Carlson, E. Davies, Z. Wang, and W. Weiss, "An Architecture for Differentiated Services", *IETF RFC 2475*, December 1998.

[RFC2675]. D. Borman, S. Deering, and R. Hinden, "IPv6 Jumbograms", *IETF RFC 2675*, August 1999.

[RFC2710]. S. Deering, W. Fenner, and B. Haberman, "Multicast Listener Discovery (MLD) for IPv6", *IETF RFC 2710*, October 1999.

[RFC2711]. C. Partridge and A. Jackson, "IPv6 Router Alert Option", *IETF RFC 2711*, October 1999.

[RFC3168]. K. Ramakrishnan, S. Floyd, and D. Black, "The Addition of Explicit Congestion Notification (ECN) to IP", *IETF RFC 3168*, September 2001.

[RFC3810]. R. Vida and L. Costa, "Multicast Listener Discovery Version 2 (MLDv2) for IPv6", *IETF RFC 3810*, June 2004.

[RFC4271]. Y. Rekhter, T. Li, and S. Hares, Eds., "A Border Gateway Protocol 4 (BGP-4)", IETF RFC 4271, January 2006.

[RFC4291]. R. Hinden and S. Deering, "IP Version 6 Addressing Architecture", *IETF RFC 4291*, February 2006.

[RFC4301]. S. Kent and K. Seo, "Security Architecture for the Internet Protocol", *IETF RFC 4301*, December 2005.

[RFC4302]. S. Kent, "IP Authentication Header", *IETF RFC 4302*, December 2005.

[RFC4303]. S. Kent, "IP Encapsulating Security Payload (ESP)", *IETF RFC 4303*, December 2005.

[RFC4443]. A. Conta, S. Deering, and M. Gupta, Eds., "Internet Control Message Protocol (ICMPv6) for the Internet Protocol Version 6 (IPv6) Specification", *IETF RFC 4443*, March 2006.

[RFC4760]. T. Bates, R. Chandra, D. Katz, and Y. Rekhter, "Multiprotocol Extensions for BGP-4", *IETF RFC 4760*, January 2007.

[RFC5095]. J. Abley, P. Savola, and G. Neville-Neil, "Deprecation of Type 0 Routing Headers in IPv6", *IETF RFC 5095*, December 2007.

[RFC6275]. C. Perkins, D. Johnson, and J. Arkko, Eds., "Mobility Support in IPv6", *IETF RFC 6275*, July 2011.

[RFC6241]. R. Enns, M. Bjorklund, J. Schoenwaelder, and A. Bierman, Eds., "Network Configuration Protocol (NETCONF)", *IETF RFC 6241*, June 2011.

[RFC6398]. F. Le Faucheur, Ed., "IP Router Alert Considerations and Usage", *IETF RFC 6398*, October 2011.

[RFC6437]. S. Amante, B. Carpenter, S. Jiang, and J. Rajahalme, "IPv6 Flow Label Specification", *IETF RFC 6437*, November 2011.

[RFC6554]. J. Hui, J.P. Vasseur, D. Culler, and V. Manral, "An IPv6 Routing Header for Source Routes with the Routing Protocol for Low-Power and Lossy Networks (RPL)", *IETF RFC 6554*, March 2012.

[RFC6936]. G. Fairhurst and M. Westerlund, "Applicability Statement for the Use of IPv6 UDP Datagrams with Zero Checksums", *IETF RFC 6936*, April 2013.

[RFC7112]. F. Gont, V. Manral, and R. Bonica, "Implications of Oversized IPv6 Header Chains", *IETF RFC 7112*, January 2014.

[RFC8200].   S. Deering and R. Hinden, "Internet Protocol, Version 6 (IPv6) Specification", *IETF RFC 8200*, July 2017.

[RFC8201].   J. McCann, S. Deering, J. Mogul, and R. Hinden, Eds., "Path MTU Discovery for IP version 6", *IETF RFC 8201*, July 2017.

[RFC8402].   C. Filsfils, S. Previdi, L. Ginsberg, B. Decraene, S. Litkowski, and R. Shakir, "Segment Routing Architecture", *IETF RFC 8402*, July 2018.

[RFC8754].   C. Filsfils, D. Dukes, S. Previdi, J. Leddy, S. Matsushima, and D. Voyer, Eds., "IPv6 Segment Routing Header (SRH)", *IETF RFC 8754*, March 2020.

[RFC8883].   T. Herbert, "ICMPv6 Errors for Discarding Packets Due to Processing Limits", *IETF RFC 8883*, September 2020.

[RFC9168].   D. Dhody, A. Farrel, and Z. Li, "Path Computation Element Communication Protocol (PCEP) Extension for Flow Specification", *IETF RFC 9168*, January 2022.

[RFC9631].   R. Bonica, Y. Kamite, A. Alston, D. Henriques, and L. Jalil, "The IPv6 Compact Routing Header (CRH)", *IETF RFC 9631*, August 2024.

[SUNACMSIG77].   Carl A. Sunshine, "Source Routing in Computer Networks", *ACM SIGCOMM Computer Communication Review*, Vol. 7, No. 1, pp. 29–33, 1 January 1977.

3 IPv6 Addressing Architecture

3.1 INTRODUCTION

A significant effort was put into defining the addressing architecture of the IP version 6 protocol, resulting in the latest specification in **[RFC4291]**. Unlike IPv4 addresses, which are 32 bits long, IPv6 addresses are 128 bits long and serve as identifiers for network interfaces and sets of interfaces in an IPv6 internetwork. IPv6 has three basic types of addresses: unicast, multicast, and anycast. Unlike IPv4, IPv6 does not support broadcast addresses; their function is instead replaced by various types of special IPv6 multicast addresses.

An interface in the IPv6 internetwork may be assigned different types of IPv6 addresses. However, an IPv6 unicast address identifies a single interface. Since any given interface belongs to a single IPv6 node, a node may use any of its interface IPv6 unicast addresses as its identifier.

This chapter discusses the IPv6 addressing architecture, representations of IPv6 addresses in textual form, definitions of various types of IPv6 addresses (unicast, multicast, and anycast), and the different types of addresses maintained by IPv6 hosts and routers. The discussion includes details about the basic formats for IPv6 addresses (unicast, anycast, and multicast) and how they are used by nodes in an IPv6 internetwork.

3.2 GLOBAL IPv6 ADDRESS ALLOCATION

This section describes the IPv6 address space for globally unique addresses and the different types of IPv6 addresses that can be allocated within this space. Subsequent sections examine in detail the different IPv6 address types within this space: unicast, multicast, and anycast. It should be noted that IPv6 does not support the concept of broadcast addresses as in IPv4. As will be discussed later in this chapter, IPv6 uses special multicast addresses such as the IPv6 Solicited-Node multicast address and the IPv6 all-device multicast addresses in place of broadcast addresses.

3.2.1 TOTAL IPv6 ADDRESS SPACE

The 128-bit IPv6 address space provides as many as 340 undecillion possible addresses, specifically, $2^{128} = 340{,}282{,}366{,}920{,}938{,}463{,}463{,}374{,}607{,}431{,}768{,}211{,}456$ addresses. Undecillion (in the United States) is a number equal to 1 followed by 36 zeros, that is, $10^{36} = 1{,}000{,}000{,}000{,}000{,}000{,}000{,}000{,}000{,}0 00{,}000{,}000{,}000{,}000$. One undecillion is one trillion trillion trillion. A trillion is $1{,}000{,}000{,}000{,}000$ (10^{12}). The 32-bit IPv4 address space, on the other hand, provides 4.29 billion possible addresses, that is, $2^{32} = 4{,}294{,}967{,}296$.

The extremely large IPv6 address space eliminates the need for Network Address Translation (NAT) devices. Removing NAT from the communication path allows direct device-to-device communication, providing greater communication speed and reliability. NAT device processing (often implemented as a gateway between two networks) can slow down data transfer performance.

Of the entire IPv6 address space, the Internet Assigned Numbers Authority (IANA) has allocated only a small portion for actual use. IANA allocated IPv6 addresses that start with (i.e., the leading leftmost bits) 001 as IPv6 Global Unicast addresses. A small portion of the IPv6 addresses with leading leftmost bits of 000 and 111 are allocated for special IPv6 address types (000 for IPv6 Unspecified, Loopback, and Embedded IPv4 addresses, and 111 for IPv6 Link-Local, Unique-Local, and Multicast addresses). The remaining possible IPv6 addresses that start with

DOI: 10.1201/9781003710646-3

010, 011, 100, 101, and 110 are reserved by the IANA for future use and are currently not allocated. A 128-bit IPv6 address serves as a Network Layer identifier for a single IPv6-enabled interface.

3.2.2 IPv6 Address Allocation

IANA oversees the allocation of globally unique IPv4 and IPv6 addresses, Autonomous System Numbers (ASNs), as well as the management of the root zone in the Domain Name System (DNS), and other Internet protocol–related resources (e.g., maintaining a registry of protocols and their parameters and coordinating the registration of protocols). IANA is responsible for allocating globally unique IP addresses and administering the domain names in root nameservers that sit at the top of the hierarchical DNS tree. IANA allocates IP address blocks to the Regional Internet Registries (RIRs) that represent different regions of the world, as shown in Figure 3.1. Each RIR then oversees the allocation of IP addresses from the IP address blocks assigned to it by the IANA to different users in its region.

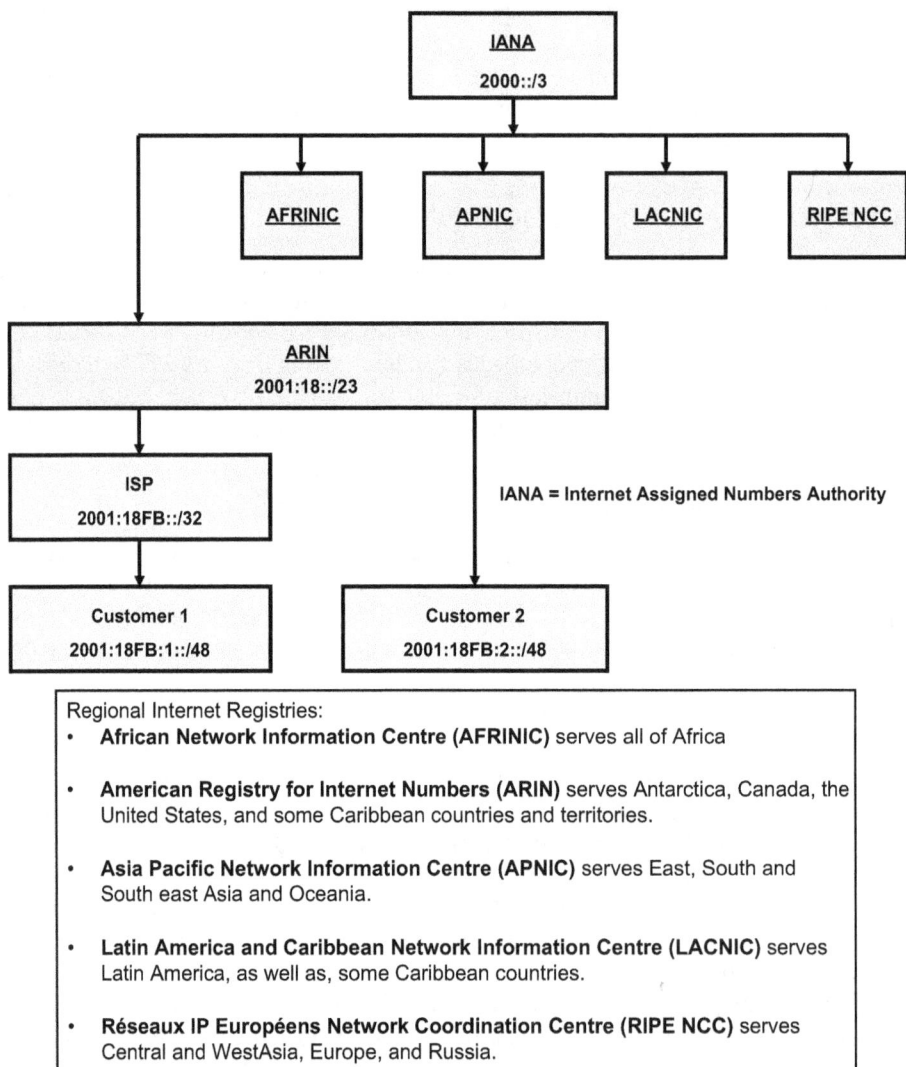

FIGURE 3.1   IANA and RIR IPv6 address allocation.

Each of the five RIRs divide and allocate IP address resources to local users, which include Local Internet Registries (LIRs), Internet Service Providers (ISPs), and end-user organizations. An LIR is an organization that assigns IP address blocks allocated to it to other local customers. In many cases, most LIRs are also ISPs. The IANA maintains the global registry for IPv4 and IPv6 addresses and ASNs, which includes all the IP address ranges and ASN blocks that are allocated for use on the Internet, as well as those allocated to each RIR. IANA, using the Classless Inter-Domain Routing (CIDR) system, typically allocates IPv4 address space to users in /8 CIDR prefix blocks and IPv6 addresses from the 2000::/3 block, in /23 to /12 CIDR prefix blocks to requesting RIRs as needed.

3.3   TEXT REPRESENTATION OF IPv6 ADDRESSES

IPv4 addresses are usually represented using *dotted-decimal notation*. In this notation, a 32-bit IPv4 address is divided into 8-bit blocks or groups. Each group of 8 bits is converted to its equivalent decimal value and separated from adjacent groups by a dot or period (.), for example, the IPv4 address 11000000 10101000 00001010 00000001 in binary form is represented as 192.168.10.1 in dotted-decimal notation. The boundary between groups is indicated by a dot. The 32-bit IPv4 addresses are shorter and easier to grasp and work with compared to the 128-bit IPv6 addresses.

A number of rules have been defined to allow the shortening of IPv6 addresses and make them easier to work with. The 128-bit IPv6 address, by convention, is written as eight 16-bit groups ($8 \times 16 = 128$), with each group represented as four hexadecimal digits, as shown in Figures 3.2 and 3.3. The convention for representing IPv6 addresses in a readable format is to divide the 128-bit IPv6 address along 16-bit boundaries, and then convert each 16-bit block into a four-digit hexadecimal number. Each adjacent four-digit hexadecimal number is separated by a colon (:). The resulting IPv6 address is called the *colon-hexadecimal* representation **[RFC4291]**.

As shown in Figures 3.2 and 3.3, each hexadecimal digit is equivalent to four binary bits, and each 16-bit group consists of four hexadecimal digits. Each group of four hexadecimal digits (representing 16 bits in total) is separated from the other groups by a colon (:). Hexadecimal digits are not case-sensitive, allowing an address to be written in either lowercase or uppercase; both address representations are equivalent.

To further elaborate, the eight 16-bit groups of the IPv6 address consist of a total of 32 hexadecimal digits ($8 \times 4 = 32$), each digit consisting of four bits, resulting in a total of 128 bits in the address. Given that IPv6 addresses are long and can be difficult for users to remember and work with, several rules have been defined that significantly shorten the representation of IPv6 addresses when expressed in the colon-hexadecimal notation **[RFC4291] [RFC5952]**.

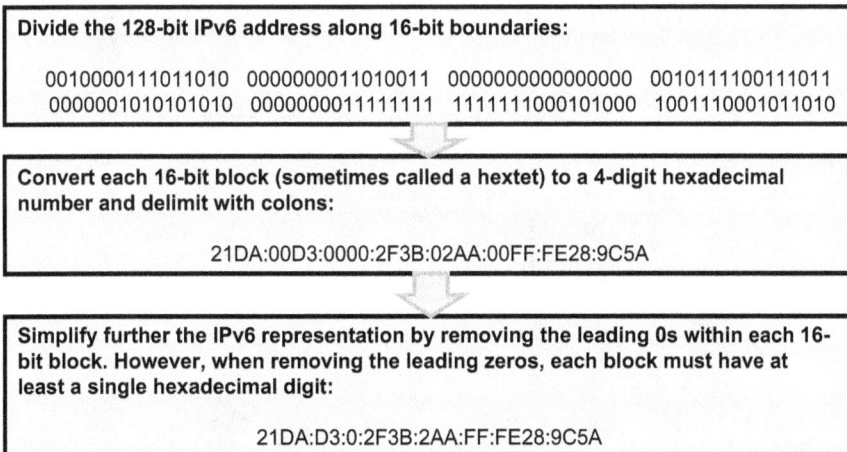

Divide the 128-bit IPv6 address along 16-bit boundaries:

0010000111011010 0000000011010011 0000000000000000 0010111100111011
0000001010101010 0000000011111111 1111111000101000 1001110001011010

Convert each 16-bit block (sometimes called a hextet) to a 4-digit hexadecimal number and delimit with colons:

21DA:00D3:0000:2F3B:02AA:00FF:FE28:9C5A

Simplify further the IPv6 representation by removing the leading 0s within each 16-bit block. However, when removing the leading zeros, each block must have at least a single hexadecimal digit:

21DA:D3:0:2F3B:2AA:FF:FE28:9C5A

FIGURE 3.2   Expressing IPv6 addresses.

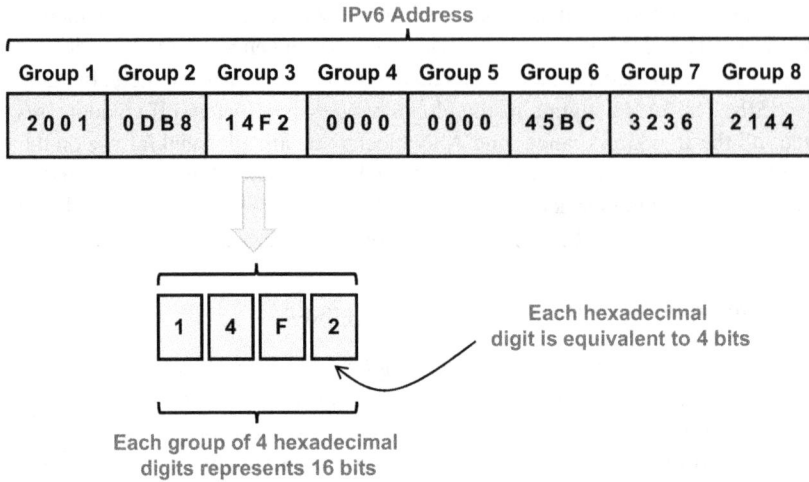

FIGURE 3.3 IPv6 address example.

The preferred form of an IPv6 address is x:x:x:x:x:x:x:x, where each "x" is a 16-bit group of the IPv6 address that can be represented by one to four hexadecimal digits (called a *hextet*). There are eight 16-bit groups in an IPv6 address. The following are additional IPv6 address examples:

- 2001:DB8:0:0:8:600:200C:234E
- ABCD:EF01:6789:2345:ABCD:EF01:2345:6789

However, in many cases, there is a need to shorten the IPv6 textual representations to make them easier to understand and work with, as discussed below (removing leading zeros and compressing a sequence of zeros).

3.4 COMPRESSING IPv6 ADDRESSES

This section discusses the rules that IPv6 address users employ to reduce the length of IPv6 address representations (see also Figure 3.4 and Table 3.1). It is important to understand that these rules only shorten the representation of the IPv6 address, while the address itself remains 128 bits long.

> **Rule 1: Omit Leading Zeros:** In this rule, leading zeros in any group of four hexadecimal digits can be omitted. *This rule applies only to leading zeros in the IPv6 address and not trailing zeros.* Even if an address group consists of four zeros (0000), the rule allows only the leading three zeros to be omitted. We illustrate this rule in the following example:

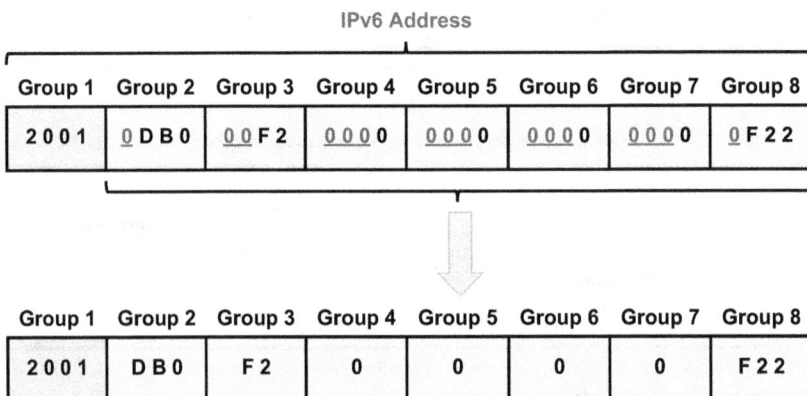

In this example, we note that Groups 2–8 all have one or more leading zeros. For Groups 2, 3, and 8, the leading zeros are straightforward, and no further compression is required. However, Groups 4, 5, and 6 can be further reduced according to Rule 2 below. *Deleting trailing 0s in the IPv6 address would lead to an incorrect interpretation of the address. Only leading 0s can be removed to ensure that there is only one correct recreation of the address.*

Rule 2: Omit Groups of All Zeros: This rule (called the Zero Compression rule) states that a *double colon* (::) can be used to replace a single, contiguous string of one or more address groups (i.e., a set of four hexadecimal digits) consisting of all 0s. The example shown below illustrates the use of this rule:

In this IPv6 address, we see that Groups 4, 5, 6, and 7 are all zeros; as a result, they can be replaced with a single double colon. *Note that a double colon (::) can be applied only once in an IPv6 address*; otherwise, the shortened IPv6 address representation would become ambiguous (and hard to interpret). Using more than one double colon makes it almost impossible to recreate the original IPv6 address from the shortened address representation.

Given the IPv6 address 2001:0DB0:00F2:0000:0000:06BB:0000:0F22, we see that there are two contiguous strings of zeros in Groups 4 and 5, and Group 7. In this case, only one double colon (::) can be used to replace either Groups 4 and 5 or Group 7, but not both.

2001:0DB0:00F2::06BB:0000:0F22 or

2001:0DB0:00F2:0000:0000:06BB::0F22

Combining Rule 1 and Rule 2: Some types of IPv6 addresses, even after applying Rule 1, still contain long sequences of zeros in the colon-hexadecimal format. In this case, to further simplify the IPv6 address representation, a contiguous sequence of 16-bit blocks that have been set to 0 can be compressed to :: (known as *double colon*).

Therefore, further IPv6 address compression can be achieved by combining both Rules 1 and 2. The resulting address representation is significantly shorter by applying these two rules, as shown below:

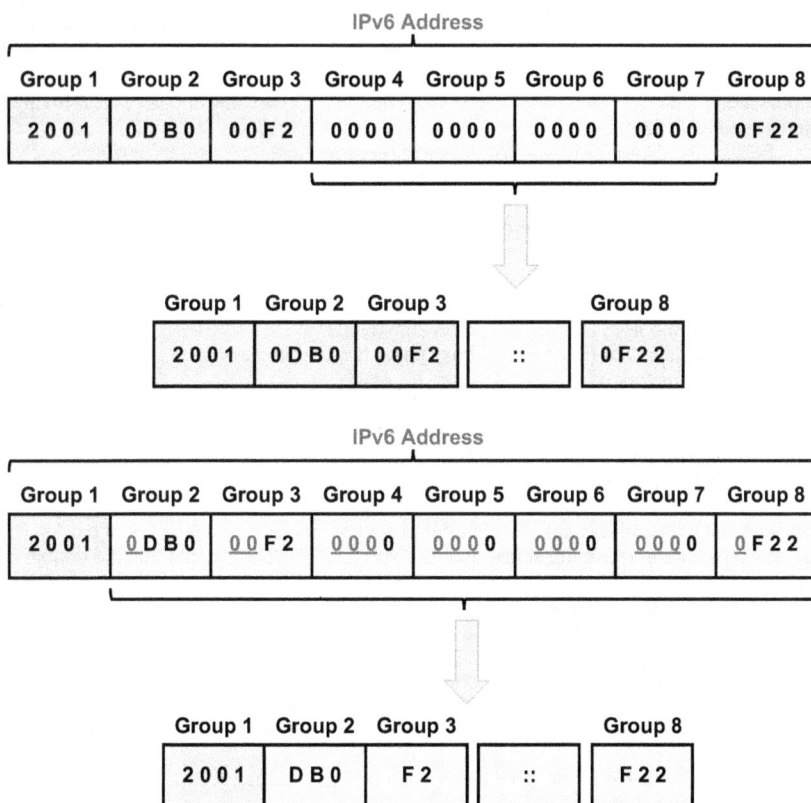

As another example, the IPv6 Link-Local address FE80:0:0:0:2BB:FF:FE9A:4CC2 can be compressed to FE80::2BB:FF:FE9A:4CC2. The IPv6 multicast address FF02:0:0:0:0:0:0:2 in compressed format is FF02::2. *Zero compression can only be applied to a single contiguous series of 16-bit blocks in an IPv6 address expressed in colon-hexadecimal notation. Zero compression cannot be applied to a portion of a 16-bit block.* For example, the IPv6 address FF02:30:0:0:0:0:0:5 cannot be expressed as FF02:3::5.

3.4.1 IPv6 Addresses with Multiple Contiguous String of All-0s Hextets

As shown in Figure 3.4, a double colon can represent only groups/segments with a single contiguous string of all-0s to avoid the address being ambiguous and hard to interpret. As explained in

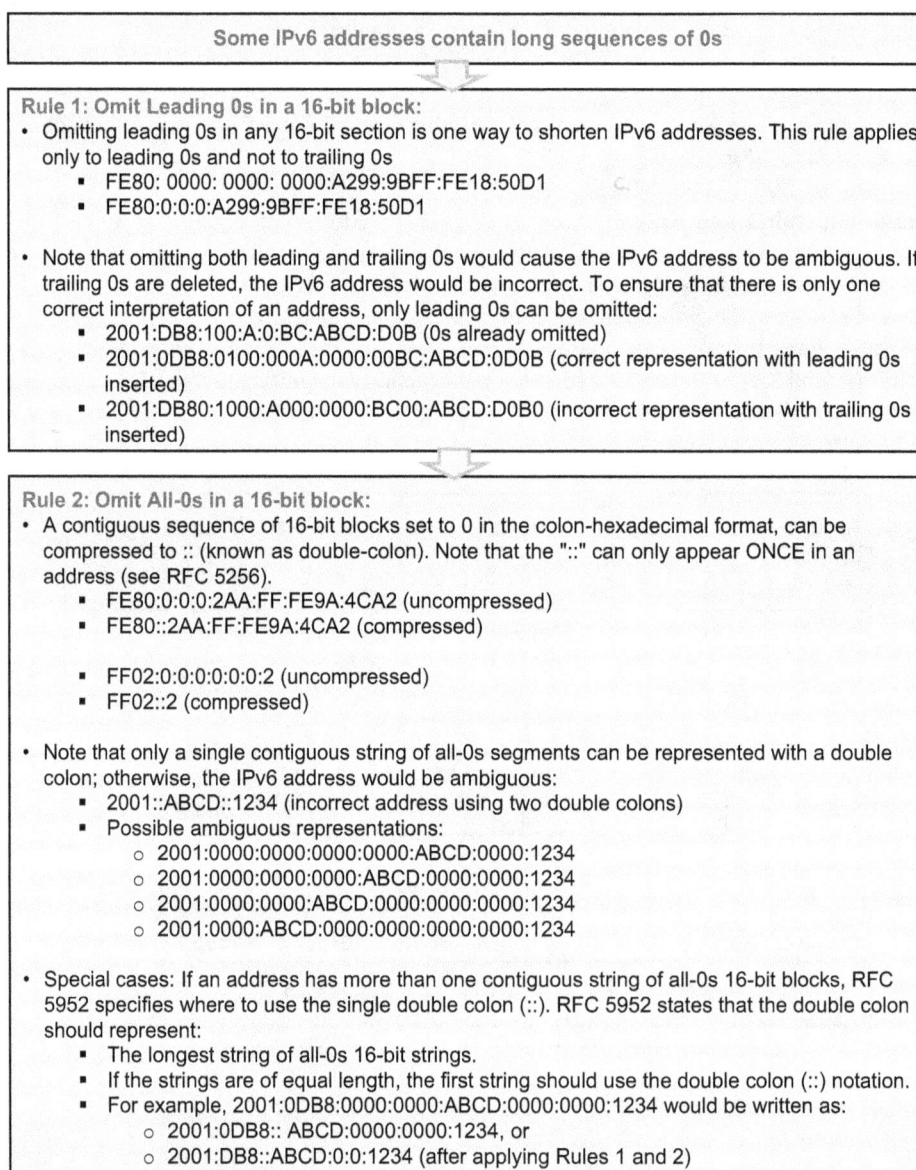

FIGURE 3.4   Compressing zeros in the IPv6 colon-hexadecimal address format.

TABLE 3.1

Examples of IPv6 Address Compression

Uncompressed IPv6 Address	Omitting Leading 0s in a 16-Bit Block	Omitting All 0s 16-Bit Blocks
0000:0000:0000:0000:0000:0000:0000:0000	0:0:0:0:0:0:0:0	::
0000:0000:0000:0000:0000:0000:0000:0001	0:0:0:0:0:0:0:1	::1
0000:0000:0000:0000:0000:0000:13.1.68.3	0:0:0:0:0:0:13.1.68.3	::13.1.68.3
0000:0000:0000:0000:0000:FFFF:129.144.52.38	0:0:0:0:0:FFFF:129.144.52.38	::FFFF:129.144.52.38
FF01:0000:0000:0000:0000:0000:0000:0101	FF01:0:0:0:0:0:0:101	FF01::101
FF02:0000:0000:0000:0000:0000:0000:0001	FF02:0:0:0:0:0:0:1	FF02::1
FE80:0000:0000:0000:A299:9BFF:FE18:50D1	FE80:0:0:0:A299:9BFF:FE18:50D1	FE80::A299:9BFF:FE18:50D1
2001:0DB8:1111:000A:00B0:0000:9000:0200	2001:DB8:1111:A:B0:0:9000:200	2001:DB8:1111:A:B0::9000:200
2001:0DB8:0000:0000:ABCD:0000:0000:1234	2001:DB8:0:0:ABCD:0:0:1234	2001:DB8::ABCD:0:0:1234
2001:0DB8:AAAA:0001:0000:0000:0000:0100	2001:DB8:AAAA:1:0:0:0:100	2001:DB8:AAAA:1::100
2001:0DB8:AAAA:0001:0000:0000:0000:0200	2001:DB8:AAAA:1:0:0:0:200	2001:DB8:AAAA:1::200

Figure 3.4, using two double colons leads to multiple possible address interpretations, making it impossible to know which address is the correct one.

Reference **[RFC5952]** explains how to compress an IPv6 address with more than one contiguous string of all-0s hextets. Let us consider, for example, the address 2001:0DB8:0000:0000:AAAA:0000:0000:BBBB. In this case, **[RFC5952]** recommends using the single double colon (::) as follows:

- Use the double colon on the longest string of all-0s hextets.
- Use the double colon on the first string if the strings are of equal length.

Therefore, the address 2001:0DB8:0000:0000:AAAA:0000:0000:BBBB would be written as 2001:0db8::AAAA:0000:0000:BBBB. Applying both Rules 1 and 2 to this IPv6 address yields 2001:DB8::AAAA:0:0:BBBB. However, most operating systems, including Microsoft Windows and Cisco IOS, allow a single double colon (::) to be placed in any valid location (not necessarily on the longest string or the first string if the strings are of equal length).

3.4.2 EXPANDING A COMPRESSED IPV6 ADDRESS

To expand an IPv6 address that has been compressed, we first determine how many 0 bits are represented by the :: in the address. We do this by counting the number of four-digit hexadecimal blocks in the compressed IPv6 address and then subtracting this number from 8 (the number of four-digit hexadecimal or 16-bit blocks in the 128-bit IPv6 address). This resulting number is then multiplied by 16.

For example, the IPv6 address FF02::2 has two four-digit hexadecimal blocks (the FF02 block and the 2 block). The resulting number (2) is subtracted from 8 and then multiplied by 16, giving 96 bits of zeros represented by the :: in the address (i.e., $96 = (8-2) \times 16$). It is important to emphasize that zero compression can only be applied once in a given IPv6 address; otherwise, the number of 0 bits represented by a double colon (::) cannot be determined.

3.4.3 COMMON MISTAKES IN IPV6 ADDRESS COMPRESSION

Some common mistakes may arise when the IPv6 compression rules are not properly applied. Below are some examples that highlight the key points of IPv6 address compression.

Original IPv6 address:

- 2001:0AA0:0000:0000:0BB0:0000:0000:0CCC

Correct Shortened forms:

- 2001:AA0::BB0:0:0:CCC
- 2001:AA0:0:0:BB0::CCC

Common Mistake 1 (using :: twice):

- 2001:AA0::BB0::CCC

Common Mistake 2 (removing trailing zeros):

- 2001:AA::BB:0:0:CCC

In this example, Groups 3 and 4, and Groups 6 and 7, of the original IPv6 address have two consecutive strings of zeros. One may be tempted to replace both sets with a double colon, resulting in the shortened address having two double colons. This mistake creates an ambiguous address representation. Another common mistake is removing trailing zeros in an address group; for example, removing the trailing zero in Group 2 (0AA0); only the leading zero can be removed.

3.5 IPv6 ADDRESS PREFIXES AND PREFIX LENGTHS

A prefix is the portion of an IPv4 or IPv6 address that indicates the bits that have fixed values or represent a network identifier. In IPv4, the network portion of the address is represented in CIDR notation. For example, an IPv4 address with the CIDR notation /24 indicates that the first 24 bits of the address are the network portion (also called the *IPv4 prefix*). The dotted-decimal network mask 255.255.255.0 can also be written in CIDR notation as /24, indicating the prefix as the first 24 bits of the IPv4 address.

The IPv4 prefix can be expressed as

Ipv4-address/prefix-length,

where the decimal value *prefix-length* indicates the number of leftmost contiguous bits of the IPv4 address that identify the network portion (i.e., prefix) of the IPv4 address. The *prefix-length* is also used with unicast IPv4 addresses to identify where the prefix portion of the IPv4 address ends and the host interface ID starts.

IPv6 also uses CIDR notation, and an IPv6 address with CIDR notation /48 indicates that the first 48 bits of the IPv6 address are the network portion (also called *IPv6 prefix*). IPv6 and IPv4 address prefixes can both be represented in CIDR notation.

The IPv6 prefix can be expressed as

ipv6-address/prefix-length,

where *prefix-length* is a decimal value that specifies the number of leftmost bits of the IPv6 address that constitute the network portion (see Figure 3.5 and Table 3.2). For example, the IPv6 address 2001:AAAA:BBBB:CCCC:0:0:0:10/64 has a *prefix length* of 64. In this address, the network portion (subnet) is 2001:AAAA:BBBB:CCCC::/64, with 2001:AAAA:BBBB:CCCC::22 being the address of a specific interface on this IPv6 subnet. Considering another example, the IPv6 prefix 21DA:D5::/48 represents an IPv6 network or route prefix, and 21DA:D5:0:2FBB::/64 represents an IPv6 subnet prefix.

An IPv6 interface address and the interface's address prefix (e.g., the IPv6 subnet prefix of the interface) can be combined as follows:

- **IPv6 interface address|:** 2001:DB8:0:AB30:123:4567:80CD:23EF
  a. **IPv6 subnet prefix:** 2001:DB8:0:AB30::/60
  b. **IPv6 subnet prefix:** 2001:DB8:0:AB30:123:4567:80CD:23EF/60

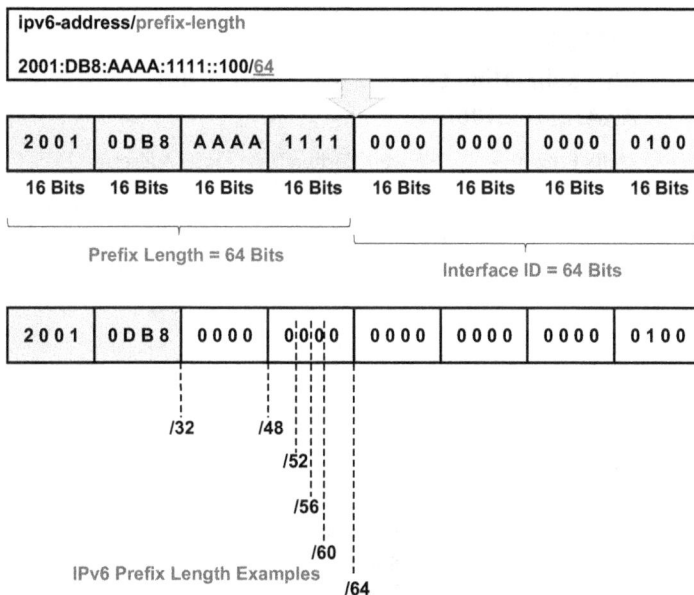

ipv6-address/prefix-length
2001:DB8:AAAA:1111::100/64

2001	0DB8	AAAA	1111	0000	0000	0000	0100
16 Bits	16 Bits	16 Bits	16 Bits	16 Bits	16 Bits	16 Bits	16 Bits

Prefix Length = 64 Bits

Interface ID = 64 Bits

2001	0DB8	0000	0000	0000	0000	0000	0100

/32   /48
      /52
     /56
    /60
IPv6 Prefix Length Examples
   /64

- **ipv6-address**: This is an IPv6 address in any of the notations.
- **prefix-length**: This is a decimal value specifying how many of the leftmost contiguous bits of the IPv6 address comprise the prefix.
- The prefix is the part of the IPv6 address that indicates the bits that belong to the network identifier.
- IPv6 prefixes for routes and subnet identifiers are expressed in the same way as the IPv4 Classless Inter-Domain Routing (CIDR) notation.
- An IPv6 prefix is typically written in ipv6-address/prefix-length notation.
  - For example, 21DA:D3::/48 is a route prefix and 21DA:D3:0:2F3B::/64 is a subnet prefix.
  - A subnet mask is not used in IPv6. Only prefix-length notation is supported.

FIGURE 3.5   IPv6 prefix length notation.

In both IPv6 and IPv4, the number of interfaces that can be on a network depends on the *prefix-length*. However, the 128-bit IPv6 address length generally eliminates the need for address space conservation that is necessary with IPv4 public addresses. Figure 3.5 and Table 3.2 show several examples of IPv6 prefix lengths: /32, /48, /52, /56, /60, and /64. It is important to note that all of these prefixes align with a nibble (i.e., 4-bit) boundary. However, IPv6 prefix lengths do not necessarily have to conform to a 4-bit boundary. Prefix lengths are also permitted to fall within a nibble; for example, one can create prefix lengths of /61, /62, or /63 as needed.

In practice, network engineers using IPv6 typically choose prefix lengths that are multiples of 4 bits. Such prefix lengths simplify subnetting and prefix assignments, making them easier to understand without the use of a subnet calculator (e.g., when using IPv6 Global Unicast addresses and performing IPv6 prefix allocation and subnetting). For example, in Figure 3.5 and Table 3.2, each additional 4 bits in the prefix length shifts the network portion of the IPv6 address one hexadecimal digit to the right. Figure 3.6 shows examples of legal and illegal representations of IPv6 prefixes. Table 3.3 presents the IPv6 address ranges for some IPv6 address prefix lengths.

3.6   IPv6 ADDRESS TYPES

This section and the subsequent ones examine in more detail the different types of IPv6 unicast, multicast, and anycast addresses. Particularly, the IPv6 Global Unicast addresses, Link-Local addresses, and multicast addresses are discussed in greater detail.

TABLE 3.2
IPv6 Subnetting Example (e.g., 2001:0DB8:
AAAA:1111::100/64)

Prefix Length	Network Portion	Total Addresses
/4	2::	2^{124}
/8	20::	2^{120}
/12	200::	2^{116}
/16	2001::	2^{112}
/20	2001:0::	2^{108}
/24	2001:0D::	2^{104}
/28	2001:0DB::	2^{100}
/32	2001:0DB8::	2^{96}
/36	2001:0DB8:A::	2^{92}
/40	2001:0DB8:AA::	2^{88}
/44	2001:0DB8:AAA::	2^{84}
/48	2001:0DB8:AAAA::	2^{80}
/52	2001:0DB8:AAAA:1::	2^{76}
/56	2001:0DB8:AAAA:11::	2^{72}
/60	2001:0DB8:AAAA:111::	2^{68}
/64	2001:0DB8:AAAA:1111::	2^{64}

The following are legal representations of the 60-bit prefix **2001 0DB8 0000 AB3** (hexadecimal):
- **2001:0DB8:0000:AB30**:0000:0000:0000:0000/60
- **2001:0DB8::AB30**:0:0:0:0/60
- **2001:0DB8:0:AB30::**/60

The following are NOT legal representations of the above prefix:
- **2001:0DB8:0:AB3**/60 (leading zeros may be dropped, but not trailing zeros, within any 16-bit block of the address)
- **2001:0DB8::AB30**/60 (address to left of "/" expands to **2001:0DB8**:0000:0000:0000:0000:0000:**AB30** which is NOT correct)
- **2001:0DB8::AB3**/60 (address to left of "/" expands to **2001:0DB8**:0000:0000:0000:0000:0000:**0AB3** which is NOT correct)

FIGURE 3.6   Examples of legal and illegal representations of IPv6 prefixes.

As shown in Figure 3.7, the IPv6 address space is divided into eight groups based on the leading 3 bits of the IPv6 address (000, 001, 010, 011, 100, 101, 110, and 111). As discussed earlier, the IANA allocated IPv6 addresses that start with 001 as IPv6 Global Unicast addresses (see Figure 3.7). The IPv6 addresses with leading bits of 000 are allocated for IPv6 Unspecified, Loopback, and Embedded IPv4 addresses, while those starting with 111 are allocated for IPv6 Link-Local, Unique-Local, and Multicast addresses, as shown in Figure 3.7.

The three main types of IPv6 addresses are as follows (see also Figure 3.8 and Table 3.4):

- **Unicast**: This is a Network Layer address that uniquely identifies a single IPv6-enabled interface. IPv6 packets sent with the destination address set to an IPv6 unicast address are delivered to the interface configured with that address. The source IPv6 address of packets must always be a unicast address. IPv6 unicast addresses are used for *one-to-one communication*.

TABLE 3.3

Address Ranges for Some IPv6 Address Prefixes

IPv6 Address with Prefix Length	Host IPv6 Address Range
2001:DB8:ABCD:0012::0/64	2001:0DB8:ABCD:0012:**0000:0000:0000:0000** to 2001:0DB8:ABCD:0012:**FFFF:FFFF:FFFF:FFFF**
2001:DB8:ABCD:0012::0/80	2001:0DB8:ABCD:0012:0000:**0000:0000:0000** to 2001:0DB8:ABCD:0012:0000:**FFFF:FFFF:FFFF**
2001:DB8:ABCD:0012::0/96	2001:0DB8:ABCD:0012:0000:0000:**0000:0000** to 2001:0DB8:ABCD:0012:0000:0000:**FFFF:FFFF**
2001:DB8:ABCD:0012::0/112	2001:0DB8:ABCD:0012:0000:0000:0000:**0000** to 2001:0DB8:ABCD:0012:0000:0000:0000:**FFFF**
2001:DB8:ABCD:0012::0/128	2001:0DB8:ABCD:0012:0000:0000:0000:0000

- **Multicast**: This is a Network Layer identifier for a group of IPv6-enabled interfaces that may belong to different nodes in the IPv6 internetwork. IPv6 packets sent to an IPv6 multicast address are delivered to all interfaces identified by that address. IPv6 multicast addresses are used for *one-to-many communication*.
- **Anycast**: This is a Network Layer identifier for a group of IPv6-enabled interfaces that belong to different nodes in the IPv6 internetwork. IPv6 packets sent to an IPv6 anycast address are delivered to the "nearest" interface identified by that address. "Nearest" here means the interface in the group with the best routing metric according to the IPv6 routing protocol used. IPv6 anycast addresses are used for *one-to-nearest (or one-to-closest) interface communication* sometimes called *one-to-any communications*. IPv6 anycast addresses are syntactically indistinguishable from IPv6 unicast addresses and are taken from the IPv6 unicast address space (of any network scope).

The concept of broadcast addresses does not exist in IPv6. Instead, IPv6 nodes implement the broadcast functionality using specially defined IPv6 multicast addresses.

The following IPv6 addresses correspond to the categories in Figure 3.8 and Table 3.4:

- **Unicast address**
  2001:DB8:0:0:8:800:200C:234E compressed to 2001:DB8::8:800:200C:234E
- **Multicast address**
  FF01:0:0:0:0:0:0:101 compressed to FF01::101
- **Loopback address**
  0:0:0:0:0:0:0:1 compressed to ::1
- **Unspecified address**
  0:0:0:0:0:0:0:0 compressed to ::

A single interface in the IPv6 internetwork may be assigned multiple IPv6 addresses of different types (unicast, multicast, and anycast) or network scopes. Interfaces that are on the same link (subnet) do not need to use IPv6 unicast addresses with a network scope greater than link-scope as the origin or destination of any IPv6 packets when communicating with each other (i.e., for on-link communications); addresses with greater scope are used between non-neighbors (i.e., interfaces on different links). IPv6 unicast addresses with link-scope (IPv6 Link-Local unicast addresses) are meant for on-link communication and are also more convenient for point-to-point interfaces.

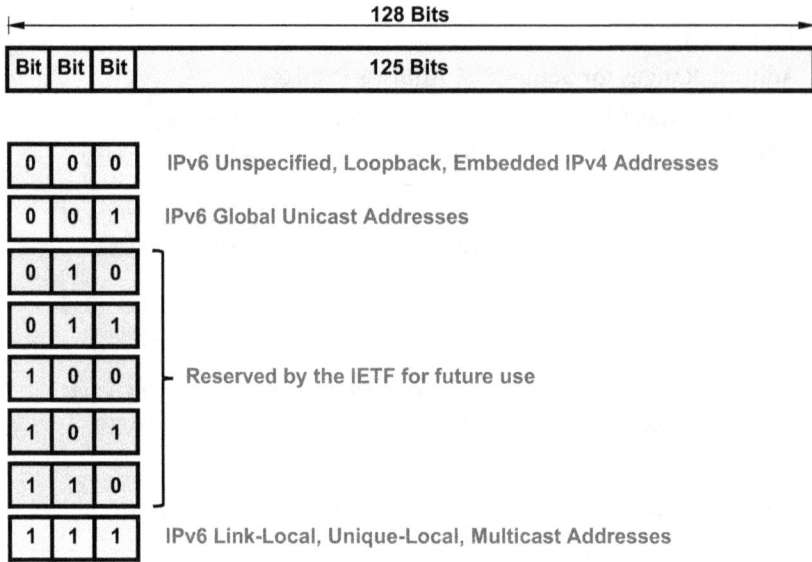

FIGURE 3.7   IANA's allocation of IPv6 address space.

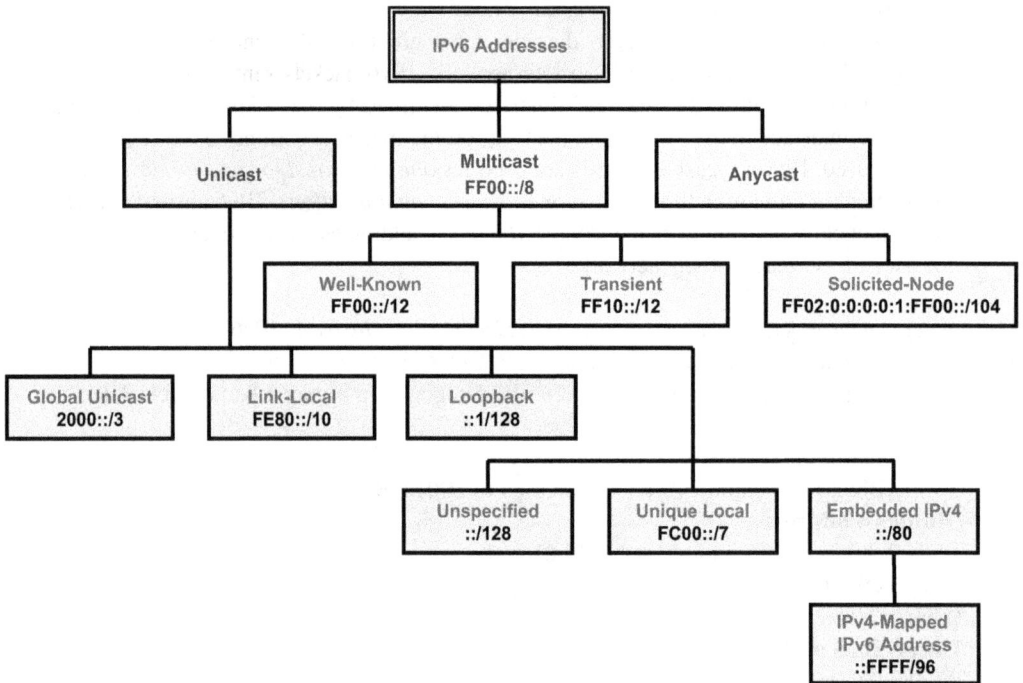

FIGURE 3.8   IPv6 address types.

IPv6 addresses with global scope (IPv6 Global Unicast addresses) are meant for communication between interfaces on different links (i.e., for off-link communications).

Table 3.5 lists the different IPv4 address types and their IPv6 equivalents to highlight the main differences between these IP addressing concepts.

TABLE 3.4
IPv6 Address Type Identification

IPv6 Address Type	Binary Prefix (Leading Bits)	IPv6 Notation	Range of First Hextet (xxxx:...)
Unspecified	00...0 (128 bits)	::/128	–
Loopback	00...1 (128 bits)	::1/128	–
Multicast	1111 1111	FF00::/8	FF00 to FFFF
Link-Local Unicast	1111 1110 10	FE80::/10	FE80 to FEBF
Global Unicast	001x	2000::/3	2000 to 3FFF
Unique-Local Unicast	1111 110x	FC00::/7	FC00 to FDFF

TABLE 3.5
IPv4 Addresses and Their Equivalents in IPv6

IPv4 Address	IPv6 Address
Initially, used address classes but later used classless addressing based on VLSM and CIDR	Not applicable in IPv6. IPv6 was designed from the onset to use VLSM and CIDR
Multicast addresses (224.0.0.0/4)	IPv6 multicast addresses (FF00::/8)
Broadcast addresses	Not applicable in IPv6
Unspecified address (0.0.0.0)	Unspecified address (::)
Loopback address (127.0.0.1)	Loopback address (::1)
IPv4 Internet uses Public IP addresses	IPv6 Internet uses Global Unicast addresses
Private IP addresses (10.0.0.0/8, 172.16.0.0/12, and 192.168.0.0/16)	Unique-Local addresses (FC00::/7)
Autoconfigured addresses (169.254.0.0/16)	Link-local addresses (FE80::/64)
Text representation: Dotted-decimal notation	Text representation: Colon-hexadecimal format with suppression of leading zeros and zero compression. IPv4-compatible addresses are expressed in dotted-decimal notation
Network bits representation: Subnet mask in dotted-decimal notation or prefix length notation	Network bits representation: Prefix length notation only

CIDR = Classless Inter-Domain Routing
VLSM = Variable Length Subnet Mask

3.7 IPv6 UNICAST ADDRESSES

An IPv6 unicast address is one that identifies a single interface within the network scope of the IPv6 unicast address type it belongs to. Using the appropriate IPv6 unicast routing protocol (e.g., RIPng, OSPFv3), IPv6 packets addressed to an IPv6 unicast address are delivered to a single interface in the network. IPv6 supports the following types of unicast IPv6 addresses (see also Figure 3.8) **[RFC4291]**: Global Unicast addresses, Link-Local addresses, Unique-Local addresses, and Special addresses (Unspecified address, Loopback addresses, and Compatibility addresses, also called IPv6 Addresses with Embedded IPv4 addresses (IPv4-Mapped IPv6 addresses)).

IPv6 unicast addresses that can be applied to an interface attached to an IPv6 link have the following scopes:

- **Link-Local Scope**: IPv6 addresses with this scope can only be used to communicate with IPv6 nodes on the attached link; Link-Local addresses have this scope.
- **Unique-Local Scope**: IPv6 addresses with this scope can only be used to communicate with IPv6 nodes within a specific administrative domain or site that contains distinct links; Unique-Local addresses have this scope.

- **Global Scope**: IPv6 addresses with this scope can be used to communicate with any IPv6 node across the global IPv6 Internet; Global Unicast addresses have this scope.

These IPv6 address scopes define network domains and are hierarchical, starting from the smallest scope, the link-local scope, to the largest scope, the global scope.

Depending on the role an IPv6 node plays in the IPv6 internetwork (for instance, an IPv6 host versus an IPv6 router), the node may have considerable or minimal knowledge of the internal structure of the IPv6 addresses it encounters. At a minimum, an IPv6 node may consider the IPv6 unicast addresses it sees (including its own configured IPv6 unicast addresses) as having no internal structure, as shown in Figure 3.9 (top figure). An IPv6 host with a somewhat sophisticated understanding of IPv6 address structures may additionally be aware of the IPv6 subnet prefix(es) for the link(s) to which it is attached, where different values for n may apply to different IPv6 addresses, as illustrated in Figure 3.9 (bottom figure). The bottom figure shows that an IPv6 address consists of an address prefix and an interface identifier (ID). This structure is equivalent to the Network ID and the host ID in an IPv4 address.

Although a very simple IPv6 router may not be aware of the internal structure of IPv6 unicast addresses, many IPv6 routers (through CIDR address aggregation or route summarization) will have knowledge of one or more of the address/routing hierarchies when running routing protocols. The address hierarchies known will vary from router to router, depending on the router's position in the routing hierarchy. Except for the purpose of knowing IPv6 subnet boundaries, IPv6 nodes should not make any assumptions regarding the structure of the IPv6 addresses they encounter.

A network operator may assign an IPv6 unicast address or a set of IPv6 unicast addresses to multiple physical interfaces in the IPv6 internetwork if those interfaces are treated as logically one interface when routing traffic on the Internet. A typical application is load sharing over multiple physical interfaces, sometimes called *equal cost multipath routing* (ECMP) *or unequal cost multipath routing (UCMP)* (depending on the routing protocol used). Protocols such as RIP, OSPF, and IS-IS support ECMP routing, while protocols such as Enhanced Interior Gateway Routing Protocol (EIGRP) support both ECMP and UCMP routing when multiple paths exist to a given destination.

3.7.1 ASSIGNING MULTIPLE IPv6 SUBNET PREFIXES TO THE SAME LINK

In IPv6, as in IPv4, a subnet prefix is associated with one link in the network. However, a network operator may assign multiple subnet prefixes to the same link, for example, when the link supports multiple logical sub-interfaces, a node has multiple virtual (logical) routers (routing engines), or an interface is configured with primary and secondary IPv6 addresses.

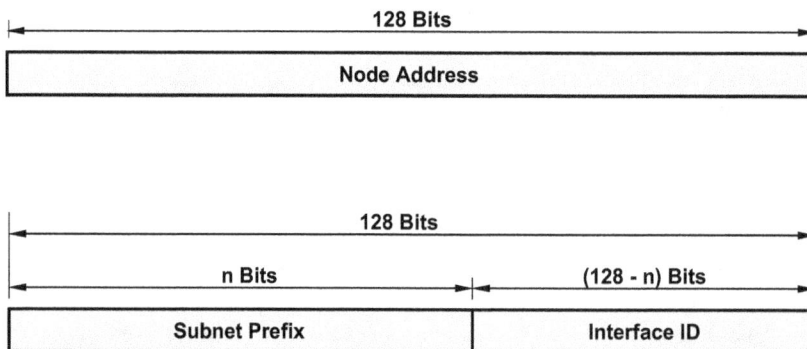

FIGURE 3.9   IPv6 unicast addresses.

3.7.1.1 Physical Interface with Multiple Sub-interfaces

A network can have one or more physical network interfaces. Multiple *sub-interfaces*, also called *virtual interfaces*, can be created by dividing a single physical interface on an IP node (e.g., router) into multiple smaller logical interfaces (see Figure 3.10) **[AWEYA1BK18]**. Virtual interfaces are intangible and exist only within the host node's software. The sub-interfaces send and receive data over the parent physical interface on which they are created. Just as a single physical interface can be assigned a subnet prefix, each of those smaller logical interfaces can be assigned its own subnet prefix. In this case, a single physical link may have an overlay of multiple subnet prefixes, each behaving like a physical link.

A different IP address, prefix length, and VLAN ID can be assigned to each sub-interface (virtual interface) on the parent physical interface. An IP router can use the multiple sub-interfaces or virtual interfaces (on a single physical interface) to connect different VLANs. The sub-interfaces support multiple VLANs on the same trunk port of the IP router; each sub-interface is a sub-part of a Layer 3 interface. Virtual interfaces allow multiple VLANs to utilize the same physical interface on an IP router.

If multiple VLANs are configured, each will have its own IP subnet prefix and VLAN ID. This is because each VLAN operates as a separate logical/virtual Layer 2 (broadcast) domain and requires a unique IP address and prefix length. When configuring virtual interfaces, multiple IP addresses and prefix lengths must be assigned to a single physical interface. Most modern routers support virtual interfaces to provide Layer 3 functionality for VLANs.

Note that a VLAN provides a mechanism for the separation or segmentation of a larger Layer 2 network into smaller logical *Layer 2 (broadcast) domains*. Traffic between any two VLANs (*inter-VLAN communication*) can only go through a routing device **[AWEYFCDM22]**. Whereas physical interfaces generally have uniquely assigned MAC addresses that are burned into their interface hardware, the MAC addresses of virtual interfaces are generated (logically) by the host node's virtualization software (i.e., software-based or virtual network interface cards (NICs)).

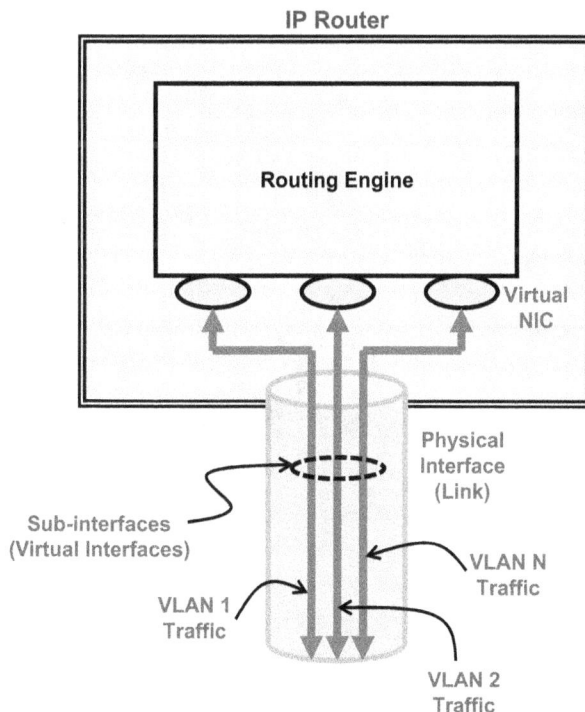

FIGURE 3.10 Physical interface with multiple sub-interfaces.

3.7.1.2 Node with Multiple Virtual Routers (Routing Engines)

A virtual router (VR) is a software function that resides in a network node and provides the functionality of a hardware-based routing device. It is a software-based routing framework that delivers the functionality of a physical router within a virtual environment. The virtualization software on a host machine allows the creation of multiple, isolated duplicates of a hardware router (see Figure 3.11). The use of VRs (which perform the same functions as a physical router) enhances network design flexibility, scalability, and reduces network infrastructure costs.

A physical IP router or a software-based server may allow multiple VRs (virtual machines (VMs)) to run simultaneously in an environment where computing resources are virtualized. Each VR may have one or more virtual NICs (each with its unique IP address, subnet mask, and logical MAC address) depending on the capabilities of the host node they are running on. Traffic to the host node is routed by IP address prefix to the correct VR.

A VR can be configured with Layer 3 interfaces to participate in dynamic routing protocols such as RIP, OSPF, and BGP, as well as use static routes. A VR can perform different types of routing in networks: static routing, default routing, and dynamic routing. Similar to physical routers, a VR can be deployed as virtual machine instances on servers (through a virtualization platform) to provide routing, switching, security, VPN services, and other network functions and to offer network communication services to users.

In many cases, VRs are created in a network functions virtualization (NFV) framework, where the functions of the traditional hardware-based router are implemented in software that can run on standard commercial off-the-shelf hardware. The cost-effectiveness of VRs (which operate like routers) makes them an attractive choice for enterprises and service providers.

3.7.1.3 Interface with Primary and Secondary IPv6 Addresses

A router running a Protocol Independent Multicast (PIM) protocol originates a Hello message with the Address List Option [AWEMULT24] [RFC7761] on an interface to advertise all secondary IP addresses associated with that interface. A router must include this Option in all Hello messages if it

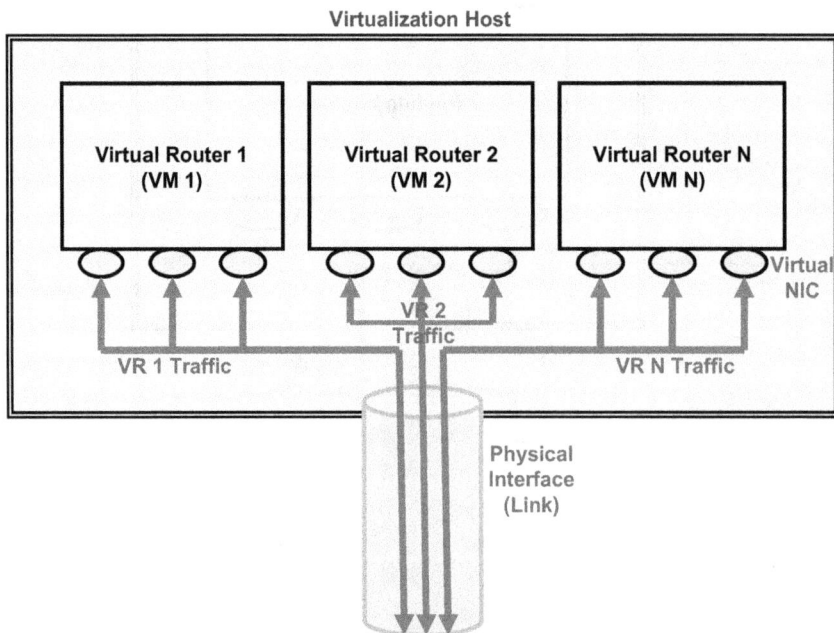

FIGURE 3.11   Node with multiple virtual routers (routing engines).

has secondary IP addresses associated with that interface, and may omit it if no secondary addresses are configured on the interface. The primary IP address of a PIM neighbor is the IP address that the neighbor uses as the source IP address in the PIM Hello messages it sends. The primary IP address must be unique among the IP addresses of all PIM neighbors on a specific PIM router interface.

It is necessary for a router to communicate its interface's secondary IP addresses to PIM neighbors to provide them with a mechanism for mapping next-hop information obtained through their multicast routing information base (MRIB) to a primary IP address that can be used as the destination address for sending PIM Join/Prune messages. A router can obtain the primary IP address of a PIM neighbor's interface from the source IP address field in the IP packets carrying PIM Hello messages. PIM routers use the Address List Option in the Hello message to advertise their secondary IP addresses. A PIM router must not list the primary IP address of the source interface within the Address List Option.

3.7.2 IPv6 Global Unicast Address Format

IPv6 Global Unicast addresses can be viewed as equivalent to public (or Internet-wide) IPv4 addresses. Just like IPv4 addresses that are globally routable and reachable on the IPv4 Internet, IPv6 Global Unicast addresses function the same on the IPv6 Internet. Using the CIDR convention, IPv6 Global Unicast addresses with prefixes of arbitrary bit length can be aggregated (summarized), similar to the use of CIDR in IPv4 addresses. IPv6 Global Unicast addresses play a significant role in the IPv6 addressing architecture. By designing IPv6 Global Unicast addresses to be aggregatable, a more efficient routing infrastructure can be achieved. IPv6 has been designed from the outset to support efficient, hierarchical addressing and routing. The uniqueness and scope of an IPv6 Global Unicast address encompass the entire IPv6 Internet.

Figure 3.12 shows the structure of the IPv6 Global Unicast address. This structure does not define any specific sizes for the three parts following the address prefix (i.e., the first 3 bits of the address). The address prefix begins with the binary value 001, resulting in the first hexadecimal digit taking the value of 2 or 3. Currently, all IPv6 Global Unicast addresses start with the binary value 001, equivalent to the IPv6 prefix, 2000::/3, in IPv6 address representation. Typically, the IPv6 Global Unicast address has a structure that consists of a 48-bit IPv6 Global Routing Prefix and a 16-bit Subnet ID.

The IANA has designated IPv6 addresses with the prefix 2000::/3 as IPv6 Global Unicast addresses that can be divided and allocated to the RIRs. Currently, the following parts of this IPv6 address space have been allocated to ARIN:

- 2001:0400::/23
- 2001:1800::/23
- 2001:4800::/23
- 2600:0000::/12
- 2610:0000::/23
- 2630:0000::/12

ARIN may allocate sub-parts of the 2001:1800::/23 address space (e.g., 2001:18FB::/32) to an ISP or a large customer (see also Figure 3.1). The ISP in turn may allocate the prefix 2001:18FB:1::/48 to Customer 1 and 2001:18FB:2::/48 to Customer 2.

All IPv6 Global Unicast addresses except those starting with the binary value 000 have an Interface ID field that is 64 bits long (i.e., $n+m=64$). No such constraint on the size or structure of the Interface ID field is placed on IPv6 Global Unicast addresses that start with the binary value 000. IPv6 addresses with embedded IPv4 addresses (discussed below) are examples of IPv6 Global Unicast addresses that start with the binary value 000.

An interface on a link can be configured with an IPv6 Global Unicast address through one of several methods: manual configuration, Stateless Address Autoconfiguration (SLAAC) **[RFC4862]**,

Prefix: 2000::/3

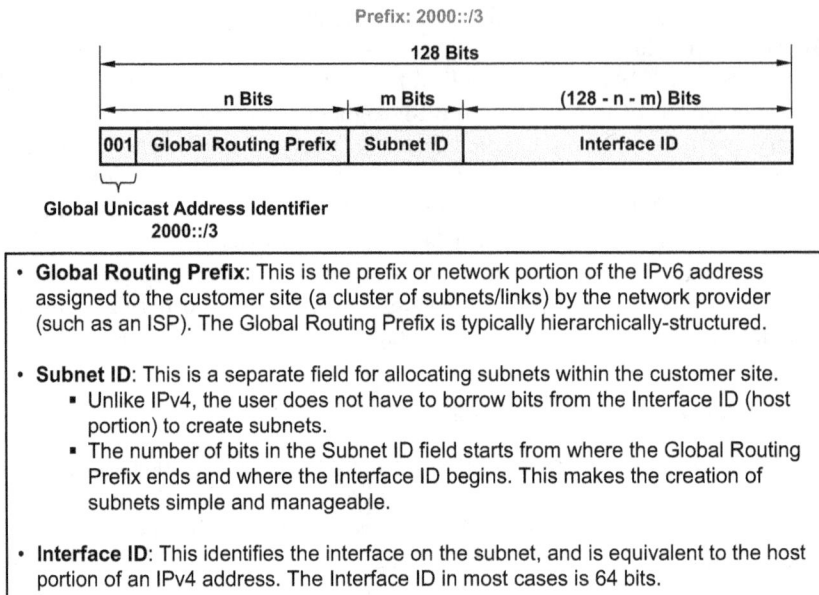

Global Unicast Address Identifier
2000::/3

- **Global Routing Prefix**: This is the prefix or network portion of the IPv6 address assigned to the customer site (a cluster of subnets/links) by the network provider (such as an ISP). The Global Routing Prefix is typically hierarchically-structured.

- **Subnet ID**: This is a separate field for allocating subnets within the customer site.
    - Unlike IPv4, the user does not have to borrow bits from the Interface ID (host portion) to create subnets.
    - The number of bits in the Subnet ID field starts from where the Global Routing Prefix ends and where the Interface ID begins. This makes the creation of subnets simple and manageable.

- **Interface ID**: This identifies the interface on the subnet, and is equivalent to the host portion of an IPv4 address. The Interface ID in most cases is 64 bits.

Example

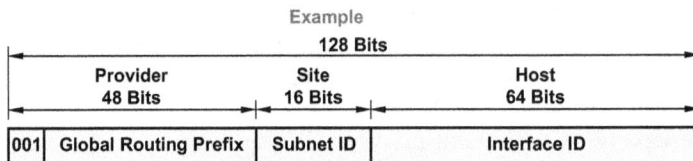

FIGURE 3.12   IPv6 Global Unicast address format.

and Stateful DHCPv6 **[RFC8415]**. A node may obtain more than one IPv6 Global Unicast address for various purposes; however, it is desirable for a node to only obtain one of these addresses from a Stateful DHCPv6 server to ensure proper address assignment and management.

Let us now consider an IPv6 Global Unicast address with a 48-bit Global Routing Prefix and a 16-bit Subnet ID. Subnetting this IPv6 address space involves using well-established techniques to divide the Subnet ID portion of the address. An organization may use this approach to delegate address spaces to different segments of an IPv6 intranet, allowing for route summarization to the IPv6 Internet. For this IPv6 Global Unicast address, the first 48 bits are fixed and are usually allocated by an ISP. Subnetting the Subnet ID portion of a Global Unicast address space involves determining the number of bits to be used for subnetting (16 bits in this case) and enumerating the new subnetted network prefixes for use in different segments of the IPv6 intranet.

3.7.3   IPv6 LINK-LOCAL UNICAST ADDRESS FORMAT

The IPv6 Link-Local address is a special type of IPv6 unicast address with link-local scope and is used only on a single link **[RFC4291]**. These addresses are used between on-link IPv6 neighbors (i.e., adjacent nodes) when communicating with each other and do not extend beyond the local link. Note that in IPv6, a link generally refers to a Layer 2 multiaccess network or point-to-point link. IPv6 nodes on a single link (i.e., with no intervening IPv6 router) use Link-Local addresses to communicate with each other, but only on that local link.

The delivery of an IPv6 packet with a destination address that is a Link-Local address is confined to the local link or subnet. A Link-Local address only needs to be unique on the local link and not beyond that link. IPv6 routers, therefore, do not forward IPv6 packets with a destination address set to a Link-Local address. Nodes on a link can use the Duplicate Address Detection (DAD) mechanism **[RFC4862]** to determine the uniqueness of the Link-Local addresses they create. *IPv6 nodes are required to use DAD on all IPv6 unicast addresses before assigning them to interfaces, regardless of whether those addresses are obtained through manual configuration, stateless autoconfiguration, or DHCPv6.*

The structure of the IPv6 Link-Local address is shown in Figure 3.13. An IPv6-enabled interface may autoconfigure this address type using a combination of the IPv6 Link-Local prefix FE80::/10 (the starting 10 bits of the address equal 1111 1110 10) and the MAC address of the interface. *Each interface in the IPv6 internetwork is required to have one IPv6 Link-Local address, which serves as a "bootstrap" address when the interface is powered up and starts IPv6 communications. When IPv6 is enabled on an interface, an IPv6 Link-Local address is immediately assigned to it; an IPv6-enabled interface must always have a Link-Local address.*

IPv6 Link-Local addresses are usually autoconfigured but can also be manually configured. *Although it is common to bind an IPv6 Link-Local address to the interface's MAC address (expressed in the modified Extended Unique Identifier (EUI)-64 format), this is not always necessary; any identifier can be used in place of the interface ID as long as the Link-Local address is unique on the local link and the local node can track the usage of its* identifiers. The identifier used could be any node-specific token such as a serial number or a randomly generated value (using a pseudorandom addressing mechanism) that ensures IPv6 address uniqueness on the local link.

IPv6 defined Link-Local addresses so that IPv6 nodes can use them for interface addressing and communication on a single link for various purposes, such as IPv6 Global Unicast address configuration (via SLAAC or Stateful DHCPv6) and neighbor discovery (see **[RFC4861]**), which

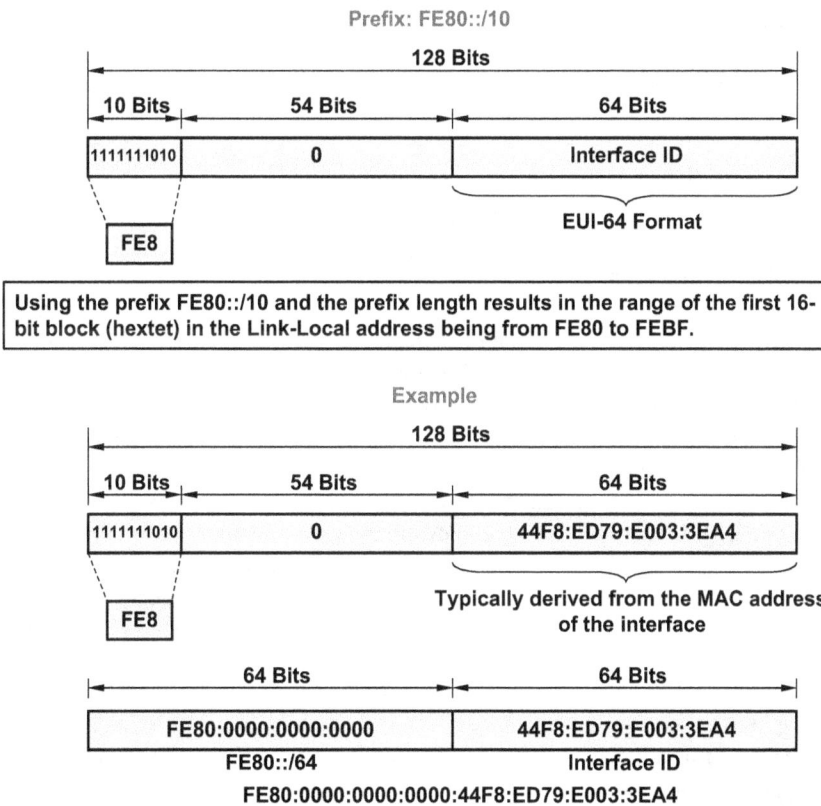

FIGURE 3.13 IPv6 Link-Local unicast address format.

includes discovering if IPv6 routers are present on the link. IPv6 Link-Local addresses are not routable because they have significance only on the link on which they are configured; such addresses do not appear in the IPv6 routing table. IPv6 routers must not forward any IPv6 packets with a source or destination address that is a Link-Local address to other links; they are restricted to the local link.

IPv6 defines Link-Local addresses to enable IPv6 nodes attached to a link to communicate without requiring IPv6 Global Unicast addresses. A similar concept exists in IPv4, where the IPv4 address block 169.254.0.0/16 (169.254.0.0 to 169.254.255.255) was reserved by the Internet Engineering Task Force (IETF) for link-local addressing (a Microsoft feature called Automatic Private IP Addressing (APIPA)). When several IPv6-enabled nodes are connected to a Layer 2 switch, they will each autoconfigure their connecting interfaces with IPv6 Link-Local addresses, discover each other, and be ready to communicate. *The scope of an IPv6 Link-Local address is limited to the respective link (i.e., local link) on which it is* configured. IPv6 nodes use Link-Local addresses for the neighbor discovery process (see **Chapter 4**) **[RFC4861]**, and these addresses are always automatically configured, even in the absence of any other IPv6 unicast addresses. As noted above, IPv6 routers never forwards packets with Link-Local addresses beyond the local link.

The key features of IPv6 Link-Local addresses are summarized as follows:

- *For an interface on a node to be IPv6-enabled, it must first be configured with an IPv6 Link-Local address.* The node does not necessarily have to be assigned an IPv6 Global Unicast address, but it must have a Link-Local address.
- An interface on a link can have only one Link-Local address.
- Link-Local addresses are only required to be unique on the local link. A node with different interfaces on different links may use the same Link-Local address on each of those interfaces.
- Link-Local addresses are not routable beyond the local link and IPv6 routers do not forward IPv6 packets with Link-Local addresses.

A node can dynamically (automatically) create an IPv6 Link-Local address on its own for an interface on a link upon startup, or the Link-Local address can be manually configured.

3.7.3.1 Configuring and Using IPv6 Link-Local Addresses

IPv6 allows a node to create an IPv6 Link-Local address completely on its own, without using the services of a DHCPv6 server or any form of manual configuration. This enables the IPv6 node to immediately start communicating with other nodes on the local link (to discover IPv6 neighbors and services). As stated above, an IPv6 node only needs a unique Link-Local address for communication with other nodes on the same link. A node may use its Link-Local address to communicate with an IPv6 router or a DHCPv6 server to obtain information (IPv6 prefixes) for creating an IPv6 Global Unicast address. The node can then use this globally unique and routable address to communicate with nodes on other networks (i.e., beyond the local link and on the IPv6 Internet).

The use of Link-Local addresses solves the IPv4 address configuration problem during node startup: *How does an IPv4 node contact a DHCP server for an IPv4 address when it first needs to have an IPv4 address before it can communicate with the server to request one?* This is a classic example of the chicken or egg problem. Which comes first? To solve this problem, IPv4 allows a node to use a DHCP Discover message with the IPv4 source address set to 0.0.0.0. With IPv6, a node during startup automatically configures itself with a unique Link-Local address on that link. It can then use this address to communicate with any IPv6 node on the same link, including a DHCPv6 server and any attached IPv6 router, if necessary. Note that an IPv6 router transmits ICMPv6 Router Advertisement messages on a link that allow nodes on that link to obtain globally unique IPv6 prefixes for configuring IPv6 Global Unicast addresses, with or without using the services of DHCPv6.

After an IPv6 node has autoconfigured a Link-Local address on an interface, it uses it for various purposes including the following:

- When the node starts up and before it obtains an IPv6 Global Unicast address, it uses the configured IPv6 Link-Local address as the source address of IPv6 packets when communicating with other nodes on the same link, including any local IPv6 routers or DHCPv6 servers.
- An IPv6 node on the link uses the Link-Local address of a discovered local IPv6 router as its default IPv6 gateway address.
- IPv6 routers exchange dynamic routing protocol (e.g., RIPng, OSPFv3) messages using their IPv6 Link-Local addresses. Note that the network between any two adjacent routers is a Layer 2 network.
- IPv6 routers populate their routing table entries (from routing information obtained from dynamic routing protocols) using the IPv6 Link-Local address as the next-hop address.

3.7.4 IPv6 Unique-Local Unicast Address Format

IPv6 has a special type of globally unique private address called the IPv6 Unique-Local address, which has the IPv6 address prefix FC00::/7 [RFC4193]. Figure 3.14 shows the format of this address type. Unique-Local addresses are conceptually similar to IPv4 private addresses (defined in [RFC1918]) and are not routable in the IPv6 Internet. However, unlike IPv4 private addresses that can be statefully translated to a global IPv4 unicast address, IPv6 Unique-Local addresses are not intended for stateful translation in the same manner.

IPv6 Unique-Local addresses are unicast addresses that can be used similarly to IPv6 Global Unicast addresses, but only as private addresses within a well-defined domain and should not be routed in the global IPv6 Internet. Unique-Local addresses are meant for use within a limited domain, such as a company site, or for routing between a small number of domains under the same administrative entity. These addresses are designed for use as private addresses on IPv6 devices that will never use them to access the Internet nor need them to be accessible from the global IPv6 Internet.

The IPv6 Unique-Local address has the following characteristics [RFC4193]:

- These addresses have a globally unique IPv6 prefix (FC00::/7), similar to the global unique prefix of the IPv6 Global Unicast addresses. If an IPv6 Unique-Local address is accidentally leaked outside the organization in which it is configured, it will not cause conflicts with other IPv6 global prefixes.
- This address type has a well-known structure (as shown in Figure 3.14), which allows for easy identification and filtering at organizational boundaries. Any incoming or outgoing IPv6 Unique-Local routes are filtered out by boundary and Internet routers.
- Using this address type, different sites can be interconnected without creating any IPv6 address conflicts. Combining or interconnecting different sites with this address type will not cause address conflicts or require address renumbering.
- Addresses in this IPv6 address space can be used by an ISP, and different ISPs can independently use this address space without causing address overlaps with any other ISP.
- A company site can use this address space independently of the IPv6 Global Unicast addresses assigned to it by any ISP.
- Applications treat addresses in this address space like regular global IPv6 addresses, even though they are not routable on the global IPv6 Internet.

Prefix: FC00::/7

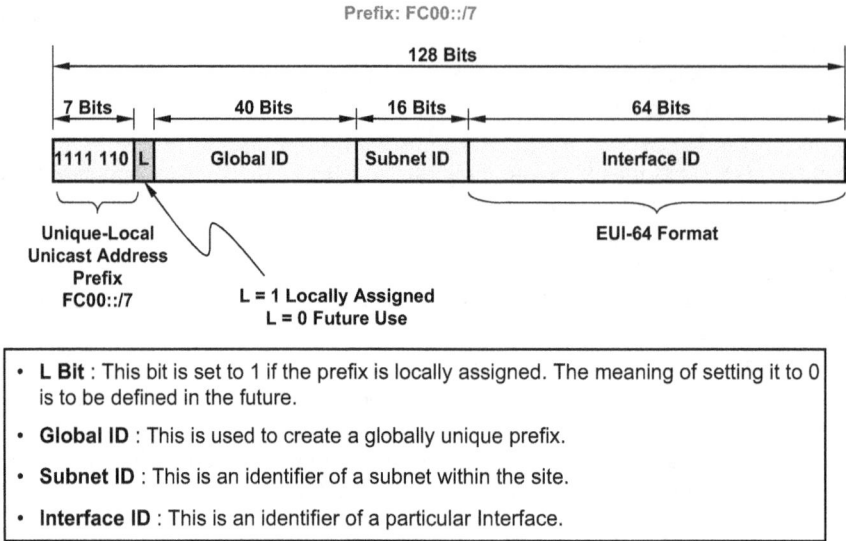

FIGURE 3.14   IPv6 Unique-Local unicast address format (see [RFC4193]).

The first 7 bits of the IPv6 Unique-Local address space are 1111 110x, which gives the prefix FC00::/7. As shown in Figure 3.14, the eighth bit (x) is known as the local or L Flag and can be either 0 or 1. With this, the Unique-Local address range is divided into two parts:

- FC00::/8 (1111 1100): When the L Flag is set to 0, there is currently no interpretation of IPv6 addresses with this Flag setting, although it may be defined in the future.
- FD00::/8 (1111 1101): When the L Flag is set to 1, the associated IPv6 address is locally assigned.

With the L Flag equal to 1 being the only legitimate value currently used, the only valid IPv6 Unique-Local addresses today have the IPv6 prefix FD00::/8.

3.7.4.1   Algorithm for Pseudorandom Global ID Generation

Reference [RFC4193] specifies a mechanism for generating unique Global IDs for Unique-Local addresses without them being administered by a central authority. A Pseudorandom Global ID Algorithm is defined in [RFC4193], which allows IPv6 nodes to pseudo-randomly generate locally assigned Global IDs that are unique with a very high probability. To ensure a high probability of uniqueness in Global IDs, it is important for all sites using the Global IDs for their Unique-Local addresses to use the same pseudorandom algorithm for generating the IDs.

The following six steps summarize the pseudorandom algorithm for generating locally assigned Global IDs as described in [RFC4193]. The resulting Global ID is then used in the appropriate address prefix field in Figure 3.14:

- Read the current time of day represented in 64-bit Network Time Protocol format [RFC1305].
- Obtain a local EUI-64 identifier (i.e., system-specific identifier) on the node running the pseudorandom algorithm if one exists. If the node does not have an EUI-64 identifier, it can create one from a 48-bit MAC address as described in Section 3.9.3. If an EUI-64 cannot be obtained or derived from the 48-bit MAC address, the node can use a suitable local unique identifier such as a system serial number.
- Create a 128-bit key by concatenating the 64-bit Network Time Protocol (NTP) time of day with the 64-bit system-specific identifier.

- Compute an SHA-1 digest on the 128-bit key as specified in **[FIPS1995] [RFC3174]**. The resulting value of the SHA-1 digest is 160 bits.
- Use the least significant 40 bits of the 160-bit digest as the Global ID.
- Create a locally assigned Unique-Local address prefix by concatenating FC00::/7, the L bit (which is set to 1), and the newly created 40-bit Global ID.

This algorithm is primarily used for Unique-Local addresses with a /48 prefix and does not work well for addresses with larger IPv6 prefixes or when contiguous prefixes are needed. This algorithm enables an IPv6 node to create a reasonably unique Global ID, which can then be used to generate a locally assigned IPv6 Unique-Local address.

3.7.5   IPv6 Addresses with Embedded IPv4 Addresses

Two types of IPv6 addresses, the *IPv4-Compatible IPv6 address* and the *IPv4-Mapped IPv6 address*, were defined to carry an IPv4 address in the low-order 32 bits of the 128-bit IPv6 address space **[RFC4291]**. These two address types were created to allow an IPv4 address to be represented within an IPv6 address.

The IPv4 address embedded in the last 32 bits to create the IPv4-Compatible IPv6 address must be a globally unique IPv4 unicast address. The IPv4-Compatible IPv6 address was defined as an addressing mechanism to assist in the transition from IPv4 to IPv6. This address type is now deprecated because such addresses are no longer used by current IPv6 transition mechanisms. This section describes only the IPv4-Mapped IPv6 address.

3.7.5.1   IPv4-Mapped IPv6 Address

IPv4-Mapped IPv6 addresses can be used by a device that supports dual-stack IPv4/IPv6 software and needs to send IPv6 packets to another device that supports an IPv4-only stack. The IPv4-Mapped IPv6 address embeds an IPv4 address in the last 32 bits of the 128-bit IPv6 address space **[RFC4291]** and uses the reserved IPv6 address prefix ::FFFF. *This address type is only used for representing the IPv4 address of an IPv4 node in the IPv6 address format.*

IPv4-Mapped IPv6 addresses are not actual IPv6 addresses but only allow the representation of IPv4 addresses in the standard IPv6 address format, as shown in Figure 3.15. For example, these addresses are not meant to be entered in a web browser for locating resources and do not function when used in that manner. A node should never use the IPv4-Mapped IPv6 address as a source or destination address of an IPv6 packet **[IANAIPv6SPREG]**. Packets with these addresses cannot be forwarded and are not globally routable. Figure 3.15 shows the structure of the IPv4-Mapped IPv6 address and a mapping example.

An IPv4-Mapped IPv6 address is an IPv6 unicast address that has all zeros in the first 80 bits, FFFF (hexadecimal) in the next 16 bits, and *an IPv4 unicast address in the last 32 bits represented*

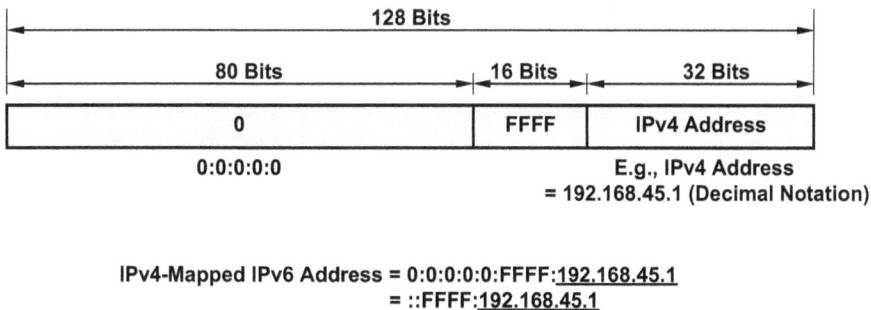

FIGURE 3.15   IPv4-Mapped IPv6 address format.

in dotted-decimal notation, as shown in Figure 3.15. This means the first 96 bits of the address space are represented as hexadecimal values, and *the last 32 bits containing the IPv4 address are expressed in dotted-decimal notation*. The IPv4 address carried in an IPv4-Mapped IPv6 address does not have to be globally unique.

When the IPv4 address w.x.y.z (in dotted-decimal notation) is embedded in an IPv4-Mapped IPv6 address, it becomes 0:0:0:0:0:FFFF:w.x.y.z, shortened to ::FFFF:w.x.y.z. The high-order 96 bits consist of the IPv6 fixed prefix ::FFFF, while the low-order 32 bits of the IPv6 address contain the IPv4 address in dotted-decimal notation. The prefix ::FFFF: is simply added in front of the IPv4 address. The use of these types of IPv6 addresses is described in **[RFC4038]**. The IPv4 address 192.168.20.10, when carried in an IPv4-Mapped IPv6 address, gives the address representation ::FFFF:192.168.20.10.

3.7.5.1.1   Using IPv4-Mapped IPv6 Addresses in an IPv4/IPv6 Dual-Stack Node

A node cannot use IPv4-Mapped IPv6 addresses in IPv6 packets but can only use them to represent IPv4 addresses in IPv6 software. For example, a host that has both IPv4 and IPv6 may run software designed exclusively for IPv6, possibly because the network administrator finds it easier to support software for only one IP protocol (IPv6) rather than for two protocols (IPv6 and IPv4). If the IPv6-based software listens on the IPv6 Unspecified address ::/128 (i.e., the source IP address of incoming packets), it can still accept connections from IPv4 clients.

However, because the software is written only for IPv6, it can only handle IPv6 addresses. In this case, the host's operating system would use the IPv4-Mapped IPv6 address ::FFFF:w.x.y.z to represent the IPv4 address w.x.y.z of an IPv4 client (see Figure 3.16). It is important to note that the software is designed to run on IPv6 but is meant to handle only IPv4 clients (using the IPv4 address embedded in the IPv4-Mapped IPv6 address).

This software does not handle IPv6 clients; it runs on IPv6 but only processes IPv4 clients. With the mapping (using the IPv4-Mapped IPv6 address format), this IPv6 software (that handles only IPv4 clients) is usable solely on IPv6. It is therefore impossible for this IPv6-only node to use these

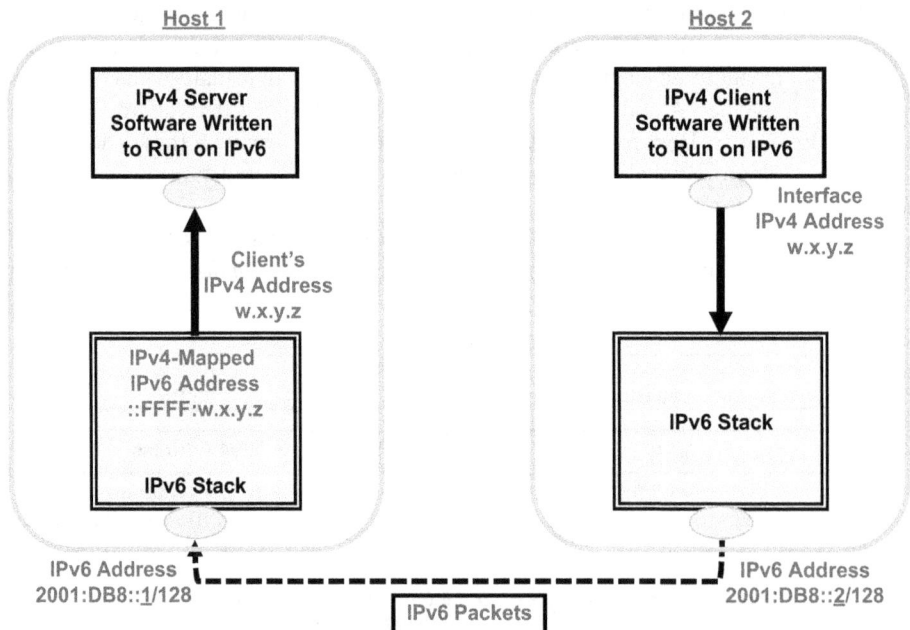

FIGURE 3.16   Using IPv4-Mapped IPv6 addresses in an IPv4/IPv6 dual-stack node.

IPv4-Mapped addresses in IPv6 packets when communicating with another IPv6 system because, internally to the IPv6-only node (Figure 3.16), these addresses are exclusively associated with IPv4 connections. It is important to note that IPv4-Mapped IPv6 addresses are meant to assist with the transition to IPv6, and network engineers should not view them as a permanent solution or replacement for full IPv6 connectivity.

3.7.5.1.2   Using IPv4-Mapped IPv6 Addresses in an IPv4/IPv6 Multiprotocol BGP Topology

The discussion above shows how IPv4-Mapped IPv6 addresses can be used in a dual IPv4/IPv6 stack environment where both protocols are in use and there is a need to facilitate communication between entities that use these protocols (see Figure 3.16). Another special case where an IPv4 address needs to be represented in the IPv6 address format is when both IPv4 and IPv6 are used in a Multiprotocol BGP (MBGP) topology, as shown in Figure 3.17. In this example, two IPv6 routers with dual-stack, Router 1 and Router 2, create an IPv4 adjacency but exchange IPv6 prefixes.

The routers use IPv4-Mapped IPv6 addresses to represent the Router IDs, which are expressed in IPv4 dotted-decimal notation. The IPv6 routers need this address representation to identify the next-hop addresses associated with the IPv4 adjacency created between them. Figure 3.17 shows the IPv6 BGP table of Router 1 (the local router) with the next-hop set to Router 2 (with Router ID of 192.168.10.2) expressed as an IPv4-Mapped IPv6 address (::FFFF:192.168.10.2). The IPv6 BGP table of Router 1 has next-hop addresses expressed in the IPv6 address format, even though an IPv4 adjacency is formed with Router 2.

When Router 1 and Router 2 exchange IPv6 prefixes over the IPv4 peering connection, they indicate the next-hop address of IPv6 routes using an IPv4-Mapped IPv6 address. This is because the two routers establish the BGP session between themselves over the IPv4 adjacency using IPv4 addresses, meaning they must represent the next-hop IPv4 addresses for IPv6 routes in the IPv6 address format, that is, using IPv4-Mapped IPv6 addresses.

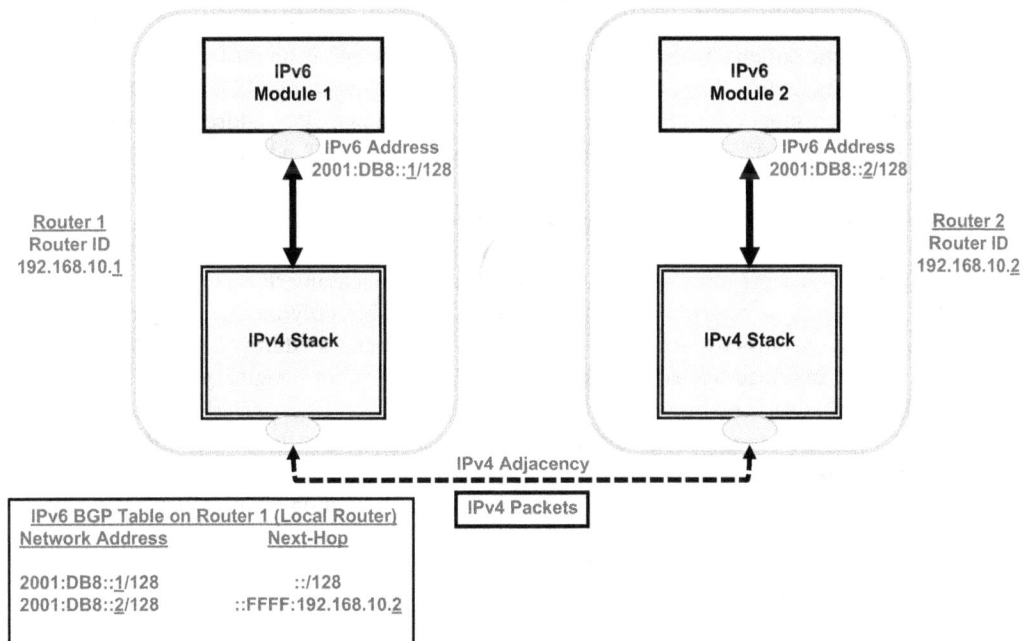

FIGURE 3.17   Using IPv4-Mapped IPv6 addresses in a IPv4/IPv6 Multiprotocol BGP (MBGP) topology.

3.7.6 IPv6 Unspecified Address

Both IPv4 and IPv6 have a special type of address called the *Unspecified address*, which has all of its binary bits set to 0. The IPv4 Unspecified address is 0.0.0.0/32, while the corresponding address for IPv6 is 0:0:0:0:0:0:0:0 (shortened as ::/128) **[RFC4291]**. An IP node uses the Unspecified address only to indicate the absence of a source IP address. Nodes typically use the Unspecified address as the source address in IP packets to indicate the lack of an address and when verifying the uniqueness of a tentative IP address. Operating systems generally use the Unspecified address in the absence of any valid source IP address, for example, when running IP address assignment applications like DHCP.

The characteristics of the IPv4/v6 Unspecified address are summarized as follows:

- IPv4/v6 routers must never forward packets that have their source or destination address set to the IPv4/v6 Unspecified address.
- This address is never used as a destination IP address, in IPv6 Routing headers, or assigned to an interface.
- This address cannot be assigned to a physical interface.
- This address, when used as a source address, indicates the absence of an address.

3.7.7 IPv6 Loopback Address

Both IPv4 and IPv6 have the concept of *loopback addresses* that identify logical interfaces on a node **[RFC4291]**. A loopback address does not represent a physical interface (only a logical one) and is always up and running on the node on which it is configured as soon as the node is powered up. A node uses a loopback address to send an IPv6 packet to itself. Packets addressed with a destination address that is a loopback address are looped (returned) on the same interface. Loopback addresses are typically used for testing and troubleshooting the TCP/IP stack on a node. Specifically, the loopback address identifies a loopback interface on a node, enabling the node to send IP packets (to the loopback interface) that will be returned to itself.

IPv6 reserves the IPv6 address space 0:0:0:0:0:0:0:1/128 (shortened to ::1/128) for loopback addresses. The IPv6 Loopback address (a type of unicast address) is an all-0s address except for the last bit, which is set to 1. IPv4 reserves the entire IPv4 address range 127.0.0.0/8 for loopback addresses. However, most operating systems use the well-known IPv4 address 127.0.0.1 (called "localhost") by default. The remaining addresses in the 127.0.0.0/8 address space are typically not used.

The characteristics of loopback addresses are summarized as follows:

- The loopback address must never be assigned to any physical interface.
  - This address is treated as if it has link-local scope, but only on the local node itself. One may view this address as a type of link-local unicast address that is assigned to a virtual interface (called the "loopback interface") on an imaginary link within the IPv6 node that leads nowhere.
- An IPv6 node must not use the loopback address as the source address for IPv6 packets that are sent outside of that node.
- An IPv6 node must never send an IPv6 packet with a destination address that is the loopback address outside of that node.
- An IPv6 router must never forward IPv6 packets with a destination address that is a loopback address; such packets must not be forwarded by an IPv6 router.
- An IPv6 node that receives an IPv6 packet on an interface with a destination address set to the loopback address must drop that packet.

3.8   IPv6 MULTICAST ADDRESSES

IP multicast is a form of communication where a sender transmits data simultaneously to a group of subscribers called a *multicast group* (*one-to-many communication*) [AWEMULT24]. Each data piece is transmitted as the payload of an *IP multicast packet* whose source IP address field is set to the IP address of the sender and whose destination address field is set to the IP address of the multicast group, known as the *multicast group address*. Only hosts that belong to the multicast group will receive and process the multicast packets sent to the specified multicast group address. The destination hosts are actually interfaces in the internetwork. Additionally, the multicast destinations may be multiple interfaces on the same device, but typically they are interfaces on different devices that may be geographically dispersed. Each multicast group is assigned a unique (reserved) recognizable IP address. Note that unicast communication (using a unicast destination address) involves sending a single packet to a single destination (*one-to-one communication*).

The set of hosts that belong to a multicast group continuously listen on a specific multicast address for multicast traffic. As noted above, the destination of a multicast packet consists of a set of interfaces (typically on different nodes), identified by a single multicast address that represents a multicast group. By using an appropriate unicast routing protocol to discover the network topology, a multicast distribution tree can be constructed, allowing packets addressed to a multicast group address to be delivered to all interfaces associated with that address. Multicast addresses cannot be used as the source IP address of any IP packet.

Hosts join an IPv6 multicast group by sending group membership messages (using the Multicast Listener Discovery (MLD) protocol [RFC2710] [RFC3810]) to their neighboring IPv6 multicast routers. IPv6 multicast routers also use MLD to determine active multicast group membership on a network segment. Both IPv6 hosts and multicast routers send MLD messages, which are special Internet Control Message Protocol for IPv6 (ICMPv6) messages defined for managing IPv6 multicast group memberships [RFC4443]. IPv6 multicast routers and multicast group members (i.e., listeners) on a network segment use MLD to exchange multicast membership status information. Host members of a multicast group report their individual memberships, while the multicast group membership status of hosts is periodically polled by the IPv6 multicast routers.

Multicast group membership is dynamic, meaning hosts can join and leave a group at any time. Additionally, a host does not have to belong to a multicast group to send traffic to that group. IP multicast groups are not limited by size or geographical location; members can be spread across multiple locations and network segments as long as there are connecting multicast routers to forward group membership information and multicast traffic. Multicast routers use *multicast routing protocols* [AWEMULT24] to learn about nodes that require multicast traffic and to build the *multicast distribution tree* of receiving interfaces.

IPv6 assigns multicast addresses from the reserved IPv6 address prefix 1111 1111 (0xFF), which constitutes the leftmost 8 bits of the IPv6 address space as shown in Figure 3.18 [RFC4291]. IPv6 multicast addresses are uniquely identified by the prefix 0xFF to distinguish them from all other IPv6 address types. The IPv6 prefix value 1111 1111 (0xFF) always identifies an address as an IPv6 multicast address. The equivalent IPv4 multicast address space is 224.0.0.0/4. The following two important rules apply to both IPv4 and IPv6 multicast:

- The source address of all IP packets, including those sent to a multicast group, must always be a unicast address.
- A multicast address cannot be used as the source address of any IP packet.

The value in the 4-bit multicast Scope field (Figure 3.18) is used to limit the scope of the multicast group. Multicast routers use this scope to constrain IPv6 multicast traffic to stay within the

Prefix: FF00::/8

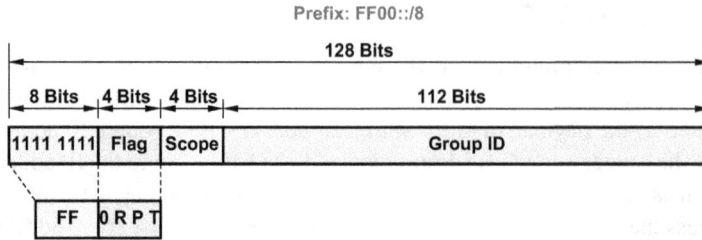

- **11111111**: This binary string at the start of the address identifies the address as being a multicast address.

- **High-Order Flag Bit**: This is reserved, and must be initialized to 0.

- **T Bit**:
  - Setting T to 0 indicates a permanently-assigned ("well-known") multicast address, assigned by the Internet Assigned Numbers Authority (IANA).
  - Setting T to 1 indicates a non-permanently-assigned ("transient" or "dynamically" assigned) multicast address.

- **P Bit**:
  - Setting P to 0 indicates a multicast address that is not assigned based on the network prefix.
  - Setting P to 1 indicates a multicast address that is assigned based on the network prefix. If P is set to 1, T MUST be set to 1

- **R Bit**:
  - When the highest-order bit is 0, setting R to 1 indicates a multicast address that embeds the address on a Rendezvous Point (RP).
  - Then P MUST be set to 1, and consequently T MUST be set to 1, as specified in RFC 3306. In effect, this implies the prefix FF70::/12. In this case, the last 4 bits of the previously reserved field are interpreted as embedding the interface ID of the RP, as specified in RFC 3956.
  - Setting R to 0 indicates a multicast address that does not embed the address of an RP and follows the semantics defined in RFC 3513 and RFC 3306.

- **Scope**: This is a 4-bit multicast scope value used to limit the scope of the multicast group (see RFC 4291).

- **Group ID**: This identifies the multicast group, either permanent or transient, within the given scope.

FIGURE 3.18   IPv6 multicast address format (see **[RFC4291]** and **[RFC3956]**).

appropriate multicast domain. The following scope values (in hexadecimal) have been defined in **[RFC4291]**:

- **1 = Interface-Local Scope**: This scope spans only a single interface on an IPv6 node and is mainly used for the loopback transmission of IPv6 multicast packets.
- **2 = Link-Local Scope**: This scope spans the same topological region as the corresponding IPv6 unicast address scope. The IPv6 Solicited-Node multicast address has link-local scope.
- **4 = Admin-Local Scope**: This scope is the smallest scope that must be administratively configured for a multicast transmission. It is not automatically derived from the physical connectivity of network nodes in the IPv6 internetwork or from other non-multicast-related configuration information.
- **5 = Site-Local Scope**: This scope is intended to span a single organizational site.

- **8 = Organization-Local Scope**: This scope is intended to span multiple sites belonging to a single organization.
- **E = Global Scope**: This scope spans the entire IPv6 Internet.

IPv6 multicast addresses must not be used as the source address of any IPv6 packet or appear in the IPv6 Routing header of IPv6 packets. IPv6 routers must not forward any multicast packet beyond the scope indicated in the 4-bit Scope field of the packet's destination multicast address.

IPv6 does not support the concept of broadcast addresses. Instead, it uses special multicast group addresses, such as the IPv6 All-devices multicast addresses and Solicited-Node multicast addresses, to provide this functionality.

The well-known IP addresses are predefined addresses reserved for special use by the IETF. The IPv4 well-known multicast addresses are in the range 224.0.0.0/24. The IPv6 well-known multicast addresses start with the IPv6 address prefix FF00::/12; the first three hexadecimal digits of these addresses are always FF0.

The following are examples of IANA-reserved and -registered IPv6 multicast addresses:

- FF02::1 – The IPv6 All-Nodes multicast address used to reach all nodes on the same network segment, also known as a link or subnet.
- FF02::2 – The IPv6 All-Routers multicast address used to reach all routers on the same network segment.
- FF02::5 – The IPv6 All-OSPF Routers multicast address used to reach all OSPF routers on the same network segment.
- FF02::6 – The IPv6 All-OSPF Designated Routers multicast address used to reach all OSPF Designated Routers on the same network segment.
- FF02::D – The All-PIM-Routers multicast address.
- FF02::16 – The All-MLDv2-Capable Routers multicast address.
- FF02::1:FFxx:xxxx – The IPv6 Solicited-Node multicast address used during the IPv6 address resolution process (see **Chapter 4**). A node uses this address to resolve the IPv6 address of a link-local node (i.e., target node) to its corresponding Link-Layer address. As shown in Figure 3.19, the transmitting node sets the last 24 bits (xx:xxxx) of the Solicited-Node multicast address to the last 24 bits of the IPv6 unicast address of the target link-local node.

3.8.1 IPV6 SOLICITED-NODE MULTICAST ADDRESS

The IPv6 Solicited-Node multicast address is a special type of IPv6 multicast address that provides a more efficient mechanism for implementing the IPv4 broadcast delivery functionality. This address type allows an IPv6 node to contact another node on the same link, knowing only its IPv6 unicast address. IPv6 nodes use the Solicited-Node multicast address for Layer 3-to-Layer 2 address resolution, similar to the use of Address Resolution Protocol (ARP) **[RFC826]** in IPv4 (see Section 4.5.1.1 **and for IPv4 in Appendix C**).

An IPv6 node generates a Solicited-Node multicast address on an interface automatically using the IPv6 unicast or anycast address of the interface. A node automatically creates Solicited-Node multicast addresses for every unicast address configured on it. As described in Figure 3.19, an IPv6 Solicited-Node multicast address consists of the fixed IPv6 prefix FF02::1:FF00:0/104 and the last 24 bits of the corresponding IPv6 unicast address **[RFC4291]**.

When an IPv6-enabled interface on a node is configured with an IPv6 unicast address, the node uses this address to automatically generate an IPv6 Solicited-Node multicast address for the interface, and then proceeds to join the associated multicast group. This means every IPv6 unicast address on an interface has a corresponding IPv6 Solicited-Node multicast address for that

Prefix: FF02::1:FF00:0000/104

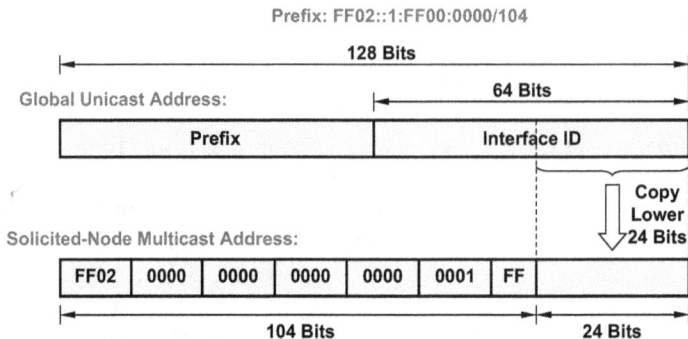

FIGURE 3.19   Solicited-Node multicast address format.

interface. The IPv6 node uses this auto-generated multicast group for various functions such as IPv6 Address Resolution, Neighbor Discovery **[RFC4861]**, and DAD, as discussed in **Chapter 4**.

Therefore, for all IPv6 unicast and anycast addresses that have been configured (manually or automatically) on the interfaces of an IPv6 node, the node is required to compute and join the associated IPv6 Solicited-Node multicast addresses *on those interfaces. It is important to note that, given the structure of the IPv6 Solicited-Node multicast address as shown in* Figure 3.19 *(i.e., using the prefix FF02::1:FF00:0/104 and only the last 24 bits of the corresponding IPv6 unicast address), a single Solicited-Node multicast address can represent (i.e., map to) multiple IPv6 unicast addresses, creating multiple multicast address overlaps.* This means multiple nodes could be listening on their interfaces for a particular Solicited-Node multicast address even if this address was not generated from any of their unicast addresses.

3.8.1.1   Example Use Case: Using the IPv6 Solicited-Node Multicast Address in IPv6-to-MAC Address Resolution

In IPv4, a node sends an ARP Request as a MAC-level broadcast, distributing the request to all nodes on the network segment, including those not running IPv4. We have already noted that IPv6 does not support broadcast addresses. Additionally, IPv6 does not support ARP as seen in IPv4 **[RFC826]**. To implement IPv4-like ARP functionality in IPv6, the IPv6 Neighbor Discovery Protocol **[RFC4861]** is used for IPv6-to-MAC address resolution (see **Chapter 4**). This protocol provides a more secure and efficient method for handling IPv6-to-MAC address resolution using

IPv6 multicast messages instead of the broadcast-based messages used in IPv4. In both IPv4 and IPv6, the term neighbor or neighbor node refers to nodes that are attached to the same Layer 2 (e.g., Ethernet) broadcast domain, such as an IP subnet or VLAN.

When an IPv6 node needs to resolve the MAC address associated with a known IPv6 address, it must send an address resolution request similar to IPv4. In the IPv6 address resolution request packet (an ICMPv6 Neighbor Solicitation message as discussed in **Chapter 4**), the sending IPv6 node sets the destination IPv6 address to the IPv6 Solicited-Node multicast address corresponding to the target node's IPv6 unicast address, and the destination MAC address to the multicast MAC address that corresponds to (i.e., is derived from) the IPv6 Solicited-Node multicast address (see Section 3.10). Note that in IPv4, the target IPv4 address in the ARP Request is 0.0.0.0.

Only the target IPv6 node "listens" on the link for this IPv6 Solicited-Node multicast address (which contains the last 24 bits of its IPv6 unicast address). This means the address resolution request will be processed only by the target IPv6 node and not by other IPv6 nodes attached to the link, similar to what happens with broadcast ARP Requests in IPv4. *Note that due to possible multicast address overlaps when an IPv6 unicast address is mapped to a corresponding Solicited-Node multicast address, multiple nodes may be listening to a Solicited-Node multicast address, but only the node with the IPv6 address indicated in the Target Address field of the Neighbor Solicitation message will respond with the requested MAC address (see details in **Chapter 4**).*

IPv6 nodes use the ICMPv6 Neighbor Solicitation message for IPv6-to-MAC address resolution. However, instead of using the IPv6 All-Nodes address (FF02::1, which has local-link scope) as the destination address of the Neighbor Solicitation message – which would flood and unnecessarily disturb all IPv6 nodes on the local link – the IPv6 Solicited-Node multicast address (derived from the target's IPv6 Link-Local address) is used. Note that only IPv6 nodes on the link that join a particular Solicited-Node multicast address (via MLD) will listen to that address in order to receive IPv6 packets sent to that address, avoiding the message flooding problem that would occur if the IPv6 All-Nodes address were used as the destination address of the Neighbor Solicitation message.

Let us assume that a target node on a link has the IPv6 Link-Local address FE80::2AA:FF:FE28:8ABC, and its corresponding Solicited-Node address is derived as FF02::1:FF28:8ABC. To resolve the IPv6 Link-Local address FE80::2AA:FF:FE28:8ABC to its corresponding MAC address, another node on the same network segment (i.e., a requester on the link) sends a Neighbor Solicitation message to the target node's IPv6 Solicited-Node address FF02::1:FF28:8ABC.

The target node with the Link-Local address FE80::2AA:FF:FE28:8ABC is listening for multicast traffic on its Solicited-Node address FF02::1:FF28:8ABC. Note that a node always registers its IPv6 multicast addresses with its network adapter. Upon receiving the Neighbor Solicitation message, the target node can respond to the sender by sending a Neighbor Advertisement message containing the MAC address corresponding to the IPv6 Link-Local address FE80::2AA:FF:FE28:8ABC. Using the Solicited-Node multicast address ensures that no other network nodes are disturbed by unwanted traffic during the IPv6 address resolution process.

3.8.2 IPv6 Unicast-Prefix-Based Multicast Address

Reference **[RFC3306]** defines an extension to the IPv6 multicast addressing architecture in **[RFC4291]** that allows the generation of globally unique IPv6 multicast addresses based on an IPv6 unicast prefix (i.e., IPv6 Unicast-Prefix-Based configuration of IPv6 multicast addresses). Using this technique, a globally unique IPv6 multicast address is configured at the same time an IPv6 unicast prefix is delegated to an IPv6 host, without the network having to run a multicast address allocation protocol. The scope of the IPv6 Unicast-Prefix-Based multicast address should not be greater than the scope of the allocated (and embedded) IPv6 unicast prefix (see Figure 3.20).

The IPv6 addressing architecture in **[RFC4291]** does not provide built-in support for dynamic IPv6 multicast address allocation. Thus, **[RFC3306]** introduces a mechanism for encoding information in an IPv6 multicast address, allowing IPv6 multicast addresses and IPv6 source-specific multicast

Prefix: FF3x::/96

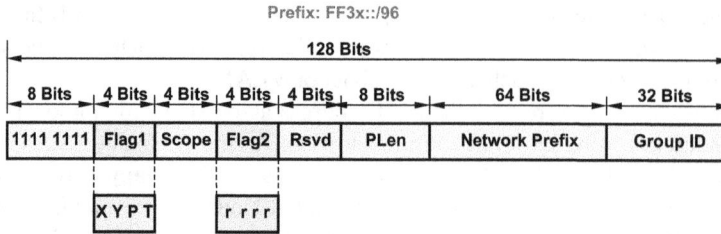

- **Flag1**:
  - Bits X and Y may each be set to 0 or 1 but X is reserved for future assignment. The meaning of Y is defined in RFC 3956 (Y = R in RFC 3956).
  - Setting P to 0 indicates a multicast address that is not assigned based on the network prefix. This indicates a multicast address as defined in RFC 4291.
  - Setting P to 1 indicates a multicast address that is assigned based on the network prefix.
  - If P is set 1, T MUST be set to 1; otherwise, the setting of the T bit is defined in Section 2.7 of RFC 4291.
  - If the flag bits in Flag1 are set to 0011, these settings create an PIM-SSM range of FF3x::/32 (where 'x' is any valid scope value).
    - The source address field in the IPv6 header identifies the owner of the multicast address. FF3x::/32 is not the only allowed SSM prefix range. For example, if the most significant flag bit in Flag1 is set, then we would get the SSM range FFBx::/32.
  - Setting Y = R to 1 indicates a multicast address that embeds the address of the Rendezvous Point (RP).
    - Then, P MUST be set to 1, and consequently T MUST be set to 1, according to RFC 3306, as this is a special case of Unicast-Prefix-Based addresses. This implies that, for instance, prefixes FF70::/12 and FFF0::/12 are embedded RP prefixes. When the R-bit is set, the last 4 bits of the field that were reserved in RFC 3306 are interpreted as embedding the RP interface ID, as specified in RFC 7371.
    - Setting R to 0 indicates a multicast address that does not embed the address of the RP and follows the semantics defined in RFC 3513 and RFC 3306.

- **Scope**: The scope of the unicast-prefix based multicast address MUST NOT exceed the scope of the unicast prefix embedded in the multicast address.

- **Flag2**: The four bits "rrrr" are reserved for future assignment as additional flag bits. The r bits MUST each be sent as 0 and MUST be ignored on receipt.

- **Rsvd**: This is a reserved field and MUST be set to zero.

- **Plen**: This indicates the actual number of bits in the network prefix field that identify the subnet when bit P is set to 1.

- **Network Prefix**: This identifies the network prefix of the unicast subnet owning the multicast address. If P is set to 1, this field contains the unicast network prefix assigned to the domain owning, or allocating, the multicast address. All non-significant bits of the network prefix field SHOULD be zero.

- **Group ID**: This identifies the multicast group, either permanent or transient, within the given scope. The Group ID is set based on the guidelines outlined in RFC 3307.

FIGURE 3.20   Unicast-Prefix-Based multicast address format (see **[RFC7371]**, **[RFC3956]**, and **[RFC3306]**).

addresses to be dynamically allocated to IPv6 hosts. **[RFC3306]** proposes the IPv6 Unicast-Prefix-Based multicast address generation mechanism by defining a new address format that enables the generation of an IPv6 multicast address through the incorporation of IPv6 unicast prefix information.

Reference **[RFC3956]** extends the IPv6 Unicast-Prefix-Based addressing method defined in **[RFC3306]** for creating an IPv6 multicast group address with an Embedded-RP address. Specifically,

[RFC3956] defines an address allocation policy in which the IPv6 address of a Rendezvous Point (RP) in a PIM – Sparse Mode (PIM-SM) network is embedded in an IPv6 multicast group address (i.e., an Embedded-RP address). The Embedded-RP address in a PIM-SM network serves as a multicast group-to-RP mapping mechanism (see related discussion in [AWEMULT24]). The use of an Embedded-RP address facilitates the deployment of scalable inter-domain PIM-SM multicast and simplifies the configuration of intra-domain PIM-SM multicast.

Reference [RFC7371] updates the IPv6 multicast addressing architecture proposed in [RFC4291] and the IPv6 Unicast-Prefix-Based multicast addressing method proposed in [RFC3306] and [RFC3956] by redefining the reserved bits in the address format as generic flag bits. Reference [RFC7371] also provides clarifications related to the meaning and use of the redefined flag bits. Figure 3.20 shows the final IPv6 Unicast-Prefix-Based multicast address format proposed in [RFC7371].

The following summarizes the meaning of the settings of the T, P, and Y = R bits in Figure 3.20:

- The lower-order T bit (defined in [RFC4291]) is set to 0 to indicate that the IPv6 multicast address is permanently assigned by IANA (i.e., a well-known multicast address). T is set to 1 to indicate that the address is a non-permanently assigned (i.e., "transient" or "dynamically" assigned) IPv6 multicast address.
- The P bit (defined in [RFC3306]) is set to 1 to indicate that the IPv6 multicast address is based on an IPv6 unicast prefix; otherwise, it is set to 0.
  - Because the IPv6 unicast address on which the IPv6 multicast address is based is considered to have a limited lifetime, the generated multicast address cannot be permanently assigned. This means that if P is set to 1, then T must also be set to 1.
- The R bit (defined in [RFC3956]) is set to 1 to indicate that the IPv6 multicast address contains the IPv6 unicast address of a PIM-SM Rendezvous Point for that multicast group; otherwise, it is set to 0.

3.9   IPv6 INTERFACE IDENTIFIERS

IPv6 unicast addresses contain interface IDs that are used to identify the interfaces attached to an IPv6 subnet (link). Interface IDs must be unique within a given IPv6 subnet prefix. Thus, it is important to ensure that the same interface ID is not assigned to different interfaces on the same link. A network operator may also decide to make interface IDs unique over a broader network scope. In some cases, an IPv6 node may be configured to derive an interface ID directly from the Link-Layer (e.g., Ethernet MAC) address of an interface. Multiple interfaces on a single IPv6 node may use the same interface ID, as long as those interfaces are attached to different IPv6 subnets (in which case, they have different IPv6 prefixes).

It is important to note that the uniqueness of interface IDs and the uniqueness of IPv6 addresses are independent issues. For example, an IPv6 node may have an IPv6 Global Unicast address with an interface ID that has a local scope and an IPv6 Link-Local address with an interface ID that has a universal scope.

Typically, the starting 64 bits of the IPv6 address are used as the network prefix, while the last 64 bits carry a unique interface ID. An interface ID uniquely identifies an interface on a network segment and is 64 bits long. Usually, the following methods are used to determine the interface ID on an IPv6 node:

- The interface ID may be manually configured by the network administrator.
- In IEEE 802.3 networks (e.g., Ethernet networks), the interface ID is derived from the 48-bit MAC address of the interface.
- Reference [RFC4291] requires all IPv6 unicast addresses that have prefixes 001 through 111 to use a 64-bit interface ID that is derived from the IEEE EUI-64 address (called the Modified EUI-64 Address format).

• Reference **[RFC8981]** describes how the 64-bit interface ID can be obtained from a randomly generated value that changes over time to provide some level of anonymity to a user communicating on the IPv6 Internet.
• The 64-bit interface ID may be assigned through a DHCPv6 server during stateful address autoconfiguration **[RFC8415]**.

3.9.1 IDENTIFIERS IN THE IEEE 802 MAC ADDRESS FORMAT

The Institute of Electrical and Electronics Engineers (IEEE) defined the 64-bit EUI-64 address that can be used to identify network interfaces. The IEEE assigns EUI-64 addresses to manufacturers of network adapters, or the EUI-64 addresses can be derived from the IEEE 802 MAC addresses that are already assigned to network interfaces (commercial Ethernet adapters typically come with embedded 48-bit MAC addresses).

Traditionally, manufacturers use a 48-bit MAC address (also called an IEEE 802 MAC address) as the interface ID for network adapters they sell (see Figure 3.21). This address consists of a 24-bit IEEE-administered *company ID* (also called the *manufacturer ID*) and a 24-bit *manufacturer-selected extension ID* (also called the *board ID*) **[AWEYA1BK18] [AWEYFCDM22]**. The company ID assigned to each manufacturer of network adapters is unique, while the extension (or board) ID assigned to each network adapter at the time of manufacture is also unique. The combination of the IEEE-administered company ID and the manufacturer-selected extension ID produces a globally unique 48-bit MAC address. This 48-bit MAC address is also often referred to as the hardware, physical, or MAC address of the network adapter.

The seventh bit of the first byte of the company ID, called the U/L bit, is used to indicate whether the MAC address is *universally* or *locally administered*. The U/L bit is set to 0 to indicate that the company ID is uniquely assigned by the IEEE (i.e., an IEEE-administered company ID). The U/L bit is set to 1 to indicate that the MAC address is locally administered by the network administrator

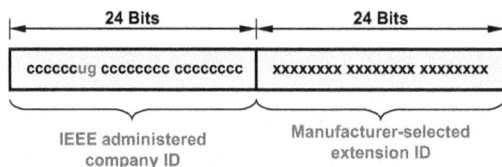

• **Universal/Local (U/L) Bit**: This bit (shown as "u") is the seventh bit of the first byte and is used to determine whether the address is universally or locally administered.
  ▪ If the U/L bit is set to 0, the IEEE has administered the address, through the designation of a unique company ID.
  ▪ If the U/L bit is set to 1, the address is locally administered. This means the network administrator has overridden the manufactured address and specified a different address.

• **Individual/Group (I/G) Bit**: This bit (shown as "g") is the low order bit of the first byte and is used to determine whether the address is an individual (unicast) address, or a group (multicast) address.
  ▪ When set to 0, the address is a unicast address.
  ▪ When set to 1, the address is a multicast address.

• **"x" Bits**: Bits of the manufacturer-selected extension identifier.

In the typical IEEE 802 MAC address for a network adapter, both the U/L and I/G bits are set to 0, which means the address is a universally administered, unicast MAC address.

FIGURE 3.21   Identifiers in the IEEE 802 MAC address format.

deploying the network adapter. In the latter case, the network administrator has overridden the manufacturer-assigned MAC address with a specified and different MAC address.

The low-order bit of the first byte of the company ID, called the I/G bit, indicates whether the MAC address is an *individual address* (*unicast address*) or a *group address* (*multicast address*). This bit is set to 0 to indicate that the MAC address is a unicast address and set to 1 to indicate that the MAC address is a multicast address.

Typically, the MAC addresses of network adapters with IEEE 802-assigned company IDs have both the U/L and I/G bits set to 0, resulting in *universally administered, unicast MAC addresses*. However, the device drivers of these network adapters still allow a network administrator to configure locally administered MAC addresses when needed. In such cases, the locally administered MAC address is used for addressing MAC frames.

3.9.2 IDENTIFIERS IN THE EUI-64 ADDRESS FORMAT

To extend the MAC address space, the IEEE created the EUI-64 address. This new address represents a new standard for addressing Link-Layer interfaces. The company ID (seen in the IEEE 48-bit MAC address) remains at 24 bits in length, while the extension ID is increased to 40 bits, creating a much larger MAC address space for network adapter manufacturers (see Figure 3.22). The uses of the U/L and I/G bits in the EUI-64 address remain the same as in the IEEE 802 MAC address.

3.9.3 MAPPING IEEE 802 MAC ADDRESSES TO EUI-64 ADDRESSES

To derive an EUI-64 address from an IEEE 802 MAC address, the creator inserts the 16-bit pattern 11111111 11111110 (0xFFFE) between the company ID and the extension ID in the IEEE 802 MAC address, as shown Figure 3.23. This figure details the conversion of a 48-bit IEEE 802 MAC address to a corresponding EUI-64 address.

An IPv6 node creates the IEEE EUI-64 identifier for an interface from its IEEE 48-bit MAC identifier by inserting the two bytes, with hexadecimal values of 0xFF and 0xFE, between the company ID and the manufacturer-supplied ID (i.e., in the middle of the 48-bit MAC address). Network adapters released by a manufacturer usually come with a 48-bit IEEE MAC address that has global scope. When an interface already has an IEEE 802 48-bit MAC address, an IPv6 node may use it to create the interface ID due to its uniqueness. Creating an EUI-64 address from a 48-bit MAC address involves the following steps (Figure 3.23):

- Take the 48-bit MAC address and insert the 16-bit binary number 1111111111111110 (hexadecimal value FFFE) after the 24th high-order bit.
- Invert the seventh high-order bit, known as the universal/local (U/L) bit. This operation ensures that the created EUI-64 identifier has the same local or global significance as the original 48-bit MAC address.

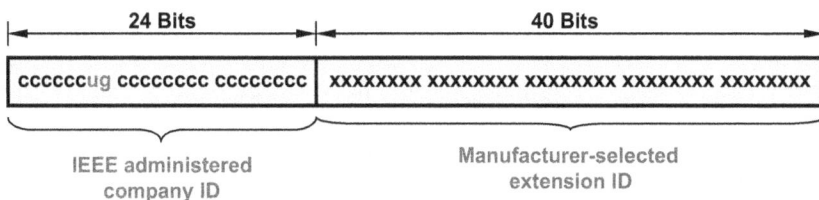

FIGURE 3.22   Identifiers in the EUI-64 address format.

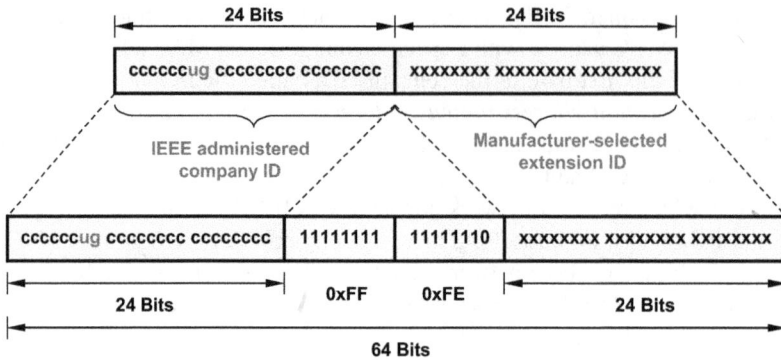

FIGURE 3.23   Mapping IEEE 802 MAC addresses to EUI-64 addresses.

3.9.4   Mapping EUI-64 Addresses to IPv6 Interface Identifiers

All IPv6 unicast addresses, except those that start with the value 000 (in binary), are required to have interface IDs that are 64 bits long, and these identifiers must be constructed in the Modified EUI-64 format. Interface *IDs based on the Modified EUI-64 format may have universal scope when derived from a universal token (e.g., a 48-bit IEEE 802 MAC address or IEEE EUI-64 identifiers), may have local scope in the absence of a global token (e.g., tunnel endpoints, serial links), or may have local scope where global tokens are undesirable* (e.g., the use of temporary tokens for privacy reasons as discussed in **Chapter 4**).

To obtain the 64-bit interface ID (known as the Modified EUI-64 format interface ID) for an IPv6 unicast address (with a given 64-bit prefix) using an EUI-64 address, the U/L bit of the EUI-64 address is complemented or inverted (i.e., if the U/L bit is 1, it is set to 0, and if it is 0, it is set to 1). Figure 3.24 describes in detail the mapping of an IEEE universally administered, unicast EUI-64 address (i.e., a globally unique IEEE EUI-64 identifier) to an IPv6 interface ID. Inverting the U/L bit is the only change required to transform an IEEE EUI-64 identifier into an IPv6 interface ID.

Thus, an IPv6 node forms the Modified EUI-64 format interface ID from an IEEE EUI-64 identifier for an interface by inverting the U/L bit. In the resulting Modified EUI-64 format interface ID (see Figure 3.24), the IPv6 node sets the U/L bit to 1 to indicate universal scope, and sets it to 0 to indicate local scope. Note that in the unmodified (native) EUI-64 format interface ID (see Figures 3.21 and 3.22), setting the U/L bit to 0 indicates universal scope, while setting it to 1 indicates local scope.

The motivation for inverting the U/L bit when creating the IPv6 interface ID for an interface (from the EUI-64 format identifier) is to make it easy for network administrators to manually configure interface IDs that are non-global when hardware tokens (e.g., a 48-bit IEEE 802 MAC address or IEEE EUI-64 identifiers) are not available **[RFC4291]**. This is most likely the case, for example, when configuring IPv6 interface IDs for serial links and tunnel endpoints.

The U/L bit is used in the Modified EUI-64 format identifier to facilitate the development of future technologies that can take advantage of IPv6 interface IDs with universal scope. IPv6 nodes are not required to validate that IPv6 addresses with interface IDs created from modified EUI-64 identifiers (e.g., IEEE EUI-64 tokens) and with the U/L bit set to universal are unique.

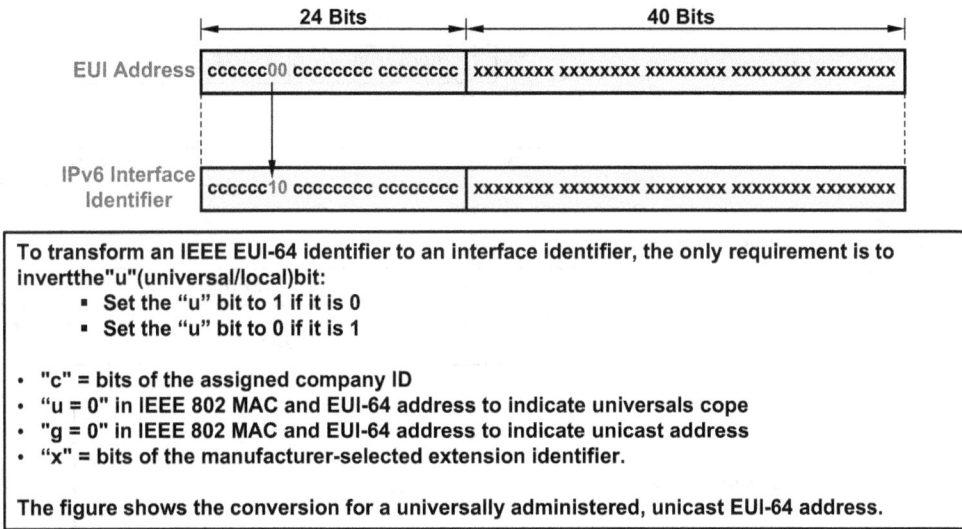

FIGURE 3.24   Mapping EUI-64 addresses to IPv6 interface identifiers.

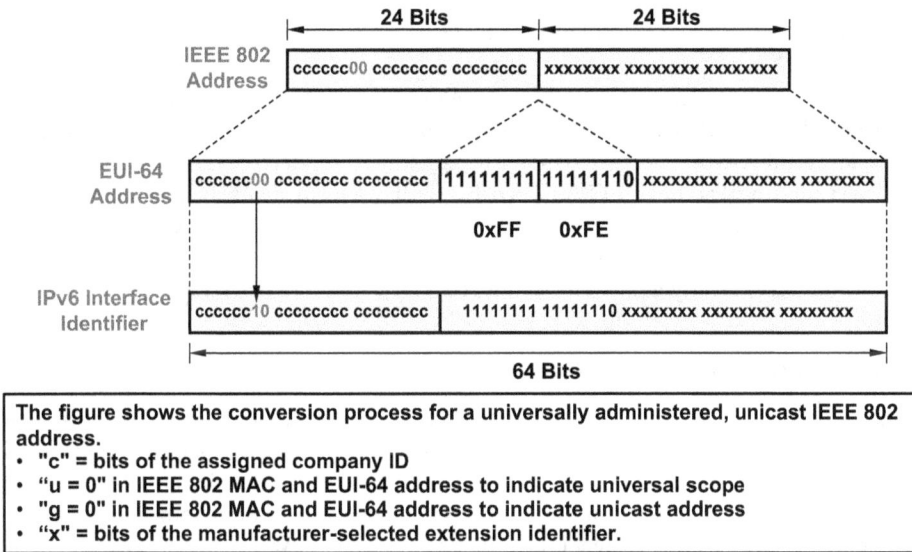

FIGURE 3.25   Mapping IEEE 802 MAC addresses to IPv6 interface identifiers.

3.9.5 MAPPING IEEE 802 MAC ADDRESSES TO IPV6 INTERFACE IDENTIFIERS

To obtain an IPv6 interface ID from an IEEE 802 MAC address, the IEEE 802 MAC address must first be mapped to an EUI-64 address, and then the U/L bit is complemented or inverted. Figure 3.25 describes the address mapping process for an IEEE universally administered, unicast IEEE 802 MAC address.

Assuming an IPv6 node has the 48-bit Ethernet MAC address of 00-AA-00–3F-2A-1C (see Figure 3.26), the IPv6 node converts this MAC address to EUI-64 format by inserting FF-FE between the third and fourth bytes, yielding 00-AA-00-FF-FE-3F-2A-1C. Next, the IPv6 node complements or inverts the seventh bit in the first byte, the U/L bit. The first byte in this MAC address

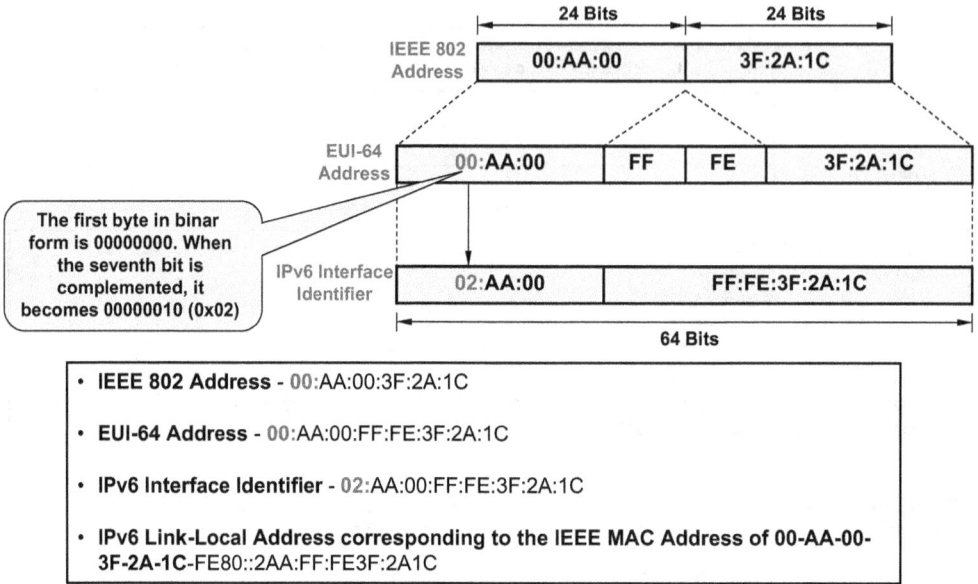

FIGURE 3.26   IEEE 802 MAC address to IPv6 interface identifier conversion example.

is 0x00 (in hexadecimal) and 00000000 (in binary). After inverting the seventh bit, it becomes 00000010 (or 0x02 in hexadecimal).

The resulting IPv6 interface ID becomes 02-AA-00-FF-FE-3F-2A-1C, 02AA:00FF:FE3F:2A1C, or 2AA:FF:FE3F:2A1C when converted to colon-hexadecimal notation. For a network adapter with the MAC address 00-AA-00–3F-2A-1C, the corresponding IPv6 interface ID is 2AA:FF:FE3F:2A1C, and the IPv6 Link-Local address is FE80::2AA:FF:FE3F:2A1C. It should be noted that when inverting the U/L bit, 0x2 should be added to the first byte if the EUI-64 address is IEEE universally administered (i.e., U/L bit is 0 before inversion), and 0x2 should be subtracted from the first byte if the EUI-64 address is locally administered (i.e., U/L bit is 1 before inversion).

3.9.6   HANDLING IPV6 LINKS WITHOUT IDENTIFIERS

A number of links, such as serial links and configured tunnels, do not have any built-in identifier. This means interfaces attached to such links must choose interface IDs that are unique within the IPv6 subnet prefix they are using. When an interface on an IPv6 node lacks a built-in identifier, the preferred approach is for the node to use a universal interface ID from another interface that has an identifier, or to use a locally assigned identifier that is unique. When a node uses this approach, it must ensure that no other interface connected to the same IPv6 subnet prefix uses that identifier.

If an IPv6 node has no universal interface ID for an interface, it needs to create an interface ID with local scope, while ensuring that the identifier is unique within the IPv6 subnet prefix being used. *An IPv6 node may also use other methods to select a unique interface ID within an IPv6 subnet prefix, including a manually configured identifier, a serial number on the node, or any other node-specific token.* The specific algorithm used by the IPv6 node in this case is link- and implementation-dependent. It is strongly recommended that the IPv6 node implement a collision detection algorithm (DAD) as part of any automatic interface ID configuration algorithm used.

If an interface does not have a globally unique (IEEE assigned) interface ID, the node may generate an IPv6 Link-Local (and possibly Global Unicast) address on that interface as follows:

- The IPv6 node may query its local pool of MAC addresses for a MAC address.
- If no MAC addresses are available, the IPv6 node may use a local serial number to form the interface ID and Link-Local address.

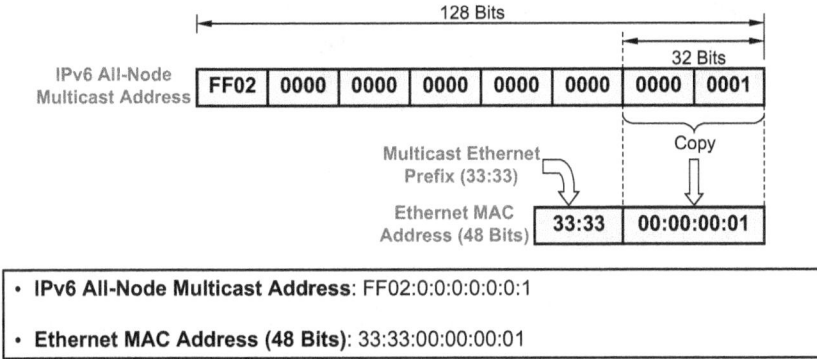

FIGURE 3.27   Example: IPv6 multicast address mapping to an IEEE 802 MAC address: IPv6 All-Nodes multicast address example.

- If a local serial number cannot be used to form the Link-Local address, the IPv6 node may use a suitable random number generator or a Message Digest 5 (MD5) hash function to generate an interface ID.

3.10   MAPPING IPv6 MULTICAST ADDRESSES TO ETHERNET MAC ADDRESSES

On Layer 2 networks, such as those based on Ethernet technologies, IPv6 packets with multicast addresses are carried in Ethernet frames with corresponding MAC multicast addresses. These MAC multicast addresses enable the switches in the Ethernet LAN to forward the encapsulated IPv6 multicast packets to all potential receivers in the multicast group. The last-hop router of a multicast group attached to an Ethernet LAN is responsible for encapsulating the IPv6 multicast packet in Ethernet frames and mapping the destination IPv6 multicast address to its corresponding destination Ethernet MAC multicast address. The Ethernet LAN switches use the mapped MAC multicast address to direct the encapsulated IPv6 packets to all host receivers on the LAN.

Thus, to enable multicast transmission at the Link Layer (particularly on multiaccess broadcast networks based on Ethernet technologies), IPv6 multicast addresses are mapped to corresponding MAC multicast addresses, as shown in Figure 3.27. This figure illustrates the address mapping process for the IPv6 All-Nodes multicast address FF02::1 **[AWEMULT24]**. The mapping process involves using 0x3333 as the prefix for the destination (multicast) MAC address.

To map an IPv6 multicast address, the lower-order 32 bits of the Ethernet MAC address are set to the lower-order 32 bits of the IPv6 multicast address. For example, the IPv6 multicast address FF02::D maps to the multicast MAC address 33-33-00-00-00-0D, and the address FF05::1:3 maps to the multicast MAC address 33-33-00–01-00–03. Figure 3.27 describes the address mapping process for all IPv6 multicast addresses.

Given that the Group ID in an IPv6 multicast address (see Figure 3.18) is 112 bits long, theoretically 2^{112} ($= 5.1922969 \times 10^{33}$) Group IDs can be created. However, when mapping IPv6 multicast addresses to Ethernet multicast MAC addresses, the Group ID is taken from the low-order 32 bits of the IPv6 multicast address, while the remaining bits of the original Group ID are set to 0, as described in Figure 3.27. Unlike in IPv4 multicast address mapping **[AWEMULT24]**, using only the low-order 32 bits as the Group ID, results in each Group ID mapping to a unique Ethernet multicast MAC address.

3.11   IPv6 ANYCAST ADDRESSES

An IPv6 anycast address is an identifier assigned to a group of IPv6-enabled interfaces (more than one interface) typically belonging to different nodes in the IPv6 internetwork **[RFC4291]**. IPv6 packets with the destination address set to an IPv6 anycast address are forwarded to the "nearest"

IPv6 interface identified by that address. The term "nearest" refers to the interface that the IPv6 routing protocol (or, equivalently, the routing table) indicates has the best path (i.e., routing metric), as illustrated in Figure 3.28.

IPv6 anycast addresses are taken from the IPv6 unicast address space, making them essentially indistinguishable from IPv6 Global Unicast addresses. An IPv6 anycast address can be obtained simply by assigning and configuring the same IPv6 unicast address to multiple IPv6-enabled interfaces in the network. Nodes assigned an IPv6 anycast address must be explicitly configured to recognize that the address is used for anycast communication, as shown in Figure 3.28. Given that IPv6 anycast addresses are syntactically indistinguishable from IPv6 unicast addresses, any IPv6 unicast address assigned to multiple interfaces in the network effectively becomes an IPv6 anycast address.

Generally, an IPv6 anycast address belongs to a long prefix P that identifies the topological region in which the multiple interfaces using that anycast address reside. Within the topological region identified by prefix P, the IPv6 nodes assigned the anycast address maintain that address as a separate entry in their routing table (the entry commonly referred to as a "host route"). Outside the topological region identified by prefix P, IPv6 nodes may aggregate the IPv6 anycast address associated with prefix P into the routing entry.

The following are some use case examples of IPv6 anycast addresses:

- An IPv6 anycast address may be used to identify the set of routers belonging to a particular organization that provides access to different ISPs. Such an address could serve as the intermediate address in the IPv6 Routing header of customer traffic, directing IPv6 packets to be delivered via a particular ISP or sequence of ISPs.
- An IPv6 anycast address may be used to identify the set of routers attached to a specific IPv6 subnet or the set of IPv6 routers that provide access to a particular routing domain.

In Figure 3.28, each participating server is configured with the same anycast address. Servers A, B, and C may be DHCPv6 servers with direct IPv6 connectivity to the network to which the host is attached. Let us assume these servers advertise the same anycast address using OSPFv3. The IPv6 router closest to the host would then forward IPv6 request packets to the nearest server identified in its routing table.

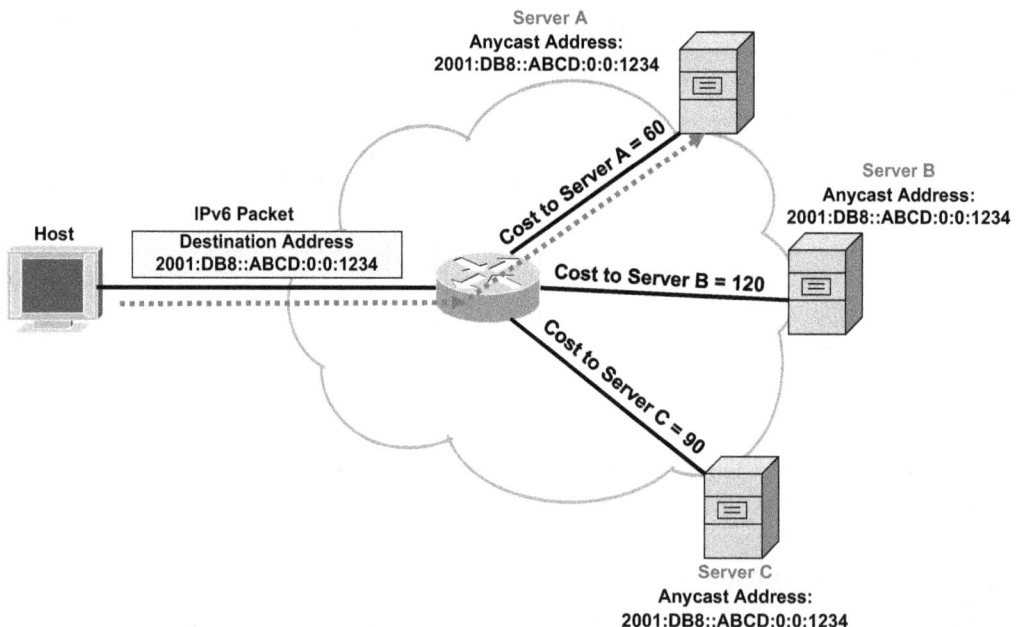

FIGURE 3.28   Example use of anycast addressing.

3.11.1   IPV6 REQUIRED ANYCAST ADDRESS: THE IPV6 SUBNET-ROUTER ANYCAST ADDRESS

The IPv6 Subnet-Router Anycast address is defined in **[RFC4291]** as an address that is required on every IPv6 subnet (link). An IPv6 node creates this address on an interface using the IPv6 subnet prefix for the subnet to which the interface is attached. To create the IPv6 Subnet-Router Anycast address for an interface, the node places the n bits of the subnet prefix in the Subnet Prefix field and sets the remaining $(128-n)$ bits to 0, as shown in Figure 3.29. The value in the Subnet Prefix field of this anycast address is the prefix that identifies the specific link (subnet) to which the interface is attached. All IPv6 router interfaces attached to an IPv6 subnet (link) are assigned the Subnet-Router Anycast address for that subnet; the address is the same for all interfaces attached to the subnet.

An IPv6 node uses the IPv6 Subnet-Router Anycast address for communication with any one of the multiple routers attached to the subnet/link associated with that anycast address. This anycast address is syntactically the same as the IPv6 unicast address of any interface attached to that link, except that the interface ID is set to zero. IPv6 packets sent with the destination address set to the IPv6 Subnet-Router Anycast address will most likely reach all IPv6 routers on the subnet, but the sender will only use the first responding router for communication. Each IPv6 router is required to support the IPv6 Subnet-Router Anycast addresses for all subnets to which it has interfaces.

3.11.1.1   Using the IPv6 Subnet-Router Anycast Address

An IPv6 node uses the Subnet-Router Anycast address (essentially a network address prefix) when it needs to communicate with any one of the set of routers attached to the subnet. For example, considering the prefix for the subnet 2001:DB8:10:40::/64, the IPv6 Subnet-Router Anycast address for that subnet is 2001:DB8:10:40::. Note that IPv6 Subnet-Router Anycast addresses can use subnet addresses of any size, not necessarily limited to /64 subnets, except for the special /127 subnets **[RFC6164]**, which are used on inter-router point-to-point links (i.e., point-to-point links between two routers with no attached hosts).

When an IPv6 node wishes to communicate with any one of multiple routers on the local subnet, it sends a Neighbor Solicitation message with the destination address set to the IPv6 Subnet-Router Anycast address. All routers on the subnet respond to the received Neighbor Solicitation message **[RFC4861]**, but the sending node uses the first router that responds with a Neighbor Advertisement message. Once a router on the subnet receives the Neighbor Solicitation message with this destination address, it will reply with a Neighbor Advertisement message **[RFC4861]**. The source address of this message is the IPv6 address of the responding router's interface, and the destination address is the IPv6 address of the node that sent the Neighbor Solicitation message.

However, when responding to Neighbor Solicitation messages with the IPv6 Subnet-Router Anycast address, it is recommended that the receiving routers randomize their responses to prevent all routers on the subnet from sending Neighbor Advertisement messages at the same time. Preferably, routers on the subnet should wait a small random amount of time before sending the Neighbor Advertisement message upon receiving Neighbor Solicitation messages.

Neighbor Advertisement messages sent in response to Neighbor Solicitation messages with Subnet-Router Anycast addresses do not have the Override flag (O-bit) set **[RFC4861]**, so the IPv6 node that sent the Neighbor Solicitation message should not switch between different routers on the subnet unnecessarily when trying to communicate with any router. If the sending IPv6 node detects

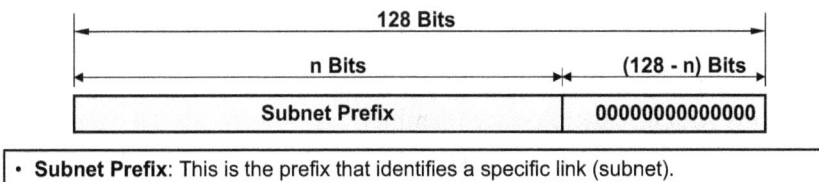

```
                              128 Bits
        |<---------------------------------------------------->|
        |                                                      |
        |<----------------- n Bits --------------->|<--(128 - n) Bits-->|
        |                                          |           |
        |              Subnet Prefix               | 00000000000000     |
        |                                          |           |
```

| **Subnet Prefix**: This is the prefix that identifies a specific link (subnet). |

FIGURE 3.29   IPv6 Subnet-Router Anycast address (see **[RFC4291]**).

that the selected router on the subnet becomes unreachable, it simply sends another Neighbor Solicitation message and waits for a response from another router.

As noted in **[RFC4861]**, an IPv6 node sets the O Flag (to 1) to indicate that the information in a Neighbor Advertisement message *should* override an existing entry in the receiver's Neighbor Cache and update the cached Link-Layer address. When the O Flag is not set (i.e., it is 0), the information in the message will not update a cached Link-Layer address; however, it will update an existing entry in the receiver's Neighbor Cache whose Link-Layer address is unknown. The O Flag *should not* be set in solicited Neighbor Advertisement messages when responding to Neighbor Solicitation messages with IPv6 anycast addresses, and in solicited proxy Neighbor Advertisement messages. However, the O Flag *should* be set in other solicited Neighbor Advertisement and unsolicited Neighbor Advertisement messages.

IPv6 hosts on a subnet can use the IPv6 Subnet-Router Anycast addressing mechanism to implement a default gateway without the need to configure a specific default gateway on the hosts. Any IPv6 router on the subnet is configured to respond to the Neighbor Solicitation messages received on the Subnet-Router Anycast address. Using this mechanism, IPv6 hosts can communicate with any of the routers present on the link.

3.11.2 IPv6 Reserved Subnet-Router Anycast Addresses

Reference **[RFC2526]** defines a set of IPv6 anycast addresses that are reserved for use within the Subnet Prefix field of the IPv6 Subnet-Router Anycast address space discussed above. These special IPv6 anycast addresses are reserved for use only within the Subnet-Router Anycast address type. As discussed above, **[RFC4291]** defines the Subnet-Router Anycast address as a new type of IPv6 anycast address that allows an IPv6 packet to be routed to the "nearest" interface belonging to one of a number of different IPv6 nodes, all assigned the same IPv6 unicast address. An IPv6 anycast address may be assigned to one or more IPv6 node network interfaces, with the network delivering an IPv6 packet addressed to this address to the nearest interface based on the best routing metric as determined by the IPv6 routing protocol in use.

In addition to the use cases discussed above, the concept of IPv6 anycast addressing may be used in the following cases **[RFC2526]**:

- To allow IPv6 nodes to access one of a set of servers belonging to a service provider (e.g., an ISP) that provides a well-known service, without having to manually configure each of those IPv6 nodes with the list of servers they can access.
- Used in a source routing context to force traffic from an IPv6 node to be routed through a specific ISP, without having to use a single specific router to provide access to that ISP; one out of a set of IPv6 routers using an IPv6 Subnet-Router Anycast address can be used to route traffic to that ISP.

The special IPv6 *Reserved* Subnet-Router Anycast addresses defined in **[RFC2526]** are an additional set of addresses that can be defined within the Subnet Prefix field of the IPv6 *Required* Subnet-Router anycast address type. Any of these addresses can be used by all routers within a specific IPv6 subnet prefix. Specifically, Reference **[RFC2526]** allows additional IPv6 anycast addresses to be taken from the IPv6 unicast address space (i.e., the IPv6 Required Subnet-Router anycast address type) as discussed below.

3.11.2.1 IPv6 Reserved Anycast Address Format – Unicast Address with EUI-64 Interface Identifier

For IPv6 address types that have 64-bit interface IDs in the EUI-64 format, an IPv6 node constructs the IPv6 *Reserved* Subnet Anycast addresses by setting the Universal/Local (U/L) bit to 0

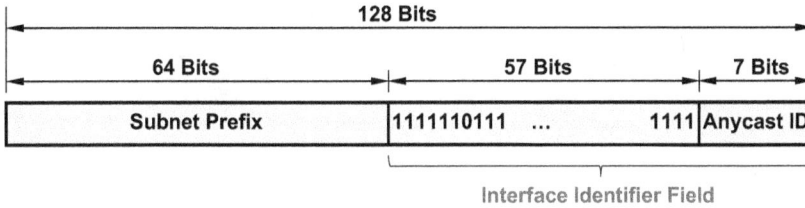

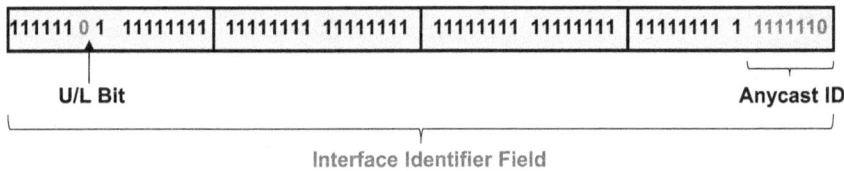

FIGURE 3.30   IPv6 Reserved Anycast address format – Unicast address with EUI-64 interface identifier (see **[RFC2526]**).

(i.e., Local), indicating that the interface ID in the Interface Identifier field is not globally unique. Reference **[RFC2526]** specifies IPv6 addresses of this type to have prefixes 001 through 111, except for multicast addresses that have the prefix 1111 1111.

The IPv6 subnet prefix in Figure 3.30 consists of the higher-order 64-bit field of the IPv6 address space. The Interface Identifier field consists of two sub-parts: a 57-bit field with a special pattern (see Figure 3.30), and a 7-bit Anycast ID field. Note that the interface ID in the EUI-64 format has the U/L bit be set to 0. *For the reserved Mobile IPv6 Home-Agents Subnet Anycast address defined in* **[RFC2526]***, the 7-bit Anycast ID is 1111110 (binary), 7E (hexadecimal), or 126 (decimal).* Mobile IPv6 **[RFC6275]** is discussed in detail in **Chapter 6**.

3.11.2.2   IPv6 Reserved Anycast Address Format – Unicast Address with Non-EUI-64 Interface Identifier

For IPv6 address types that have the interface ID in the non-EUI-64 format and may have lengths that are not 64 bits, an IPv6 node constructs the IPv6 *Reserved* Subnet Anycast addresses as shown in Figure 3.31. Even in this format, an interface ID may still be 64 bits long, although interface IDs of lengths other than 64 bits may be used in the IPv6 *Reserved* Subnet Anycast addresses.

Here, we consider for comparison purposes that the interface ID is 64 bits long. In this case, an IPv6 node constructs the reserved Mobile IPv6 Home-Agents Subnet Anycast address by using the 64-bit Subnet Prefix, followed by the 57-bit (all 1s field) and the 7-bit Anycast ID (1111110), as shown in the example in Figure 3.31.

```
                           128 Bits
|<------------------------------------------------------------------------>|
|         n Bits                  |    (121 - n) Bits        |  7 Bits  |
|<------------------------------->|<------------------------>|<-------->|
|            Subnet               | 1111111111  ...   1111 |Anycast ID|
                                  |                                     |
                                  _____ _____/
                                                       |
                                          Interface Identifier Field
```

| • The interface ID is not in EUI-64 format and may be other than 64 bits in length. |

Example:

```
| 11111111 11111111 | 11111111 11111111 | 11111111 11111111 | 11111111 1 1111110 |
                                                                         \___ ___/
                                                                             |
                                                                        Anycast ID
_____ _____/
                                      |
                          Interface Identifier Field
```

**(In this example, we assume that the length of the interface ID is 64 bits,
although interface IDs of lengths other than 64 bits can be used)**

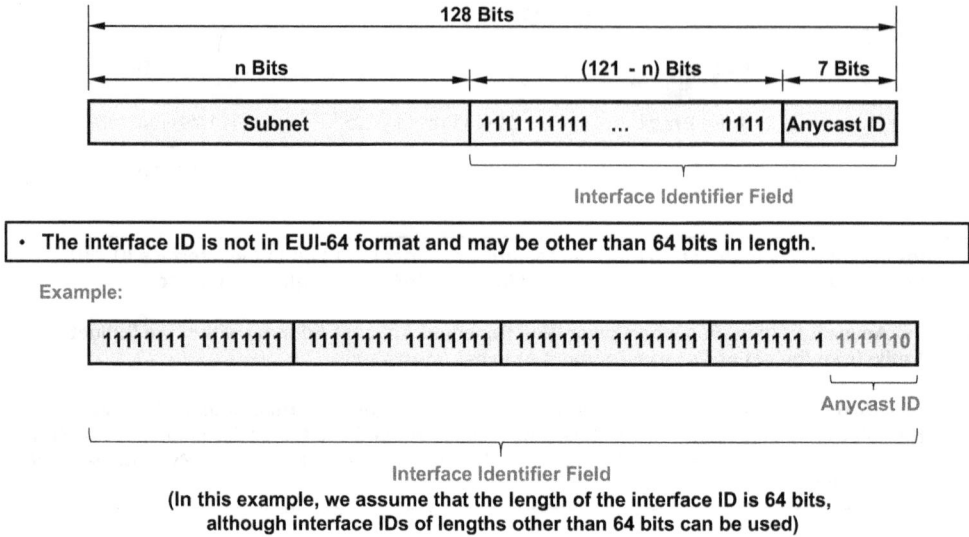

FIGURE 3.31   IPv6 Reserved Anycast address format - Unicast address with non-EUI-64 interface identifier (see **[RFC2526]**).

3.12   IPv6 ADDRESSES ON HOSTS AND ROUTERS

This section discusses the IPv6 addresses supported on IPv6 hosts and routers.

3.12.1   IPv6 ADDRESSES ON HOSTS

A single network interface on an IPv4 host typically has a single IPv4 address assigned to it. However, a single interface on an IPv6 host usually has multiple IPv6 addresses. An IPv6 host interface is assigned the following IPv6 unicast addresses:

- Unicast address and any anycast addresses that have been configured (manually or automatically)
- Link-Local address
- Loopback address (::1) for its loopback interface

IPv6 hosts can be seen as logically multihomed because they are typically configured with at least two IPv6 addresses which they can use to send and receive packets. Each IPv6 host has a Link-Local address (which has significance only on the local link) and a routable Global Unicast address.

An IPv6 host may additionally support the following IPv6 multicast addresses:

- The IPv6 All-Nodes address (FF01::1), which has *interface-local or (node-local) scope.*
  - IPv6 packets with this destination address must remain within the current node and may not be sent over any network link.
- The IPv6 All-Nodes address (FF02::1), which has *link-local scope.*
  - IPv6 packets with this destination address must remain only on the local link, that is, stay within the subnet that the sending host is connected to and not be routed anywhere.
- The IPv6 Solicited-Node address for each IPv6 unicast address configured on each interface.
- The IPv6 multicast addresses of multicast groups that the host has joined on each interface.

3.12.2   IPV6 ADDRESSES ON ROUTERS

An IPv6 router is typically configured with the following IPv6 unicast addresses:

- An IPv6 Link-Local address for each interface.
- An IPv6 Global Unicast address for each interface.
- An IPv6 Loopback address (::1) for the loopback interface.

An IPv6 router is configured with the following required and optional IPv6 anycast addresses:

- An IPv6 Subnet-Router Anycast address for each subnet it is attached to (required).
- Any other IPv6 Anycast addresses as required by the network administrator (optional).

Additionally, an IPv6 router listens for traffic on the following IPv6 multicast addresses:

- The IPv6 All-Nodes address (FF01::1) with interface-local scope.
- The IPv6 All-Routers address (FF01::2) with interface-local scope.
- The IPv6 All-Nodes address (FF02::1) with link-local scope.
- The IPv6 All-Routers address (FF02::2) with link-local scope.
- The IPv6 All-Routers address (FF05::2) with site-local scope.
  - IPv6 packets with this destination address are restricted to the local site (these addresses are equivalent to IPv4 private addresses and have now been deprecated).
- The IPv6 Solicited-Node address for each IPv6 unicast address on each interface.
- The IPv6 multicast addresses of multicast groups joined on each interface.

REVIEW QUESTIONS

3.1.   What is an IP unicast address?

3.2.   What is an IP multicast address?

3.3.   What is an IP anycast address?

3.4.   What is an IP address prefix?

3.5.   What is an IP address prefix length?

3.6.   Write the following IPv6 address in its most compressed format: 2001:0DB8:CAB0:0234:0034:0004:0000:0000.

3.7.   Write the following IPv6 address in its most compressed format: 2001:0DB8:0CAB:0000:0000:0000:0001:0000.

3.8.   Write the following IPv6 address in its most compressed format: 2001:0DB8:0CAB:4000:0230:1200:0034:0000.

3.9.   Write the following IPv6 address in its most compressed format: 2001:0000:0000:0000:1234:0000:0000:0000.

3.10. Write the following IPv6 address in its most compressed format: 2001:0DB8:0000:0000:1234:0000:0000:1000.

3.11. Expand the following compressed IPv6 address to its complete form: 2001:DB8:CAB::1.

3.12. Expand the following compressed IPv6 address to its complete form: 2001:DB8:0:0:234::.

3.13. Derive the prefix for the IPv6 address 2001:DB8:BB8A:F390::1/32.

3.14. Derive the prefix for the IPv6 address 2001:DB8:80F:F425:250:56FF:FE83:ECC/48.

3.15. Derive the prefix for the IPv6 address FE80::250:56FF:FE83:ECC/64.

3.16. Derive the prefix for the IPv6 address 2001:DB8:80F:F425::230/48.

3.17. Derive the prefix for the IPv6 address 2001:DB8:80F:F425:250:56FF:FE83:ECC/64.

3.18. Derive the prefix for the IPv6 address 2001:DB8:80F:F425::230/64.

3.19. What is the scope of an IPv6 address?

3.20. What are the differences between the following IPv6 address scopes: link-local, unique-local and global scope?

3.21. What is the purpose of the IPv6 Global Unicast address?

3.22. What is the purpose of the IPv6 Link-Local address?

3.23. What is the purpose of the IPv6 Unique-Local address?

3.24. What is the purpose of the IPv6 Unspecified address?

3.25. What is the purpose of the IPv6 Loopback address?

3.26. What is the purpose of the IPv4-Mapped IPv6 address?

3.27. What is the purpose of the IPv6 Solicited-Node multicast address?

3.28. What is an IPv6 Unicast-Prefix-Based multicast address?

3.29. Which type of IPv6 address is required for an interface to be IPv6-enabled?

3.30. Which IPv6 unicast address type provides functions similar to IPv4 private addresses?

3.31. Which IPv6 unicast address is an all-0s address?

3.32. Which IPv6 multicast address is used in Layer 3-to-Layer 2 address resolution similar to ARP in IPv4?

3.33. What are the two main parts of an IEEE-administered MAC address?

3.34. What is the purpose of the Universally/Local (U/L) bit in an Ethernet MAC address?

3.35. What is the purpose of the Individual/Group (I/G) bit in an Ethernet MAC address?

3.36. How do you convert a 48-bit Ethernet MAC address to an EUI-64 address?

3.37. How do you convert an EUI-64 address to an IPv6 interface ID?

3.38. When is it necessary to convert an IPv6 multicast address to a corresponding Ethernet MAC address?

3.39. How do you convert an IPv6 multicast address to a corresponding Ethernet MAC address?

3.40. What is the purpose of the IPv6 Subnet-Router Anycast address?

REFERENCES

[AWEYA1BK18].   J. Aweya, *Switch/Router Architectures: Shared-Bus and Shared-Memory Based Systems*, Wiley-IEEE Press, ISBN 9781119486152, 2018.

[AWEYFCDM22].   James Aweya, *Designing Switch/Routers: Fundamental Concepts and Design Methods*, CRC Press, Taylor & Francis Group, ISBN 9781032317694, October 2022.

[AWEMULT24].   James Aweya, *IP Multicast Routing Protocols: Concepts and Designs*, CRC Press, Taylor & Francis Group, ISBN 9781032701929, May 2024.

[FIPS1995].   "Federal Information Processing Standards Publication", (FIPS PUB) 180–1, Secure Hash Standard, 17 April 1995.

[IANAIPv6SPREG].   IANA IPv6 Special-Purpose Address Registry.

[RFC826].   D. C. Plummer, "An Ethernet Address Resolution Protocol", *IETF RFC 826*, November 1982.

[RFC1305].   D. L. Mills, "Network Time Protocol (Version 3) Specification, Implementation and Analysis", *IETF RFC 1305*, March 1992.

[RFC1918].   Y. Rekhter, B. Moskowitz, D. Karrenberg, G. J. de Groot, and E. Lear, "Address Allocation for Private Internets", *IETF RFC 1918*, February 1996.

[RFC2526].   D. Johnson and S. Deering, "Reserved IPv6 Subnet Anycast Addresses", *IETF RFC 2526*, March 1999.

[RFC2710].   S. Deering, W. Fenner, and B. Haberman, "Multicast Listener Discovery (MLD) for IPv6", *IETF RFC 2710*, October 1999.

[RFC3174].   D. Eastlake 3rd and P. Jones, "US Secure Hash Algorithm 1 (SHA1)", *IETF RFC 3174*, September 2001.

[RFC3306].   B. Haberman and D. Thaler, "Unicast-Prefix-based IPv6 Multicast Addresses", *IETF RFC 3306*, August 2002.

[RFC3810].   R. Vida and L. Costa, "Multicast Listener Discovery Version 2 (MLDv2) for IPv6", *IETF RFC 3810*, June 2004.

[RFC3956].   P. Savola and B. Haberman, "Embedding the Rendezvous Point (RP) Address in an IPv6 Multicast Address", *IETF RFC 3956*, November 2004.

[RFC4038].	M.-K. Shin, Ed., Y.-G. Hong, J. Hagino, P. Savola, and E. M. Castro, "Application Aspects of IPv6 Transition", *IETF RFC 4038*, March 2005.
[RFC4193].	R. Hinden and B. Haberman, "Unique Local IPv6 Unicast Addresses", *IETF RFC 4193*, October 2005.
[RFC4291].	R. Hinden and S. Deering, "IP Version 6 Addressing Architecture", *IETF RFC 4291*, February 2006.
[RFC4443].	A. Conta, S. Deering, and M. Gupta, Ed., "Internet Control Message Protocol (ICMPv6) for the Internet Protocol Version 6 (IPv6) Specification", *IETF RFC 4443*, March 2006.
[RFC4861].	T. Narten, E. Nordmark, W. Simpson, and H. Soliman, "Neighbor Discovery for IP Version 6 (IPv6)", *IETF RFC 4861*, September 2007.
[RFC4862].	S. Thomson, T. Narten, and T. Jinmei, "IPv6 Stateless Address Autoconfiguration", *IETF RFC 4862*, September 2007.
[RFC5952].	S. Kawamura and M. Kawashima, "A Recommendation for IPv6 Address Text Representation", *IETF RFC 5952*, August 2010.
[RFC6164].	M. Kohno, B. Nitzan, R. Bush, Y. Matsuzaki, L. Colitti, and T. Narten, "Using 127-Bit IPv6 Prefixes on Inter-Router Links", *IETF RFC 6164*, April 2011.
[RFC6275].	C. Perkins, Ed., D. Johnson, and J. Arkko, "Mobility Support in IPv6", *IETF RFC 6275*, July 2011.
[RFC7371].	M. Boucadair and S. Venaas, "Updates to the IPv6 Multicast Addressing Architecture", *IETF RFC 7371*, September 2014.
[RFC7761].	B. Fenner, M. Handley, H. Holbrook, I. Kouvelas, R. Parekh, Z. Zhang, and L. Zheng, "Protocol Independent Multicast - Sparse Mode (PIM-SM): Protocol Specification (Revised)", IETF RFC 7761, March 2016.
[RFC8415].	T. Mrugalski, M. Siodelski, B. Volz, A. Yourtchenko, M. Richardson, S. Jiang, T. Lemon, and T. Winters, "Dynamic Host Configuration Protocol for IPv6 (DHCPv6)", *IETF RFC 8415*, November 2018.
[RFC8981].	F. Gont, S. Krishnan, T. Narten, and R. Draves, "Temporary Address Extensions for Stateless Address Autoconfiguration in IPv6", *IETF RFC 8981*, February 2021.

4 IPv6 Neighbor Discovery, Address Configuration, and IPv6 Routing Table

4.1 INTRODUCTION

This chapter describes the IPv6 Neighbor Discovery protocol **[RFC4861]**, a key protocol within the IPv6 suite of protocols. The IPv6 Neighbor Discovery protocol supports several functions that replace important IPv4 protocols such as Address Resolution Protocol (ARP), ICMPv4 Router Discovery, and ICMPv4 Redirect. It also provides many improvements over these IPv4 protocols. Specifically, the IPv6 Neighbor Discovery protocol offers various capabilities that allow IPv6 nodes on the same network segment (IP subnet or Virtual LAN (VLAN)) to advertise their presence to neighboring nodes and to learn about the presence of other active neighbors, including attached routers.

IPv6 routers and hosts (both referred to as nodes) use Neighbor Discovery protocol messages to determine the Link-Layer (or MAC) addresses of neighbors on the attached network segment and to purge or overwrite invalid Neighbor Cache entries when addressing information changes. IPv6 nodes use this protocol to actively keep track of the reachable IPv6 neighbors and to detect if any node has a changed Link-Layer address.

An IPv6 node requesting the Link-Layer address of a target node sends a Neighbor Solicitation message via multicast, including the target address. The target node replies with a Neighbor Advertisement message containing the requested Link-Layer address. IPv6 nodes use Neighbor Solicitation and Advertisement messages to detect the existence of duplicate IPv6 unicast addresses on the same link. An IPv6 node can use an IPv6 address only after configuration and only if there is no duplicate address on that link. The Duplicate Address Detection function that IPv6 hosts use to verify the uniqueness of unicast IPv6 addresses on a link is a key requirement for IPv6 address autoconfiguration.

IPv6 nodes also use Neighbor Solicitation and Advertisement messages for neighbor unreachability detection, which involves a node verifying the presence and reachability of a target IPv6 node on a given link when necessary. An IPv6 router sends Redirect messages to inform a host on the same link of a better next-hop router to a particular destination or to indicate that the destination is indeed a neighbor on the same link. This feature is similar to the ICMPv4 Redirect function in IPv4. Using this feature, an IPv6 router employs the ICMPv6 Redirect message to inform an IPv6 host on the same link of a better next-hop for a given destination. The goal of this feature is to enable IPv6 routers on a link to assist hosts in making more efficient local routing decisions.

IPv6 hosts also use the Neighbor Discovery protocol to discover neighboring IPv6 routers that can forward packets on their behalf to external destinations. In particular, IPv6 nodes use Router Solicitation and Advertisement messages to actively monitor the availability and reachability of routers on the same network segment. When the path to an IPv6 router or the router itself fails, IPv6 nodes use these router discovery messages to actively search for functioning alternative routers and paths to reach external IPv6 destinations.

The IPv6 routing table contains sufficient information about a local network and the IPv6 internetwork, allowing IPv6 nodes to determine the best routes for forwarding IPv6 packets to their destinations. The discussion in this chapter also includes the IPv6 routing table and how routing table entries are created.

Because the IPv6 Neighbor Discovery protocol utilizes the built-in multicast capabilities of Link-Layer technologies such as Ethernet (multiaccess link technologies) for most of its services,

DOI: 10.1201/9781003710646-4

these services cannot be implemented on Link-Layer technologies based on Non-Broadcast Multi-Access (NBMA) links or networks. NBMA refers to a link/network in which multiple interfaces can be attached, but the link does not support multicast or broadcast natively as in multi-access Ethernet networks. When using NBMA links, alternative protocols or mechanisms must be employed for the services provided by the Neighbor Discovery protocol. The Neighbor Discovery services that do not directly depend on multicast, such as next-hop determination, Redirects, and Neighbor Unreachability Detection, work over both multiaccess and NBMA links and use the IPv6 Neighbor Discovery protocol as specified in **[RFC4861]**.

4.2 ON-LINK AND OFF-LINK IPv6 ADDRESSES

In IPv6, *network segments* or *subnets* are referred to simply as *links*, primarily due to the IPv6 addressing architecture, which differs from IPv4 (e.g., the use of link scope, site scope, and global scope addresses, along with their corresponding address types: Link-Local, Unique-Local Unicast, and Global Unicast addresses). IPv6 also includes the concept of on-link and off-link addresses **[RFC5942]**.

An *on-link* IPv6 address is assigned to an interface on the same link (or subnet) and can be reached by any node on that link (subnet) without going through a next-hop node or default router. An *off-link* IPv6 address is one that is not assigned to any interfaces on the specified link; it belongs to another link in the IPv6 internetwork.

According to **[RFC4861]**, an IPv6 node on a particular link considers an IPv6 Global Unicast address to be on-link if it satisfies one of the following criteria:

- The address is covered by one of the link's IPv6 prefixes (e.g., as indicated by the 1-bit L (on-link) Flag in the Prefix Information Option that may be included in ICMPv6 Router Advertisement messages); only routers on the same link can send such messages.
- A neighboring IPv6 router specifies the address as the Target Address in an ICMPv6 Redirect message, indicating that the target is a neighbor on the same link.
- The IPv6 node received an ICMPv6 Neighbor Advertisement message from this address; such a message can only be sent by a neighbor on the local link.
- The IPv6 node received any IPv6 Neighbor Discovery message from the address; only neighbors can exchange Neighbor Discovery messages.

However, Reference **[RFC5942]** clarifies the rules used by IPv6 nodes to designate a given IPv6 Global Unicast address as on-link or off-link. *This reference argues that an IPv6 host should not consider an IPv6 address to be on-link solely based on the existence of a corresponding on-link IPv6 prefix. Reference [RFC5942] discusses the additional information a host needs to consider when determining whether an IPv6 address is on-link or off-link, as well as how the host's Prefix List is populated.* An IPv6 host maintains and uses a Prefix List to identify the ranges of IPv6 addresses that are considered to be on-link. Reference **[RFC5942]** outlines the rules IPv6 hosts must follow to correctly process IPv6 packets with on-link and off-link destinations.

The term "neighbor" or "neighboring node" in our discussion refers to IPv6 nodes that are attached to the same Layer 2 network domain, specifically a broadcast domain such as those based on Ethernet technologies. A Layer 2 network or broadcast domain, which may be an IP subnet or VLAN, is also referred to as a link in IPv6 terminology.

4.3 IPv6 NEIGHBOR DISCOVERY

The IPv6 Neighbor Discovery protocol **[RFC4861]** consists of a set of ICMPv6 messages and processes that are used to manage communication between IPv6-enabled neighboring nodes on a link/subnet. This protocol replaces the IPv4 protocols ARP, ICMPv4 Router Discovery, and ICMPv4 Redirect. IPv6 Neighbor Discovery provides additional functionality beyond those IPv4 protocols.

Unlike IPv4, which has some capabilities (like ARP) implemented below the IP layer, the IPv6 Neighbor Discovery protocol is implemented entirely within ICMPv6. Implementing the IPv6 Neighbor Discovery protocol within ICMPv6 allows the various features of Neighbor Discovery to benefit from the many services provided by the IP layer, such as security (via the IPv6 Authentication and Encapsulation Security Payload headers as discussed in **Chapter 2**) and multicast.

For Layer 3-to-Layer 2 address resolution (similar to ARP in IPv4), IPv6 Neighbor Discovery provides a more secure and efficient way of performing this process using IPv6 multicast messages instead of the broadcast-based messages used in IPv4 ARP. Address resolution in both IPv4 (using ARP) and in IPv6 (using Neighbor Discovery) involves determining the Link-Layer address corresponding to a known IPv6 address. There is no dedicated protocol like ARP in IPv6. In IPv6, address resolution is accomplished using various ICMPv6 messages carried in IPv6 packets, whereas ARP in IPv4 uses ARP Request and ARP Reply messages that are encapsulated directly in Ethernet frames.

IPv6 hosts use Neighbor Discovery for the following:

- Discovering IPv6 routers attached to the local link (i.e., neighboring routers). Router discovery involves how an IPv6 host identifies IPv6 routers on the attached link.
- Discover Link-Layer addresses of neighboring nodes, IPv6 address prefixes of on-link destinations, and other configuration parameters such as link MTU and Hop Limit values. This process includes how an IPv6 host discovers address prefixes for local link destinations and prefixes for destinations that can only be reached through an attached router (Prefix Discovery). It also encompasses how an IPv6 node learns various link and Internet parameters that can be used for communication with external (off-link) destinations (Parameter Discovery).

IPv6 routers use Neighbor Discovery for the following:

- Advertise their presence to nodes on the attached link and provide the nodes with information about various link and Internet parameters, host configuration parameters such as link MTU and Hop Limit values, and IPv6 address prefixes of on-link nodes.
- Inform IPv6 hosts on the attached link of a better first-hop node (router) address for forwarding packets to a specific IPv6 destination.

IPv6 nodes (hosts and routers) use Neighbor Discovery for the following:

- Resolve the Link-Layer address of a neighboring node (given its IPv6 address) to which an IPv6 packet is to be forwarded. This process involves how an IPv6 node uses the IPv6 address of a node's interface on the attached link to determine its corresponding Link-Layer address (Address Resolution).
- Determine whether a tentatively generated IPv6 address is already in use by another node (Duplicate Address Detection).
- Check whether a neighboring node is still reachable via its cached Link-Layer address.
- Detect when the Link-Layer address of a node on the same link has changed.
- Assess whether a neighboring node is still reachable. This process includes how an IPv6 node determines if a neighbor is reachable or no longer reachable on the link (Neighbor Unreachability Detection).

Table 4.1 summarizes the Neighbor Discovery processes described in **[RFC4861]**. Table 4.2 presents the mechanisms supported by IPv6 hosts and routers in the IPv6 Neighbor Discovery protocol.

TABLE 4.1

IPv6 Neighbor Discovery Processes

IPv6 Neighbor Discovery Feature	Description	Equivalent IPv4 Feature
Router Discovery	This is the process by which IPv6 hosts discover routers on the attached link.	ICMPv4 Router Discovery [RFC1256]
Prefix Discovery	This is the process by which IPv6 hosts discover the set of network prefixes that define which destinations are on-link for the local link. Nodes use address prefixes to distinguish destinations that reside on-link from those only reachable through a router.	This is similar to the ICMPv4 Address Mask Request/Reply [RFC950] [RFC6918]
Parameter Discovery	This is the process by which IPv6 hosts learn link parameters (such as the link MTU) and the default Hop Limit for outgoing packets.	Path MTU Discovery [RFC1191]
Address Autoconfiguration	This is the process by which IPv6 nodes configure an IPv6 address for an interface in a stateless manner, either in the presence or absence of a server that provides stateful address configuration using a protocol such as DHCPv6.	–
Address Resolution	This is the process by which IPv6 nodes resolve the IPv6 address of an on-link destination (a neighbor) to its Link-Layer address. A node determines the Link-Layer address of a neighbor given only its IPv6 address. This is the IPv6 equivalent of ARP in IPv4.	ARP [RFC826]
Next-hop Determination	This is the process by which IPv6 nodes determine the IPv6 address of the neighbor (i.e., next node) to which a packet is to be forwarded based on the destination address. The forwarding or next-hop address is either the final destination address or the address of an on-link default router.	Use ARP Cache for on-link destinations, otherwise use default router
Neighbor Unreachability Detection	This is the process by which IPv6 nodes determine that a neighbor is no longer receiving packets (i.e., unreachable). For neighbors that are routers, alternate default routers can be tried. For both routers and hosts, address resolution can be performed again.	Dead Gateway Detection [RFC816] [RFC1122]
Duplicate Address Detection (DAD)	This is the process by which IPv6 nodes determine whether an IPv6 address considered for use (i.e., tentative address) is already in use by a neighboring node.	Gratuitous ARP [RFC5227]
Redirect function	This is the process by which a router informs an IPv6 host of a better first-hop IPv6 address to reach a particular destination.	IPv4 ICMP Redirect [RFC792]
Neighbor Discovery Proxying	This is the process by which an IPv6 node accepts packets on a link on behalf of other IPv6 nodes that have gone off-link.	Proxy ARP [RFC1027]
Selection of default gateway and more-specific routes	This involves IPv6 routers sending information to multihomed IPv6 hosts to enable them to select better default routers and more-specific routes.	–

4.3.1 Interface Initialization and IPv6 Solicited-Node Multicast Addresses

An IPv6 host performs IPv6 unicast address autoconfiguration (for IPv6 Link-Local and Global Unicast addresses) on multicast-capable interfaces (e.g., those based on Ethernet technologies) and on a per-interface basis. Multihomed IPv6 hosts will perform IPv6 address autoconfiguration (as well as address uniqueness checks using Duplicate Address Detection) independently on each interface.

When an IPv6 node enables a multicast-capable interface, it must join the IPv6 All-Nodes multicast address (FF02::1) on that interface, as well as the IPv6 Solicited-Node multicast address corresponding to each of the IPv6 unicast addresses assigned to the interface. As discussed in Chapter 3, *the purpose of the IPv6 Solicited-Node multicast address is to provide a more efficient mechanism for implementing the IPv4 broadcast delivery functionality without using broadcast addresses and packets for* IPv6. IPv6 does not support broadcast addresses as in IPv4; instead, it uses a number of special IPv6 multicast addresses for broadcast functionality.

TABLE 4.2

**Mechanisms Supported by IPv6 Hosts and Routers in
IPv6 Neighbor Discovery Protocol**

Entities and Interactions	Mechanisms
IPv6 host	• Default router selection
	• Next-hop determination
IPv6 host-host communication	• Neighbor Unreachability Detection
	• Duplicate Address Detection
IPv6 host-router communication	• Router Discovery
	• Default router selection
	• Prefix Discovery
	• Parameter Discovery
	• More-specific routes
IPv6 node-node communication	• Address Resolution
	• Redirect

It is important to note that broadcast traffic can create an excessive load on a network, leading to unnecessary bandwidth consumption and network congestion, as well as making the network more vulnerable to security attacks and breaches. Furthermore, networks that support broadcasts do not scale well (one of the reasons VLANs were introduced to limit broadcast traffic) and can be inefficient for real-time (voice and video) communication; such communications do not use data retransmissions, and excessive delays are unacceptable.

The set of IPv6 addresses assigned to an interface of an IPv6 node may change over time. The interface may have old IPv6 addresses removed and new IPv6 addresses added through IPv6 Stateless Address Autoconfiguration (SLAAC). In such cases, the node must use the IPv6 Multicast Listener Discovery (MLD) protocols (MLDv1 **[RFC2710]** or MLDv2 **[RFC3810]**) to join and leave the IPv6 Solicited-Node multicast address corresponding to the new and old IPv6 unicast addresses, respectively.

Note that in some (even many) cases, multiple IPv6 unicast addresses may map to the same IPv6 Solicited-Node multicast address, meaning a node must not leave the IPv6 Solicited-Node multicast group until it has removed all assigned IPv6 unicast addresses corresponding to that IPv6 multicast address.

As discussed in **Chapter 3**, an IPv6 Solicited-Node multicast address is a link-local scope IPv6 multicast address constructed from a specific IPv6 unicast address. The method for constructing the multicast address (FF02::1:FFxx:xxxx, where xx:xxxx is the last six hexadecimal values of the IPv6 unicast address) are the last six hexadecimal values of the IPv6 unicast address) is designed such that IPv6 addresses that differ only in the most significant bits (e.g., a node with multiple IPv6 prefixes associated with different service providers) *will map to the same IPv6 Solicited-Node address, thereby reducing the overall number of IPv6 multicast addresses a node must join at the Link Layer*. Recall that an IPv6 Link-Local address is an IPv6 unicast address with link-only scope that can be used to reach neighbors (on the same link). All IPv6 interfaces on a link must have an IPv6 Link-Local address.

4.3.2 NEIGHBOR DISCOVERY MESSAGES

The IPv6 Neighbor Discovery protocol uses the ICMPv6 messages described in this section to perform all its functions. IPv6 Neighbor Discovery **[RFC4861]** defines the following five types of ICMPv6 messages that can be carried directly in IPv6 packets:

• Router Solicitation (ICMPv6 Type 133)
• Router Advertisement (ICMPv6 Type 134)

- Neighbor Solicitation (ICMPv6 Type 135)
- Neighbor Advertisement (ICMPv6 Type 136)
- Redirect Message (ICMPv6 Type 137)

Table 4.3 summarizes the most important features of the IPv6 Neighbor Discovery messages. The various ICMPv6 message types used by the IPv6 Neighbor Discovery protocol are carried in IPv6 packets with the Next Header field value in the IPv6 header or in the IPv6 extension header immediately preceding a message set to 58. This indicates that the data following the IPv6 header or the preceding IPv6 extension header is an ICMPv6 message. When an IPv6 packet is carried in an Ethernet frame, the EtherType is set to 0x86DD. The EtherType for IPv4 is 0x0806.

In IPv4, ARP packets are encapsulated directly in Ethernet frames because ARP is a protocol that operates between Layer 2 (Ethernet) and Layer 3 (IPv4). Note that ICMP runs directly over IP; ICMPv4 over IPv4 and ICMPv6 over IPv6. Thus, since the IPv6 Neighbor Discovery protocol messages are ICMPv6 messages, they are all carried in IPv6 packets with the Next Header field set to 58. Note that when ICMPv4 messages are carried in IPv4 packets, the Protocol Number or Identifier field in the IPv4 header is set to 1.

Because all IPv6 Neighbor Discovery messages use a Hop Limit of 255 in the IPv6 header, the protocol is not susceptible to spoofing attacks originating from off-link IPv6 nodes. In contrast, off-link IPv4 nodes can send ICMPv4 Redirect messages. Off-link IPv4 nodes can also send ICMPv4 Router Advertisement messages.

Another important feature of the IPv6 Neighbor Discovery protocol is that it places IPv6 Address Resolution and other functions at the ICMPv6 layer, making the protocol more media-independent than IPv4 ARP. Consequently, IPv6 Neighbor Discovery can use standard IPv6 authentication and security mechanisms such as IPSec **[RFC4301]**.

The following IPv6 address types are used in the IPv6 packets that carry Neighbor Discovery messages:

- IPv6 Link-Local address (prefix FE80::/10): Source or destination address
- IPv6 Unspecified address (::): Source address only
- IPv6 All-Nodes multicast address (FF02::1): Destination address only
- IPv6 All-Routers multicast address (FF02::2): Destination address only
- IPv6 Solicited-Node multicast address (prefix FF02::1:FF00:0/104): Destination address only

4.3.2.1   Router Solicitation Message (Type 133)

IPv6 hosts send Router Solicitation messages (ICMPv6 Message Type 133) via multicast to discover IPv6 routers present on an attached link (Figure 4.1). When an interface becomes enabled, IPv6 hosts send these messages to prompt IPv6 routers to respond with Router Advertisement messages immediately, rather than at their next scheduled time (i.e., waiting for the attached routers to send periodic Router Advertisement messages).

IPv6 routers send Router Advertisement messages periodically; however, when an IPv6 node connects to a link, it sends out a Router Solicitation message on the link to request IPv6 routers to generate Router Advertisement messages immediately rather than at their next scheduled time. Router Solicitation messages have their destination IPv6 address set to the IPv6 All-Routers multicast address (FF02::2), indicating that only IPv6 routers on the local link are the target of these Router Solicitation messages.

4.3.2.2   Router Advertisement Message (Type 134)

IPv6 routers attached to a link advertise their presence periodically using ICMPv6 Router Advertisement messages (ICMPv6 Message Type 134). IPv6 routers send this ICMPv6 message on a link either periodically or in response to Router Solicitation messages from IPv6 hosts (Figure 4.2). The information contained in Router Advertisement messages is required by hosts to determine

TABLE 4.3

Important Features of IPv6 Neighbor Discovery Messages

IPv6 Neighbor Discovery Message	Sender	Target	IPv6 Neighbor Discovery Message Options
Router Solicitation (ICMPv6 Type 133)	IPv6 node	All IPv6 routers	Source Link-Layer Address Option [RFC4861]
Router Advertisement (ICMPv6 Type 134)	IPv6 router	Sender of the Router Solicitation message or all IPv6 nodes	Source Link-Layer Address Option [RFC4861]; MTU Option [RFC4861]; Prefix Information Option [RFC4861]; Advertisement Interval Option [RFC6275]; Route Information Option [RFC4191]; Recursive DNS Server Option [RFC8106]; DNS Search List Option [RFC8106]; Home Agent Information Option [RFC6275];
Neighbor Solicitation (ICMPv6 Type 135)	IPv6 node	Solicited-Node multicast address corresponding to Target Address, or Target Address itself	Source Link-Layer Address Option [RFC4861]
Neighbor Advertisement (ICMPv6 Type 136)	IPv6 node	Sender of the Neighbor Solicitation message, or all IPv6 nodes	Target Link-Layer Address Option [RFC4861]
Redirect (ICMPv6 Type 137)	IPv6 router	IPv6 host that triggered the redirect	Target Link-layer Address Option [RFC4861]; Redirected Header Option [RFC4861]

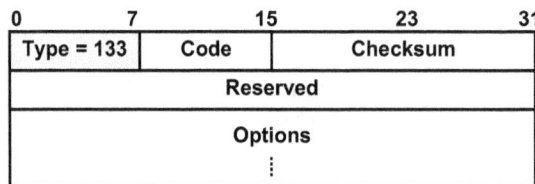

IPv6 Header:
- **Source Address:**This is the IPv6 address assigned to the sending interface, or the IPv6 Unspecified address if no address is assigned to the sending interface.
- **Destination Address:** Typically, set to the IPv6 All-Routers multicast address (FF02::2).
- **Hop Limit:** 255

ICMPv6 Fields:
- **Type (8 Bits):** 133
- **Code (8 Bits):** 0
- **Checksum (16Bits):**This is a16-bit ICMPv6 checksum which is calculated as the ones complement of the ones complement sum of the entire ICMPv6 message, which starts at the Type field of the message. The 'entire' message includes the IPv6 header and any IPv6 extension header fields.
- **Reserved (32 Bits):** This field is unused and MUST be initialized to zero by the sender and MUST be ignored by the receiver.

Valid Options:
- **Source Link-Layer Address:** This is the Link-Layer address of the sending interface, if known. It MUST NOT be included if the Source Address field of the IPv6 packet carrying the ICMPv6 message is the IPv6 Unspecified address. Otherwise, this Option SHOULD be included on Link Layers that have Link-Layer addresses.

FIGURE 4.1   Router Solicitation message format (ICMPv6 Message Type 133).

IPv6 link prefixes, link MTUs, and whether the hosts should use IPv6 address autoconfiguration on the interfaces (i.e., SLAAC) [RFC4862]). The information in these messages also includes the duration for which hosts should consider the addresses created through address autoconfiguration to be both valid and preferred.

The Router Advertisement messages that routers send on a link contain a list of IPv6 prefixes that attached IPv6 hosts use for address autoconfiguration, maintain a database of on-link IPv6 prefixes, and perform Duplicate Address Detection. If a destination IPv6 node is on-link, IPv6 packets originating from the same link are sent directly to that node. If the destination node is off-link, IPv6 packets are sent to the best attached router that leads to that remote node.

As shown in Figure 4.2, each IPv6 prefix in the Prefix List of a Router Advertisement message (prefixes are included in the Prefix Information Option in the message) contains an IPv6 Prefix Length, Valid Lifetime, and Preferred Lifetime for the IPv6 prefix, as well as various flags for address configuration [RFC4861]. The information provided by Router Advertisement messages enables IPv6 nodes on a particular link to perform address autoconfiguration and set link parameters such as Hop Limit and link MTU size. The Prefix Information Option is described in a section below.

The IPv6 router sends periodic (unsolicited) Router Advertisement messages with the destination IPv6 address of the messages set to the IPv6 All-Nodes multicast address (FF02::1), indicating that the messages are meant for all IPv6 nodes on the link. Router Advertisement messages contain several fields as indicated in Figure 4.2, and a number of possible message options that include the Source Link-Layer Address, MTU, and Prefix Information Options. IPv6 nodes use Router Advertisement messages for services such as SLAAC, as discussed in a section below.

4.3.2.2.1   Using ICMPv6 Router Advertisements

Each IPv6 router attached to a link transmits a Router Advertisement message periodically to the IPv6 All-Nodes multicast address to announce its presence to nodes on the link.

4.3.2.2.1.1   IPv6 Router Discovery   IPv6 hosts on a link use Router Discovery to locate routers attached to the link and learn IPv6 prefixes and configuration parameters that can be used for IPv6 SLAAC. Each router attached to the link transmits Router Advertisement messages indicating whether it is willing to serve as a default router. An IPv6 host on the link receives Router Advertisement messages transmitted by all attached routers and builds a *Default Router List* (a list of default routers on the link).

The attached routers transmit Router Advertisement messages frequently enough for the IPv6 hosts on the link to learn of their availability, but not so slowly that hosts interpret the absence of Router Advertisements as router failure. IPv6 Neighbor Discovery provides a separate mechanism, the Neighbor Unreachability Detection algorithm, for hosts to detect router failure.

Each router joins the IPv6 All-Routers multicast address (FF01::2) on each of its advertising interfaces and responds to Router Solicitation messages sent to this address. The router also verifies the consistency of Router Advertisement messages sent by neighboring routers. It transmits periodic (unsolicited multicast) as well as solicited (unicast) Router Advertisement messages on its *advertising interfaces* onto the attached links. An advertising interface is any functioning interface that is IPv6-enabled, has at least one unicast IPv6 address configured on it, and has the *AdvSendAdvertisements* Flag set to TRUE [RFC4861].

When an IPv6 host enables an interface for IPv6, it may be unwilling to wait for the next periodically transmitted unsolicited Router Advertisement message on the link to locate default routers or learn IPv6 prefixes. In such cases, the host transmits Router Solicitation messages to the IPv6 All-Routers multicast address. The host sets the source IPv6 address of the message to either one of the interface's unicast IPv6 addresses or to the IPv6 Unspecified address (::). If the source IPv6 address is not the IPv6 Unspecified address, the host includes the Source Link-Layer Address Option containing the host's Link-Layer address.

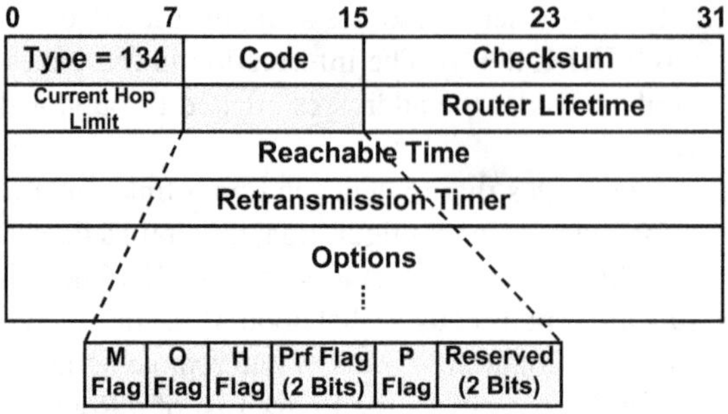

```
0          7          15          23          31
┌─────────────┬───────────┬─────────────────────────┐
│  Type = 134 │   Code    │        Checksum         │
├─────────────┼───────────┼─────────────────────────┤
│ Current Hop │           │      Router Lifetime    │
│    Limit    │           │                         │
├─────────────┴───────────┴─────────────────────────┤
│              Reachable Time                        │
├───────────────────────────────────────────────────┤
│              Retransmission Timer                  │
├───────────────────────────────────────────────────┤
│                   Options                          │
│                     ⋮                              │
└───────────────────────────────────────────────────┘
```

M Flag	O Flag	H Flag	Prf Flag (2 Bits)	P Flag	Reserved (2 Bits)

IPv6 Header:
- **Source Address**: This MUST be the IPv6 Link-Local address assigned to the interface from which this message is sent.
- **Destination Address**: Typically, set to the Source Address of the node that sent the Router Solicitation message or the IPv6 All-Nodes multicast address (FF02::1).
- **Hop Limit**: 255

ICMPv6 Fields:
- **Type (8 Bits)**: 134
- **Code (8 Bits)**: 0
- **Checksum (16 Bits)**: The ICMPv6 checksum.
- **Current Hop Limit (8 Bit)**: This is the default value that should be placed in the Hop Count field of the IPv6 header for outgoing IPv6 packets. A value of zero means unspecified (by this router).
- **M Flag (1 Bit)**: This is called the "Managed Address Configuration" Flag. When set, it indicates that IPv6 addresses are available via DHCPv6. If the M flag is set, the O flag is redundant and can be ignored because DHCPv6 will return all available configuration information.
- **O Flag (1 Bit)**: This is called the "Other Configuration" Flag. When set, it indicates that other configuration information is available via DHCPv6. Examples of such information are DNS-related information, or information on other servers within the network .Note that if neither the M nor O Flags are set, this indicates that no information is available via DHCPv6.
- **Reserved (6 Bits)**: This field is unused and MUST be initialized to zero by the sender and MUST be ignored by the receiver.
- **Router Lifetime (16 Bits)**: This is the lifetime (in seconds) associated with the default router. This field can contain values up to 65535 and receivers should handle any value, while the sending rules in Section 6 of RFC 4861 limit the lifetime to 9000 seconds. A Lifetime of 0 indicates that the router is not a default router and SHOULD NOT appear on the Default Router List. The Router Lifetime applies only to the router's usefulness as a default router; it does not apply to information contained in other message fields or options. Options that need time limits for their information include their own lifetime fields.
- **Reachable Time (32 Bits)**: This is the time (in milliseconds) that a node assumes a neighbor is reachable after having received a reachability confirmation. This is used by the Neighbor Unreachability Detection algorithm. A value of zero means unspecified (by this router).
- **Retransmission Timer (32 Bit)**: This is the time (in milliseconds) between retransmitted Neighbor Solicitation messages. This is used by the IPv6 Address Resolution and the Neighbor Unreachability Detection functions. A value of zero means unspecified (by this router).

Possible Options:
- **Source Link-Layer Address**: This is the Link-Layer address of the interface from which the Router Advertisement is sent. This is only used on Link Layers that have addresses. A router MAY omit this Option in order to enable inbound load sharing across multiple Link-Layer addresses.
- **MTU**: This SHOULD be sent on links that have a variable MTU (as specified in the document that describes how to run IP over the particular link type). This MAY be sent on other links.
- **Prefix Information**: These Options specify the IPv6 prefixes that are on-link and/or are used for IPv6 Stateless Address Autoconfiguration (SLAAC). A router SHOULD include all of its on-link prefixes (except the Link-Local prefix), so that multihomed hosts have complete prefix information about on-link destinations for the links to which they attach. If complete information is lacking, a host with multiple interfaces may not be able to choose the correct outgoing interface when sending traffic to its neighbors.

FIGURE 4.2 Router Advertisement message format (ICMPv6 Message Type 134).

4.3.2.2.1.2   IPv6 Prefix Discovery   IPv6 Prefix Discovery is the process through which an IPv6 host on a link learns the ranges of IPv6 addresses that are on the local link and can be reached directly (i.e., on-link addresses) without going through a router. Router Advertisement messages also contain one or more Prefix Information Options (one Option for each included IPv6 prefix) that list the set of IPv6 prefixes identifying the IPv6 addresses that can be used on the local link (on-link addresses).

Router Advertisement messages contain a list of IPv6 prefixes (in the Prefix Information Option) that IPv6 hosts use for the following:

- on-link IPv6 address determination (indicated by the 1-bit L (on-link) Flag in the Prefix Information Option), and/or
- autonomous (stateless) IPv6 address configuration (indicated by the 1-bit A (autonomous address configuration) Flag in the Prefix Information Option).

These two Flags, associated with the IPv6 prefixes (carried in the Prefix Information Option), specify to the receiving IPv6 node the intended uses of a particular advertised IPv6 prefix. When an IPv6 host receives a Prefix Information Option that has the L Flag set, the host interprets this Option as containing an IPv6 prefix that identifies a range of on-link IPv6 addresses.

Each IPv6 host uses the on-link IPv6 prefixes advertised to construct and maintain a Prefix List, a small database that it uses to determine whether the destination IPv6 address of a particular packet is on-link or off-link (beyond a local router). Note that the destination IPv6 address of a transmitted packet can be an on-link address even if it does not belong to any of the advertised on-link IPv6 prefixes. In such cases, an attached router, upon receiving such an IPv6 packet (which the sender believes has an off-link destination), can send an ICMPv6 Redirect message to inform the sender that the destination is a neighbor.

4.3.2.2.1.3   IPv6 Address Configuration   Through Router Advertisement messages (and the IPv6 address and parameter configuration M and O Flags in these messages as shown in Figure 4.2), attached routers can inform IPv6 hosts on the link how to perform IPv6 address autoconfiguration. For example, routers can send Router Advertisement messages (with appropriate settings of the per-prefix Flags) to specify whether hosts on the link should configure interface IPv6 addresses using Stateful Dynamic Host Configuration Protocol for IPv6 (DHCPv6) and/or SLAAC. DHCPv6 is described in greater detail in **Chapter 5**.

4.3.2.2.1.4   Internet Parameter Configuration   The IPv6 routers also include Internet parameters such as the Hop Limit in the Router Advertisement messages they send, which the IPv6 hosts use in the Hop Limit field of outgoing IPv6 packets (see **Chapter 2**). The routers optionally include link parameters such as the link MTU in the messages, allowing hosts to appropriately size outgoing IPv6 packets. The link MTU is the maximum packet size (in bytes) that can be transmitted on a particular link in one piece without requiring fragmentation. Including such information in Router Advertisement messages allows the network operator to centralize the administration of critical network parameters and set them on routers to be automatically propagated to all hosts on a link.

4.3.2.2.1.5   Change in IPv6 Link-local Address   The IPv6 Link-Local addresses on the interfaces of a router are normally statically configured and should rarely change, if ever. This is because if a particular router on a link sends multiple IPv6 packets containing different source IPv6 Link-Local addresses, IPv6 nodes on the link will assume that these packets come from different routers, leading to undesirable network behavior. Note that the IPv6 Global Unicast addresses on routers are usually manually or statically configured (as part of the IPv6 addressing plan of the network).

For example, Redirect messages sent by a router to an IPv6 node on a link will be ignored if that router is not the node's current first-hop router. Thus, the source IPv6 Link-Layer address that Router A uses in the Router Advertisement messages it sends must be identical to the target IPv6 Link-Layer address that Router B uses in a Redirect message when Router B redirects packets to Router A. Using the IPv6 Link-Local address to uniquely identify the routers originating IPv6 packets on a link has the benefit that the IPv6 address that a router is known by should not change even when IPv6 address renumbering occurs on a site.

If the IPv6 Link-Local address on a router interface changes, the router should inform the IPv6 hosts on the link of this change by multicasting a few Router Advertisement messages using the old Link-Local address as the source IPv6 address, with the message's Router Lifetime field set to zero. The router should also multicast a few Router Advertisement messages using the new IPv6 Link-Local address as the source IPv6 address. This procedure has the same effect as when one interface on a router stops being an advertising interface, and a different interface on the same router starts being the advertising interface.

4.3.2.2.2   The 1-Bit Home Agent (H) Flag

Mobile IPv6 [RFC6275] is a protocol that allows an IPv6 node (called a Mobile Node) to leave its Home Link and roam on Foreign Links on the IPv6 Internet while using its Home IPv6 Address and a Care-of IPv6 Address, and still remain reachable as if it were on its Home Link (see Section 6.3). A Home Agent is an IPv6 router on the Home Link of the Mobile Node with which the Mobile Node registers its current Foreign Link associated Care-of IPv6 Address.

An IPv6 router on the Home Link sets the 1-bit Home Agent (H) Flag [RFC6275] in the Router Advertisement message (see Figure 4.2) it sends on a link to indicate that it is also functioning as a Mobile IPv6 Home Agent on the link. Mobile IPv6 [RFC6275] modified the Router Advertisement message format [RFC4861] with the addition of the H Flag to enable a router to use the Router Advertisement message to inform IPv6 hosts on the link that it is also serving as a Home Agent.

4.3.2.2.3   The 2-Bit Prf Flag: Default Router Preferences and More-Specific Routes

Reference [RFC4191] defined an optional extension to the ICMPv6 Router Advertisement message (a 2-bit Flag) and the IPv6 Route Information Option (Option Type 24), which allows IPv6 routers attached to a link to communicate Default Router Preferences and more-specific routes to IPv6 hosts (see Figure 4.2). The optional extensions (in [RFC4191]) include the definition of a new 2-bit *Default Router Preference* (Prf) Flag for the Router Advertisement message itself (to be used in addition to the original M and O Flags defined in [RFC4861], the H Flag defined in [RFC6275], and the P Flag defined in [RFC4389]), and the new IPv6 Route Information Option, which contains a 2-bit *Route Preference* (Prf) Flag.

The IPv6 Route Information Option is discussed in more detail in a section below. Note that the 2-bit Prf Flag defined for the Router Advertisement message itself is called the Default *Router* Preference Flag, while the Flag defined within the Route Information Option is called the Default *Route* Preference Flag; the two Flags may be confused.

These improvements allow an IPv6 host on a link to select an appropriate IPv6 router, especially when the IPv6 host is multihomed and the attached IPv6 routers are on different links. *The Preference values and specific routes that the attached IPv6 routers advertise (via the 2-bit Flag in the Router Advertisement message and the 2-bit Flag in the Route Information Option) to hosts on the link require administrative configuration (by the network operator); the IPv6 routers do not automatically derive these values from the IPv6 routing* tables.

An IPv6 router can set the Prf Flag (Default *Router* Preference) in the Router Advertisement message (see Figure 4.2) to Low (1), Medium (0), or High (3). When an IPv6 node on a link receives Router Advertisement messages from multiple attached IPv6 routers, it uses the setting of the Default *Router* Preference in the messages to determine which router (via its Link-Local address) to prefer as a default gateway. The network operator is responsible for setting the Default *Router* Preference values on the attached routers.

4.3.2.2.4   The 1-Bit Proxy (P) Flag

An IPv6 Neighbor Discovery Proxy is an IPv6 router on a link that listens for all Neighbor Discovery messages sent on the link on behalf of destination nodes that are off-link. This router responds unconditionally on behalf of the destination IPv6 hosts by sending Neighbor Advertisement messages when it receives Neighbor Solicitation messages and Neighbor Unreachability Detection messages on the link. Reference **[RFC4389]** defines a new 1-bit Proxy (P) Flag for the Router Advertisement message (see Figure 4.2) to be used when an IPv6 Neighbor Discovery Proxy is present on a link. A Proxy processes Router Advertisement messages as follows:

- When a Router Advertisement message with the P Flag set to 0 arrives on the upstream interface of a Proxy, it sets the P Flag to 1 when proxying the Router Advertisement message out all other (downstream) interfaces (called *proxy interfaces*).
- If a Router Advertisement message arrives on a given interface on the Proxy (including the upstream interface) with the P Flag set to 1 within the last 60 minutes, the Proxy must NOT use that interface as a proxy interface (i.e., the Proxy disables proxy functionality on that interface).
- If any Router Advertisement message (regardless of the setting of the P Flag) arrives on a downstream proxy interface within the last 60 minutes, the Proxy must NOT use that interface as a proxy interface.

The Proxy also processes a received Router Advertisement message locally and proxies it as described above, unless such proxying is disabled on the interface.

4.3.2.3   Neighbor Solicitation Message (Type 135)

IPv6 hosts send Neighbor Solicitation messages (ICMPv6 Message Type 135) to discover the Link-Layer addresses of IPv6 nodes that are on-link (Figure 4.3). These ICMPv6 messages include the sender's Link-Layer address (included in the Source Link-Layer Address Option). Hosts send these messages via multicast to determine the Link-Layer address associated with a known IPv6 address and via unicast to verify that a neighboring node is still reachable through a locally cached Link-Layer address (in the Neighbor Cache). These messages are also used for IPv6 Duplicate Address Detection.

The following sub-sections present the typical uses of Neighbor Solicitation messages (IPv6 Address Resolution and Duplicate Address Detection) and the IPv6 and MAC addresses used in these messages.

4.3.2.3.1   Using Neighbor Solicitations in IPv6 Address Resolution

An IPv6 node uses the IPv6 Address Resolution process **[RFC4861]** to determine the Link-Layer address (e.g., Ethernet MAC address) of another IPv6 node on the same link, given only its IPv6 address. IPv6 nodes never perform Address Resolution on IPv6 multicast addresses. An IPv6 node performs Address Resolution only on IPv6 unicast addresses that belong to the local link (i.e., on-link IPv6 addresses) and for which the node does not know the corresponding Link-Layer addresses.

When an IPv6 node on a link wants to resolve (i.e., determine) the Link-Layer address corresponding to the known IPv6 address of another node on the same link, it multicasts a Neighbor Solicitation message for this IPv6 address on the link, requesting the target node to return its Link-Layer address. The Target Address field of this ICMPv6 message contains the IPv6 address the sending node wishes to find the corresponding Link-Layer address for. The Neighbor Solicitation message is sent to the IPv6 Solicited-Node multicast address associated with the target node's

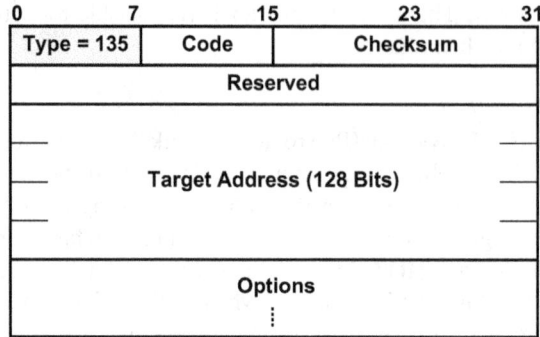

```
0             7         15         23         31
┌──────────────┬──────────┬─────────────────────┐
│  Type = 135  │   Code   │      Checksum        │
├──────────────┴──────────┴─────────────────────┤
│                   Reserved                     │
├─                                             ─┤
│                                                │
│─                                             ─│
│             Target Address (128 Bits)         │
│─                                             ─│
│                                                │
├─                                             ─┤
│                   Options                      │
│                      ⋮                         │
└────────────────────────────────────────────────┘
```

IPv6 Header:
- **Source Address**: This is either an IPv6 address assigned to the interface from which this message is sent, or (if Duplicate Address Detection is in progress) the IPv6 Unspecified address.
- **Destination Address**: This is either the IPv6 Solicited-Node multicast address corresponding to the target IPv6 address, or the target IPv6 address.
- **Hop Limit**: 255

ICMPv6 Fields:
- **Type (8 Bits)**: 135
- **Code (8 Bits)**: 0
- **Checksum (16 Bits)**: The ICMPv6 checksum.
- **Reserved (32 Bits)**: This field is unused and MUST be initialized to zero by the sender and MUST be ignored by the receiver.
- **Target Address (128 Bits)**: This is the IPv6 address of the target of the Neighbor Solicitation message. It MUST NOT be a multicast address.

Valid Options:
- **Source Link-Layer Address**: This is the Link-Layer address of the sending interface. It MUST NOT be included when the Source Address of the IPv6 packet carrying the ICMPv6 message is the IPv6 Unspecified address (::). Otherwise, Link Layers that have Link-Layer addresses MUST include this Option in multicast Solicitations and SHOULD include in unicast Solicitations.

FIGURE 4.3   Neighbor Solicitation message format (ICMPv6 Message Type 135).

IPv6 address. The target node responds by returning a unicast Neighbor Advertisement message directly to the requester containing the corresponding Link-Layer address.

The Neighbor Solicitation message is part of the address resolution mechanism that IPv6 uses instead of the IPv4 ARP and ARP Request message **[RFC826]**. However, the use of the IPv6 Neighbor Solicitation message, which involves multicast transmission, allows for more secure and efficient address resolution compared to the broadcast-based IPv4 ARP. Using an ICMPv6 Type 135 message explicitly indicates to the receiving node that the message being sent is a Neighbor Solicitation message.

4.3.2.3.2   Using Neighbor Solicitations in IPv6 Duplicate Address Detection

Neighbor Solicitation messages are also used for IPv6 Duplicate Address Detection, where an IPv6 node wishes to determine if more than one node on the link has been assigned the unicast IPv6 address that the node intends to use (i.e., a tentative address). When performing Duplicate Address Detection, an IPv6 node sends Neighbor Solicitation messages on the link targeting its own "tentative" IPv6 address, with the source IPv6 address of each message set to the IPv6 Unspecified address. These messages prompt IPv6 nodes on the link that are already using the requester's tentative IPv6 address to respond with a multicast Neighbor Advertisement message indicating that the IPv6 address is already in use.

4.3.2.3.3   Source and Destination IPv6 Address in the IPv6 Packet
Carrying the Neighbor Solicitation Message

The ICMPv6 Neighbor Solicitation (Type 135) message is encapsulated in an IPv6 packet with the source IPv6 address set to the Link-Local address (with prefix FE80::/10) of the sending interface. The destination IPv6 address of this ICMPv6 message contains the IPv6 Solicited-Node multicast address (with prefix FF02::1:FF00:0/104), which is derived from the Link-Local address of the target node's interface (i.e., the IPv6 address to be resolved). The use of the Solicited-Node multicast address is key to the improved security and efficiency of IPv6 address resolution compared to the broadcast-based ARP in IPv4.

As discussed in **Chapter 3**, every IPv6 node joins a multicast group identified by the IPv6 Solicited-Node multicast address FF02::1:FFxx:xxxx, where xx:xxxx are the last 6 hexadecimal values of an IPv6 unicast address. For each IPv6 unicast address configured on an IPv6 node (whether Link-Local or Global unicast address), the node needs to join the corresponding auto-generated IPv6 Solicited-Node multicast group. The sending IPv6 node transmits the Neighbor Solicitation message to the on-link node configured with the Target Address (to be resolved). Note that the target node must have joined (as required by IPv6) the IPv6 Solicited-Node multicast group generated from the Target Address it was configured with (i.e., the IPv6 address being resolved by the sending node). *The target node must join the Solicited-Node multicast address for each of its IPv6 unicast addresses to receive multicast messages sent to those Solicited-Node multicast addresses.*

4.3.2.3.4   Source and Destination MAC Address in the Ethernet
Frame Carrying the Neighbor Solicitation Message

After the sending node has created an IPv6 packet containing a Neighbor Solicitation message, it encapsulates the packet in an Ethernet frame. The source MAC address of this departing Ethernet frame is set to the MAC address of the sending interface. The destination MAC address of this frame is set to a multicast MAC address created by mapping the IPv6 Solicited-Node multicast address in the destination field of the departing IPv6 packet to a corresponding multicast MAC address (the "Solicited-Node multicast MAC address"). As noted above, each IPv6 interface must have an IPv6 Solicited-Node multicast address configured for each of the interface's IPv6 unicast addresses. Additionally, each IPv6 node must listen to the Solicited-Node multicast MAC addresses on all active interfaces configured with IPv6 unicast addresses.

Chapter 3 explains that the multicast MAC address corresponding to an IPv6 multicast address is created as 3333.xxxx.xxxx (in hexadecimal digits), where xxxx:xxxx are the last 8 hexadecimal digits in the IPv6 multicast address. The source MAC address of the departing frame is a unicast MAC address of the sending interface, while the destination MAC address (3333.xxxx.xxxx) is generated from the destination IPv6 address of the encapsulated IPv6 packet, which is an IPv6 multicast address (in this case, the Solicited-Node multicast address).

4.3.2.4   Neighbor Advertisement Message (Type 136)

IPv6 nodes (hosts and routers) send *unsolicited* Neighbor Advertisement messages when necessary and *solicited* (ICMPv6 Message Type 136) in response to Neighbor Solicitation messages from on-link hosts (Figure 4.4). Unsolicited Neighbor Advertisement messages are sent by nodes to inform neighboring nodes of changes in their Link-Layer addresses. The information contained in Neighbor Advertisement messages is required by neighboring nodes to determine the sender's Link-Layer address, and the sender's role on the network (the R Flag in Figure 4.4 indicates whether the sender is an IPv6 router).

When an IPv6 node receives a Neighbor Solicitation message from a node on the same link, it checks the address in the Target Address field of the message's (ICMPv6) header and compares it against its own configured IPv6 addresses. If the Target Address matches the receiver's IPv6 Link-Local address, it will reply to the sending node with a Neighbor Advertisement message. This message functions like the IPv6 equivalent of the ARP Reply message in IPv4 **[RFC826]**.

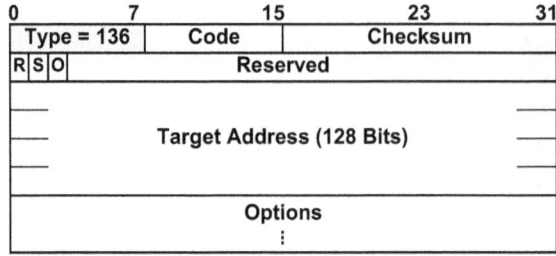

FIGURE 4.4   Neighbor Advertisement message format (ICMPv6 Message Type 136).

In the message's ICMPv6 header, the sender sets the Type field to 136, indicating that the message is a Neighbor Advertisement message. For a *solicited* Neighbor Advertisement message, the sender sets the message's Target Address field (Figure 4.4) to the IPv6 address indicated in the received Neighbor Solicitation message (i.e., the sender's own Link-Local address). For an *unsolicited* Neighbor Advertisement message, the sender sets the Target Address field to the IPv6 address corresponding to the sender's own local Link-Layer address that has changed. In the Target Link-Layer

Address Option placed in the message, the sender sets the Target Link-Layer address field to the Link-Layer address corresponding to the IPv6 address in the message's Target Address field.

4.3.2.4.1 Using ICMPv6 Neighbor Solicitations and Advertisements in IPv6 Address Resolution

This section describes how IPv6 nodes on a particular link use Neighbor Solicitation and Advertisement messages in IPv6 Address Resolution.

4.3.2.4.1.1 Sending and Receiving Neighbor Solicitations When an IPv6 node has an IPv6 unicast packet to send to another node on the same link (neighbor or target node) but does not know the target node's Link-Layer address, it performs Address Resolution. This involves the sending node creating a Neighbor Cache entry, setting its state to INCOMPLETE, and then transmitting a Neighbor Solicitation message targeted at the neighbor. The IPv6 node sends the Neighbor Solicitation message to the IPv6 Solicited-Node multicast address corresponding to the neighbor's IPv6 address.

The following conditions are considered when sending a Neighbor Solicitation message:

- If the IPv6 address of the source entity sending the IPv6 packet with the Neighbor Solicitation message is the same as one of the IPv6 addresses assigned to the outgoing interface, the IPv6 node uses that address in the Source IPv6 Address field of the IPv6 packet containing the outgoing Neighbor Solicitation message. Otherwise, the IPv6 node uses any of the IPv6 addresses assigned to the interface. Using the IPv6 address of the source entity, when possible, ensures that the IPv6 node receiving the Neighbor Solicitation message will install in its Neighbor Cache the IPv6 address that is highly likely to be used in subsequent IPv6 packets returned to the source of the received packet.
- If the IPv6 node is sending the Neighbor Solicitation message to the IPv6 Solicited-Node multicast address of the neighbor, it must include its own Link-Layer address (if one exists) in a Source Link-Layer Address Option. Including the Source Link-Layer Address in a Neighbor Solicitation message sent as a multicast solicitation ensures that the target node has an IPv6 address to which it can return the Neighbor Advertisement message. For a unicast Neighbor Solicitation message, an implementation may decide to omit the Source Link-Layer Address Option altogether. The assumption here is that if the sender of the unicast Neighbor Solicitation message has the target node's Link-Layer address in its Neighbor Cache, there is a high probability that the target node will also have an entry in its Neighbor Cache for the sender. Consequently, the sender need not send the Source Link-Layer Address Option.
- If the sending node does not receive a Neighbor Advertisement message after sending the maximum number of Neighbor Solicitation messages (MAX_MULTICAST_SOLICIT), Address Resolution has failed. In this case, the sender MUST return an ICMPv6 Destination Unreachable indication with Code 3 (meaning "Address Unreachable") for each queued IPv6 packet waiting for Address Resolution.

The following conditions are considered at the receiver of the Neighbor Solicitation message:

- If the Source IPv6 Address of the IPv6 packet carrying the Neighbor Solicitation message is not the IPv6 Unspecified address (and the transmission is on a Link Layer that uses Link-Layer addresses), and the Solicitation message includes a Source Link-Layer Address Option, then the receiving node should create or update its Neighbor Cache entry for the Source IPv6 Address of the Neighbor Solicitation message.
  - If the Neighbor Cache does not already have an entry for this IPv6 address, the receiving node should create a new entry and set its reachability state to STALE.

- If the Neighbor Cache already has an entry, and the cached Link-Layer address is different from the one in the received Source Link-Layer Option, the receiving node should replace the cached Link-Layer address with the received Link-Layer address and set the entry's reachability state to STALE.
- If the Source IPv6 Address of the IPv6 packet carrying the Neighbor Solicitation message is the IPv6 Unspecified address, the receiving node must not create or update the entry in the Neighbor Cache. After making the necessary updates to the Neighbor Cache, the receiving node returns a Neighbor Advertisement message in response to the sender of the Neighbor Solicitation message.

4.3.2.4.1.2 Sending and Receiving Solicited Neighbor Advertisements   Upon receiving a valid Neighbor Solicitation message from an IPv6 node on the local link targeting one of its assigned IPv6 addresses, the receiving node returns a Neighbor Advertisement message in response to the sending node. The Target Address field value of the Neighbor Advertisement message is copied from the Target Address field of the Neighbor Solicitation message. The responding node processes the Neighbor Advertisement message as follows before transmitting it:

- If the Destination IPv6 Address of the Neighbor Solicitation message is not an IPv6 multicast address (i.e., it is an IPv6 unicast address), the responding node may omit the Target Link-Layer Address Option in the Neighbor Advertisement message, as the receiver's cached Link-Layer address must already be current in the sender's Neighbor Cache for the Neighbor Solicitation message to have been received.
- If the Destination IPv6 Address of the Neighbor Solicitation message is an IPv6 multicast address, the responding node must include the Target Link-Layer Address Option in the Neighbor Advertisement message. Furthermore, if the responding node is a router, it must set the R (Router) Flag to 1 (see Figure 4.4); otherwise, it must set the Flag to 0.
- If the value in the Target Address field of the Neighbor Solicitation message is either an IPv6 unicast address or an IPv6 Anycast address for which the responding node is providing a proxy service, or if the responding node has not included the Target Link-Layer Address Option in the Neighbor Advertisement message, the responding node sets the O (Override) Flag to 0. Otherwise, the node sets the O Flag to 1. Properly setting the O Flag ensures that IPv6 nodes on the local link give preference to non-proxy Neighbor Advertisements, even when these Advertisements are received after proxy Neighbor Advertisements, and also ensures that the first Neighbor Advertisement message for an IPv6 Anycast address is preferred (i.e., wins).
- If the source IPv6 address of the Neighbor Solicitation message is the IPv6 Unspecified address, the responding node must set the S (Solicited) Flag of the Neighbor Advertisement message to 0 and multicast this message to the IPv6 All-Nodes multicast address. Otherwise, the responding node must set the S Flag to 1 and unicast the Neighbor Advertisement message to the Source IPv6 Address of the Neighbor Solicitation message.

Because IPv6 nodes are not required to include a Source Link-Layer Address Option in unicast Neighbor Solicitation messages, it is possible that an IPv6 node sending a solicited Neighbor Advertisement message to a particular node on the link may not have a corresponding Link-Layer address for that node in its Neighbor Cache. In such situations, the sender of the solicited Neighbor Advertisement message will first need to use IPv6 Neighbor Discovery to determine the Link-Layer address of the neighbor (i.e., transmit a multicast Neighbor Solicitation message).

When an IPv6 node on the link receives a valid (solicited or unsolicited) Neighbor Advertisement message, it searches its Neighbor Cache for the target node's entry (i.e., the entry for the sender of the Advertisement message). If no entry exists, the receiver silently discards the Neighbor Advertisement message. The receiver does not need to create an entry if none exists, since it has apparently not initiated any communication with the sender of the Neighbor Advertisement message.

However, if the receiver of the Neighbor Advertisement message finds the appropriate Neighbor Cache entry, the specific actions it takes depend on the state of the target node's entry in the Neighbor Cache, the Flags in the Neighbor Advertisement message, and the actual Link-Layer address received. If the entry in the Neighbor Cache for the target node is in the INCOMPLETE state when the Neighbor Advertisement message is received, the receiving node performs various actions, including the following: recording the Link-Layer address in the Neighbor Cache entry; setting the state of the entry to REACHABLE if the S Flag in the Neighbor Advertisement message is set; otherwise, setting the state to STALE (see Section 7.2.5 of **[RFC4861]** for more details).

4.3.2.4.2   Sending Unsolicited Neighbor Advertisements when a Link-Layer Address Changes

An IPv6 node may be designed to determine when its Link-Layer address has changed (e.g., when an interface card is hot-swapped). When this happens, the IPv6 node may want to inform its neighbors of the new Link-Layer address immediately. When the Link-Layer address has changed, the IPv6 node multicasts a small number of unsolicited Neighbor Advertisement messages to all nodes on the link (using the IPv6 All-Nodes multicast address) to quickly update the Link-Layer addresses cached on the IPv6 nodes (in their Neighbor Caches) that have become invalid.

Note that the sending of unsolicited Neighbor Advertisement messages to update a node's Link-Layer address is simply a mechanism for enhancing network performance and does not guarantee that all nodes will reliably receive these messages or discover the updated Link-Layer address. The transmitted unsolicited Neighbor Advertisement messages might not be received by all IPv6 nodes on the link, and their transmission does not guarantee that the Neighbor Caches on all nodes will be reliably updated. The sending of such messages should be viewed only as a performance optimization tool to quickly update the Neighbor Caches on most nodes on the link. The IPv6 Neighbor Unreachability Detection function, on the other hand, ensures that all nodes on the link will reliably learn and obtain the new (reachable) Link-Layer address, although this process may incur a somewhat longer delay.

The sending IPv6 node sets the Target Address field in the unsolicited Neighbor Advertisement message to the IPv6 address of the sending interface and fills the Target Link-Layer Address Option of the message with the new Link-Layer address. The node sets the S Flag to 0 (indicating an unsolicited message) to avoid making it difficult for the Neighbor Unreachability Detection algorithm to interpret node reachability; a solicited Neighbor Advertisement message (which is used in this algorithm) has the S Flag set to 1. If the message sender is a router, it sets the R (Router) Flag to 1; otherwise, it sets the R Flag to 0.

The node may set the O (Override) Flag to either 0 or 1. In either case, nodes on the local link (upon receiving the Neighbor Advertisement message) will immediately change the state of the entries in their Neighbor Caches for the Target Address to STALE, causing them to (use the Neighbor Unreachability Detection algorithm to) verify the path to the message sender for reachability. If the O Flag is set to 1, receiving nodes will install the new Link-Layer address in their Neighbor Caches; the new address will override existing cache entries for the message sender. Otherwise (i.e., if the O Flag is 0), the nodes will ignore the new Link-Layer address and instead (send unicast Neighbor Solicitation messages) to probe the cached Link-Layer address; the nodes will invoke the Neighbor Unreachability Detection algorithm to verify the reachability of the message sender.

An IPv6 node that has multiple IPv6 addresses assigned to an interface may multicast a separate Neighbor Advertisement message (to the IPv6 All-Nodes multicast address) for each of those IPv6 addresses.

4.3.2.4.3   Using IPv6 Anycast Addresses

The IPv6 Neighbor Discovery protocol **[RFC4861]** treats IPv6 Anycast addresses similarly to IPv6 unicast addresses in most cases. Since an IPv6 Anycast address is syntactically identical to an IPv6 unicast address, nodes treat an IPv6 Anycast address as if it were an IPv6 unicast address when performing Address Resolution or Neighbor Unreachability Detection; an IPv6 Anycast address does not require special processing.

An IPv6 Anycast address typically identifies a set of IP nodes that provide a common service in a network (e.g., DNS Servers belonging to an ISP). In this scenario, multiple IPv6 nodes on the same link may be configured with the same IPv6 Anycast address. IPv6 Neighbor Discovery handles IPv6 Anycast addresses on a link by expecting the IPv6 nodes on the link with those addresses to send multiple Neighbor Advertisement messages for the same target IPv6 address in response to a single transmitted Neighbor Solicitation message.

All the Neighbor Advertisement messages for a given IPv6 Anycast address are tagged (through the 1-bit O (Override) Flag in Figure 4.4) as non-Override messages. *A non-Override Neighbor Advertisement message (with the O Flag set to 0) does not update or replace/override in the Neighbor Cache the Link-Layer address and any related information installed by another Neighbor Advertisement* message. IPv6 nodes that have an IPv6 Anycast address configured on an interface treat that address exactly like an IPv6 unicast address, except that the O Flag in Neighbor Advertisement messages should be set to 0 (indicating non-Overriding). This ensures that when nodes on the link receive multiple Advertisement messages, they use the first received Advertisement message rather than the most recently received one. Specific rules must be provided to the IPv6 hosts on the link to enable them to determine which of the multiple Neighbor Advertisement messages to use.

Also, an IPv6 node configured to belong to an IPv6 Anycast address may multicast unsolicited Neighbor Advertisement messages (to the IPv6 All-Nodes multicast address) with the Target Address field set to the IPv6 Anycast address when its Link-Layer address changes. As with IPv6 unicast addresses, an IPv6 node uses the Neighbor Unreachability Detection algorithm to quickly detect when the current Link-Layer address for an IPv6 Anycast address becomes invalid.

4.3.2.4.4 Using IPv6 Proxy Neighbor Advertisements

An IPv6 node (particularly a router) on a link may be configured to act as an IPv6 Proxy Neighbor Discovery agent to accept IPv6 packets on behalf of a target IPv6 address on the same link that is unable to respond to Neighbor Solicitation messages. The target node has moved off-link and cannot accept packets directly, but the Proxy is willing to accept packets not explicitly addressed to it. The IPv6 node (the Proxy) can issue non-Override Neighbor Advertisement messages on behalf of the target IPv6 address (node).

IPv6 Proxy Advertisements are sent by a Mobile IPv6 Home Agent on a link to prevent the use of a Mobile Node's Home IPv6 Address (by another on-link node) when the Mobile Node moves off-link (i.e., is visiting a Foreign Network), and the Home Agent is willing to accept IPv6 packets on behalf of the off-link Mobile Node. Mobile IP is discussed in detail in **Chapter 6**.

The IPv6 Proxy Neighbor Discovery uses an MLD protocol such as MLDv1 or MLDv2 to join the IPv6 Solicited-Node multicast address(es) corresponding to the IPv6 address(es) assigned to the IPv6 node for which it is proxying (i.e., the IPv6 node that has moved off-link). The Proxy sends all solicited Proxy Neighbor Advertisement messages with the O Flag set to 0. This ensures that if the off-link node itself moves back to the Home Link, the Neighbor Advertisement messages it sends (with the O Flag set to 1) will take precedence over any Neighbor Advertisement messages received from the Proxy. The Proxy may transmit unsolicited Neighbor Advertisement messages with the O Flag set to 1, but doing so may cause the Proxy Neighbor Advertisement messages to override a valid Neighbor Cache entry created by the IPv6 node itself (which is now on-link).

An IPv6 Proxy Neighbor Discovery (e.g., a Mobile IPv6 Home Agent) may multicast Neighbor Advertisement messages (to the IPv6 All-Nodes multicast address) when its Link-Layer address changes or when it is configured (by system management or other mechanisms) to act as a Proxy for an IPv6 address. If the local link has multiple IPv6 nodes that are configured to provide proxy services for the same set of IPv6 addresses, a mechanism should be provided to the proxies to prevent them from multicasting Neighbor Advertisement messages for any given IPv6 address at the same time, in order to reduce the chances of generating excessive multicast traffic on the link.

4.3.2.4.5 Source and Destination Addresses in the IPv6 and Ethernet
Packets Carrying the Neighbor Advertisement Message

In the IPv6 header of an IPv6 packet carrying a solicited Neighbor Advertisement message, the sender sets the source IPv6 address to the Link-Local address of the sending interface and the destination IPv6 address to the Link-Local address of the target node. However, for an unsolicited Neighbor Advertisement message, the sender sets the destination IPv6 address to the IPv6 All-Nodes multicast address (FF02::1), since this message is advertised to all nodes on the link.

In the Ethernet header of the frame carrying the IPv6 packet with the solicited Neighbor Advertisement message, the sender sets the source MAC address to the Link-Layer address of the sending interface and the destination MAC address to the Link-Layer address of the sender of the Neighbor Solicitation message. In this case, the Ethernet frame carries a unicast Neighbor Advertisement message sent directly to the sender of the Neighbor Solicitation message. For an Ethernet header carrying an unsolicited Neighbor Advertisement message, the sender sets the destination MAC address to the multicast MAC address derived from the IPv6 All-Nodes multicast address (FF02::1). **Chapter 3** describes how IPv6 multicast addresses are mapped to corresponding MAC addresses.

4.3.2.5 Redirect Message (Type 137)

IPv6 routers send Redirect messages (ICMPv6 Message Type 137) to inform a host on a link of a better first-hop node (address) that leads to a specific destination (Figure 4.5). Routers send such messages only to hosts that are sending unicast traffic; *only hosts process* Redirect *messages*. IPv6 hosts do not send Redirect messages.

A router can redirect an IPv6 host to a better first-hop, but it can also use a redirect to inform a host that the destination is, in fact, a neighbor (on the same link). In the latter case, the router sets the value in the Target Address field of the Redirect message equal to the value in the Destination Address field of the message; both fields contain the same address, the IPv6 address of the neighbor. The Target Address field contains the IPv6 address of a local node (a first-hop router or neighbor) to which the host that triggered the sending of the Redirect message should send subsequent IPv6 packets for the destination.

The Destination Address field of the Redirect message contains the destination IPv6 address of the packet that triggered the redirection, specifically the address in the Destination Address field of the original IPv6 packet that initiated the redirection (Figure 4.5). This address could be an off-link or on-link destination. The router performing the redirection will normally forward the received IPv6 packet, if possible, and then specify in the Target Address field of the Redirect message the IPv6 address to which subsequent IPv6 packets for that destination should be sent.

The redirecting router determines (by some means not specified in **[RFC4861]**, considered out of scope) that a better first-hop router resides on the local link as the sending node for the redirected destination IPv6 address (the packet's destination address). For an on-link destination, the redirecting router uses the on-link IPv6 prefixes to ascertain whether the packet's destination is a neighbor on the local link. The sender of the original IPv6 packet, upon receiving the Redirect message, sends subsequent IPv6 packets to the redirected node (specified in the Target Address field of the Redirect message).

The following sections describe the processing of Redirect messages in IPv6 routers and hosts on a given link.

4.3.2.5.1 IPv6 Router Processing

IPv6 routers attached to a link send Redirect messages to direct IPv6 hosts on the link to use a better first-hop router when sending IPv6 packets to a specific IPv6 destination or to inform the hosts that a particular IPv6 destination is, in fact, an on-link destination (i.e., a neighbor). The routers accomplish on-link destination redirection by setting the IPv6 address in the Target Address of the Redirect message equal to the address in the Destination Address field of the message.

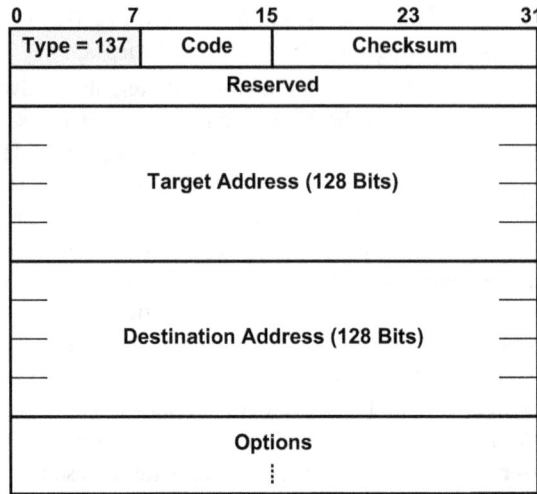

```
0          7        15              23          31
┌──────────┬────────┬────────────────────────────┐
│ Type = 137│  Code  │         Checksum           │
├──────────┴────────┴────────────────────────────┤
│                   Reserved                      │
├─                                              ─┤
│                                                 │
│─              Target Address (128 Bits)       ─│
│                                                 │
├─                                              ─┤
│                                                 │
│─           Destination Address (128 Bits)     ─│
│                                                 │
├─                                              ─┤
│                   Options                       │
│                     ⋮                           │
└─────────────────────────────────────────────────┘
```

IPv6 Header:
- **Source Address**: This MUST be the IPv6 Link-Local address assigned to the interface from which this message is sent.
- **Destination Address**: This is the Source Address of the IPv6 packet that triggered the Redirect message to be sent.
- **Hop Limit**: 255

ICMPv6 Fields:
- **Type (8 Bits)**: 137
- **Code (8 Bits)**: 0
- **Checksum (16 Bits)**: The ICMPv6 checksum.
- **Reserved (32 Bits)**: This field is unused and MUST be initialized to zero by the sender and MUST be ignored by the receiver.
- **Target Address (128 Bits)**: This is the same as the address in the Destination Address field of this message if the packet's destination is a neighbor (i.e., a node on the same link); in this case the Target Address and Destination Address are the same. If the target is not a neighbor, then this is the address of an attached router which is a better first-hop node. In the latter, the target is a better first-hop router and the Target Address MUST be the router's IPv6 Link-Local address.
- **Destination Address (128 Bits)**: This is the IPv6 address of the packet's destination (i.e., the destination that triggered there direction). If the destination is a neighbor, then this address will also be used as the Target address.

Possible Options:
- **Target Link -Layer Address**: This is the Link-Layer address for the target (neighbor or best first-hop router). It SHOULD be included (if known). Note that on NBMA (non-broadcast multiple access) links, hosts may rely on the presence of the Target Link-Layer Address Option in Redirect messages as the means for determining the Link-Layer addresses of neighbors. In such cases, the Option MUST be included in Redirect messages.
- **Redirected Header**: This contains all or part of the IPv6 packet that caused the redirection to be performed without making the Redirect message exceed the IPv6 minimum link MTU of 1280 bytes.

FIGURE 4.5   Redirect message format (ICMPv6 Message Type 137).

An IPv6 router on a link must be able to determine the IPv6 Link-Local address of each of the other routers attached to the link to ensure that the IPv6 address used in the Target Address field of a Redirect message identifies the correct neighboring router using its IPv6 Link-Local address. For static routing, this requirement implies that the sender of the Redirect message should specify the IPv6 address of the (best) next-hop router (in the Target Address field) using its IPv6 Link-Local address. For dynamic routing, all IPv6 routing protocols allow neighboring routers to exchange their IPv6 Link-Local addresses.

An IPv6 router on a link sends a Redirect message to an IPv6 host on the same link whenever the router forwards an IPv6 packet from that host that is not explicitly addressed to the router itself (i.e., an IPv6 packet that is not meant to be source-routed through the router). Note that a router also sends a Redirect message only when the Source IPv6 Address field of the received IPv6 packet identifies a neighbor and the destination IPv6 address field of the packet does not contain an IPv6 multicast address. The router creates the Redirect message with the following contents:

- The source IPv6 address of the Redirect message is the IPv6 Link-Local address of the router's sending interface. Note that routers must use their IPv6 Link-Local address as the source IPv6 address for Redirect and Router Advertisement messages they send, so that IPv6 hosts on the link can uniquely identify the sending routers.
- The IPv6 Hop Limit field value is set to 255, preventing the packet from being forwarded by a router.
- A valid checksum is computed for the message and the message's Code field is set to 0 (see Figure 4.5).
- The Destination Address field of the Redirect message does not contain an IPv6 multicast address; it contains the destination IPv6 address of the received IPv6 packet being redirected.
- The Target Address field of the Redirect message contains either an IPv6 Link-Local address (when redirecting to another router on the link, the best next-hop router) or the same value as the Destination Address field of the message (when redirecting to an on-link destination). In the latter case, the Target Address field contains the destination IPv6 address of the original packet that triggered the redirection, which is the IPv6 address of a neighbor.
- The router includes all Options in the Redirect message, each with a length greater than zero:
  - The Target Link-Layer Address Option contains the Link-Layer address of the target node (the first-hop router or neighbor), if known.
  - The Redirected Header Option contains as much of the redirected packet as possible without the Redirect message exceeding the IPv6 minimum MTU of 1280 bytes **[RFC8200]**.

4.3.2.5.2   IPv6 Host Processing

An IPv6 host, upon receiving a valid Redirect message, updates its Destination Cache accordingly so that it can send subsequent IPv6 packets to the specified target node (the best first-hop router or neighbor). If the host has no entry in its Destination Cache for the redirected IPv6 destination, it creates one. The Destination Cache contains both on-link and off-link destinations to which the host recently sent traffic. This Cache maps a destination IPv6 address to the IPv6 address of the next-hop neighbor or a local on-link neighbor **[RFC4861]**.

If the received Redirect message includes a Target Link-Layer Address Option (containing the Link-Layer address of the target node), the IPv6 host either updates an existing entry or creates a new entry in the Neighbor Cache for the target node. In both cases, the IPv6 host copies the Link-Layer address from the Target Link-Layer Address Option to cache it in the Neighbor Cache. If the host has created a Neighbor Cache entry for the target node, the host sets the reachability state of that entry to STALE. If a Neighbor Cache entry already exists and the host has updated it with a different Link-Layer address, the host also sets the entry's reachability state to STALE. If the received Link-Layer address in the Option is the same as that already in the Neighbor Cache, the host leaves the entry's state unchanged.

If the host finds that the addresses in the Target Address and Destination Address fields of the Redirect message are the same, it treats the target node as on-link. If the value in the Target Address field differs from that in the Destination Address field, the host sets the *IsRouter* Flag to TRUE for the target node. The *IsRouter* Flag **[RFC4861]** is set to TRUE to indicate that a particular interface has IPv6 routing enabled. However, if the addresses in the Target Address and Destination Address fields are the same, the IPv6 host cannot reliably determine whether the target node is a router.

Consequently, when the host creates new Neighbor Cache entries, it should set the *IsRouter* Flag to FALSE, while leaving the Flag unchanged for existing Neighbor Cache entries. If the target node is a router, the host will update the *IsRouter* Flag accordingly when it receives subsequent Neighbor Advertisement or Router Advertisement messages from it.

The Redirect message that an IPv6 host receives applies to all IPv6 packets being sent to a particular IPv6 destination. Upon receiving a Redirect message for a specific IPv6 address (indicated in the message's Destination Address field), the host updates all Destination Cache entries for that address to use the specified next-hop router (indicated in the message's Target Address field), regardless of the contents of the Flow Label field in the IPv6 header that appears in the truncated original IPv6 packet in the Redirected Header Option (i.e., information in the Option's "IP Header+Data" field).

4.3.3 Purpose of the Hop Limit in Neighbor Discovery Messages

All Neighbor Discovery messages are sent with the IPv6 header Hop Limit set to 255 (the maximum legal value) to ensure that these messages are sent by a node on the local link to another node on the same link. When a node receives a Neighbor Discovery message, it checks the Hop Limit field in the IPv6 header. If the value in the field is not 255, the node silently discards the message. Neighbor Discovery messages are verified to have an IPv6 header Hop Limit of 255 to provide protection from network attacks based on Neighbor Discovery and launched from nodes that are off-link.

Note that Neighbor Discovery messages with a Hop Limit of 255 prevent an IPv6 router from forwarding such messages from off-link nodes onto a particular local link. IPv6 routers decrement the IPv6 header's Hop Limit by one when forwarding IPv6 packets. Thus, accidentally forwarding an IPv6 packet with a Neighbor Discovery message will result in a Hop Limit of 254, making it unacceptable for the link on which it is forwarded. This means that an IPv6 packet containing a Neighbor Discovery message with a Hop Limit of 255 (the maximum legal value for IPv6 packets carrying Neighbor Discovery messages) must have been sent by a node on the local link (a neighbor). This mechanism reduces the exposure of the IPv6 Neighbor Discovery protocol to external threats in the absence of authentication by allowing IPv6 routers to ignore Neighbor Discovery messages received from off-link senders (i.e., messages with a Hop Limit less than 255).

4.3.4 Neighbor Discovery Options

This section describes the Options that have been defined to be included in Neighbor Discovery messages [**RFC4861**]. IPv6 Neighbor Discovery [**RFC4861**] defines the following Option types that can be carried in Neighbor Discovery ICMPv6 messages:

- Source Link-Layer Address (Option Type 1)
- Target Link-Layer Address (Option Type 2)
- Prefix Information (Option Type 3)
- Redirected Header (Option Type 4)
- MTU (Option Type 5)

IPv6 Neighbor Discovery messages can contain zero or more Options, and an IPv6 node may include some of these Options multiple times in the same message. The sending node should pad an Option when necessary to ensure that it ends on its natural 64-bit boundary.

Given that the original Neighbor Discovery protocol [**RFC4861**] is vulnerable to various attacks if not secured, [**RFC3971**] specifies security mechanisms (and Options) for the Neighbor Discovery protocol (SEcure Neighbor Discovery (SEND)) that are not based on IPSec. Note that the Neighbor Discovery protocol [**RFC4861**] specification calls for the use of IPSec to protect Neighbor Discovery protocol messages; however, IPSec requires manual configuration of security associations.

4.3.4.1 Source/Target Link-layer Address

Figure 4.6 shows the format of the Neighbor Discovery message Type 1 and 2 Options. An IPv6 node must silently ignore these options when carried in other Neighbor Discovery messages.

- **Source Link-Layer Address Option (Type 1)**: This Option (which may be included in Neighbor Solicitation, Router Solicitation, and Router Advertisement messages) contains the Link-Layer address of the sender of the Neighbor Discovery message. This Option is not included in a Neighbor Discovery message when the source address of the message is the IPv6 Unspecified address (::).
- **Target Link-Layer Address Option (Type 2)**: This Option (which may be included in Neighbor Advertisement and Redirect messages) contains the Link-Layer address of the target neighboring node.

Chapter 3 describes that an IPv6 node uses the IPv6 Unspecified address, a reserved IPv6 address, when it lacks an IPv6 address (e.g., when the IPv6 address is unknown) for use as the source address of an IPv6 packet under certain conditions. The IPv6 Unspecified address has a value of 0:0:0:0:0:0:0:0 (or ::). This address is never used as a destination IPv6 address but may be used as a source IPv6 address if the sender does not (yet) know its own IPv6 address (e.g., while the sender is verifying that a tentative IPv6 address is unused during IPv6 SLAAC). A Neighbor Discovery message in an IPv6 packet with the source address set to the IPv6 Unspecified address does not include the Source Link-Layer Address Option.

It is possible for an IPv6 host to receive a Neighbor Solicitation, a Router Advertisement, or a Redirect message that does not contain a Link-Layer Address Option. IPv6 hosts must not create or update Neighbor Cache entries when they receive such messages. If an IPv6 host does not have an entry in its Neighbor Cache for the sender of such a message, it will perform Address Resolution before it can begin unicast IPv6 communications with that IPv6 address.

4.3.4.2 Prefix Information Option (Type 3)

This Option (sent only in Router Advertisement messages) contains IPv6 address prefixes and other information that IPv6 hosts on the attached link use for IPv6 SLAAC (Figure 4.7). Multiple Prefix Information Options (one Option for each IPv6 prefix) can be included in each Router Advertisement message to indicate multiple IPv6 address prefixes. Note that only IPv6 routers send Router Advertisement messages.

4.3.4.3 Redirected Header Option (Type 4)

This Option (sent in Redirect messages) contains all or part of the original IPv6 packet that caused a router to send a Redirect message (Figure 4.8). The Redirected Header Option includes all or part

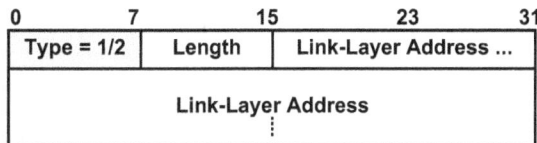

- **Type (8 Bits)**:
  - 1 = Source Link-layer Address
  - 2 = Target Link-layer Address
- **Length (8 Bits)**: This is the length of the Option (including the Type and Length fields) in units of 8 bytes. For example, the Length for IEEE 802 addresses is 1.
- **Link-Layer Address (Variable Length)**: The content and format of this field depends on the Link Layer over which IPv6 is operating.

FIGURE 4.6 Source/Target Link-Layer Address Option format (Type 1/2).

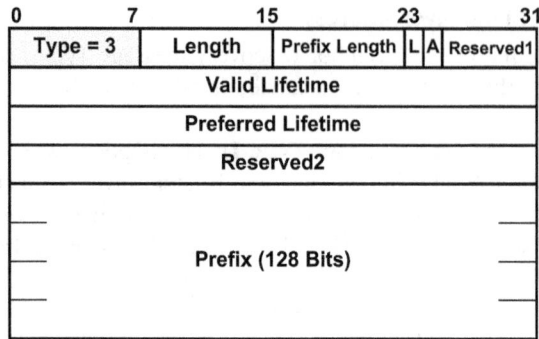

0	7	15	23			31
Type = 3	Length	Prefix Length	L	A	Reserved1
Valid Lifetime					
Preferred Lifetime					
Reserved2					
Prefix (128 Bits)					

- **Type (8 Bits)**: 3
- **Length (8 Bits)**: 4
- **Prefix Length (8 Bits)**: This is the number of leading bits (ranging from 0 to 128) in the IPv6 Prefix that are valid. The Prefix Length field provides necessary information for on-link address determination (when combined with the L Flag in the Prefix information Option). It also assists with address autoconfiguration as specified in RFC 4862 ("IPv6 Stateless Address Autoconfiguration"), for which there may be more restrictions on the Prefix Length.
- **L (1 Bit)**: This is called the on-link Flag. When set, it indicates that this prefix can be used for on-link address determination. When not set, the advertisement makes no statement about on-link or off-link properties of the prefix. In other words, if the L Flag is not set, a host MUST NOT conclude that an address derived from the prefix is off-link. That is, it MUST NOT update a previous indication that the address is on-link.
- **A (1 Bit)**: This is called the Autonomous Address-Configuration Flag. When set, it indicates that this prefix can be used for Stateless Address Autoconfiguration as specified in RFC 4862.
- **Reserved1 (6 Bits)**: This MUST be initialized to zero by the sender and MUST be ignored by the receiver.
- **Valid Lifetime (32 Bits)**: This is the length of time in seconds (relative to the time the packet is sent) that the prefix is valid for the purpose of on-link determination.Avalueofall onebits(0xFFFFFFFF)representsinfinity.TheValidLifetimeisalsousedbyRFC4862.
- **Preferred Lifetime (32 Bits)**: This is the length of time in seconds (relative to the time the packet is sent) that addresses generated from the prefix via Stateless Address Auto configuration remain preferred [RFC 4862]. A value of all one bits (0xFFFF FFFF) represents infinity. Note that the value of this field MUST NOT exceed the Valid Lifetime field value to avoid preferring addresses that are no longer valid.
- **Reserved2 (32 Bits)**: This field is unused and MUST be initialized to zero by the sender and MUST be ignored by the receiver.
- **Prefix (128 Bits)**: This is an IPv6 address or a prefix of an IPv6 address. The Prefix Length field contains the number of valid leading bits in the prefix. The bits in the prefix after the prefix length are reserved and MUST be initialized to zero by the sender and ignored by the receiver. A router SHOULD NOT send a Prefix Information Option for the Link-Local prefix and a host SHOULD ignore such an Option.

FIGURE 4.7   Prefix Information Option format (Type 3).

of the original IPv6 packet, depending on the size of that packet. The redirecting router includes as much of the original IPv6 packet that triggered the transmission of the Redirect message while ensuring that the Redirect packet does not exceed the IPv6 minimum link MTU of 1,280 bytes.

4.3.4.4   MTU Option (Type 5)

This Option (sent in Router Advertisement messages) contains the recommended IPv6 MTU for a link (Figure 4.9). In cases where a link MTU is not well-known by all nodes on a link, an IPv6 router includes this Option in Router Advertisement messages to ensure that all nodes use the same MTU value. The link MTU in the MTU Option sent by the IPv6 router overrides the IPv6 MTU reported by the host's interface hardware. Note that, in IPv4, hosts on the same network segment may use different MTU values.

```
0          7          15         23         31
+-----------+-----------+----------------------+
| Type = 4  |  Length   |      Reserved        |
+-----------+-----------+----------------------+
|               Reserved                       |
+----------------------------------------------+
|            IP Header + Data                  |
|                   ⋮                          |
+----------------------------------------------+
```

- **Type (8 Bits)**: 4
- **Length (8 Bits)**: This is the length of the Option in units of 8 bytes.
- **Reserved (48 Bits)**: This field is unused and MUST be initialized to zero by the sender and MUST be ignored by the receiver.
- **IP Header + Data**: This is the original IPv6 packet truncated to ensure that the size of the Redirect message does not exceed the minimum MTU required to support IPv6 as specified in RFC 8200.

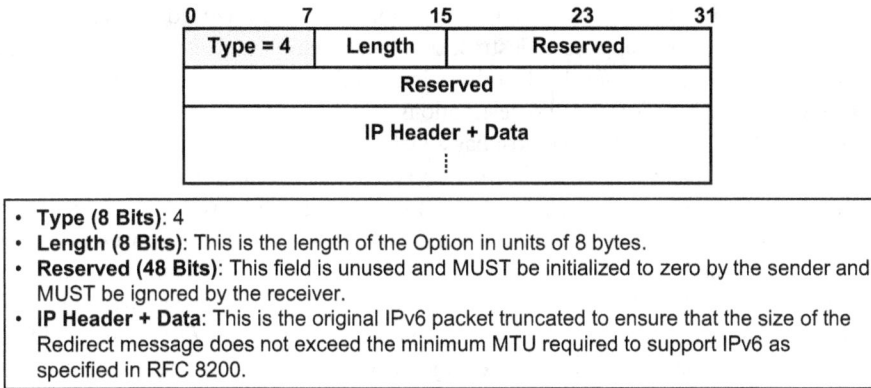

FIGURE 4.8 Redirected Header Option format (Type 4).

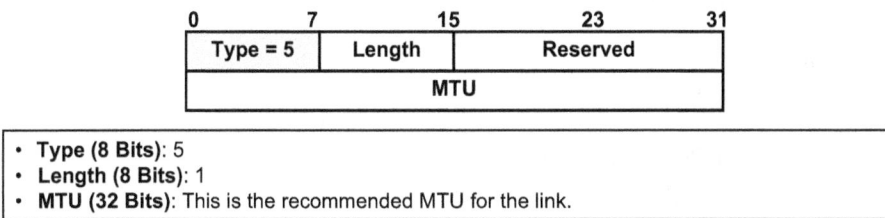

```
0          7          15         23         31
+-----------+-----------+----------------------+
| Type = 5  |  Length   |      Reserved        |
+-----------+-----------+----------------------+
|                  MTU                         |
+----------------------------------------------+
```

- **Type (8 Bits)**: 5
- **Length (8 Bits)**: 1
- **MTU (32 Bits)**: This is the recommended MTU for the link.

FIGURE 4.9 MTU Option format (Type 5).

In Layer 2 network configurations where heterogeneous Link-Layer technologies are bridged together, the maximum supported MTU may differ between network segments with specific Link-Layer technologies. The Layer 2 network segments may have different Link-Layer technologies, each with different Link-Layer MTUs. Given that Layer 2 switches or bridges generally do not generate ICMPv6 Packet Too Big messages (ICMPv6 Type 2 messages), nodes sending IPv6 packets will not be able to use IPv6 Path MTU Discovery **[RFC8201]** to dynamically discover the appropriate MTU on a per-neighbor basis. The MTU Option, which allows a router to communicate a common MTU for all nodes on a link (Layer 2 domain) to use, becomes very useful in such cases.

Specifically, IPv6 Path MTU Discovery **[RFC8201]** cannot be used to discover the differences in IPv6 MTUs between nodes on the same network. In these cases, IPv6 routers attached to the heterogeneous Link-Layer network can be configured to send Router Advertisement messages with the MTU Option to specify the maximum MTU value supported by all of those network segments. An IPv6 router uses the MTU Option to indicate the maximum IPv6 MTU supported by all Link-Layer technologies on that network segment.

4.3.4.5 IPv6 Route Information Option (Type 24)

An IPv6 router includes this Option in the Router Advertisement messages it sends on an attached link to communicate its Default Router Preference and more-specific routes to hosts on the link **[RFC4191]**. Sending Router Advertisement messages with this Option enhances the ability of each IPv6 host to select an appropriate default router, especially when the host is multihomed and connected to routers on different links. Figure 4.10 shows the structure of the IPv6 Route Information Option (Type 24).

IPv6 Neighbor Discovery **[RFC4861]** specifies various mechanisms for IPv6 hosts to maintain a Default Router List and a Prefix List. IPv6 hosts send Router Solicitation messages on the local link and receive Router Advertisement messages from attached routers. Each IPv6 host populates its

Default Router List and Prefix List based on the information in the received Router Advertisement messages. An IPv6 host then applies a destination determination algorithm to the Prefix List to determine if a particular destination IPv6 address is on-link or not. It uses the Default Router List to select a default router for off-link IPv6 destinations.

In network topologies where an IPv6 host has a Default Router List with multiple routers, selecting the right router for an off-link IPv6 destination is crucial, as one router may provide a significantly better route for a destination than another. In some cases, choosing the wrong router may result in communication failure or poor data transfer. The Route Information Option (Type 24), when included in Router Advertisement messages, provides essential information to attached IPv6 hosts to enable them to select the best default router when multiple routers are available.

The Route Information Option (Option Type 24) has a 2-bit Prf (*Route Preference*) field as shown in Figure 4.10. The Router Advertisement message itself (ICMPv6 Message Type 134) also has a 2-bit Prf (*Default Router Preference*), as shown in Figure 4.2. The Default Router Preference value (in the ICMPv6 message itself) for determining the best default router and the Route Preference value (in the Option) for more-specific routes are encoded the same way. Both Preference values are encoded as a two-bit signed integer, as follows:

- 01 = High
- 00 = Medium (default)
- 11 = Low
- 10 = Reserved - MUST NOT be sent

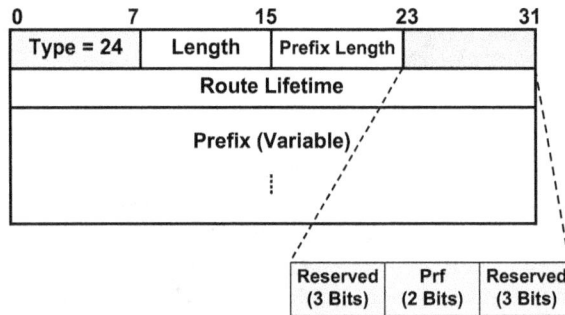

- **Type (8 Bits)**: 24
- **Length (8 Bits)**: This is the length of the Option (including the Type and Length fields) in units of 8 bytes. The Length field is 1, 2, or 3 depending on thePrefix Length. If Prefix Length is greater than 64, then Length must be 3. If Prefix Length is greater than 0, then Length must be 2 or 3. If Prefix Length is zero, then Length must be 1, 2, or 3.
- **Prefix Length (8 Bits)**: This is the number of leading bits in the Prefix that are valid. The value ranges from 0 to 128. The Prefix field is 0, 8, or 16 bytes depending on Length.
- **Prf (Route Preference) (2 Bits)**: This indicates whether to prefer the IPv6 router associated with this prefix over others, when multiple identical prefixes (for different routers) have been received. If the Reserved (10) value is received, the Route Information Option MUST be ignored.
- **Reserved (3 Bits)**: These fields MUST be initialized to zero by the sender and MUST be ignored by the receiver.
- **Route Lifetime (32 Bits)**: This is the length of time in seconds (relative to the time the packet is sent) that the prefix is valid for route determination. A value of all one bits (0xFFFFFFFF) represents infinity.
- **Prefix (Variable-length)**: This field contains an IPv6 address or a prefix of an IPv6 address. The Prefix Length field contains the number of valid leading bits in the prefix. The bits in the prefix after the Prefix Length (if any) are reserved, and MUST be initialized to zero by the sender and ignored by the receiver.

FIGURE 4.10   Route Information Option (Type 24).

A Router Advertisement message (with Default Router Preference and Router Lifetime field values, Figure 4.2) can contain a Route Information Option (with Route Preference and Route Lifetime field values, Figure 4.10).

The procedures described in **[RFC4191]** are applicable to IPv6 hosts only and do not affect the forwarding algorithm used by routers (including IPv6 hosts with IPv6 forwarding enabled). According to Reference **[RFC4191]**, *the Preference values and specific routes advertised in the Route Information Option of Router Advertisement messages to IPv6 hosts require explicit administrative configuration by the network operator. Both Default Router Preference and Route Preference values are not automatically derived from the IPv6 routing tables.* It is also important to note that the Preference values communicated by IPv6 routers are not routing metrics. Furthermore, Reference **[RFC4191]** does not recommend that routers "dump out" their entire IPv6 routing tables to attached hosts to enable proper use of the Preference values.

4.3.4.6   Other Options for ICMPv6 Router Advertisement Messages

Reference **[RFC8106]** specifies two Options (the Recursive DNS Server Option and DNS Search List (DNSSL) Option) that can be included in IPv6 Router Advertisement messages to allow IPv6 routers to advertise DNS information to IPv6 hosts on a link. These Options are mainly used by routers to enhance DNS configuration on hosts without referring them to DHCPv6 Servers for such information. Sending DNS configuration information via Router Advertisement messages enables IPv6 hosts on a link to perform full configuration of basic networking information without requiring DHCPv6. This feature allows IPv6 hosts to obtain the DNS configuration (i.e., the recursive DNS Server addresses and DNSSL) for the links to which they are connected. IPv6 hosts are able to learn DNS configuration information from the same Router Advertisement messages that provide IPv6 prefix configuration information for a link.

The IPv6 Router Advertisement Options provide a useful alternative capability in IPv6 networks where IPv6 hosts can autoconfigure their addresses through IPv6 SLAAC and where either of the following conditions exists:

- the infrastructure has no DHCPv6 services at all, or
- some IPv6 hosts do not support a DHCPv6 Client.

The goal of this Option is to enable IPv6 hosts to perform full configuration of basic networking information without requiring DHCPv6. This Option is mainly applicable in the above cases. However, in reality, DHCPv6 is more likely to be employed in IPv6 networks that need to distribute additional information, making IPv6 Router Advertisement-based DNS configuration unnecessary.

4.3.4.6.1   The Recursive DNS Server Option (Type 25)

This Option allows IPv6 hosts on a link to obtain recursive DNS Server address information from Router Advertisement messages they receive, instead of through a DHCPv6 Server. A recursive DNS Server (also called a resolver) is an intermediary server between a DNS client device and other DNS Servers in the wider DNS, handling the resolution of domain names to corresponding IP addresses. The recursive DNS Server manages, on behalf of the DNS client, the complex process of sending DNS queries to multiple DNS Servers until a domain name is resolved to the correct IP address or the name resolution fails. In this case, an IPv6 router is configured to send Router Advertisement messages with the Recursive DNS Server Option to provide DNS Server information to IPv6 hosts. Upon receiving such Router Advertisement messages, IPv6 hosts on the link will be able to use IPv6 SLAAC while still obtaining their DNS Server information from these messages without having to consult a DHCPv6 Server. IPv6 SLAAC is particularly useful when a network infrastructure does not have a DHCPv6 Server.

4.3.4.6.2   The DNSSL Option (Type 31)

This option allows IPv6 hosts on a link to obtain DNS suffix information from received Router Advertisement messages instead of through a DHCPv6 Server. A DNS suffix refers to that part of a domain name (e.g., aweya.com) that is appended to a host name, also called the *unqualified host name* (e.g., server1), to create a *fully qualified domain name (FQDN)* (server1.aweya.com) for a DNS name query. In this example, the DNS suffix of the host name is "aweya.com," the unqualified host name is "server1," and the FQDN to query is "server1.aweya.com." A DNS Server resolves a query for the FQDN to an IP address. Essentially, the DNS suffix (aweya.com) identifies a specific server or website within the domain (server1).

When a user is seeking the IP address of a host, it uses the DNS suffix to create a FQDN and then sends a DNS query with the FQDN to a DNS Server. Typically, DHCP is used to configure a DNS suffix on each host on a network. However, in some cases, an IPv6 router can be configured to send Router Advertisement messages with the DNSSL Option, allowing IPv6 hosts on a link to obtain DNS suffix information. Using this option, IPv6 hosts can use SLAAC and still obtain their DNS suffix information from an IPv6 router. This method is also useful when the IPv6 network infrastructure does not support a DHCPv6 Server.

A DNSSL is a list of DNS suffix domain names that IPv6 hosts use when they send DNS queries to search for short, unqualified domain names. The DNSSL Option included in Router Advertisement messages may contain one or more domain names. All the domain names listed in a DNSSL Option share the same lifetime value, which specifies the maximum time (in seconds) the receiving nodes may use the DNSSL for name resolution. If different lifetime values need to be indicated for domain names, multiple DNSSL Options must be included.

4.4   HOST SPECIFICATION AND DATA STRUCTURES

To store information for the Neighbor Discovery processes and to facilitate interactions between neighboring nodes, **[RFC4861]** defined the following data structures for IPv6 hosts (i.e., these are example data structures of a conceptual model of an IPv6 host). Each IPv6 host maintains the following data structures for each of its interfaces:

- **Neighbor Cache**: This stores, among other information, the IPv6 unicast address of each on-link neighbor (to which IPv6 packets have recently been sent), its corresponding Link-Layer address, a flag indicating whether the neighbor is a host or a router, and an indication of the state of reachability of that neighbor (the state is maintained by the Neighbor Unreachability Detection algorithm). This cache is equivalent to the ARP Cache in IPv4.
- **Destination Cache**: This stores information about the next-hop IPv6 addresses for destinations to which the host recently sent IPv6 packets. Each entry in the Destination Cache includes the destination IPv6 address (either on-link or off-link), the previously resolved next-hop IPv6 address, and the Path MTU for that destination. The Destination Cache maintains a mapping between a destination IPv6 address and its next-hop (neighbor) IPv6 address.
- **Prefix List**: This is a list of IPv6 prefixes that define the IPv6 addresses on the local link (on-link addresses). Each entry in this list defines a range of IPv6 addresses for destinations that are directly reachable on the link (i.e., nodes on the local link or on-link neighbors). The IPv6 host populates this list from IPv6 prefixes that attached routers advertise in their Router Advertisement messages. Each entry in the list is associated with an invalidation timer value (taken from the Router Advertisement message) that the IPv6 host uses to expire received IPv6 prefixes when they become invalid.

    The list uses a special "infinity" timer value that specifies that a particular IPv6 prefix remains valid forever unless the IPv6 host receives a new (finite) value in a subsequent Router Advertisement message. The host enters an IPv6 Link-Local prefix in the Prefix

List with an infinite invalidation timer, regardless of whether an attached router advertised an IPv6 prefix for it. Router Advertisement messages that the host receives should not modify the Link-Local prefix's invalidation timer.

- **Default Router List**: This is a list of IPv6 addresses corresponding to on-link IPv6 routers (i.e., routers attached to the local link) that send Router Advertisement messages and are eligible to be default routers. Each entry in the list is also associated with an invalidation timer value (taken from Router Advertisement messages) that the IPv6 host uses to delete entries that are no longer advertised.

These data structures are just example structures, and an IPv6 implementation is not required to create them exactly, as long as the external behavior of the host is consistent with **[RFC4861]**.

4.4.1 IPv6 NEXT-HOP DETERMINATION

When an IPv6 node has an IPv6 packet to send to a destination, it uses a combination of the Prefix List, the Default Router List, and the Destination Cache to determine the IPv6 address of the appropriate next-hop. This process is known as IPv6 next-hop determination. Once the node has determined the IPv6 address of the next-hop, it consults the Neighbor Cache for Link-Layer information for that neighbor.

An IPv6 node performs the next-hop determination for a given IPv6 unicast destination as follows:

- The IPv6 node takes the packet's destination IPv6 address and performs a longest prefix matching (LPM) search in the Prefix List to determine whether the destination is on-link or off-link.
- If the destination IPv6 address is on-link, the next-hop IPv6 address is the same as the packet's destination IPv6 address.
- Otherwise, the IPv6 node selects a router from the Default Router List as the next-hop for the packet's destination.

4.4.1.1 Using the Neighbor Cache and Destination Cache during IPv6 Next-Hop Determination

To improve packet processing efficiency, an IPv6 node does not perform next-hop determination on every IPv6 packet that it sends. Instead, after performing a next-hop determination, the node stores the results in the Destination Cache. Note that the node also stores updates it learns from Redirect messages in the Destination Cache. Then, when the node has an IPv6 packet to send, it first checks the Destination Cache to see if there is an entry for the packet's destination IPv6 address. If no entry exists for the destination, the node initiates next-hop determination to find the next-hop and create a Destination Cache entry for the destination.

Once the IPv6 node has determined the IPv6 address of the next-hop node, it inspects the Neighbor Cache for the Link-Layer information for that neighbor. If the node finds no entry for the neighbor, it creates one and sets the entry's state to INCOMPLETE. The node then initiates IPv6 Address Resolution and queues the IPv6 packet pending the completion of the IPv6 Address Resolution process. IPv6 Address Resolution involves the node sending a Neighbor Solicitation message and waiting for a response in the form of a Neighbor Advertisement message. When the node receives a Neighbor Advertisement message, it creates an entry for the Link-Layer address in the Neighbor Cache and then queues the IPv6 packet for transmission.

Each time the IPv6 node examines a Neighbor Cache entry while sending a unicast IPv6 packet, it also checks information related to the Neighbor Unreachability Detection mechanism, according to the Neighbor Unreachability Detection procedures. Checking the unreachability of a neighbor may result in the IPv6 node transmitting a unicast Neighbor Solicitation message on the local link to verify that the neighbor is still reachable.

The IPv6 node performs next-hop determination the first time it sends IPv6 packets to a destination and populates the Destination Cache. However, as long as the node successfully sends subsequent IPv6 packets to that destination, it continues to use the corresponding Destination Cache entry. If at some point the node determines that it cannot communicate with the packet's destination, as indicated by the Neighbor Unreachability Detection algorithm, the node may need to reperform next-hop determination. This need may arise, for example, when the node has to switch to a functioning router after the current router fails and is unable to forward IPv6 packets.

Note that when the IPv6 node reperforms next-hop determination, it does not have to discard the complete Destination Cache entry. This is because retaining cached information in the Destination Cache entry, such as the path MTU and round-trip timer values, can be beneficial.

4.4.1.2   Selecting a Default Router

The algorithm that an IPv6 host uses to select a default router (when multiple routers are attached to the local link) depends in part on whether the host has determined that a particular router is reachable. The host initiates the default router selection process during next-hop determination when there is no entry in the Destination Cache for an IPv6 destination that is off-link, or when the current router that the host is communicating through appears to have failed. Under normal conditions, the IPv6 host selects a router the first time it sends IPv6 packets to a destination and sends subsequent packets to that destination using the same router as indicated in the Destination Cache, barring any changes to the Destination Cache caused by Redirect messages.

4.5   NEIGHBOR DISCOVERY PROCESSES AND MESSAGE EXCHANGES

The IPv6 Neighbor Discovery protocol **[RFC4861]** defines a set of ICMPv6 messages and behaviors that IPv6 nodes use to perform various important functions. IPv6 nodes exchange Neighbor Discovery protocol messages for various processes, including the following: Address Resolution, Duplicate Address Detection, Router Discovery, Redirect Function, Neighbor Unreachability Detection, and Proxy Neighbor Advertisements. These processes are described in this section. IPv4, on the other hand, defines dedicated protocols for some of these functions, as discussed below.

Table 4.4 lists the IPv6 Neighbor Discovery protocol messages with their corresponding source and destination IPv6 addresses. The IPv6 multicast addresses used in the destination address field of IPv6 packets carrying Neighbor Discovery protocol messages are mapped to corresponding MAC addresses to be placed in the destination MAC address field of the Ethernet frames carrying the protocol messages.

4.5.1   IPV6 ADDRESS-TO-LINK LAYER ADDRESS RESOLUTION

IPv6 nodes on the same link/subnet exchange Neighbor Solicitation and Neighbor Advertisement messages to determine (resolve) the Link-Layer address corresponding to a given IPv6 address **[RFC4861]**. Address resolution involves resolving a Layer 3 address to a corresponding Layer 2 address, as done in IPv4 ARP **[RFC826]**. Thus, address resolution here relates to the process through which an IPv6 node determines the Link-Layer address of a neighbor (i.e., on the same link/subnet) given only its IPv6 address. IPv4 has a dedicated protocol for IPv4-to-MAC address resolution called ARP **[RFC826]** (see the IPv4 ARP discussion in Appendix C).

In both IPv6 and IPv4 address resolution, an IP node knows only the IP address of the destination (target node) but requires its Link-Layer address to send Link-Layer packets (e.g., Ethernet frames) to the target node. Note that communication between nodes on the same link/subnet (a broadcast domain) is done via Link-Layer packets, requiring neighboring nodes to know each other's Link-Layer addresses. Communication between nodes on different links/subnets is done via IP packets. Address resolution allows a node on a link to determine the Link-Layer address of a neighboring node so that it can initiate Layer 2 communication on the same link/subnet with that neighbor.

TABLE 4.4

IPv6 Neighbor Discovery Protocol Messages with Corresponding Source and Destination Addresses

IPv6 Neighbor Discovery Message	Source IPv6 Address	Destination IPv6 Address
Router Solicitation	Link-Local address of sending interface, or the IPv6 Unspecified address (::) if the interface is not assigned an address	IPv6 All-Routers multicast address (FF02::2)
Solicited Router Advertisement	Link-Local address of sending interface	Link-Local address of the sender of the Router Solicitation message, or the IPv6 All-Nodes multicast address if the sender used the IPv6 Unspecified address (::)
Unsolicited Router Advertisement	Link-Local address of sending interface	IPv6 All-Nodes multicast address (FF02::1)
Neighbor Solicitation	Link-Local address of sending interface (during IPv6 Address Resolution), or the IPv6 Unspecified address (during Duplicate Address Detection)	IPv6 Solicited-Node multicast address corresponding to the Target Address, or the Target Address itself
Solicited Neighbor Advertisement	Link-Local address of sending interface	Link-Local address of the sender of the Router Solicitation message, or the IPv6 All-Nodes multicast address if the sender used the IPv6 Unspecified address (::)
Unsolicited Neighbor Advertisement	Link-Local address of sending interface	IPv6 All-Nodes multicast address (FF02::1)
Redirect	Link-Local address of sending interface	Link-Local address of the host that triggered the redirect

4.5.1.1 IPv6 Address Resolution Process

The source node sends a Neighbor Solicitation message to the IPv6 Solicited-Node multicast destination address of the target node. This Solicited-Node multicast address is derived from the IPv6 unicast address (i.e., Link-Local address) of the target node. Only the target node, always listening on the multicast group address corresponding to its Solicited-Node multicast address (derived from its IPv6 unicast address), will respond with a Neighbor Advertisement message, providing its Link-Layer address to the requesting node. The requesting node then uses the received information to create a Neighbor Cache entry.

In the address resolution process (see Figures 4.11 and 4.12), Host 1 must resolve Host 3's Link-Layer address to send IPv6 traffic to Host 3. Host 1 has an Ethernet MAC address of 00-AA-00–11-11-11 and a corresponding IPv6 Link-Local address of FE80::2AA:FF:FE11:1111. Host 3 has an Ethernet MAC address of 00-AA-00–33-33-33 and a corresponding IPv6 Link-Local address of FE80::2AA:FF:FE33:3333.

The IPv6 address-to-Link Layer address resolution process can be described as follows:

1. Host 1 sends a multicast Neighbor Solicitation message on a link/interface to resolve the Link-Layer address corresponding to an IPv6 address (FE80::2AA:FF:FE33:3333). The destination IPv6 address of this Neighbor Solicitation message is a multicast address, specifically the Solicited-Node multicast address (FF02::1:FF33:3333) of the target node, Host 3, derived from the target node's IPv6 Link-Local (unicast) address (FE80::2AA:FF:FE33:3333) (see **Chapter 3**). Host 1 uses the Source Link-Layer Address Option to include its Link-Layer address (00-AA-00–11-11-11) in the Neighbor Solicitation message.

```
Ethernet Header:
   Source MAC = 00-AA-00-11-11-11
   Destination MAC =33-33-FF-33-33-33 (Host 3's Solicited-Node Address Mapped to a MAC Address)
IPv6 Header:
   Source Address = FE80::2AA:FF:FE11:1111
   Destination Address = FF02::1:FF33:3333 (Host 3's Link-Local Address
                                            Mapped to a Solicited-Node Multicast Address)
   Hop Limit = 255
Neighbor Solicitation Message Header (ICMPv6 Message Type 135, Code 0):
   Target Address = FE80::2AA:FF:FE33:3333 (Host 3's Link-Local Address)
Neighbor Discovery Option:
   Source Link-Layer Address Option:
      Source Link-Layer Address = 00-AA-00-11-11-11 (Host 1's Link-Layer Address)
```

Host 1
MAC = 00-AA-00-11-11-11
Interface ID = 02AA:00FF:FE11:1111
Link-Local = FE80::2AA:FF:FE11:1111

Router 1
MAC = 00-AA-00-44-44-44
Link-Local = FE80::2AA:FF:FE44:4444

Neighbor Solicitation Message

Host 2
MAC = 00-AA-00-22-22-22
Link-Local = FE80::2AA:FF:FE22:2222

Host 3
MAC = 00-AA-00-33-33-33
Link-Local = FE80::2AA:FF:FE33:3333

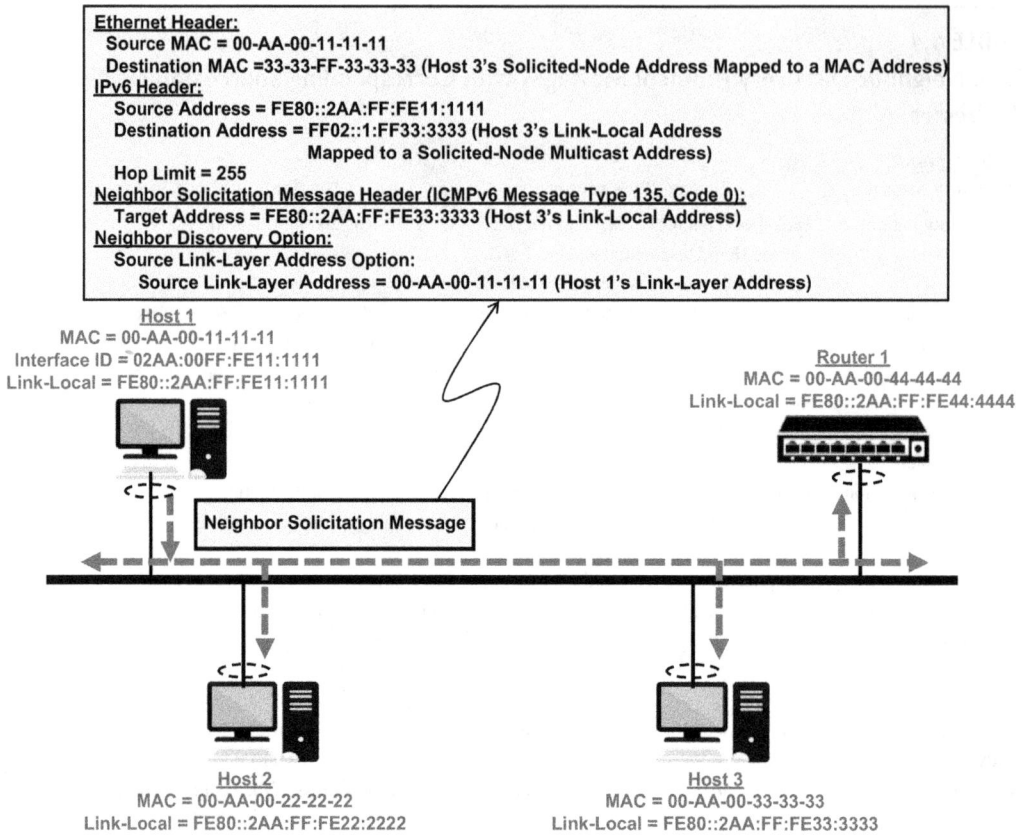

FIGURE 4.11 Sending multicast Neighbor Solicitation message for Address Resolution.

2. The target host, Host 3, having registered its multicast MAC address (33-33-FF-33-33-33) with its Ethernet adapter (derived from its IPv6 Solicited-Node multicast address (FF02::1:FF33:3333)), receives and processes the Neighbor Solicitation message. Host 3 updates its Neighbor Cache based on the source IPv6 address of the Neighbor Solicitation message (FE80::2AA:FF:FE11:1111) and the Link-Layer address in the Source Link-Layer Address Option (00-AA-00–11-11-11).

3. Next, the target host, Host 3, sends a unicast Neighbor Advertisement directly to the sender of the Neighbor Solicitation message, Host 1. This Neighbor Advertisement message includes the Target Link-Layer Address Option containing the Link-Layer address of Host 3 (00-AA-00–33-33-33), corresponding to Host 3's IPv6 Link-Local address FE80::2AA:FF:FE33:3333.

4. After receiving the Neighbor Advertisement from Host 3, Host 1 updates its cache with an entry for Host 3 based on the information in the Target Link-Layer Address Option. At this point, Host 1 (the sending host) and Host 3 (the target host) can send unicast IPv6 traffic to each other.

4.5.1.2 Forwarding of Neighbor Solicitation Messages in the Presence of IPv6 MLD Snooping in Layer 2 Switches

In some cases, the IPv6 nodes in Figures 4.11 and 4.12 may be connected through Layer 2 devices that support IPv6 MLD Snooping, which is similar to the IPv4 Internet Group Management Protocol (IGMP) Snooping described in **[AWEBKMULT]**. The following observation can be made depending on whether the intervening Layer 2 network connecting the devices in Figures 4.11 and 4.12 supports MLD Snooping.

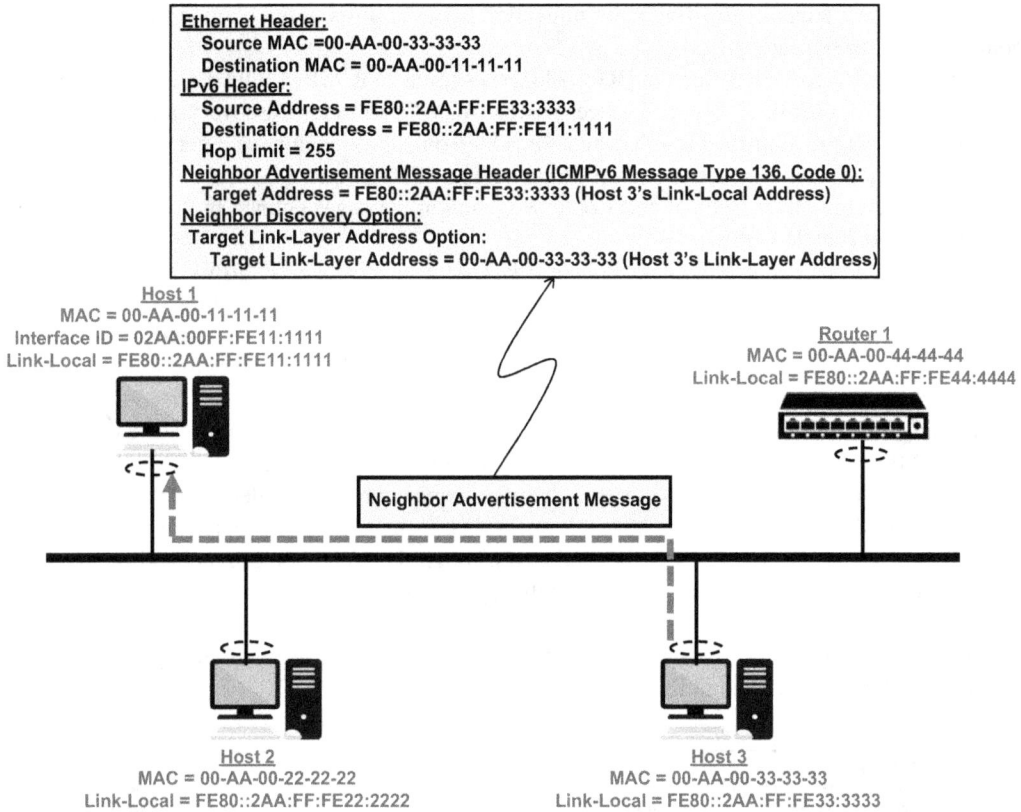

FIGURE 4.12 Responding with unicast Neighbor Advertisement message for Address Resolution.

In Figure 4.11, when Host 1 transmits a Neighbor Solicitation message on the link, two possible scenarios exist depending on whether the intervening Layer 2 network supports IPv6 MLD Snooping:

- If the Layer 2 switches on the link support MLD Snooping, they will determine that only Host 3 has subscribed to the IPv6 Solicited-Node multicast group (FF02::1:FF33:3333), enabling them to forward the Ethernet frame carrying the Neighbor Solicitation message only to Host 3.
- If the Layer 2 switches on the link are not running MLD Snooping, they will broadcast the Ethernet frame to all nodes on the link, similar to how ARP frames are sent in IPv4. However, even with the Ethernet frame being broadcast, only Host 3 will accept and process it because only Host 3 has subscribed to the IPv6 Solicited-Node multicast group (FF02::1:FF33:3333). All other nodes on the link that receive the Ethernet frame containing the Neighbor Solicitation message will discard it, as they are not listening to the Solicited-Node address FF02::1:FF33:3333.

4.5.2 IPv6 Router Discovery

Communication between IP hosts on different network segments (i.e., IP subnets/VLANs) goes through an IP router. Router Discovery in both IPv4 and IPv6 is the process by which IP hosts discover the set of IP routers attached to the local link/subnet. For an IP host to communicate with another host outside the local network segment, it must first discover the IP routers attached to its local segment. For network segments based on Ethernet technologies, an IP subnet or VLAN is a

Layer 2 broadcast domain, allowing communication between hosts in the domain to occur without going through an IP router.

IPv6 Router Discovery (defined in **[RFC4861]**) is similar to ICMPv4 Router Discovery for IPv4 (defined in **[RFC1256]**). A key difference between ICMPv4 Router Discovery and IPv6 Router Discovery is the mechanism through which IP nodes on a link change or determine the default router when the current one becomes unavailable. The IPv6 Router Discovery function is based on ICMPv6 Router Advertisement and Router Solicitation messages defined in the IPv6 Neighbor Discovery protocol **[RFC4861]**.

In ICMPv4 Router Discovery, the Router Advertisement message (ICMPv4 Message Type 9, Code 0) includes an (Advertisement) Lifetime field that indicates the maximum time (in seconds) that an IPv4 router's addresses may be considered valid (i.e., available) after the router sends its last Router Advertisement message; the IPv4 router's addresses are considered invalid after the Lifetime. In the worst case, a router on the link may become unavailable, and hosts on the link will not attempt to discover a new default router until the Lifetime in the ICMPv4 Router Advertisement message has elapsed.

The ICMPv6 Router Advertisement message used in IPv6 has a Router Lifetime field that indicates the length of time (in seconds) that the advertising router can be considered a default router (see Figure 4.2, ICMPv6 Message Type 134). However, if the current default router becomes unavailable, IPv6 hosts on the link detect this condition through the Neighbor Unreachability Detection function (discussed below), rather than through the Router Lifetime field in the ICMPv6 Router Advertisement message. Because the Neighbor Unreachability Detection function allows hosts to determine that an attached router is no longer reachable, hosts can immediately choose a new default router from their Default Router List.

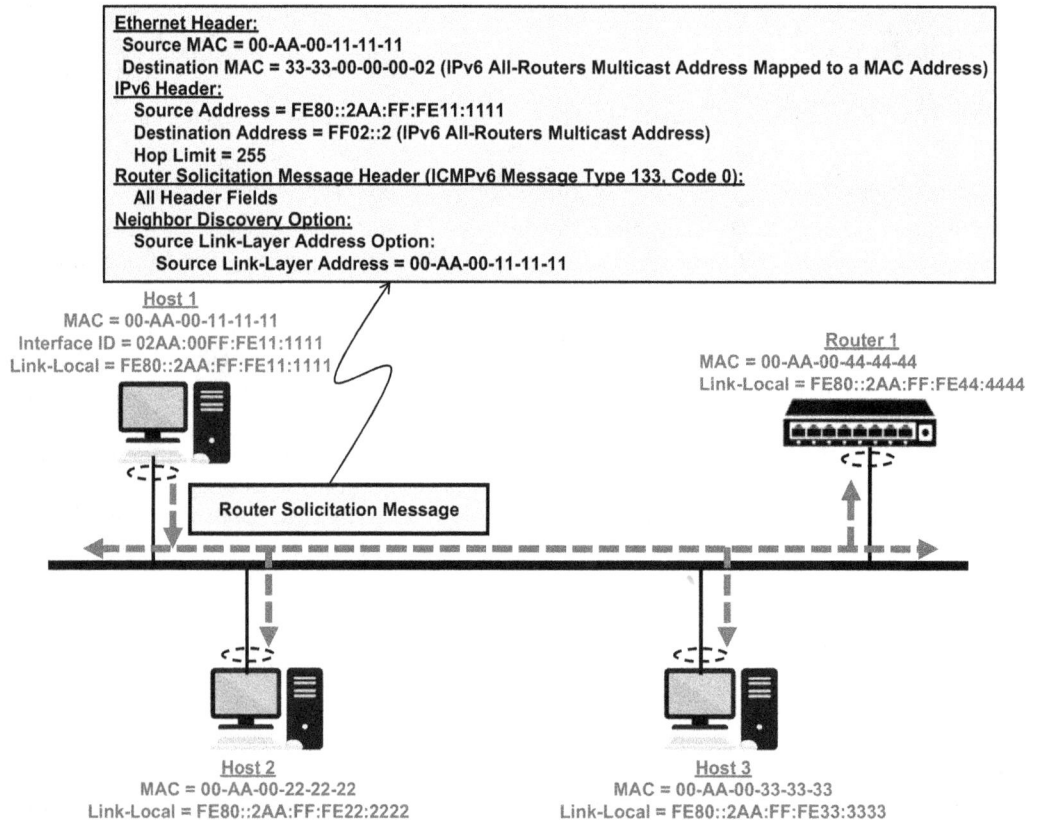

FIGURE 4.13   Sending IPv6 Router Solicitation message for Router Discovery.

IPv6 routers on a link periodically multicast (i.e., unsolicited) Router Advertisement messages, announcing their availability. IPv6 hosts on the link listen for these advertisement messages to learn IPv6 address prefixes for autoconfiguration and to discover the Link-Local addresses of the neighboring routers. When an IPv6 host on the link starts up, it multicasts a Router Solicitation message to request immediate transmission of Router Advertisement messages. These router discovery messages do not constitute routing protocol messages and are not exchanged between IPv6 routers. They only enable IPv6 hosts on a link to discover the existence of IPv6 routers attached to the link, but are not used by routers to determine how best to reach a particular destination.

In addition to providing IPv6 hosts on a link with the mechanism they require for configuring a default router, IPv6 Router Discovery also enables hosts to configure the following:

- The default value to be used in the Hop Limit field in the IPv6 header of packets sent by the hosts.
- An indication of whether the hosts should use SLAAC with Stateless DHCPv6 or Stateful DHCPv6 for obtaining IPv6 addresses and other configuration parameters.
- The timer values (i.e., Router Lifetime, Reachable Time, Retransmission Timer included in Router Advertisement messages, Figure 4.2) used in IPv6 node reachability detection and the retransmission of ICMPv6 Neighbor Solicitation messages.
- The list of IPv6 prefixes defined for the local link, with each network prefix containing both the IPv6 prefix and its Valid and Preferred Lifetimes. If the M Flag in the Router Advertisement message indicates that Stateless DHCPv6 should be used (M=0), the host uses the advertised network prefix combined with the interface identifier (ID) to create a stateless IPv6 address configuration for the receiving interface (i.e., the host uses SLAAC). Each IPv6 prefix provided also defines the range of IPv6 addresses for hosts on the local link.
- The MTU (included in the MTU Option) for the local link.

The IPv6 Router Discovery process can be summarized as follows:

- IPv6 routers (Router 1 in Figures 4.13 and 4.14) periodically transmit Router Advertisement messages on the local link, advertising their presence as IPv6 routers. These advertisements also provide configuration parameters to attached IPv6 hosts, such as default Hop Limit, link MTU, and IPv6 prefixes. These periodic (unsolicited) Router Advertisement messages are sent to the IPv6 All-Nodes multicast address (FF02::1).
- Active IPv6 hosts on the local link use the information contained in received Router Advertisement messages to maintain their Default Router Lists, IPv6 Prefix Lists, and other configuration parameters.
- An IPv6 host (Host 1) that is starting up on the link transmits a Router Solicitation message to the IPv6 All-Routers multicast address (FF02::2) with link-local scope (see Figure 4.13).
- Upon receipt of the Router Solicitation message, each router on the local link (Router 1) responds with a Router Advertisement message to the IPv6 node that sent the Router Solicitation message, Host 1 (Figure 4.14). The destination address of the Router Advertisement message may also be the IPv6 All-Nodes multicast address (FF02::1).
- The sending IPv6 node (Host 1) receives the Router Advertisement messages and uses the information contained in them to build its Default Router and IPv6 Prefix Lists and to set other configuration parameters.

4.5.3 IPv6 Duplicate Address Detection

After an IPv6 host has autoconfigured a tentative IPv6 address on an interface (Link-Local or Global unicast address), it must use the IPv6 Duplicate Address Detection function [RFC4862] to ensure that the address is unique and not used by any other node on the local link. Although the

```
Ethernet Header:
  Source MAC = 00-AA-00-44-44-44
  Destination MAC = 33-33-00-00-00-01 (IPv6 All-Nodes Multicast Address Mapped to a MAC Address)
IPv6 Header:
  Source Address = FE80::2AA:FF:FE44:4444
  Destination Address = FF02::1 (IPv6 All-Nodes Multicast Address)
  Hop Limit = 255
Router Advertisement Message Header (ICMPv6 Message Type 134, Code 0):
  All Header Fields
Neighbor Discovery Options:
  Source Link-Layer Address Option:
    Source Link-Layer Address = 00-AA-00-44-44-44
  MTU Option:
    MTU = 1500
  Prefix Information Option:
    Prefix Length = 64
    Prefix = 2001:1244:A:B:: (All On-link Prefixes (Except the Link-Local Prefix))
```

Host 1
MAC = 00-AA-00-11-11-11
Interface ID = 02AA:00FF:FE11:1111
Link-Local = FE80::2AA:FF:FE11:1111

Router 1
MAC = 00-AA-00-44-44-44
Link-Local = FE80::2AA:FF:FE44:4444

Router Advertisement Message

Host 2
MAC = 00-AA-00-22-22-22
Link-Local = FE80::2AA:FF:FE22:2222

Host 3
MAC = 00-AA-00-33-33-33
Link-Local = FE80::2AA:FF:FE33:3333

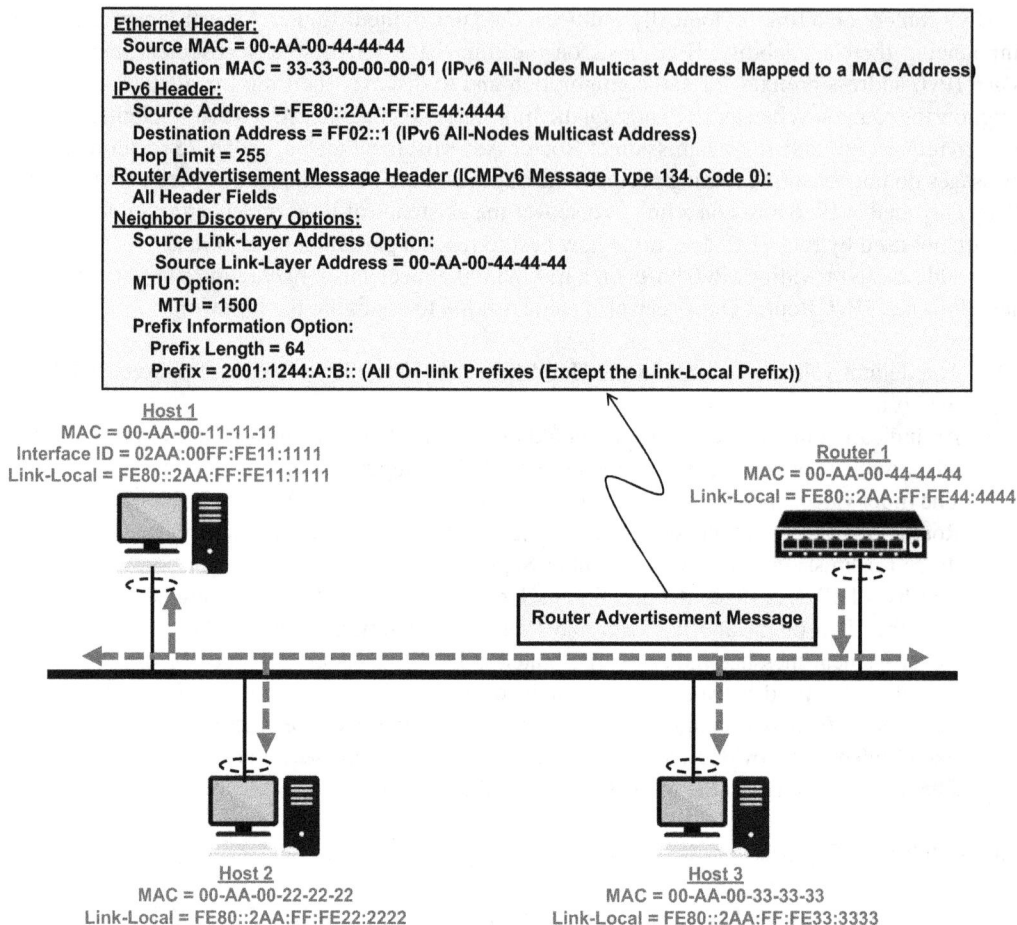

FIGURE 4.14   Responding with IPv6 Router Advertisement message for Router Discovery.

chances of another node using the exact same address are remote, performing Duplicate Address Detection is recommended. This process allows an IPv6 host to verify the ownership of an IPv6 unicast address after configuration.

Configuring an IPv6 address based on a globally unique interface ID (such as a 48-bit or 64-bit MAC address/identifier) significantly reduces the chances of address conflicts. Additionally, configuring an IPv6 Global Unicast address via a Stateful DHCPv6 Server makes the Duplicate Address Detection process largely unnecessary since the DHCPv6 Server maintains the state of each IPv6 address assigned to hosts. However, the use of Duplicate Address Detection is still recommended for the reasons presented below.

Note that duplicate IPv6 addresses on a link can occur during manual IPv6 address configuration and stateless IPv6 address autoconfiguration, particularly when no special measures are taken to avoid assigning the same interface ID (used in IPv6 unicast addresses, such as Link-Local and Global Unicast addresses) to multiple nodes. Duplicate Address Detection is particularly necessary if IPv6 addresses are autoconfigured. An IPv6 unicast address for an interface is considered a tentative address when it has not yet been verified by Duplicate Address Detection. *IPv6 Duplicate Address Detection is similar to Gratuitous ARP in IPv4* **[RFC5227]** (**see the IPv4 Gratuitous ARP discussion in Appendix D**).

It is important to note that only IPv6 hosts (and not routers) perform Duplicate Address Detection during the IPv6 configuration process. Routers are typically manually (statically) configured as part of the overall network IP addressing plan. However, IPv6 routers may choose to generate IPv6 Link-Local addresses using the IPv6 Stateless Autoconfiguration mechanism. *Reference [RFC4862] recommends the use of the IPv6 Duplicate Address Detection function on all IPv6 unicast addresses, whether manually configured, obtained via IPv6 stateless autoconfiguration, or assigned through DHCPv6, to ensure that all addresses are unique on a given link before they are assigned to interfaces.* IPv6 nodes do not perform Duplicate Address Detection on IPv6 Anycast addresses.

During stateless address assignment, IPv6 nodes are responsible for resolving any duplicate address conflicts using the following procedure:

1. Generate a tentative IPv6 unicast address using a specified interface ID.
2. Run the Duplicate Address Detection function.
3. If the generated tentative IPv6 address is in use, attempt to generate another one using an alternative interface ID (e.g., a device serial number, a node-specific token, or a randomly generated interface ID, if supplied by system management), and run the Duplicate Address Detection function again. This process may be repeated several times (using interface IDs supplied by system management) until a unique address is obtained, or until autoconfiguration fails, at which point the address may be manually configured (if system management permits or indicates this).

IPv6 nodes use an IPv6 Solicited-Node multicast address (as the IPv6 destination) when performing Duplicate Address Detection. After configuring an IPv6 address on an interface, an IPv6 node joins the multicast group identified by the Solicited-Node multicast address FF02::1:FFxx:xxxx, where xx:xxxx represent the last six hexadecimal values in the IPv6 unicast address to be verified. Every IPv6 node joins the auto-generated Solicited-Node multicast address for each configured unicast

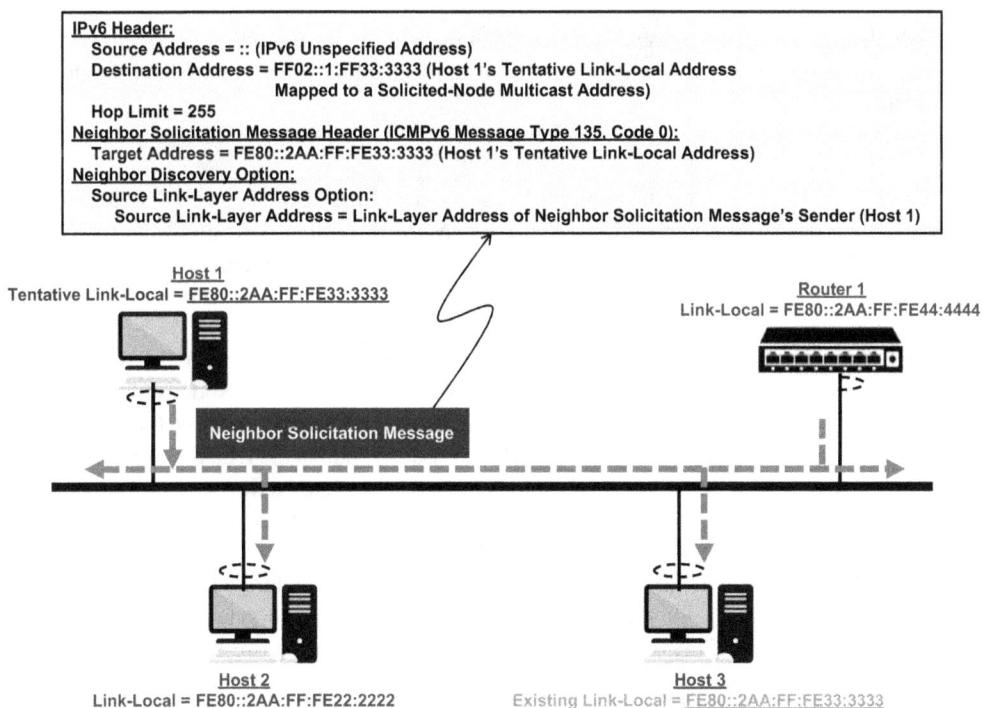

FIGURE 4.15   IPv6 Duplicate Address Detection: sending Neighbor Solicitation message.

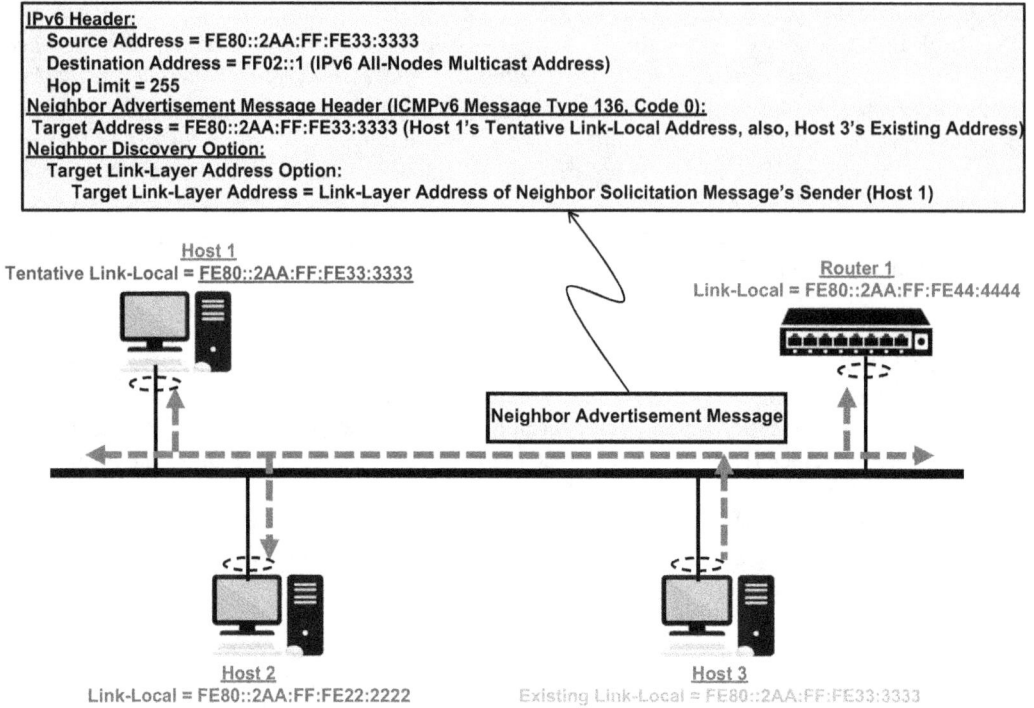

FIGURE 4.16 IPv6 Duplicate Address Detection: responding with Neighbor Advertisement message if a duplicate address exists.

address, whether Link-Local or Global Unicast. Each node joins the respective Solicited-Node multicast group upon configuring a new (tentative) IPv6 unicast address and then performs Duplicate Address Detection.

4.5.3.1 Performing IPv6 Duplicate Address Detection

In Figure 4.15, IPv6 Host 1 creates the tentative Link-Local address FE80::2AA:FF:FE33:3333 on an interface and then joins the corresponding IPv6 Solicited-Node multicast group FF02::1:FF33:3333 (the last 6 hexadecimal values xx:xxxx are 33:3333). We assume here that Host 1 created this tentative IPv6 address using an interface ID through other means and not based on one generated from a globally unique identifier such as an IEEE-assigned MAC address.

To check for any duplicate addresses on the link, Host 1 sends an ICMPv6 Neighbor Solicitation message with the destination address set to the IPv6 Solicited-Node multicast address FF02::1:FF33:3333 and the source address set to the IPv6 Unspecified address (::), as shown in Figure 4.15. The Target Address field of this ICMPv6 message contains the tentative IPv6 Link-Local address FE80::2AA:FF:FE33:3333. Host 1 then transmits this message on the local link to verify that the prospective IPv6 address is not already being used by another IPv6 node on the link. After verifying uniqueness, Host 1 can assign the tentative Link-Local address to the transmitting interface.

If another IPv6 host on the local link is using the same Link-Local address FE80::2AA:FF:FE33:3333, it will also be listening for messages on the corresponding auto-generated Solicited-Node multicast group FF02::1:FF33:3333. Only IPv6 nodes on the link that are listening to this exact auto-generated Solicited-Node multicast group will accept and process the Neighbor Solicitation message; all other nodes will discard it. If any node on the link is using an IPv6 address that has the same last 6 hexadecimal digits (33:3333), it will examine the Neighbor Solicitation message and check if the address in the message's Target Address field (FE80::2AA:FF:FE33:3333) matches any of its own IPv6 addresses. If a match is found, the IPv6 host (Host 3) will reply with a Neighbor Advertisement message with the Target Address field set to this IPv6 address (FE80::2AA:FF:FE33:3333), indicating that the address is already in use (see Figure 4.16). If Host 1 receives no replies, it will conclude that the tentative IPv6 address (FE80::2AA:FF:FE33:3333) is unique and available for use and will proceed to assign it to the transmitting interface.

The specific behavior of Host 3 upon receiving the Neighbor Solicitation message may be one of the following (see Section 4.10.4 for details):

- If FE80::2AA:FF:FE33:3333 is a tentative address on Host 3, it will not use this address on its interface and will not respond with a Neighbor Advertisement message.
- If FE80::2AA:FF:FE33:3333 is a tentative address on Host 3 (meaning that Host 3 is also attempting to use the same address), it may continue verifying this address for its interface by retransmitting its own Neighbor Solicitation messages and will not respond with a Neighbor Advertisement message.
  - The number of transmissions or retransmissions of the Neighbor Solicitation message, as well as the delay between consecutive solicitations, are specific to the link.
    In general, Host 3 will not use this address and will not respond to the Neighbor Solicitation message, as stated in the first bullet.
- If FE80::2AA:FF:FE33:3333 is in use by Host 3, it will respond with a Neighbor Advertisement message addressed to the IPv6 All-Nodes multicast address (FF02::1), with the Target Address set to FE80::2AA:FF:FE33:3333. This allows Host 1 to mark the duplicate tentative address FE80::2AA:FF:FE33:3333 as an address that cannot be used.

If an IPv6 node determines that the tentative IPv6 Link-Local address for an interface is not unique, it stops the address autoconfiguration process. At that point, the Link-Local address must be manually configured on the interface. To simplify the address configuration process, an alternate interface ID can be supplied to override the default interface ID. This allows the IPv6 host to resume the autoconfiguration process using the new, presumably unique, interface ID. When the IPv6 host determines that the tentative Link-Local address is unique, it assigns the address to the transmitting interface. At this point, the IPv6 host has IPv6-level connectivity with other IPv6 nodes on the same link.

Note that IPv6 address autoconfiguration is performed only by IPv6 hosts. An IPv6 node must always run the Duplicate Address Detection algorithm before assigning a tentative address to an interface. IPv6 address autoconfiguration applies only to IPv6 hosts and not to routers. *Because the address autoconfiguration information that IPv6 hosts use is advertised by IPv6 routers, address configuration on routers must be done through other* means. Routers may autogenerate Link-Local addresses just like IPv6 hosts, but IPv6 Global Unicast prefixes on routers are usually manually configured, as such prefixes are allocated as part of the IPv6 addressing plan of a network. Moreover, IPv6 routers are expected to successfully pass the Duplicate Address Detection process on all IPv6 addresses before assigning them to interfaces.

4.5.4 IPv6 Redirect Function

IPv6 routers on a link use the IPv6 Redirect function to inform hosts on the same link of a better first-hop neighboring router to which traffic for a specific IPv6 destination should be sent **[RFC4861]**. IPv6 routers use the IPv6 Redirect function primarily for the following purposes:

- An IPv6 router informs an IPv6 host on a link of the IPv6 address of a local router that is "closer" to a specific destination (i.e., the best first-hop router). The term "closer" refers to the best routing metric used to reach that destination from the local network segment. This redirect condition can occur when multiple routers exist on the link to a destination, and the source host chooses a default router that is not the best first-hop to reach that destination.

- A router informs an IPv6 host on a link that the destination is also a neighboring node (i.e., it is on the same link as the source host). This redirect condition can occur when the IPv6 Prefix List of the source host does not include the IPv6 prefix of the destination (which is also on the same link). Because the source host cannot match the destination address with an IPv6 prefix in its Prefix List, it forwards the IPv6 packet to its default router, which then causes the packet redirection to take place.

The IPv6 Redirect process can be described by the following steps (Figures 4.17 and 4.18):

1. The source host (Host 1) sends a unicast IPv6 packet to its default router (Router 1).
2. The default router (Router 1) processes the IPv6 packet and detects that the IPv6 address of the originating host (Host 1) is a neighboring node. Additionally, the default router notices that both the originating host (Host 1) and the next-hop (which can be either an on-link destination or the best first-hop router) are on the same link.
3. The default router (Router 1) forwards the IPv6 packet to the appropriate next-hop address, which may be either an on-link destination or the best first-hop router.
4. The default router (Router 1) sends a Redirect message to the source host (Host 1). The Target Address field of the Redirect message contains the next-hop address of the node to which the source host (Host 1) should send IPv6 packets addressed to the destination.
5. For IPv6 packets redirected to a neighboring host (Host 2 in Figure 4.17), the Target Address field is set to the destination IPv6 address of the original IPv6 packet that triggered the redirection process (in this case, the address of Host 2). For IPv6 packets redirected to a best first-hop router (Router 2 in Figure 4.18), the Target Address field is set to the IPv6 Link-Local address of the first-hop router.

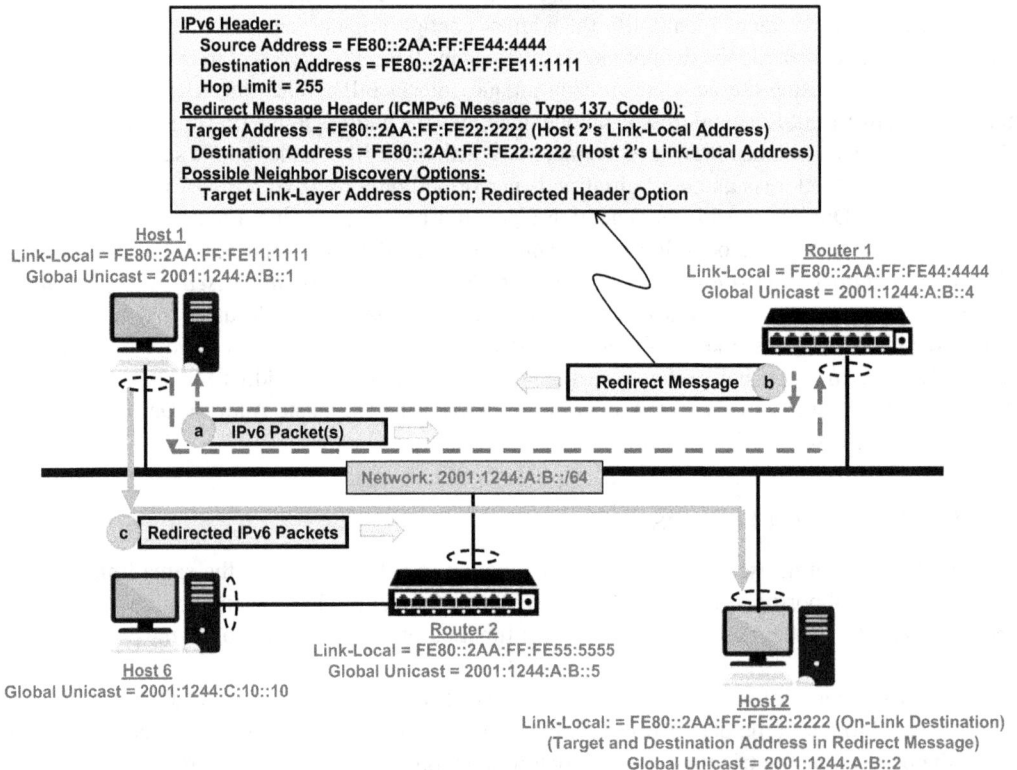

FIGURE 4.17   IPv6 packet redirection: On-link destinations.

6. The Redirect message in both the on-link and off-link destination cases includes the Redirected Header Option. This message may also include the Target Link-Layer Address Option.

7. Upon receiving the Redirect message, the source host (Host 1) uses the address in the Target Address field to update the destination IPv6 address entry in its Destination Cache. If the Redirect message includes the Target Link-Layer Address Option, the information in this Option is used to create or update the corresponding Link-Layer address entry in the source host's Neighbor Cache.

The Destination Cache [RFC4861], a (conceptual) data structure maintained by an IPv6 node on a link (in addition to the Neighbor Cache), consists of a set of entries about IPv6 destinations to which IPv6 traffic was recently sent. The Destination Cache includes both on-link and off-link IPv6 destinations and provides a level of indirection into the Neighbor Cache also maintained by an IPv6 node. The entries of the Destination Cache map a destination IPv6 address to the IPv6 address of the next-hop neighbor.

An IPv6 node updates its Destination Cache with information learned from ICMPv6 Redirect messages. An IPv6 implementation may choose to store additional information not directly related to IPv6 Neighbor Discovery in its Destination Cache entries, such as the Path MTU associated with links and the round-trip timers maintained by Transport Layer protocols.

Only the first router on the path between the source host and the packet's destination (usually the default router) sends ICMPv6 Redirect messages, and (like ICMPv6 error messages) these Redirect messages are rate limited. IPv6 hosts never send ICMPv6 Redirect messages, and IPv6 routers never update their routing tables based on the information contained in any received Redirect message.

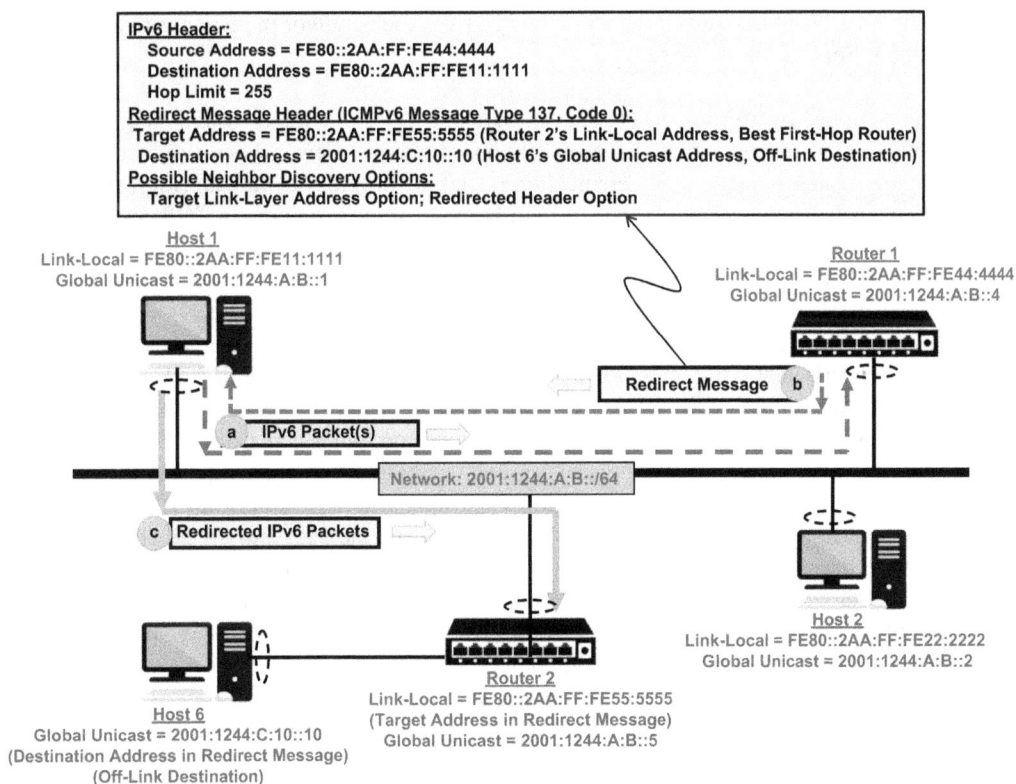

FIGURE 4.18 IPv6 packet redirection: Off-link destinations.

4.5.5   IPv6 Neighbor Unreachability Detection

Communication between two IPv6 nodes on the same link may fail at any time for various reasons (e.g., hardware failure, cable damage, hot-swapping of an interface card, etc.). However, failure of the destination node itself means total communication failure with that node. If, on the other hand, the path to the destination node fails, communication recovery may be possible. Thus, IPv6 Neighbor Discovery allows an IPv6 node to actively track the reachability "state" of other nodes on the same link (neighbors) to which it is sending or may send IPv6 packets.

IPv6 nodes on the same link (host-to-host, host-to-router, and router-to-host) use Neighbor Unreachability Detection. Routers (router-to-router) may also use Neighbor Unreachability Detection, but this is not usually necessary if an equivalent mechanism is available; for example, routers usually run routing protocols and do not need this mechanism. An IPv6 node performs Neighbor Unreachability Detection only for neighbors to which it is sending IPv6 unicast packets; it is not used when the node is sending IPv6 packets to multicast addresses.

An IPv6 node considers another node on the same link (neighbor) to be reachable if it has recently sent IPv6 packets to the neighbor and has received confirmation that those packets were received by the neighbor's IP layer. An IPv6 node uses the IPv6 Neighbor Unreachability Detection function to determine if a neighbor (on the same link) has failed or if the data forwarding path to the neighbor has failed. To make this determination, the node requires positive confirmation that the IPv6 packets it sends to the neighbor are actually being delivered and processed properly by the neighbor's IP layer.

Neighbor Unreachability Detection uses two sources of neighbor reachability confirmation:

1. Indications from upper-layer protocols (e.g., TCP) that a connection is making progress in data forwarding (e.g., TCP Acknowledgments), or
2. Receipt of a Neighbor Advertisement message from the neighbor in response to a unicast Neighbor Solicitation message.

In some cases, upper-layer protocols (such as those using TCP) provide a positive neighbor reachability confirmation through data delivery acknowledgments. New acknowledgments recently received by the sender indicate that a connection is making progress in data delivery; that is, data that was previously sent is acknowledged to have been delivered correctly. In TCP, for example, a node receiving a new acknowledgment from the neighbor indicates that data it previously sent has reached the neighbor. Similarly, the receipt of new (non-duplicate) data from the neighbor indicates that earlier acknowledgments the node sent to the neighbor are being delivered.

Additionally, if the IPv6 packets that a node sends are reaching a neighbor, they must also be reaching the sender's next-hop router, which is also a neighbor on the same link. In this case, such progress in data forwarding confirms that the next-hop router is reachable. For destinations that are off-link, progress in data forwarding implies that the first-hop router is reachable. When available, the sending IPv6 node should use the upper-layer confirmation information.

In the absence of such positive confirmation from upper-layer protocols, an IPv6 node sends unicast Neighbor Solicitation messages (which serve as probe messages) to the neighbor to solicit Neighbor Advertisement messages as neighbor reachability confirmation. To reduce unnecessary link traffic, the source node transmits these unicast probe messages only to the neighbors (via unicast transmission) to which the node is actively sending IPv6 packets; multicast Neighbor Solicitation messages are not considered probes for neighbor reachability confirmation.

4.5.5.1   Reachability in IP Routing

Reachability in IP routing is generally defined as the ability to deliver an IP packet to its destination in the IP internetwork. Reachability in the context of IPv6 Neighbor Discovery **[RFC4861]** is defined as the ability to send an IPv6 packet to a neighboring node on a link and have the IPv6 layer of that neighboring node receive and process that IPv6 packet. This definition of reachability does not require delivery to a remote node across a router; it applies only to a neighboring host or router. When an IP node sends a packet to an IP router attached to the local link that is reachable, the IP packet is delivered to the router's IPv6 layer, which processes and then forwards the packet to the next-hop; note that the packet's destination may also be a local entity on the router itself, referred to as local delivery. When an IPv6 node sends a packet to a neighboring IPv6 host, the packet is delivered to the host's IPv6 layer.

When an IPv6 node on a link detects that a neighbor on the link has become unreachable, it identifies this condition and attempts to correct it. As stated above, to enable an IPv6 node to determine whether a neighbor is reachable or not, IPv6 relies on either upper-layer protocols (like TCP) that indicate the progress of the communication or on the receipt of an ICMPv6 Neighbor Advertisement message that has been sent in response to a received unicast Neighbor Solicitation message.

For TCP traffic, the progress of communication with a destination is indicated when a node receives new data or acknowledgment segments for previously sent data. For UDP traffic, there is no indication of communication progress at the UDP layer (though it might be present in upper layers). Reachability information may not be readily available from upper-layer protocols, for example, in UDP-based protocols and when routers are forwarding IPv6 packets to hosts. In the absence of reachability indications, an IPv6 node actively probes the neighbor by sending unicast Neighbor Solicitation messages to the (next-hop) neighbor to monitor its ongoing reachability.

4.5.5.2　Proof of Reachability in IPv6 Neighbor Unreachability Detection: What Constitutes Reachability Confirmation

IPv6 Neighbor Discovery considers proof of reachability to occur only when a node receives a (solicited) Neighbor Advertisement message from the neighboring node in response to a sent unicast Neighbor Solicitation message (a reachability probe). An IPv6 node sends a solicited Neighbor Advertisement message (with the S (Solicited) Flag set to 1, see Figure 4.4) only in response to a Neighbor Solicitation message. IPv6 Neighbor Discovery does not consider the receipt of *unsolicited* Neighbor Advertisement (i.e., with the S Flag set to 0) or Router Advertisement messages as proof of neighbor reachability; these messages are not considered as reachability confirmation.

4.5.5.2.1　Symmetric versus Asymmetric Reachability and Proof of Reachability

The Neighbor Unreachability Detection in IPv6 Neighbor Discovery detects *symmetric reachability*. In symmetric reachability, IPv6 packets must be able to travel to and from the desired source and destination neighboring node. In this case, the (symmetric) path between the neighboring nodes is confirmed when a unicast Neighbor Solicitation message is sent and a solicited Neighbor Advertisement message is received. However, when an unsolicited Neighbor Advertisement or Router Advertisement message is sent, only the path from the sender to the message receiver is confirmed.

Receipt of unsolicited Neighbor Advertisement messages (with the S Flag set to 0) only confirms that the one-way path from the sender to the receiver is functioning. This second type of neighbor reachability is called *asymmetric reachability*. Note that receipt of a solicited Neighbor Advertisement message indicates that both directions are functional (*symmetric reachability*). This means the unicast Neighbor Solicitation message must have reached the neighbor, prompting it to generate a solicited Neighbor Advertisement message.

For a specific local destination node on a link, only the node that sent a unicast Neighbor Solicitation message and receives a Neighbor Advertisement message can confirm the reachability of the neighboring node. The IPv6 node that sent the Neighbor Advertisement message receives no confirmation that this message has reached the intended neighboring IPv6 node. *Thus, two neighboring nodes on the same link can determine each other's reachability when each node separately exchanges Neighbor Solicitation and Neighbor Advertisement messages.*

However, *from the perspective of an IPv6 node using the Neighbor Unreachability Detection algorithm, only the reachability of the neighbor at the other end of the forward path is of interest to that node; the reachability of the reverse path is of interest only to the neighbor.* Therefore, an IPv6 node using the Neighbor Unreachability Detection algorithm is only required to keep track of the reachability of the forward path to a neighbor from its perspective, not the neighbor's perspective.

The receipt of a Neighbor Advertisement message from the neighbor (after sending a unicast Neighbor Solicitation message) indicates that the path from the neighbor (i.e., the reverse path) is also functioning. The sender of the Neighbor Advertisement message (the neighbor) has no direct way of knowing that the message it sent actually reached the intended receiver, but this is not relevant to the receiver when it is performing Neighbor Unreachability Detection (only the reachability of the forward path to the sender of the Neighbor Advertisement message is relevant).

4.5.5.2.2 Dead Gateway Detection

The IPv6 host requirements [RFC4861] specify some possible algorithms for *dead gateway detection*, one of which is the Neighbor Unreachability Detection algorithm. The Neighbor Unreachability Detection function allows IPv6 hosts on a link to perform dead default gateway detection more efficiently. The receipt of a solicited Neighbor Advertisement message serves as neighbor reachability confirmation, since a neighbor sends a Neighbor Advertisement message (with the S Flag set to 1) only in response to a unicast Neighbor Solicitation message.

Neighbor Unreachability Detection can detect asymmetric reachability between neighbors on a link (it is able to detect the absence of symmetric reachability). An IPv6 node, after running the Neighbor Unreachability Detection, avoids all paths to a neighbor without symmetric reachability. The Neighbor Unreachability Detection algorithm will typically discover all such half-connectivity paths, allowing the IPv6 node to avoid using those paths.

4.5.5.3 Advantages of IPv6 Neighbor Unreachability Detection

The IPv6 Neighbor Unreachability Detection function improves IPv6 packet delivery even when routers on the link are failing. Additionally, for links that are partially failing or partitioned, this capability enhances the delivery of IPv6 packets over such links. Using Neighbor Unreachability Detection, IPv6 nodes can detect half-link failures, allowing them to avoid sending IPv6 traffic to neighbors when there is no two-way connectivity. This function also improves IPv6 packet delivery to nodes that have changed their Link-Local addresses. For example, a mobile IPv6 node can move off-link and still maintain connectivity with its Home Link because its Neighbor Cache does not become stale. There is no equivalent method for Neighbor Unreachability Detection in IPv4.

An IPv6 node determines the reachability of a neighboring node by monitoring the state of the entry for that node in the Neighbor Cache. The states of a Neighbor Cache entry are described in Table 4.5 and Figure 4.19.

4.6 IPv6 NEIGHBOR CACHE

The IPv6 Neighbor Cache on an IPv6 node maintains information for each neighbor on the link, including the IPv6 address and its corresponding Link-Layer address [RFC4861]. This cache is equivalent to the ARP Cache in IPv4. The IPv6 Neighbor Unreachability Detection process maintains the information contained in the Neighbor Cache and tracks the states of each entry.

An entry in the Neighbor Cache can be in one of five states (called *neighbor discovery reachability states*): INCOMPLETE, REACHABLE, STALE, DELAY, and PROBE (see Table 4.5 and Figure 4.19). Each entry has a well-defined state at any given time. An IPv6 host can send IPv6 packets to a destination in all Neighbor Cache entry states, except the INCOMPLETE state or when there is no corresponding Neighbor Cache entry. In the INCOMPLETE state, the node queues data packets pending completion of the IPv6 Address Resolution process.

Figure 4.19 shows the state diagram of an entry in the Neighbor Cache of an IPv6 node. If the unreachable neighboring node is a router, the originating IPv6 host selects another local IPv6 router from its Default Router List and performs both Address Resolution (as described above) and Neighbor Unreachability Detection on that router.

TABLE 4.5

Neighbor Cache Entry States

State	Description
INCOMPLETE	In this state, address resolution is in progress and the Link-Layer address of the neighbor has not yet been determined.
REACHABLE	In this state, the neighbor is known to have been reachable recently (within the last tens of seconds).
STALE	In this state, the neighbor is no longer known to be reachable, but until traffic is sent to the neighbor, the local node should make no attempt to verify its reachability.
DELAY	The neighbor is no longer known to be reachable, and traffic has recently been sent to the neighbor. Rather than probe (i.e., send a unicast Neighbor Solicitation message to) the neighbor immediately, the local node delays sending probes for a short while to give upper-layer protocols a chance to provide reachability confirmation.
PROBE	In this state, the neighbor is no longer known to be reachable, and the local node is sending unicast Neighbor Solicitation messages (probes) to verify its reachability.

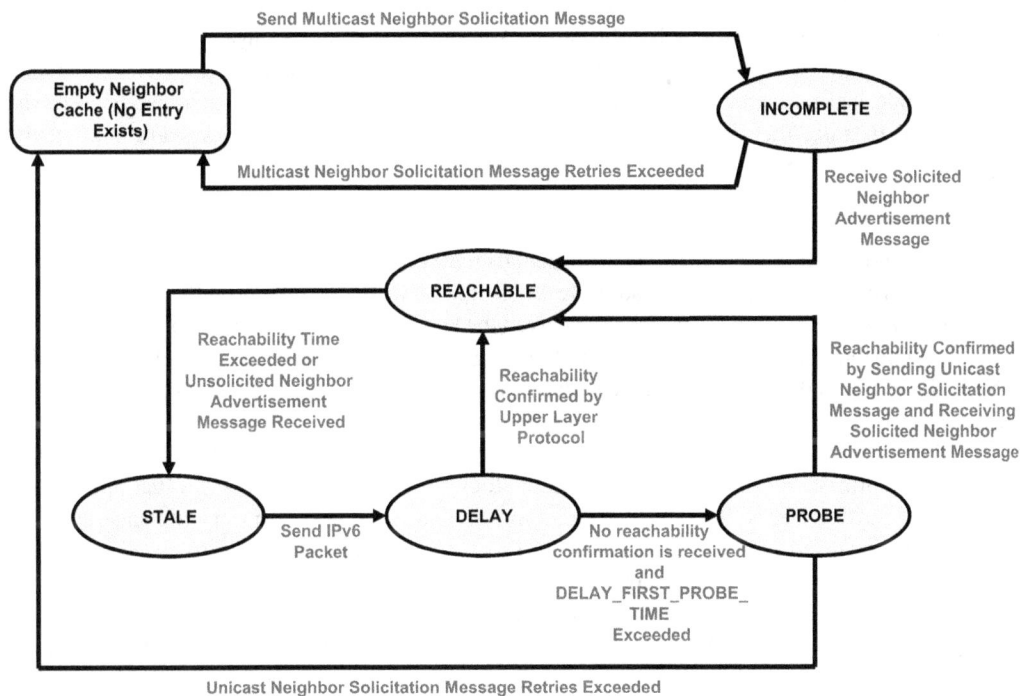

FIGURE 4.19   State diagram of an entry in the Neighbor Cache.

4.6.1 NEIGHBOR CACHE ENTRY STATES

An IPv6 node operates the Neighbor Unreachability Detection algorithm in parallel with sending IPv6 packets to a neighbor. While the node is reassessing the reachability of a neighbor, it continues sending IPv6 packets to that neighbor using the corresponding Link-Layer address in the Neighbor Cache. If the node is not sending IPv6 packets to a neighbor, it also does not send probes (which are unicast Neighbor Solicitation messages) to that neighbor. This section describes the five states of an entry in the Neighbor Cache.

4.6.1.1 INCOMPLETE State

When an IPv6 node needs to perform IPv6 Address Resolution on the IPv6 address of a node on the same link, it creates an entry in the Neighbor Cache, sets its state to INCOMPLETE, and then initiates Address Resolution. In this state, the IPv6 node is performing Address Resolution on the entry in its Neighbor Cache. Specifically, the node has sent a Neighbor Solicitation message to the IPv6 Solicited-Node multicast address of the target node but has not yet received the corresponding Neighbor Advertisement message from the target node.

If the IPv6 node determines that Address Resolution has failed, it deletes the entry from the Neighbor Cache so that subsequent IPv6 packets it sends to that neighbor will trigger the next-hop determination procedure again. Triggering next-hop determination at this point causes the IPv6 node to try alternate default routers.

4.6.1.2 REACHABLE State

In this state, the IPv6 node has received positive confirmation within the last *ReachableTime* milliseconds that the path leading to the target node (neighbor) is working correctly. When the IPv6 node has received a neighbor reachability confirmation (either through an upper-layer protocol entity indication or a solicited (unicast) Neighbor Advertisement message), it changes the entry's state in the Neighbor Cache to REACHABLE.

The only exception is that reachability confirmation from an upper-layer protocol entity has no effect on Neighbor Cache entries that are in the INCOMPLETE state (e.g., entries for which the IPv6 node has no cached Link-Layer address). While the Neighbor Cache entry is in the REACHABLE state, the IPv6 node takes no special action as IPv6 packets are sent to the neighbor.

4.6.1.3 STALE State

In this state, more than *ReachableTime* milliseconds have elapsed since the IPv6 node last received positive confirmation that the path leading to the neighbor was working correctly. The IPv6 node waits *ReachableTime* milliseconds since it received the last reachability confirmation for a neighbor, and if no confirmation is received, it changes the Neighbor Cache entry's state from REACHABLE to STALE. While in the STALE state, the IPv6 node takes no action until an IPv6 packet is sent to the neighbor.

An IPv6 node enters the STALE state upon receiving an unsolicited Neighbor Discovery message (i.e., a multicast Neighbor Advertisement or Router Advertisement message) that updates the cached Link-Layer address. Receipt of such an unsolicited Neighbor Discovery message does not confirm neighbor reachability, and entering the STALE state ensures that the IPv6 node can quickly verify neighbor reachability if the Neighbor Cache entry is actually being used. However, the IPv6 node does not verify neighbor reachability until the entry is used.

An IPv6 node places a Neighbor Cache entry in the STALE state when it receives IPv6 Neighbor Discovery messages that differ from solicited Neighbor Advertisement messages (i.e., Router Solicitations, Router Advertisements, Redirects, and unsolicited Neighbor Advertisements). These ICMPv6 messages contain the Link-Layer address of either the sender or, in the case of Redirect messages, the Link-Layer address of the target node being redirected to. However, receipt of these Link-Layer addresses (contained in the message Options) does not constitute reachability confirmation of the forward path to the message sender.

Placing a newly created Neighbor Cache entry and its known Link-Layer address in the STALE state ensures that the IPv6 node will quickly detect path failures. In addition, if a cached Link-Layer address is modified due to the IPv6 node receiving one of the unsolicited Neighbor Discovery messages mentioned above, the IPv6 node also sets the state of the corresponding entry to STALE, prompting verification that the forward path to the new Link-Layer address is functioning properly.

4.6.1.4   DELAY State

In this state, more than *ReachableTime* milliseconds have elapsed since the IPv6 node last received a positive confirmation that the path leading to the neighbor was functioning correctly, and the node sent an IPv6 packet to the neighbor within the last DELAY_FIRST_PROBE_TIME seconds. The first time the IPv6 node transmits an IPv6 packet to a neighbor whose Neighbor Cache entry is in the STALE state, the sending node changes the state to DELAY and starts a timer that is set to expire in DELAY_FIRST_PROBE_TIME seconds. If the node finds that the entry is still in the DELAY state when the timer expires, it changes the entry's state to PROBE.

Specifically, if the IPv6 node receives no neighbor reachability confirmation within DELAY_FIRST_PROBE_TIME seconds of the Neighbor Cache entry entering the DELAY state, it sends a unicast Neighbor Solicitation message to the neighbor and changes the entry's state to PROBE. If the IPv6 node receives neighbor reachability confirmation before the timer expires, it changes the entry's state to REACHABLE.

The DELAY state serves as an optimization mechanism that gives upper-layer protocols on the local IPv6 node additional time to provide neighbor reachability confirmation in cases where *ReachableTime* milliseconds have elapsed since the node received the last reachability confirmation due to a lack of recent IPv6 packets. Without this optimization mechanism, opening a TCP connection on the local IPv6 node after a pause in IPv6 traffic flow would cause the node to initiate the sending of probes (i.e., unicast Neighbor Solicitation messages) to the neighbor, even though the subsequent TCP three-way handshake mechanism would provide a neighbor reachability confirmation almost immediately.

4.6.1.5   PROBE State

In this state, the IPv6 node is actively seeking neighbor reachability confirmation by retransmitting unicast Neighbor Solicitation messages (probes) to the neighbor every *RetransTimer* milliseconds until it receives a neighbor reachability confirmation.

When a Neighbor Cache entry enters the PROBE state, the IPv6 node transmits a unicast Neighbor Solicitation message to the neighbor using the neighbor's cached Link-Layer address. While the Neighbor Cache entry remains in the PROBE state, the node retransmits unicast Neighbor Solicitation messages (probes) every *RetransTimer* milliseconds until it obtains neighbor reachability confirmation.

The IPv6 node retransmits probes even if it sends no additional IPv6 packets to the neighbor. If the node receives no response from the neighbor after waiting *RetransTimer* milliseconds after sending MAX_UNICAST_SOLICIT unicast Neighbor Solicitation messages (probes), it ceases retransmissions and deletes the Neighbor Cache entry. Sending subsequent IPv6 packets to that neighbor allows the IPv6 node to recreate the Neighbor Cache entry and perform IPv6 Address Resolution again.

4.7   IPv6 NEIGHBOR DISCOVERY PROXY

In some situations, an IPv6 router may be configured to act as a Neighbor Discovery Proxy for one or more other IPv6 nodes on a link. The router, through the Neighbor Advertisement messages it sends on a link, may indicate to nodes on the link that it is willing to accept IPv6 packets that are *not* explicitly addressed to it **[RFC4389] [RFC4861]**. For example, an IPv6 router (acting as a Neighbor Discovery Proxy) may be configured to accept IPv6 packets on behalf of a Mobile Node that is a neighbor on a particular link but has moved off-link, as discussed below (see Figure 4.20). The router, acting as a proxy, responds to IPv6 Neighbor Discovery query messages on behalf of the off-link node.

With the IPv6 Neighbor Discovery Proxy feature, a host may be configured, for example, to belong to a particular link (IPv6 subnet/VLAN) on an organization's IPv6 network, while still being able to move or roam seamlessly to other links on the network without relying on upper-layer protocol connectivity methods such as those based on or requiring WiFi login and authentication. For security, the IPv6 host may use IPSec, since IPv6 specifies IPSec as its Network Layer security mechanism. IPSec provides mechanisms for authentication and encryption of IPv6 packets to ensure secure communication between two devices. The use of IPSec does not preclude the implementation of other (upper-layer) security mechanisms when needed. The IPv6 Neighbor Discovery Proxy feature and Mobile IPv6 allow an IPv6 host to roam to a Foreign Network while still maintaining connectivity with hosts on the Home Network (see **[RFC5944]** for Mobile IPv4 and **[RFC6275]** for Mobile IPv6). Mobile IP (for IPv4 and IPv6) is discussed in detail in **Chapter 6**.

A Neighbor Discovery Proxy also enables IPv6 hosts on different network segments or broadcast domains (IPv6 subnets/VLANs) to communicate with each other as if they are on the same network segment. Another scenario where a Neighbor Discovery Proxy is needed is when intra-VLAN communication is required on a Layer 2 switch with Port Isolation. In this case, hosts on isolated Layer 2 ports (i.e., Isolated Ports in the same VLAN) can still communicate through the IPv6 Neighbor Discovery Proxy. Note that hosts on different Isolated Ports, by default, cannot communicate with each other in the absence of a router or Proxy (see the **Private VLAN and Port Isolation discussion in Appendix F**). The IPv6 Neighbor Discovery Proxy is conceptually similar to Proxy ARP in IPv4 networks (see the **IPv4 Proxy ARP discussion in Appendix E**).

The main features of the IPv6 Neighbor Discovery Proxy are as follows:

- An interface on a Neighbor Discovery Proxy responds to an IPv6 Neighbor Discovery request on behalf of an IPv6 host connected to another interface.
- An egress interface on a Neighbor Discovery Proxy modifies the source Link-Layer information in the Neighbor Discovery message with its own Link-Layer address, and updates the Link-Layer address in the Layer 2 header with its own Link-Layer address.
- The presence of an entry for a neighbor in the Neighbor Cache of an IPv6 host in the REACHABLE state verifies the neighbor's recent reachability status.
- The Neighbor Discovery Proxy uses the ICMPv6 Neighbor Solicitation and Neighbor Advertisement messages to determine the Link-Layer address of a neighbor.
- The Neighbor Discovery Proxy uses a Neighbor Solicitation message to determine the Link-Layer address of a neighboring host by sending the message to the IPv6 Solicited-Node multicast address of that host.
- The Neighbor Discovery Proxy sends a unicast Neighbor Advertisement message as a reply to a received Neighbor Solicitation message.

When an IPv6 Neighbor Discovery Proxy is set up, its configured proxy interfaces respond with proxy Neighbor Advertisement messages on behalf of IPv6 hosts located on different physical network segments when Neighbor Solicitation messages are received on those interfaces.

4.7.1 Use Case: Handling Proxy Neighbor Discovery Messages on Behalf of a Neighboring Mobile IPv6 Node That Has Moved Off-Link

An IPv6 router may be configured to accept IPv6 packets on behalf of a target address and to issue non-override Neighbor Advertisement messages. In this case, the IPv6 router accepts IPv6 packets for a target address that is unable to respond directly to Neighbor Solicitation messages (see Figure 4.20). A Neighbor Discovery Proxy can be used to handle cases where a mobile IPv6 node (Host 5) has moved off-link. A typical use case is Mobile IPv6 **[RFC6275]**, where an IPv6 Neighbor Discovery Proxy running on a Home Agent enables a Mobile Node roaming on a Foreign Network to maintain connectivity with its Home Network (see Mobile IPv6 discussion in **Chapter 6**).

In Figure 4.20, the Proxy (Router 1) must join the IPv6 Solicited-Node multicast address(es) corresponding to the IPv6 address(es) assigned to Host 5, the IPv6 node for which it is proxying. Router 1 joins this multicast group using the MLD protocol (MLDv1 **[RFC2710]** or MLDv2 **[RFC3810]**).

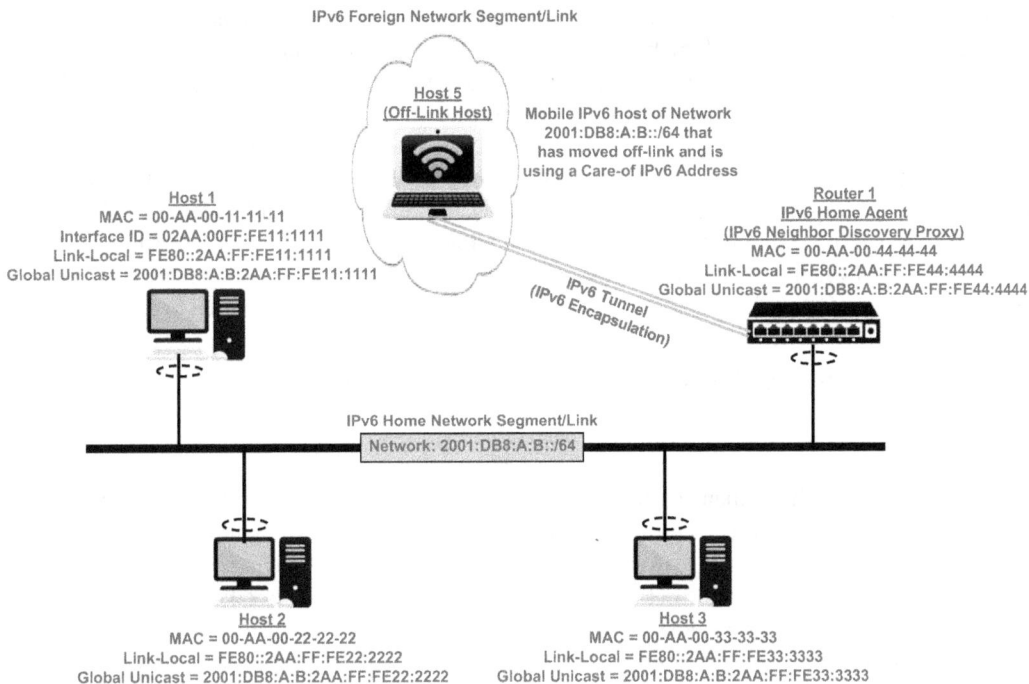

FIGURE 4.20 Accepting IPv6 Proxy Neighbor Discovery messages on behalf of a mobile IPv6 node that has moved off-link.

The Proxy, Router 1, must send all solicited proxy IPv6 Neighbor Advertisement messages on the link with the Override (O) Flag set to 0. Doing this ensures that if Host 5 itself is present on the link (i.e., moves back to its Home Link), its Neighbor Advertisement messages (with the O Flag set to 1) will take precedence over any Neighbor Advertisement messages received from the Proxy, Router 1. The Proxy may send unsolicited Neighbor Advertisement messages with the O Flag set to 1, but doing so would be problematic and may cause the proxy Neighbor Advertisement messages to override a valid entry created by Host 5 itself.

Furthermore, when the Proxy, Router 1, sends a proxy Neighbor Advertisement message in response to a Neighbor Solicitation message from a neighbor, it should delay the response by a random time between 0 and MAX_ANYCAST_DELAY_TIME seconds to avoid message collisions when multiple responses are sent by several proxies on the link. However, in cases where only one Proxy is present on the link (e.g., when using Mobile IPv6), such message delays are not necessary.

In Figure 4.20, the Home Agent, running IPv6 Proxy Neighbor Discovery, intercepts IPv6 packets on the Home Link that are addressed to the Home IPv6 Address of Host 5, and tunnels them (using IPv6 encapsulation) to Host 5's Care-of IPv6 Address on the Foreign Network Segment (Foreign Link). When using IPv6 encapsulation, the destination IPv6 address in the outer IPv6 header is Host 5's Care-of IPv6 Address, while the destination IPv6 address of the inner IPv6 header (i.e., the original or encapsulated IPv6 packet) is the Home IPv6 Address of Host 5. The intercepted IPv6 packets on the Home Link could be from a local (on-link) host or from an off-link host communicating with Host 5.

Let us assume that Host 1 wishes to communicate with Host 5 and sends an IPv6 Neighbor Solicitation message seeking Host 5's MAC address. Router 1 (the Home Agent) receives this message and sees that Host 5 is visiting a Foreign Network, and there is a registered Mobility Binding in Router 1's Mobility Binding Cache (there is an entry for Host 5's Care-of and Home IPv6 Addresses). Note that, in Mobile IPv6, each Home Agent must maintain a Mobility Binding Cache that holds mobility information for its Mobile Nodes **[RFC6275]**. Router 1 then responds by sending a Neighbor

Advertisement message to Host 1 containing its own MAC address. Host 1 can then send IPv6 packets destined for Host 5 to Router 1, which tunnels them to Host 5 on the Foreign Network.

Host 1 also updates its Neighbor Cache by associating Host 5's Home IPv6 Address with Router 1's MAC address, a mapping that Host 1 uses for further communication with the off-link Host 5. The Ethernet frames sent by Host 1 that contain Host 5's IPv6 packets have the destination MAC address set to Router 1's MAC address and the source MAC address set to Host 1's own MAC address. Host 5 stops using its Care-of IPv6 Address and relies solely on its Home IPv6 Address when it returns to its Home Network Segment (see **Chapter 6**). The Care-of IPv6 Address is only relevant and used when Host 5 is visiting the corresponding Foreign Network Segment; each Foreign Network assigns a Care-of IPv6 Address from its routable IPv6 addressing space to a visiting host.

4.7.2   GENERAL IPV6 NEIGHBOR DISCOVERY PROXY OPERATIONS

IPv6 nodes use IPv6 Neighbor Discovery to determine the Link-Layer addresses of neighbors on the same link, keep track of which neighbors are reachable, and update the Link-Layer addresses in their Neighbor Caches that have changed. IPv6 nodes advertise their own MAC addresses along with the corresponding IPv6 addresses, and they also solicit such addressing information from neighboring nodes. IPv6 Neighbor Discovery also supports the concept of a Neighbor Discovery Proxy, where an IPv6 node has a neighboring node (a Proxy) that can accept and forward packets on its behalf.

In practice, when a network device (e.g., switch, switch/router, router, firewall) is configured to act as an IPv6 Neighbor Discovery Proxy for IPv6 addresses (specified and maintained in a "Proxy Address List," which may be implemented as part of the IPv6 routing table), the Proxy sends proxy Neighbor Advertisement messages in response to Neighbor Solicitation messages from hosts (on an "upstream" proxy interface) that are seeking the MAC addresses of IPv6 prefixes assigned to hosts behind the Proxy (i.e., on "downstream" proxy interfaces).

Note that in Mobile IPv6, the Proxy Address List is equivalent to the Mobility Binding Cache maintained by a Home Agent that contains the Home IPv6 Addresses, Care-of IPv6 Addresses, timers, and related information for Mobile Nodes that are visiting Foreign Networks [**RFC6275**]. Each Mobile Node, when visiting a Foreign Network, registers with a Home Agent, which creates a Mobility Binding Cache entry for the Mobile Node (see **Chapter 6** for details).

Typically, the Proxy can also be configured with IPv6 addresses for which it will not respond to proxy requests (i.e., "denied" or "negated" IPv6 addresses). The Proxy responds to Neighbor Discovery messages sent to specified Proxy IPv6 addresses, and not to denied/negated Proxy IPv6 addresses. The reception of Neighbor Discovery messages causes the Proxy to save the MAC addresses and IPv6 addresses of neighbors in its Neighbor Cache.

When an interface with Neighbor Discovery Proxy enabled receives a Neighbor Solicitation message requesting the MAC address corresponding to an IPv6 address, it performs the following operations:

- The Proxy searches the Neighbor Cache to ensure that the IPv6 address in the Target Address field of the message is not there. If the address exists, the Proxy ignores the Neighbor Solicitation message.
- If the source IPv6 address of the Neighbor Solicitation message is the IPv6 Unspecified address, it indicates that the message is a Duplicate Address Detection message, and the Proxy ignores the Neighbor Solicitation message.
- The Proxy takes the address in the Target Address field of the Neighbor Solicitation message and performs an LPM search in the Proxy Address List to find the best matching entry. If a best match is found but is marked as denied/negated, the Proxy drops the Neighbor Solicitation message.
- If the LPM search matches an entry in the Proxy Address List, and that matched address is not denied/negated, the Proxy responds to the Neighbor Solicitation message with a Neighbor Advertisement, providing its own MAC address as the MAC address of the next-hop leading to the target node (address).

The Proxy generates and sends proxy Neighbor Solicitation messages on the proxy interfaces when the target address is not in the Neighbor Cache. It searches for routes for the target address in its routing table. The routing table lookup provides the routes that point to the target address, enabling the Proxy to send proxy Neighbor Solicitation messages on the appropriate proxy interface.

To successfully support the IPv6 Neighbor Discovery protocol, the Proxy does not perform Neighbor Discovery Proxy for Duplicate Address Detection messages and addresses in the Proxy's Neighbor Cache (because these addresses belong to discovered neighbors, not the Proxy). It is important to note that the Neighbor Discovery Proxy functionality is different from the Duplicate Address Detection Proxy functionality discussed in Section 4.8.

4.7.3   USE CASE: IPv6 NEIGHBOR DISCOVERY PROXY FOR BRIDGING IPv6 HOSTS IN DIFFERENT BROADCAST DOMAINS WITH IDENTICAL IPv6 SUBNET PREFIXES

This section describes how an IPv6 Neighbor Discovery Proxy enables IPv6 hosts in different broadcast domains with identical IPv6 subnet prefixes to communicate with each other.

4.7.3.1   Scenario 1

In Figure 4.21, Host 1 wants to communicate with Host 2 in a different broadcast domain (VLAN) that is directly connected to the Proxy, Router 1. Host 2 is on a different VLAN, but from its IPv6 prefix configuration and routing table, Host 1 sees that Host 2 is on the same network segment and shares the same IPv6 subnet prefix. However, Host 1 does not know the Link-Layer address of the destination, Host 2. By implementing a Neighbor Discovery Proxy on Router 1, IPv6 hosts in different broadcast domains but with identical IPv6 subnet prefixes (based on the IPv6 prefix length settings) can communicate with each other. The Proxy, Router 1, is configured to intercept and accept IPv6 packets on VLAN 10 on behalf of Host 2 on VLAN 20; Router 1 acts as a Proxy for Host 2.

A *Switch Virtual Interface* (SVI) (also called *VLAN Interface* or *Routed VLAN Interface* (RVI) by some vendors) represents a logical Layer 3 (IP) or virtual routed interface on a switch/router (i.e., an integrated Layer 2/Layer 3 device) that connects a VLAN to the device's Layer 3 (IP) routing engine. Only one SVI or RVI can be associated with a particular VLAN (or Secondary VLAN when Private VLANs are used, **as discussed in Appendix F**). An SVI or RVI is required for a VLAN only when there is a need to perform routing between VLANs (or Secondary VLANs).

Note that a switch/router is a device capable of performing Layer 2 forwarding (bridging) and Layer 3 forwarding (routing) depending on the destination of a packet (intra-VLAN/Secondary VLAN or inter-VLAN/Secondary VLAN communication when required). A switch/router is also called an Integrated Routing and Bridging (IRB) device by some vendors. When VLANs terminate directly on an IP router, the terminating interfaces are referred to as routed interfaces; these interfaces are simple router ports that handle routed traffic.

4.7.3.1.1   *Sending ICMPv6 Neighbor Solicitation Messages*

Host 1 on VLAN 10 wants to communicate with Host 2 on VLAN 20 through Router 1, the Neighbor Discovery Proxy (Figure 4.21). Host 1 first performs a local IPv6 routing table lookup on the (destination) IPv6 address of Host 2. Host 1 finds that this destination address matches its on-link IPv6 subnet prefix, so it creates a Destination Cache entry for this address, as well as a Neighbor Cache entry, setting its state to INCOMPLETE. Before Host 1 can send traffic to Host 2, it needs to resolve Host 2's IPv6 address to a corresponding MAC address.

Therefore, Host 1 multicasts an ICMPv6 Neighbor Solicitation message on the local link to discover the MAC address of Host 2. The destination MAC address of the Ethernet frame carrying this message is set to the Solicited-Node multicast MAC address derived from the IPv6 Solicited-Node multicast address of Host 2. The Target Address field of the Neighbor Solicitation message is set to the IPv6 address of Host 2. The Source Link-Layer Address Option included in the Neighbor Solicitation message contains Host 1's own MAC address. The Ethernet frame containing this Neighbor Solicitation message is multicast on the local link to all listening nodes. The Ethernet frame and IPv6 packet carrying the Neighbor Solicitation message contain the following information:

- **Source MAC Address**: MAC address of Host 1(00-AA-00–11-11-11)
- **Destination MAC Address**: Solicited-node multicast MAC address of destination, Host 2 (33-33-FF-22-22-22) derived from Host 2's IPv6 Solicited-Node multicast address
- **Source IPv6 Address**: Globally unique IPv6 address of Host 1 (2001:DB8:A:B1:2AA:FF :FE11:1111) or Host 1's IPv6 Link-Local address (FE80::2AA:FF:FE11:1111)
- **Destination IPv6 Address**: IPv6 Solicited-Node multicast address of destination, Host 2 (FF02::1:FF22:2222) derived from Host 2's IPv6 address
- **Target Address Field**: Globally unique IPv6 address of Host 2 (2001:DB8:A:B2:2AA:F F:FE22:2222)

Router 1 receives the multicast Ethernet frame (with the Neighbor Solicitation message) and processes it as it would any multicast MAC frame and IPv6 multicast packet. Router 1 extracts the IPv6 packet containing the Solicitation message and performs an IPv6 routing table lookup on the packet's destination address, which is the IPv6 address of Host 2 on VLAN 20. Router 1 finds a matching IPv6 subnet prefix in the routing table and determines that this destination IPv6 address requires proxying (i.e., the address is in the Proxy List).

Router 1 creates a Neighbor Cache entry for Host 1 on Port 1 and records its MAC address. It also creates a Neighbor Cache entry for Host 2 (on an arbitrary proxy interface) and sets the entry's state to INCOMPLETE. Note that Router 1 updates its Neighbor Cache using the information in Host 1's Neighbor Solicitation message. We assume that Router 1 does not have a recent entry for Host 2 in its Neighbor Cache. The outgoing interface of the Proxy (Router 1) modifies the received Neighbor Solicitation packet before multicasting it on the proxy interface. The proxy interface (Port 2 of Router 1) generates a proxy Neighbor Solicitation message with the source MAC address of the Ethernet frame carrying this message changed to the MAC address of the proxy-enabled interface (Port 2), which

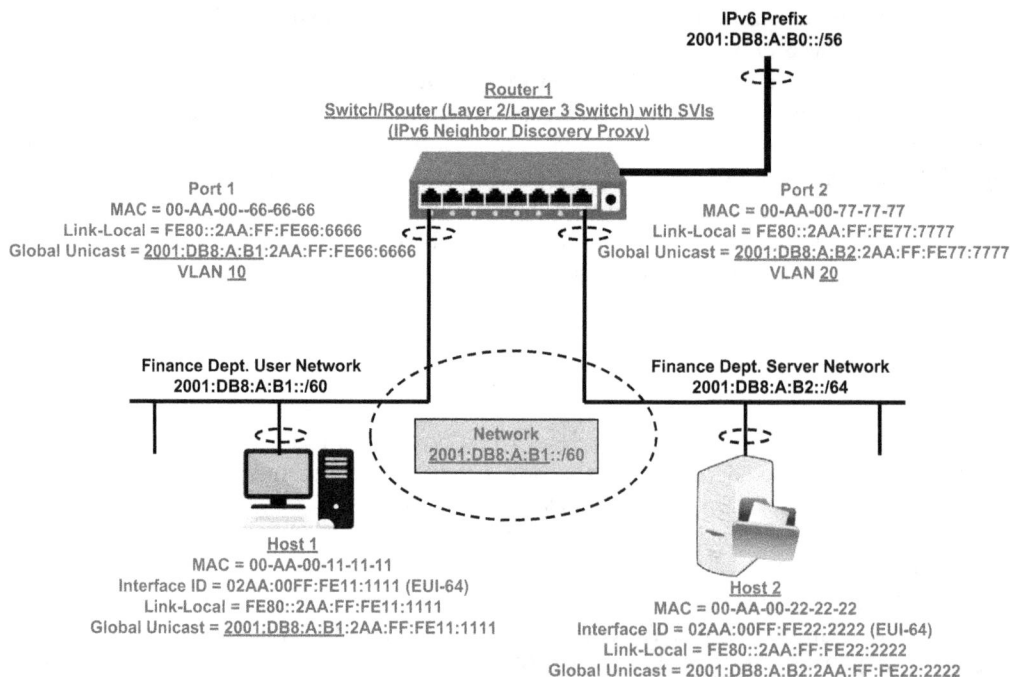

FIGURE 4.21 IPv6 Neighbor Discovery Proxy for bridging IPv6 hosts in different broadcast domains with identical IPv6 subnet prefixes: Scenario 1.

is 00-AA-00–77-77-77. Router 1 also replaces the MAC address in the Source Link-Layer Address Option with its own MAC address, that of Port 2. The Ethernet frame and IPv6 packet carrying the generated proxy Neighbor Solicitation message contain the following information:

- **Source MAC Address**: The MAC address of Host 1 will be changed to the MAC address of the proxy interface, Port 2 (00-AA-00–77-77-77)
- **Destination MAC Address**: The Solicited-Node multicast MAC address of the destination, Host 2 (33-33-FF-22-22-22), remains unchanged
- **Source IPv6 Address**: The IPv6 Link-Local address of the proxy interface, Port 2 (FE80::2AA:FF:FE77:7777)
- **Destination IPv6 Address**: The IPv6 Solicited-Node multicast address of the destination, Host 2 (FF02::1:FF22:2222), remains unchanged
- **Target Address Field**: The globally unique IPv6 address of Host 2 (2001:DB8:A:B2:2AA :FF:FE22:2222), or the IPv6 Link-Local address of Host 2

The proxy interface (Port 2) transmits the proxy Neighbor Solicitation message to the Solicited-node multicast address of the target node, Host 2. Host 2 is expected to receive and reply to this proxy Neighbor Solicitation message because the Solicited-Node multicast IPv6 and MAC addresses (FF02::1:FF22:2222 and 33-33-FF-22-22-22, respectively) are derived from Host 2's own IPv6 address (2001:DB8:A:B2:2AA:FF:FE22:2222).

4.7.3.1.2   Sending ICMPv6 Neighbor Advertisement Messages

The target node, Host 2, receives the proxy Neighbor Solicitation message and processes it as usual. Host 2 creates a Neighbor Cache entry for Host 1 by mapping Host 1 to the MAC address of Port 2 of Router 1. Host 2 then responds with a Neighbor Advertisement message sent to Host 1 containing Host 2's own MAC address. The Neighbor Advertisement message is sent using Host 1's Neighbor Cache entry, that is, to the MAC address of Port 2 of Router 1. Host 2's Neighbor Advertisement message includes the Target Link-Layer Address Option, which contains Host 2's own MAC address information. The Neighbor Advertisement message reaches Router 1, which updates its Neighbor Cache. The Ethernet frame and IPv6 packet carrying Host 2's Neighbor Advertisement message contain the following information:

- **Source MAC Address**: MAC address of Host 2 (00-AA-00–22-22-22)
- **Destination MAC Address**: MAC address of the proxy interface, Port 2 (00-AA-00–77-77-77)
- **Source IPv6 Address**: Globally unique IPv6 address of Host 2 (2001:DB8:A:B2:2AA:FF :FE22:2222)
- **Destination IPv6 Address**: MAC address of the proxy interface, Port 2 (FE80::2AA: FF:FE77:7777)

The Neighbor Advertisement message reaches Router 1, which processes it as it would any unicast ICMPv6 message. Router 1 inspects the message to determine if it requires proxying. Since it is a Neighbor Advertisement message, Router 1 updates its Neighbor Cache entry state for Host 2 to be REACHABLE and records Host 2's MAC address. Router 1 then replaces the Link-Layer address in the Target Link-Layer Address Option with its own MAC address, that of the outgoing interface, Port 1. The Neighbor Advertisement message is then sent out Port 1. Router 1 sends this message on Port 1 based on its Neighbor Cache. Note that Router 1 sends the proxy Neighbor Advertisement message via unicast to Host 1. The Ethernet frame and IPv6 packet carrying this proxy Neighbor Advertisement message contain the following information:

- **Source MAC Address**: MAC address of the proxy interface (Port 1) instead of the MAC address of Host 2 (00-AA-00--66-66-66)
- **Destination MAC Address**: MAC address of Host 1 (00-AA-00–11-11-11)

- **Source IPv6 Address**: IPv6 Link-Local address of the egress interface, Port 1 (FE80::2AA:FF:FE66:6666)
- **Destination IPv6 Address**: IPv6 Link-Local address of Host 1 (FE80::2AA:FF:FE11:1111)

Host 1 receives this unicast Neighbor Advertisement message and processes it as usual. Host 1 updates the state of the Neighbor Cache entry for Host 2 (on Port 2 of Router 1) to REACHABLE, and associates Host 2's IPv6 address with the MAC address of Port 1. After Host 1 receives the proxy Neighbor Advertisement message, both Host 1 and Host 2, which are on different network segments of Router 1, can now communicate with each other.

Host 1 forwards all IPv6 packets addressed to Host 2 to the Port 1 MAC address of Router 1. Since Router 1 knows how to reach Host 2, it forwards the IPv6 packet to Host 2. Additionally, the Neighbor Caches of all IPv6 hosts on Host 1's IPv6 link are populated with the MAC address of Port 1 of Router 1 for communication with Host 2. Host 1 and all hosts on its local link see Port 1 of Router 1 as the owner of Host 2's IPv6 address. Hence, all IPv6 packets destined for Host 2 are sent to Router 1 to be forwarded to Host 2 on VLAN 20.

4.7.3.2 Scenario 2

Figure 4.22 shows another scenario where an IPv6 Neighbor Discovery Proxy is deployed on a router to enable IPv6 hosts on different VLANs (or hosts that are part of a Private VLAN or an Isolated VLAN) with identical IPv6 subnet prefixes to communicate with each other. In Figures 4.22 and 4.23, a Neighbor Discovery Proxy is used to internetwork two separate VLANs with identical IPv6 subnet prefixes.

The Neighbor Discovery Proxy is implemented on Router 1 to enable its proxy interfaces to facilitate communication between hosts in VLAN 10 and VLAN 20. Router 1 maintains a Proxy Address List that indicates the host IPv6 addresses that require proxying. In Figure 4.22, Host 1 and

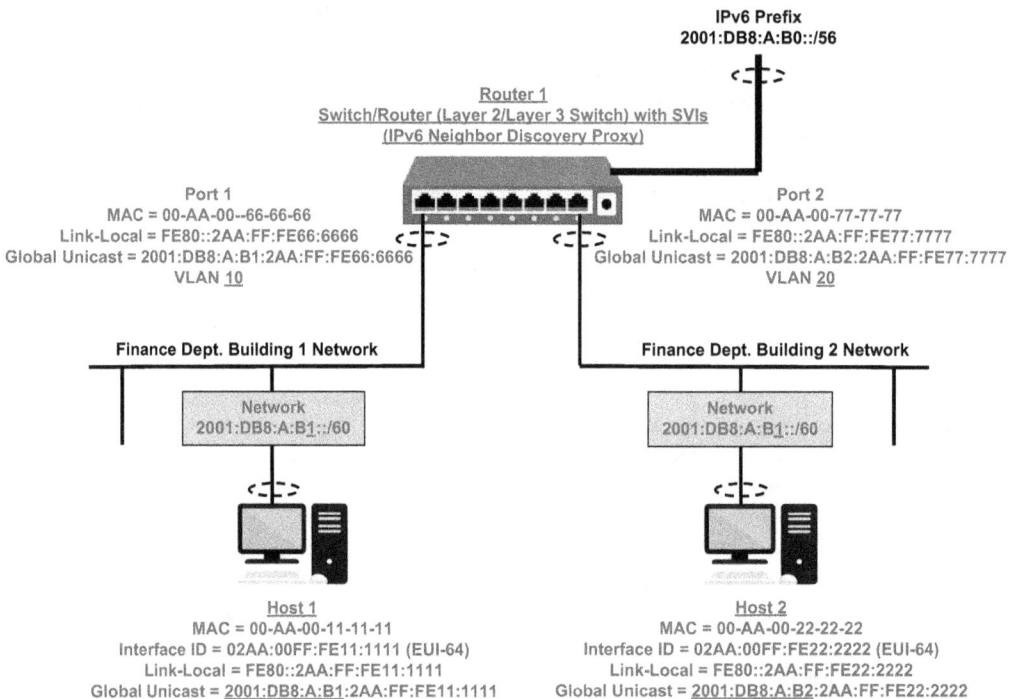

FIGURE 4.22 IPv6 Neighbor Discovery Proxy for bridging IPv6 hosts on different VLANs with identical IPv6 subnet prefixes: Scenario 2.

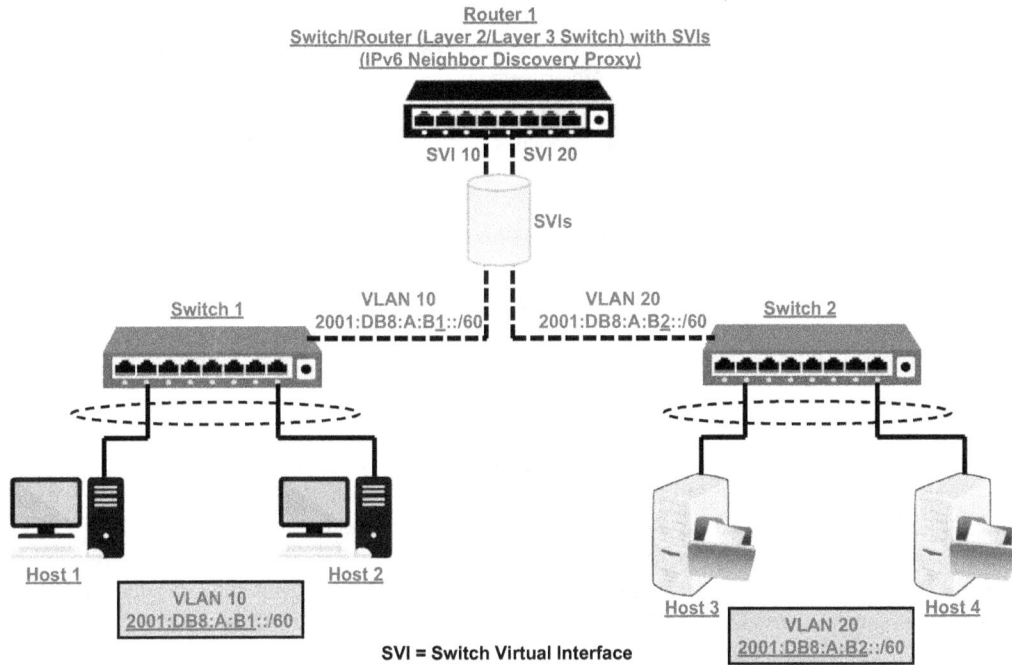

FIGURE 4.23 SVIs on a switch/router providing routing between two VLANs.

Host 2 share the same IPv6 subnet prefix but are on different VLANs; Host 1 is in VLAN 10 and Host 2 is in VLAN 20. Host 1 sends a Neighbor Solicitation message directly to Host 2 to request its MAC address because Host 1 sees that they share the same IPv6 subnet prefix. However, because Host 1 and Host 2 reside on different VLANs, Host 2 will not receive the Neighbor Solicitation message. The Neighbor Discovery Proxy is implemented on the interfaces of Router 1 to allow it to forward Neighbor Discovery messages between Host 1 and Host 2. The generation of the proxy Neighbor Advertisement packet works as explained in Scenario 1 above.

4.7.4 USE CASE: NEIGHBOR DISCOVERY PROXY FOR INTRA-VLAN COMMUNICATION ON A LAYER 2 SWITCH WITH PORT ISOLATION

Generally, Layer 2 networks (particularly those based on multiaccess network technologies such as Ethernet) are divided into multiple smaller broadcast domains called VLANs to limit broadcasts, create manageable network segments, enhance network security, and provide network operators the flexibility to design more efficient Layer 2 networks. Hosts in a VLAN can directly communicate with each other since a VLAN is a flat broadcast-based network segment [AWEYFCDM22]. However, hosts on different VLANs (just like in different IP subnets) can only communicate through an IP router.

Additionally, some switch ports in the same VLAN can be restricted from communicating with each other at Layer 2, using the technique of Port Isolation even in a VLAN that normally allows unrestricted intra-VLAN communication (see **Private VLANs and Port Isolation in Appendix F**). Hosts in the same VLAN but residing on switch ports that implement Port Isolation (i.e., on a Private VLAN) cannot communicate with each other, although they belong to the same VLAN. That is, hosts on ports configured in the same Port Isolation group cannot communicate at Layer 2 even though a VLAN is a single broadcast domain. However, in some cases, hosts on the same VLAN but on isolated ports may still need to communicate with each other, just like hosts on different VLANs or IP subnets may need to.

A Neighbor Discovery Proxy can be deployed on a VLAN with Port Isolation to enable connectivity between hosts on different isolated ports (see Figures 4.24 and 4.25). Currently, there are Layer 2 switches that support Proxy Neighbor Advertisements. The Neighbor Discovery Proxy enables intra-VLAN communication where hosts needing to communicate with each other belong to the same VLAN, but Port Isolation is configured on the switch ports to which the hosts are connected.

As discussed above, if Port Isolation is configured on switch ports in a VLAN, hosts on those ports (even though they are in the same VLAN) cannot communicate with each other. However, configuring an intra-VLAN Neighbor Discovery Proxy on a switch within the VLAN with the Port Isolation feature enables communication between the affected hosts but at Layer 3 (i.e., via routing, just as routing facilitates inter-VLAN communication). In Figures 4.24 and 4.25, Host 1 and Host 2 are in the same VLAN (VLAN 10) but are on isolated ports, Port 1 and Port 2, respectively. As a result, Host 1 and Host 2 cannot communicate at Layer 2 because Port 1 and Port 2 have VLAN Port Isolation implemented.

However, if an intra-VLAN Neighbor Discovery Proxy is configured on Router 1 (in Figures 4.24 and 4.25), Host 1 and Host 2 will be able to communicate at Layer 3. Router 1 must be config- ured to accept packets on behalf of specific hosts on isolated ports (i.e., act as a Proxy for those host IPv6 addresses). In this case, Router 1 maintains a Proxy Address List that contains the host IPv6 addresses requiring proxying. Let us assume Port 1 on Router 1 receives a Neighbor Solicitation message from Host 1, whose destination IPv6 address is not Router 1's own IPv6 address, but an address that requires proxying (an IPv6 address in the message's Target Address field that is also in Router 1's Proxy Address List).

Router 1 does not discard the Neighbor Solicitation message but searches for a recent Neighbor Cache entry that matches the target address, the IPv6 address of Host 2. If Router 1 finds that a recent Neighbor Cache entry for Host 2 exists, it sends its MAC address to Host 1 and then acts as a

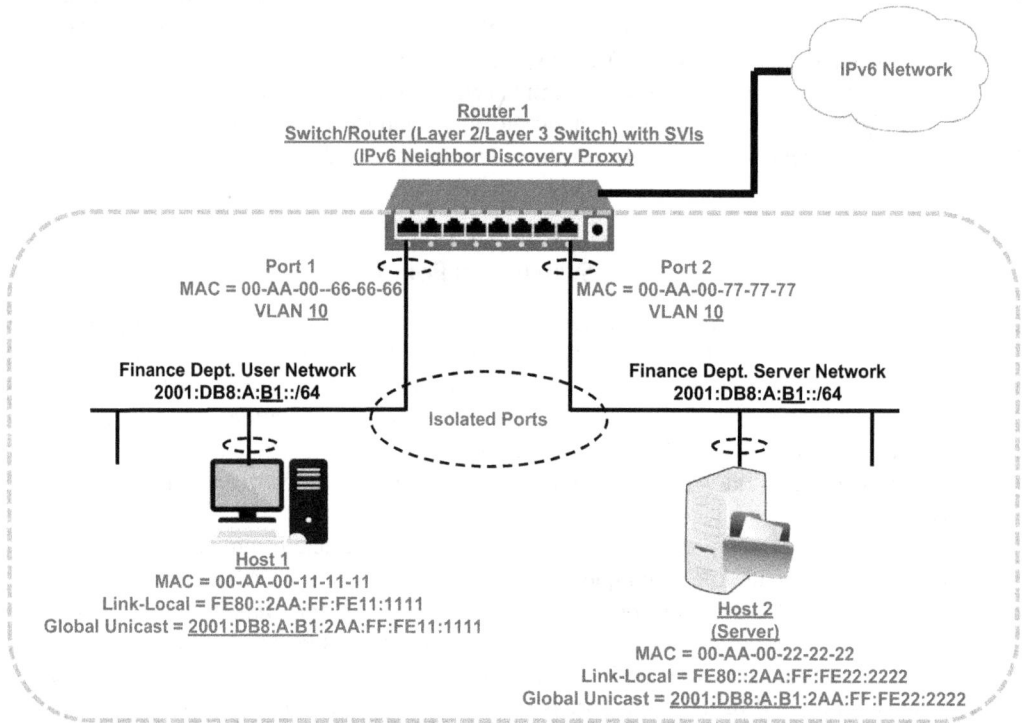

FIGURE 4.24 IPv6 Neighbor Discovery Proxy for intra-VLAN communication on a switch/router with Port Isolation: Architecture 1.

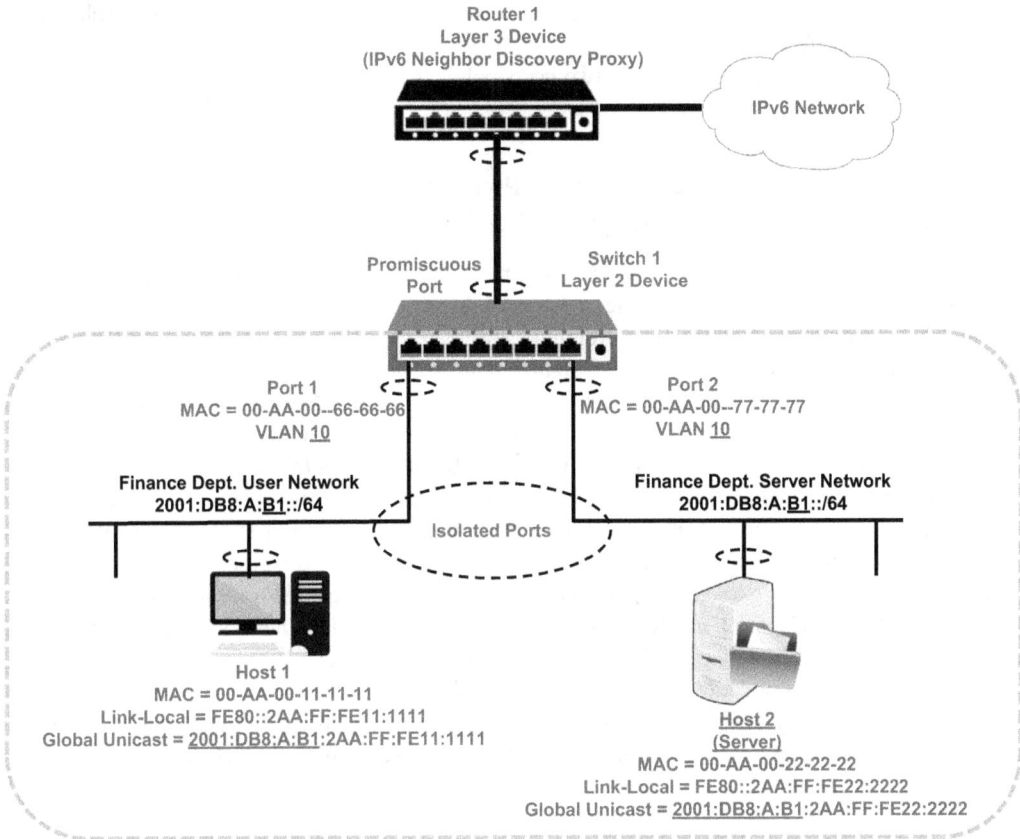

FIGURE 4.25 IPv6 Neighbor Discovery Proxy for intra-VLAN communication on a router with Port Isolation: Architecture 2.

proxy for Host 2, intercepting and accepting IPv6 packets on behalf of Host 2. If no recent Neighbor Cache entry exists for Host 2, Router 1 sends a proxy Neighbor Solicitation message on the proxy interfaces, requesting the MAC address associated with the target address, Host 2. Router 1, acting as a proxy for Host 2, receives a Neighbor Advertisement message with Host 2's MAC address on Port 2 and then proxies it as a unicast message to Host 1 on Port 1. Host 1 then has the necessary information to send IPv6 traffic through Router 1 to Host 2 as if it were communicating with Host 2 on the same network segment. The Neighbor Discovery Proxy operations presented in the previous section for Scenarios 1 and 2 also apply here and are not repeated.

As discussed above, a Neighbor Discovery Proxy enables a router to respond to a Neighbor Solicitation message that requests the Link-Layer address of an IPv6 host on another network segment. With the Neighbor Discovery Proxy, IPv6 hosts in different broadcast domains can communicate with each other as they would when located in the same network. *Note that the IPv6 Neighbor Discovery Proxy (Router 1) may also implement network filtering policies using access control lists (ACLs) to deny or permit certain devices on isolated/restricted ports from communicating with each other.*

The Neighbor Discovery Proxy facilitates Layer 3 (IPv6) communication in the following cases when two IPv6 hosts want to communicate (see details in **Appendix F**):

- Two hosts connect to separate ports on the same switch and the ports are on different VLANs.
- Two hosts connect to different Isolated Ports on the same switch.

- Two hosts connect to separate Layer 2 switch ports, but the ports are in the same isolation group of a VLAN.
- A super VLAN is created, and the two hosts belong to different sub-VLANs.
- A Private VLAN is created, and the two hosts belong to different Secondary VLANs.

4.7.5 Use Case: IPv6 Neighbor Discovery Proxy for Bridging Network Segments within a Network Using IPv6 Subnet Prefix Delegation

An IPv6 Neighbor Discovery Proxy can be used to bridge network segments within an IPv6 subnet prefix when bridging is not possible at Layer 2. This section describes how this is done (see Figure 4.26). As noted earlier, the IPv6 Neighbor Discovery Proxy feature is similar to Proxy ARP in IPv4 [RFC1027]. In Figure 4.26, the Neighbor Discovery Proxy runs on a Customer Premises Equipment (CPE) device (Router 2) and acts as a proxy for IPv6 Neighbor Discovery messages exchanged between the Provider Edge (PE) router (Router 1) and the CPE device.

The Neighbor Discovery Proxy allows Router 2 to function as both the router for the customer network and a proxy for handling Neighbor Discovery messages. This setup is particularly useful in cases where an ISP (through the PE Router 1) provides only limited IPv6 address delegation (e.g., Router 1 sends a single /48 IPv6 prefix to the CPE). By using a Neighbor Discovery Proxy, such limitations can be bypassed, allowing the CPE network to use the ISP-provided /48 IPv6 prefix.

The IPv6 Prefix Delegation mechanism for DHCPv6 is specified in [RFC3633] and [RFC8415] and further discussed in **Chapter 5**. IPv6 Prefix Delegation is a DHCPv6 mechanism through which an IPv6 delegating router (a DHCPv6 Server) delegates a long-lived IPv6 prefix across an administrative boundary to an IPv6 requesting router (a DHCPv6 Client), with the delegating router not required to know the topology of the links in the network to which the delegated IPv6 prefixes will be assigned.

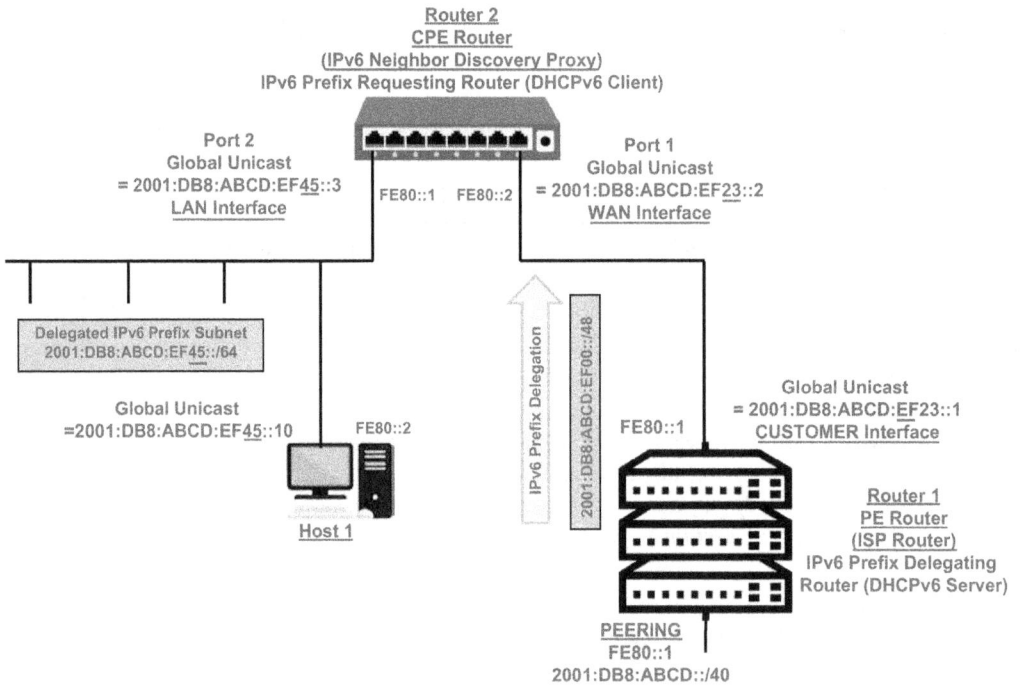

FIGURE 4.26 IPv6 Neighbor Discovery Proxy for bridging network segments within an IPv6 subnet using a delegated IPv6 prefix.

In IPv6, internal networks use IPv6 Global Unicast addresses, avoiding the need for Network Address Translation (NAT) for Internet traffic. An organization can also use site-scoped, yet globally unique IPv6 addresses, known as Unique-Local addresses, without needing NAT mechanisms (see **Chapter 3**). In Figure 4.26, the IPv6 subnet prefix 2001:DB8:ABCD:EF45::/64 is associated with the IPv6 subnet on Port 2 of Router 2. In this scenario, a Neighbor Solicitation message sent by Router 1 would not reach the client, Host 1, since it is in a different Layer 2 network segment. To solve this problem, the IPv6 Neighbor Discovery Proxy can be deployed on Router 2 to bridge the two IPv6 network segments (on the WAN and LAN interfaces of Router 2).

If Router 1, with IPv6 address 2001:DB8:ABCD:EF23::1/128 on its CUSTOMER interface, sends an ICMPv6 Neighbor Solicitation message to resolve the Layer 2 address of Host 1 with IPv6 address 2001:DB8:ABCD:EF45::10/128, the Neighbor Discovery Proxy (Router 2) will reply to this message on Port 1 by sending a Neighbor Advertisement message containing the MAC address of Port 1 as a substitute. This will allow Router 1 to communicate with Host 1 by forwarding its traffic to Router 2. In Figure 4.26, the Neighbor Discovery Proxy is configured on Router 2, allowing it to proxy for nodes on Port 1 and Port 2.

4.7.5.1 IPv6 Neighbor Discovery Proxy Configuration Requirements

In Figure 4.26, the WAN interface, Port 1 (i.e., the listening interface on CPE Router 2), must be set to *promiscuous mode*. If this interface is connected to a VLAN, it must be set as the *parent interface* of the VLAN. Otherwise, CPE Router 2 cannot join the appropriate IPv6 multicast groups to respond to Neighbor Solicitation messages for IPv6 hosts on the CPE LAN. Additionally, the WAN interface (Port 1 on Router 2) and LAN interface (Port 2 on Router 2) must not be configured with an IPv6 Global Unicast address in the same /64 delegated IPv6 prefix. If a Global Unicast address on the WAN interface (Port 1) is required, it must have a /128 IPv6 prefix. Router 1 can use the DHCPv6 Prefix Exclude Option to assign a sub-prefix from the delegated IPv6 prefix for the PE-CPE link (see discussion below).

All IPv6 hosts on the CPE LAN network will autogenerate a Global Unicast address using SLAAC and will use Router 2 as their default gateway. Router 1 (the ISP or PE router) delegates the 2001:DB8:ABCD:EF00::/48 network prefix to the downstream CPE Router 2 (using the DHCPv6 Prefix Delegation mechanism **[RFC3633] [RFC8415]**). Router 2 will configure 2001:DB8:ABCD:EF23::2/128 on its WAN interface and a default IPv6 route to the Link-Local address configured on the CUSTOMER interface of PE Router 1. The CPE Router 2, which is connected to the downlink of PE Router 1, will receive the delegated /48 IPv6 prefix on its WAN interface (Port 1). The goal is to allow Router 2 to use a sub-prefix from this /48 prefix on the LAN interface and proxy Neighbor Discovery messages between its LAN and WAN interfaces. If an IPv6 host powers up on the CPE Router 2's LAN, the host will autoconfigure an IPv6 Global Unicast address within the delegated /48 IPv6 prefix, using the sub-prefix 2001:DB8:ABCD:EF45::10/64.

4.7.5.2 The IPv6 Neighbor Discovery Proxy Message Flow Process in a Network Using DHCPv6 Prefix Delegation

1. **LAN Client (IPv6 Host 1)**: Host 1 on the CPE LAN (with IPv6 address 2001:DB8:ABCD:EF45::10/64) initiates a conversation with a destination on the IPv6 Internet. Host 1 sends an IPv6 packet to its default gateway, the LAN interface of CPE Router 2.

2. **CPE Router 2**: Router 2 receives the IPv6 packet on its LAN interface and forwards it on its WAN interface (with IPv6 Global Unicast address 2001:DB8:ABCD:EF23::2/128 and Link-Local address FE80::2) toward PE Router 1. Since the IPv6 packet received from Host 1 is destined for an external destination in the IPv6 Internet, CPE Router 2 consults its IPv6 routing table to send the IPv6 packet. Router 2 has a default route that points to the CUSTOMER interface (downlink) of Router 1 as the next-hop.

3. **PE Router 1**: The PE Router 1 receives Host 1's IPv6 packet on its CUSTOMER interface and forwards it toward the intended destination in the IPv6 Internet. The external

destination host receives the IPv6 packet and responds with an IPv6 packet, which is routed back to PE Router 1. To deliver the reply IPv6 packet to the LAN client, Host 1 (with address 2001:DB8:ABCD:EF45::10/128), PE Router 1 must resolve Host 1's IPv6 address to a corresponding Link-Layer (MAC) address. Thus, PE Router 1 sends an ICMP6 Neighbor Solicitation message on its CUSTOMER interface addressed to 2001:DB8:ABCD:EF23::2/128, the WAN interface of CPE Router 2.

4. **Actions of the Neighbor Discovery Proxy on CPE Router 2**:
   a. The Neighbor Discovery Proxy on CPE Router 2 listens for Neighbor Discovery messages on both its WAN and LAN interfaces.
   b. When a Neighbor Solicitation is received on the WAN interface of CPE Router 2, the Neighbor Discovery Proxy intercepts it and proxies it to the LAN interface.
   c. Host 1 receives the Neighbor Solicitation message and responds with a Neighbor Advertisement message containing its MAC address.
   d. The Neighbor Discovery Proxy proxies the received Neighbor Advertisement message back to Router 2's WAN interface, sending it to the CUSTOMER interface of PE Router 1.
   e. PE Router 1 now has the necessary MAC address information to forward the IPv6 reply packet from the external IPv6 host to the LAN client, Host 1.

4.7.5.3   Using IPv6 Prefix Exclusion During DHCPv6 Prefix Delegation

The DHCPv6 Prefix Exclude Option (Option Code 67) **[RFC6603]** allows a DHCPv6 Server (delegating router) to delegate IPv6 prefixes to a DHCPv6 Client (requesting router) while excluding a specific IPv6 sub-prefix from the delegated IPv6 prefixes to be used on the Client's uplink to the DHCPv6 Server (WAN interface in Figure 4.26). Without the DHCPv6 Prefix Exclude Option, the DHCPv6 Server would have to delegate two IPv6 prefixes: one for the Client's downlink(s) and the other for the uplink to the DHCPv6 Server. DHCPv6 Prefix Delegation and the use of the Prefix Exclude Option are discussed in greater detail in **Chapter 5**.

A requesting router (the CPE with a DHCPv6 Client in Figure 4.26) includes an Option Request Option (Option Code 6) containing the Prefix Exclude Option in a SOLICIT, REQUEST, RENEW, or REBIND message to inform the delegating router (the PE router with a DHCPv6 Server) about its support for the DHCPv6 Prefix Delegation functionality. The delegating router may also include the Prefix Exclude Option in an Option Request Option carried in a RECONFIGURE message to instruct the requesting router to initiate IPv6 prefix exclusion from the delegating router.

The delegating router (PE) receives the DHCPv6 message from the requesting router (CPE) and adds the IPv6 sub-prefix that is excluded from the delegated IPv6 prefix set in the Prefix Exclude Option. This Option is carried in a REPLY message sent to the requesting router. Upon receiving the REPLY message with the excluded IPv6 sub-prefix, the requesting router must not assign it to any of its downstream interfaces. The requesting router is free to allocate sub-prefixes (other than the excluded prefix) from the delegated IPv6 prefix to its downstream links as it wishes.

The delegating router and the requesting router both use the excluded IPv6 prefix on the link through which they exchange DHCPv6 messages. *The excluded IPv6 prefix is a single prefix taken from the same delegated IPv6 prefix set and has a prefix length greater than that of the delegated IPv6 prefix; the excluded IPv6 prefix is a sub-prefix of the delegated IPv6* prefix.

The following are the IPv6 prefixes and addresses used in Figure 4.26:

IPv6 prefix delegated to CPE (Router 2) by PE (Router 1):	2001:DB8:ABCD:EF00::/48
Excluded IPv6 prefix sent to CPE by PE:	2001:DB8:ABCD:EF23::/64
IPv6 prefix used on Port 2 (LAN) of CPE:	2001:DB8:ABCD:EF45::/64
IPv6 address configured on the WAN interface of CPE:	2001:DB8:ABCD:EF23::2
IPv6 address configured on the CUSTOMER interface of PE:	2001:DB8:ABCD:EF23::1

4.7.5.4   Configuring a Default Route from the CPE to the PE Router

In an IPv6 network where the service provider directly controls and manages the CPE, the provider can use a sub-prefix from the delegated IPv6 prefix to configure an IPv6 address on the loopback interface of the CPE. The provider can use this IPv6 loopback address to manage the CPE. The CPE can then use this IPv6 address to communicate with the PE; it can also use this as the source IPv6 address of packets when communicating with the PE.

The PE and the CPE are connected through a single link. Therefore, a default route can simply be configured in the CPE's IPv6 routing table, pointing to the PE. This default route points to the IPv6 address of the PE's downlink interface as the next-hop. It is also desirable to configure a */48 route* (called a *black hole route*) toward the CPE's *Null0 interface* for the delegated IPv6 prefix, to ensure that the CPE has (i.e., owns) routing information for the entire delegated IPv6 prefix address block (see discussion on the Null0 interface and black hole route on page 100 of **[CISCPOPOC]**).

In the absence of this black hole route, the CPE (requesting router) will forward IPv6 packets along the default route to the PE for parts of the delegated /48 prefix that the CPE has not yet assigned to its downlinks. The PE (delegating router) also configures a routing entry in its IPv6 routing table for the delegated /48 prefix toward the CPE, which means that, in the absence of the black hole route, there could be a routing loop on the PE-CPE link. The PE can install the delegated IPv6 prefix assigned to the CPE as a static route in its routing table, with the next-hop set to the IPv6 Link-Layer address of the CPE's uplink. Typically, the delegating router uses a binding database or table to record and maintain the state of all the IPv6 prefixes delegated to requesting routers (see the binding table in **Chapter 5**).

4.7.6   IPv6 Neighbor Discovery Proxy for Bridging IPv6 Hosts on Network Segments with Dissimilar Link-Layer Technologies

Figure 4.27 shows another use case where an IPv6 Neighbor Discovery Proxy is used to bridge IPv6 hosts on network segments that share an IPv6 prefix but use different Link-Layer technologies (e.g., Ethernet and WiFi). In this scenario, Host 1 on Port 1 of Router 1 and Host 2 on the wireless link of Router 2 belong to the same IPv6 network segment. Router 1 serves as an IPv6 Neighbor Discovery Proxy to connect these IPv6 hosts sharing the IPv6 prefix.

4.7.6.1   Bridging Network Segments with Dissimilar Link-Layer Technologies

The goal of this architecture is to ensure that the hosts on Port 1 of Router 1 and those on Router 2's wireless network belong to the same logical IPv6 network segment with a common IPv6 prefix. All these hosts appear to be part of that common (logical) IPv6 network segment, even though they use different Link-Layer technologies (Ethernet and wireless). Furthermore, we assume that a subnet/VLAN is created for the IPv6 hosts on Port 1 of Router 1 (a subnet/VLAN associated with the IPv6 subnet prefix 2001:DB8:A:BC1::/56).

This architecture (using an IPv6 Neighbor Discovery Proxy and appropriately configured IPv6 prefixes) allows the IPv6 hosts on the wireless link to appear as if they belong to the IPv6 subnet/VLAN on Port 1, despite the fact that the hosts use different Link-Layer technologies. It is well-understood in networking that bridging multiple links (or Layer 2 domains) at the Link-Layer into a single entity provides several operational benefits; for example, a single IP prefix can support multiple Layer 2 domains and simplifies network configuration and management. However, it is either impossible or very challenging to bridge certain types of Link-Layer technologies or media at the Link-Layer, thereby requiring the use of Network Layer mechanisms to accomplish this (in the form of IPv6 Neighbor Discovery Proxy **[RFC4389]**) as described in the example in Figure 4.27.

Discussion: Ethernet (IEEE 802.3) and WiFi (IEEE 802.11) have different Link-Layer characteristics and behaviors, making it challenging, if not impossible, to bridge networks that implement these technologies at the Link-Layer (Layer 2). This means such networks can only be bridged at the

Network Layer (Layer 3) using mechanisms such as IPv6 Proxy Neighbor Discovery **[RFC4389]**. IPv6 Proxy Neighbor Discovery can be used to bridge network segments that implement these technologies, making them appear as a single logical network segment, as shown in Figure 4.27. Note that Mobile IPv6 **[RFC6275]**, as illustrated in Figure 4.20, uses IPv6 Proxy Neighbor Discovery to bridge a Mobile Node's Home Link (which uses a multiaccess network technology such as Ethernet) and its Foreign Link (when visiting that link), regardless of the type of Link-Layer technology used by the Foreign Link (e.g., WiFi).

This approach may also be a useful tool for defining the perimeter of an IPv6 network segment that includes both Ethernet and WiFi portions (dissimilar Link-Layer technologies). Although this topology may not have wide practical utility, it serves to further illustrate the applicability of the IPv6 Neighbor Discovery Proxy in IPv6 networks. The IPv6 prefix length used in this architecture (/56) is purely for illustrative purposes; in practice, other IPv6 prefix lengths (greater or smaller than /56) may typically be used depending on the IPv6 subnet size.

4.7.6.2   DHCPv6 Prefix Delegation to Router 2 (WiFi Router)

In Figure 4.27, Router 1 acts as a DHCPv6 delegating router (DHCPv6 Server), while Router 2 functions as a DHCPv6 requesting router (DHCPv6 Client) **[RFC8415]**. Both Router 1 (the delegating router with DHCPv6 Server) and Router 2 (the requesting router with DHCPv6 Client) must support the Prefix Exclude Option **[RFC6603]** for IPv6 prefix exclusion to be performed. Using this Option, Router 1 selects a single IPv6 sub-prefix from its delegated IPv6 prefix set and sends this prefix information to Router 2. Router 1 and Router 2 use addresses from the excluded IPv6 prefix on the link connecting them (the uplink of Router 1). Router 2 (the WiFi router) assigns IPv6 addresses and sub-prefixes (other than the excluded IPv6 prefix) from the delegated IPv6 prefix to its WiFi clients and other local wired IPv6 links.

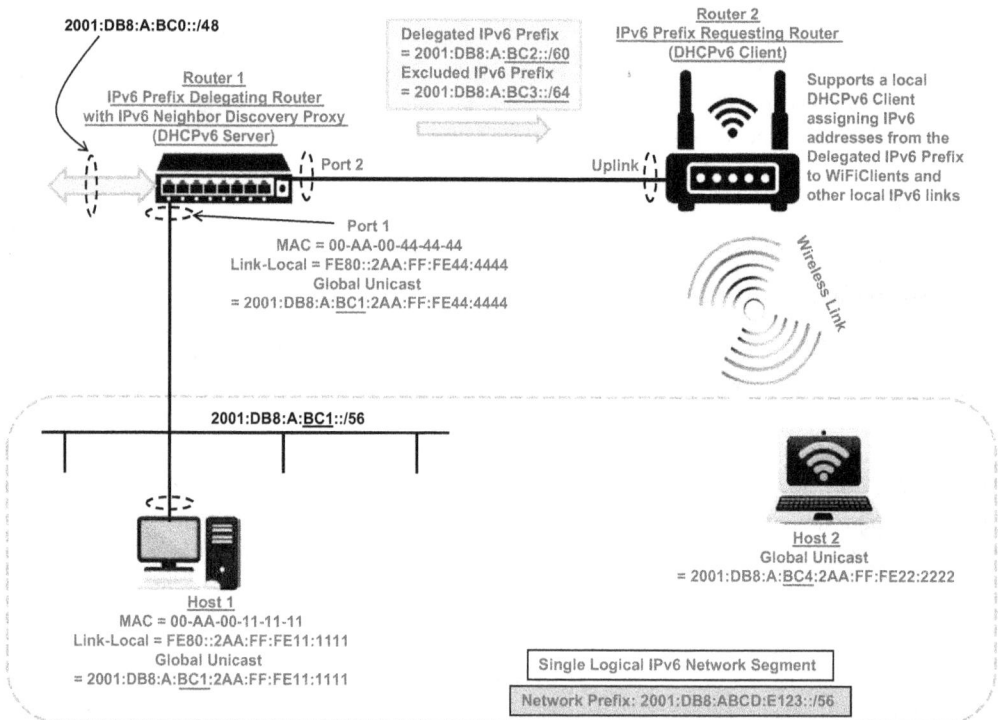

FIGURE 4.27   IPv6 Neighbor Discovery Proxy for bridging IPv6 hosts on network segments with dissimilar Link-Layer technologies but with the same IPv6 prefix.

Note that a WiFi router typically has multiple wired (Ethernet) interfaces/ports and a wireless (air) interface (with multiple logical sub-interfaces) that also support multiple wireless clients. The wireless interface on the WiFi router has multiple channels that can be viewed as multiple logical interfaces or ports to which clients connect via their air interfaces. The WiFi router must assign IPv6 addresses from its delegated IPv6 prefix to clients on any of its wired and wireless client ports.

The following are the IPv6 prefixes and addresses used in Figure 4.27:

IPv6 prefix delegated to Router 2 (DHCPv6 Client):	2001:DB8:A:BC2::/60
Excluded IPv6 prefix sent to Router 2 by Router 1 (DHCPv6 Server):	2001:DB8:A:BC3::/64
IPv6 address configured on the uplink of Router 2:	2001:DB8:A:BC3::2
IPv6 address configured on Port 2 of Router 1:	2001:DB8:A:BC3::1
IPv6 prefix used on Port 1 (LAN) of Router 1:	2001:DB8:A:BC1::/56

Notice that the excluded IPv6 prefix (2001:DB8:A:BC3::/64) is exactly a single sub-prefix taken from the same delegated IPv6 prefix set (2001:DB8:A:BC2::/60) and has a prefix length (/64) that is greater than the delegated IPv6 prefix length (/56). Router 1 (the delegating router) creates the excluded IPv6 prefix as a sub-prefix of the delegated IPv6 prefix.

4.7.6.3 The IPv6 Neighbor Discovery Proxy Message Flow Process in an IPv6 Network with Dissimilar Link-Layer Technologies

In Figure 4.27, when Host 1 has an IPv6 packet to send to Host 2, it first checks its IPv6 prefix configuration and routing table for the IPv6 address of Host 2 and sees that Host 2 is on the same IPv6 network segment. Host 1 then checks its Neighbor Cache to see if there is a MAC address entry corresponding to Host 2's IPv6 address. If no entry exists, Host 1 sends a Neighbor Solicitation message on the attached network segment seeking Host 2's MAC address. However, Host 2 is not on Host 1's local network segment (broadcast domain), and IPv6 routers do not forward Neighbor Discovery messages.

Router 1 receives the Neighbor Solicitation message from Host 1 and sees that Host 2 is in its Proxy Address List and can be reached via one of its interfaces (the route to Router 2). We assume Router 1 maintains a Proxy Address List that specifies the IPv6 addresses for which proxying is required (see the discussion in Section 4.7.2). The Proxy Address List may be a standalone list or logically part of Router 1's IPv6 routing table. Router 1 realizes that it has an entry for Host 2 and decides to respond to the Neighbor Solicitation message. We assume that Router 1 has a route in its IPv6 routing table that points to the correct outgoing interface for Host 2.

Router 1 sends a Neighbor Advertisement message to Host 1 containing the MAC address of Port 1, associating it with Host 2's IPv6 address. Host 1 is then able to send IPv6 packets destined for Host 2 to Router 1 (via Port 1), which routes them to Host 2 on Router 2's wireless network. Host 1 also updates its Neighbor Cache by associating Host 2's IPv6 address with Port 1's MAC address, a mapping that can be used for further communication with Host 2. The route to Host 2's network in Router 1's routing table may be a static route to Router 2, with the next-hop set to Router 2's IPv6 Link-Layer address.

Router 1 and Router 2 are connected through a single link; no other path exists to Router 2. Therefore, it is straightforward to configure a default route on Router 2 pointing to Router 1. This default route uses the IPv6 address of Router 1's downlink interface (Port 2) as the next-hop. IPv6 packets sent by Host 2 and destined for Host 1 are routed normally through Router 2 and Router 1 to Host 1. Note that Host 2 connects to Router 2 and sends all IPv6 packets directly to Router 2. Router 1 has an entry for Host 1's IPv6 address in its IPv6 routing table, as well as corresponding entries in its Neighbor and Destination Caches. The mapping between Host 1's IPv6 and MAC addresses is in Router 1's Neighbor Cache.

4.8   IPv6 DUPLICATE ADDRESS DETECTION PROXY

The Neighbor Discovery Proxy feature enables IPv6 packet forwarding among IPv6 hosts that reside in the same IPv6 subnet/VLAN but are restricted from communicating directly with each other because they are on isolated ports (see the **Private VLANs and Port Isolation discussion in Appendix F**). Particularly, a VLAN using Port Isolation configures Neighbor Discovery Proxy to enable IPv6 hosts on different physical segments with the same IPv6 subnet prefix to communicate without an additional IPv6 gateway and prefix. The Neighbor Discovery Proxy functions on a switch or router placed between multiple physical segments of a single VLAN using the same IPv6 prefix. When a Neighbor Discovery Proxy is implemented as discussed in the previous sections, the configured proxy interfaces send proxy Neighbor Advertisement messages on behalf of hosts on the different physical segments when Neighbor Solicitation messages are received.

The Duplicate Address Detection Proxy feature enables an IPv6 node (router or switch) to respond to Duplicate Address Detection queries (i.e., Neighbor Solicitation messages) on behalf of an IPv6 node on the same IPv6 subnet/VLAN that cannot directly communicate or respond to the queries from the sending nodes (Figure 4.28). In this case, using the Duplicate Address Detection Proxy feature allows IPv6 hosts (on the same IPv6 subnet but restricted from communicating directly with the sending nodes) to safely configure and use IPv6 addresses without causing address conflicts. The Duplicate Address Detection Proxy feature detects the presence of duplicate IPv6 addresses on the VLAN using proxy Neighbor Solicitation messages. This feature functions similarly to the Gratuitous ARP mechanism in IPv4 discussed in **Appendix D**.

For example, in Figure 4.28, the IPv6 Duplicate Address Detection Proxy on Router 1 of VLAN 10 responds to Duplicate Address Detection queries on behalf of any IPv6 host on Port 2 of Router 1 that is using a queried address generated on Port 1, and vice versa. The IPv6 Duplicate Address Detection Proxy uses a *binding table* or *local tracking database* to ensure the uniqueness of IPv6 addresses on the common VLAN 10:

- When the Proxy receives a Duplicate Address Detection request (i.e., Neighbor Solicitation message) from a host (on the upstream interface) for a target IPv6 address, it performs a lookup in the binding table (i.e., local tracking database). If the lookup returns a matching

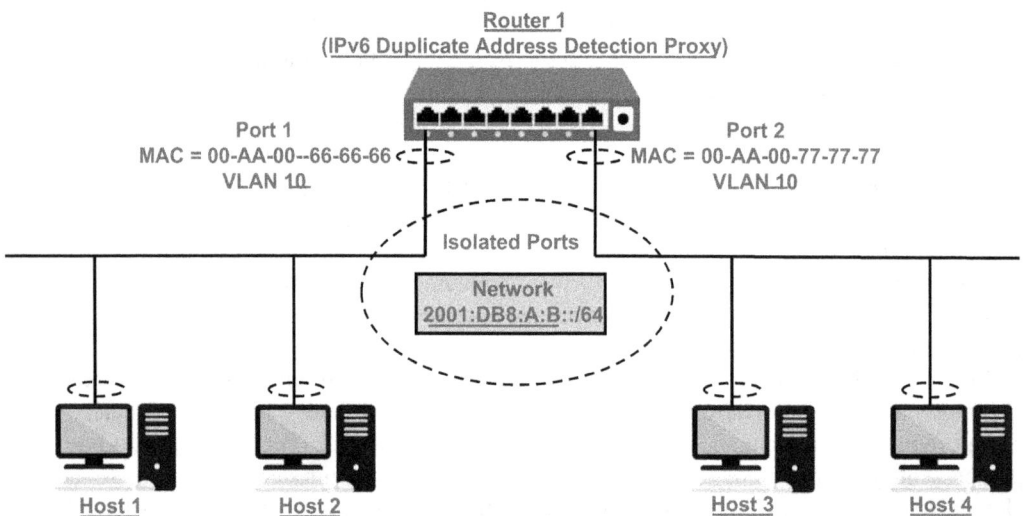

FIGURE 4.28   IPv6 Duplicate Address Detection Proxy.

entry, the Proxy sends a unicast Neighbor Solicitation message on the downstream or proxy interface(s) as part of the Neighbor Unreachability Detection function to verify whether the target IPv6 address is still being used.

- If any IPv6 host (on the downstream interface) using the target IPv6 address replies to the Neighbor Unreachability Detection message, the Proxy sends back a Neighbor Advertisement message to the querying host (on the upstream interface), indicating that the target IPv6 address is already in use.
- If no host (on the downstream interface) responds to the Neighbor Unreachability Detection message, the Proxy does not send any response to the querying host (on the upstream interface).

The IPv6 Duplicate Address Detection Proxy (using the tracking database) can respond to Duplicate Address Detection queries on behalf of any IPv6 node currently using the queried IPv6 unicast address.

4.8.1 Main Operating Steps of the Duplicate Address Detection Proxy

An IPv6 node (router or switch) configured with the Duplicate Address Detection Proxy feature detects the usage of IPv6 duplicate addresses on a link by sending proxy Neighbor Solicitation messages according to the following operations:

- The Proxy generates a proxy Neighbor Advertisement message on behalf of other hosts as a reply when it receives a Neighbor Solicitation message (i.e., Duplicate Address Detection request), and the Solicitation message contains a tentative IPv6 address that is being used and is reachable through another proxy interface.
- When a Duplicate Address Detection request (Neighbor Solicitation message) arrives at the Proxy and the tentative IPv6 address is not available or is in the STALE state in the Proxy's Neighbor Cache, the Proxy initiates Neighbor Unreachable Detection on all other proxy interfaces except the interface on which the message was received.
- If a Duplicate Address Detection request is received from an IPv6 host querying a tentative IPv6 address that is already in the middle of a Duplicate Address Detection process by another host, the Proxy replies with a Neighbor Advertisement message to both IPv6 hosts.

4.9   IPv6 ADDRESS ASSIGNMENT

An IPv6 node, upon startup, must have an IPv6 Link-Local address on an interface to communicate with other nodes on the local link. Without such an address at startup, the node will not be able to communicate with other nodes (like routers and DHCPv6 Servers) to obtain configuration information, such as IPv6 Global Unicast prefixes and addresses, as well as other configuration details from DHCPv6 Servers (e.g., DNS Server addresses and domain names). Thus, to communicate with IPv6 nodes outside the local network segment (or link) and the broader IPv6 Internet, each IPv6 node needs an IPv6 Global Unicast address (a globally unique IPv6 address as discussed in **Chapter 3**). IPv6 nodes use the methods discussed in the following sub-sections to obtain Global Unicast addresses (see also Figure 4.29).

An IPv6 node can use any of the three methods (manual configuration, SLAAC with Stateless DHCPv6 Server, or Stateful DHCPv6 Server) to configure an interface with a Global Unicast address, default gateway, and DNS Server and domain name (see the DHCPv6 discussion in **Chapter 5**). Whenever possible, using SLAAC with Stateless DHCPv6 Server or Stateful DHCPv6 Server is preferred over manual configuration (except on routers as discussed below).

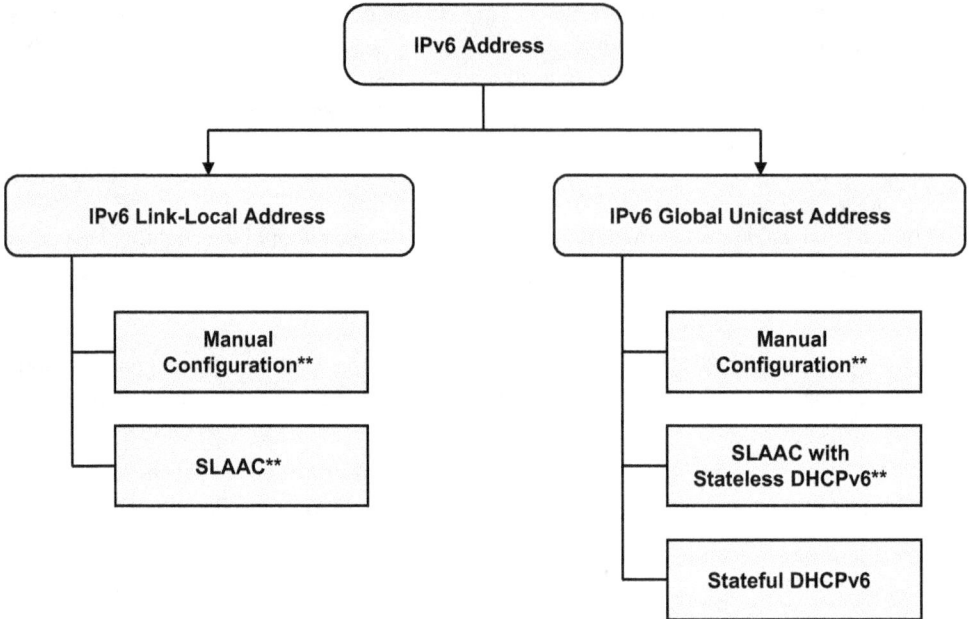

FIGURE 4.29 IPv6 address assignment methods.

4.9.1 MANUAL IPv6 ADDRESS ASSIGNMENT

The network administrator may manually configure any IPv6 node with an IPv6 address. The main disadvantage of this approach is that if the IPv6 network under consideration has many nodes and interfaces, the network administrator must manually configure each interface with the appropriate IPv6 addresses and all additional information needed to get the interface IPv6-enabled and ready for IPv6 communication. This approach, however, is not scalable and is also prone to human error.

It should be noted that IPv6 addresses, both Global Unicast and Link-Local addresses, are generally configured manually on IPv6 routers. In particular, IPv6 Global Unicast addresses on routers are assigned as part of the general network addressing plan. Additionally, given that routers must be up and running as soon as they are powered on and IPv6 routing is enabled, prior manual configuration of addresses makes sense. Similarly, IPv6 addresses on data servers are beneficially manually configured since, once powered up, they remain running and process requests from clients. Typically, a server, once manually configured with an address, will not need address reconfiguration unless the network addressing plan changes.

Note that, in some scenarios (mostly in service provider networks), a CPE router (or an edge router) acting as a DHCPv6 requesting router (i.e., DHCPv6 Client) may be delegated IPv6 prefixes for long-term use by a PE router acting as a DHCPv6 delegating router (i.e., DHCPv6 Server). In such cases, the DHCPv6 Server sets the Valid Lifetime of the delegated IPv6 prefixes to 0xFFFFFFFF ("infinity"), indicating to the Client that the delegated IPv6 prefixes are permanently assigned to the Client, and the Client does not have to worry about renewing the assigned IPv6 prefixes.

4.9.2 IPv6 STATELESS ADDRESS AUTOCONFIGURATION (SLAAC)

The SLAAC mechanism was designed to provide a simpler and more straightforward method for automatic IPv6 addressing of interfaces using the ICMPv6 Router Advertisement messages sent by IPv6 routers attached to a link **[RFC4862]**. SLAAC provides a lightweight IPv6 address configuration method, allowing each host on an IPv6 network segment to automatically configure a unique

IPv6 address on an interface without any other device (DHCPv6 Server) on the network keeping track of the addresses assigned to the network nodes and the addresses that are still available for assignment. IPv6 hosts that use SLAAC are responsible for resolving any duplicate IP address conflicts using the IPv6 Duplicate Address Detection mechanism discussed above and in **[RFC4861]**.

SLAAC does not support the provisioning of DNS Server addresses to hosts (it does not provide DNS and domain name information). To solve this problem, IPv6 nodes using SLAAC on the network segment can contact a Stateless DHCPv6 Server to obtain the needed DNS and domain name information (DNS Server list and domain names). The use of SLAAC requires the advertising routers to set the O Flag in the Router Advertisement messages. However, in simpler network topologies where IPv6 hosts do not support a DHCPv6 Client, routers attached to a link may be configured to send Router Advertisement messages with the Recursive DNS Server Option and DNS Search List Option to advertise DNS information to IPv6 hosts on the link (see Section 4.3.4.6).

Using a Stateless DHCPv6 Server means that maintaining any dynamic state for the IPv6 addresses configured on individual IPv6 nodes (using SLAAC) is not required. Stateful IPv6 address assignment, on the other hand, involves deploying a dedicated device (DHCPv6 Server) on the network to keep track of the state of each host's IPv6 address assignment. The DHCPv6 Server tracks the IPv6 address pool to see which addresses are available and resolves duplicate address conflicts. It also logs every IPv6 address assigned along with its expiration time.

4.9.3 DYNAMIC HOST CONFIGURATION PROTOCOL VERSION 6 (DHCPV6)

A DHCPv6 Server may be deployed on a network to dynamically assign IPv6 prefixes/addresses as well as other configuration information to hosts (see the discussion in **Chapter 5** and also in **[RFC8415]**). As noted above, a Stateless DHCPv6 Server does not assign IPv6 prefixes/addresses at all; it only provides additional information such as DNS Server lists and domain names to SLAAC users. A Stateless DHCPv6 Server **[RFC3736]** works in conjunction with SLAAC, enabling users to obtain other configuration information from a DHCPv6 Server after auto-generating IPv6 Global Unicast addresses.

A Stateful DHCPv6 Server **[RFC8415]**, on the other hand, assigns IPv6 prefixes/addresses and provides additional information to hosts. This DHCPv6 Server also keeps track of the state of each IPv6 prefix/address assigned from its prefix/address pool(s), monitors the IPv6 prefixes/addresses still available for assignment, and resolves duplicate IPv6 address conflicts in the prefix/address pool(s). It also keeps a log of every IPv6 prefix/address assigned and its expiration time. The main difference between DHCPv6 and DHCPv4 is that a DHCPv4 server typically provides the IPv4 addresses of default gateways to hosts, while in IPv6, only IPv6 routers sending ICMPv6 Router Advertisement messages can dynamically provide the IPv6 addresses of default gateways.

4.10 UNDERSTANDING IPv6 STATELESS ADDRESS AUTOCONFIGURATION SLAAC

A key feature of IPv6 is the ability of an IPv6 host to automatically configure an IPv6 address on an interface without the use of a stateful configuration protocol, such as DHCPv6 **[RFC8415]**. By default, IPv6 requires hosts to configure an IPv6 Link-Local address for each interface to communicate with other IPv6 nodes on the same link **[RFC4862]**. Note that IPv6 Link-Local addresses (which are autoconfigured) have only local link scope and are not globally unique in the IPv6 Internet. They are unique only on the local link and can only be used to communicate with other nodes on the same link, not beyond it. The IPv6 Link-Local address on an interface serves more as a bootstrap address, allowing a node to initiate IPv6 communication on that interface.

Particularly, since IPv6 does not support broadcast addresses (unlike IPv4), any node that starts up (without being previously configured manually with an IPv6 address) must first be assigned a Link-Local address to communicate with any other node on the local link, and then be configured with a globally unique address to communicate with nodes outside the link. The absence of broadcast addresses makes the IPv6 address autoconfiguration feature more important and evident.

The IPv6 SLAAC feature does not require a network administrator to manually configure IPv6 hosts with globally unique IPv6 unicast addresses. It involves minimal (if any) configuration of the IPv6 routers on the link for IPv6/prefix assignment and requires no additional IPv6 addressing servers for that purpose. Using the SLAAC mechanism, an IPv6 host can generate its own IPv6 Global Unicast addresses using a combination of local network interface information (i.e., interface IDs) and IPv6 prefix information that attached routers advertise via ICMPv6 Router Advertisement messages.

Routers attached to a link use Router Advertisement messages to advertise IPv6 prefixes that identify the IPv6 subnet(s) associated with the local link. Each IPv6 host on a link can generate an interface ID that uniquely identifies the interface attached to the link. The IPv6 host on the link then forms a globally unique IPv6 unicast address for the interface by combining the advertised IPv6 prefix and the interface ID. Note that in the absence of routers on a link (to supply unique IPv6 prefixes), the local IPv6 hosts can only generate IPv6 Link-Local addresses for communicating with only on-link nodes; these addresses cannot be used for communicating with off-link nodes.

Using the IPv6 Router Discovery mechanism (discussed above), an IPv6 host on a link can discover and determine the addresses of local IPv6 routers in order to obtain IPv6 prefixes/addresses and other configuration parameters. The Router Advertisement message that an attached IPv6 router sends indicates whether the receiving IPv6 host should use a stateful address configuration protocol (DHCPv6) or not.

A site uses the SLAAC mechanism when the network administrator is not particularly concerned with the exact IPv6 unicast addresses that the local IPv6 hosts will use but only wants these addresses to be unique and routable. On the other hand, a site generally uses DHCPv6 **[RFC8415]** when the network administrator requires tighter control over how IPv6 addresses are assigned to hosts. It is not uncommon for a site to use both SLAAC and DHCPv6 simultaneously.

4.10.1 TYPES OF IPV6 ADDRESS AUTOCONFIGURATION

With the exception of IPv6 Link-Local addresses, only IPv6 hosts may use autoconfiguration for IPv6 Global Unicast addresses when instructed to do so. IPv6 routers, on the other hand, must obtain IPv6 unicast addresses and configuration parameters through another means, usually through manual configuration, because they have to adhere to the network operator's addressing plans.

IPv6 host address configuration falls under one of the following three methods:

- **Stateless Autoconfiguration**: In this mode, an IPv6 host uses the information contained in Router Advertisement messages sent by an attached router for address autoconfiguration. These messages include IPv6 address prefixes and other information that require stateless maintenance and require hosts on the link not to use a stateful address configuration protocol such as a Stateful DHCPv6 Server (see **Chapter 5**). In this mode, there is sufficient information in the Router Advertisement messages for an IPv6 node to create a Global Unicast address; however, the uniqueness of the address still has to be verified through IPv6 Duplicate Address Detection.
- **Stateful Autoconfiguration**: In this mode, address configuration depends on a stateful address configuration protocol, such as DHCPv6, to obtain all IPv6 prefixes/addresses and other required configuration parameters. In this case, IPv6 hosts on a link use the address configuration information provided by a Stateful DHCPv6 Server. IPv6 hosts receive Router Advertisement messages from a local router that do not include IPv6 prefixes, thereby requiring the hosts to use a stateful address configuration protocol, DHCPv6. An IPv6 host will typically use a stateful address configuration protocol (DHCPv6 Server) when no routers are present on the local link to provide SLAAC information, or when the network administrator requires tighter control over the assignment of IPv6 addressing information.

- **Both Stateless and Stateful Autoconfiguration**: In this mode, address configuration is based on Router Advertisement messages received from a local router. These messages include stateless IPv6 address prefixes, but require the IPv6 hosts on the link to use a stateful address configuration protocol (Stateful DHCPv6 Server) to obtain additional configuration information. In this case, a host may statelessly autoconfigure an IPv6 Global Unicast address while consulting a Stateful DHCPv6 Server for DNS and other configuration information. It is possible for IPv6 hosts on a link to obtain IPv6 address information using both SLAAC and DHCPv6 if both are enabled on the link.

However, it is important to note that in all of these address configuration methods, an IPv6 host must always configure an IPv6 Link-Local address for each of its interfaces when it starts up, allowing the host to communicate with any attached entity for further address configuration, most importantly, configuring global IPv6 addresses **[RFC4862]**. As noted above, an IPv6 Link-Local address is required upon power-up to enable the node to communicate with other nodes on the attached link. An IPv6 node can only start communicating with any other node on the local link when the relevant interface has a Link-Local address. **Chapter 3** discusses in detail the structure of IPv6 Link-Local addresses and how they are used.

Figure 4.30 summarizes the two main phases of IPv6 address configuration on IPv6 hosts (not routers). SLAAC allows IPv6 hosts to autoconfigure globally unique IPv6 addresses using the IPv6

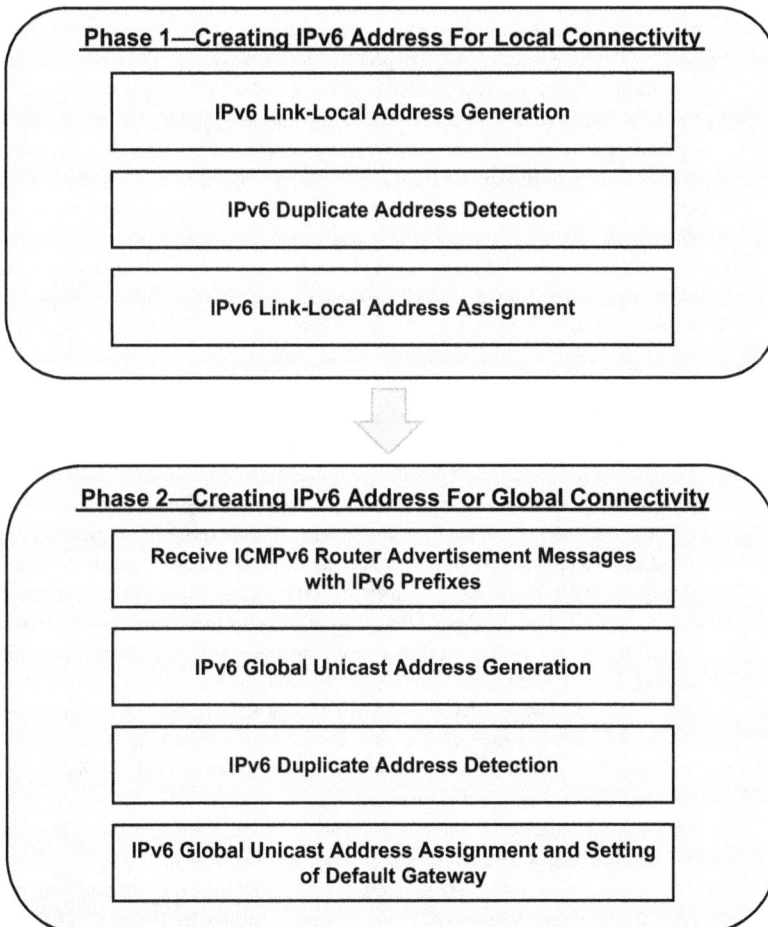

FIGURE 4.30   Phases of IPv6 address configuration on host interfaces.

prefixes provided by attached routers in the Router Advertisement messages they send. The use of SLAAC removes the need to explicitly configure IPv6 host interfaces on a given link via manual configuration or a Stateful DHCPv6 Server. At the end of the configuration process in Figure 4.30, each IPv6-enabled interface on the host will have two IPv6 addresses: a Link-Local address and a Global Unicast address.

4.10.2 AUTOCONFIGURED IPv6 ADDRESS STATES

An autoconfigured IPv6 address on an IPv6 node takes on the states described in Table 4.6 and Figure 4.31 [RFC4862]. Figure 4.31 shows the relationship between the states of an IPv6 autoconfigured address and its Preferred and Valid Lifetimes. Each IPv6 host on a given link maintains a list of IPv6 addresses with their corresponding Lifetimes in its IPv6 Prefix List. This list contains both autoconfigured IPv6 addresses (Global Unicast and Link-Local addresses) and manually configured IPv6 addresses.

TABLE 4.6
States and Lifetimes of an IPv6 Address

Parameter	Description
Tentative Address	This is an address that an IPv6 node is in the process of verifying for uniqueness, prior to assigning it to an interface. The host performs verification through the IPv6 Duplicate Address Detection function. An interface that receives IPv6 packets addressed to a Tentative Address discards them but accepts Neighbor Discovery packets used in Duplicate Address Detection of the Tentative Address.
Preferred Address	An address for which the IPv6 node has verified its uniqueness, assigned to an interface, and has unrestricted use by upper-layer protocols. A Preferred Address may be used as the source (or destination) address of IPv6 packets sent from (or to) the interface. An IPv6 node can send and receive unicast traffic to and from a Preferred Address. Router Advertisement messages include the duration that an address can remain in the Tentative and Preferred states.
Deprecated Address	This is an address that the IPv6 node assigns to an interface, but its use is discouraged, though not forbidden. This address should no longer be used as a source address in new communications, but IPv6 packets sent from or to such an address are delivered as expected. An IPv6 node may continue to use such an address as a source address in IPv6 packets where switching to a Preferred Address is problematic for a specific upper-layer activity (e.g., an existing TCP connection).In such cases, existing communication sessions can continue to use a Deprecated Address; IPv6 nodes can send and receive unicast traffic to and from Deprecated Addresses.
Valid Address	This is an address from which unicast traffic can be sent and received. A Valid Address is either a Preferred or Deprecated Address. An IPv6 node can use a Valid Address as the source or destination address of an IPv6 packet, and the Internet routing system is expected to deliver packets sent to a Valid Address to their intended recipients. The Valid State (Figure 4.31) covers both the Preferred and Deprecated states. Router Advertisement messages include the length of time that an address remains in the Valid State. The Valid Lifetime must be longer than or equal to the Preferred Lifetime.
Invalid Address	This is an IPv6 address for which an IPv6 node can no longer send or receive unicast traffic; an address that is not assigned to any interface. A Valid Address becomes invalid when its Valid Lifetime expires. An Invalid Address should not be used as the destination or source address of an IPv6 packet. In the former case, the Internet routing system will not be able to deliver the packet; in the latter case, the recipient of the packet will not be able to respond to it. An address enters the Invalid State after the Valid Lifetime expires.
Preferred Lifetime	This is the length of time that a Valid Address is preferred (i.e., the time until it is deprecated). When the Preferred Lifetime of the address expires, it becomes deprecated.
Valid Lifetime	This is the length of time that an address remains in the Valid State (i.e., the time until it is invalidated). The Valid Lifetime must be greater than or equal to the Preferred Lifetime. When the Valid Lifetime of the address expires, it becomes invalid.

When an IPv6 address is leased to an IPv6 host interface, that address may be used for a fixed (i.e., finite) length of time. In some cases, the IPv6 address may be used indefinitely (a permanent address). This means each IPv6 address assigned to a host interface has a Lifetime associated with it that indicates how long the interface can use that IPv6 address. When a Lifetime expires, the IPv6 address binding on the interface is marked as invalid, and the address is free to be reassigned to another interface in the network.

To ensure that IPv6 address bindings expire gracefully, an IPv6 address assigned to a host interface goes through two distinct phases or states (Preferred and Deprecated) while still on that interface (Table 4.6 and Figure 4.31). Initially, the IPv6 address is marked as Preferred on the interface, indicating that the address has unrestricted use in arbitrary communication with other nodes. Later, the IPv6 address is marked as Deprecated on the interface, with the prospect of its current binding on the interface becoming invalid. An IPv6 node deprecates a Preferred Address when its Preferred Lifetime expires. It is not strictly forbidden for an interface to use an IPv6 address in the Deprecated state, but its use is generally discouraged.

An IPv6 host should use a Preferred Address (i.e., an IPv6 address in the Preferred state) whenever possible (as the source IPv6 address) when initiating new communication with another node (e.g., opening a new TCP connection). An IPv6 host should use a Deprecated Address (i.e., an IPv6 address in the Deprecated state) only for applications that are still actively using that IPv6 address for communication and would find it difficult to switch to another IPv6 unicast address without disrupting the functioning of the applications (e.g., an application using an existing TCP connection).

4.10.2.1 Using Preferred and Deprecated IPv6 Addresses

A mechanism to time out IPv6 addresses assigned to interfaces is normally provided when those addresses are leased to IPv6 hosts. Current implementations of upper-layer protocols, such as TCP, do not support changing endpoint IP addresses while a connection is open. If the IP address of an endpoint of an active TCP connection becomes invalid, that connection will break, and all communication on the connection to the invalid IP address will fail. Even when UDP is used by an application, the IP addresses for the endpoints must generally remain the same during communication between the endpoints.

Note that an active connection between TCP or UDP endpoints is defined by the 5-tuple {Transport Layer Protocol Type, Source IP Address, Destination IP Address, Source Port Number, Destination Port Number}. This means that changing the Source or Destination IP Address completely redefines a connection. The IP address of an active TCP or UDP endpoint cannot be changed while the connection is active.

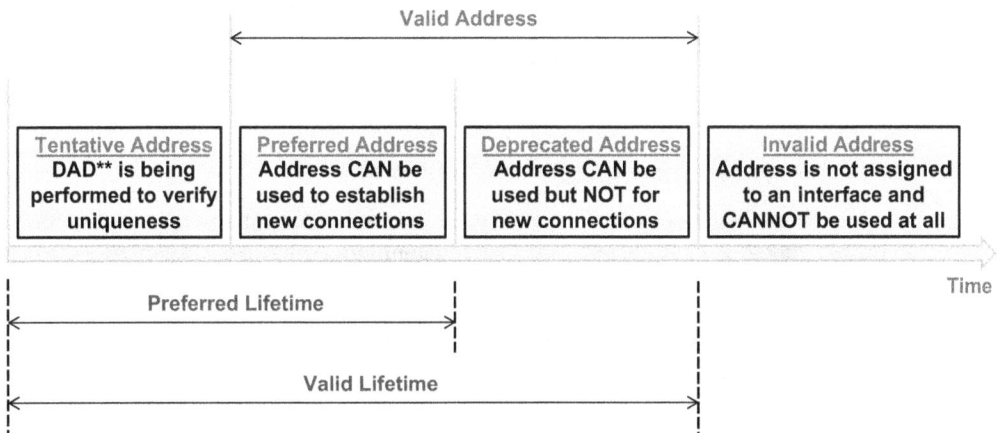

FIGURE 4.31   States of an autoconfigured IPv6 address.

Categorizing valid IPv6 addresses into Preferred and Deprecated, provides a mechanism for an IPv6 host to indicate to its upper-layer protocol entities that a valid IPv6 address may become invalid shortly, and that future communication using that IPv6 address will fail if the Valid Lifetime of the address expires before communication ends. To avoid communication failure, a Preferred Address should be used by the IPv6 host's upper-layer protocol entities to increase the chances that an IPv6 address will remain valid for the duration of the communication.

The network administrator has to set appropriate Lifetimes for IPv6 prefixes to minimize the impact of communication failure when IPv6 address renumbering occurs. The network administrator should set the deprecation duration (or time interval) of an IPv6 address to be long enough such that, at the time an IPv6 address expires and becomes invalid, most, if not all, communications on the associated IPv6 host will be using the new IPv6 address. The IPv6 layer of hosts should support a mechanism for upper-layer protocol entities (including applications) to select the most appropriate source IPv6 address for a given IPv6 destination.

4.10.2.2 Handling Tentative IPv6 Addresses

A tentative IPv6 address is one that the Duplicate Address Detection procedure is trying to determine for its uniqueness and can only be assigned to an interface after the procedure has completed successfully and verified it is unique. How an IPv6 host uses a Tentative Address assigned to an interface depends on the IPv6 packet carrying that address. An interface must accept Neighbor Solicitation and Advertisement messages whose Target Address field contains a Tentative Address, but such messages are processed differently from those whose Target Address field contains an IPv6 address that is already assigned to the interface.

The IPv6 node should silently discard "other packets" addressed to the Tentative Address. The term "other packets" includes Neighbor Solicitation and Advertisement messages that have the destination IPv6 address set to an IPv6 unicast Tentative Address and whose Target Address field contains the Tentative Address. Such cases should not occur during normal operation, since IPv6 nodes will multicast these messages during the Duplicate Address Detection process.

An IPv6 node performs Duplicate Address Detection on an IPv6 address prior to assigning it to an interface to prevent multiple IPv6 nodes on the local link from using the same IPv6 address simultaneously. If an IPv6 node (the first node) starts using an IPv6 address while performing Duplicate Address Detection on that address, and another node (the second node) on the link is already using that IPv6 address, the first node will erroneously process IPv6 packets intended for the second node, potentially resulting in negative network and node behavior, such as the resetting of open TCP connections.

If the Duplicate Address Detection function on an IPv6 node discovers that another IPv6 node on the link is already using a tentative IPv6 address (indicating a duplicate address exists), that IPv6 address cannot be assigned to the intended interface. If the IPv6 node derived the IPv6 address from an interface ID and this resulted in an IPv6 address conflict on the link, the node will need to assign a new interface ID to the interface, or the IPv6 address for the interface will have to be manually configured.

4.10.3 Role of Duplicate Address Detection in IPv6 SLAAC

IPv6 nodes (hosts and routers) perform IPv6 address autoconfiguration only on multicast-capable interfaces (links). A node begins address autoconfiguration when it enables IPv6 on a multicast-capable interface (e.g., during system startup).

4.10.3.1 Phase 1: Autoconfiguration of IPv6 Link-Local
Address and Duplicate Address Detection

A node (host or router) starts the IPv6 address autoconfiguration process by generating an IPv6 Link-Local address for the interface (see Figure 4.30). It forms the IPv6 Link-Local address by appending the interface ID (usually 64 bits long) to the well-known IPv6 link-local prefix, FE80::/64.

Before an IPv6 node assigns a tentative IPv6 Link-Local address to an interface for communication, it must first verify that the address is not already being used by another node on the link. The IPv6 node transmits a Neighbor Solicitation message containing the tentative IPv6 address in the message's Target Address field (see Figure 4.3). If another node on the link is already using that IPv6 Link-Local address, it will respond with a Neighbor Advertisement indicating that the address is already taken.

If another node on the same link is also attempting to use the same IPv6 Link-Local address, it will respond by sending a Neighbor Solicitation message for that target IPv6 Link-Local address. The number of times an IPv6 node will (re)transmit a Neighbor Solicitation message and the time interval (i.e., spacing) between consecutive Neighbor Solicitation messages is link-specific and may be set by system management.

If the IPv6 node determines from the responses that the tentative IPv6 Link-Local address is not unique, it stops the IPv6 address autoconfiguration process and resorts to manual configuration of the interface. However, to simplify recovery and ensure that address autoconfiguration can still continue in this case, the network administrator may supply an alternate interface ID (e.g., based on a device serial number or any suitable node-specific token) that overrides the default (previous) interface ID, allowing the IPv6 address autoconfiguration mechanism to resume using this new (presumably unique) interface ID. Alternatively, the network administrator may decide to manually configure the IPv6 Link-Local and other addresses on the interface.

Once the IPv6 node has ascertained the uniqueness of its tentative IPv6 Link-Local address, it assigns the address to the target interface. At this point, the node is able to communicate with other nodes on the link since it now has IPv6-level connectivity with neighboring nodes. After autoconfiguration of an IPv6 Link-Local address on an interface, *only hosts will autoconfigure an IPv6 Global Unicast address on the interface; IPv6 unicast addresses on router interfaces are typically configured through other means (usually manual configuration). It is important to note that IPv6 autoconfiguration applies primarily to IPv6 hosts; however, both IPv6 hosts and routers can autogenerate IPv6 Link-Local addresses and then perform Duplicate Address Detection on those addresses prior to assigning them to* interfaces.

4.10.3.2 Phase 2: Receiving ICMPv6 Router Advertisement Messages, IPv6 Global Unicast Address Configuration, and Duplicate Address Detection

In the next phase of IPv6 address autoconfiguration, the IPv6 node receives Router Advertisement messages from attached routers if present on the link. Routers attached to the link send Router Advertisement messages that specify how IPv6 hosts on the link can perform IPv6 Global Unicast address configuration. IPv6 hosts on the link may use a DHCPv6 service for IPv6 Global Unicast address configuration if available, even if no routers are present on the link.

Routers transmit Router Advertisement messages periodically to the IPv6 All-Nodes multicast address (FF01::1), but the time interval (spacing) between successive messages will generally be greater than the time an IPv6 host performing IPv6 address autoconfiguration on the link may want to wait **[RFC4861]**. To enable an IPv6 host to obtain a Router Advertisement message quickly, the host sends one or more Router Solicitation messages addressed to the IPv6 All-Routers multicast address (FF01::2).

Each Router Advertisement message sent includes zero or more Prefix Information Options (Option Type 3) **[RFC4861]** that contain information used by IPv6 hosts on the link for stateless IPv6 Global Unicast address autoconfiguration. IPv6 hosts on the link may use both IPv6 SLAAC and DHCPv6 simultaneously. The Prefix Information Option contains the 1-bit A (Autonomous Address Configuration) Flag field that indicates whether the IPv6 prefix included in the Option can be used for IPv6 SLAAC. If the A Flag is set to 1, the Option contains an IPv6 prefix with corresponding Valid and Preferred Lifetime values that indicate how long IPv6 addresses generated from the included IPv6 prefix will remain preferred and valid. An IPv6 host creates an IPv6 Global Unicast address for an interface by appending an interface ID (typically 64 bits long) to an

IPv6 prefix of appropriate length received in a Router Advertisement message's Prefix Information Option.

Routers send (unsolicited) Router Advertisement messages periodically on a link, allowing IPv6 hosts on the link to continually receive new Advertisement messages. IPv6 hosts continuously process the information contained in the received Advertisement messages, building on and refreshing existing information from previous Advertisement messages.

By default, an IPv6 host checks a generated IPv6 Global Unicast address for uniqueness prior to assigning it to an interface. Reference **[RFC4862]** recommends that *an IPv6 host checks all IPv6 addresses for uniqueness (using Duplicate Address Detection), whether they are manually configured, configured using IPv6 SLAAC, or via DHCPv6.*

To speed up the IPv6 address autoconfiguration process on an IPv6 host, a host may create an IPv6 Link-Local address for an interface (and verify its uniqueness using Duplicate Address Detection) in parallel while waiting for a Router Advertisement message. Because routers generally take time (a few seconds) to respond to a Router Solicitation message, the total time that an IPv6 host takes to complete IPv6 Global Unicast address autoconfiguration can be significantly longer if the host performs IPv6 Link-Local address creation (along with uniqueness verification) first and then waits for a router to send a Router Advertisement message (i.e., if these two steps are done sequentially).

4.10.4 SENDING AND RECEIVING IPV6 NEIGHBOR DISCOVERY MESSAGES DURING DUPLICATE ADDRESS DETECTION

This section describes the sending and receiving of Neighbor Solicitation or Advertisement messages and the tests an IPv6 node performs when verifying the uniqueness of a Tentative Address. Once an IPv6 node determines that an IPv6 address is unique, it may assign the address to an interface.

4.10.4.1 Sending ICMPv6 Neighbor Solicitation Messages

Before an IPv6 node sends a Neighbor Solicitation message on an interface, it must first join the IPv6 All-Nodes multicast address (FF01::1) and the IPv6 Solicited-Node multicast address associated with the Tentative Address. The node performs the former to ensure that it receives Neighbor Advertisement messages from other on-link nodes already using the Tentative Address. The node performs the latter to ensure that any other on-link nodes attempting to use the same address simultaneously would detect the sender's presence.

The sender of the Neighbor Solicitation message sets the message's Target Address field to the Tentative Address, the source IPv6 address of the IPv6 packet carrying the message to the IPv6 Unspecified address (::), and the destination IPv6 address to the IPv6 Solicited-Node multicast address associated with the Target Address (i.e., the Tentative Address). For the first Neighbor Solicitation message on an interface, the node joins the IPv6 Solicited-Node multicast address.

An IPv6 node joins an IPv6 multicast address by sending an MLD Report message **[RFC2710]** **[RFC3810]** to that multicast address. In the case of Duplicate Address Detection, the IPv6 node sends an MLD Report message to inform MLD-Snooping switches (instead of routers) of the presence of multicast listeners, allowing them to correctly forward IPv6 multicast packets on the interface. To improve the robustness of the Duplicate Address Detection procedure on an interface, an IPv6 node must receive and process IPv6 packets sent to the IPv6 All-Nodes multicast address or the IPv6 Solicited-Node multicast address of the Tentative Address.

4.10.4.2 Receiving ICMPv6 Neighbor Solicitation Messages

The behavior of an IPv6 node upon receiving a valid Neighbor Solicitation message on an interface depends on whether the message's Target Address field contains an IPv6 address that is a Tentative Address at the receiving node. If the Target Address is NOT a Tentative Address at the message's receiver (i.e., the receiver has already assigned the address to the receiving interface), the Neighbor Solicitation message is processed by the receiver as follows:

- If the source IPv6 address of the message is not the IPv6 Unspecified address and the message includes a Source Link-Layer Address Option, then the receiver updates or creates the Neighbor Cache entry for the message's source IPv2 address.
- If the Neighbor Cache does not already have an entry, the receiver creates a new entry and sets the entry's reachability state to STALE.
- If the Neighbor Cache already has an entry and the cached Link-Layer address is different from the address in the received Source Link-Layer Option, the receiver replaces the cached Link-Layer address with the received Link-Layer address and sets the entry's reachability state to STALE.

If the message's Target Address field contains an IPv6 address that is a Tentative Address at the receiver, and the message's source IPv6 address is an IPv6 unicast address, then the receiver sees the message's sender as performing Address Resolution on the Target Address. In this case, the receiver should silently ignore the Neighbor Solicitation message. Otherwise (i.e., if the address is the receiver's Tentative Address but the source IPv6 address is NOT an IPv6 unicast address), the receiver interprets the IPv6 address in the Target Address field of the message (i.e., the Tentative Address) as a duplicate, and neither node should use that IPv6 address. In this case, the source IPv6 address of the message is the IPv6 Unspecified address, meaning the message is from a node performing Duplicate Address Detection. *In all cases, the receiver must not respond to a Neighbor Solicitation message that contains a Tentative Address in the Target Address* field.

The receiving node uses the following checks to determine when a Tentative Address that it has locally generated is NOT unique:

- If the node received a Neighbor Solicitation message for a Tentative Address for the receiving interface before the node itself sends such a message, then the Tentative Address is considered a duplicate. This situation occurs when two IPv6 nodes on the local link run the Duplicate Address Detection procedure simultaneously but send initial Neighbor Solicitation messages at different times (e.g., the nodes have selected different random delay values before joining the IPv6 Solicited-Node multicast address for the Tentative Address and transmitting the initial Neighbor Solicitation message).
- If the actual number of Neighbor Solicitation messages that the IPv6 node has received is greater than the number of messages expected, the node considers the Tentative Address a duplicate. This situation occurs when two IPv6 nodes on the local link run the Duplicate Address Detection procedure simultaneously and send Neighbor Solicitation messages around the same time.

4.10.4.3 Receiving ICMPv6 Neighbor Advertisement Messages

The behavior of an IPv6 node, upon receiving a valid Neighbor Advertisement message on an interface depends on whether the IPv6 address in the message's Target Address field is a Tentative Address or matches an IPv6 unicast or Anycast address assigned to the receiving interface:

- If the IPv6 address in the message's Target Address field is a Tentative Address on the receiving interface, then this address is not unique.
- If the IPv6 address in the Target Address field matches an IPv6 unicast address already assigned to the receiving interface, this may indicate that the IPv6 address is a duplicate, but the Duplicate Address Detection procedure has not detected this (note that the Duplicate Address Detection procedure is not completely reliable). Reference **[RFC4862]** does not provide a solution to this situation.

- Otherwise, the receiving IPv6 node processes the Neighbor Advertisement message as described in Section 4.3.2.4.1.2.

If either the sending or receiving IPv6 node determines a Tentative Address to be a duplicate, it does not assign it to an interface and should log a system management error.

If the Tentative Address is an IPv6 Link-Local address generated from an interface ID based on the interface's MAC (hardware) address, which is supposed to be universally unique (e.g., an EUI-64 interface ID derived from a universally unique Ethernet MAC address for an interface), the IPv6 node should disable IPv6 operation on that interface. In this case, duplication of the IPv6 address most likely indicates that a duplicate MAC address exists on the local link. The solution to this problem requires the network administrator to trace the source of the IPv6 address (equivalently, the MAC address) causing the duplication and take the necessary steps to rectify this situation before further network anomalies arise.

4.10.5 IPv6 SLAAC Process

In IPv6 SLAAC, an IPv6 node self-configures an IPv6 unicast address on an interface without using a DHCPv6 Server that keeps track of the IPv6 addresses that have been assigned and those that are still available for assignment (i.e., Stateful DHCPv6 Server). This method of address configuration requires the IPv6 node to resolve any duplicate address conflicts (using IPv6 Duplicate Address Detection) after IPv6 address generation, as described in this section.

4.10.5.1 Autoconfiguration of IPv6 Link-Local Addresses

An IPv6 node absolutely needs a Link-Local address on each of its interfaces to be able to communicate with any other node on the link. *Note that the process of configuring a Link-Local address is not exactly part of the stateless IPv6 address autoconfiguration feature, but without first configuring a Link-Local address, an IPv6 node would not be able to communicate at the IPv6 protocol layer with any other IPv6 node.* Configuring a Link-Local address on an interface is a pre-requisite for everything else the node does on a link.

An IPv6 node autoconfigures an IPv6 Link-Local address for an interface whenever it is enabled. The following events may cause an interface to become enabled, resulting in an IPv6 Link-Local address being autoconfigured on it:

- The IP6 node initializes the interface at system startup.
- The IPv6 node reinitializes the interface after it has temporarily failed or after system management has temporarily disabled it.
- The interface is connected to a particular link for the first time. This includes the case where the interface dynamically changes to another link, for example, when the interface has moved to another access point of a wireless network.
- System management has enabled the interface after it was administratively disabled.

The following sub-sections summarize the address autoconfiguration process for Link-Local addresses on IPv6 nodes.

4.10.5.1.1 Configuring an IPv6 Link-Local Address on an IPv6 Node

When an IPv6 node first connects to an IPv6 network and the connecting interface has not been previously configured manually with an IPv6 Link-Local address, it first autoconfigures that interface with a Link-Local address. The purpose of this Link-Local address is to enable the IPv6 module on the connecting node to communicate with other IPv6 nodes on the local link.

The most widely used IPv6 Link-Local address autoconfiguration method combines the Link-Local prefix FE80::/64 with the interface ID in the modified EUI-64 format (typically generated from the interface's 48-bit MAC address). *The IPv6 Link-Local address prefix is FE::/10, but FE::/64 is used because the bits between the prefix FE80 and the modified EUI-64 interface ID are set to zero, as described in* ***Chapter 3***. The modified EUI-64 interface ID can also be randomly generated, as discussed in a section below.

The following steps describe how an IPv6 Link-Local address is generated from the 48-bit MAC address 00-DE-00–1A-2B-3C (in hexadecimal):

1. Take the 48-bit MAC address 00-DE-00–1A-2B-3C.
2. Insert 0xFFFE in the middle of this 48-bit MAC address, resulting in 00DE:00FF:FE1A:2B3C.
3. Invert the seventh bit in the first leading byte of the resulting value. The first byte is 00 in hexadecimal and 00000000 in binary. Inverting the seventh bit gives 00000010, which is 02 in hexadecimal. The interface address in the modified EUI-64 interface is then 02DE:00FF:FE1A:2B3C.
4. Prepend the IPv6 Link-Local prefix FE80:: to the modified EUI-64 interface ID, giving the IPv6 Link-Local address FE80::2DE:FF:FE1A:2B3C.

The above steps show how an IPv6 node creates a fully functional IPv6 Link-Local address with an interface ID in the modified EUI-64 format. Note that the EUI-64 interface ID can also be a manually configured identifier, created from a node serial number, or a randomly generated value, as discussed in a section below.

Other examples:

- The MAC address D7-AA-00-BB-CC-DD (leading byte = 1101 0111) in the modified EUI-64 format is D5AA:FF:FEBB:CCDD (leading byte = 1101 0101), resulting in the IPv6 Link-Local address FE80::D5AA:FF:FEBB:CCDD.
- The MAC address AB-AA-00-BB-CC-DD (leading byte = 1010 1011) in the modified EUI-64 format is A9AA:FF:FEBB:CCDD (leading byte = 1010 1001), resulting in the IPv6 Link-Local address FE80::A9AA:FF:FEBB:CCDD.

An IPv6 node assigns an infinite Preferred and Valid Lifetime to each IPv6 Link-Local address generated; it is never timed out.

4.10.5.1.2   Performing Duplicate Address Detection for the IPv6 Link-Local Address

To check if the IPv6 Link-Local address FE80::2DE:FF:FE1A:2B3C generated above is already in use by another IPv6 node on the local link, the source node sends an ICMPv6 Neighbor Solicitation message with the destination address set to the corresponding auto-generated IPv6 Solicited-Node multicast address FF02::1:FF1A:2B3C and the source address set to the IPv6 Unspecified address (::). The Target Address field of this ICMPv6 message is set to the generated (tentative) IPv6 address FE80::2DE:FF:FE1A:2B3C.

Only IPv6 nodes on the link that are listening to this exact auto-generated multicast group (FF02::1:FF1A:2B3C) will receive and process the ICMPv6 message; all other nodes will simply discard it. If any node on the link is using the tentative IPv6 address FE80::2DE:FF:FE1A:2B3C, it will reply using a Neighbor Advertisement message, indicating that this IPv6 address is already in use. If no node replies, the source node will conclude that this address is unique and available for use on the sending interface.

4.10.5.1.3   Obtaining a IPv6 Router Advertisements and Prefix Configuration Information

After IPv6 Link-Local address autoconfiguration, the next step involves the IPv6 host obtaining Router Advertisement messages to determine if IPv6 routers are present on the local link. If IPv6 routers are present, they transmit Router Advertisement messages that specify the type of address configuration IPv6 hosts on the link should perform.

The Router Advertisement messages are sent periodically (unsolicited messages); however, the time interval between successive messages is generally longer than the time an IPv6 host performing address configuration can wait. Thus, to speed up the process of obtaining router advertisements, an IPv6 host sends one or more Router Solicitation messages to the IPv6 All-Routers multicast address (FF02::2).

Router Advertisement messages also contain IPv6 prefix information, allowing IPv6 hosts on the link to use SLAAC to generate IPv6 prefixes. A Router Advertisement message can contain multiple Prefix Information Options that are processed independently by receiving hosts. An Option contains IPv6 prefix information and the 1-bit A (Autonomous Address Autoconfiguration) Flag, which indicates whether the Option applies to SLAAC. If the Option applies to SLAAC, additional fields in the Option contain an IPv6 prefix for the link along with Lifetime values. These Lifetime values indicate the length of time that IPv6 addresses created from the Option's IPv6 prefix can remain preferred and valid on the link.

Because IPv6 routers periodically send (unsolicited) Router Advertisement messages on a link, attached IPv6 hosts continually receive new advertisements. IPv6 hosts on the link process the information contained in each advertisement and refresh their local information obtained from previous advertisements.

IPv6 hosts use Link-Local addresses to uniquely identify IPv6 routers on a link, enabling them to maintain the necessary IPv6 router associations. Identifying IPv6 routers is essential for hosts to respond correctly to Router Advertisement and Redirect messages. IPv6 hosts need to maintain router associations to effectively use newly advertised IPv6 global prefixes. IPv4 does not support a corresponding method for dynamically identifying IPv4 routers on a link (via unsolicited Router Advertisements and link-scope interface addresses).

4.10.5.1.4   IPv6 Neighbor Solicitation and Unreachability

IPv6 nodes use Neighbor Solicitation messages to determine if any other node on a link is assigned the same IPv6 unicast address (Duplicate Address Detection). They also use the IPv6 Neighbor Unreachability Detection function to detect the failure of a neighboring node or the failure of the packet forwarding path to a neighbor. The Neighbor Unreachability Detection process requires positive confirmation that IPv6 packets sent to a neighbor are actually reaching that neighbor. This process also verifies that IPv6 packets sent by an IPv6 node are being processed properly by the neighbor's IPv6 layer.

The Neighbor Unreachability Detection function relies on confirmation from two sources: confirmation from upper-layer protocols and confirmation through the receipt of Neighbor Solicitation messages. When possible, an upper-layer protocol (e.g., TCP) may provide a positive confirmation that a connection is actively receiving and processing packets. For example, when an IPv6 host receives new TCP acknowledgments for data sent, this confirms that previously sent data has been delivered correctly.

When an IPv6 node does not receive positive confirmation from upper-layer protocols after data are sent, the node sends unicast Neighbor Solicitation messages to solicit the sending of Neighbor Advertisement messages. These unicast Neighbor Solicitation messages are sent to confirm the reachability of the neighboring node. To reduce unnecessary traffic on the link, an IPv6 node sends these probe messages (unicast Neighbor Solicitation messages) only to neighbors to which it is actively sending IPv6 packets.

4.10.5.1.5   Change in IPv6 Link-Local Address

If the Link-Local address on an IPv6 node has changed, the node can multicast unsolicited Neighbor Advertisement messages on the link to announce the change. The node can send these messages to the IPv6 All-Nodes multicast address (FF02::1) to update cached Link-Local addresses on the local link that have become invalid due to the change. Allowing nodes to send unsolicited Neighbor Advertisement messages serves as a network performance enhancement. The Neighbor

Unreachability Detection mechanism ensures that all IPv6 nodes on the link can reliably discover the new Link-Local address, although the discovery delay might be somewhat longer.

4.10.5.1.6   *Load Balancing over Multiple Layer 3 Interfaces with Separate IPv6 Link-Local Addresses to an IPv6 Host*

An IPv6 node, such as a server, may be configured with multiple Layer 3 interfaces for the purpose of balancing traffic (the concept of Equal Cost Multipath (ECMP) routing). In Figure 4.32, The IPv6 node then load balances IPv6 packets across the multiple Layer 3 network interfaces on the same link. In Figure 4.32, the IPv6 node has multiple IPv6 Link-Local addresses, one assigned to each interface. For instance, a single network bonding driver on the IPv6 server (using a Layer 3 NIC bonding/teaming driver) and the IPv6 routing table in the IPv6 router (using IPv6 ECMP routing) may represent multiple physical network interface cards (NICs) as a single logical Layer 3 interface, with each interface assigned an IPv6 Link-Local address. Most modern IP routers and servers support network drivers for bonding Layer 3 and Layer 2 interfaces to perform load balancing.

Most IP routers support ECMP routing, allowing multiple routes to a single destination to be installed in the routing table as one logical route for load balancing. Load balancing/sharing over Layer 3 is typically achieved through the ECMP routing feature in RIP, OSPF, and IS-IS **[AWE2BK21V1]** **[AWE2BK21V2]**. Note that EIGRP supports both ECMP and Unequal Cost Multipath (UCMP) routing. Load balancing/sharing over Layer 2 is generally accomplished using IEEE 802.3ad Link Aggregation (now IEEE 802.1AX). In this book, we abbreviate IS-IS for IPv6 as IS-ISv6.

The IPv6 router performs load balancing across multiple Layer 3 interfaces by omitting the source IPv6 Link-Local address from the Router Advertisement messages it sends on these interfaces (the source IPv6 address is set to the IPv6 Unspecified address (::)). Consequently, a neighbor (i.e., the IPv6 server) connected to the multiple interfaces must use Neighbor Solicitation messages to learn the IPv6 Link-Local addresses of the IPv6 router. The Neighbor Advertisement messages returned by the attached IPv6 router contain IPv6 Link-Local addresses that may differ, depending on which server interface issued the Neighbor Solicitation message. In this scenario, each router interface/link has its own autoconfigured or manually configured IPv6 Link-Local address, and the interface ID (in the modified EUI-64 format) in the IPv6 Link-Local address may be based on the interface's MAC address or any suitable node-specific token.

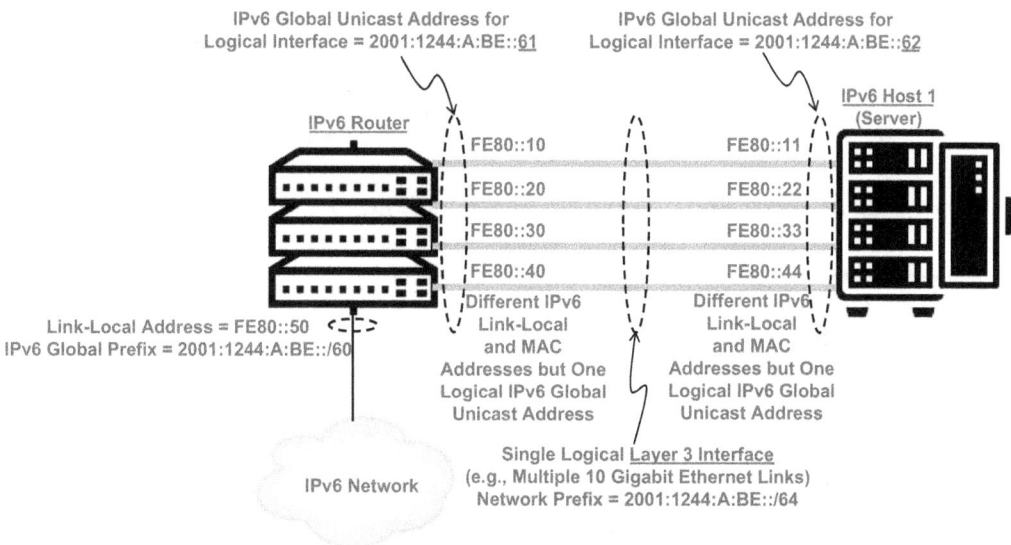

FIGURE 4.32   Load balancing over multiple Layer 3 interfaces with different IPv6 Link-Local addresses to an IPv6 host.

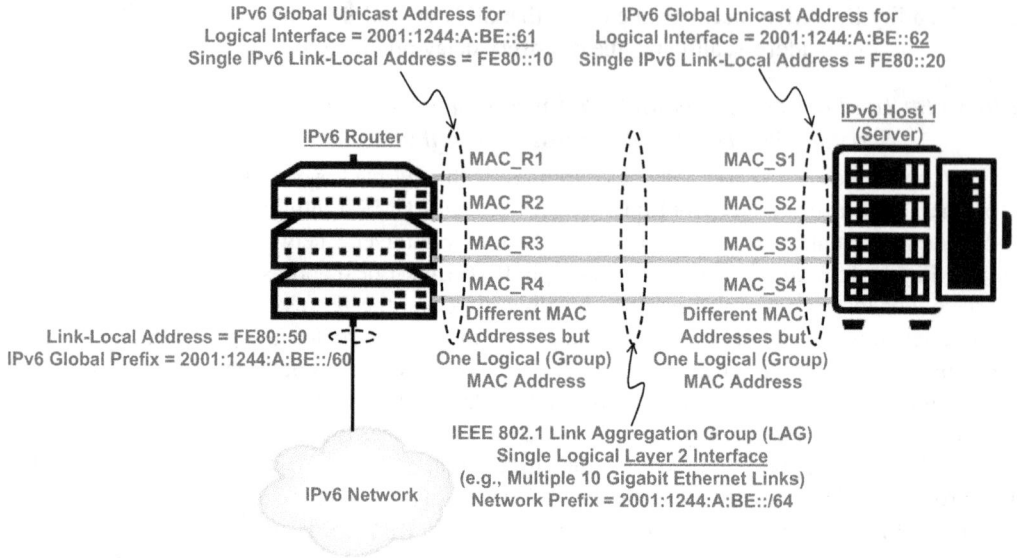

IPv6 Global Unicast Address for
Logical Interface = 2001:1244:A:BE::61
Single IPv6 Link-Local Address = FE80::10

IPv6 Global Unicast Address for
Logical Interface = 2001:1244:A:BE::62
Single IPv6 Link-Local Address = FE80::20

IPv6 Host 1
(Server)

IPv6 Router

MAC_R1   MAC_S1
MAC_R2   MAC_S2
MAC_R3   MAC_S3
MAC_R4   MAC_S4

Different MAC   Different MAC
Addresses but   Addresses but
One Logical (Group)   One Logical (Group)
MAC Address   MAC Address

Link-Local Address = FE80::50
IPv6 Global Prefix = 2001:1244:A:BE::/60

IEEE 802.1 Link Aggregation Group (LAG)
Single Logical Layer 2 Interface
(e.g., Multiple 10 Gigabit Ethernet Links)
Network Prefix = 2001:1244:A:BE::/64

IPv6 Network

FIGURE 4.33   Load balancing over an IEEE 802.1 Link Aggregation Group (LAG) to an IPv6 host.

In Figure 4.32, Ethernet frames sent on each physical interface of the logical Layer 3 link have the source MAC address set to the MAC address of the sending physical interface, and the destination MAC address set to the MAC address of the receiving physical interface. The destination IPv6 address of IPv6 packets sent to the server is the single IPv6 Global Unicast address of the receiving side of the logical Layer 3 (IPv6) link.

4.10.5.1.7   Load Balancing over Multiple Layer 2 Interfaces to an IPv6 Host

Note that the architecture in Figure 4.32, where Router 1 and Host 1 (the server) are connected by multiple links with different IPv6 Link-Local addresses, represents a Layer 3 multipath routing architecture. This differs from an architecture where Router 1 and the server (Host 1) are connected by an Ethernet (Layer 2) Link Aggregation Group (LAG), as shown in Figure 4.33. IEEE 802.1AX Link Aggregation is a technique that allows multiple parallel physical Ethernet (Layer 2) links to be combined (aggregated) to create a single, larger logical Layer 2 link. Link Aggregation is used to increase the total traffic-carrying capacity of a connection beyond what a single connection could provide and offers link redundancy between two nodes, allowing all but one of the physical links in the LAG to fail without losing connectivity.

The use of an IEEE 802.1AX LAG to a destination is not ECMP routing but rather single-path routing over a Layer 2 link that consists of several bonded physical links to the same destination. The bundle of physical links in the LAG is seen by both end devices as a single logical Layer 2 link, similar to any other single-path physical link in the routed network. A LAG is effectively a single path with multiple physical lanes.

To use a LAG, both the router and the server must support Layer 2 network bonding/teaming drivers that make the different physical interfaces/NICs appear as a single logical Layer 2 interface (a LAG), as discussed in Chapter 4 of **[AWEYFCDM22]**. *Each interface/NIC in the LAG has its own MAC address, but the LAG itself appears as a single logical interface with its own MAC* address. The NIC teaming driver combines multiple NICs to function together as a single logical NIC. The Layer 2 network bonding/teaming driver is responsible for configuring the MAC address for the logical Layer 2 interface (the LAG).

In Figure 4.33, Ethernet frames sent on each physical interface of the LAG have the source MAC address set to the logical group MAC address of the sending LAG interface, and the destination

MAC address set to the logical group MAC address of the receiving LAG interface. The destination IPv6 address of IPv6 packets sent to the server is the single IPv6 Global Unicast address of the receiving side of the LAG.

4.10.5.2 Stateless Autoconfiguration of IPv6 Global Unicast Addresses

After an IPv6 node has configured a Link-Local address on an interface to communicate with any other node on the attached link, it needs an IPv6 Global Unicast address on the interface to communicate with other nodes beyond that local link. The steps for configuring an IPv6 Global Unicast address on an interface in a stateless manner can be described by the following steps (see Figures 4.34 and 4.35). The details of using Stateless or Stateful DHCPv6 for address configuration are described in other sections below. This section discusses the stateless autoconfiguration of an IPv6 Global Unicast address on an interface to set the context for the discussion on the use of Stateless and Stateful DHCPv6 addressing on an interface.

The general steps for stateless IPv6 Global Unicast address autoconfiguration on an interface of an IPv6 node are as follows:

1. The IPv6 node derives a tentative IPv6 Link-Local address for the interface based on the Link-Local address prefix of FE80::/64 and the 64-bit interface ID. The interface ID may be based on an EUI-64 ID generated from the MAC address of the interface or may be a randomly generated interface ID (as discussed in a section below).

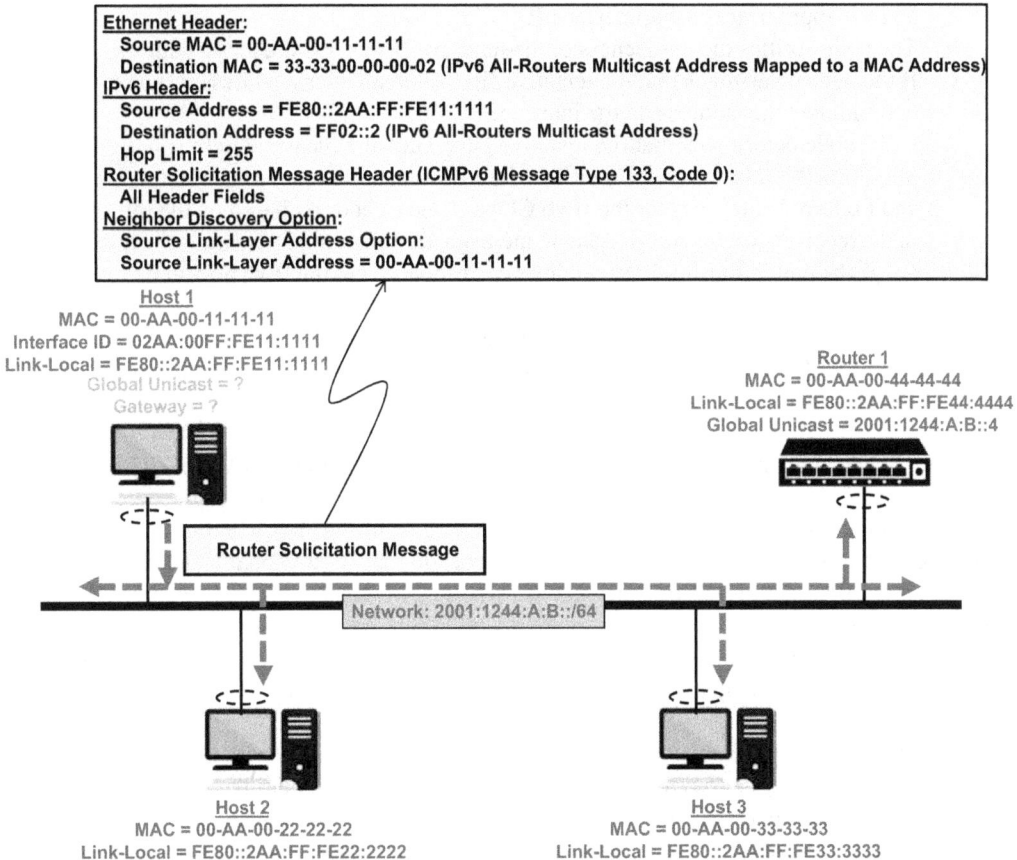

FIGURE 4.34 Stateless Autoconfiguration of IPv6 Global Unicast address: sending Router Solicitation message.

2. The node performs Duplicate Address Detection to verify the uniqueness of the tentative IPv6 Link-Local address.

   a. If the IPv6 address already exists and is in use by another on-link interface, the interface ID must be configured manually or randomly regenerated if this feature is supported.

   b. If the IPv6 address does not exist on the link, the tentative Link-Local address is assumed to be unique and valid and is initialized on the interface. The node then proceeds to generate a corresponding IPv6 Solicited-Node multicast address for the configured Link-Local address.

   c. The node then maps the Solicited-Node multicast address to a corresponding multicast Link-Layer address, and registers it with the interface's network adapter.

3. The IPv6 host transmits a Router Solicitation message as described in Figure 4.34.

4. If the IPv6 host receives no Router Advertisement messages from an attached IPv6 router, it may use a stateful address configuration protocol (i.e., Stateful DHCPv6 Server) to obtain IPv6 addresses and other configuration parameters.

5. If the IPv6 host receives a Router Advertisement message from an attached IPv6 router (see Figure 4.35), it proceeds to configure an IPv6 Global Unicast address for the interface based on the information in this message.

6. The Router Advertisement message includes the following information for each stateless IPv6 address prefix it contains, and the IPv6 node performs the following actions when required:

   a. The node derives a tentative IPv6 Global Unicast address from the IPv6 address prefix and the appropriate 64-bit interface ID.

   b. The node verifies the uniqueness of the tentative IPv6 Global Unicast address.

   c. If the node determines that the tentative IPv6 Global Unicast address is in use, it does not initialize this address on the interface.

   d. If the node determines that the tentative IPv6 Global Unicast address is not in use, it initializes this address on the interface. Initialization involves the node setting the Valid and Preferred Lifetimes for the IPv6 Global Unicast address based on the information in the received Router Advertisement message. Initialization also entails the host registering the multicast Link-Layer address corresponding to the IPv6 Solicited-Node with the interface's network adapter.

7. If the received Router Advertisement message specifies a stateful address configuration protocol (i.e., Stateful DHCPv6 Server) to obtain additional addresses or configuration parameters, the host uses this information.

After Host 1 has autoconfigured an IPv6 Link-Local address (FE80::2AA:FF:FE11:1111) on an interface, it proceeds to autoconfigure an IPv6 Global Unicast address on the same interface using SLAAC (see Figure 4.34). Host 1 begins this process by transmitting an ICMPv6 Router Solicitation message on the link to all attached IPv6 routers, requesting an IPv6 Global Unicast prefix to use. The destination IPv6 address of this message is the IPv6 All-Routers multicast address (FF02::2), and the source IPv6 address is Host 1's sending Link-Local address (FE80::2AA:FF:FE11:1111). Only IPv6 routers subscribe to the multicast group FF02::2, meaning only Router 1 on the link will receive and process the Router Solicitation message, while all other nodes on the local link will discard it.

Router 1 receives the Router Solicitation message and responds with an ICMPv6 Router Advertisement message (see Figure 4.35). This ICMPv6 message includes the IPv6 Global Unicast prefix for the link (2001:1244:A:B::) and its prefix length (/64). The source IPv6 address of this Router Advertisement message is Router 1's own Link-Local address (FE80::2AA:FF:FE44:4444), and the destination IPv6 address is the IPv6 All-Nodes multicast address (FF02::1).

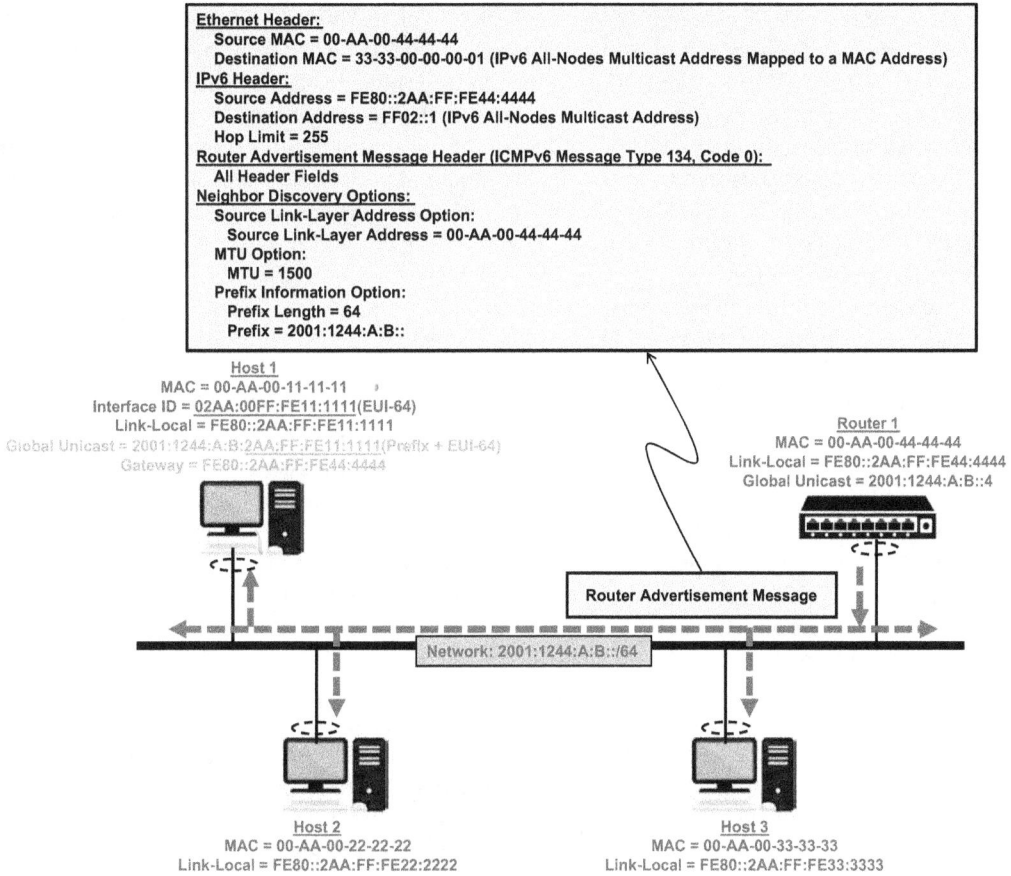

FIGURE 4.35 Stateless Autoconfiguration of IPv6 Global Unicast address: responding with Router Advertisement message.

Host 1 receives the Router Advertisement message from Router 1, combines the IPv6 prefix 2001:1234:A:B::/64 with its modified EUI-64 interface ID (02AA:00FF:FE11:1111), resulting in the IPv6 Global Unicast address 2001:1244:A:B:2AA:FF:FE11:1111 for the interface. Because the Router Advertisement message was sent by Router 1, Host 1 sets its IPv6 default gateway to Router 1's Link-Local address FE80::2AA:FF:FE44:4444.

Host 1 now has an auto-generated IPv6 Global Unicast address (2001:1244:A:B:2AA:FF: FE11:1111) and a default gateway (FE80::2AA:FF:FE44:4444). However, Host 1 must ensure that this address is unique on the local link. Host 1 accomplishes this by performing Duplicate Address Detection on this IPv6 address.

After Host 1 has auto-generated this IPv6 Global Unicast address (2001:1244:A:B:2AA:FF: FE11:1111), it immediately joins the corresponding auto-generated IPv6 Solicited-Node multicast group FF02::1:FF11:1111 (the last 6 hexadecimal values 11:1111 are derived from the Global Unicast address). To ensure that no other IPv6 node is using this address, Host 1 transmits an ICMPv6 Neighbor Solicitation message with the destination address set to the IPv6 Solicited-Node address FF02::1:FF11:1111 and waits to see if another IPv6 node will reply with a Neighbor Advertisement message indicating that the address is already in use. If no reply is received, Host 1 concludes that this address is unique and can assign it to the interface for communication with IPv6 nodes outside the local link, including on the IPv6 Internet.

4.10.5.2.1   Relevance of the Flags in the ICMPv6 Router Advertisement Message

After an IPv6 node has successfully autoconfigured an IPv6 Global Unicast address and a default gateway via SLAAC, it still lacks DNS information to resolve domain names to IPv6 addresses, which is necessary to use many services accessed over the Internet. SLAAC, by default, does not provide DNS information, and without DNS, many services that require resolution from domain names to IPv6 addresses cannot be accessed. The Router Advertisement message header contains several fields (Flags) designed to allow an IPv6 host to obtain further configuration from DHCPv6 Servers. These fields (in the Router Advertisement message) indicate to IPv6 nodes where DNS information can be obtained.

The Router Advertisement message includes several Flags, as shown in Figure 4.2: the M, O, and Prf Flags. The relevance of the M and O Flags is noted below:

- *The M Flag is set to 1 to indicate to IPv6 hosts on the link that IPv6 addresses are available via a Stateful DHCPv6 Server.* The IPv6 router sets this Flag to direct IPv6 nodes to contact a Stateful DHCPv6 Server for all IPv6 prefixes/addresses and DNS information. If the M Flag is set to 1, IPv6 hosts can ignore the O Flag, because the Stateful DHCPv6 Server will provide all available information.
- *The O Flag is set to 1 to indicate to IPv6 hosts that only DNS information is available via a Stateless DHCPv6 Server.* The IPv6 router sets this Flag to 1 to inform the IPv6 nodes to autoconfigure an IPv6 address via SLAAC and then consult a Stateless DHCPv6 Server for DNS information.

If neither the M nor O Flags are set in the Router Advertisement message, this indicates to the IPv6 nodes that no DHCPv6 Server is available on the link. If a DHCPv6 Server is present on the link, the IPv6 router would set either the M Flag or the O Flag in the Router Advertisement message. Typically, when an IPv6 router is enabled to perform IPv6 unicast routing, it starts sending periodic (unsolicited) Router Advertisement messages via all interfaces configured with IPv6 Global Unicast addresses.

4.11   IPv6 GLOBAL UNICAST ADDRESS AUTOCONFIGURATION WITH STATELESS DHCPv6

Note that the configuration of an IPv6 Link-Local address is by design stateless, because an IPv6 node needs such an address to initiate communication with any other node on a link. IPv6 SLAAC allows an IPv6 node to autogenerate a Global Unicast address on an interface, using information contained in Router Advertisement messages sent by an IPv6 router attached to the local link. However, the information provided to an IPv6 node during SLAAC, does not include DNS and domain name information. To resolve this problem and allow IPv6 nodes to obtain further configuration information, the transmission of the Router Advertisement messages includes setting the special O Flag to 1 (see Figure 4.2). Setting this Flag indicates to the IPv6 nodes on the link to contact a Stateless DCHPv6 Server to obtain the required DNS and domain name information **[RFC3736]**.

IPv6 hosts consult a Stateless DHCPv6 Server to obtain other information, such as a list of DNS Servers and domain names, and in some cases, Network Time Protocol (NTP) Server addresses to obtain time references for their local clocks, and Session Initiation Protocol (SIP) Server addresses for multimedia (voice and video) communication with other IPv6 hosts. Such information does not require the maintenance of any dynamic state on individual IPv6 hosts on the link. An IPv6 host that uses Stateless DHCPv6 **[RFC3736]** must have first obtained its IPv6 addresses (Global Unicast addresses) through some other means, usually through SLAAC. Stateless DHCPv6 is discussed in detail in **Chapter 5**.

4.11.1 CONFIGURING IPv6 GLOBAL UNICAST ADDRESSES THROUGH SLAAC WITH STATELESS DCHPV6

This section describes how an IPv6 host dynamically configures an IPv6 Global Unicast address on an interface using SLAAC and contacts a Stateless DHCPv6 Server to obtain DNS and domain name information (see Figures 4.36–4.38).

1. **Send Router Solicitation Message**: Host 1, unwilling to wait for the next scheduled (periodic, unsolicited) Router Advertisement message from an attached router after powering up, sends a Router Solicitation message to discover all IPv6 routers on the local link (Figure 4.36). This ICMPv6 Type 133 message is destined for the IPv6 All-Routers multicast address FF02::2.

2. **Receive Router Advertisement Message**: Router 1 responds with this message upon receiving the Router Solicitation message. This message contains configuration information for Host 1. This ICMPv6 Type 134 message is destined for the IPv6 All-Nodes multicast address FF02::1, and is therefore received by all IPv6 nodes on the local link. The following fields and values are set in the ICMPv6 message header (Figure 4.37):

   a. The M Flag (Managed Address Configuration) is set to 0, indicating to all IPv6 nodes on the link that Stateful DHCPv6 is not needed.

   b. The O Flag (Other Configuration) is set to 1, indicating to all IPv6 nodes on the link that they can use a Stateless DHCPv6 Server to obtain other information such as DNS Servers and domain name information.

   c. The IPv6 Prefix Length is set to 64.

   d. The IPv6 Prefix is set to 2001:1234:A:B::.

   e. The MTU value is set to 1500.

   f. The A Flag (Address Autoconfiguration) is set to 1, indicating to all IPv6 nodes on the link that they can use SLAAC for auto-addressing.

3. **Perform SLAAC**: Host 1 uses the information in the received Router Advertisement message to autoconfigure an IPv6 Global Unicast address on an interface. The flags in the message instruct Host 1 to use a Stateless DHCPv6 Server to obtain DNS information and other required details. Upon receiving this information from Router 1, Host 1 performs the following:

   a. Uses the IPv6 prefix 2001:1234:A:B::/64 and the modified EUI-64 Interface ID to create one or more IPv6 Global Unicast addresses.

   b. The interface ID may be generated from the interface's 48-bit MAC address in the modified EUI-64 format or based on a randomly generated 64-bit value. Host 1 may generate its IPv6 address from the IPv6 prefix plus the modified EUI-64 identifier.

   c. Host 1 sets its default gateway to the IPv6 Link-Local address of Router 1 (the source of the Router Advertisement message).

4. **Perform Duplicate Address Detection**: Host 1 performs this action to determine if any other node on the link is already using the generated Global Unicast address.

   a. This action ensures that the IPv6 address (created using SLAAC) is unique and not used by other nodes on the link. Host 1 performs Duplicate Address Detection by sending a Neighbor Solicitation message. If no node replies, Host 1 concludes that the IPv6 address is unique.

   b. At this point, Host 1 has an IPv6 address that is globally unique, and Router 1 is the default gateway. Host 1 has all the local addressing information it needs to communicate with nodes outside its local network segment, including nodes on the IPv6 Internet.

   c. However, Host 1 does not have a DNS Server or domain name, meaning services that require domain name-to-IPv6 address resolution cannot be accessed. Because Router

1 has set the O Flag in the Router Advertisement message to 1, Host 1 understands that there is a Stateless DHCPv6 service available from which it can obtain DNS Server and domain name information.

5. **Send DHCPv6 SOLICIT Message**: Host 1 sends this message on the link looking for a DHCPv6 Server. The O Flag in the Router Advertisement message was set to 1 to indicate that additional information is available from a Stateless DHCPv6 Server. Host 1 transmits a DHCPv6 SOLICIT message destined for the IPv6 All DHCPv6 Relay Agents and Servers multicast address FF02::1:2 (see **Chapter 5**).

6. **Receive DHCPv6 ADVERTISE Message**: A DHCPv6 Server sends this message announcing its presence on the network. Upon receiving the DHCPv6 SOLICIT message, the DHCPv6 Server replies with a DHCPv6 ADVERTISE indicating that the service is available. This is a unicast message sent to the IPv6 Link-Local address of Host 1.

7. **Send DHCPv6 INFORMATION-REQUEST Message**: Host 1 sends this message to the DHCPv6 Server to request DNS and domain name information. This message is also sent to the IPv6 All DHCPv6 Relay Agents and Servers address FF02::1:2.

8. **Receive DHCPv6 REPLY Message**: The DHCPv6 Server responds with a message containing a list of DNS Servers and a domain name. This is a unicast message sent to Host 1's Link-Local address.

At the end of the above process, if successful, Host 1 should have an IPv6 Global Unicast address, a default gateway (Router 1), a DNS Server, a domain name, and possibly NTP and SIP Server addresses.

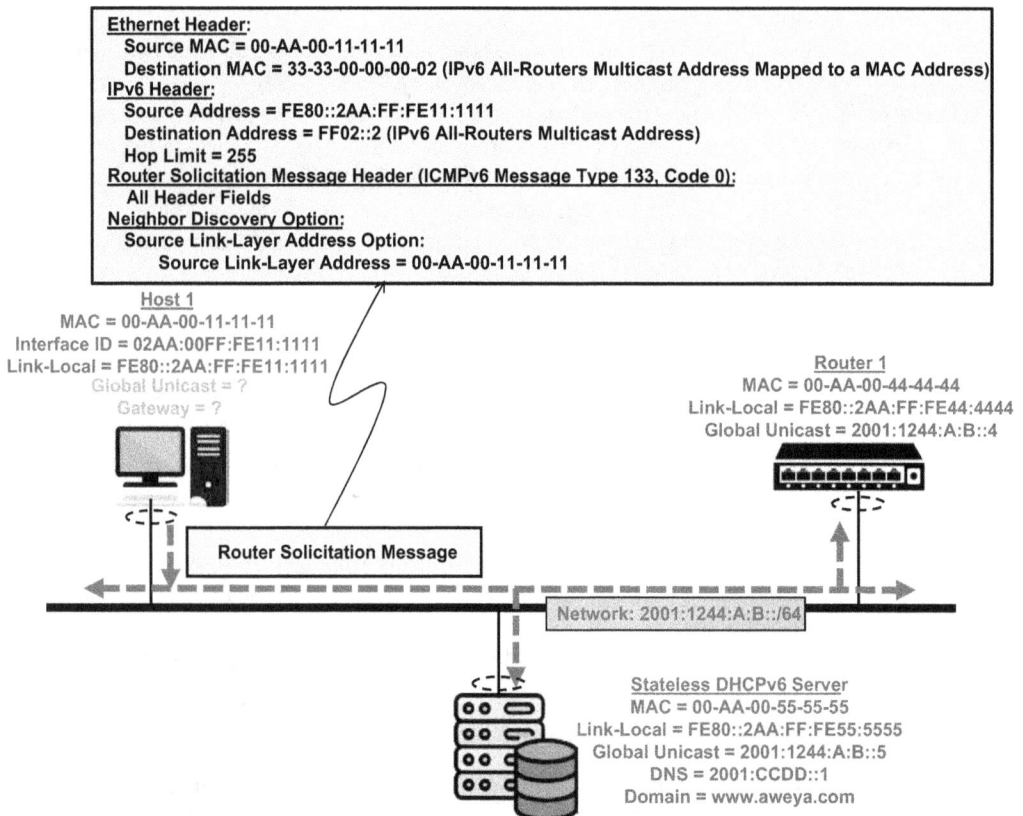

FIGURE 4.36 IPv6 Global Unicast address configuration with Stateless DHCPv6: sending Router Solicitation message.

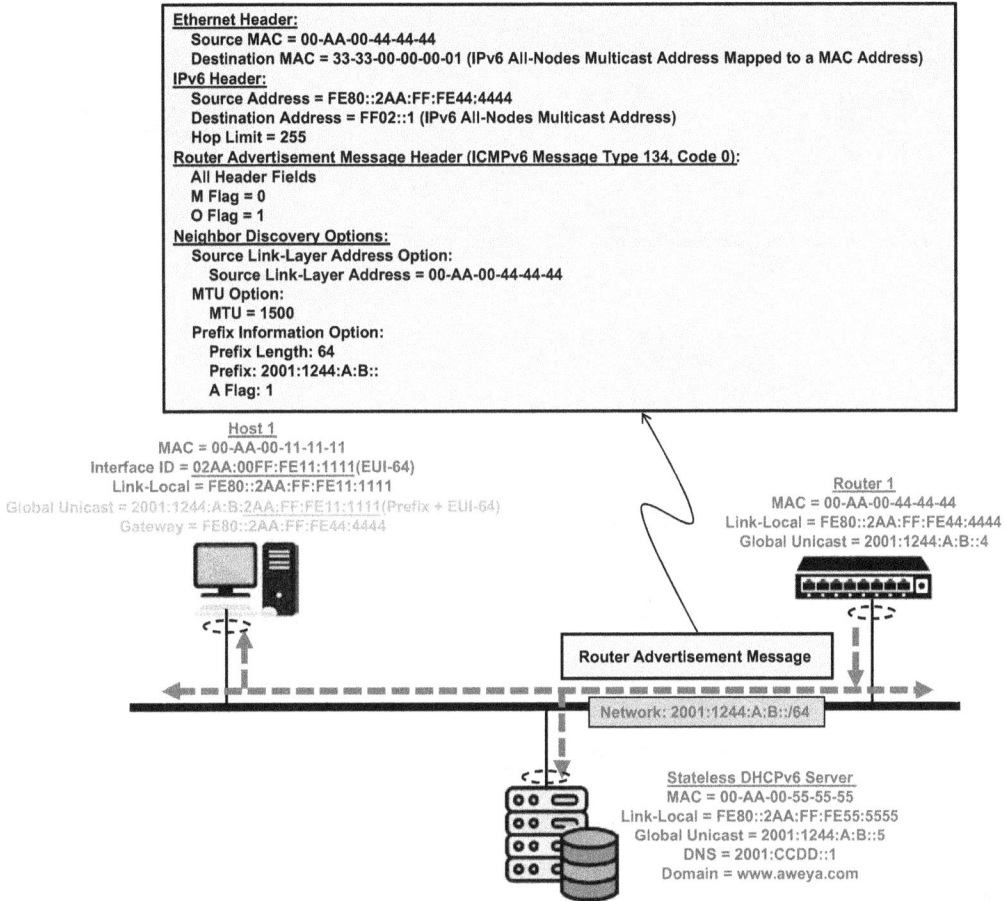

```
Ethernet Header:
    Source MAC = 00-AA-00-44-44-44
    Destination MAC = 33-33-00-00-00-01 (IPv6 All-Nodes Multicast Address Mapped to a MAC Address)
IPv6 Header:
    Source Address = FE80::2AA:FF:FE44:4444
    Destination Address = FF02::1 (IPv6 All-Nodes Multicast Address)
    Hop Limit = 255
Router Advertisement Message Header (ICMPv6 Message Type 134, Code 0):
    All Header Fields
    M Flag = 0
    O Flag = 1
Neighbor Discovery Options:
    Source Link-Layer Address Option:
        Source Link-Layer Address = 00-AA-00-44-44-44
    MTU Option:
        MTU = 1500
    Prefix Information Option:
        Prefix Length: 64
        Prefix: 2001:1244:A:B::
        A Flag: 1
```

Host 1
MAC = 00-AA-00-11-11-11
Interface ID = 02AA:00FF:FE11:1111(EUI-64)
Link-Local = FE80::2AA:FF:FE11:1111
Global Unicast = 2001:1244:A:B:2AA:FF:FE11:1111(Prefix + EUI-64)
Gateway = FE80::2AA:FF:FE44:4444

Router 1
MAC = 00-AA-00-44-44-44
Link-Local = FE80::2AA:FF:FE44:4444
Global Unicast = 2001:1244:A:B::4

Router Advertisement Message

Network: 2001:1244:A:B::/64

Stateless DHCPv6 Server
MAC = 00-AA-00-55-55-55
Link-Local = FE80::2AA:FF:FE55:5555
Global Unicast = 2001:1244:A:B::5
DNS = 2001:CCDD::1
Domain = www.aweya.com

FIGURE 4.37 IPv6 Global Unicast address configuration with Stateless DHCPv6: responding with Router Advertisement message.

4.11.2 CONFIGURING SLAAC WITH STATELESS DHCPV6 ON AN IPV6 NETWORK SEGMENT

Implementing SLAAC with Stateless DHCPv6 on a network segment typically requires the network administrator to perform the following operations:

- Set up the IPv6 router to send IPv6 Router Advertisement messages
- Set up the O Flag in the Router Advertisement messages
- Configure a Stateless DHCPv6 Server on the network segment

A dedicated Stateless DHCPv6 Server may be configured on the network segment, or another IPv6 router on the segment may function as the DHCPv6 Server. In the latter case, Router 1 sends Router Advertisement messages on the segment, and the other IPv6 router acts as the Stateless DHCP Server, providing DNS and domain name information to IPv6 hosts on the link.

It should be noted that IPv6 unicast routing must first be enabled on the routers on the link before Router 1 can send Router Advertisement messages to attached hosts. After enabling the IPv6 routing process on Router 1, an IPv6 Link-Local and Global Unicast address must be configured on the router interface attached to the link of Host 1, as well as on all IPv6-enabled interfaces on Router 1 (typically through manual configuration by the network administrator).

Once the IPv6 router interface is configured and enabled with Link-Local and Global Unicast addresses, the router starts advertising its presence on the link through unsolicited, periodic Router Advertisement messages. The A Flag in Router Advertisement messages, when set to 1, indicates

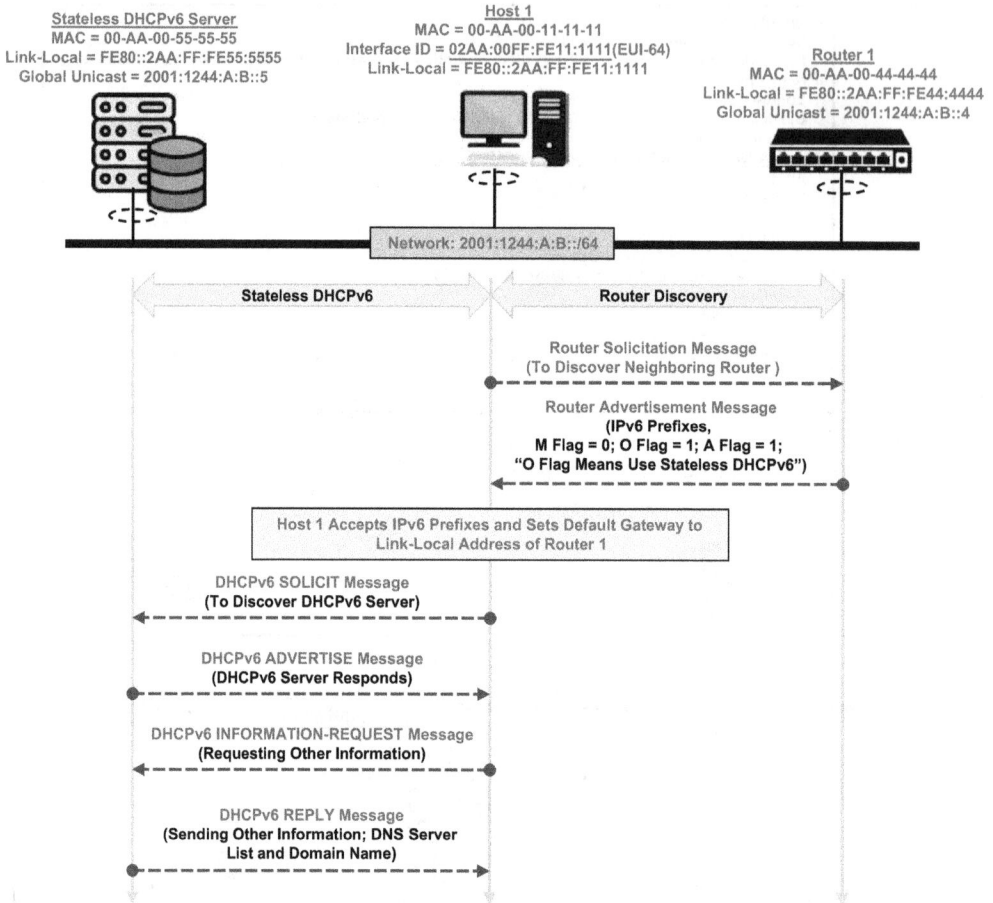

FIGURE 4.38   IPv6 Global Unicast address configuration with Stateless DHCPv6: message exchange.

to IPv6 hosts on the link that they can use SLAAC for auto-addressing. The O Flag is set to 1 to indicate to the hosts to obtain other configuration information from a Stateless DHCPv6 Server (DNS Server list and domain name, and possibly NTP and SIP Server addresses).

4.12   IPv6 GLOBAL UNICAST ADDRESS CONFIGURATION WITH STATEFUL DHCPv6

Stateful DHCPv6 for IPv6 Global Unicast address configuration is similar in functionality to DHCPv4 in IPv4 [**RFC2131**]. However, some major differences exist, particularly in the way DHCP messages are exchanged and the type of configuration information provided to DHCP Clients. This section describes how hosts obtain IPv6 prefixes/addresses and other configuration information from a Stateful DHCPv6 Server. **Chapter 5** describes in greater detail Stateful DHCPv6.

4.12.1   Configuring IPv6 Global Unicast Addresses through Stateful DCHPv6

In this section, we describe the steps an IPv6 host takes to configure an IPv6 Global Unicast address, default gateway, and DNS information using a Stateful DHCPv6 Server (see also Figure 4.39):

1. **Send Router Solicitation Message**: Host 1 transmits this message with the destination address set to the IPv6 All-Routers multicast address FF02::2.

2. **Receive Router Advertisement Message**: Upon receiving the Router Solicitation from Host 1, Router 1 sends a Router Advertisement message with the M Flag set to 1, and the O and A Flags set to 0. This indicates to Host 1 that it cannot use SLAAC on this link and must consult a Stateful DHCPv6 Server for IPv6 addressing and other configuration information. The Router Advertisement messages are sent to the IPv6 All-Nodes multicast address FF02::1 and are received by all IPv6 nodes on the local link.

3. **Set Default Gateway**: Upon receiving the Router Advertisement message, Host 1 sets the source IPv6 address (i.e., Link-Local address FE80::2AA:FF:FE44:4444) of Router 1 as its default gateway. Because the A Flag in the message is set to 0, Host 1 does not use SLAAC for address configuration.

4. **Send DHCPv6 SOLICIT Message**: Because the M Flag in the Router Advertisement message is set to 1, Host 1 transmits a DHCPv6 SOLICIT message to the All DHCPv6 Relay Agents and Servers address FF02::1:2, seeking a DHCPv6 Server.

5. **Receive DHCPv6 ADVERTISE Message**: The DHCPv6 Server receives the SOLICIT message and responds with a DHCPv6 ADVERTISE message. The ADVERTISE message is sent as a unicast directly to the IPv6 Link-Local address of Host 1 (FE80::2AA:FF:FE11:1111).

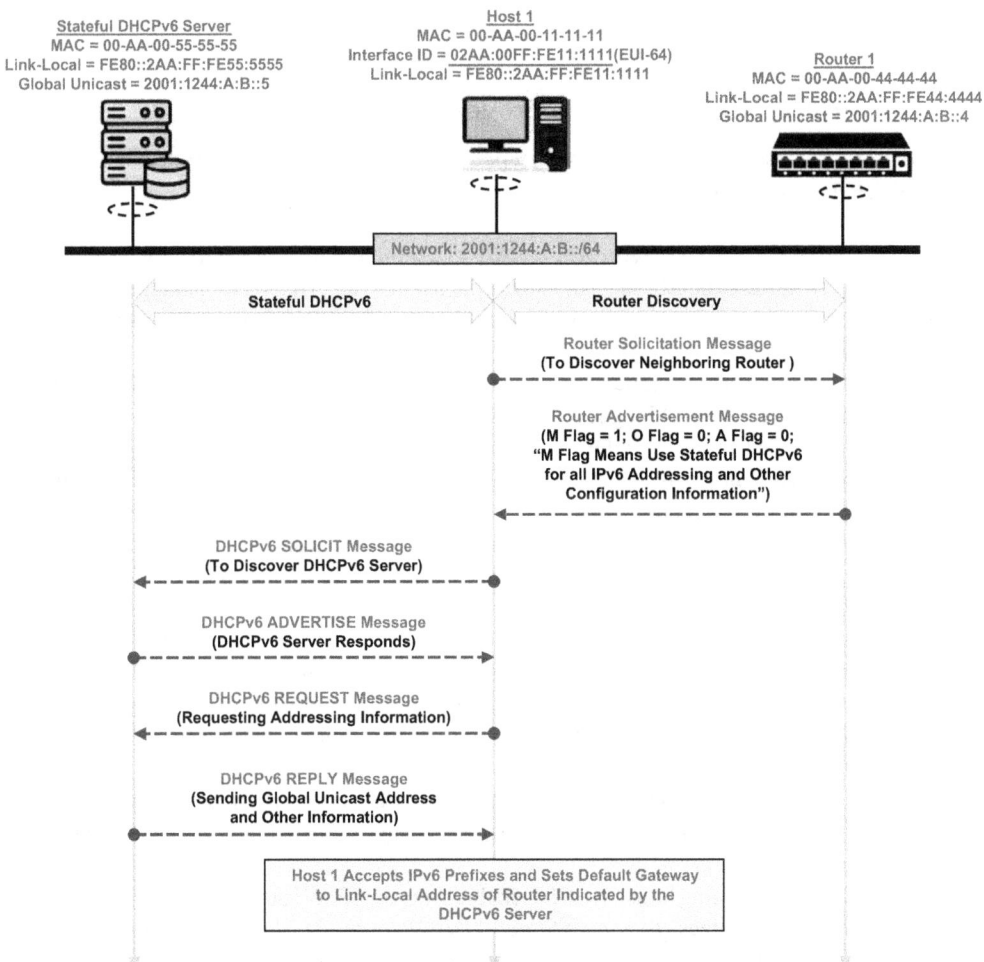

FIGURE 4.39 IPv6 Global Unicast address configuration with Stateful DHCPv6.

6. **Send DHCPv6 REQUEST Message**: Host 1 receives the DHCPv6 ADVERTISE message and sees that DHCPv6 service is available on the link. Host 1 then sends a DHCPv6 REQUEST message to the DHCPv6 Server, requesting IPv6 addressing and other configuration information.

7. **Receive DHCPv6 REPLY Message**: The DHCPv6 Server receives the REQUEST message from Host 1 and responds with a DHCPv6 REPLY message that contains the IPv6 Global Unicast prefix/address and all other information needed by Host 1.

At the end of the above process, Host 1 may optionally perform Duplicate Address Detection on the received IPv6 Global Unicast address to ensure that it is unique. This may be necessary to avoid address conflicts when some interfaces on the link are manually or autoconfigured via SLAAC with IPv6 addresses. Generally, a Stateful DHCPv6 Server assigns IPv6 addresses without conflicts. Typically, IPv6 hosts perform Duplicate Address Detection on all IPv6 addresses, whether manually configured or configured via SLAAC or Stateful DHCPv6.

It is important to note that, although DHCPv6 is a separate service, it works with the message exchange process of the IPv6 Neighbor Discovery protocol **[RFC4861]** to accomplish IPv6 host addressing. Although the DHCPv6 Server provides the IPv6 Global Unicast address along with all other information needed by Host 1, it is the IPv6 router (Router 1) that provides the default gateway required by Host 1.

4.12.2 CONFIGURING IPv6 ADDRESSING WITH STATEFUL DHCPv6 ON AN IPv6 NETWORK SEGMENT

In this section, we discuss the three main steps involved in configuring IPv6 addressing with Stateful DHCPv6 on a network segment:

- **Configure IPv6 Router to Send Router Advertisement Messages with the M Flag Set to 1**: IPv6 routers use the M Flag (set to 1) in the Router Advertisement messages to inform IPv6 hosts on the local network segment that there is a DHCPv6 Server that provides both IPv6 addressing and other configuration information.
  - Setting the M Flag to 1 indicates that IPv6 addresses are available via DHCPv6. If the M Flag is set to 1, the O Flag is redundant and can be ignored because all configuration information is available via DHCPv6.
- **Configure IPv6 Router to Send Router Advertisement Messages with the A Flag Set to 0**: Setting the A Flag is not a mandatory step if the M Flag is set to 1. However, setting the A Flag to 1 is problematic because this will cause IPv6 hosts to obtain an IPv6 Global Unicast address from a DHCPv6 Server (because the M Flag = 1) and will also lead them to autogenerate an address using SLAAC (because the A Flag = 1). This results in IPv6 hosts configuring at least two IPv6 Global Unicast addresses. *Therefore, for security policy reasons and to correctly track IP address assignment on a network, when the M Flag is set to 1, IPv6 hosts should NOT be allowed to autogenerate Global Unicast addresses simultaneously. Thus, it is a best practice to set the A Flag to 0 to disable the SLAAC process on IPv6 hosts when the M Flag is set to 1.*
- **Set up a Stateful DHCPv6 Server on the Network Segment**: A dedicated DHCPv6 Server or an IPv6 router in the network must be configured to act as the DHCPv6 Server.

Note that IPv6 unicast routing must first be enabled on an IPv6 router for it to begin sending Router Advertisement messages. *To enable Stateful DHCPv6, the M Flag must be set to 1 in Router Advertisement messages (and both O and A Flags must be set to 0 to disable SLAAC).* This causes IPv6 hosts to obtain all parameters such as IPv6 prefixes, DNS Servers, and domain names from a DHCPv6 Server.

4.13   IPv6 NEIGHBOR DISCOVERY SNOOPING IN A VLAN OR VXLAN

A VLAN is a logical Layer 2 (broadcast) overlay network on a shared physical LAN that groups together a subset of devices, with the goal of isolating broadcast traffic within that logical network from other logical broadcast networks. A VLAN is simply a Layer 2 (broadcast) domain that confines broadcast traffic generated in that domain to stay within that domain. Communication between hosts on different VLANs must go through an IP router.

A VXLAN (Virtual eXtensible Local Area Network) is a tunneling method used to encapsulate Ethernet frames generated in one part of a VLAN in UDP datagrams and tunnel them over an IP network to a remote part of the same VLAN. VXLAN interconnects physically separate parts of VLANs over a UDP/IP tunnel, making these parts appear as one larger logical Layer 2 network. VXLAN, which uses the 24-bit VNID (VXLAN Network Identifier), also called Network Segment ID, was developed to address the scalability limitations of VLAN technology (which uses the 12-bit VLAN Tag) and to provide a more robust tool for scaling an Ethernet (Layer 2) network across IP network boundaries.

When IPv6 Neighbor Discovery Snooping is configured on an Ethernet switch in a Layer 2 network, the switch learns the source MAC addresses, source IPv6 addresses, input switch interfaces/ports, and the VLANs/VXLANs associated with arriving Neighbor Discovery messages and Ethernet frames, to build the Neighbor Discovery Snooping table.

The entries in the Neighbor Discovery Snooping table can be used by a *Neighbor Discovery detection* mechanism on a switch to prevent spoofing attacks. Ethernet LAN switches, in particular, are vulnerable to spoofing attacks that involve forging the source MAC or source IPv6 addresses of traffic. Hosts connected to untrusted access interfaces on an Ethernet switch may send spoofed packets. The entries in the Neighbor Discovery Snooping table can be used by a mechanism like an *IPv6 source guard* to prevent spoofing attacks. IPv6 source guard is a Layer 2 switch feature that allows a switch to examine the source address of IPv6 packets and then check if the packet's source IPv6 address exists in the switch's *IPv6 binding table*, also known as the *DHCPv6 Snooping table* (see Section 5.10).

Through the Neighbor Discovery detection mechanism, the switch processes the Neighbor Discovery messages received on trusted and untrusted Neighbor Discovery interfaces as follows:

- The Neighbor Discovery detection function forwards all Neighbor Discovery messages received on a trusted Neighbor Discovery interface.
- The Neighbor Discovery detection function compares all Neighbor Discovery messages received on an untrusted Neighbor Discovery interface with the Neighbor Discovery Snooping entries, except for ICMPv6 Router Advertisement and Redirect messages.

This process allows an Ethernet switch to validate the source of IPv6 traffic and block any packets from unknown sources. For example, the switch blocks a source that is not already entered in the IPv6 binding table or has not been previously learned through IPv6 Neighbor Discovery or DHCP gleaning. The switch denies traffic originating from an IPv6 address that is not stored in the IPv6 binding table.

The IPv6 source guard mechanism does not inspect Neighbor Discovery or DHCP messages; instead, it works in conjunction with an inspection mechanism based on IPv6 Neighbor Discovery or IPv6 address gleaning. Both of these mechanisms detect IPv6 addresses as packets are forwarded on a link and enter them into the IPv6 binding table. A switch using the IPv6 source guard mechanism can deny IPv6 traffic from unknown sources or unallocated IPv6 addresses, such as IPv6 traffic sent by sources not assigned by a local DHCPv6 Server.

4.13.1   How IPv6 Source Guard and Neighbor Discovery Inspection Work in a VLAN

This section describes how an Ethernet switch in a VLAN uses IPv6 source guard and Neighbor Discovery inspection to protect against IPv6 address spoofing attacks. The switch employs these mechanisms along with the DHCPv6 Snooping (IPv6 binding) table to mitigate the risk of IPv6 address spoofing attacks. The switch populates its DHCPv6 Snooping table with valid IPv6-to-MAC address bindings.

When the switch receives an IPv6 packet from a host attached to an untrusted access interface, it uses the IPv6 source guard mechanism to verify the packet's source IPv6 address and MAC address against the entries in the DHCPv6 Snooping table. If the table has no matching entry, the switch discards the packet. Additionally, using the Neighbor Discovery inspection function, the switch verifies IPv6 Neighbor Discovery messages exchanged between IPv6 nodes on the same link against the entries in the DHCPv6 Snooping table, discarding messages if there are no matching entries.

4.13.2 How IPv6 Neighbor Discovery Snooping Works

The Neighbor Discovery Snooping switch tracks IPv6 host liveness on a link, allowing the Neighbor Discovery Snooping table to be updated in a timely manner. The Neighbor Discovery Snooping switch uses the following mechanisms to create, update, and delete Neighbor Discovery Snooping entries.

- **Creation of Neighbor Discovery Snooping Entries**: When the switch receives a Neighbor Discovery message or IPv6 packet from an unknown source, it creates a Neighbor Discovery Snooping entry in INVALID status and performs Duplicate Address Detection for the message's source IPv6 address. The switch sends Neighbor Solicitation messages several times from the trusted Neighbor Discovery interfaces on the VLAN.
  - If the switch does not receive a Neighbor Advertisement message within the "invalid entry lifetime," it marks the entry as valid.
  - If the switch receives a Neighbor Advertisement message within the "invalid entry lifetime," it deletes this entry; the entry is deemed invalid.
- **Updating Neighbor Discovery Snooping Entries**: When an untrusted Neighbor Discovery interface on the switch receives a Neighbor Discovery message with a source IPv6 address that does not match an entry for an IPv6 address already in the table, the switch performs Duplicate Address Detection for the entry by sending Neighbor Solicitation messages several times on the VLAN.
  - If the switch does not receive a Neighbor Advertisement message within the "invalid entry lifetime," it updates the entry by associating it with the new receiving interface.
  - If the switch receives a Neighbor Advertisement message within the "invalid entry lifetime," it leaves the Neighbor Discovery Snooping entry unchanged; the arriving source IPv6 address is deemed valid.
- **Deleting Neighbor Discovery Snooping Entries**:
  - When a trusted Neighbor Discovery interface on the switch receives a Neighbor Discovery message from an IPv6 address that the switch previously learned and created a Neighbor Discovery Snooping entry, it performs Duplicate Address Detection for the entry. The switch sends Neighbor Solicitation messages several times on the VLAN.
    - If the switch does not receive a Neighbor Advertisement message within the "invalid entry lifetime," it deletes the entry.
    - If the switch receives a Neighbor Advertisement message within the "invalid entry lifetime," it leaves the Neighbor Discovery Snooping entry unchanged.
  - If a Neighbor Discovery Snooping entry has no matching Neighbor Discovery messages sent within the "valid entry lifetime," the switch marks that entry as invalid. The switch then performs Duplicate Address Detection for the entry by sending Neighbor Solicitation messages several times from the interface associated with the entry.
    - If the switch does not receive a Neighbor Advertisement message within the "invalid entry lifetime," it deletes the entry.
    - If the switch receives a Neighbor Advertisement message within the "invalid entry lifetime," it leaves the Neighbor Discovery Snooping entry unchanged, meaning it remains valid.

A switch in a VXLAN that is configured to use Neighbor Discovery Snooping learns the source MAC addresses, source IPv6 addresses, Virtual Switching Instance name, and link IDs to build the Neighbor Discovery Snooping table. The Neighbor Discovery detection and IPv6 source guard mechanisms in the switch use the Neighbor Discovery Snooping entries to prevent spoofing attacks.

Each Neighbor Discovery Snooping entry is assigned an "aging time." If the switch does not receive a matching packet before the end of the entry's "aging time," it sets the entry to TENTATIVE status. At the same time, the switch sends a Neighbor Solicitation message for the entry. If the source IPv6 and source MAC addresses in the received Neighbor Discovery message match the Neighbor Discovery Snooping entry, the switch sets the entry to VALID and resets the "aging time." When the "aging time" of a Neighbor Discovery Snooping entry is reached, the switch deletes the entry.

4.14 RANDOMIZED INTERFACE IDENTIFIERS FOR IPv6 ADDRESSES

Typically, in IPv6 (as discussed in **Chapter 3**), the first 64 bits of the IPv6 address are used as the network prefix, while the last 64 bits carry a unique interface ID for an interface (see Figure 4.40). According to [RFC4291], all IPv6 unicast addresses with prefixes 001 through 111 must use a 64-bit interface ID that may be derived from the MAC address of the interface using the Modified IEEE Extended Unique Identifier (EUI)-64 address format. The IPv6 interface ID may also be manually configured by the network administrator, or generated after IPv6 router discovery when the host is creating an IPv6 address for the interface using SLAAC [RFC3736], or stateful address configuration via a DHCPv6 Server [RFC8415].

In the case where an IPv6 node has no universal interface ID (such as an IEEE 802 MAC address) for creating a modified EUI-64 ID for an interface, it needs to create one with local scope while ensuring that the interface ID is unique within the IPv6 subnet prefix used. An IPv6 node may use various methods to select a unique interface ID within an IPv6 subnet prefix. These include using a manually configured identifier, a serial number on the node, or any other node-specific token, such as one generated using a 64-bit random number generator, as illustrated in Figure 4.41.

The specific algorithm used for generating the 64-bit interface ID is link- and implementation-dependent. It is strongly recommended that the IPv6 node implements an IPv6 address collision detection algorithm as part of any automatic interface ID configuration algorithm used. Generally, an IPv6 node is required to perform Duplicate Address Detection after creating an IPv6 address through manual configuration, SLAAC, or Stateful DHCPv6.

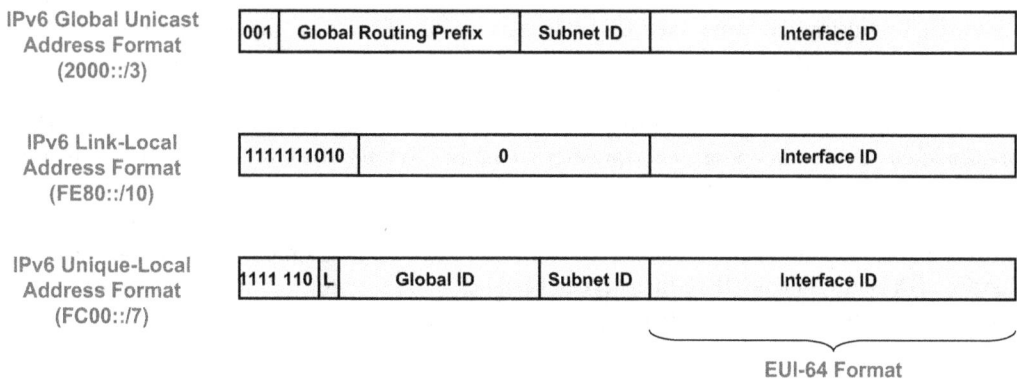

FIGURE 4.40 IPv6 Link-Local address with interface identifier in EUI-64 format.

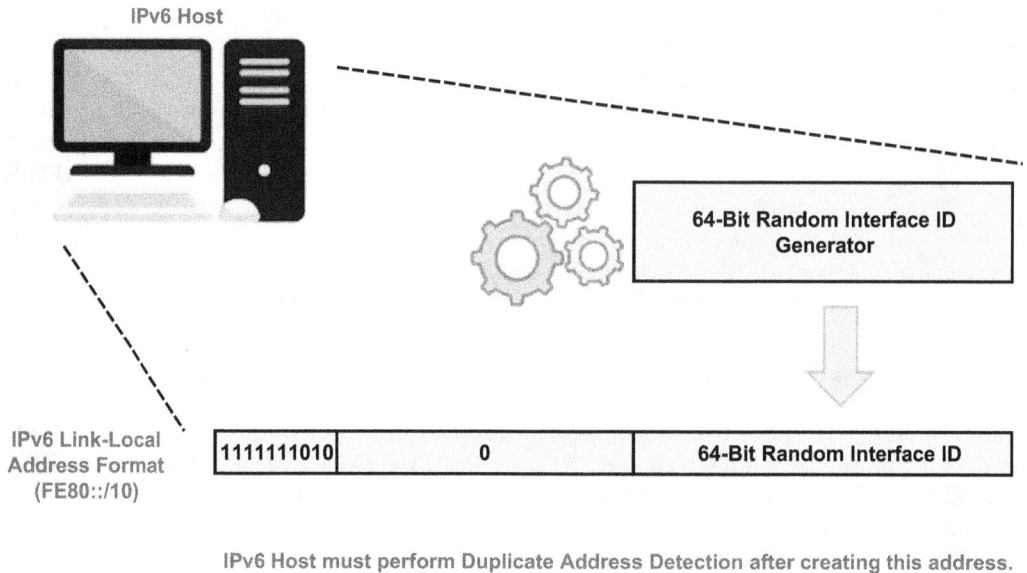

FIGURE 4.41   IPv6 Link-Local address with randomized interface identifier.

4.14.1   Rationale for Using Randomized Interface Identifiers

Typically, IPv6 hosts use only MAC addresses (usually globally unique) to create modified EUI-64 interface IDs for IPv6 Global Unicast and Link-Local addresses. An IPv6 host creates these addresses using the network segment's IPv6 prefix plus the modified EUI-64 interface ID generated from the globally unique MAC address associated with the host interface. However, with rising concerns about network security, using a fixed modified EUI-64 interface ID based on a globally unique MAC address presents security vulnerabilities, as a configured IPv6 address can easily be tied to the MAC address configured on an interface, given that it uniquely identifies a physical device.

Let us assume, for example, that an IPv6 host connects to one network in the IPv6 Internet with Global Unicast prefix x:x:x:x::/64. If the host autoconfigures an interface using SLAAC, the globally unique IPv6 address x:x:x:x:EUI-64 is generated using the EUI-64 interface ID. Let us assume again that the IPv6 host later connects to another network in the IPv6 Internet with a Global Unicast prefix y:y:y:y::/64. In this case, the host will generate an IPv6 Global Unicast address y:y:y:y:EUI-64 using the same fixed EUI-64 interface ID. If the host connects again to the IPv6 Internet using the IPv6 prefix z:z:z:z::/64, it will generate the IPv6 address z:z:z:z::EUI-64 using the same EUI-64 interface ID.

This example clearly shows that using the fixed EUI-64 interface ID based on the fixed interface MAC address creates an opportunity for external entities to track the host. Every network that the host connects to involves using an EUI-64 interface ID for the globally unique IPv6 address generated by the host, that remains the same. This means the host cannot connect anonymously to any network in the IPv6 Internet, as an external entity can track the host simply by knowing its EUI-64 interface ID. Entities on the IPv6 Internet can easily exploit this vulnerability in various ways (e.g., when a user visits websites) by associating or correlating the different IPv6 addresses of a particular host with its fixed EUI-64 interface ID.

Two interface ID assignment methods have been introduced to improve a user's privacy: Randomized Interface Identifiers and Temporary IPv6 Addresses. This section has already covered the first method, Randomized Interface Identifiers. The next section discusses the second approach. Using these methods, whenever an IPv6 host generates an IPv6 address using SLAAC, it uses an interface ID that is randomly generated. Recall that an IPv6 host can configure an IPv6 address on an interface using one of three methods: manual configuration, SLAAC, or Stateful DHCPv6 (see also **Chapter 5**).

The following is a simple example algorithm for generating randomized interface IDs for an IPv6 address:

1. Obtain a random number from a pseudorandom number generator that can produce random numbers of at least the number of bits required for the Interface ID (typically, 64 bits for IPv6 addresses).
2. Obtain the interface ID by taking 64 bits from the random number obtained in the previous step.
3. Compare the resulting interface ID against the reserved IPv6 interface IDs **[RFC5453]** **[IANA-RESERVED-IID]** and against the interface IDs already used in an IPv6 address of the same network interface and the same IPv6 prefix. If the interface ID is unacceptable, generate a new interface ID by repeating the algorithm from the first step.

Reference **[RFC8981]** also describes the generation of interface IDs using some example pseudorandom functions.

4.15   TEMPORARY IPv6 ADDRESSES

This section describes the use of temporary IPv6 addresses as a method for providing user privacy when IPv6 address assignments are done through SLAAC. The main idea behind using temporary IPv6 addresses is to allow an IPv6 host to autoconfigure a public IPv6 address that is randomized (in EUI-64 interface ID), has a relatively short lifetime, and can be used for setting up anonymous outgoing connections. With this feature, each time an IPv6 host powers up or reboots its IPv6 stack, or when the Preferred Lifetime of a temporary address expires, it regenerates a temporary address using a *Randomized Interface Identifier*. This allows the IPv6 host to initiate different outgoing connections using different temporary IPv6 addresses, which minimizes the chances of an entity on the IPv6 Internet tracking the host by associating the IPv6 Global Unicast address with a physical device or user (i.e., by correlating the IPv6 address with the MAC address of the device).

In many practical implementations, an IPv6 host may establish certain connections to websites on the IPv6 Internet using fixed public (global) IPv6 addresses that do not change (with corresponding incoming connections made to those addresses). However, a host may want to initiate connections to certain websites anonymously using different temporary IPv6 addresses (client-server communication), especially connections through an Internet service provider to those websites. In such cases, multiple temporary IPv6 addresses could be set up by the host at a given time, as illustrated in Figure 4.42. A public (global) IPv6 address is an address that uses the IPv6 address prefix in the Router Advertisement message and a fixed interface ID usually created from the globally unique MAC address of the interface. A temporary IPv6 address is an address that uses the IPv6 address prefix in the Router Advertisement message and a randomized interface ID generated through an appropriate algorithm **[RFC8981]**.

Note that in IPv4, each time a user connects to a network after an unusually long pause (in cases where an IPv4 address is not statically assigned), a different IPv4 address may be assigned to the user (by DHCPv4). This method of address assignment, combined with the fact that IPv4 addresses do not contain interface IDs, makes it difficult to track a user's traffic on the IPv4 Internet based solely on their IPv4 address. IPv4 addresses lack embedded interface IDs, unlike IPv6 addresses (as discussed in **Chapter 3**).

As mentioned above, for IPv6 connections based on, for example, a 64-bit prefix, a user may be assigned an IPv6 address through router discovery and SLAAC, or stateful address configuration. However, it has been observed that if the interface ID is consistently based on the EUI-64 address (typically derived from the statically assigned IEEE 802 MAC address of the interface), it becomes easier for entities on the IPv6 Internet to identify and track the IPv6 traffic of a specific node, regardless of the IPv6 prefix used. The fixed interface ID (based on a unique MAC address) in the IPv6 address facilitates tracking a specific user and their use of the IPv6 Internet. To address this concern and provide some level of anonymity when users connect to the IPv6 Internet, **[RFC8981]** provides an alternative approach for randomly generating IPv6 interface IDs for an IPv6 address and changing the interface IDs over time as needed (see Figure 4.42).

Reference **[RFC8981]** describes a technique for randomly generating a 64-bit interface ID and changing it over time to provide some level of anonymity to the user. The initial IPv6 interface ID on an interface is generated using a random number generator. This technique is defined as an extension to IPv6 SLAAC, allowing IPv6 hosts to create temporary IPv6 addresses on an interface with randomized interface IDs for each IPv6 prefix advertised, with IPv6 SLAAC enabled on the interface.

By changing its IPv6 addresses over time, an IPv6 host limits the duration during which other network entities can eavesdrop and perform IPv6 address-based correlation when the same IPv6 address and interface ID are used by the IPv6 host for multiple transactions on the IPv6 Internet. Additionally, this reduces the IPv6 host's exposure window even when the host is actively communicating on the Internet using an IPv6 address that becomes revealed (through its IPv6 prefix and interface ID).

For IPv6 systems that cannot store any historical information for future interface ID generation, the user generates a new randomized interface ID each time the IPv6 protocol is initialized. For IPv6 users that can store such historical interface information, a previous interface ID value is retained, and when the IPv6 protocol is initialized, a new interface ID for a temporary IPv6 address is generated using various pseudorandom functions described in **[RFC8981]**.

The IPv6 address generated from this process, based on the randomized interface ID, is known as a temporary IPv6 address. Typically, a user generates temporary IPv6 addresses for public

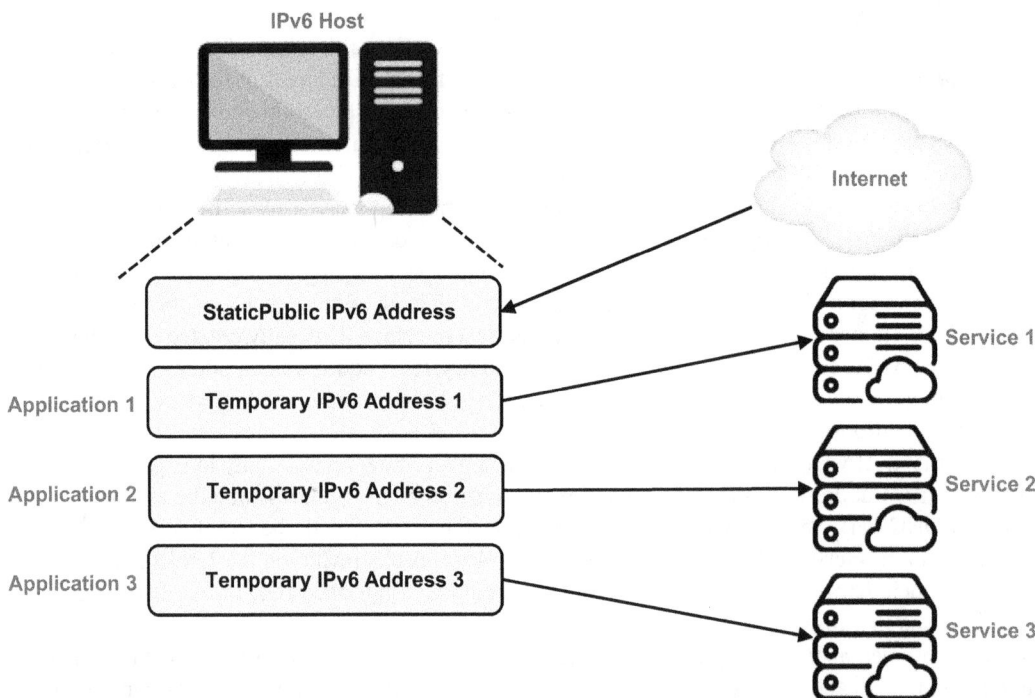

FIGURE 4.42   Use of temporary IPv6 addresses.

(global) IPv6 address prefixes that employ IPv6 SLAAC. The lifetime of temporary IPv6 addresses is determined by the lower of the Valid and Preferred Lifetime values:

- The Lifetime values included in the Valid Lifetime field (TEMP_VALID_LIFETIME) and Preferred Lifetime field (TEMP_PREFERRED_LIFETIME) of the Prefix Information Option carried in the received Router Advertisement message (see Figures 4.2 and 4.7).
- Local default values of 2 days for the Valid Lifetime, and 1 day for the Preferred Lifetime.

The user generates a new interface ID and temporary IPv6 address after the Valid Lifetime of a temporary IPv6 address expires.

4.16 IPv6 ROUTING TABLE ENTRIES

IP routers maintain information about neighboring routers, other IP networks, and destination nodes in a database called the routing table (also known as the *routing information base* (RIB)). The routing table keeps information about how to reach remote networks and hosts from the current node. Each network segment (IP subnet) is identified by an *IP prefix* and *prefix length* indication, the latter also called a *network mask length* in IPv4. Additionally, a routing table may support information about each directly attached host (see "on-link IPv6 addresses" below). A directly attached host on a router can be viewed as a specific instance of a network segment (with a more specific IP prefix and prefix length, /128 in IPv6 and /32 in IPv4).

When powered up or rebooted, an IP router automatically includes directly connected networks and hosts (loopback addresses/interfaces and destination addresses on the router itself) in its routing table. The router adds other routes to its routing table as they are discovered and determined by dynamic routing protocols (i.e., best routes) to each given destination. Typically, an IPv6 routing table (in hosts and routers) consists of the following entries or columns (let us consider the local IPv6 node in Figure 4.43):

- **IPv6 Prefix**: An IPv6 prefix identifies a particular network learned through a routing protocol or manually configured on a router (i.e., a static route). The IPv6 prefix is the contiguous, high-order bits in the destination IPv6 address field of a received packet that must match the IPv6 prefix in a routing table entry. For example:
  - Address: 2001:DB8:1AD:0:218:71FF:FEDD:CF00/64
    Prefix: 2001:DB8:1AD:0/64
  - Address: 2001:17B:1:1: 218:71FF:FEDD:CF00/48
    Prefix: 2001:17B:1/48
    As discussed in **Chapter 3**, an IPv6 address consists of 8 hextet groups separated by colons. Each hextet is 4 bits, and there are four hexadecimal digits in a group (equivalent to 16 bits in a group).
- **Route Type:**
  - **Directly Connected Route**: This is an IPv6 destination address configured on the router itself, which may include any one of the following:
    - Manually configured loopback addresses/interfaces (or routes) on the router itself (with IPv6 prefix ::1/128)
    - Link-Local addresses (with IPv6 prefix FE80::/10) and Global Unicast addresses (with IPv6 prefix 2000::/3) configured on the router itself
    - Host routes, which are directly connected interfaces or hosts on the router itself (e.g., data servers, media servers), are defined as *host routes* that lead to a single connected host (IPv6 prefix length equal to 128). In contrast, a *network (subnet) route* leads to a connected network segment with more than one node (IPv6 prefix length is less than 128). The destination address for a host route may be an IPv6 Link-Local or

Global Unicast address configured on the directly connected interface. The default Administrative Distance of a host route is "0" (see Section 1.5).

The router automatically installs these destination addresses in its routing table when powered up. For each of the locally configured IPv6 routes, the router assigns a default Administrative Distance of "0" and a routing metric of "1." In many cases, a network administrator manually configures IPv6 loopback interfaces in the routing table, with the gateway (i.e., the loopback interface (lo0)) being the special IPv6 address ::1/128 (see Section 3.6).

- **Static Route**: This is a manually configured route to a destination on another router. Typically, the default Administrative Distance and routing metric for statically configured routes are both "1" (see **Chapter 1**).
- **Dynamic Route (e.g., RIPng, OSPFv3, IS-ISv6, and MBGP)**: This is a route discovered by a dynamic routing protocol running on the router itself. The type (i.e., source) of a dynamic route must be specified when it is entered into the IPv6 routing table (e.g., OSPFv3). For example, if a router is running OSPFv3, it learns routes from the OSPFv3 advertisements received from other OSPFv3 routers. If the router discovers that an OSPFv3 route has a lower Administrative Distance than any other routes from different routing information sources to the same destination, it enters the OSPFv3 route into the IPv6 routing table.
  - **Subtype**: Some routing protocols, such as OSPFv3 and IS-ISv6, also specify a route's subtype. IS-ISv6 may specify the subtypes IS-IS Level 1, IS-IS Level 2, IS-IS Inter-area, or IS-IS Summary. OSPFv3 may specify the subtypes OSPF Intra-Area, OSPF Inter-Area, OSPF External 1, OSPF External 2, OSPF NSSA External 1, or OSPF NSSA External 2 (see **[AWE2BK21V2]**).
- **Next-Hop IPv6 Address (Gateway to Network Prefix)**: This is the IPv6 address of a directly connected interface (e.g., a locally configured internal router interface or an attached host like a server) or the next relaying node (called the *next-hop router*) to which the packet should be forwarded in order to reach its ultimate destination. The latter is the next node that lies on the optimal path to the destination address indicated in the IPv6 packet.
  - Most often, this address is the IPv6 address of the next directly connected router (i.e., the next-hop router) that lies on the best outgoing interface for forwarding packets toward its actual (final) destination. In either case, the IPv6 address used can be either the IPv6 Link-Local or Global Unicast address of the receiving interface on the directly connected host or next-hop router.
  - When a local interface connects to a directly attached host or a next-hop router, the router (upon startup or reboot) automatically enters the corresponding network address in its routing table. The addresses in the routing table include destinations with Link-Local or Global unicast addresses on the router interfaces. In addition to the IPv6 routing table, a router also maintains a Neighbor Cache and a Destination Cache, as discussed in Section 4.4.
- **Outgoing Interface**: This is the routing interface (i.e., interface number) on the router through which IPv6 packets matching an address prefix in the IPv6 routing table are forwarded. This is the best local interface that leads to the destination of an IPv6 packet.
  - Note that some routing protocols, such as BGP (MBGP), do not specify an outgoing interface for a given destination IPv6 prefix in the routing table but rather an IPv6 address prefix associated with the destination (i.e., an IPv6 address that points to the packet's destination). In this case, the router must perform a recursive lookup on the outgoing IPv6 address to find the actual local router interface leading to the specified (outgoing) address (see Chapter 3 of **[AWE2BK21V2]** for a detailed discussion on routing table recursive lookups).
  - This means the information placed in the outgoing interface column of the routing table can be either the local outgoing routing interface or the IPv6 address of the next

directly connected router that can forward traffic toward the packet's destination. If an IPv6 address is associated with the outgoing interface information, it can be either the IPv6 Link-Local or Global Unicast address of the receiving interface on the next-hop router.

- **Routing Metric or Cost**: This is the cost of the route leading to the packet's destination IPv6 address/prefix. Lower routing metric numbers indicate preferred routes. The routing metric is used to compare different routes learned by the same routing protocol to a given destination (e.g., RIPng, OSPFv3), allowing the router to select the best overall route to that destination. Each routing protocol has its own routing metric type, as discussed in **[AWE2BK21V1] [AWE2BK21V2]**.

- **Administrative Distance (also Called Route Preference by Some Router Vendors)**: This is a preference value assigned by a routing information source to a route (see Section 1.5). A router uses this to select a route when multiple routing information sources provide routes to the same IPv6 prefix.
  - When there are multiple routes to a given destination, the router enters only the route with the best preference value (lowest Administrative Distance value) in the routing table and uses that route to forward packets to that destination. Generally, when Administrative Distance values are used, the route with the lowest value is preferred. However, when Route Preference values are used, the route with the highest value is preferred.
  - The default Administrative Distance for connected routes is 0. The default Administrative Distance for static routes is 1. Generally, the Administrative Distances of static and dynamic routes are configurable.

- **Lifetime**: This is the total time a route (i.e., a specified IPv6 address prefix) is available for use before it is deprecated. Each configured IPv6 unicast address/prefix in the routing table is assigned a Lifetime value that determines how long that address prefix is available for use before it must be refreshed or removed.
  - An address may have a Lifetime setting of "*permanent*," meaning, it does not expire. Other addresses may have both a Lifetime setting of "*preferred*" and "*valid*" along with the duration of their use and availability.
  - A *Valid Lifetime* is the total length of time an IPv6 address is allowed to remain available for use on a particular router interface. A *Preferred Lifetime* is the duration for which the router intends to use an IPv6 address on an interface, and this value must be less than or equal to the Valid Lifetime setting of the address/prefix (see the discussion in Section 4.10.2).

- **Route Advertisement**: This indicates whether the route (a specified IPv6 address prefix) is published (i.e., advertised in a Routing Advertisement message).

- **Route Aging Method**: This describes how long a route is allowed to remain in the routing table before it is removed.

- **Default Route**: This is the IPv6 address used to forward packets to a remote network destination in the absence of a direct route or the best matching route in the routing table. An *on-link address* means the destination address exists on a link connected to the local device (i.e., a neighboring node sharing a link with the router).
  - The IPv6 address of the local default route is ::/0 (which is the same as the IPv6 Unspecified address described in **Chapter 3**). The default route (::/0) is usually a static route configured in the IPv6 routing table that is used for all IPv6 packets with destination addresses not reachable through any other route in the routing table.

The contents of the IPv6 routing tables of hosts (e.g., end-systems like computers or servers running IPv6) and routers are very similar in many ways. Hosts typically use the default route (a route with a prefix of ::/0 in their IPv6 routing tables) to forward an IPv6 packet to a default

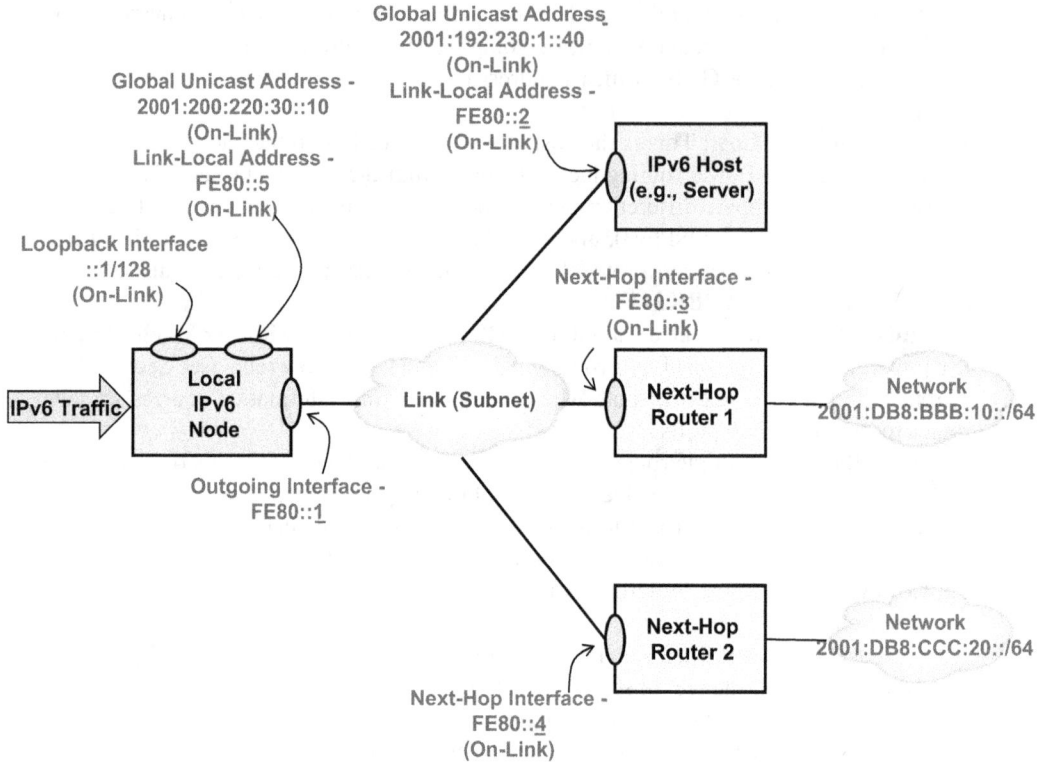

FIGURE 4.43 Example IPv6 network with various interface types and address prefixes.

(gateway) router on the local link (network segment). The default router is expected to contain routing information for the IPv6 prefixes (i.e., other IPv6 subnets) within the larger IPv6 inter-network, and packets sent to it are forwarded to other (next-hop) routers until they are eventually delivered to their destinations.

An IPv6 routing table may contain routing information specific to a routing protocol (e.g., RIPng, OSPFv3, IS-ISv6). Link-state routing protocols such as OSPFv3 and IS-ISv6 maintain their own database of IPv6 routes, from which the router selects the route with the lowest Administrative Distance for placement in the IPv6 routing table when multiple routing information sources provide routes to a given destination.

Typically, routers (like those used in aggregation and core networks) do not support entries like a default route (or gateway) in their routing tables. These routers implement destination address look-ups in the IPv6 routing table using the *LPM* method, and typically, IPv6 packets with unmatched destination addresses are simply discarded (because default routes are not supported). When for-warding IPv6 packets, the router searches its routing table (using LPM) for the entry that is the most specific match to the destination IPv6 address of the packet.

4.17   IPv6 ROUTING PROCESS STARTUP AND ROUTING TABLE INITIALIZATION

Before an IPv6 router interface can start participating in any IPv6 routing protocol and begin for-warding IPv6 packets, IPv6 routing must be enabled on the interface. This process also activates the transmission of ICMPv6 Router Advertisement messages **[RFC4861]** on the interface and triggers the interface to subscribe to a number of IPv6 multicast groups. An IPv6 router periodically sends out ICMPv6 Router Advertisement messages, or in response to an ICMPv6 Router Solicitation message from IPv6 nodes. The IETF base specification for ICMPv6 is **[RFC4443].**

IPv6 routers attached to a network segment periodically transmit (unsolicited) ICMPv6 Router Advertisement messages to announce their presence and availability for IPv6 routing and to convey relevant information to neighboring IPv6 nodes, enabling them to automatically configure various IPv6 addresses on their interfaces. The ICMPv6 Router Advertisement messages sent to hosts on the network segment (addressed to the IPv6 All-Nodes multicast address FF02::1) include important information about IPv6 prefixes and the method the hosts should use to configure their IPv6 addresses (through the setting of certain Flag bits in the messages). As shown in Figure 4.2, ICMPv6 Router Advertisement messages contain several Flag bits that the IPv6 host on the link must closely examine **[RFC4861]**.

IPv6 hosts send ICMPv6 Router Solicitation messages to inquire about the presence of IPv6 routers on the local network. Essentially, a host sends these messages to any IPv6 routers on the attached (local) network segment (link) as a way of requesting them to advertise their presence on the network segment.

Particularly, when IPv6 is enabled on an interface, an IPv6 Link-Local address is first configured on it, and the interface also joins three well-known IPv6 multicast groups: the IPv6 All-Nodes multicast group (FF02::1), the IPv6 All-Routers multicast group (FF02::2), and the IPv6 Solicited-Node multicast group address with the prefix FF02::1:FFxx:xxxx, where the x's represent the least significant hexadecimal digits of the interface's IPv6 unicast address. For every IPv6 unicast address configured on an interface, a corresponding IPv6 Solicited-Node multicast address is automatically created.

IPv6 routers on the local network segment listen on FF02::2 (the IPv6 All-Routers multicast address) to receive ICMPv6 Router Solicitation messages from hosts. In response to an ICMPv6 Router Solicitation message, the router immediately sends an ICMPv6 Router Advertisement message to all nodes on the network (using the IPv6 All-Nodes multicast address FF02::1). The router also sends ICMPv6 Router Advertisement messages periodically (typically every 200 seconds) to keep the attached nodes informed of any changes to the IPv6 addressing information for the network segment.

ICMPv6 Router Advertisement messages facilitate the bootstrapping of the IPv6 connectivity process on an attached node when IPv6 is enabled **[RFC4861]**. These messages inform the hosts on the network segment how to acquire their IPv6 Global Unicast addresses and start IPv6 routing on the network. They also provide hosts with information about local IPv6 routers and their ability to function as a default gateway to off-link nodes.

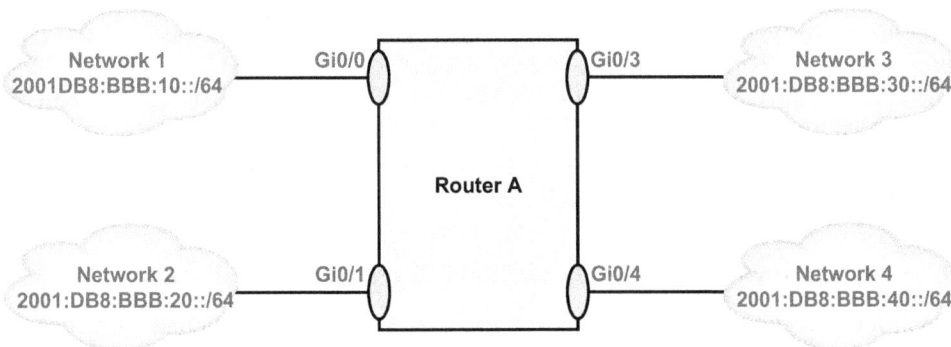

FIGURE 4.44 Example IPv6 network with connected routes.

4.18   ACTIVATING THE IPv6 ROUTING PROCESS

Unlike IPv4 routing, which is typically enabled by default on an interface, IPv6 must be manually enabled on most routers. This is because when IPv6 routing is enabled on an interface, the router starts sending ICMPv6 Router Advertisement messages immediately. Typically, most IPv6 hosts on a link are configured to actively listen for these ICMPv6 Router Advertisement messages, and upon receiving one, will automatically configure themselves with an IPv6 Global Unicast address and a default gateway. This means configuring IPv6 routing by default on an interface can significantly impact the network traffic load and may present some security concerns. For these reasons, IPv6 is normally enabled manually; however, network administrators must still understand the implications of activating the IPv6 process on a link.

When the IPv6 routing process is enabled on an interface and address assignment on the interface has been completed, the router goes through the following process:

- Starts listening for messages addressed to the IPv6 All-Routers multicast address FF02::2.
- Starts forwarding IPv6 packets based on information from the IPv6 routing table.
- Starts sending IPv6 Router Advertisement messages on all connected links to announce itself to attached nodes.
- Starts participating in any dynamic routing protocol (RIPng, OSPF3, IS-ISv6, MBGP) if the router is configured to do so.

4.18.1   HANDLING IPv6 DIRECTLY CONNECTED AND LOCAL ROUTES

When an IPv6 Global Unicast address is configured on a router interface and the interface is up, the router performs the following operations:

- Adds a Connected route entry (denoted as C) in its IPv6 routing table for the configured IPv6 Global Unicast address.
- Adds a Local route entry (denoted as L) in the IPv6 routing table for the configured IPv6 Global Unicast address.
- Removes both Connected and Local routing entries if the interface status changes to down.

It is important to note that the router only creates Connected and Local routes in its IPv6 routing table when an interface is configured with an IPv6 Global Unicast address. IPv6 routers do not create these entries in the IPv6 routing table when an interface is configured with only an IPv6 Link-Local address.

Let us assume, for example, that interface Gi0/0 on Router A in Figure 4.44 is configured with the IPv6 Global Unicast address 2001:DB8:BBB:10::1/128. This interface is directly connected to Network 1 with the IPv6 prefix 2001:DB8:BBB:10::/64; interface Gi0/0's IPv6 address is part of this IPv6 address prefix. Router A, therefore, creates in its IPv6 routing table the Connected route (C) 2001:DB8:BBB:10::/64 and the Local route (L) 2001:DB8:BBB:10::1/128, all associated with router interface Gi0/0. IPv6 packets addressed to the IP prefix 2001:DB8:BBB:10::/64 (Connected route) are forwarded directly through interface Gi0/0. IPv6 packets addressed to 2001:DB8:BBB:10::1/128 (Local route) are handled by Router A itself.

4.19   ROLE OF IPv6 LINK-LOCAL ADDRESSES IN IPv6 ROUTING

It is important to understand how IPv6 routing uses Link-Local addresses on links between routers in an IPv6 network (also called Infrastructure Links [RFC7404]). In IPv6, links between routers (i.e., router-to-router links or Infrastructure Links) generally do not require unique IPv6 Global

Unicast addresses. The advantages of using only Link-Local addresses on Infrastructure Links are as follows:

- **Fewer IPv6 Routing Table Entries Because IPv6 Link-Local Addresses Are Not Advertised in the IPv6 Internet**: Given that IPv6 routing protocols do not advertise IPv6 Link-Local addresses (as they are only significant on the link where they are configured), such addresses will not appear in the IPv6 routing table. This reduces routing table size, memory requirements, and increases the speed of routing protocol convergence. IPv6 Link-Local addresses are not routable, and IPv6 routers do not forward IPv6 packets with a source or destination address that is a Link-Local address to other links.
- **Better Global IPv6 Address Management Because Only IPv6 Global Unicast Address Are Advertised in the IPv6 Internet**: A router requires only one IPv6 Global Unicast address associated with the loopback interface to have all IPv6 services operational. This leads to simpler and more efficient address management compared to IPv4.
- **More Secure Links Because IPv6 Link-Local Addresses Are Restricted to the Local Link/Subnet**: Each IPv6 Global Unicast address configured on a router represents a potential attack point for distributed denial-of-service and other attacks. Thus, using only IPv6 Link-Local addresses on Infrastructure Links makes them invisible and unreachable remotely, and these links do not need to be protected from the outside network as would be necessary when Global Unicast addresses are used.
- **Reuse of IPv6 Link-Local Addresses Because These Addresses Are Restricted to the Local Link/Subnet**: Since Link-Local addresses have local significance, Link-Local addresses configured on one link can be reused on other links without causing addressing and routing conflicts on each link (see Figure 4.45).

Despite these important advantages of IPv6 Link-Local addresses, there are a few noteworthy disadvantages [RFC7404]. If an interface is not configured with a routable IPv6 Global Unicast address, that interface (address) can only be pinged from nodes directly attached to the same link. It is not possible to ping interfaces with only IPv6 Link-Local addresses from outside that link. The use of network utility tools such as traceroute faces the same challenges when IPv6 Link-Local addresses are used. IPv6 Link-Local addresses are, in particular, used by IPv6 routing protocols as next-hop addresses since any two adjacent routers share a link, the interconnecting link (e.g., RIPng, OSPFv3).

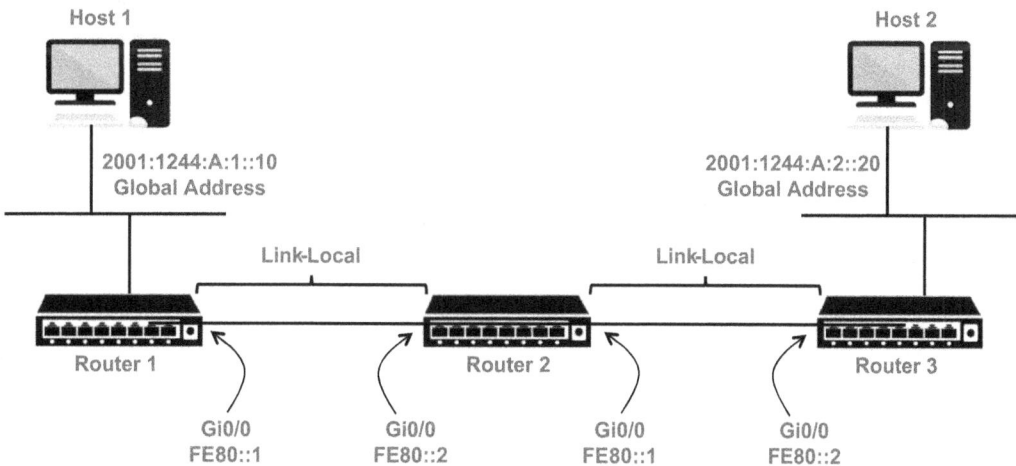

FIGURE 4.45 Reuse of IPv6 Link-Local addresses.

4.20   STATIC ROUTING IN IPv6

The discussion above shows that there are three methods to add entries to the IPv6 routing table:

- **Automatically Adding Connected Routes**: When a router interface configured with an IPv6 prefix (address and prefix length) is enabled for IPv6 routing, the router automatically adds that IPv6 prefix to its routing table as a Connected route.
- **Adding Static Routes**: In this method, a network administrator manually configures an IPv6 route, which the router then enters into the IPv6 routing table.
- **Adding Dynamic Routes**: In this method, a routing protocol running on the router (e.g., RIPng, OSPFv3) exchanges routing information with other routers in the network, and the learned routes are automatically entered into the router's IPv6 routing table.

The main benefits of using IPv6 static routes are as follows:

- **Better Security**: Static routing does not require the security mechanisms used in dynamic routing protocols. Dynamic routing protocols are relatively less secure when used natively without additional security mechanisms, due to the broadcast and/or multicast methods they use to propagate routing updates. The interfaces used by dynamic routing protocols to send out routing updates require additional mechanisms for authenticating routing protocol exchanges (see **[AWE2BK21V1] [AWE2BK21V2]**).
- **More Efficient Router Processor and Memory Usage**: Dynamic routing protocols consume more of a router's processing and memory resources for protocol operations. Static routing requires fewer resources because no processor cycles are needed to compute the network topology, as no messages are exchanged between routers. Static routing does not require routing update algorithms and mechanisms, nor does it need route advertisements over the network.

However, the main disadvantage of static routing is the lack of automatic re-routing around network failures and unintended topology changes. An important concern is preventing the configuration of routing loops when using static routes. Dynamic routing protocols allow routers to automatically exchange routing information when changes in the network topology or state occur. This automatic exchange of routing information enables routers to discover new routes to remote networks and determine alternate paths when existing paths to network destinations become unavailable.

Using Cisco routing systems as the reference platform, we describe in this section different methods for adding a static route to the IPv6 routing table.

4.20.1   Configuring IPv6 Static Routes

Static routes define an explicit path between two network devices; they are manually configured by the network administrator. To configure an IPv6 static route in the IPv6 routing table, the following minimum configuration information is needed in global configuration command mode:

```
ipv6 route [destination_prefix] [outgoing_interface] [next_hop]
[admin_distance]
```

Some parameters in the general command structure above are optional, and various combinations can be used when configuring an IPv6 static route. Different methods of configuring IPv6 static routes are available depending on the specified parameters: next-hop, outgoing interface, and Administrative Distance. The router behaves differently based on the parameter combination used in the command **[CISCIPv6STR]**.

4.20.1.1   Directly Attached Static Routes

To configure a directly attached static route, only the output interface is specified as follows:

```
ipv6 route [destination_prefix] [outgoing_interface]
ipv6 route 2001:DB8:200:10::/64 Gi0/1
```

The destination (the IPv6 host in Figure 4.46) is assumed to be directly attached to interface Gi0/1 of Router A; thus, the IPv6 destination address of the packet is used as the next-hop address. In this example, all IPv6 destinations with the IPv6 prefix 2001:DB8:200:10::/64 are directly reachable through interface Gi0/1 of Router A. A router can only enter directly attached static routes in its IPv6 routing table if they refer to a valid IPv6 interface, meaning an interface that is both up and has IPv6 enabled.

This method of configuring static routes is used on point-to-point links (e.g., devices directly attached to the router, like servers) that do not require next-hop resolution. This method is not applicable if the outgoing link is a multiaccess broadcast network, such as those based on Ethernet technologies.

4.20.1.2   Recursive Static Routes

To configure a recursive static route in the IPv6 routing table, only the next-hop is specified as follows:

```
ipv6 route [destination_prefix] [next_hop]
ipv6 route 2001:DB8::/32 2001:DB8:60::10
```

The addresses in this command are arbitrarily chosen and are not shown in Figure 4.46. The local router derives the outgoing interface from the next-hop router's IPv6 address 2001:DB8:60::10 (by performing a recursive lookup on this address in the routing table to find the actual local outgoing interface). Any route in the routing table that has only a next-hop address associated with a destination IPv6 prefix (whether a recursive static or dynamic route) requires one or more recursive lookups

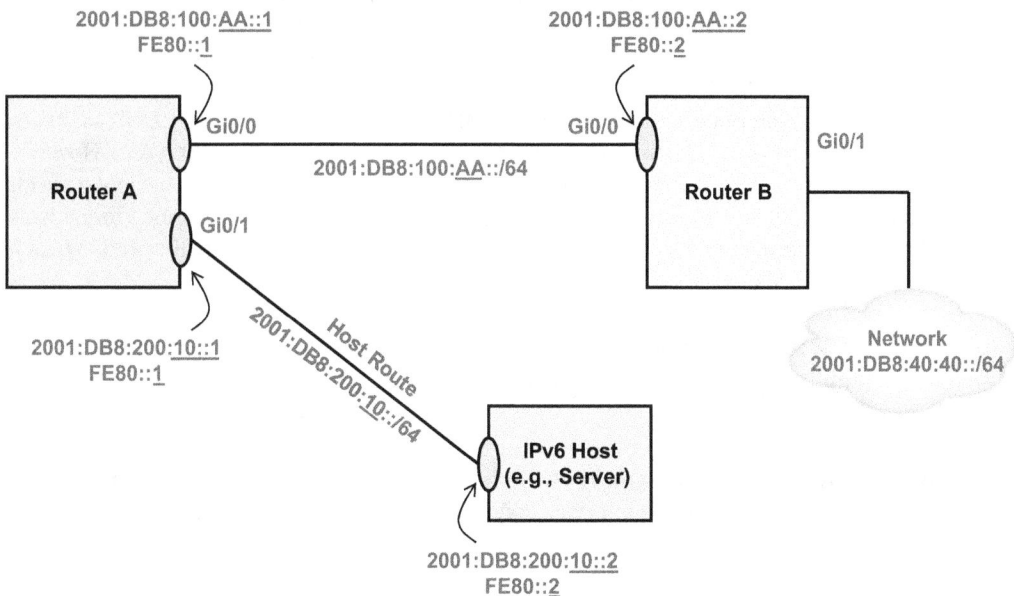

FIGURE 4.46   Illustrating IPv6 static routing – directly attached static route.

to determine the outgoing interface for the route (see **Chapter 3** of **[AWE2BK21V2]**). The router derives the outgoing interface by performing another routing lookup using the next-hop *address*. *Typically, this method of configuring static routes is used when the status of the static route does not have to depend on the status of the outgoing* interface. In this example, all IPv6 destinations with IPv6 prefix 2001:DB8::/32 are reachable via the router with IPv6 address 2001:DB8:60::10; however, the actual local interface to this next-hop address (2001:DB8:60::10) must be determined through a recursive lookup in the routing table.

A router inserts a recursive static route in the IPv6 routing table (i.e., the route is valid) only if the following conditions are met:

- The specified next-hop IPv6 address resolves, either directly or indirectly, to a valid local router outgoing interface.
- The route does not self-recurse (i.e., the route itself is not used to resolve its own next-hop; that is, it does not self-recursive).
- The recursion depth (i.e., the number of times the recursive lookups are performed in the routing table to find the outgoing interface) is not allowed to surpass the maximum IPv6 forwarding recursion depth.

Transient network topology changes and the routes learned through a dynamic routing protocol may cause a recursive static route that has been inserted in the IPv6 routing table to become self-recursive. When a router detects that a static route has become self-recursive, it will delete that route from the IPv6 routing table but not from the configuration. The router maintains the route in the configuration because subsequent network changes may cause the static route to no longer be self-recursive, in which case, the router will reinsert it into the IPv6 routing table.

This configuration example refers to Figure 4.46:

```
ipv6 route [destination_prefix] [IPv6_Global_Unicast_Address_Next_Hop]
ipv6 route 2001:DB8:40:40::/64 2001:DB8:100:AA::2
```

In this example, only the IPv6 Global Unicast address of the next-hop is specified. Configuring the static route without specifying an outgoing interface requires the router to perform a recursive lookup (i.e., another IPv6 routing table lookup) to determine the link to which this IPv6 Global Unicast address is attached.

Because an outgoing interface is not specified, when IPv6 packets destined for 2001:DB8:40:40::/64 arrive at the router, it knows that it must forward them to the next-hop 2001:DB8:100:AA::2. However, to determine the correct outgoing interface, it must perform another IPv6 routing table lookup using this next-hop address. This command instructs the router to send IPv6 packets destined for network 2001:DB8:40:40::/64 to next-hop 2001:DB8:100:AA::2, but it must perform another routing table lookup to find the corresponding outgoing interface to the next-hop.

4.20.1.3 Fully Specified Static Routes

To configure a fully specified static route in the IPv6 routing table, both the output interface and the next-hop must be specified.

- **Using the outgoing interface and IPv6 Global Unicast address of the next-hop:**
  In this method, the outgoing interface and IPv6 Global Unicast address of the next-hop are specified:

```
ipv6 route [destination_prefix] [outgoing_interface]
[IPv6_Global_Unicast_Address_Next_Hop]
ipv6 route 2001:DB8:40:40::/64 Gi0/0 2001:DB8:100:AA::2
```

This command instructs the router to send IPv6 packets destined for network 2001:DB8:40:40::/64 out on interface Gi0/0 to next-hop 2001:DB8:100:AA::2. *This is the recommended method for specifying static routes if all nodes on the link have IPv6 Global Unicast addresses.*

- **Using the outgoing interface and IPv6 Link-Local of next-hop:**

    In this method, the outgoing interface and IPv6 Link-Local address of the next-hop are specified:

```
ipv6 route [destination_prefix] [outgoing_interface]
[IPv6_Link_Local_Address_Next_Hop]
ipv6 route 2001:DB8:40:40::/64 Gi0/0 FE80::2
```

This command instructs the router to send IPv6 packets destined for network 2001:DB8:40:40::/64 out on interface Gi0/0 to next-hop FE80::2. *This second method is typically used when the next-hop is on a multiaccess (Ethernet) segment with no IPv6 Global Unicast addresses configured. Note that only devices on the same link can reach IPv6 Link-Local addresses configured on the same link. Therefore, if an IPv6 Link-Local address is used for the next-hop, it is necessary to specify an outgoing interface, as the same Link-Local address may exist on another link.*

The fully specified static route is the recommended method for configuring static routing entries in the IPv6 routing table. A router adds a fully specified static route to the IPv6 routing table (i.e., the route is considered valid) only when the specified IPv6 interface is IPv6-enabled and up. Fully specified static routes (both configuration cases above) are used when the output interface is connected to a multiaccess network (like those based on Ethernet technologies). In such cases, it is necessary to explicitly identify the next-hop, which must also be directly attached to the same multiaccess network to which the specified output interface is connected.

4.20.1.4 Floating Static Routes

A floating static route is a static route configured as a backup to a dynamic route learned through the routing protocols running on the network. To allow the routes learned through the dynamic routing protocol to be used under normal network conditions, the network operator configures a floating static route with a higher Administrative Distance than the dynamic route. The floating route is assigned a higher Administrative Distance than the default value of 1, which is normally assigned to a static route (see Figure 4.47). This preference ensures that the dynamic route is always favored over the floating static route. However, when the dynamic route fails and becomes unavailable, the floating static route is used instead. The following example shows how to configure a floating static route (see Figure 4.47):

- **Using the IPv6 Global Unicast address of next-hop:**

    In this method, the IPv6 Global Unicast address of the next-hop is specified:

```
ipv6 route [destination_prefix] [outgoing_interface] [IPv6_Global_
Unicast_Address_Next_Hop] [admin_distance]
```

    Primary static route:

```
ipv6 route 2001:DB8:40:40::/64 Gi0/1 2001:DB8:100:BB::2 1
```

    If an Administrative Distance value is not specified, the command defaults to 1.
    Floating (backup) static route:

```
ipv6 route 2001:DB8:40:40::/64 Gi0/0 2001:DB8:100:AA::2 210
```

    In this example, the floating (backup) static route is configured with an Administrative Distance value of 210, which is larger than the default value of 1 but smaller than the "Unknown (Other)" Administrative Distance value of 255 shown in Figure 4.47.

- **Using the IPv6 Link-Local address of the next-hop:**
  In this method, the IPv6 Link-Local address of the next-hop is specified:

  ipv6 route [destination_prefix] [outgoing_interface] [IPv6_Link_Local_Address _Next_Hop] [admin_distance]

  Primary static route:

  ipv6 route 2001:DB8:40:40::/64 Gi0/1 FE80::2 1

  Floating (backup) static route:

  ipv6 route 2001:DB8:40:40::/64 Gi0/0 FE80::2 210

This second method is used on network segments where no IPv6 Global Unicast addresses are configured.

Typically, a network operator configures a fully specified static route as a backup for a primary route to a particular destination. This is useful in scenarios where the operator has two routes to a specific destination and wants to designate one as the primary route and the other as the backup route. The Administrative Distance of this backup route is set to a value greater than that of the primary route for the destination.

A network operator can use any of the three IPv6 static routing methods discussed above (directly attached static route, recursive static route, or fully specified static route) to configure a floating static route to a destination. The floating route configuration may use various combinations of the outgoing interface, IPv6 Global Unicast address, and IPv6 Link-Local address, as discussed above. Note that an outgoing interface must be specified when using the next-hop's IPv6 Link-Local address.

A floating static route must be configured with a larger Administrative Distance value than that of the dynamic routing protocol because routes with smaller Administrative Distances are preferred. The default Administrative Distance value of static routes is smaller than that of dynamic routes, allowing static routes to be preferred over dynamic routes (see **Chapter 1**).

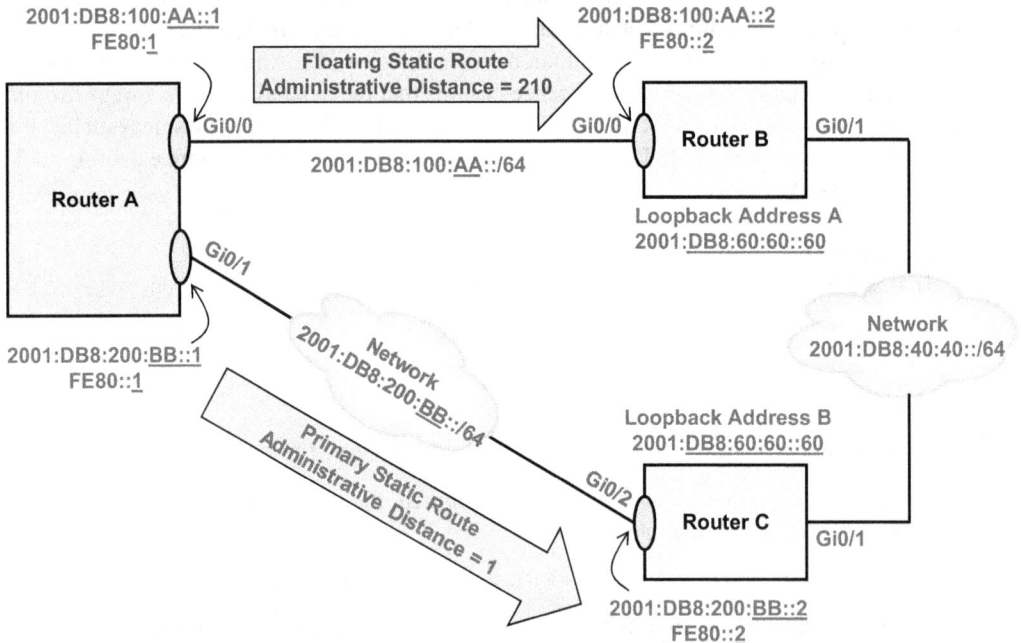

FIGURE 4.47 Illustrating IPv6 static routing – floating static route.

4.20.1.5   Static Default Route

A network operator may want to configure static default routes; a default route consists only of zeroes in its IPv6 address (::) and has a /0 prefix length. This can be done using an outgoing interface, IPv6 Global Unicast address, or IPv6 Link-Local address as described below:

- **Using the outgoing interface only:**
  ipv6 route [default_route] [outgoing_interface]
  ipv6 route ::/0 Serial0/0
- **Using the IPv6 Global Unicast address of next-hop:**
  ipv6 route [default_route] [IPv6_Global_Unicast_Address_Next_Hop]
  ipv6 route ::/0 2001:DB8:2:2::2
- **Using the IPv6 Link-Local address of next-hop:**
  ipv6 route [default_route] [outgoing_interface]
  [IPv6_Link_Local_Address_Next_Hop]
  ipv6 route ::/0 Serial0/0 FE80::2

4.21   IPv6 FORWARDING TABLE

IPv6 routers forward IPv6 packets using routing information that is either manually configured or dynamically learned through a routing protocol (e.g., RIPng, OSPFv3). A network administrator manually configures static routes in the routing table when there is a need to define an explicit path between two network devices. Unlike dynamic routing protocols, which automatically update routes when the network topology changes, static routes must be manually reconfigured when such changes occur.

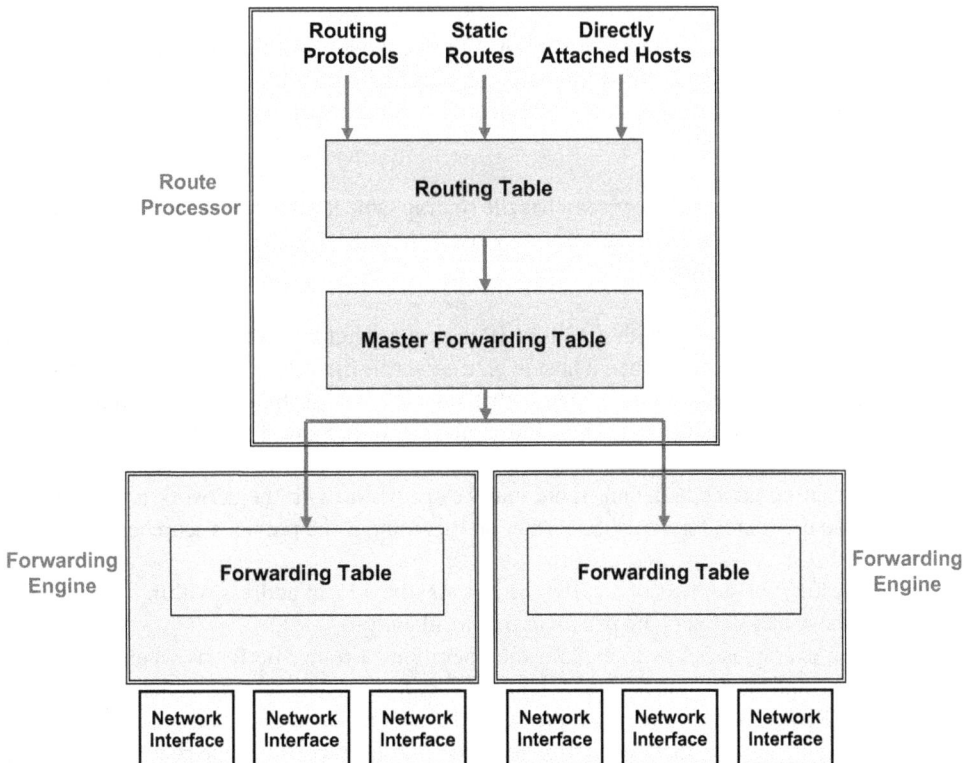

FIGURE 4.48   Routing table and forwarding tables in a routing device.

The IPv6 forwarding table (also called the forwarding information base (FIB) is derived from the IPv6 routing table. The forwarding table contains the same routing information as the routing table but is structured in a compact and optimized format for actual packet forwarding (see Figure 4.48). Anytime there is a routing or network topology change, the routing protocol updates the routing table, and those changes are then reflected in the forwarding table.

The router updates the forwarding table when one of the following occurs: the routing table entry for a network prefix changes or is removed; the routing table entry for the next-hop changes or is removed; or the Neighbor Cache entry for the next hop times out, changes, or is removed. The routing and forwarding tables contain essentially the same information needed for packet forwarding; the forwarding table only removes information that is not directly necessary or relevant for packet forwarding (e.g., the routing metric associated with a route is not listed in the forwarding table).

Because of the use of VLSM and CIDR in today's networks, the IPv6 prefixes in the routing table and forwarding table can be of variable lengths. This means that address lookups in the routing table and forwarding table are based on LPM instead of exact matching. Note that the forwarding table does not contain recursive routes (and as a result, does not require recursive lookups) because all recursive routes in the routing table are resolved before they are installed in the forwarding table.

4.22 IPv6 PACKET FORWARDING

For each IPv6 packet received, an IPv6 router examines (parses) the destination IPv6 address (in the IPv6 packet header), compares it to the routing information in the locally maintained IPv6 routing table or forwarding table, and takes appropriate action. Note that, typically, medium- to large-sized routers (particularly aggregation and core routers) use the more compact forwarding table for packet forwarding because it allows for more efficient and faster forwarding plane implementations. Depending on the routing information, the router does one of the following:

- Passes the IPv6 packet to a local upper-layer protocol entity within the router.
- Forwards the IPv6 packet through one of its attached network interfaces to another network segment (via a *next-hop* router) or directly to an attached host.
- Discards the packet entirely.

To forward an IPv6 packet, the router searches the routing table for the route (IPv6 prefix) that is the best match to the destination IPv6 address in the packet. Typically, the router determines the best (or most specific) route as follows:

- A host route (i.e., a route with a 128-bit IPv6 prefix length) that matches the destination IPv6 address. This occurs when a host (e.g., a server) is directly attached to the router.
- A route with the longest prefix length that matches the destination IPv6 address (this lookup method is called LPM). The LPM method will find a host route if one exists in the routing table.
- In some routing tables, a default route may be specified (with the network prefix ::/0), in which case the router forwards the packet on this route if the previous searches fail.

Note that the destination address of an IPv6 packet may be a local address within the router itself, in which case the router delivers the packet to that local entity.

We use some examples below to explain the operations a router performs when it receives an IPv6 packet that requires a routing table lookup and forwarding. The router matches the destination address of the IPv6 packet to a network prefix in the routing table and then forwards the packet to the next-hop indicated for that destination address. The IPv6 prefix in the router's routing table defines how many leftmost contiguous bits (i.e., high-order bits) are used when matching the destination address of an IPv6 packet to an IPv6 prefix in the routing table.

- Let us consider, for example, that an IPv6 routing table has the entry:
  2001:DB8:0:1AD:0:F1:7A:0/112
- This routing table entry applies to all IPv6 packets received with destination addresses for which the first 112 (leftmost contiguous or high-order) bits are:
  2001:DB8:0:1AD::F1:7A
- If the destination address of an arriving IPv6 packet matches more than one entry in the IPv6 routing table, the router using LPM determines the most specific route (i.e., the route with the longest prefix) among the matching routes. The matching entry is considered to be the most accurate route for that IPv6 packet. For example, let us consider the following destination address of an arriving packet and the IPv6 routing table entries:
  - Destination address of the IPv6 packet: 2001:DB8:0:1D5:A15::F:101/64
  - Entry with 72 bits in the routing table: 2001:DB8:0:1D5:A10::/72
  - Entry with 64 bits in the routing table: 2001:DB8:0:1D5::/64
- Both routing table entries apply to the arriving IPv6 packet, but using LPM, the 72-bit entry is the more-specific route and will be selected for the packet.

4.23 COMMUNICATION BETWEEN HOSTS IN IP NETWORKS

This section describes how IPv4 and IPv6 hosts on the same subnet/VLAN (i.e., broadcast domain) or on different subnets/VLANs communicate with each other. The mechanisms used by IPv6 hosts and IPv4 hosts for such communications have some notable differences, as described below.

4.23.1 COMMUNICATION BETWEEN HOSTS IN IPV4 NETWORKS

We use Figure 4.49 as the basis for our IPv4 discussion here. We assume that all IPv4 router interfaces have been appropriately configured (usually manually) with the IPv4 addresses required for global communication, and all IPv6 hosts have acquired their IPv4 global addresses and default gateways through manual configuration or from a DHCPv4 Server. The discussion here involves communication between IPv4 hosts on the same network segment (subnet or VLAN) and between hosts on different network segments.

4.23.1.1 How an IPv4 Host Sends IPv4 Packets to Another Host on the Same Network Segment

In this example (see Figure 4.49), we assume that IPv4 Host 1, with the IPv4 address 172.16.10.11, wants to send IPv4 packets to Host 3 on the same network segment (172.16.10/24). Host 1 first checks its local ARP Cache to see if there is a matching MAC address associated with the IPv4 address 172.16.10.33, which is the IPv4 address of Host 3. Host 1 searches its local ARP Cache for a matching entry to avoid broadcasting an ARP Request if a MAC address exists.

Host 1 finds that there is no matching entry for this IPv4 address in its local ARP Cache. Therefore, Host 1 performs the following actions:

1. Host 1 sends an Ethernet broadcast frame containing an ARP Request message on the local network (172.16.10/24), requesting the MAC address associated with the IPv4 address of Host 3, the target IPv4 address 172.16.10.33.
   a. The Ethernet frame containing the ARP Request message has the destination MAC address set to the well-known broadcast MAC address FF-FF-FF-FF-FF-FF (indicating one-to-all Layer 2 communication, but only the owner of the target IPv4 address will send an ARP Reply). The target MAC address in the ARP Request message is set to 00-00-00-00-00-00.
2. All hosts on the network segment receive a copy of Host 1's broadcast ARP Request message.

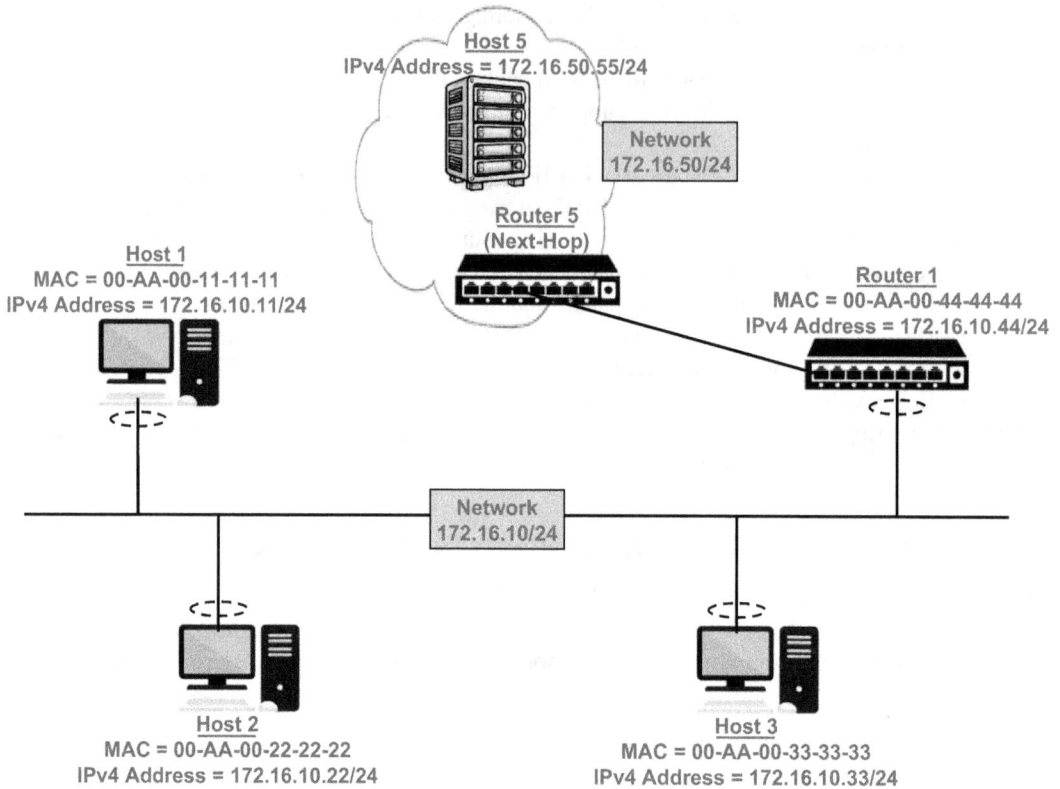

FIGURE 4.49 Example IPv4 network with hosts and routers.

3. Host 3, which owns the Target IPv4 Address 172.16.10.33, replies by sending a unicast Ethernet frame containing an ARP Reply that includes the MAC address 00-AA-00–33-33-33 (associated with the Target IPv4 Address). All other hosts on the network segment may see this unicast Ethernet frame but will drop the ARP Reply.

    a. The source and destination MAC addresses of the Ethernet frame containing the ARP Reply message are both unicast MAC addresses (indicating one-to-one Layer 2 communication between the ARP requestor and replier, with no broadcasts involved).

    b. Host 3 would also cache the IPv4 and MAC address mapping (or binding) in its ARP Cache so that when it needs to send an IPv4 packet to Host 1 later, it will not have to send an ARP Request searching for Host 1's MAC address. Typically, every IPv4 node maintains a local ARP Cache that maps IPv4 addresses to corresponding MAC addresses.

4. Host 1 receives the ARP Reply with Host 3's MAC address and is now able to send IPv4 packets encapsulated in Ethernet frames on the local network segment (172.16.10.0/24) addressed to Host 3's MAC address (00-AA-00–33-33-33). The source IPv4 address of Host 1's IPv4 packet is 172.16.10.11 and the destination address is 172.16.10.33.

    a. Additionally, Host 1 caches Host 3's IPv4-to-MAC address mapping in its ARP Cache for sending future IPv4 packets to Host 3's IPv4 address.

4.23.1.2 How an IPv4 Host Sends IPv4 Packets to Another Host on a Different Network Segment

Now, let us look at the case where Host 1, with IPv4 address 172.16.10.11 (on network 172.16.10.0/24) in Figure 4.49, wants to send IPv4 packets to an IPv4 host on a different network segment (Host 5 with IPv4 address 172.16.50.55 on external network 172.16.50.0/24). Host 1 first uses its own IPv4 address, the destination IPv4 address, and its prefix length (network mask) to check if the destination host is a neighbor on the local network segment or on a different network. The process below assumes that Host 1 has determined that the destination host (Host 5) is on a different network:

1. Host 1 finds that the default gateway for the IPv4 address of Host 5 is Router 1's IPv4 address 172.16.10.44.
2. We assume that Host 1 finds no matching entry for Router 1's IPv4 address 172.16.10.44 in its local ARP Cache.
3. Host 1 sends an ARP Request on the network segment seeking the MAC address of the default gateway with the IPv4 address 172.16.10.44.
4. All IPv4 hosts on the network segment receive a copy of the ARP Request including Router 1.
5. Router 1 replies to Host 1 with an ARP Reply message that contains its MAC address, 00-AA-00-44-44-44.
6. Host 1 receives the ARP Reply with Router 1's MAC address and is now able to send IPv4 packets encapsulated in Ethernet frames on the local network segment (172.16.10/24) addressed to Router 1's MAC address (00-AA-00-44-44-44).
7. Router 1 receives an IPv4 packet from Host 1 and uses the packet's destination IPv4 address (172.16.50.55) to perform an LPM search in its IPv4 routing table to determine the next-hop IPv4 address and outgoing interface for this destination.
8. Router 1 determines that the next-hop IPv4 address and outgoing interface for the destination IPv4 address (172.16.50.55) in its routing table point to an interface on Router 5.
9. When necessary, Router 1 may send an ARP Request message on the next-hop network segment to determine the MAC address associated with the receiving interface of the next-hop IPv4 address.
10. Router 1 forwards the IPv4 packet encapsulated in an Ethernet frame to Router 5, and this process may be repeated until the IPv4 packet finally reaches Host 5 (with the IPv4 address 172.16.50.55). Note that the Ethernet frame sent by Router 1 to Router 5 has its source MAC address set to Router 1's sending interface MAC address and the destination MAC address set to the receiving interface of Router 5.

The process of Router 1 sending an IPv4 packet from an external network to Host 1 involves Router 1 using a host route or directly connected network in its IPv4 routing table. The Link-Layer data transfer process to Host 1 is similar to the intra-network segment process described above.

4.23.2 COMMUNICATION BETWEEN HOSTS IN IPV6 NETWORKS

The IPv6 discussion here is based on Figure 4.50. We assume that all IPv6 router interfaces have been appropriately configured (usually manually) with the required IPv6 Link-Local addresses for local (on-link) communication and the required IPv6 Global Unicast addresses for off-link communication. We assume that all IPv6 hosts have auto-generated IPv6 Link-Local addresses on their local interfaces and either auto-generated the IPv6 Global Unicast addresses on those interfaces or acquired them through a DHCPv6 Server.

The process of configuring globally unique IPv6 unicast addresses includes assigning the default gateways for those IPv6 Global Unicast addresses. The discussion here involves communication between IPv6 hosts on the same network segment (subnet or VLAN) and between hosts on different network segments.

Through the exchange of one or more IPv6 Neighbor Discovery messages (Neighbor Solicitation, Neighbor Advertisement, Router Solicitation, and Router Advertisement), IPv6 nodes on a link can discover neighboring nodes (hosts and routers) and their IPv6-to-MAC address mappings (to be maintained in the Neighbor Cache). IPv6 hosts on a link can also obtain IPv6 prefixes, default gateways, and other information via unsolicited and solicited ICMPv6 Router Advertisement messages from attached IPv6 routers. IPv6 hosts also discover neighbors or best next-hop routers (gateways) for external destinations through ICMPv6 Redirect messages sent by attached routers.

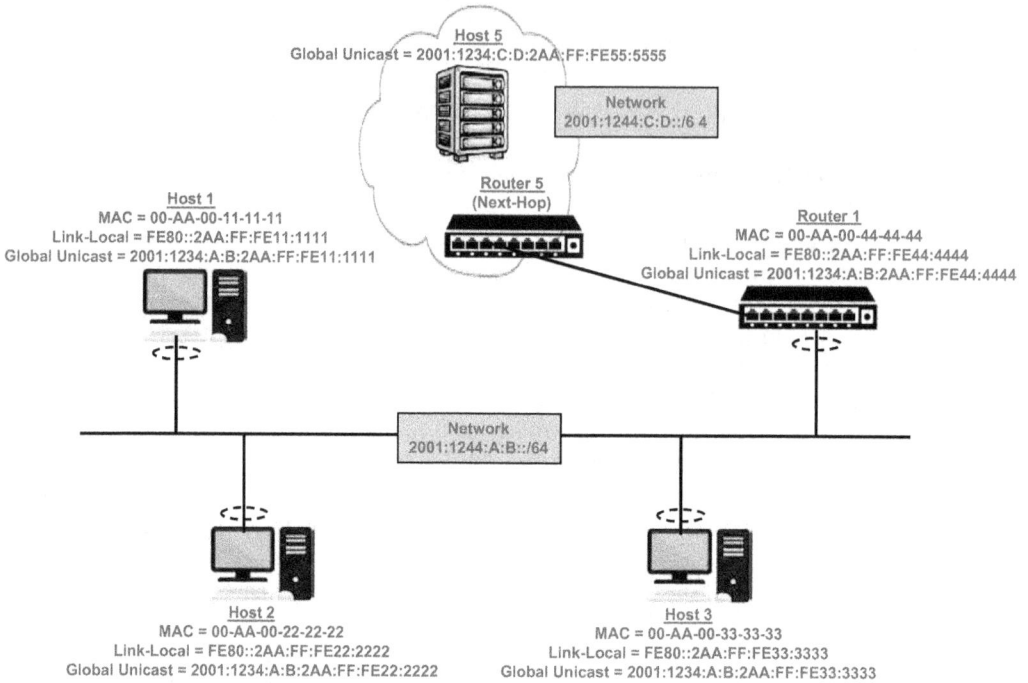

FIGURE 4.50   Example IPv6 network with hosts and routers.

4.23.2.1   How an IPv6 Host Sends IPv6 Packets to Another Host on the Same Network Segment

Unlike in IPv4, IPv6 hosts on a link are always aware of the active neighboring hosts on the link through the Neighbor Solicitation and Neighbor Advertisement messages exchanged, and they are also aware of routers through the Router Advertisement messages. In IPv6, all nodes on a link have multiple ways of discovering active nodes, allowing them to effectively and continuously update their Neighbor Cache entries and IPv6 routing tables with appropriate IPv6 prefixes, default gateways, and other configuration parameters.

In this example (see Figure 4.50), we assume that IPv6 Host 1 wants to send IPv6 packets to Host 3 on the same IPv6 network segment, 2001:1244:A:B::/64. Host 1 first checks its local Neighbor Cache to see if there is a matching MAC address associated with the IPv6 address FE80::2AA:FF:FE33:3333, which is the IPv6 Link-Local address of Host 3. Host 1 searches its local Neighbor Cache for a matching entry so that it does not have to multicast a Neighbor Solicitation message on the link if a MAC address exists.

Host 1 has several ways to determine if Host 3 is on-link or off-link, including examining its Neighbor Cache (populated through transmitted Neighbor Discovery messages), Destination Cache, and Prefix List (as described in Section 4.4). Specifically, when Host 1 has an IPv6 packet to send to a destination, it uses a combination of its Prefix List, the Default Router List, and the Destination Cache to determine if the destination address is on-link (the next-hop is a neighbor) or off-link (in which case the appropriate next-hop router must be determined). The IPv6 next-hop determination process was described earlier. Once Host 1 has determined the IPv6 address of the next-hop, it consults its Neighbor Cache for Link-Layer information about that neighbor.

Let us assume that Host 1 has determined that Host 3 is on-link but finds that there is no matching entry for Host 3's IPv6 address in its local Neighbor Cache. Therefore, Host 1 performs the following actions:

1. Host 1 sends a multicast Neighbor Solicitation message on the link to determine the MAC address corresponding to the IPv6 address FE80::2AA:FF:FE33:3333. The destination IPv6 address of this Neighbor Solicitation message is a multicast address, specifically the IPv6 Solicited-Node multicast address (FF02::1:FF33:3333) of Host 3, derived from Host 3's IPv6 Link-Local address (FE80::2AA:FF:FE33:3333). The Neighbor Solicitation message includes the MAC address of Host 1 (00-AA-00–11-11-11) in the Source Link-Layer Address Option.

2. Host 3, having registered its multicast MAC address (33-33-FF-33-33-33) with its Ethernet adapter (derived/mapped from its IPv6 Solicited-Node multicast address (FF02::1:FF33:3333)), receives and processes the Neighbor Solicitation message. Host 3 updates its own Neighbor Cache based on the source IPv6 address of the Neighbor Solicitation message (FE80::2AA:FF:FE11:1111) and the MAC address in the Source Link-Layer Address Option (00-AA-00–11-11-11).

3. Next, Host 3 sends a unicast Neighbor Advertisement to the sender of the Neighbor Solicitation message, Host 1. This Neighbor Advertisement message includes the Target Link-Layer Address Option containing the MAC address of Host 3 (00-AA-00–33-33-33) corresponding to Host 3's IPv6 Link-Local address FE80::2AA:FF:FE33:3333.

4. After receiving the Neighbor Advertisement from Host 3, Host 1 updates its Neighbor Cache with an entry for Host 3 based on the information in the Target Link-Layer Address Option. At this point, Host 1 (the sending host) and Host 3 (the target host) can send unicast IPv6 traffic to each other.

5. Host 1 sends IPv6 packets encapsulated in Ethernet frames on the local link addressed to Host 3's MAC address (00-AA-00–33-33-33). The source IPv6 address of Host 1's IPv6 packet is FE80::2AA:FF:FE11:1111 and the destination address is FE80::2AA:FF:FE33:3333.

4.23.2.2 How an IPv6 Host Sends IPv6 Packets to Another Host on a Different Network Segment

In IPv6, the receipt of periodic (unsolicited) Router Advertisement messages allows IPv6 nodes on a link to refresh their knowledge of attached routers, their Link-Layer addresses, IPv6 prefixes, and other network configuration information. Additionally, the transmission of Router Solicitation messages by IPv6 hosts and the receipt of Router Advertisement messages enables the hosts to obtain the latest such information.

Now, we consider the case where Host 1 (on network 2001:1244:A:B::/64) in Figure 4.50 wants to send IPv6 packets to an IPv6 host on a different network segment (Host 5 on the external network 2001:1244:C:D::/64). Host 1 first uses a combination of its Prefix List, the Default Router List, and the Destination Cache to determine if the destination host is a neighbor on the local network segment or on a different network. The process below assumes that Host 1 has determined that the destination host (Host 5) is on a different network:

1. Host 1 finds that the default gateway for the IPv6 address of Host 5 is Router 1's IPv6 Link-Local address FE80::2AA:FF:FE44:4444.

2. We assume that Host 1 finds that there is no matching entry for Router 1's IPv6 address FE80::2AA:FF:FE44:4444 in its local Neighbor Cache.

3. Host 1 sends a Neighbor Solicitation message on the link seeking the MAC address of the default gateway IPv6 address FE80::2AA:FF:FE44:4444.

4. All IPv6 hosts on the link receive a copy of the Neighbor Solicitation message, including Router 1.

5. Router 1 replies to Host 1 with a Neighbor Advertisement message that contains its MAC address 00-AA-00-44-44-44.

6. Host 1 receives the Neighbor Advertisement message with Router1's MAC address, and is now able to send IPv6 packets encapsulated in Ethernet frames on the local link addressed to Router 1's MAC address (00-AA-00–44-44-44).

7. Router 1 receives an IPv6 packet from Host 1 and uses the destination IPv6 address (2001:1234:C:D:2AA:FF:FE55:5555) to perform a LPM search in its IPv6 routing table to determine the next-hop IPv6 address and outgoing interface for this destination IPv6 address.

8. Router 1 determines that the next-hop IPv4 address and outgoing interface for the destination IPv6 address (2001:1234:C:D:2AA:FF:FE55:5555) in its IPv6 routing table point to an interface on Router 5.

9. When necessary, Router 1 may send a Neighbor Solicitation message on the next-hop network segment to determine the MAC address associated with the receiving interface of the next-hop IPv6 address.

10. Router 1 forwards the IPv6 packet encapsulated in an Ethernet frame to Router 5, and the processes may be repeated until the IPv6 packet finally reaches Host 5 (with IPv4 address 2001:1234:C:D:2AA:FF:FE55:5555). Note that the Ethernet frame sent by Router 1 to Router 5 has its source MAC address set to the MAC address of Router 1's sending interface, and the destination MAC address set to the receiving interface of Router 5.

The process of Router 1 sending an IPv6 packet from an external network to Host 1 involves Router 1 using a host route or a directly connected network in its IPv6 routing table. The Link-Layer data transfer process to Host 1 is similar to the intra-network segment (on-link) process already described above.

REVIEW QUESTIONS

4.1. What are on-link and off-link IPv6 addresses?

4.2. Why does IPv6 Neighbor Discovery use IPv6 Solicited-Node multicast addresses as destination addresses for messages?

4.3. Why do all IPv6 Neighbor Discovery messages use a Hop Limit of 255 in the IPv6 header?

4.4. What are the advantages of placing all of the IPv6 Neighbor Discovery protocol functions, such as Address Resolution and other functions, at the ICMPv6 layer?

4.5. What is IPv6 Router Discovery, and what IPv6 Neighbor Discovery protocol message(s) are used for this process?

4.6. What is IPv6 Prefix Discovery, and what IPv6 Neighbor Discovery protocol message(s) are used for this process?

4.7. What is IPv6 Parameter Discovery, and what IPv6 Neighbor Discovery protocol message(s) are used for this process?

4.8. What is IPv6 Address Autoconfiguration, and what IPv6 Neighbor Discovery protocol message(s) are involved in this process? Your answer should include when IPv6 Address Autoconfiguration is necessary on an IPv6 node.

4.9. What is IPv6 Address Resolution, and what IPv6 Neighbor Discovery protocol message(s) are used for this process?

4.10. What is IPv6 next-hop determination, and what IPv6 Neighbor Discovery protocol database(s) are used for this process?

4.11. What is IPv6 Neighbor Unreachability Detection, and what IPv6 Neighbor Discovery protocol message(s) are used for this process?

4.12. How does an IPv6 node confirm the reachability of a neighboring node on the same link?

4.13. How does an IPv6 host on a link perform dead gateway (default router) detection?

4.14. What is IPv6 Duplicate Address Detection, and what IPv6 Neighbor Discovery protocol message(s) are used for this process?

4.15. What is IPv6 Redirect, and what IPv6 Neighbor Discovery protocol message(s) are used for this process?

4.16. How does an IPv6 node on a link inform other neighboring nodes when its Link-Layer address has changed? Include in your answer what could cause the Link-Layer address of an interface to change.

4.17. What is the purpose of the Source Link-Layer Address Option in the IPv6 Neighbor Discovery protocol?

4.18. What is the purpose of the Target Link-Layer Address Option in the IPv6 Neighbor Discovery protocol?

4.19. What is the purpose of the Prefix Information Option in the IPv6 Neighbor Discovery protocol?

4.20. What is the purpose of the Redirected Header Option in the IPv6 Neighbor Discovery protocol?

4.21. What is the purpose of the MTU Option in the IPv6 Neighbor Discovery protocol?

4.22. What is the purpose of the IPv6 Route Information Option in the IPv6 Neighbor Discovery protocol?

4.23. What is the purpose of the Recursive DNS Server Option in the IPv6 Neighbor Discovery protocol?

4.24. What is the purpose of the DNS Search List (DNSSL) Option in the IPv6 Neighbor Discovery protocol?

4.25. What is an IPv6 Neighbor Discovery Proxy?

4.26. What is the longest prefix match (LPM) and what is its purpose in IPv6 routing?

4.27. What is the purpose of the Neighbor Cache on an IPv6 node?

4.28. What is the purpose of the Destination Cache on an IPv6 node?

4.29. What is the purpose of the Prefix List on an IPv6 node?

4.30. What is the purpose of the Default Router List on an IPv6 node?

4.31. What is IPv6 Stateless Address Autoconfiguration (SLAAC)?

4.32. What is an IPv6 Duplicate Address Detection Proxy?

4.33. What is a Randomized Interface Identifier in an IPv6 Address?

4.34. What is the purpose of Temporary IPv6 Addresses?

4.35. Explain the main difference between the IP routing table and the IP forwarding table.

4.36. What is the next-hop IP address in the routing table?

4.37. What is a static route?

4.38. What is a recursive static route?

4.39. What is a floating static route?

4.40. What is a default static route?

REFERENCES

[AWE2BK21V1].   J. Aweya, *IP Routing Protocols: Fundamentals and Distance Vector Routing Protocols*, CRC Press, Taylor & Francis Group, ISBN 9780367710415, 2021.

[AWE2BK21V2].   J. Aweya, IP Routing Protocols: *Link-State and Path-Vector Routing Protocols*, CRC Press, Taylor & Francis Group, ISBN 9780367710361, 2021.

[AWEBKMULT].   J. Aweya, *IP Multicast Routing Protocols: Concepts and Designs*, CRC Press, Taylor & Francis Group, ISBN 9781032701929, May 2024.

[AWEYFCDM22].   J. Aweya, *Designing Switch/Routers: Fundamental Concepts and Design Methods*, CRC Press, Taylor & Francis Group, ISBN 9781032317694, October 2022.

[CISCPOPOC].   Ciprian Popoviciu, Eric Levy-Abegnoli, and Patrick Grossette, *Deploying IPv6 Networks*, Cisco Press, 2006.

[CISCIPv6STR].   Cisco Systems, *IPv6 Routing: Static Routing, Feature Information for IPv6 Routing: Static Routing.*

[IANA-RESERVED-IID].   IANA (Internet Assigned Numbers Authority), Reserved IPv6 Interface Identifiers.

[RFC792].   J. Postel, "Internet Control Message Protocol", *IETF RFC 792*, September 1981.

[RFC816].   D. D. Clark, "Fault Isolation and Recovery", *IETF RFC 816*, July 1982.

[RFC826].   D. C. Plummer, "An Ethernet Address Resolution Protocol", *IETF RFC 826*, November 1982.

[RFC950].   J. Mogul and J. Postel, "Internet Standard Subnetting Procedure", *IETF RFC 950*, August 1985.

[RFC1027].   S. Carl-Mitchell and J. S. Quarterman, "Using ARP to Implement Transparent Subnet Gateways", *IETF RFC 1027*, October 1987.

[RFC1122].   R. Braden, Ed., "Requirements for Internet Hosts – Communication Layers", *IETF RFC 1122*, October 1989.

[RFC1191].   J. Mogul and S. Deering, "Path MTU Discovery", IETF RFC 1191, November 1990.

[RFC1256].   S. Deering, Ed., "ICMP Router Discovery Messages", *IETF RFC 1256*, September 1991.

[RFC2131].   R. Droms, "Dynamic Host Configuration Protocol", *IETF RFC 2131*, March 1997.

[RFC2710].   S. Deering, W. Fenner, and B. Haberman, "Multicast Listener Discovery (MLD) for IPv6", *IETF RFC 2710*, October 1999.

[RFC3633].   O. Troan and R. Droms, "IPv6 Prefix Options for Dynamic Host Configuration Protocol (DHCP) Version 6", *IETF RFC 3633*, December 2003.

[RFC3736].   R. Droms, "Stateless Dynamic Host Configuration Protocol (DHCP) Service for IPv6", *IETF RFC 3736*, April 2004.

[RFC3810].   R. Vida and L. Costa, "Multicast Listener Discovery Version 2 (MLDv2) for IPv6", *IETF RFC 3810*, June 2004.

[RFC3971].   J. Arkko, Ed., J. Kempf, B. Zill, and P. Nikander, "SEcure Neighbor Discovery (SEND)", *IETF RFC 3971*, March 2005.

[RFC4191].   R. Draves and D. Thaler, "Default Router Preferences and More-Specific Routes", *IETF RFC 4191*, November 2005.

[RFC4291].   R. Hinden and S. Deering, "IP Version 6 Addressing Architecture", *IETF RFC 4291*, February 2006.

[RFC4301].   S. Kent and K. Seo, "Security Architecture for the Internet Protocol", *IETF RFC 4301*, December 2005.

[RFC4389].   D. Thaler, M. Talwar, and C. Patel, "Neighbor Discovery Proxies (ND Proxy)", *IETF RFC 4389*, April 2006.

[RFC4443].   A. Conta, S. Deering, and M. Gupta, Ed., "Internet Control Message Protocol (ICMPv6) for the Internet Protocol Version 6 (IPv6) Specification", *IETF RFC 4443*, March 2006.

[RFC4861].   T. Narten, E. Nordmark, W. Simpson, and H. Soliman, "Neighbor Discovery for IP Version 6 (IPv6)", *IETF RFC 4861*, September 2007.

[RFC4862].   S. Thomson, T. Narten, and T. Jinmei, "IPv6 Stateless Address Autoconfiguration", *IETF RFC 4862*, September 2007.

[RFC5227].   S. Cheshire, "IPv4 Address Conflict Detection", *IETF RFC 5227*, July 2008.

[RFC5453].   S. Krishnan, "Reserved IPv6 Interface Identifiers", *IETF RFC 5453*, February 2009.

[RFC5942].   H. Singh, W. Beebee, and E. Nordmark, "IPv6 Subnet Model: The Relationship between Links and Subnet Prefixes", *IETF RFC 5942*, July 2010.

[RFC5944].   C. Perkins, Ed., "IP Mobility Support for IPv4, Revised", *IETF RFC 5944*, November 2010.

[RFC6275].   C. Perkins, Ed., D. Johnson, and J. Arkko, "Mobility Support in IPv6", *IETF RFC 6275*, July 2011.

[RFC6603].   J. Korhonen, Ed., T. Savolainen, S. Krishnan, and O. Troan, "Prefix Exclude Option for DHCPv6-based Prefix Delegation", *IETF RFC 6603*, May 2012.

[RFC6918].   F. Gont and C. Pignataro, "Formally Deprecating Some ICMPv4 Message Types", *IETF RFC 6918*, April 2013.

[RFC7404].   M. Behringer and E. Vyncke, "Using Only Link-Local Addressing inside an IPv6 Network", *IETF RFC 7404*, November 2014.

[RFC8200].   S. Deering and R. Hinden, "Internet Protocol, Version 6 (IPv6) Specification", *IETF RFC 8200*, July 2017.

[RFC8201].   J. McCann, S. Deering, J. Mogul, and R. Hinden, Ed., "Path MTU Discovery for IP version 6", *IETF RFC 8201*, July 2017.

[RFC8106].   J. Jeong, S. Park, L. Beloeil, and S. Madanapalli, "IPv6 Router Advertisement Options for DNS Configuration", *IETF RFC 8106*, March 2017

[RFC8415].   T. Mrugalski, M. Siodelski, B. Volz, A. Yourtchenko, M. Richardson, S. Jiang, T. Lemon, and T. Winters, "Dynamic Host Configuration Protocol for IPv6 (DHCPv6)", *IETF RFC 8415*, November 2018.

[RFC8981].   F. Gont, S. Krishnan, T. Narten, and R. Draves, "Temporary Address Extensions for Stateless Address Autoconfiguration in IPv6", *IETF RFC 8981*, February 2021.

5 Dynamic Host Configuration Protocol for IPv6 (DHCPv6)

5.1 INTRODUCTION

This chapter describes the Dynamic Host Configuration Protocol for IPv6 (DHCPv6) **[RFC8415]**, a Client/Server protocol that enables IPv6 nodes on a link to obtain IPv6 addresses and prefixes, as well as other network configuration parameters such as Domain Name System (DNS) Server addresses and domain names. IPv6 hosts need configuration information to configure IPv6 addresses on their interfaces, perform domain name-to-IPv6 address mapping, obtain time references (from a Network Time Protocol (NTP) Server) for synchronizing their local clocks, and acquire other information such as Session Initiation Protocol (SIP) Server addresses for multimedia (voice and video) communication with other IPv6 hosts.

DHCPv6 is used when a network operator wants a network entity (a DHCPv6 Server) to assign and record IPv6 addresses and prefixes, facilitating automatic configuration of interfaces and management of a network. IPv6 nodes can obtain IPv6 addresses and parameters using Stateless DHCPv6 **[RFC3736]** or Stateful DHCPv6 **[RFC8415]**, which assigns one or more IPv6 addresses and/or prefixes in a stateful manner. IPv6 nodes can rely entirely on DHCPv6 for IPv6 address assignment (i.e., Stateful DHCPv6) or use DHCPv6 in conjunction with Stateless Address Autoconfiguration (SLAAC), a method often referred to as Stateless DHCPv6. SLAAC allows an IPv6-enabled node to configure an IPv6 address on its interface independently, without address assignment from a DHCPv6 Server or without manual configuration (a process commonly referred to broadly as IPv6 address autoconfiguration).

A DHCPv6 Server on a link provides managed (and automated) configuration of IPv6 prefixes, addresses, and network parameters on IPv6 nodes (referred to as DHCPv6 Clients) on the same link. The DHCPv6 Relay Agent functionality acts as an intermediary mechanism that enables communication between a DHCPv6 Server and Clients that are not on the same link.

A DHCPv6 Server uses various well-defined (DHCPv6) options to provide nodes (Clients) with IPv6 addresses/prefixes and other configuration information. DHCPv6 defines various types of Options to be included in DHCPv6 messages for carrying specific and optional information needed for DHCPv6 operations. Clients and Servers add Options to DHCP messages as needed, depending on the type of configuration information requested by the Clients. The use of Options also allows DHCPv6 to be readily extended when the need arises, to accommodate new features and capabilities without the need to define new DHCPv6 messages.

A DHCPv6 Client is an IPv6 node on a link that sends requests to one or more DHCPv6 Servers to obtain network configuration parameters. A DHCPv6 Server can be a standalone server or an IPv6 node, such as a router on a link (running a DHCPv6 Server), that responds to requests from DHCPv6 Clients. A DHCPv6 Server may or may not reside on the same link as the DHCPv6 Client(s).

In networks where the DHCPv6 Clients and Servers are not on the same link (i.e., a network segment like an Ethernet LAN), the DHCPv6 Relay Agent is an IPv6 node on a link that acts as an intermediary to pass on DHCPv6 messages exchanged between DHCPv6 Clients and Servers. The main function of a DHCPv6 Relay Agent is to relay DHCPv6 messages between DHCPv6 Clients and Servers. Some network configurations may support more than one DHCPv6 Relay Agent between Clients and Servers, where a Relay Agent may pass on DHCPv6 messages to another Relay Agent to be sent to Clients or Servers.

DOI: 10.1201/9781003710646-5

DHCPv6 also supports a mechanism that allows automated delegation of IPv6 prefixes to DHCPv6 Clients **[RFC3633] [RFC8415] [RFC7084]**. An IPv6 *delegating router* (running a DHCPv6 Server) uses a *DHCPv6 prefix delegation mechanism* to delegate IPv6 prefixes to *requesting routers* (running a DHCPv6 Client software). A delegating router performs the functions of a DHCPv6 Server, responding to requests for delegated IPv6 prefixes from requesting routers. A DHCPv6 Client may act as a requesting router for IPv6 prefixes if the Client, in turn, supports the delegation of IPv6 prefixes to other IPv6 nodes (end devices such as desktops, laptops, smartphones, and WiFi access points). When a DHCPv6 Server supports the DHCPv6 prefix delegation mechanism for delegating IPv6 prefixes to requesting routers, it functions as an IPv6 prefix delegating router.

DHCPv6 can also be used to supply other DHCPv6 configuration Options (i.e., DHCPv6 Options that do not carry IPv6 prefixes or addresses) to Clients on a link that already have autoconfigured IPv6 addresses on their interfaces. In this mode of operation, called Stateless DHCPv6, the DHCPv6 Server is not required to track IPv6 prefix/address assignment states. Stateless DHCPv6 **[RFC3736]** requires fewer mechanisms to implement compared to Stateful DHCPv6. A *Lease* in DHCPv6 is the agreement or commitment between a DHCPv6 Server and a Client when the Server grants an IPv6 address or delegates an IPv6 prefix to the Client for use during a specified period of time.

The IPv6 addressing architecture **[RFC4291]** defines different IPv6 address types and their address scopes for use in IPv6 networks of various sizes and types. This architecture also provides various configuration guidelines for designing IPv6 networks using the different IPv6 address spaces. IPv6 requires support for multicast on links (e.g., links based on Ethernet technologies), since multicast allows IPv6 nodes on a link to efficiently reach other nodes on the same link after creating their IPv6 Link-Local addresses during IPv6 initialization. The IPv6 nodes (acting as Clients) then use their IPv6 Link-Local addresses and the well-known IPv6 Link-Local Scope multicast address (FF02::1:2) to discover and communicate with DHCPv6 Servers or Relay Agents on the local link. The address FF02::1:2, reserved for DHCPv6 use, is called the IPv6 All_DHCP_Relay_Agents_and_Servers multicast address.

5.1.1 DHCPv6 Terminology

Table 5.1 presents some terminology specific to DHCPv6 **[RFC8415]**. An IPv6 node configured as a DHCPv6 Server performs the following key functions:

- **Assigns Non-temporary and Temporary IPv6 Addresses to IPv6 Hosts (DHCPv6 Clients)**: A DHCPv6 Server assigns and may renew normal (non-temporary) IPv6 addresses to Clients. It assigns temporary IPv6 addresses to Clients for a limited time (Lease time); such addresses are usually allocated for privacy reasons (see the **discussion in Chapter 4**).
- **Delegates IPv6 Prefixes to DHCPv6 Clients**: A DHCPv6 Server may delegate IPv6 prefixes to Clients, who in turn assign IPv6 addresses and subnet prefixes from the delegated prefixes to their interfaces and links (subnets). Similar to IPv4 addresses, a DHCPv6 Server can use part of the bits of a delegated IPv6 prefix to indicate an IPv6 subnet prefix (e.g., 2001:DB8:AB34::/64 can be a subnet of the IPv6 prefix 2001:DB8:AB34:/48). The Client can then append a modified EUI64 interface identifier (ID) to a /64 prefix to create an IPv6 address for an interface.

A DHCPv6 Server and a Client use an IA to identify and manage a group of IPv6 addresses or delegated IPv6 prefixes that are related. Each IA consists of an Identity Association ID (IAID) (which uniquely identifies the IA) and its associated configuration information. A DHCPv6 Server creates a Binding for a Client to record the configuration information assigned to the Client, which includes the IPv6 addresses/prefixes, Client's DUID, IAID, and Preferred and Valid Lifetimes. The Server uses the tuple <DUID, IA-type, IAID> to index a Binding containing information about a specific IA (where IA type is the type of Lease in the IA, for example, temporary). The Server uses <DUID>

TABLE 5.1

DHCPv6 Terminology

Terminology	Description
Binding	This is a group of DHCPv6 Server data records containing the information that the Server has about the IPv6 addresses or delegated IPv6 prefixes in an Identity Association (IA), or configuration information explicitly assigned to a DHCPv6 Client.
Configuration parameter	This is an element of the configuration information configured on the DHCPv6 Server that is sent to a Client through DHCPv6. The parameter contains information that the Client uses to configure its network subsystem in order to enable communication on a link or internetwork.
Container Option	This is a DHCPv6 Option that encapsulates (or contains) other Options (e.g., the IA_NA Option).
DHCP domain	This is a set of links managed by DHCPv6 and operated by a single administrative entity.
DUID (DHCP Unique Identifier)	This is a DHCPv6 Unique Identifier for a DHCPv6 participant. Each DHCPv6 Client and Server is assigned only one DUID.
Encapsulated Option	This is a DHCPv6 Option that is usually only contained in another DHCPv6 Option (e.g., the IA Address Option is contained in the IA_NA or IA_TA Options).
IA (Identity Association)	This is a collection of Leases that the DHCPv6 Server assigns to a DHCPv6 Client.
IA Option(s)	This includes one or more of the following Options: IA_NA, IA_TA, and/or IA_PD Options defined in [RFC8415].
IAID (Identity Association Identifier)	This is an identifier for an IA, selected by the DHCPv6 Client. Each IA has an IAID, which is selected to be unique among the IAIDs for IAs of a specific type that belong to that Client.
IA_NA (Identity Association for Non-temporary Addresses)	This is an IA that contains IPv6 addresses assigned by the DHCPv6 Server that are NOT Temporary Addresses (see IA_TA).
IA_PD (Identity Association for Prefix Delegation)	This is an IA that contains IPv6 prefixes delegated by the DHCPv6 Server.
IA_TA (Identity Association for temporary Addresses)	This is an IA that contains Temporary Addresses assigned by the DHCPv6 Server.
Singleton Option	This is an Option that is allowed to appear only once as a top-level Option, or at any encapsulation level. Most DHCPv6 Options are Singletons.
T1	This is the time interval after which the DHCPv6 Client is expected to contact the Server to extend (using RENEW message) the Lifetimes of the IPv6 addresses (obtained via IA_NA Option(s)) and/or delegated IPv6 prefixes (obtained via IA_PD Option(s)) assigned to the Client.
T2	This is the time interval after which the DHCPv6 Client is expected to contact any available DHCPv6 Server to extend (using REBIND message) the Lifetimes of the IPv6 addresses (obtained via IA_NA Option(s)) and/or delegated IPv6 prefixes (obtained via IA_PD Option(s)) assigned to the Client.
Top-Level Option	This is an Option directly carried in a DHCPv6 message (i.e., not encapsulated in any other Option).
Transaction ID	This is an opaque value used to match DHCPv6 responses with replies initiated by either a DHCPv6 Client or a Server.

in general to index a Binding containing configuration information for a Client. It should be noted, however, that regarding the creation of DHCPv6 Bindings, the configuration information that a DHCPv6 Server returns to a DHCPv6 Client through a DHCPv6 policy, such as the information returned to all Clients on a given link, does not require the creation of a Binding.

A DHCPv6 Server uses DUIDs to identify Clients when selecting the Clients' configuration parameters and associating IAs with Clients. A DHCP Client uses DUIDs to identify a Server when receiving and processing DHCPv6 messages where identifying the associated Server is necessary. The DHCPv6 Client Identifier Option carries the DUID for identifying a particular Client, while the DHCPv6 Server Identifier Option contains the DUID for identifying a specific Server. The creation of a DUID may be based on any one of the following [RFC8415]: a Link-Layer address plus time of creation, a vendor-assigned unique ID based on an Enterprise Number, a Link-Layer address, or a Universally Unique Identifier (UUID).

Each IA has an IAID associated with it. The DHCPv6 Server may assign more than one IA to a Client (e.g., one IA assigned to each of the Client's interfaces). Each IA contains one type of Lease; for example, an IA for Temporary Addresses (IA_TA) contains temporary IPv6 addresses, while an IA for Prefix Delegation (IA_PD) contains delegated IPv6 prefixes. Reference [RFC8415] defines three types of IA: IA_NA, IA_TA, and IA_PD (see Table 5.1).

The parameter T1 is expressed in seconds and is transmitted to a DHCPv6 Client in IA Container Options ([RFC8415] defines the IA_NA and IA_PD Container Options). The Client interprets T1 as the time interval since the reception of the DHCPv6 message. The T1 value is stored in the T1 field of the IA Options. The T1 time refers to the actual moment when the timer expires from the time the DHCPv6 message was received. T2, also expressed in seconds, is transmitted to the DHCPv6 Client in IA Container Options (IA_NA and IA_PD Options). The Client interprets T2 as the time interval since the reception of the DHCPv6 message. The T2 value is stored in the T2 field of the IA Options. T2 time is similarly the actual moment when the timer expires from the time the DHCPv6 message was received.

Setting the Lifetime of an IPv6 address/prefix or the value for the T1 or T2 parameters to 0xFFFFFFFF means "infinity" in time. Setting the Valid Lifetime of an IPv6 address or a delegated IPv6 prefix to 0xFFFFFFFF (i.e., infinity) signifies that the IPv6 address or delegated IPv6 prefix is being permanently assigned to a DHCPv6 Client. A DHCPv6 Server should only use the infinity setting when there is a genuine need to assign an IPv6 address or delegated IPv6 prefix permanently to a Client.

5.2 DHCPv6 MESSAGE AND OPTION TYPES

Table 5.2 describes the messages used by DHCPv6, while Table 5.3 details the various DHCPv6 Options defined in [RFC8415]. Reference [RFC8415] outlines the formats of these DHCPv6 messages and Options. *DHCPv6 employs different types of Options in messages to convey specific and optional information necessary for DHCPv6 operations. Options also make DHCPv6 easily extensible to accommodate additional (new) features and capabilities without the need to define new messages.* Defining new DHCPv6 messages that may serve only a limited purpose adds to the complexity and bulk of DHCPv6. Options act as containers for packing information into DHCPv6 messages as needed, facilitating the interaction between DHCPv6 Servers and Clients, and enabling Servers to appropriately process the configuration information requested by Clients.

5.2.1 DHCPv6 MESSAGES

All DHCPv6 messages exchanged between Clients and Servers have a common fixed-format header and a variable-length portion that contains DHCPv6 Options. The data in the DHCPv6 message header and Options is organized in network byte (i.e., Big-Endian) order. In network byte order (or Big-Endian), the first (leftmost) byte in each field of the message header or Option is the most significant byte of the data, while the last byte is the least significant byte; the most significant byte is transmitted first (see **Appendix A** for a discussion on Big-Endian data ordering).

The Options placed in the Options field of a DHCPv6 message are stored sequentially (or back-to-back) with no padding added between them. Each Option is internally byte-aligned, but the Options in a DHCPv6 message are not aligned in any other way (such as on 2-byte or 4-byte boundaries).

TABLE 5.2
DHCPv6 Message Types

Message	Type	Description
SOLICIT	1	A **Client** sends this message to locate DHCPv6 Servers, that is, to discover DHCPv6 Servers configured to assign Leases or return other configuration parameters on the link to which the Client is attached.
ADVERTISE	2	A **DHCPv6 Server** sends this message to indicate that it is available for DHCPv6 service, in response to a SOLICIT message received from a Client.
REQUEST	3	A **Client** sends this message to request configuration parameters, including addresses and/or delegated prefixes, from a specific DHCPv6 Server.
CONFIRM	4	A **Client** sends this message to any available DHCPv6 Server to determine whether the addresses it was assigned are still appropriate for the link to which the Client is connected.
RENEW	5	A **Client** sends this message to the DHCPv6 Server that originally provided the Client's leases and configuration parameters, to extend the Lifetimes of the Leases and to update other configuration parameters.
REBIND	6	A **Client** sends this message to any available DHCPv6 Server to extend the Lifetimes on the Leases assigned to the Client and to update other configuration parameters; this message is sent after a Client receives no response to a RENEW message.
REPLY	7	A **Server** sends this message containing assigned Leases and configuration parameters in response to a SOLICIT, REQUEST, RENEW, or REBIND message received from a Client. A Server sends a REPLY message containing configuration parameters in response to an INFORMATION-REQUEST message. A Server sends a REPLY message in response to a CONFIRM message to confirm or deny that the addresses assigned to the Client are appropriate for the link to which the Client is connected. A Server sends a REPLY message to acknowledge receipt of a RELEASE or DECLINE message.
RELEASE	8	A **Client** sends this message to the DHCPv6 Server that assigned Leases to the Client to indicate that the Client will no longer use one or more of the assigned leases.
DECLINE	9	A **Client** sends this message to a DHCPv6 Server to indicate that the Client has determined that one or more addresses assigned by the Server are already in use on the link to which the Client is connected.
RECONFIGURE	10	A **DHCPv6 Server** sends this message to a Client to inform the Client that the Server has new or updated configuration parameters and that, the Client is to initiate a RENEW/REPLY, REBIND/REPLY, or INFORMATION-REQUEST/REPLY transaction with the Server in order to receive the updated information.
INFORMATION-REQUEST	11	A **Client** sends this message to a DHCPv6 Server to request configuration parameters without the assignment of any Leases to the Client.
RELAY-FORWARD	12	A **Relay Agent** sends this message to relay messages to DHCPv6 Servers, either directly or through another Relay Agent. The received message, either a Client message or a RELAY-FORWARD message from another Relay Agent, is encapsulated in an Option in the RELAY-FORWARD message.
RELAY-REPLY	13	A **DHCPv6 Server** sends this message to a Relay Agent containing a message that the Relay Agent delivers to a Client. The RELAY-REPLY message may be relayed by other Relay Agents for delivery to the Relay Agent closest (next) to the Client. The Server encapsulates the Client message as an Option in the RELAY-REPLY message, which the Relay Agent extracts and relays to the Client.

During the DHCPv6 lifecycle of IPv6 address and delegated IPv6 prefix assignment, a DHCPv6 Client uses SOLICIT, REQUEST, CONFIRM, RENEW, REBIND, RELEASE, DECLINE, and INFORMATION-REQUEST messages. The DHCPv6 Server uses ADVERTISE, REPLY, and RECONFIGURE messages during DHCPv6 message exchanges.

A DHCPv6 Relay Agent relays a DHCPv6 message from a Client to a Server using a RELAY-FORWARD message, and a Relay Agent can relay that message to another Relay Agent using another RELAY-FORWARD message. A DHCPv6 Server relays a DHCPv6 message through a Relay Agent to a Client using a RELAY-REPLY message, and a Relay Agent can relay that message to another Relay Agent using another RELAY-REPLY message.

5.2.2   IPv6 Multicast Addresses for DHCPv6 and UDP Port Numbers

DHCPv6 uses the following reserved, well-known IPv6 multicast addresses [**RFC8415**]:

- **The IPv6 All_DHCP_Relay_Agents_and_Servers Multicast Address (FF02::1:2)**: This is an IPv6 link-scope multicast address used by a DHCPv6 Client to exchange DHCPv6 messages with on-link (i.e., neighboring) DHCPv6 Servers and Relay Agents. All DHCPv6 Servers and Relay Agents that are active on a link join this multicast group. A DHCPv6 module enabled on a node listens to this IPv6 address.
- **The IPv6 All_DHCP_Servers Multicast Address (FF05::1:3)**: This is an IPv6 site-scope multicast address used by a DHCPv6 Relay Agent to exchange DHCPv6 messages with on-link (i.e., neighboring) Servers. A DHCPv6 Relay Agent uses this IPv6 multicast address either to transmit DHCPv6 messages to all Servers on a site or because it does not know the IPv6 unicast addresses (usually the IPv6 Global Unicast or Unique-Local addresses) of the Servers. Note that for the Relay Agent to use this IPv6 site-scope multicast address, it must have an IPv6 unicast address of sufficient scope (IPv6 Global Unicast or Unique-Local addresses) to be reachable by all the on-site DHCPv6 Servers. All active on-site DHCPv6 Servers must join this IPv6 multicast group on all interfaces within the site.

DHCPv6, like all IPv6 nodes and applications, uses multicast addresses to implement broadcast functionality because IPv6 does not support broadcast addresses. DHCPv6 also uses IPv6 unicast addresses under certain conditions. IPv6 multicast addresses provide equivalent functionality to IPv4 broadcast addresses. An IPv4/v6 multicast address identifies a group of interfaces, and IPv4/v6 packets with a multicast destination address are sent to all interfaces in that group.

It is important to note that the source IPv6 address of all IPv6 packets containing a DHCPv6 message sent by a DHCPv6 participant (Client, Server, or Relay Agent) is usually set to the IPv6 Link-Local address of the sending interface. The IPv6 packet's destination address is, in most cases, set to one of the above IPv6 well-known multicast addresses (see also the DHCPv6 unicast transmission discussion below). The IPv6 Link-Local address of an interface is autoconfigured as soon as a device powers up or reboots (see **Chapters 3 and 4**).

DHCPv6 uses the User Datagram Protocol (UDP) as its Transport Layer protocol. DHCPv6 Clients listen on UDP port 546 for DHCPv6 messages, while DHCPv6 Servers and Relay Agents listen on UDP port 547 for DHCPv6 messages.

- A DHCPv6 Client sends DHCPv6 messages to a DHCPv6 Server or Relay Agent using destination UDP port 547 in the messages.
- A DHCPv6 Server or Relay Agent responds to a DHCPv6 Client using destination UDP port 546 in the response messages.
- A DHCPv6 Client and Server/Relay Agent exchange DHCPv6 messages over UDP ports 547 and 546, Client to Server/Relay Agent port and Server/Relay Agent to Client port, respectively.

5.2.3 DHCPv6 OPTIONS

The DHCPv6 specification **[RFC8415]** defines a wide range of Options for various DHCPv6 operations that can be included in DHCPv6 messages. Additional Options are defined in other IETF specifications. DHCPv6 uses Options in DHCPv6 messages to convey additional information and parameters to DHCPv6 participants. All Options share a common base format as described in **[RFC8415]**. The values placed in the fields of all Options are represented in network byte order (Big-Endian).

Unless otherwise specified for a particular Option, each Option may appear only once in a DHCPv6 message and may only be included in the message's Options area. If an Option appears multiple times in a DHCPv6 message, each instance is considered separate from the others, and the sender must not concatenate or otherwise combine the data areas of the multiple Options. Options that can appear only once in a DHCPv6 message are called "Singleton Options" (e.g., IA_NA, IA_TA, Vendor Class, Vendor-specific Information, and IA_PD Options). The IA Address and IA Prefix may appear more than once in their respective IA Options.

The scope of a DHCPv6 Option is defined by its encapsulation in a message. Some Options are specific to an IA, some are specific to the IPv6 addresses specified in an IA, and some apply in general to the Client.

TABLE 5.3
DHCPv6 Option Types

Option	Code	Description
Client Identifier Option	1	Used to carry a DHCP Unique Identifier (DUID) that identifies a DHCPv6 Client.
Server Identifier Option	2	Used to carry a DUID that identifies a DHCPv6 Server.
Identity Association for Non-temporary Addresses (IA_NA) Option	3	Used to carry an IA_NA, the parameters associated with the IA_NA (IAID, T1, and T2), and the non-temporary IPv6 addresses associated with the IA_NA. IPv6 addresses appearing in an IA_NA Option are non-temporary addresses for the Client.
Identity Association for Temporary Addresses (IA_TA) Option	4	Used to carry an IA_TA, the parameters associated with the IA_TA, and the IPv6 addresses associated with the IA_TA. IPv6 addresses in this Option are temporary addresses for the Client
IA Address Option	5	Used to specify an IPv6 address associated with an IA_NA or an IA_TA. This Option must be encapsulated in the IA_NA-options field of an IA_NA Option or the IA_TA-options field of an IA_TA Option. The IAaddr-options field of this Option encapsulates those other Options that are specific to this IPv6 address.
Option Request Option	6	Used to identify a list of Options in a DHCPv6 message exchanged between a Client and a Server.
Preference Option	7	Sent by a Server to a Client to control the selection of a Server by the Client.
Elapsed Time Option	8	A Client must include an Elapsed Time Option in DHCPv6 messages to indicate how long the Client has been trying to complete a DHCPv6 message exchange.
Relay Message Option	9	This Option is used to relay verbatim a DHCPv6 message in a RELAY-FORWARD or RELAY-REPLY message to a DHCPv6 participant.
Authentication Option	11	This carries authentication information for authenticating the identity and contents of DHCPv6 messages.
Server Unicast Option	12	The DHCPv6 Server sends this Option to a Client to indicate to the Client that it is allowed to unicast DHCPv6 messages to the Server.
Status Code Option	13	This Option is used to return a status indication related to the DHCPv6 message or Option in which it appears.

(Continued)

TABLE 5.3 (*Continued*)
DHCPv6 Option Types

Option	Code	Description
Rapid Commit Option	14	Sent by a DHCPv6 participant to signal its readiness to use the DHCPv6 two-message exchange for IPv6 address assignment.
User Class Option	15	Used by a DHCPv6 Client to identify the type or category of users or applications it represents.
Vendor Class Option	16	Used by a DHCPv6 Client to identify the vendor that manufactured the hardware on which the Client is running. The information contained in the vendor-class-data field of this Option is carried in one or more opaque fields that identify details of the hardware configuration.
Vendor-specific Information Option	17	Used by DHCPv6 Clients and Servers to exchange vendor-specific information.
Interface-ID Option	18	A Relay Agent may send this Option to identify the interface on which the Client message was received. If a Relay Agent receives a RELAY-REPLY message with this Option, the Relay Agent relays the message to the Client through the interface identified by this Option.
Reconfigure Message Option	19	A DHCPv6 Server includes this Option in a RECONFIGURE message to indicate to the Client whether the Client is to respond with a RENEW message, a REBIND message, or an INFORMATION-REQUEST message.
Reconfigure Accept Option	20	A DHCPv6 Client uses this Option to announce to the Server whether the Client is willing to accept RECONFIGURE messages, and a Server uses this Option to inform the Client whether or not to accept RECONFIGURE messages. In the absence of this Option, the default behavior is that the Client is unwilling to accept RECONFIGURE messages.
Identity Association for Prefix Delegation (IA_PD) Option	25	Used to carry a DHCPv6 prefix delegation IA, the parameters associated with the IA_PD, and the IPv6 prefixes associated with it.
IA Prefix Option	26	Used to specify an IPv6 prefix associated with an IA_PD. This Option must be encapsulated in the IA_PD-options field of an IA_PD Option.
Information Refresh Time Option	32	This Option is requested by a DHCPv6 Client and returned by a Server to specify an upper bound for how long the Client should wait before refreshing information retrieved from the DHCPv6 Server. It is only used in REPLY messages in response to INFORMATION-REQUEST messages.
SOL_MAX_RT Option	82	A DHCPv6 Server sends this Option to a Client to override the default value of SOL_MAX_RT. One use for this Option is to set a higher value for SOL_MAX_RT; this reduces the SOLICIT message traffic from a Client that has not received a response to its SOLICIT messages.
INF_MAX_RT Option	83	A DHCPv6 Server sends this Option to a Client to override the default value of INF_MAX_RT. One use for this Option is to set a higher value for INF_MAX_RT; this reduces the INFORMATION-REQUEST message traffic from a Client that has not received a response to its INFORMATION-REQUEST messages.

DHCPv6 Clients include the Information Refresh Time Option (Option Code 32) in an INFORMATION-REQUEST message sent to a Server to request the upper bound on how long the Client should wait before contacting the DHCPv6 Server to refresh information it retrieved from the Server. A DHCPv6 Client places this Option in the Option Request Option (Option Code 6), which is included in the INFORMATION-REQUEST message. The Server returns a REPLY message with the "information-refresh-time" field of the Information Refresh Time Option, specifying the maximum time limit for the Client. This Option is only used in INFORMATION-REQUEST and REPLY messages. Other DHCPv6 messages typically contain time information (e.g., T1 and T2 time intervals and Lifetimes) that indicate when the Client should contact the Server. DHCPv6 participants normally use this Option when configuration parameters change or during an

IPv6 address renumbering event, allowing Clients operating in DHCPv6 SLAAC mode to update their configuration parameters.

DHCPv6 Clients and Servers use status codes (included in the DHCPv6 Status Code Option with Option Code 13) to communicate the success or failure of operations requested in DHCPv6 messages. Clients and Servers also use Status Codes to provide additional information about the specific cause of any request failure indicated in a DHCPv6 message. If a DHCPv6 message, which could include the Status Code Option, does not contain this Option, then the status of the request indicated in the message is assumed to be Success.

The SOL_MAX_RT parameter (with a default value of 3,600 seconds) represents the maximum timeout value for a SOLICIT message. The INF_MAX_RT parameter (also with a default value of 3,600 seconds) is the maximum timeout value for an INFORMATION-REQUEST message. Reference [RFC8415] provides a detailed list of the parameter values used to describe the behavior of Clients and Servers during DHCPv6 message transmission. A DHCPv6 participant (Client or Server) may adjust some of these time values by a randomization factor and backoff values to randomize DHCPv6 message transmission times, thus avoiding synchronized message departure times. Some message transmissions may also be rate-limited by the DHCPv6 participant.

5.3 DHCPv6 SERVER AND CLIENT FUNCTIONALITY

This section describes the key functionalities of the DHCPv6 Server and Client, their identification in a network, and the main elements of the Client configuration information renewal and rebinding processes. This discussion is based on the DHCPv6 Server and Client implementations in [ALLIEDDHCPv6] [CISCODHCPv6] [H3CDHCPv6]. It primarily addresses issues related to DHCPv6 implementation.

5.3.1 DHCPv6 Server and Client Identification

Each DHCPv6 participant (Client or Server) in a network is identified by a DHCPv6 Unique Identifier (DUID). The DUID of a DHCPv2 participant consists of a 2-byte Type Code represented in network byte order, followed by a variable-length value representing the actual ID [RFC8415]. The length of the DUID (excluding the Type Code) can range from 1 to 128 bytes. The DUID of a DHCPv2 Client or Server can be created from a Link-Layer address plus time (Type 1 DUID, DUID-LLT), a vendor-assigned unique ID based on an Enterprise Number (Type 2 DUID, DUID-EN), a Link-Layer address (Type 3 DUID, DUID-LL), or a UUID as defined in [RFC6355] (Type 3 DUID, DUID-UUID).

5.3.1.1 DHCPv6 Unique Identifier (DUID)

A DHCPv6 Client sends the Client Identifier Option (Option Code 1) containing its DUID to a Server to identify itself. In turn, a Server sends a Server Identifier Option (Option Code 2) containing its DUID to a Client for identification purposes. The DUID is unique and stable for each Client and Server in the network; it is distinct across all DHCPv6 Servers and Clients. As noted above, a DUID may be based on the Link-Layer address of a Client or Server interface. In such cases, the Client or Server uses the Medium Access Control (MAC) address of the interface to determine its DUID.

DHCPv6 considers IPv6 prefixes (assigned or to be assigned) to belong to different Clients when a particular Client requests two IPv6 prefixes from a Server on different Client interfaces with the same Client DUID but different IAIDs. For all the IAs of a specific type that belong to a Client, the Client selects an IAID for each IA to ensure uniqueness among the IAIDs chosen for those IAs.

5.3.1.2 Identity Associations (IA_PD, IAID, and IA_NA)

A DHCPv6 Client creates an IA, identified by a unique IAID, as a construct through which the Client manages the IPv6 addresses/prefixes and other configuration parameters provided by a Server. A Client may create multiple IAs (with corresponding IAIDs), one for each of its interfaces, to facilitate the management of the IPv6 addresses, prefixes, and other configuration parameters assigned by the Server to those interfaces. The Client ensures that the IAID of an IA is unique within the Client.

Specifically, a DHCPv6 Client uses an IAID to identify each IA associated with an interface that is configured with information from a DHCPv6 Server. An IA on an interface contains the IAID and the configuration information for that interface. When the Client sends requests to the Server for configuration information for a particular interface, it includes the IAID to identify the IA and the interface.

An IA_PD is a set of IPv6 prefixes assigned by a delegating device (delegating router) to a requesting device (requesting router). A requesting device may be assigned more than one IA_PD if it intends to assign an IA_PD for each of its interfaces when the device has multiple interfaces requiring configuration information.

Each IA_PD is identified by an IAID, and the requesting device ensures that the IAIDs are unique among the IA_PD IAIDs it uses. IAIDs remain consistent after the device reloads or reboots using configuration information on the associated interface that is permanently stored on the device.

5.3.1.3   Using IA_PD, IAID, and IA_NA with DHCPv6 Prefix Delegation

When performing subscriber LAN IPv6 addressing, a network provider may use DHCPv6 with IPv6 address and/or prefix delegation to provision IPv6 Global Unicast addresses for subscribers on the LAN. To accomplish this, the network provider must first configure IA_PD or IA_NA delegation pools on a DHCPv6 Prefix Delegation Server. The Server stores in various IPv6 address/prefix delegation pools, the IPv6 prefixes or addresses to be allocated to Clients.

As discussed in **Chapter 4**, IPv6 routers attached to a link transmit ICMPv6 Router Advertisement messages containing configuration information to be used by Client(s) for configuring their interfaces with IPv6 addresses/prefixes, default gateways, and default IPv6 route(s). The information in the Router Advertisement messages may instruct Clients to use either SLAAC, SLAAC with Stateless DHCPv6, or Stateful DHCPv6 for parameter configuration on the interfaces.

When a Client creates an IA_PD, it can then initiate IPv6 prefix delegation (as a requesting device) with the Server by including an IA_PD Option (Option Code 25) and the Client DUID in the SOLICIT messages sent to the Server. Upon receiving IPv6 prefixes from the Server, the Client automatically derives IPv6 addresses for its interfaces from the delegated IPv6 prefix information.

5.3.2   MUTUALLY EXCLUSIVENESS OF DHCPv6 CLIENT, SERVER, AND RELAY AGENT FUNCTIONALITIES ON AN INTERFACE

In DHCPv6, the Server, Client, and Relay Agent functionalities are mutually exclusive on any given interface. When a device enables one of these functions on an interface, it cannot enable the other function on the same interface. If the device tries to configure a DHCPv6 Client or Server on the same interface, a message will indicate that the first function has already been enabled on the interface: "Interface is in DHCP server mode", "Interface is in DHCP client mode", or "Interface is in DHCP relay mode."

5.3.3   DHCPv6 SERVER FUNCTIONALITY

The primary function of a DHCPv6 Server is to assign IPv6 addresses/prefixes, DNS Server IPv6 addresses, domain name suffixes, and other configuration parameters to DHCPv6 Clients on a network. A DHCPv6 Server maintains configuration parameters for Clients in various *DHCPv6 configuration pools* [CISCODHCPv6] (also called the *DHCPv6 address pools* in [H3CDHCPv6]). A Server associates a DHCPv6 configuration pool with a particular Server interface. The IPv6 prefixes that the Server delegates to a particular Client come from either a list of IPv6 prefixes preassigned to that Client or from local IPv6 prefix pools (to be shared by multiple Clients) [ALLIEDDHCPv6].

When using a DHCPv6 configuration pool, the Server references and uses the list of configured IPv6 prefixes or local IPv6 prefix pools in the DHCPv6 configuration pool associated with a Server interface/link for IPv6 address/prefix assignments to Clients on that Server interface/link.

A Server may provide configuration parameters to Clients without maintaining any dynamic state, such as when a Client has autoconfigured an IPv6 Global Unicast address on an interface and requires only DNS Server addresses and domain search lists from a Server. The Server can also be configured to perform IPv6 prefix delegation to Clients. A network administrator may enable DHCPv6 Server functionality on individual locally attached IPv6-enabled Virtual LAN (VLAN) interfaces.

A DHCPv6 Server typically maintains an *automatic binding table* to record and track the assignment of configuration parameters (such as IPv6 prefixes) to Clients. The Server may store automatic bindings semi-permanently on a local non-volatile random access memory (NVRAM) file system or on a remote Server, such as a Remote Authentication Dial-In User Service (RADIUS) or Trivial File Transfer Protocol (TFTP) Server. Normally, the transmission of ICMPv6 Router Advertisement messages is turned off on a DHCPv6 Server to facilitate the functioning of the IPv6 Neighbor Discovery protocol [RFC4861] and allow Clients to issue ICMPv6 Router Solicitation messages to discover IPv6 gateways on a link.

5.3.3.1 DHCPv6 Address Pool Types

When a DHCPv6 Server receives a request for configuration information from a Client, the Server selects IPv6 addresses, IPv6 prefixes, and other parameters from a DHCPv6 address pool, to assign to the Client.

- **Local DHCPv6 Address Pool for the Assignment of Shared IPv6 Prefixes**: This pool is used for IA_NA assignments and contains /64 IPv6 prefixes to which Clients can append their interface IDs to create /128 IPv6 addresses. The /64 IPv6 prefixes are considered simply as IPv6 addresses in the DHCPv6 address pool. The DHCPv6 Server assigns, renews, and reclaims IPv6 addresses in the local DHCPv6 address pool. Alternatively, the DHCPv6 Server may allocate an IPv6 address to a Client that already includes a 64-bit prefix and a 64-bit interface ID (EUI-64 or randomly generated), allowing the Client to automatically configure its IPv6 address. The Server may obtain the Client's interface ID from the DUID the Client sent in a Client Identifier Option (with Option Code 1) to the Server. The DUID formats contain a field that carries a unique ID for a DHCPv6 Client **[RFC8415]**. The interface ID the Server uses in the Client's IPv6 address may be based on this unique Client ID or on a randomly generated 64-bit number that is verified to be unique. In either case, the Client receives the complete IPv6 address and simply assigns it to the appropriate interface. As discussed in **Chapter 4**, the use of randomly generated interface IDs in IPv6 addresses ensures user anonymity when accessing certain services on the Internet.
- **Local DHCPv6 Prefix Delegation Pool for the Assignment of Unshared IPv6 Prefixes**: This pool is used for IPv6 prefix delegation (IA_PD) and typically contains /48 or /56 IPv6 addresses. The IPv6 prefixes assigned by a delegating device (DHCPv6 Server) may be stored in a local IPv6 prefix delegation pool. A Client may subnet the IPv6 prefixes assigned to it for its attached links. A Client creates an IPv6 Global Unicast address by appending an interface ID to an assigned IPv6 prefix.
- **DHCPv6 Address Pool on a Remote Data Server**: A DHCPv6 address pool may reside on an external source such as a RADIUS Server or on a DHCPv6 Server that can be accessed through one or more DHCPv6 Relay Agents. RADIUS is a protocol that provides authentication, authorization, and accounting (AAA) of users in a centralized manner (usually on a RADIUS Server) when users want to connect and use a network service **[RFC2865]**. The DHCPv6 Server also supports a RADIUS Client to communicate with the RADIUS Server. In this case, the DHCPv6 Server, upon receiving a Client request, contacts the external source to obtain the appropriate configuration parameters for the Client.

5.3.3.2 DHCPv6 Address Pool Contents

A DHCPv6 Server maintains in a DHCPv6 address pool the IPv6 addresses/prefixes and other configuration parameters it assigns to Clients. A DHCPv6 address pool generally contains the following information:

- Static IPv6 prefix: a prefix (with length less than /64) that is statically bound to a particular Client and can only be assigned to that Client.
- Static IPv6 address: an address (with length of /64) or an IPv6 address with an interface ID that is statically bound to a particular Client and can only be assigned to that Client.
- IPv6 prefix pool: a prefix range from which the Server dynamically assigns IPv6 prefixes to Clients.
- IPv6 subnet prefix: a range from which the Server dynamically assigns IPv6 addresses to Clients.
- DNS Server IPv6 address.
- DHCPv6 Client domain name.
- SIP Server IPv6 address or domain name.

A SIP Server is a core component of a voice over IP (VoIP) system that acts as a central hub for managing (i.e., initiating, maintaining, and terminating) calls and other communication sessions between devices.

5.3.3.2.1 DHCPv6 Prefix Delegation Construct

A DHCPv6 Server creates a Prefix Delegation (construct) to record the information for each IPv6 prefix assigned to a Client. The Prefix Delegation (also called a Lease record) typically contains the following information:

- IPv6 prefix assigned to a Client
- Client DUID
- IAID of the IPv6 prefix
- Valid Lifetime
- Preferred Lifetime
- IPv6 address (Link-Local address) of the requesting Client

5.3.3.3 IPv6 Address and Prefix Assignment Mechanisms

This section describes the IPv6 address/prefix allocation mechanisms supported by a DHCPv6 Server.

5.3.3.3.1 IPv6 Address Assignment Mechanisms

A DHCPv6 Server supports the following IPv6 address assignment mechanisms **[H3CDHCPv6]**:

- **Static IPv6 Address Assignment**: To implement the static assignment mechanism, a DHCPv6 address pool must first be created on the Server. Then, when the Server receives a request from a Client, it manually binds the DUID and IAID of the Client to an IPv6 address in the DHCPv6 address pool. Upon receiving a Client request for an IPv6 address, the Server assigns an IPv6 address from the address pool as a *static binding* to the Client.
  - If a DUID and IAID are statically bound to an IPv6 address, the DUID and IAID in a Client's request must match those in the binding before the IPv6 address can be assigned to the Client.
  - If a DUID is statically bound to an IPv6 address, the DUID in a Client's request must match the DUID in the binding before the IPv6 address can be assigned to the Client.

- **Dynamic IPv6 Address Assignment**: To implement the dynamic assignment mechanism, a DHCPv6 address pool must first be created for Clients. An IPv6 prefix must be specified for the DHCPv6 address pool, and the IPv6 prefix space divided into non-temporary and temporary IPv6 address ranges. Upon receiving a request from a Client, the Server selects an IPv6 address for assignment to the Client from the non-temporary or temporary IPv6 address range based on the IPv6 address type specified in the Client's request (in IA_NA or IA_TA Options). The DHCPv6 address pool serves as a repository in which the Server records the unassigned and assigned non-temporary and temporary IPv6 prefixes along with their parameters such as Lifetime values and Client DUIDs.

An IPv6 address in both cases may be a /64 IPv6 prefix from the DHCPv6 address pool; the Client then appends its interface ID to create the /128 IPv6 address. Alternatively, the DHCPv6 Server may be configured to allocate an IPv6 address that includes a 64-bit prefix plus a 64-bit interface ID (EUI-64 or randomly generated) to a Client, allowing it to simply configure the IPv6 address on the interface (an IPv6 address that already includes an interface ID). The DHCPv6 Server may obtain the interface ID from the Client's DUID sent in a Client Identifier Option (with Option Code 1). All the DUID formats defined in **[RFC8415]** contain a field that carries a unique ID for the DHCPv6 Client. The interface ID that the Server uses in the IPv6 address assigned to the Client may be based on this unique Client ID, or the Server may use a randomly generated 64-bit token as the interface ID.

5.3.3.3.2   IPv6 Prefix Assignment Mechanisms

A DHCPv6 Server supports the following IPv6 prefix assignment mechanisms **[H3CDHCPv6]**:

- **Static IPv6 Prefix Assignment**: To implement the static prefix assignment mechanism, a DHCPv6 address pool is first created, and when the Server receives a request from a Client, the Server manually binds the Client's DUID and IAID to an IPv6 prefix in the DHCPv6 address pool. Upon receiving a Client request, the Server assigns an IPv6 prefix from the address pool as a *static binding* to the Client.
  - If a DUID and IAID are statically bound to an IPv6 prefix, the DUID and IAID in a Client's request must match those in the binding before the IPv6 prefix can be assigned to the Client. Note that an IPv6 prefix can be bound to only one Client.
  - If a DUID is statically bound to an IPv6 prefix, the DUID in the Client's request must match the DUID in the binding before the IPv6 prefix can be assigned to the Client.
- **Dynamic IPv6 Prefix Assignment**: To implement the dynamic prefix assignment mechanism, a DHCPv6 address pool is first created. An IPv6 prefix is specified for the DHCPv6 address pool, and the IPv6 prefix pool is associated with the DHCPv6 address pool. Only one IPv6 prefix pool can be applied to a DHCPv6 address pool. Upon receiving a request from a Client, the Server *dynamically selects* an IPv6 prefix from the associated IPv6 prefix pool for the Client. The DHCPv6 address pool serves as a database in which the Server records the unassigned and assigned IPv6 prefixes and their parameters, such as IAIDs, Client DUIDs, etc.

An IPv6 prefix, in both cases, is an IPv6 prefix with a length less than /64 from the DHCPv6 address pool (e.g., /48 or /56 prefixes). The network administrator may specify different Lease times for different DHCPv6 prefix pools; however, all the IPv6 prefixes within a given DHCPv6 prefix pool must have the same Lease time. This is done to facilitate the management of DHCPv6 prefix pools on a Server and the allocation of IPv6 prefixes to Clients. Several DHCPv6 prefix pools may be created on a Server with different IPv6 prefixes and Lease times.

5.3.3.3.3   Configuring the DHCPv6 Server on an Interface

When a DHCPv6 Server is enabled on an interface, one of the following IPv6 address/prefix assignment methods is configured on the interface:

- **Apply a DHCPv6 Address Pool on the Interface**: Upon receiving a request from a Client, the Server selects an IPv6 address/prefix from the DHCPv6 address pool applied to the interface for the Client. If no assignable IPv6 address/prefix exists in the DHCPv6 address pool, the Server will not be able to assign an IPv6 address/prefix to the Client.
- **Configure an IPv6 Global Unicast Address Assignment on the Interface**: Upon receiving a Client request, the Server selects an IPv6 address/prefix from the DHCPv6 global address pool that matches the IPv6 address of the Server's interface, or from the IPv6 address of the DHCPv6 Relay Agent interface closest to the Client.

An interface cannot act as a DHCPv6 Client, Server, and Relay Agent at the same time; only one of these modes is permitted on an interface at any given time.

5.3.3.4   DHCPv6 Address Pool Selection Principles

When a DHCPv6 Server receives a request from a Client, it selects an IPv6 address or prefix from the DHCPv6 address pool for the Client according to the following principles [**H3CDHCPv6**]:

1. If a DHCPv6 address pool exists containing an IPv6 address or prefix that is statically bound to the requesting Client's DUID or IAID, this DHCPv6 address pool is selected by the Server. The Server then assigns this statically bound IPv6 address or prefix along with other configuration parameters to the Client.
2. If the interface on which the Client's request was received has a DHCPv6 address pool applied, the Server uses this DHCPv6 address pool to select an IPv6 address or prefix and other configuration parameters for the Client.
3. If the interface on which the Client's request was received has a DHCPv6 policy and the Client matches a user class in the policy, the Server selects the DHCPv6 address pool that is bound to the matching user class. Each user class in a DHCPv6 policy has a DHCPv6 address pool associated with it. If the policy has no matching user class, the Server uses the default DHCPv6 address pool to assign an IPv6 address/prefix and other configuration parameters for the Client. If the policy does not specify a default DHCPv6 address pool, or the default DHCPv6 address pool does not have IPv6 addresses that can be assigned to the Client, the IPv6 address assignment fails.
4. If the above conditions do not meet the Client's request, the Server selects a DHCPv6 address pool based on the Client's location.
   - **Client's Interface Is on the Same IPv6 Subnet as the Server's Interface**: The Server compares the IPv6 address of the interface on which the Client's request was received with the IPv6 subnets (i.e., prefixes) of all available DHCPv6 address pools. The Server then selects the DHCPv6 address pool with the longest-matching IPv6 prefix.
   - **Client's Interface Is on a Different IPv6 Subnet Than the Server's Interface**: The Server compares the IPv6 address of the DHCPv6 Relay Agent interface closest to the Client with the IPv6 prefixes of all available DHCPv6 address pools. The Server then selects the DHCPv6 address pool with the longest-matching IPv6 prefix.

To ensure that the IPv6 address allocation mechanisms work correctly, the IPv6 subnet/prefix used for dynamic assignment must match the IPv6 subnet/prefix for the interface on which the DHCPv6 Server or DHCPv6 Relay Agent resides. If a Client moves from one IPv6 subnet to another, the Server selects an IPv6 address/prefix from the DHCPv6 address pool that corresponds to the new IPv6 subnet.

5.3.3.5   DHCPv6 Prefix Delegation Pool Contents

A DHCPv6 Server uses an IPv6 prefix delegation pool to track and manage the IPv6 prefixes and related configuration parameters assigned to Clients. This pool contains information about the configuration parameters and policies available to the Server for assigning configuration parameters to Clients. The IPv6 prefix delegation pool is configured independently and then associated with a Server. Typically, the following configuration parameters and information are configured in a DHCPv6 prefix delegation pool:

- IPv6 prefix delegation information, including the name of the DHCPv6 prefix pool and the IPv6 prefixes (available for assignment to Clients) along with their configured Preferred and Valid Lifetimes.
- IPv6 addresses of DNS Servers [**RFC3646**].
- IPv6 addresses of NTP Servers [**RFC5908**].

5.3.3.6   IPv6 Address Assignment: Address Selection Process

The IPv6 addresses (i.e., /64 prefixes or addresses with interface IDs) in the DHCPv6 address pool assigned to Clients are of the following types:

- **Non-temporary IPv6 Addresses**: These are assigned to DHCPv6 Clients with Lease times and possibly renewals.
- **Temporary IPv6 Addresses**: These are IPv6 addresses used by a Client and frequently changed to improve user privacy without Lease renewal. Their interface IDs are typically randomly generated by the Server or the Client when given a /64 prefix.

An IPv6 subnet/prefix and address ranges must be specified for each of these address types in a DHCPv6 address pool.

Upon receiving a Client request, the Server performs the following operations to assign an IPv6 address (i.e., prefix length of /64 or address with interface IDs) [**H3CDHCPv6**]:

- Searches all the configured DHCPv6 address pools for a static IPv6 address bound to the Client.
- If a static IPv6 address is found in a DHCPv6 address pool, the Server assigns that IPv6 address and other configuration parameters to the Client.
- If no static IPv6 address is found, the Server selects a DHCPv6 address pool in the following order:
  1. Selects the DHCPv6 address pool applied to the interface on which the Client request was received.
  2. If the receiving interface does not have a DHCPv6 address pool applied to it, the Server selects a DHCPv6 address pool as follows:
     - If the source IPv6 address of the IPv6 packet carrying the Client request is an IPv6 Link-Local address, it indicates that the Client is on the same link as the receiving interface. In this case, the Server selects a DHCPv6 address pool that best matches the most recently configured IPv6 address of that interface.
     - If the Client request comes from a DHCPv6 Relay Agent, the Server selects a DHCPv6 address pool that best matches the IPv6 Link-Local address in the Client request (which is the IPv6 address of the Relay Agent closest to the Client).
  3. Uses the DHCPv6 address pool determined above to select an IPv6 address and other configuration parameters for the Client.

The Server manages the assignment of non-duplicate IPv6 addresses and assigns the correct IPv6 prefix to a Client based on the network/interface to which the Client is connected. The Server may assign IPv6 addresses from one or multiple IPv6 prefix pools depending on the number of prefix pools configured. In some cases, the Server may send additional information, such as DNS Server addresses and domain names, to the Client. Address pools may be configured on a Server for use on a specific Server interface or on multiple Server interfaces. Alternatively, the Server may be configured to automatically locate the appropriate DHCPv6 address pool upon receiving a Client request.

5.3.3.7 IPv6 Prefix Assignment: Prefix Selection Process

For a DHCPv6 Server to assign IPv6 prefixes to Clients, a DHCPv6 address pool must first be applied to the receiving interface of the Server, as described earlier. Upon receiving a Client request, the Server performs the following operations to assign an IPv6 prefix (i.e., prefix lengths less than /64) [H3CDHCPv6]:

- Searches all the configured DHCPv6 address pools for a static IPv6 prefix bound to the requesting Client.
- If a static IPv6 prefix exists in a DHCPv6 address pool, the Server assigns that IPv6 prefix to the Client along with other configuration parameters from the DHCPv6 address pool.
- If no static IPv6 prefix is found, the Server assigns an IPv6 prefix and other configuration parameters from the address pool applied to the interface on which the Client request was received.

A DHCPv6 Server (acting as a delegating router) may assign an IPv6 prefix to a DHCPv6 Client (acting as a requesting router), and the Client may then advertise the IPv6 prefix information in multicast ICMPv6 Router Advertisement messages, allowing IPv6 hosts on a link to automatically configure their IPv6 addresses using the advertised prefix.

As discussed above, a DHCPv6 Server uses a local IPv6 prefix pool to dynamically assign IPv6 prefixes to Clients. When the Server receives a request from a Client for IPv6 prefix assignment, it attempts to obtain unassigned IPv6 prefixes from the local IPv6 prefix pool. Additionally, whenever a Client releases (via a RELEASE message) previously assigned IPv6 prefixes, the Server returns those prefixes to the local IPv6 prefix pool for reassignment.

5.3.3.8 Obtaining IPv6 Prefixes from an External Source

After receiving a request from a DHCPv6 Client, the Server selects appropriate IPv6 prefixes from the IPv6 prefix delegation pool for assignment to the Client. The Server may select IPv6 prefixes for assignment using either static or dynamic assignment mechanisms as discussed above. The IPv6 prefixes (along with their Preferred and Valid Lifetimes) to be delegated to a requesting router (DHCPv6 Client) may be obtained from a local address pool or from an external source such as a RADIUS Server. Generally, the network administrator manually configures IPv6 prefixes with their Preferred and Valid Lifetimes for an IA_PD of a Client (identified by its DUID).

When the DHCPv6 Server receives a request for IPv6 prefix assignment from a Client, the Server checks if it has a static binding configured for the IA_PD in the Client's DHCPv6 message. If a static binding exists, the Server returns the IPv6 prefixes in that binding to the Client. If no binding exists, the Server attempts to find other sources to assign IPv6 prefixes to the Client. A DHCPv6 Server (IPv6 prefix delegating router) may use the Framed-IPv6-Prefix attribute (IPv6 RADIUS Attribute Type 97) [RFC3162] [RFC4818] [RFC6911] to obtain IPv6 prefixes from an external authority such as a RADIUS Server, to be assigned to a DHCPv6 Client (a requesting router), as illustrated in Figure 5.1.

The DHCPv6 Server (running a RADIUS Client) may send a RADIUS Access-Request packet containing addressing information to the RADIUS Server, indicating a preference for specific IPv6 prefixes. Note that the RADIUS Server is not required to honor the specific IPv6 prefixes requested. The RADIUS Server may use the RADIUS Delegated-IPv6-Prefix attribute (IPv6 RADIUS Attribute Type 123 [RFC4818], defined to carry an IPv6 prefix) to send an

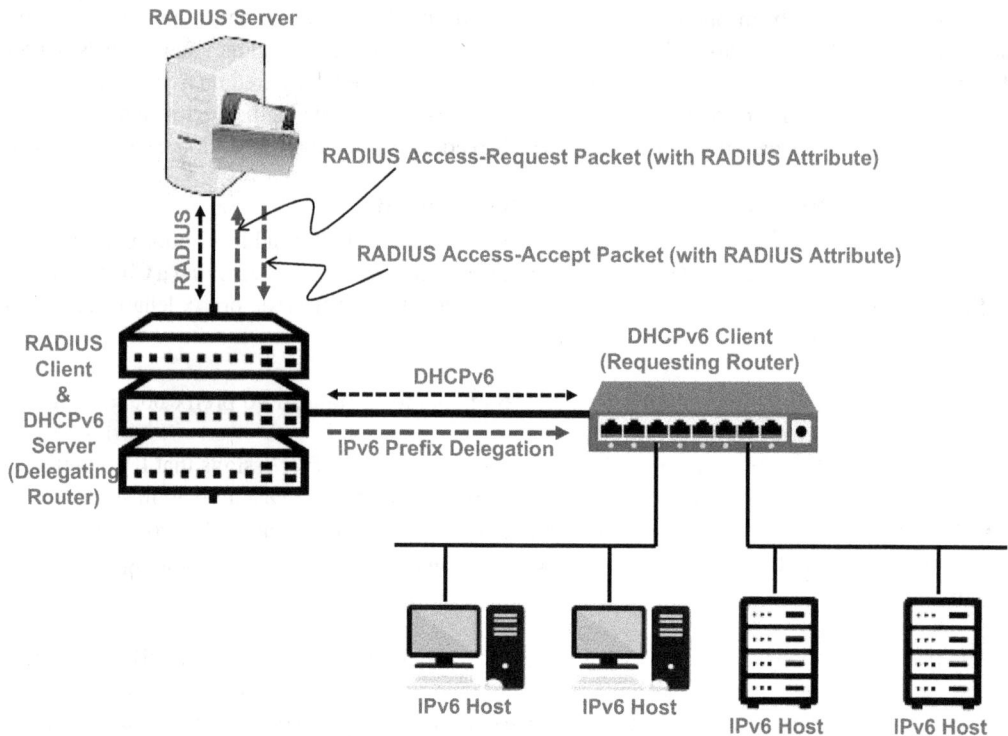

FIGURE 5.1   DHCPv6 Server obtaining configuration information from an external source.

IPv6 prefix to a DHCPv6 Server (a delegating router). This allows a DHCPv6 Server, performing DHCPv6 Prefix Delegation, to obtain IPv6 prefixes from an external source to delegate to a requesting router.

The following are possible messages exchanges between the DHCPv6 Server and the RADIUS Server:

- The DHCPv6 Server may send a RADIUS Access-Request packet (containing a Framed-IPv6-Prefix attribute) to the RADIUS Server, which replies with a RADIUS Access-Accept packet (containing a Delegated-IPv6-Prefix attribute) that includes the delegated IPv6 prefixes.
    - The RADIUS Server may also send a RADIUS Access-Accept packet (with a Framed-IPv6-Prefix attribute) containing IPv6 prefixes to the DHCPv6 Server for delegation to the DHCP Client.
- The DHCPv6 Server may send a RADIUS Access-Request packet (containing a Framed-IPv6-Pool attribute, Attribute Type 100) to the RADIUS Server, specifying the name of a DHCPv6 address pool to use for IPv6 prefix delegation **[RFC3162]**.
- The RADIUS IPv6-Delegated-Pool-Name attribute defined in **[RFC6911]**, when sent by the DHCPv6 Server, specifies the name of an IPv6 address pool configured on the RADIUS Server from which the RADIUS Server should delegate an IPv6 prefix.

Reference **[RFC6911]** provides clarifications on the use of the various RADIUS attributes defined in **[RFC3162] [RFC4818]** and **[RFC6911]**, because their use in many cases can be unclear or even confusing.

5.3.3.9   Automatic Binding Table on a DHCPv6 Server

Each DHCPv6 configuration pool configured on a Server is linked to a corresponding *automatic binding table* (also called a *binding database*). The DHCPv6 Server delegates IPv6 prefixes from the DHCPv6 configuration pool to Clients and records all assigned IPv6 prefixes in the automatic binding table. The DHCPv6 Server's permanent storage that holds the binding database is referred to as the *database agent*, typically implemented on NVRAM. A storage medium like NVRAM stores configuration information (including the IPv6 prefixes assigned to Clients by the Server) so that the information is retained even after system reboots or reloads. Each entry in the automatic binding table contains the following information:

- DUID of the Client.
- IPv6 address of the Client (Link-Local address).
- The IA_PDs associated with the Client.
- IPv6 prefixes delegated by the Server to each IA_PD.
- Preferred and Valid Lifetimes for each IPv6 prefix.
- The DHCPv6 configuration pool associated with this binding table.
- The Server interface associated with the configured DHCPv6 configuration pool.

After delegating an IPv6 prefix to a Client from the DHCPv6 configuration pool, the Server creates a corresponding entry in the binding table and updates the entry when the Client renews, rebinds, or confirms the delegation of the IPv6 prefix. The Server deletes the binding table entry when any of the following events occur:

- The Client sends a RELEASE message to release all the IPv6 prefixes in the binding.
- All Valid Lifetimes expire.
- The server administrator runs an appropriate command to clear the binding.

5.3.3.10   Binding Database and Binding Agent

The *database agent* mentioned above is a permanent storage in which the binding database is stored. A database agent can be a local file system (on the DHCPv6 Server itself) such as NVRAM, a remote host such as an FTP (File Transfer Protocol) Server, or a RADIUS Server (see Figure 5.1). The DHCPv6 Server maintains automatic bindings in local memory and can also save them to permanent storage so that configuration information (such as the IPv6 prefixes assigned to Clients) will not be lost after system reboots or reloads. The DHCPv6 Server stores the bindings as text records to facilitate easy maintenance. The following information is contained in each binding record:

- Name of the DHCPv6 pool from which the DHCPv6 Server assigned configuration information to the Client.
- Interface ID on which the DHCPv6 Server received the Client requests.
- The IPv6 address of the Client.
- The DUID of the Client.
- IAID of the IA_PD.
- IPv6 prefix delegated to the Client.
- The IPv6 prefix length.
- The Preferred Lifetime of the IPv6 prefix (in seconds).
- The Valid Lifetime of the IPv6 prefix (in seconds).
- The expiration timestamp of the IPv6 prefix.
- Optionally, the name of the local IPv6 prefix pool from which the DHCPv6 Server assigned the IPv6 prefix.

5.3.3.11   DHCPv6 Server and DNS for IPv6 Address Assignment

A DHCPv6 Server may send other configuration information, such as the default domain name and the IPv6 address of a DNS Server, to a Client. A DHCPv6 Server may be configured to use specific IPv6 address pools for address assignment on a particular interface or to automatically determine the appropriate address pool to use for a Client request.

5.3.3.12   NTP Server Functionality

NTP Server functionality is usually used with DHCPv6 to provide a list of IPv6 addresses of available NTP Servers to requesting Clients, allowing the Clients to synchronize their local system clocks to the time of a standard time server (an NTP Server). The DHCPv6 Server typically sends a list of available NTP Servers, enabling the Clients to select the NTP Servers that can provide the time reference for clock synchronization.

Some typical applications of the NTP time references on a DHCPv6 Client include the following:

- Real-time timestamping/marking of events and transactions.
- Real-time timestamping of medical records, inventory data, and log files in a system.
- Timestamping for event correlation, for example, troubleshooting, auditing, and forensics.
- Triggers for event/transaction/task scheduling and processing.
- Triggers for control/automated actions (automated provisioning of services and processing of transactions).
- Timestamping for real-time traffic profiling, server performance monitoring, health and availability monitoring, multi-level threshold-based monitoring, application performance monitoring, service monitoring, server process monitoring, event log monitoring, etc.
- Timestamping for latency measurements across networks and through software stacks.

5.3.4   DHCPv6 Client Functionality

DHCPv6 Clients may send requests to a DHCPv6 Server for the delegation of IPv6 prefixes. The Server retrieves IPv6 prefixes stored in an IPv6 prefix pool to be delegated to the requesting Clients. The delegated IPv6 prefixes (from the Server's IPv6 prefix pool) can then be used by the Clients to configure addresses on their downstream interfaces. A DHCPv6 Client is enabled and operates on a particular IPv6-enabled interface of a Server. A Client can also send a request to a Server for configuration parameters other than IPv6 prefixes, such as the IPv6 addresses of DNS Servers, a request that does not require the Server to maintain any dynamic state for individual requesting Clients.

5.3.4.1   DHCPv6 Server Selection by a DHCPv6 Client

By sending a DHCPv6 SOLICIT message and receiving ADVERTISE messages from DHCPv6 Servers, a DHCPv6 Client is able to construct a list of available Servers in a network. Servers include the DHCPv6 Preference Option (Option Code 7) in their ADVERTISE messages to signal a preference value to the Client (carried in the Option's "pref-value" field). The Client then ranks the response messages from the Servers based on the Server preference values. When a Client is interested in IPv6 prefixes for configuring its interfaces, it considers only the DHCPv6 Servers that advertise IPv6 prefixes when requesting IPv6 prefixes from Servers.

5.3.5   DHCPv6 Configuration Information Renewal and Rebinding

The DHCPv6 configuration information renewal and rebinding processes initiated by a Client rely on the following timers and Lifetime values: T1 Timer, T2 Timer, Preferred Lifetime, and Valid Lifetime:

- **T1 Timer**: This timer indicates when a DHCPv6 Client is expected to contact a Server (through sending a RENEW message) to renew IPv6 addresses or prefixes.

- **T2 Timer**: This timer indicates when a DHCPv6 Client is expected to contact a Server (through sending a REBIND message) to rebind IPv6 addresses or prefixes.
- **Preferred Lifetime**: This indicates the length of time during which preferred IPv6 addresses or prefixes are available for unrestricted use on a node's interfaces (**see Chapter 4**); these addresses/prefixes are deprecated when their Preferred Lifetime Timer expires. An IPv6 node is discouraged but not forbidden from using deprecated addresses and prefixes. IPv6 nodes should not use deprecated addresses or prefixes to form the source address of IPv6 packets but should accept IPv6 packets sent from deprecated addresses or prefixes.
- **Valid Lifetime**: This indicates the length of time after which IPv6 addresses or prefixes must be abandoned (**see Chapter 4**). When the Valid Lifetime Timer expires, the associated IPv6 addresses or prefixes become invalid and are no longer available for use on interfaces. IPv6 nodes should not use invalid IPv6 addresses or prefixes to form the source or destination address of IPv6 packets.

The following are the Client States during the DHCPv6 information renewal and rebinding processes:

- **Bound State**: Normal Client operation with an assigned Lease.
- **Renewing State**: Renewing the assigned Lease; the Client sends a REQUEST/RENEW message to the Server.
- **Rebinding State**: The Client enters this state when it has not received a REPLY message from the Server after sending a RENEW message; the Client sends a REBIND message to the Server.
- **Bound State**: The Client receives a new Lease from the Server, processes it, and finalizes its usage.

The DHCPv6 Lease renewal process is summarized as follows:

- The Client sees that the renewal T1 Timer for a Lease has expired (the default T1 Timer may be set to 50% of the Lease length).
- The Client state (see above) transitions from Bound to Renewing State.
- The Client transmits REQUEST/RENEW messages to the Server.
- The Client state transitions to Rebinding State (if the Client receives no REPLY message from the Server and the T2 Timer expires).
- The Client state transitions to Bound State (when the Client receives a REPLY message from the Server).

5.3.6 Hierarchical DHCPv6 Parameter Configuration: Hierarchical IPv6 Prefix Delegation

An Internet Service Provider (ISP) may use hierarchical DHCPv6 with stateless or stateful management to send configuration parameters to DHCPv6 Clients. In Figure 5.2, a Provider Edge (PE) router that is configured as a DHCPv6 Server (a delegating router) sends configuration parameters (from a local configuration pool) to Customer Premises Equipment (CPE) that supports a DHCPv6 Client (a requesting router). This architecture is typically seen in ISP access network deployments. A CPE with an upstream DHCPv6 Server may be configured to act as a DHCPv6 requesting router for IPv6 prefix delegation.

The CPE interface leading to the PE may support a Stateful or Stateless DHCPv6 Client. In the Stateless DHCPv6 scenario, the DHCPv6 Server provides only configuration parameters—such as DNS Server IPv6 addresses, domain names, and NTP Servers—to the DHCP Client on the CPE, without IPv6 address/prefix assignment. In most cases, the DHCPv6 Server provides configuration information specific to the ISP. The CPE may be configured to run a Stateless DHCPv6 Server on

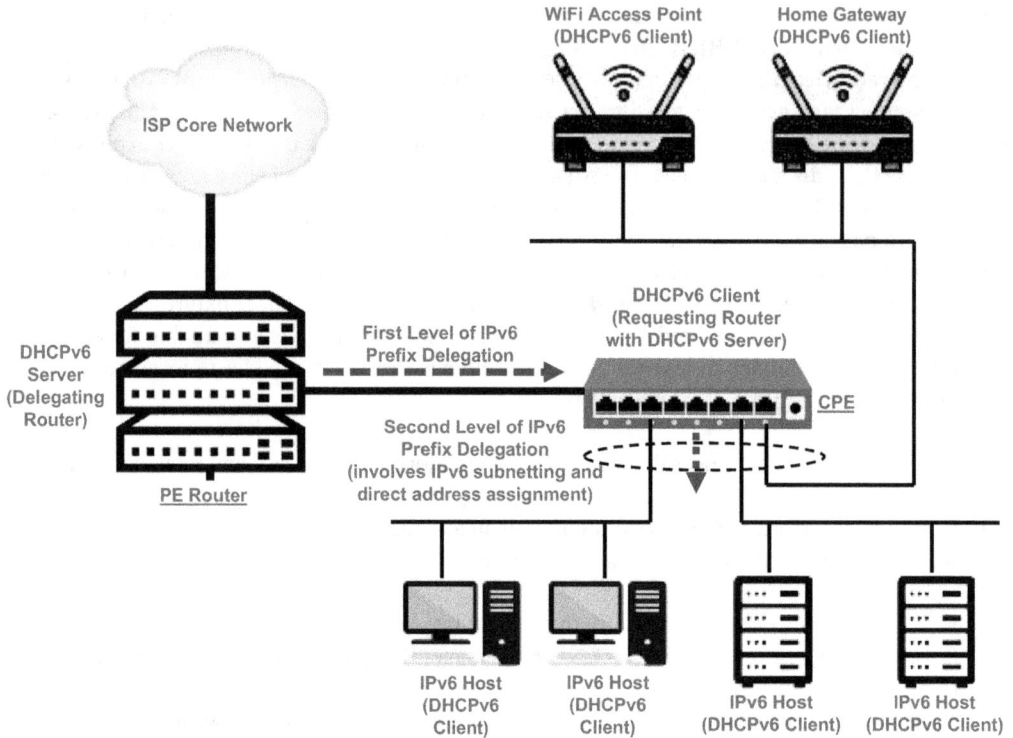

FIGURE 5.2   Example network for hierarchical IPv6 prefix delegation.

its downstream links and relay DHCPv6 non-address configuration parameters to hosts attached to those links.

In addition to having a DHCPv6 Client on the interface leading to the PE, the CPE may support a Stateful DHCPv6 Server that assigns IPv6 addresses and subnet prefixes (from the IPv6 prefixes delegated to it) to devices attached to its downstream links. These CPE-connected devices may include IPv6 hosts (e.g., computers, data servers, cameras, sensors, meters), home gateways (routers), and WiFi access points. The PE's DHCPv6 Server obtains the IPv6 prefixes to be delegated from either a local IPv6 prefix delegation pool, an external source such as a RADIUS Server, or a DHCPv6 Server that can be accessed through one or more DHCPv6 Relay Agents. Each delegated IPv6 prefix has an associated Preferred and Valid Lifetime, which the requesting router may extend. Some devices connected to the CPE may use Stateful DHCPv6 to obtain all their configuration parameters from the CPE's DHCPv6 Server. Other devices may autoconfigure IPv6 Global Unicast addresses (using SLAAC) and then consult the CPE's DHCPv6 Server to obtain specific configuration parameters, such as DNS Server IPv6 addresses, domain names, and NTP Servers.

The CPE (acting as a requesting router) and its attached devices can exchange IPv6 Neighbor Discovery messages, as described in **Chapter 4**. The CPE's DHCPv6 Server may perform IPv6 address allocation on attached links using ICMPv6 Router Advertisement messages, DHCPv6, or a combination of these two methods. The CPE may also function as a default gateway router for its attached devices. The CPE's DHCPv6 Server may send the DHCPv6 Information Refresh Option (Option Code 32) to an attached Client, specifying the maximum time the Client should wait before refreshing information obtained from the Server. The Server sends this Option in a REPLY message to the Client in response to an INFORMATION-REQUEST message containing an Option Request Option (Option Code 6) from the Client.

ISPs use the DHCPv6 prefix delegation mechanism to automate the assignment of IPv6 prefixes to CPEs. The PE (delegating router) assigns IPv6 prefixes to a CPE (requesting router), which then uses the delegated IPv6 prefixes to assign IPv6 Global Unicast addresses to the devices connected to its downstream links. The CPE may also assign IPv6 subnet addresses to the subnets attached to it. The DHCPv6 prefix delegation mechanism is useful when the delegating router (PE) lacks information about or is unconcerned with the topological details of the networks (links) connected to the request- ing router (CPE); the delegating router only requires the identity and local connecting interface of the requesting router to select suitable IPv6 prefixes for delegation. DHCPv6 prefix delegation is one of the IPv6 mechanisms that eliminates the need for Network Address Translation in IPv6.

5.4   DHCPv6 CLIENT–SERVER MESSAGE EXCHANGES

DHCPv6 Clients, Servers, and Relay Agents exchange DHCPv6 messages over UDP. A Client uses the interface's IPv6 Link-Local address or an IPv6 address configured through other means to send and receive DHCPv6 messages. A DHCPv6 Client sends most DHCPv6 messages using the well-known IPv6 link-scoped multicast destination address called the IPv6 All_DHCP_Relay_ Agents_and_Servers multicast address (FF02::1:2). This means DHCPv6 Clients on a network do not need to be configured with the IPv6 address or addresses of DHCPv6 Servers to obtain configu- ration information.

The presence of a DHCPv6 Relay Agent on a link (acting as an intermediary between DHCPv6 Clients and Servers) allows a DHCPv6 Client to send DHCPv6 messages to a DHCPv6 Server that is not attached to the same link. The DHCPv6 Relay Agent on the Client's link relays messages between the DHCPv6 Client and Server. Although attached to the Client's link and acting as an intermediary, the operation of the DHCPv6 Relay Agent is transparent to the DHCPv6 Client.

In some cases, once a DHCPv6 Client has determined the IPv6 address of a DHCPv6 Server, it may send DHCPv6 messages directly to the Server using IPv6 unicast transmission.

5.4.1   DHCPv6 CLIENT INITIATION OF MESSAGE EXCHANGE WITH A SERVER

The following are some reasons why a DHCPv6 Client would initiate a message exchange with one or more Servers to obtain or update configuration information:

- The Client initiates a DHCPv6 message exchange as part of the operating system configuration/bootstrap process.
- An Application Layer entity requests a DHCPv6 message exchange through an operating system-specific API.
- The receipt of an ICMPv6 Router Advertisement message indicates that DHCPv6 should be used for IPv6 address configuration.
- The Client initiates a DHCPv6 message exchange (using RENEW and REBIND messages) to extend the Lifetime of IPv6 address(es) and/or delegated IPv6 prefix(es).
- After receiving a RECONFIGURE message, a Client may be requested by a Server to initiate a DHCPv6 message exchange.

It should be noted that it is the DHCPv6 Client that creates IAs and then requests a Server to assign IPv6 addresses and/or delegated IPv6 prefixes to those IAs. The Client starts by creating an IA and assigning an IAID to it. The Client then includes IA Options describing the IAs in a SOLICIT message and transmits this message to any available Servers. To send such a SOLICIT message, the Client must not be using any of the IPv6 addresses or delegated IPv6 prefixes being requested.

When a DHCPv6 Client autoconfigures IPv6 Global Unicast addresses using SLAAC (meaning, it does not need to contact a DHCPv6 Server for the assignment of IPv6 addresses or delegated IPv6 pre- fixes), it can obtain other configuration information, such as a list of available DNS Servers **[RFC3646]** or NTP Servers **[RFC5908]**, through a single DHCPv6 message exchange with a DHCPv6 Server. To obtain such configuration information, the Client first transmits an INFORMATION-REQUEST message to the IPv6 multicast address FF02::1:2. Any available DHCPv6 Server will respond by sending a REPLY message containing the requested configuration information to the Client.

5.4.2 DHCPv6 Client–Server Exchange Involving Four Messages

The DHCPv6 Server is responsible for the assignment of IPv6 addresses and/or delegated IPv6 prefixes and other configuration information to DHCPv6 Clients. However, a DHCPv6 Client must first locate a DHCPv6 Server and then request the Server to assign one or more IPv6 addresses and/ or delegated IPv6 prefixes (a process called *server discovery*). A DHCPv6 Client sends a SOLICIT message to FF02::1:2 (the IPv6 All_DHCP_Relay_Agents_and_Servers multicast address) to locate available DHCPv6 Servers (see Figure 5.3). Any DHCPv6 Server that can satisfy the Client's request will respond by sending an ADVERTISE message to the Client; multiple Servers might respond.

The Client then selects one of the responding DHCPv6 Servers (according to the sequence of the ADVERTISE messages received and the server priority) and transmits a REQUEST message to the selected DHCPv6 Server, requesting the committed assignment of IPv6 addresses and/or delegated

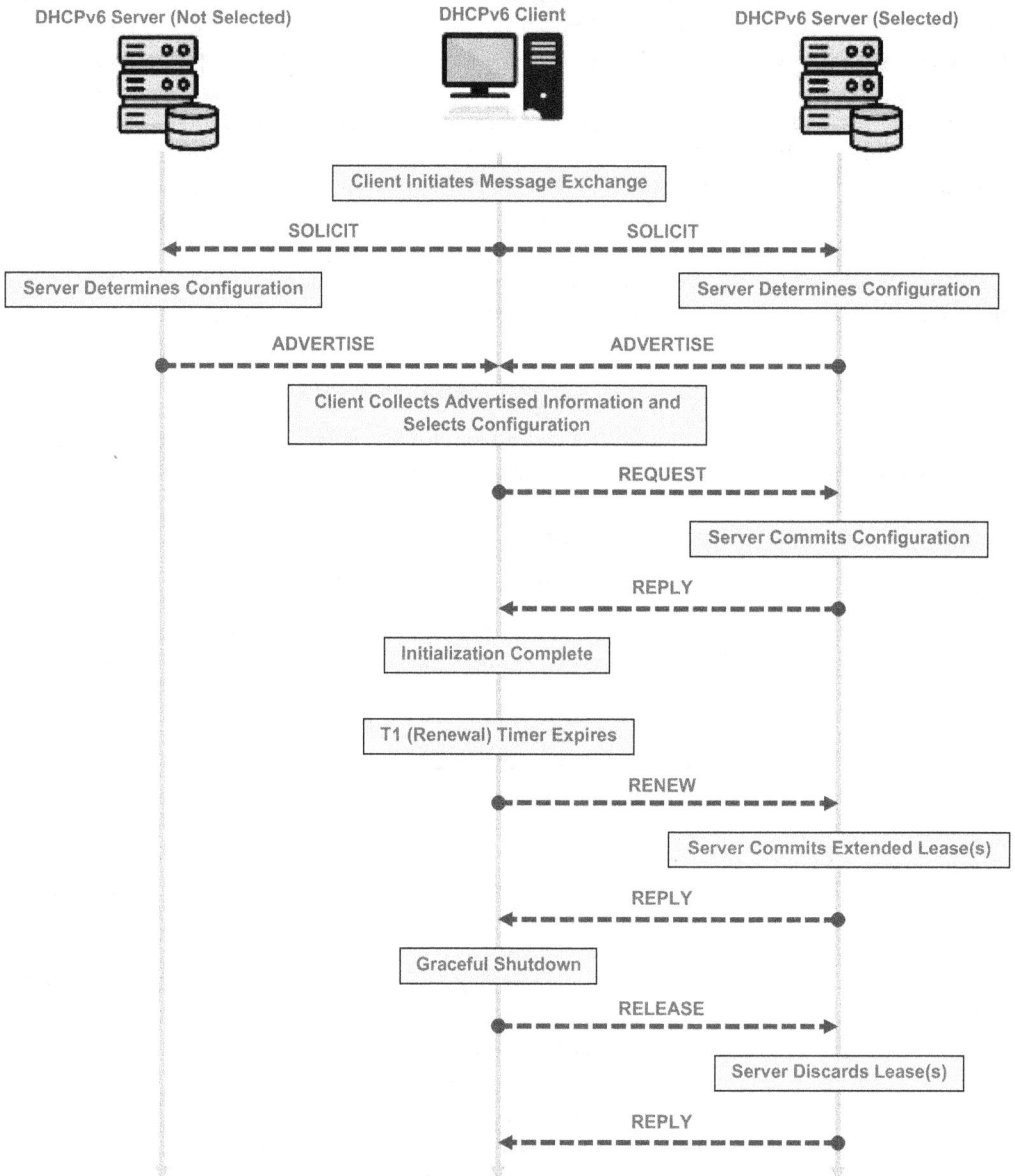

FIGURE 5.3   DHCPv6 Client–Server message exchange.

IPv6 prefixes and other configuration information. A DHCPv6 Server sends a Preference Option (Option Code 7) with the Option's "pref-value" field set to a predefined value to indicate its priority to the Client.

The DHCPv6 Server, upon receiving the Client's REQUEST message, will respond by sending a REPLY message containing the assigned IPv6 addresses, delegated IPv6 prefixes, and other configuration information. The DHCPv6 Client can request the Server to extend the Lifetimes assigned to the IPv6 addresses or delegated IPv6 prefixes (this involves a DHCPv6 two-message exchange as discussed in a section below).

5.4.2.1 Typical DHCPv6 Messages Exchanged between a Client and Two Servers for One or More Leases

Figure 5.3 shows the typical timeline of the DHCPv6 message exchange process between a Client and multiple Servers when the Client is requesting one or more Leases. This process begins with the Client and Server exchanging the four DHCPv6 messages SOLICIT/ADVERTISE/REQUEST/REPLY (called the DHCPv6 four-message exchange process), allowing the Client to obtain the Lease(s). This process may be followed by the Client and Server exchanging RENEW/REPLY messages (called the DHCPv6 two-message exchange process), which allows the Client to extend the Lifetime of the Lease(s). The entire DHCPv6 process then ends with a DHCPv6 two-message exchange of RELEASE/REPLY messages, enabling the Client to terminate the use of the Lease(s).

As discussed above, the Client requests the assignment of one or more IPv6 addresses or delegated IPv6 prefixes (Figure 5.3) by first locating a DHCPv6 Server and sending a request (via a SOLICIT message to FF02::1:2) to that Server for the assignment of IPv6 addresses/prefixes and other configuration information. The Servers respond by sending ADVERTISE messages to the Client. The Client then sends a REQUEST message to one of the Servers (selected according to the criteria described above) to obtain configuration information.

A DHCPv6 Client wishing to perform the DHCPv6 two-message exchange (using SOLICIT/REPLY message exchange) will include a Rapid Commit Option in the SOLICIT message (see discussion below) it sends to the Servers. Servers that can perform IPv6 address or delegated IPv6 prefix assignments to the Client's IAs will respond by sending an ADVERTISE or REPLY message to the Client, provided that the Client's SOLICIT message included a Rapid Commit Option and the Server is configured to accept such messages. If the Server responds by sending an ADVERTISE message, the Client will initiate a DHCPv6 configuration information exchange using REQUEST, RENEW, REBIND, RELEASE, and DECLINE messages.

A DHCPv6 Server may initiate a DHCPv6 message exchange with a Client by transmitting a RECONFIGURE message to the Client. The receipt of this message causes the Client to send a RENEW, REBIND, or INFORMATION-REQUEST message (depending on the message type indicated in the DHCPv6 Reconfigure Message Option with Option Code 19) to the Server to refresh its configuration information.

5.4.3 DHCPv6 CLIENT/SERVER EXCHANGE INVOLVING TWO MESSAGES

The DHCPv6 two-way message exchange process is a simplified mode of operation in which the DHCPv6 Clients and Servers exchange only two DHCPv6 message types when communicating with each other.

5.4.3.1 Using the DHCPv6 Two-Message Exchange for Obtaining Other Client Configuration Information

When a DHCPv6 Client autoconfigures IPv6 Global Unicast addresses (via SLAAC) without requiring IPv6 address assignment or delegated prefixes from a DHCPv6 Server, the Client can obtain other configuration information from a DHCPv6 Server, such as a list of available DNS Servers [RFC3646] or NTP Servers [RFC5908]. This mode of DHCPv6 message exchange for host configuration is referred to as Stateless DHCPv6 message exchange (see Figure 5.4). In this mode, the DHCPv6 Client obtains its configuration information (without IPv6 addresses/prefixes) through a two-message exchange with a DHCPv6 Server (using INFORMATION-REQUEST and REPLY messages).

To obtain the above configuration information from a DHCPv6 Server, the Client first transmits a DHCPv6 INFORMATION-REQUEST message to FF02::1:2, the IPv6 All_DHCP_Relay_Agents_ and_Servers multicast address. DHCPv6 Servers respond by sending a REPLY message containing the other configuration information requested by the Client.

5.4.3.2 Using the DHCPv6 Two-Message Exchange for Expedite IPv6 Address Assignment or Prefix Delegation

A DHCPv6 Client may also use the DHCPv6 two-message exchange (only SOLICIT and REPLY messages) instead of the normal DHCPv6 four-message exchange to request a DHCPv6 Server to expedite IPv6 address assignment and/or IPv6 prefix delegation (see Figure 5.5). The Client can request expedited IPv6 address/prefix assignment, but the DHCPv6 Server is not required or obligated to honor the request. A DHCPv6 Client usually requests expedited service when the local link most likely has only one DHCPv6 Server on it, the Client does not expect a second Server to be available on the link, or when the Client's priority is to complete the IPv6 address/prefix configuration process as quickly as possible.

To use the DHCPv6 two-message exchange to request expedited DHCPv6 service, a Client sends a SOLICIT message to FF02::1:2, requesting a DHCPv6 Server to assign IPv6 addresses and/or delegated IPv6 prefixes and other configuration information. This SOLICIT message includes the DHCPv6 Rapid Commit Option (see discussion below), indicating that the Client is willing to accept a REPLY message that is immediately sent by the DHCPv6 Server. A DHCPv6 Server willing to assign IPv6 addresses and/or delegated IPv6 prefixes to the Client would immediately respond by transmitting a REPLY message. The REPLY message contains configuration information along with the IPv6 addresses and/or delegated IPv6 prefixes that the Client can use immediately.

The DHCPv6 Server must be configured to support the rapid assignment of IPv6 addresses/ prefixes and other configuration parameters to Clients in order to process the SOLICIT message with the Rapid Commit Option. If the DHCPv6 Server does not support this capability, the Client and Server must communicate using the DHCPv6 four-message exchange process. Without the

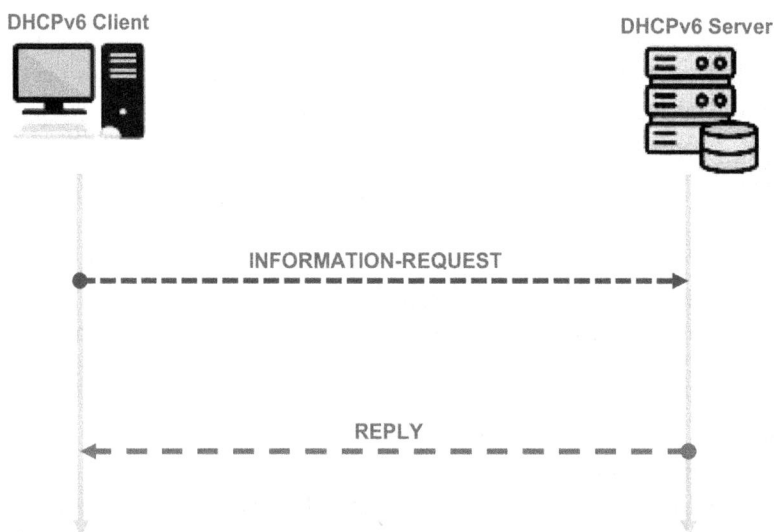

FIGURE 5.4   Stateless DHCPv6 message exchange (INFORMATION-REQUEST/REPLY message exchange).

rapid assignment capability, the DHCPv6 Server will respond with an ADVERTISE message upon receiving a SOLICIT message containing a Rapid Commit Option.

5.4.3.2.1   Extending the Lifetime of an IPv6 Address or Delegated IPv6 Prefix

For each IPv6 address or delegated IPv6 prefix that a DHCPv6 Server assigns to a Client, the Server specifies Preferred and Valid Lifetimes for it. The Client can request the Server to extend the Lifetimes assigned to an IPv6 address or delegated IPv6 prefix by sending a DHCPv6 RENEW message to the Server. The Server responds by sending a REPLY message to the Client containing the new Lifetimes (carried in the IA Address Option **[RFC8415]**), allowing the Client to continue using the IPv6 address or delegated IPv6 prefix without interrupting its operation.

If the DHCPv6 Server is not able to extend the Lifetime of an IPv6 address or delegated IPv6 prefix, it returns a REPLY message with the Lifetime of the IPv6 address or delegated IPv6 prefix set to 0, indicating its inability to satisfy the Client's request. At the same time, the Server may return a REPLY message assigning other IPv6 addresses or delegated IPv6 prefixes to the Client.

5.4.4   Using the DHCPv6 Rapid Commit Option

The default behavior of DHCPv6 is for a Client and a DHCPv6 Server to exchange four DHCPv6 messages (SOLICIT, ADVERTISE, REQUEST, and REPLY) for the Client to obtain the requested configuration information. The DHCPv6 Rapid Commit Option **[RFC8415]** reduces this communication to only two DHCPv6 message exchanges: SOLICIT and REPLY. When this Option is used, the Client sends the initial SOLICIT message with the Rapid Commit Option set (Option Code 14). This indicates to the DHCPv6 Server that the Client wants to expedite the DHCPv6 process (using the two-message exchange).

If the DHCPv6 Server is enabled to perform the Rapid Commit function, it responds directly to the Client with a REPLY message, skipping the need to send ADVERTISE and INFORMATION-REQUEST messages. If the DHCPv6 Server is not enabled for the Rapid Commit function, it responds by sending an ADVERTISE message to the Client, and the DHCPv6 process continues with the standard four-message exchange.

5.4.5   Using the DHCPv6 Reconfigure Message

The DHCPv6 Server with which a Client previously communicated may have negotiated to listen for RECONFIGURE messages sent to it. Under certain circumstances, a DHCPv6 Server may send a RECONFIGURE message to a Client, prompting the Client to send an INFORMATION-REQUEST, RENEW, or REBIND message (indicated by the "msg-type" field value in the Reconfigure Message Option with Option Code 19) to the Server to update its configuration. The Client then updates its configuration information by performing the DHCPv6 two-message exchange described above. This mechanism is typically used when there is a need to expedite changes to a Client's configuration, such as during address renumbering of a network (see **[RFC6879]**).

A DHCPv6 Client includes a Reconfigure Accept Option (with Option Code 20) in the SOLICIT messages sent to a Server if it is willing to accept RECONFIGURE messages from the Server.

5.4.6   Unicast Transmission of DHCPv6 Messages

If a DHCPv6 Client has received a Server Unicast Option (with Option Code 12) from a Server and the Client has the Server's IPv6 address of sufficient scope, the Client should unicast any REQUEST, RENEW, INFORMATION-REQUEST, RELEASE, and DECLINE messages it wishes to transmit to the Server. The Server specifies in the "server-address" field of the Server Unicast Option the IPv6 address to use when the Client wishes to send unicast DHCPv6 messages to the Server. After receiving this Option and where permissible and appropriate, the Client unicasts

DHCPv6 messages directly to the Server using this IPv6 address. DHCPv6 Clients are not allowed to unicast SOLICIT, CONFIRM, and REBIND messages, regardless of whether the Client is configured to use the Server Unicast Option.

The use of unicast for the above DHCPv6 messages is intended to avoid delays that may arise when DHCPv6 messages are being relayed by Relay Agents, as well as to reduce the overhead on Servers when DHCPv6 Client messages are delivered via multicast to multiple Servers. However, given that Clients are required to include Relay Message Option (Option Code 9) when DHCPv6 messages are relayed through a Relay Agent, a Server should enable the use of unicast only when DHCPv6 messages do not carry Relay Message Option. A DHCPv6 Server should use the Server Unicast Option only when Relay Message Option are not used.

A Server is not supposed to accept unicast DHCPv6 messages from a Client when it is not explicitly configured to do so. For example, the Client is not allowed to use unicast transmission for SOLICIT, CONFIRM, and REBIND messages, even if the Server and Client are configured to use the Server Unicast Option. The Client is only allowed to use unicast transmission for REQUEST, RENEW, INFORMATION-REQUEST, RELEASE, and DECLINE messages if it is configured to accept the Server Unicast Option.

When a Client sends a DHCPv6 message via unicast to a Server that did not previously send a Server Unicast Option (or is not currently configured to do so) to the Client, the Server discards that message. The Server then responds by sending an ADVERTISE message (when responding to a SOLICIT message) or a REPLY message (when responding to any other DHCPv6 messages) containing the following: a Status Code Option (Option Code 13) with the status code UseMulticast (Status Code 5), a Server Identifier Option (Option Code 2) containing the Server's DUID, the Client Identifier Option (Option Code 1) from the Client's DHCPv6 message (if any), but adds no other Options. The status code UseMulticast instructs the Client to send DHCPv6 messages to the Server using the IPv6 All_DHCP_Relay_Agents_and_Servers multicast address (FF02::1:2).

5.5 SENDING AND RECEIVING DHCPv6 MESSAGES

This section describes how DHCPv6 Clients and Servers send and receive the different DHCPv6 messages described above.

5.5.1 Solicit Message (Sent by a Client)

A DHCPv6 Client transmits a SOLICIT message to discover the DHCPv6 Servers that are active on the network and are configured to assign IPv6 addresses/delegated prefixes or provide other configuration parameters (such as a list of available DNS Servers and NTP Servers) on the link to which the Client is attached.

5.5.1.1 Client: Creation and Transmission of SOLICIT Messages

The Client performs the following operations when sending a SOLICIT message:

- Sets the SOLICIT message's "msg-type" field to SOLICIT and generates and inserts a Transaction ID in the "transaction-id" field.
- Includes a Client Identifier Option (Option Code 1) to identify itself to the Server. The Client includes one or more IA Options and any other appropriate Options.
- Includes an Elapsed Time Option (Option Code 8) to indicate the length of time the Client has been trying to complete the current DHCPv6 message exchange.
- Includes IA_NA Options (Option Code 3) to request the assignment of non-temporary addresses, IA_TA Options (Option Code 4) to request the assignment of temporary addresses, and IA_PD Options (Option Code 25) to request IPv6 prefix delegation. DHCPv6 messages can include IA_NA, IA_TA, or IA_PD Options, or a combination of these Options. In addition, a DHCPv6 message can include multiple instances of any IA Option type.

- May include IPv6 addresses in IA Address Options (Option Code 5) encapsulated within IA_NA and IA_TA Options, indicating to the Server the preferred IPv6 addresses of the Client.
- May include values in IA Prefix Options (Option Code 26) encapsulated within IA_PD Options, indicating the delegated IPv6 prefix and/or prefix length preferred by the Client.
- Includes an Option Request Option (Option Code 6) to request the Server to return the SOL_MAX_RT Option (Option Code 82) and any other Options the Client wishes to receive. The Client may also include instances of those Options identified in the Option Request Option, along with data values indicating to the Server the parameter values that the Client would like to receive.
- Includes a Reconfigure Accept Option (Option Code 20) if the Client is willing to accept RECONFIGURE messages from the Server.
- Includes a Rapid Commit Option (Option Code 14) if the Client wishes to use the Rapid Commit two-message exchange.
- The Client transmits the SOLICIT message according to the following parameters:
  - IRT (Initial Retransmission Time)=SOL_TIMEOUT (Initial Solicit timeout with default value of 1 second)
  - MRT (Maximum Retransmission Time)=SOL_MAX_RT (Max Solicit Timeout with default value of 3,600 seconds)
  - MRC (Maximum Retransmission Count)=0
  - MRD (Maximum Retransmission Duration)=0

5.5.1.2   Server: Receipt of SOLICIT Messages

A DHCPv6 Server sends an ADVERTISE message in response to a valid SOLICIT message received from a Client, announcing its availability to act as a Server for the Client. In most cases, a Server will respond by sending a REPLY message when it receives REQUEST, CONFIRM, RENEW, REBIND, DECLINE, RELEASE, and INFORMATION-REQUEST messages from a Client. A Server will also respond with a REPLY message when it receives a SOLICIT message with a Rapid Commit Option (Option Code 14) from a Client when the Server is configured to assign committed Leases.

The Server must include in the ADVERTISE and REPLY messages, the Server Identifier Option (Option Code 2) containing the Server's DHCP Unique Identifier (DUID), and the Client Identifier Option (Option Code 1) taken from the Client's DHCPv6 message if one was present.

If the Server receives a DHCPv6 message from a Client that contains an Option Request Option (Option Code 6), it includes appropriate Options in its response message to the Client. These included Options contain configuration parameters for all of the Options identified in the Client's Option Request Option that the Server is configured to return. The Server may also send additional Options to the Client if it has been configured to do so.

Upon receiving a SOLICIT message from a Client, the Server determines information about the Client and the link to which it is connected (through the interface on which the message is received) and checks any configured administrative policy regarding how to respond to the Client. If the Server is configured not to respond to the Client, it discards the SOLICIT message. For example, the Server discards the SOLICIT message if the administrative policy indicates that it may only respond to a Client that is willing to accept a RECONFIGURE message, but the Client does not indicate this by failing to include a Reconfigure Accept Option (Option Code 20) in the SOLICIT message.

The Server sends an ADVERTISE message to the Client if any of the following conditions occur:

- The Server is permitted to respond to the Client's SOLICIT message.
- The Client's SOLICIT message does not include a Rapid Commit Option (Option Code 14).
- The Server has not been configured to send committed assignments of Leases and other configuration parameters to the Client.

DHCPv6 Client   DHCPv6 Server

SOLICIT Message with DHCPv6 Rapid Commit Option
●- →

REPLY
←- ●

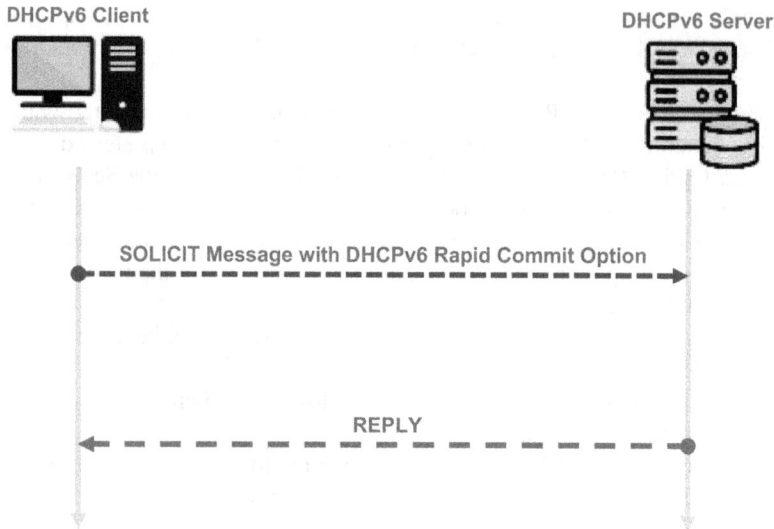

FIGURE 5.5 DHCPv6 SOLICIT/REPLY exchange for expedited IPv6 address assignment or prefix delegation (SOLICIT message with the DHCPv6 Rapid Commit Option).

The Server, upon receiving a SOLICIT message, responds with a REPLY message if the Client's SOLICIT message included a Rapid Commit Option and the Server has been configured to respond with committed assignments of Leases and other configuration parameters. The Server creates the REPLY message as it would if it had received a REQUEST message from the Client. Before sending the REPLY message to the Client, the Server first commits the assignment of any IPv6 addresses, delegated IPv6 prefixes, or other configuration information. In this case, the Server includes a Rapid Commit Option in the REPLY message to indicate to the Client that this REPLY message is sent in response to a SOLICIT message. If the Client receives responses from more than one Server, it only uses the Leases from one of those Servers, even though the other Servers have committed their Leases to the Client but will not be used by the Client.

5.5.2   REQUEST MESSAGE (SENT BY A CLIENT)

A DHCPv6 Client includes IAs with desired Leases and other configuration information in a REQUEST message sent to a Server. The REQUEST message includes one or more IA Options, and once the Server receives the message, it sends a REPLY message containing Leases and other information about the IAs to the Client.

5.5.2.1   Client: Creation and Transmission of REQUEST Messages

The Client performs the following operations when sending the REQUEST message:

- Sets the REQUEST message's "msg-type" field to REQUEST and generates and inserts a Transaction ID in the "transaction-id" field.
- Includes a Server Identifier Option (Option Code 2) containing the ID of the destination Server.
- Includes a Client Identifier Option (Option Code 1) to identify itself to the Server. The Client includes one or more IA Options and any other appropriate Options.
- Includes an Elapsed Time Option (Option Code 8) to indicate the length of time the Client is taking to complete the current DHCPv6 message exchange.
- Includes an Option Request Option (Option Code 6) to request the Server to return the SOL_MAX_RT Option (Option Code 82) and any other Options that the Client is interested in receiving.

- Includes a Reconfigure Accept Option (Option Code 20) if the Client is willing to accept RECONFIGURE messages from the Server.
- Transmits the REQUEST message according to the following parameters:
  - IRT (Initial Retransmission Time)=REQ_TIMEOUT (Initial Request Timeout with default value of 1 second)
  - MRT (Maximum Retransmission Time)=REQ_MAX_RT (Maximum Request Timeout with default value of 30 seconds)
  - MRC (Maximum Retransmission Count)=REQ_MAX_RC (Maximum Request Retry Attempts with default value of 10)
  - MRD (Maximum Retransmission Duration)=0

5.5.2.2 Server: Receipt of REQUEST Messages

After receiving a valid REQUEST message from a DHCPv6 Client, the Server creates bindings for the Client according to the administrative policy and configuration information on the Server, and then records the IAs and other information requested by the Client. The Server performs the following operations when processing the REQUEST message:

- Creates a REPLY message, sets the message's "msg-type" field to REPLY, and copies the Transaction ID from the received REQUEST message into the REPLY message's "transaction-id" field.
- Includes a Server Identifier Option (Option Code 2) in the REPLY message containing the DUID of the Server and the Client Identifier Option (Option Code 1) from the REQUEST message.
- The Server examines all the IAs in the REQUEST message, and for each IA_NA Option (Option Code 3) and IA_TA Option (Option Code 4), it checks whether the IPv6 prefixes of the included IPv6 addresses are appropriate for the link to which the Client is attached.
  - If the Server finds that any of the IPv6 prefixes of the included IPv6 addresses are not appropriate for the Client's link, it returns the IA to the Client with a Status Code Option (Option Code 13) containing NotOnLink (Status Code 4, indicating that the IPv6 prefix for the IPv6 address is not appropriate for the link to which the Client is attached).
  - If the Server does not send the Status Code NotOnLink to the Client and also cannot assign any IPv6 addresses to an IA, it returns the IA Option in the REPLY message without any IPv6 addresses in the IA and adds a Status Code Option containing NoAddrsAvail (Status Code 2, indicating that the Server has no IPv6 addresses available to assign to the IA(s)).
  - If the Server finds that it cannot assign any delegated IPv6 prefixes to any IA_PD Option in the REQUEST message, it returns the IA_PD option in the REPLY message without any IPv6 prefixes and includes a Status Code Option containing NoPrefixAvail (Status Code 6, indicating that the Server has no IPv6 prefixes available to assign to the IA_PD(s)).
- The Server may assign different IPv6 addresses and/or delegated IPv6 prefixes to an IA than those contained in the IA of the received REQUEST message.
- If the Server determines that it can assign IPv6 addresses or delegated IPv6 prefixes to any of the IAs, the REPLY message includes that IA with IPv6 addresses (for IA_NAs and IA_TAs), with IPv6 prefixes (for IA_PDs), and other configuration parameters, and then records the IA as a new Client binding. The Server does not include any IPv6 addresses or delegated IPv6 prefixes in the IA that it is not permitted to assign to the Client.
- The Server sets the T1 and T2 time intervals in each applicable IA Option for the REPLY message to their required values for all IAs (all IAs have the same T1 and T2 values). The Server determines the T1 and T2 time intervals for all applicable bindings for the Client in the REPLY message. This allows the Client to renew all of its bindings simultaneously.

- The Server should include a Reconfigure Accept Option (Option Code 19) in the REPLY message if the administrative policy configured on the Server permits the use of the Reconfigure mechanism and the Client supports it.
- If the Server determines that it already has a binding that associates an IA with the Client and that IA was included in the Client's REQUEST message, a REPLY message will be sent to the Client with the existing bindings, possibly with updated Lifetimes. The bindings may be updated according to the Server's local policies, but the response should be regenerated, and previously sent information should not simply be retransmitted, even if the REQUEST message's "transaction-id" field value matches that of a previously transmitted message. The Server must not cache the responses sent to the Client.

5.5.3   Confirm Message (Sent by a Client)

After a DHCPv6 Server has assigned only IPv6 addresses (and not delegated IPv6 prefixes) to a Client, and later the Client detects a change in its network information, the Client sends a CONFIRM message to the Server to determine if it is still connected to the same link to which the assigned IPv6 addresses belong.

5.5.3.1   Client: Creation and Transmission of CONFIRM Messages

The Client performs the following operations when sending the CONFIRM message:

- Sets the CONFIRM message's "msg-type" field to CONFIRM and generates and inserts a Transaction ID in the "transaction-id" field.
- Includes a Client Identifier Option (Option Code 1) to identify itself to the Server. The Client includes one or more IA Options and any other appropriate Options.
- Includes an Elapsed Time Option (Option Code 8) to indicate the length of time the Client is taking to complete the current DHCPv6 message exchange.
- Includes IA Options for all the IAs assigned to the sending interface of the CONFIRM message. The Client includes in the IA Options all the IPv6 addresses it currently has that are associated with those IAs. It also sets the T1 and T2 fields in any included IA_NA Options (Option Code 3) and the "preferred-lifetime" and "valid-lifetime" fields in the IA Address Options (Option Code 5) to 0, since the Server will ignore these fields upon receiving these Options.
- The first CONFIRM message to the Server on the interface is delayed by a random time interval between 0 and CNF_MAX_DELAY (i.e., the maximum delay for the first CONFIRM message, with a default value of 1 second). The message is transmitted according to the following parameters:
  - IRT (Initial Retransmission Time)=CNF_TIMEOUT (Initial Confirm Timeout with default value of 1 second)
  - MRT (Maximum Retransmission Time)=CNF_MAX_RT (Maximum Confirm Timeout with default value of 4 seconds)
  - MRC (Maximum Retransmission Count)=0
  - MRD (Maximum Retransmission Duration)=CNF_MAX_RD (Maximum Confirm Duration with default value of 10 seconds)

When a DHCPv6 Client detects that it may have moved to a new link, it sends a CONFIRM message to available DHCPv6 Servers if it was assigned only IPv6 addresses. The Client sends a REBIND message to the Server if it was delegated IPv6 prefixes (and IPv6 addresses). The Client sends INFORMATION-REQUEST messages to the Server when it needs only configuration information (not IPv6 addresses and prefixes).

5.5.3.2   Server: Receipt of CONFIRM Messages

When a DHCPv6 Server receives a CONFIRM message from a Client, it checks whether the IPv6 addresses in the message can still be used by the Client on the link to which it is connected:

- If the Server determines that all the IPv6 addresses in the CONFIRM message are still applicable to the Client's link, it returns a REPLY message to the Client with a status of Success (Status Code 0).
- If the Server finds that any of the IPv6 addresses are not applicable to the Client's link, it sends a REPLY message to the Client with a status of NotOnLink (Status Code 4, indicating that the IPv6 prefix for the assigned IPv6 address is not appropriate for the link to which the Client is connected).
- If the Server is unable to determine the applicability of the IPv6 addresses for the Client's link (e.g., if the Server lacks information about the IPv6 prefixes on the Client's link), or if any of the IAs sent by the Client contain no IPv6 addresses, the Server does not send a REPLY message to the Client.
- The Server ignores the T1 and T2 fields in the IA Options (i.e., IA_NA and IA_PD Options) and the "preferred-lifetime" and "valid-lifetime" fields in the IA Address Options.
- The Server creates a REPLY message, sets the "msg-type" field to REPLY, and copies the Transaction ID from the CONFIRM message into the REPLY message's "transaction-id" field.
- The Server includes a Server Identifier Option (Option Code 2) containing the Server's DUID in the REPLY message and adds the Client Identifier Option (Option Code 1) taken from the CONFIRM message.
- The Server includes a Status Code Option (Option Code 13) in the REPLY message indicating the status of the CONFIRM message.

5.5.4   RENEW MESSAGE (SENT BY A CLIENT)

A DHCPv6 Client sends a RENEW message to the Server from which it obtained Leases assigned to the Client's IAs to extend the Preferred and Valid Lifetimes for those Leases and to obtain new IPv6 addresses or delegated IPv6 prefixes for IAs. A DHCPv6 Server may assign an IPv6 address to a Client for a limited or unlimited time. If the Lifetime of the IPv6 address is limited, it is assigned a Preferred Lifetime and a (generally longer) Valid Lifetime. A Client has unrestricted use of Preferred IPv6 addresses or prefixes on interfaces and deprecates them when their Preferred Lifetime Timer expires.

When an IPv6 address or prefix becomes invalid (i.e., when its Valid Lifetime Timer expires), the Client can no longer use that address or prefix on an interface. The Client cannot use invalid IPv6 addresses or prefixes as the source or destination IPv6 address of IPv6 packets.

Typically, when half the time between the assignment of an IPv6 address to a Client and the address's Preferred Lifetime has passed (i.e., the T1 time interval), the Client transmits a RENEW message to the Server that assigned the IPv6 address to request an extension of the address's Lifetime. Generally, if the Client does not receive a REPLY message from the assigning Server after 80% of the Valid Lifetime of the IPv6 address has passed (i.e., the T2 time interval), the Client multicasts a REBIND message to discover another DHCPv6 Server to extend the Lifetime.

5.5.4.1   Client: Creation and Transmission of RENEW Messages

The Client performs the following operations when sending the RENEW message:

- Includes IA Options for the IAs whose Lease Lifetimes are to be extended.
- For IAs with assigned Leases, the Client includes a corresponding IA Option containing an IA Address Option (Option Code 5) for each IPv6 address assigned to the IA and an IA Prefix Option (Option Code 26) for each IPv6 prefix assigned to the IA.

- Includes IA Address Options (Option Code 5) within IA_NA (Option Code 3) and IA_TA (Option Code 4) Options for the IPv6 addresses assigned to the IAs.
- Includes IA Prefix Options (Option Code 26) within IA_PD Options (Option Code 25) for the delegated IPv6 prefixes assigned to the IAs.
- Sets the RENEW message's "msg-type" field to RENEW, generates and inserts a Transaction ID in the "transaction-id" field.
- Includes a Client Identifier Option (Option Code 1) to identify itself to the Server. The Client includes one or more IA Options and any other appropriate Options.
- Includes a Server Identifier Option (Option Code 2) containing the ID of the destination Server with which it most recently communicated.
- Includes an Elapsed Time Option (Option Code 8) to indicate the length of time the Client is taking to complete the current DHCPv6 message exchange.
- Includes an Option Request Option (Option Code 6) to request the Server to return the SOL_MAX_RT Option (Option Code 82) and any other Options that the Client is interested in receiving.
- The Client transmits the RENEW message according to the following parameters:
  - IRT (Initial Retransmission Time)=REN_TIMEOUT (Initial Renew Timeout with default value of 10 seconds)
  - MRT (Maximum Retransmission Time)=REN_MAX_RT (Maximum Renew Timeout with default value of 600 seconds)
  - MRC (Maximum Retransmission Count)=0
  - MRD (Maximum Retransmission Duration)=Remaining time until earliest T2

The DHCPv6 Server is responsible for controlling (through the T1 and T2 values assigned to an IA) the time at which the Client should contact it to extend the assigned Lease Lifetimes.

5.5.4.2   Server: Receipt of RENEW Messages

When a DHCPv6 Server receives a RENEW message from a Client, the Server takes each IA in the message, locates the Client's binding, and verifies that the information in the IA received from the Client matches the information the Server has stored locally for the Client:

- If the Server is able to locate the Client's entry for the IA, it returns a REPLY message to the Client for that IA but with new Lifetimes and, if applicable, updated T1 and T2 time intervals.
- If the Server examines the IA and is unable to extend the Lifetimes of an IPv6 address or delegated IPv6 prefix for the IA, it may choose not to include the IA Address Option (Option Code 5) in the REPLY message for that IPv6 address or to include the IA Prefix Option (Option Code 26) for that delegated IPv6 prefix.
- If the Server chooses to include the IA Address or IA Prefix Option in the REPLY message for such an IPv6 address or delegated IPv6 prefix, it sets the values of the T1 and T2 fields in the IA Option to the Valid Lifetime, unless it has also included in the REPLY message other IPv6 addresses or delegated IPv6 prefixes for which it can extend the Lifetimes under consideration. The Server sets the T1 and T2 values equal to the Valid Lifetime to inform the Client that the Leases associated with that IA will not be extended, and the Client should not attempt to request any extensions. This also avoids unnecessary DHCPv6 message traffic as the remaining Lifetime approaches 0.
- When sending the REPLY message to the Client for the received IAs, the Server may choose to change the IPv6 addresses or delegated IPv6 prefixes and the Lifetimes listed in the received IAs.
- If the Server determines that any of the IPv6 addresses listed in the received IA are not applicable to the Client's link, it returns a REPLY message to the Client with the Lifetimes of those IPv6 addresses set to 0.

When the Server examines a received IA and cannot find a related Client entry, it performs the following actions, depending on the policy and configuration information on the Server:

- If the Server is configured to create new bindings for a Client's IA in response to RENEW messages, it creates a Client binding and sends a REPLY message to the Client for the IA with assigned IPv6 addresses or delegated IPv6 prefixes, along with Lifetimes. If applicable, it also includes T1 and T2 time interval values and other information requested by the Client. If the Client's RENEW message included the IA Prefix Option within the IA_PD Option with the "IPv6-prefix" field set to 0 and the "prefix-length" field set to a non-zero value, the Server may use the "prefix-length" as a hint for determining the length of the IPv6 prefixes to be assigned to the Client.
- If the Server is configured to create new bindings for a Client's IA in response to RENEW messages but is not set to assign any Leases to an IA, it sends a REPLY message to the Client for the IA Option containing a Status Code Option (Option Code 13) with status code NoAddrsAvail (Status Code 2) or NoPrefixAvail (Status Code 6).
- If the Server is not configured to support the creation of new bindings for a Client that sent a RENEW message, or if the network administrator has disabled this behavior through policy or configuration, the Server returns a REPLY message to the Client with the IA Option containing a Status Code Option indicating NoBinding.

The Server performs the following operations when sending the REPLY message to the Client after processing the Client's RENEW message:

- Constructs a REPLY message, sets the "msg-type" field to REPLY, and copies the Transaction ID from the RENEW message into the REPLY message's "transaction-id" field.
- Includes a Server Identifier Option containing the Server's DUID in the REPLY message and adds the Client Identifier Option taken from the RENEW message in the REPLY message.
- Includes other Options containing configuration information to be sent to the Client.
- May include Options containing the IAs and other configuration parameters values in the REPLY message, even if the Client did not request those parameters in the received RENEW message.
- Sets the T1 and T2 time interval values in each applicable IA Option in the REPLY message to be the same across all IAs. The Server also determines the T1 and T2 time interval values for all applicable Client bindings in the REPLY message. This enables the Client to renew all of the bindings at the same time.

5.5.5   REBIND MESSAGE (SENT BY A CLIENT)

After waiting a time interval equal to T2, a DHCPv6 Client initiates a REBIND/REPLY message exchange with any available Server to extend the Lifetimes of Leases previously assigned to the Client and to update other configuration parameters. A Client sends a REBIND message to a Server when it receives no response to a RENEW message. Note that the end of the T2 interval will only be reached (i.e., T2 has elapsed) if the Server to which the Client sent a RENEW message at the start of the T1 interval has not responded. The Client also sends a REBIND message to the Server to verify the bindings of a delegated IPv6 prefix, but REBIND retransmissions are done with different parameters.

5.5.5.1   Client: Creation and Transmission of REBIND Messages

The Client performs the following operations when sending the REBIND message:

- Sets the message's "msg-type" field to REBIND.
- Does not include the Server Identifier Option (Option Code 2) in the message.

- The Client transmits the REBIND message according to the following parameters:
  - IRT (Initial Retransmission Time)=REB_TIMEOUT (Initial Rebind Timeout with default value of 10 seconds)
  - MRT (Maximum Retransmission Time)=REB_MAX_RT (Maximum Rebind time-out value with default value of 600 seconds)
  - MRC (Maximum Retransmission Count)=0
  - MRD (Maximum Retransmission Duration)=Remaining time until the Valid Lifetimes of all Leases in all IAs have expired

5.5.5.2 Server: Receipt of REBIND Messages

When a DHCPv6 Server receives a REBIND message from a Client containing an IA Option, it locates the local binding for the Client and checks if the information in the received IA matches the information stored for the Client.

- If the Server locates the Client entry for the IA and determines that the IPv6 addresses or delegated IPv6 prefixes in the IA are still appropriate for the Client's link according to the Server's configuration information, it sends a REPLY message to the Client containing the IA with new Lifetimes and, if applicable, T1 and T2 time interval values.
- If the Server examines an IPv6 address in the received IA and is unable to extend its Lifetimes, it may choose to send a REPLY message to the Client that does not include the IA Address Option for that IPv6 address.
- If the Server examines a delegated IPv6 prefix in the received IA and is unable to extend its Lifetimes, it may choose to send a REPLY message to the Client that does not include the IA Prefix Option for that IPv6 prefix.
- If the Server determines that the local Client entry for the received IA and any of the IPv6 addresses or delegated prefixes are no longer applicable for the Client's link according to the Server's configuration information, it sends a REPLY message to the Client with the Lifetimes of those IPv6 addresses or delegated IPv6 prefixes set to 0.

    If the Server cannot locate a Client entry for the received IA, it examines the IA to see if it contains IPv6 addresses (for IA_NA and IA_TA Options) or delegated IPv6 prefixes (for IA_PD Options). The Server checks whether the IPv6 addresses and delegated IPv6 prefixes are still applicable for the Client's link according to the Server's configuration information.
- For any IPv6 address in the IA that is not appropriate for the Client's link, the Server may send a REPLY message to the Client that includes the IA Address Option with Lifetimes of 0.
- For any delegated IPv6 prefix that is not appropriate for the Client's link, the Server may send a REPLY message to the Client that includes the IA Prefix Option with Lifetimes of 0. This message with Lifetimes of 0 is meant as an explicit notification to the Client that the specified IPv6 addresses and delegated IPv6 prefixes are no longer valid and cannot be used by the Client.
- If the Server decides not to include any IAs containing IA Address or IA Prefix Options with Lifetimes of 0 in a REPLY message to the Client, and also chooses not to include any other IAs with Leases and/or Status Code Options with status codes in the REPLY message, then the Server will not send any REPLY message at all and will discard the REBIND message.

Otherwise, if the Server cannot find a Client entry for an IA, it performs the following operations based on its policy and configuration information:

- If the Server is configured to create new bindings for a Client's IA as a result of processing REBIND messages, it creates a Client binding and sends a REPLY message to the Client for the IA with assigned Leases and Lifetimes. If applicable, it includes T1 and T2 time interval values and any other information requested by the Client. The Server does not include in the REPLY message any IPv6 addresses or delegated IPv6 prefixes in the IA that it is not assigning to the Client.

• If the Server is set up to create new bindings for a Client's IA as a result of processing REBIND messages but will not allocate any Leases to an IA, it sends a REPLY message to the Client containing the IA Option with a Status Code Option indicating NoAddrsAvail (Status Code 2) or NoPrefixAvail (Status Code 6).

• If the Server is not configured to support the creation of new bindings for a Client that sent a REBIND message, or if the network administrator has disabled this behavior through policy or configuration information on the Server, it returns a REPLY message to the Client with the IA Option containing a Status Code Option indicating NoBinding.

It is possible that while a Server is creating new bindings for a Client's IA, other Servers may also be creating bindings for the same IA as a result of receiving the same Client REBIND message. Therefore, the Server should only create new bindings for a Client's IA for a received REBIND message if it is configured to respond with a REPLY message upon receiving a Client's SOLICIT message containing the Rapid Commit Option (Option Code 14).

The Server performs the following operations when sending the REPLY message:

• Constructs a REPLY message, sets the "msg-type" field to REPLY, and copies the Transaction ID from the REBIND message into the REPLY message's "transaction-id" field.

• Includes a Server Identifier Option containing the Server's DUID in the REPLY message and adds the Client Identifier Option taken from the REBIND message.

• Includes other Options containing configuration information to be sent to the Client.

• May include Options with the IAs and other configuration parameter values in the REPLY message, even if the Client did not request those parameters in the received REBIND message.

• Sets the T1 and T2 time interval values in each applicable IA Option in the REPLY message to be consistent across all IAs. The Server also determines the T1 and T2 time interval values for all applicable Client bindings in the REPLY message, enabling the Client to renew all bindings simultaneously.

5.5.6 INFORMATION-REQUEST MESSAGE (SENT BY A CLIENT)

A DHCPv6 Client sends an INFORMATION-REQUEST message to a Server to obtain configuration information only, without requesting IPv6 addresses and/or delegated IPv6 prefixes.

5.5.6.1 Client: Creation and Transmission of INFORMATION-REQUEST Messages

The Client performs the following operations when sending the INFORMATION-REQUEST message:

• Sets the INFORMATION-REQUEST message's "msg-type" field to INFORMATION-REQUEST and generates and inserts a Transaction ID in the "transaction-id" field.

• Includes a Client Identifier Option (Option Code 1) to identify itself to the Server.

• Includes an Elapsed Time Option (Option Code 8) to indicate how long the Client has been taking to complete the current DHCPv6 message exchange.

• Includes an Option Request Option (Option Code 6) to request the INF_MAX_RT Option (Option Code 83), the Information Refresh Time Option (Option Code 32), and any other Options the Client wishes to receive. The Client may include Options with data values as indications (hints) to the Server about the parameter values it would like to receive.

• When responding to a RECONFIGURE message received from the DHCPv6 Server, the Client includes a Server Identifier Option (Option Code 2) with the Server's ID taken from the received RECONFIGURE message.

- The Client transmits the INFORMATION-REQUEST message according to the following parameters:
  - IRT (Initial Retransmission Time)=INF_TIMEOUT (Initial Information-Request Timeout with default value of 1 second)
  - MRT (Maximum Retransmission Time)=INF_MAX_RT (Maximum Information-request Timeout with default value of 3,600 seconds)
  - MRC (Maximum Retransmission Count)=0
  - MRD (Maximum Retransmission Duration)=0

5.5.6.2   Server: Receipt of INFORMATION-REQUEST Messages

When a DHCPv6 Server receives an INFORMATION-REQUEST message from a Client, this indicates that the Client is requesting configuration information without the assignment of any IPv6 addresses and/or delegated IPv6 prefixes. The Server, upon receiving this message, determines all configuration parameters that are applicable to the Client based on the configuration policies on the Server.

The Server performs the following operations when sending the REPLY message:

- Constructs a REPLY message, sets the "msg-type" field to REPLY, and copies the Transaction ID from the INFORMATION-REQUEST message into the REPLY message's "transaction-id" field.
- Includes a Server Identifier Option containing the Server's DUID in the REPLY message, and if the INFORMATION-REQUEST message included the Client Identifier Option, this Option is also added to the REPLY message.
- Includes in the REPLY message to be sent to the Client Options containing the configuration information. The Server may include in the REPLY message additional Options that the Client did not request in the INFORMATION-REQUEST message.

If a Client Identifier Option was not included in the Client's INFORMATION-REQUEST message, the Server responds with a REPLY message containing any configuration parameters that are not necessarily based on the identity of the Client.

5.5.7   RELEASE MESSAGE (SENT BY A CLIENT)

A DHCPv6 Client sends a RELEASE message to the Server to free up one or more Leases. A Client sends a RELEASE message to inform the Server that it will no longer use one or more of the IPv6 addresses assigned to it.

5.5.7.1   Client: Creation and Transmission of RELEASE Messages

The Client performs the following operations when sending the RELEASE message:

- Sets the RELEASE message's "msg-type" field to RELEASE and generates and inserts a Transaction ID in the "transaction-id" field.
- Places the ID of the DHCPv6 Server that assigned the Lease(s) in a Server Identifier Option.
- Includes a Client Identifier Option (Option Code 1) to identify itself to the Server.
- Includes an Elapsed Time Option (Option Code 8) to indicate the length of time the Client is taking to complete the current DHCPv6 message exchange.
- Includes Options containing the IAs for the Leases it is freeing up in the RELEASE message's "options" field. The Client must include the Leases to be freed in the IAs and must not include in the IAs the Leases it wishes to continue using.
- The Client transmits the message according to the following parameters:
  - IRT (Initial Retransmission Time)=REL_TIMEOUT (Initial Release Timeout with default value of 1 second)
  - MRT (Maximum Retransmission Time)=0

- MRC (Maximum Retransmission Count)=REL_MAX_RC (Maximum Release Retry Attempts with default value of 4)
- MRD (Maximum Retransmission Duration)=0

The Client must cease using all of the Leases it is releasing before beginning the RELEASE message exchange process. When releasing an IPv6 address, the Client must have removed that address from the interface. When releasing a delegated IPv6 prefix, the Client must have advertised that IPv6 prefix in a Router Advertisement message with a Preferred Lifetime and Valid Lifetime set to 0. Additionally, the Client must not use any of the IPv6 addresses being released as the source IPv6 address in the RELEASE message or in any subsequently transmitted message.

5.5.7.2 Server: Receipt of RELEASE Messages

Upon receiving a valid RELEASE message from a Client, the Server checks the validity of the received IAs and Leases in the IAs. If the Server finds that the Leases for the IAs in the RELEASE message are associated with a Client binding for the Leases that the Server previously assigned to the Client, the Server deletes those Leases from the IAs and marks them as free and available for assignment to other Clients. After processing all the Leases, the Server generates a REPLY message.

The Server performs the following operations when sending the REPLY message:

- Constructs a REPLY message, sets the "msg-type" field to REPLY, and copies the Transaction ID from the RELEASE message into the REPLY message's "transaction-id" field.
- Includes a Status Code Option with status Success (Status Code 0), a Server Identifier Option containing the DUID of the Server, and a Client Identifier Option containing the Client's DUID.

If the Server finds that it has no binding information for an IA in the RELEASE message, it includes an IA Option using the IAID from the RELEASE message and adds a Status Code Option with status NoBinding in the IA Option. The Server includes no other Options in the IA Option. The Server may choose to retain a record of the Leases and IAs it assigned to the Client after the Lease Lifetimes have expired, allowing the Server to reassign those Leases to other Clients.

5.5.8 DECLINE MESSAGE (SENT BY A CLIENT)

If a DHCPv6 Client detects that one or more of the IPv6 addresses assigned to it by a Server are already being used by another IPv6 node on the link, it transmits a DECLINE message to the Server to inform it that the assigned IPv6 address is suspect and that it wishes to decline the address. DECLINE messages are not used in IPv6 prefix delegation. Thus, the Client must not include IA_PD Options (Option Code 25) in a DECLINE message. Note that an IPv6 Client uses IPv6 Duplicate Address Detection (see **Chapter 4**) to determine whether any of the IPv6 addresses assigned by the Server are already in use on the link to which the Client is connected.

5.5.8.1 Client: Creation and Transmission of DECLINE Messages

The Client performs the following operations when sending the DECLINE message:

- Sets the DECLINE message's "msg-type" field to DECLINE and generates and inserts a Transaction ID in the "transaction-id" field.
- Places the ID of the DHCPv6 Server that assigned the IPv6 address(es) in a Server Identifier Option.
- Includes a Client Identifier Option (Option Code 1) to identify itself to the Server.
- Includes an Elapsed Time Option (Option Code 8) to indicate the length of time the Client has been taking to complete the current DHCPv6 message exchange.

- Includes Options containing the IAs for the IPv6 addresses it is declining in the DECLINE message's "options" field. The Client must include the IPv6 addresses being declined in the IAs and should not include any IPv6 addresses that it wishes to continue using. The Client must not use any of the IPv6 addresses being declined as the source IPv6 address in the DECLINE message or in any message subsequently transmitted.
- The Client transmits the DECLINE message according to the following parameters:
  - IRT (Initial Retransmission Time)=DEC_TIMEOUT (Initial Decline Timeout with default value of 1 second)
  - MRT (Maximum Retransmission Time)=0
  - MRC (Maximum Retransmission Count)=DEC_MAX_RC (Maximum Reconfigure Attempts with default value of 8)
  - MRD (Maximum Retransmission Duration)=0

5.5.8.2   Server: Receipt of DECLINE Messages

Upon receiving a valid DECLINE message from a Client, the Server checks the validity of the received IAs and their IPv6 addresses. If the Server finds that the IAs in the message are in a Client binding and that the Server assigned the indicated IPv6 addresses to those IAs, it deletes those IPv6 addresses from the IAs.

Before sending the DECLINE message, the Client must determine that the IPv6 addresses included are already in use on its link; it is declining IPv6 addresses that it is already using. Therefore, the Server marks these IPv6 addresses as declined by the Client to prevent assigning them to other Clients (avoiding duplicate addressing). The Server may also add a local notification indicating that these IPv6 addresses were declined by a Client. The Server uses local policies to decide when IPv6 addresses identified in a DECLINE message may be marked as available for assignment to Clients.

After processing all the IPv6 addresses in the DECLINE message, the Server generates a REPLY message:

- Constructs a REPLY message, sets the "msg-type" field to REPLY, and copies the Transaction ID from the DECLINE message into the REPLY message's "transaction-id" field.
- Includes a Status Code Option with status Success (Status Code 0), a Server Identifier Option containing the DUID of the Server, and a Client Identifier Option containing the Client's DUID.

If the Server finds that it has no binding information for an IA in the DECLINE message, it includes an IA Option using the IAID from the DECLINE message and adds a Status Code Option with status NoBinding in the IA Option. The Server includes no other Options in the IA Option.

5.5.9   ADVERTISE MESSAGE (SENT BY A SERVER)

A DHCPv6 Server, upon receiving a SOLICIT message from a Client, responds by sending an ADVERTISE message to indicate its availability for DHCPv6 service.

5.5.9.1   Server: Creation of ADVERTISE Messages

The Server performs the following operations when sending an ADVERTISE message:

- Constructs an ADVERTISE message, sets the "msg-type" field to ADVERTISE, and copies the Transaction ID from the SOLICIT message into the ADVERTISE message's "transaction-id" field.
- Includes a Server Identifier Option (Option Code 2) containing the Server's DUID, and copies the Client Identifier Option (Option Code 1) from the SOLICIT message into the ADVERTISE message.

- May include a Preference Value in the "pref-value" field of a Preference Option (Option Code 7) added to the ADVERTISE message. DHCPv6 Server implementations typically allow the network administrator to set a Server Preference Value. Unless otherwise configured by the server administrator, the Server Preference Value must be set to the default of 0.
- Includes a Reconfigure Accept Option (Option Code 20) if the Server wishes to indicate to the Client that it supports the Reconfigure mechanism. The Client may use this information during the Server selection process.
- Includes Options to be sent to the Client in a subsequent REPLY message. These Options contain information that the Client may use in selecting a Server if it receives ADVERTISE messages from multiple Servers. The Server includes configuration parameters in the ADVERTISE message that it has been configured to return to the Client for all of the Options identified in the SOLICIT message's Option Request Option (Option Code 6). If the Client included a Container Option (i.e., an Option that encapsulates other Options, such as the IA_NA Option) in the Option Request Option, the Server includes in the ADVERTISE message all the Options that are eligible to be encapsulated in that Container Option. The Client may use the Option Request Option to signal to the Server that it supports a particular feature even when that Option is encapsulated in the Option Request Option, as in the case of the Prefix Exclude Option (Option Code 67) **[RFC6603]**. In this case, the Server requires special processing to handle such Options. The Server may include additional Options in the ADVERTISE message to be returned to the Client if it has been configured to do so. The Prefix Exclude Option **[RFC6603]** is an optional mechanism that allows a Server (a delegating router) to signal to a Client (requesting router) to exclude one specific IPv6 prefix from a delegated IPv6 prefix set when the Server and Client are using the DHCPv6 prefix delegation mechanism.
- Examines the IAs contained in the SOLICIT message from the Client and includes IA Options in the ADVERTISE message that contains any IPv6 addresses and/or delegated IPv6 prefixes to be assigned to those IAs. If the Client included IA Address Options (Option Code 5) with IPv6 addresses in the SOLICIT message, the Server may use those addresses as hints about the IPv6 addresses that the Client wishes to receive. If the SOLICIT message included IA Prefix Options (Option Code 26), the Server may use the IPv6 prefix specified in the Option's "IPv6-prefix" field and/or the prefix length indicated in the Option's "prefix-length" field as hints about the IPv6 prefixes the Client wishes to receive. If the Server is not willing to assign an IPv6 address or delegated IPv6 prefix indicated in the received SOLICIT message, it must not include this IPv6 address or delegated IPv6 prefix in the ADVERTISE message.
- If the Server is unable to allocate any IPv6 addresses to an IA_NA or IA_TA Option included in subsequent REQUEST messages that the Client may send, it must include the IA Option in the ADVERTISE message with no IPv6 addresses in that IA, along with a Status Code Option (Option Code 13) encapsulated in the IA Option containing the status code NoAddrsAvail (Status Code 2).
- If the Server is unable to allocate any IPv6 prefixes to an IA_PD included in subsequent REQUEST messages that the Client may send, it must include the IA_PD Option (Option Code 25) in the ADVERTISE message with no IPv6 prefixes in the IA_PD Option and a Status Code Option encapsulated in the IA_PD containing the status code NoPrefixAvail.

5.5.9.2   Client: Receipt of ADVERTISE Messages

Upon receiving a valid ADVERTISE message from one or more DHCPv6 Servers, the Client selects one or more of those messages (and Servers) based on the following criteria:

- The Client prefers the ADVERTISE messages with the highest Server Preference Value among the received messages. The Client may select a Server with a lower Server Preference Value if that Server advertised a better set of parameters; for instance, if the Server provides a better set of IAs and other configuration parameters.

- When the Client receives a set of ADVERTISE messages with the same Server Preference Value, it may select a particular Server whose ADVERTISE message contains the information of greatest interest.

A DHCPv6 Server includes the Preference Option (Option Code 7) in an ADVERTISE message to enable a Client to select a Server. The 8-bit "pref-value" field of the Preference Option contains the Preference Value of that particular Server.

After the DHCPv6 Client has selected ADVERTISE message(s) and Server(s), it typically maintains a small database that contains information about each Server, such as the Server Preference Value, the IPv6 addresses advertised by the Server, the time the ADVERTISE message was received, and other relevant information. In practical implementations, a DHCPv6 Client maintains separate per-IA state machines for each selected Server. If a selected Server does not respond, the Client needs to select an alternate Server using the criteria mentioned above.

5.5.10   REPLY MESSAGE (SENT BY A SERVER)

When a DHCPv6 Server receives a SOLICIT, REQUEST, RENEW, REBIND, or INFORMATION-REQUEST message from a Client, it responds by sending a REPLY message containing assigned Leases and configuration parameters. A Server also responds to CONFIRM, RELEASE, or DECLINE messages by sending a REPLY message as explained below:

- A Server responds to an INFORMATION-REQUEST message from a Client by sending a REPLY message that contains configuration parameters.
- A Server sends a REPLY message in response to a CONFIRM message received from a Client to confirm or deny that the IPv6 addresses assigned to the Client are appropriate for the link to which the Client is attached.
- A Server acknowledges the receipt of a RELEASE or DECLINE message by sending a REPLY message to the Client.

5.5.10.1   Server: Transmission of ADVERTISE and REPLY Messages

A DHCPv6 Server sends an ADVERTISE message in response to a SOLICIT message received from a Client to indicate that it is available to provide DHCPv6 service. If a Server directly receives a DHCPv6 message from a Client that requires sending an ADVERTISE or REPLY message as a response, the Server unicasts the response message directly to the Client using the IPv6 address indicated in the source IPv6 address field of the IPv6 packet in which the Client's DHCPv6 message was received. The Server sends the ADVERTISE or REPLY message through the interface on which the Client's DHCPv6 message was received.

If the Server receives the Client's DHCPv6 message in a RELAY-FORWARD message, it constructs a RELAY-REPLY message containing a Relay Message Option (Option Code 9); the Server places a REPLY message in the payload (i.e., "DHCP-relay-message" field) of the Relay Message Option. If an Interface-Id Option (Option Code 18) was included in the RELAY-FORWARD message, the Server copies that Option to the RELAY-REPLY message. The Server then sends the RELAY-REPLY message via unicast transmission directly to the Relay Agent using the IPv6 address indicated in the source IPv6 address field of the IPv6 packet in which the RELAY-FORWARD message was received.

5.5.10.2   Client: Receipt of REPLY for SOLICIT (with Rapid Commit
Option), REQUEST, RENEW, or REBIND Messages

If a DHCPv6 Client sends a SOLICIT message (with a Rapid Commit Option) and receives a REPLY message with a Status Code Option containing a NotOnLink status from the Server, or sends a REQUEST message and receives a REPLY message, the Client can either resend the message without specifying any IPv6 addresses or restart the DHCPv6 Server discovery process. The NotOnLink status (with Status Code 4) indicates that the IPv6 prefix for the assigned IPv6 address is not appropriate for the link to which the Client is connected.

If the Client sent a SOLICIT (with a Rapid Commit option), REQUEST, RENEW, or REBIND message and received a REPLY message in response from the Server, the Client updates the information associated with the recorded IAs using the information contained in the IA Options in the REPLY message:

- Calculates T1 and T2 time intervals (using the T1 and T2 values in the REPLY message and the time the REPLY message was received), if appropriate for the IA type.
- Adds any new Leases in the received IA Option to the local IA maintained by the Client.
- Updates the Lifetimes of any Leases in the received IA Option that already exist in the Client's local IA.
- Discards any Leases in the Client's local IA that have a Valid Lifetime of 0, as indicated in the received IA Address or IA Prefix Option.
- Leaves unchanged any information about Leases in the Client's local IA that are not included in the IA received from the Server.

If the Client can use the IPv6 addresses and/or prefixes received from the Server, it does the following:

- The Client uses the assigned IPv6 addresses, delegated IPv6 prefixes, and other information in any received IAs that do not contain a Status Code Option with the status NoAddrsAvail (Status Code 2, indicating that the Server has no IPv6 addresses available to assign to the IA(s)), or NoPrefixAvail (Status Code 6, indicating that the Server has no IPv6 prefixes available for assignment to the IA_PD(s)) **[RFC8415]**.
  - The Client may include in subsequent RENEW and REBIND messages sent to the Server the IAs for which it received the status code NoAddrsAvail or NoPrefixAvail, without including IPv6 addresses or prefixes, to retry obtaining IPv6 addresses or prefixes for these IAs.
- The Client must perform IPv6 Duplicate Address Detection **[RFC4862]** (**see Chapter 4**) on each of the IPv6 addresses in any received IAs, provided that the Client did not perform Duplicate Address Detection on these IPv6 addresses during the processing of any of the previous REPLY messages sent by the Server. The Client must perform the IPv6 Duplicate Address Detection before applying these received IPv6 addresses to interfaces and for addressing any IPv6 packets. If the Client finds that any of the IPv6 addresses are in use on the link, it sends a DECLINE message to the Server for those IPv6 addresses.
- If the Client finds that it does not have any associated reachability information **[RFC4861]** for any assigned IPv6 address (**see Chapter 4**), it must not assume that the IPv6 address is reachable on the link as a result of receiving an IA_NA or IA_TA Option from the Server. The Client must not use IPv6 addresses obtained from an IA_NA or IA_TA Option to create an implicit IPv6 prefix with a length other than 128.
- For each delegated IPv6 prefix received from a Server, the Client assigns an IPv6 subnet prefix to each of its attached links. When subnetting a delegated IPv6 prefix, the Client adds extra bits to the IPv6 prefix to create unique, longer IPv6 prefixes:
  - For example, if a Client is delegated the IPv6 unique unicast address 2001:DB8:0::/48, it may generate the IPv6 subnet prefixes 2001:DB8:0:1::/64 and 2001:DB8:0:2::/64 to assign to two attached links. If the Client is delegated the IPv6 prefixes 2001:DB8:0::/48 and 2001:DB8:5::/48, it may assign the IPv6 subnet prefixes 2001:DB8:0:1::/64 and 2001:DB8:5:1::/64 to one of its attached links, and the IPv6 subnet prefixes 2001:DB8:0:2::/64 and 2001:DB8:5:2::/64 to the other attached link.

- If the Client uses a delegated IPv6 prefix to configure IPv6 addresses on directly attached interfaces or to configure IPv6 addresses on other nodes behind it, the Client must ensure that at any given time, the Preferred and Valid Lifetimes of those IPv6 addresses are not greater than the remaining Preferred and Valid Lifetimes, respectively, for the delegated IPv6 prefix. In particular, if the Client advertises a delegated IPv6 prefix or an IPv6 prefix derived from the Server's delegated IPv6 prefix for use in IPv6 SLAAC **[RFC4862]**, the Client must ensure that the advertised Preferred and Valid Lifetimes for that prefix do not exceed the corresponding remaining Lifetimes of the Server's delegated IPv6 prefix.

If the Client receives a REPLY message from a Server that contains IAs but finds no usable IPv6 addresses and/or delegated IPv6 prefixes in any of these IAs, the Client may either try contacting another Server (possibly by restarting the DHCPv6 Server discovery process) or send an INFORMATION-REQUEST message to the Server to obtain other configuration information only.

When the Client sends a RENEW or REBIND message to a Server and receives a REPLY message in response, the Client does the following:

- Sends a REQUEST message to the responding Server if any of the IAs in the REPLY message has the Status Code Option containing NoBinding (Status Code 3, indicating Client record (binding) unavailable). The Client includes IA Options in the REQUEST message for all IAs. The Client continues to use other bindings that do not have error indications from the Server.
- Sends a RENEW or REBIND message if any of the IAs the Client wants are not included in the REPLY message. This situation likely indicates that the responding Server does not support the IA type the Client wants, and thus, sending a REQUEST message immediately to the Server is unlikely to yield a different result. Therefore, the Client must rate-limit its message transmissions or may simply wait for the normal message retransmission time (as if the REPLY message had not been received). The Client continues to use other bindings for which the Server did return configuration information.
- Otherwise, the Client accepts the information in the REPLY message's IA.

Whenever a DHCPv6 Client selects an alternate Server or restarts the DHCPv6 Server discovery process, the Client should cease using all the IPv6 addresses and delegated IPv6 prefixes for which it has bindings and try contacting a new Server to obtain all required Leases. This capability allows the Client to use a single state machine for all bindings.

5.5.10.3   Client: Receipt of REPLY for RELEASE and DECLINE Messages

When a Client receives a valid REPLY message from a Server after sending a RELEASE message, the Client marks the RELEASE event as completed, regardless of the indication in the "status-code" field of the Status Code Option included in the REPLY message from the Server.

When the Client receives a valid REPLY message from a Server after sending a DECLINE message, the Client marks the DECLINE event as completed, regardless of the value in the "status-code" field of the Status Code Option(s) returned by the Server.

5.5.10.4   Client: Receipt of REPLY for CONFIRM Messages

If a Client sends a CONFIRM message and receives any REPLY messages in response, with Status Code Option(s) containing a status code (0) indicating Success (explicit or implicit), the Client can use the IPv6 addresses in the received IA and ignore any REPLY messages with Status Code Option(s) indicating NotOnLink (Status Code 4). When the Client receives one or more REPLY messages containing Status Code (4) (i.e., NotOnLink) in response to a CONFIRM message, the Client performs the DHCPv6 Server discovery process.

5.5.10.5   Client: Receipt of REPLY for INFORMATION-REQUEST Messages

As discussed above, a DHCPv6 Client includes the Information Refresh Time Option (Option Code 32) in the Option Request Option (Option Code 6), which is added to an INFORMATION-REQUEST message sent to a Server. A Client sends the Information Refresh Time Option to request that a Server specify the maximum length of time (Information Refresh Time) a Client should wait before contacting the Server to refresh information previously retrieved from it.

The Server returns the requested information in a REPLY message that also includes an Information Refresh Time Option (with Information Refresh Time in the Option's "information-refresh-time" field). The value in the Server's Information Refresh Time Option must not be less than IRT_MINIMUM (the Minimum Information Refresh Time with a default value of 600 seconds). If the REPLY message does not contain the Information Refresh Time Option, the Client must treat the REPLY message as if it contained this Option with the value IRT_DEFAULT (the Default Information Refresh Time, which is 86,400 seconds (or 24 hours)).

The Client must use the refresh time IRT_MINIMUM if the REPLY message contained the Information Refresh Time Option with a value less than IRT_MINIMUM. A value of 0xFFFFFFFF indicates "infinity," which implies that the Client should not contact the Server to refresh its configuration information unless something triggers a refresh (e.g., the Client detects movement to a new link). If the Client contacts the Server to obtain new information or refresh some existing information before the Information Refresh Time expires, it should also take this opportunity to refresh all configuration information covered by this Option.

When the Client detects that the Information Refresh Time has expired, it should send an INFORMATION-REQUEST message to the Server to update its configuration information; however, the Client must delay sending the message by a randomly selected time between 0 and INF_MAX_DELAY (which is the maximum delay for the first INFORMATION-REQUEST message, with a default value of 1 second).

It may happen that a DHCPv6 Client already has a maximum value for the Information Refresh Time, meaning the Client uses that value whenever it receives the Information Refresh Time Option from the Server with a value higher than this maximum value. The Client also uses that maximum value when it receives an Information Refresh Time value of "infinity." This maximum value may decrease the Client's vulnerability to attacks based on forged DHCPv6 messages. Without this maximum value, the Client may be compelled to use incorrect configuration information for a potentially indefinite period. However, the network administrator may have reasons for allowing a Client to use a very long Information Refresh Time; therefore, it may be desirable for this maximum value to be configurable.

5.5.11   Reconfigure Message (Sent By A Server)

A DHCPv6 Server uses a RECONFIGURE message containing the Reconfigure Message Option (Option Code 19) to inform a Client that the Server has updated or new configuration parameters. Upon receiving this message, the Client is to initiate a RENEW/REPLY or INFORMATION-REQUEST/REPLY message exchange with the Server to obtain updated information.

When a DHCPv6 Client receives a RECONFIGURE message from a Server, it responds by sending a RENEW, REBIND, or INFORMATION-REQUEST message according to the message response type indicated in the "msg-type" field of the Reconfigure Message Option. The Client may send any of these messages to the Server to update its configuration information. The Client updates its configuration through the DHCPv6 two-message exchange described below. The Client expects the Server to return a REPLY message containing IAs and/or other configuration information.

5.5.11.1   Server: Creation and Transmission of RECONFIGURE Messages

A DHCPv6 Server may be set up to send RECONFIGURE messages to a Client to initiate a DHCPv6 configuration exchange, allowing the Client to obtain new IPv6 addresses, prefixes, and other configuration information. For example, a network administrator may configure a Server to use a Server-initiated DHCPv6 configuration exchange with a Client when IPv6 address renumbering is occurring on the links in a DHCPv6 domain or when other configuration parameters are being updated, such as when Servers are added, moved, or removed.

When the Client receives the RECONFIGURE message, it sends a RENEW, REBIND, or INFORMATION-REQUEST message to the Server as indicated by the value in the "msg-type" field of the Reconfigure Message Option (Option Code 19). The Server sends a REPLY message containing IAs and/or other configuration information to the Client. The Server may include in the REPLY message Options containing the IAs and new values for other configuration parameters, even if the Client's message did not request those additional IAs and parameters.

The Server performs the following operations when sending a RECONFIGURE message:

- Constructs a RECONFIGURE message and sets the message's "msg-type" field to RECONFIGURE and the "transaction-id" field to 0.
- Includes a Server Identifier Option (Option Code 2) containing its DUID and a Client Identifier Option (Option Code 1) containing the Client's DUID in the RECONFIGURE message.
- The Server must use the DHCPv6 Authentication Option (Option Code 11) in the RECONFIGURE message because of the risk of denial-of-service (DoS) attacks against DHCPv6 Clients; DHCPv6 mandates the use of a security mechanism in RECONFIGURE messages.
- Includes a Reconfigure Message Option (Option Code 19) to indicate to the Client the kind of response required: RENEW, REBIND, or INFORMATION-REQUEST message.
- Must not include any other Options in the RECONFIGURE message, except those Options specifically permitted in the definition of an individual Option.

The Server uses an IPv6 unicast address belonging to the DHCPv6 Client and of sufficient scope to send each RECONFIGURE message to the Client. If the Server does not have an IPv6 address to directly send the RECONFIGURE message to the Client, it uses a RELAY-REPLY message to send the RECONFIGURE message to a Relay Agent, which will relay the message to the Client. The Server may use the information it has obtained about Clients it has contacted or through some external agent to obtain the IPv6 address of the Client (and the appropriate Relay Agent, if required).

To reconfigure two or more Clients, the Server sends a separate RECONFIGURE message via unicast transmission to each of the target Clients. Reconfiguration of multiple Clients may be done concurrently; for example, the Server may transmit a RECONFIGURE message to additional Clients while previously initiated reconfiguration message exchanges are still ongoing.

A Client, upon receiving a RECONFIGURE message from a Server, initiates a RENEW/REPLY, REBIND/REPLY, or INFORMATION-REQUEST/REPLY message exchange with the Server. When the Server receives a RENEW, REBIND, or INFORMATION-REQUEST message from the Client (the message type indicated in the original RECONFIGURE message), it interprets the Client's response as a result of the RECONFIGURE message request.

The Server sets the Retransmission Time to REC_TIMEOUT (i.e., the Initial Reconfigure Timeout with a default value of 2 seconds) when transmitting the RECONFIGURE message. If the Server sends a RECONFIGURE message and does not receive a RENEW, REBIND, or INFORMATION-REQUEST message from the Client before the Retransmission Time elapses, the Server retransmits the RECONFIGURE message with double the Retransmission Time value and waits again for a response. The Server continues this retransmission process until the number of unsuccessful attempts reaches REC_MAX_RC (i.e., the Maximum Reconfigure Attempts with a default value of 8), at which point the Server aborts the reconfiguration process for that Client.

5.5.11.2 Client: Receipt of RECONFIGURE Messages

A DHCPv6 Client listens on UDP port 546 for RECONFIGURE messages from a Server. These messages are sent to interfaces for which the Client has obtained configuration information through

DHCPv6. Upon receiving a valid RECONFIGURE message, the Client responds by transmitting a RENEW, REBIND, or INFORMATION-REQUEST message, as indicated by the "msg-type" field of the Reconfigure Message Option (Option Code 19). The Client ignores the "transaction-id" field of the received RECONFIGURE message, and while handling a transaction, it discards any RECONFIGURE messages it receives.

The RECONFIGURE message serves as a trigger that prompts a Client to complete a successful DHCPv6 two-message exchange. Upon receiving a RECONFIGURE message, the Client proceeds with the DHCPv6 two-message exchange (and retransmits the RENEW, REBIND, or INFORMATION-REQUEST message, if necessary). The Client ignores any additional RECONFIGURE messages it receives until it completes the DHCPv6 two-message exchange process.

5.5.12 RELAY-FORWARD AND RELAY-REPLY MESSAGES

A DHCPv6 Relay Agent may exchange messages with other Relay Agents or directly with Servers and Clients. A Relay Agent is an intermediary that relays DHCPv6 messages between Clients and Servers that are not connected to the same link. The two Relay Agent messages are the RELAY-FORWARD (Type 12) and the RELAY-REPLY (Type 13) messages (see Table 5.2). All data in the fields of the DHCPv6 message header and Options of the Relay Agent messages are also organized in network byte order:

- A Relay Agent uses a RELAY-FORWARD message to relay DHCPv6 messages from a Client, either directly to a Server or through another Relay Agent to a Server. The Relay Agent encapsulates a DHCPv6 message received from a Client or a RELAY-FORWARD message from another Relay Agent into a DHCPv6 Option that is contained in a new RELAY-FORWARD message.
- A DHCPv6 Server uses a RELAY-REPLY message to send a DHCPv6 message to a Relay Agent, which the Relay Agent then delivers to a Client. The RELAY-REPLY message containing the Server's DHCPv6 message may be relayed by other DHCPv6 Relay Agents to the Relay Agent closest to the Client. The Server encapsulates the DHCPv6 message sent to the Client in a DHCPv6 Option that is contained in the RELAY-REPLY message, and the Relay Agent closest to the Client extracts the Server's DHCPv6 message and relays it to the Client.

When a DHCPv6 Server receives any DHCPv6 message from a Client encapsulated in one or more RELAY-FORWARD messages, the Server must use the received RELAY-FORWARD message (potentially with several levels of encapsulation) to construct a RELAY-REPLY message that must be relayed through the same Relay Agents (in reverse order) that handled the original DHCPv6 message from the Client. It may also be necessary for the Server to record the Client's information in case the Server needs to send a RECONFIGURE message to the Client at a later time, unless an IPv6 address has already been configured on the Server for sending RECONFIGURE messages directly to the Client. Figure 5.6 shows the Stateful DHCPv6 message exchange between a Client, a Relay Agent, and a Server.

5.5.12.1 Relaying a Client Message or a RELAY-FORWARD Message

A DHCPv6 Relay Agent should be configured to use a list of destination IPv6 addresses that may include the All_DHCP_Servers multicast address (FF02::1:2) and other IPv6 unicast addresses assigned by the network administrator. The Relay Agent must use the IPv6 All_DHCP_Servers multicast address as the default address if it has not been explicitly configured to use a list of destination IPv6 addresses. When relaying DHCPv6 messages to the All_DHCP_Servers multicast address, or to other IPv6 multicast addresses, the Relay Agent sets the Hop Limit field of the IPv6 packet carrying the DHCPv6 message to 8.

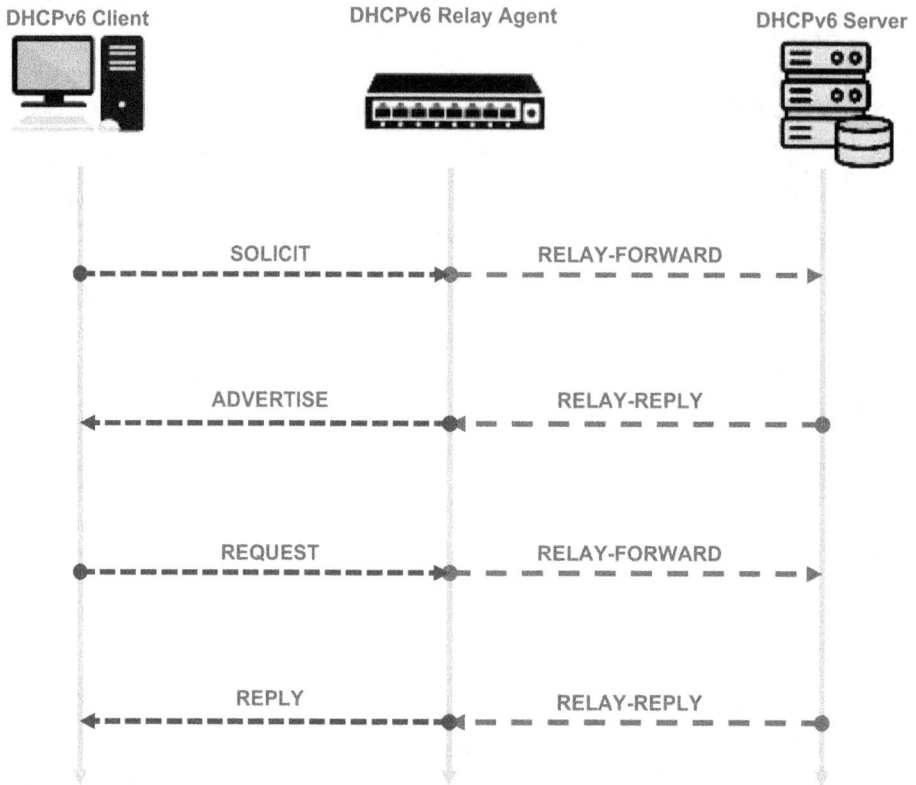

FIGURE 5.6   Stateful DHCPv6 message exchange between a Client, a Relay Agent, and a Server.

When a Relay Agent receives a DHCPv6 message from a Client or a RELAY-FORWARD message from another Relay Agent, it relays these messages either to a Server directly or to another Relay Agent to be forwarded to the target Server. When a Relay Agent receives a DHCPv6 message type that it recognizes but is not the intended target, a RELAY-FORWARD message from another Relay Agent, or a DHCPv6 message type that it does not recognize **[RFC7283]**, it constructs a new RELAY-FORWARD message to be forwarded by performing the following operations:

- Copies the source IPv6 address from the header of the IPv6 packet carrying the DHCPv6 message into the corresponding (peer) IPv6 address field of the IPv6 packet containing the new RELAY-FORWARD message.
- Copies the received DHCPv6 message (excluding any IPv6 or UDP headers encapsulating the message) into a Relay Message Option (Option Code 9) in the new RELAY-FORWARD message.
- Adds any other Options it is configured to include to the new RELAY-FORWARD message.

The new RELAY-FORWARD message is sent directly to the target Server or to another Relay Agent to be forwarded to the target Server; the Server may receive a RELAY-FORWARD message with several levels of encapsulation.

A Lightweight DHCPv6 Relay Agent (LDRA) is defined in Reference **[RFC6221]** that allows an access node (e.g., Ethernet switches and Digital Subscriber Link Access Multiplexers (DSLAM)) performing Link-Layer bridging (not IPv6 routing functions) and handling DHCPv6 message exchanges to insert Relay Message Option in those exchanges. An LDRA is located on the IPv6 link where the Client, Server, and Relay Agent are also present.

5.5.12.1.1   Relaying a DHCPv6 Message from a Client

If a Relay Agent receives a DHCPv6 message from a Client to be relayed, it writes a globally scoped IPv6 unicast address (i.e., an IPv6 Global Unicast or Unique-Local address) into the "link-address" field of the RELAY-FORWARD message. This IPv6 unicast address is taken from an IPv6 prefix assigned to the link on which Leases are assigned to the Client. If the Relay Agent has no such IPv6 address available, it may set the message's "link-address" field to an IPv6 Link-Local address configured on the interface where the original Client DHCPv6 message was received. The latter approach is not recommended, as this may require the Server to be configured with additional information.

The Server uses the IPv6 address (in the "link-address" field) to determine the IPv6 link on which the Client should be assigned Leases and other configuration information. The Relay Agent sets the "hop-count" field of the RELAY-FORWARD message to 0.

If the Relay Agent cannot use the IPv6 address in the RELAY-FORWARD message's "link-address" field to identify the interface on which it will relay the response message (RELAY-REPLY message) to the Client, it must include an Interface-Id Option (Option Code 18) in the RELAY-FORWARD message. A Relay Agent uses the Interface-Id Option (which contains an "interface-id" field) to identify the interface on which it received the Client's DHCPv6 message. The value in the "interface-id" field is an arbitrary value generated by the Relay Agent to identify each of its interfaces. When the Relay Agent receives a RELAY-REPLY message with an Interface-Id Option (also included by the Server), it relays the DHCPv6 message through the interface identified by the Option to the Client.

The Server, when sending the RELAY-REPLY message to the Client, will include the Interface-Id Option (taken from the RELAY-FORWARD message) in this outgoing message. The Relay Agent sets the RELAY-REPLY message's "link-address" field as described above, regardless of whether the Relay Agent included an Interface-Id Option in the RELAY-FORWARD message.

5.5.12.1.2   Relaying a DHCPv6 Message from a Relay Agent

If a Relay Agent receives a RELAY-FORWARD message from another Relay Agent that has a "hop-count" field equal to HOP_COUNT_LIMIT (with a default value of 8), the Relay Agent will process and then discard that message. The Relay Agent prepares a new RELAY-FORWARD message to be relayed to another Relay Agent or the target Server. The Relay Agent copies the source IPv6 address from the IPv6 packet carrying the received message into the corresponding IPv6 address field of the IPv6 packet containing the new RELAY-FORWARD message and sets the "hop-count" field of the new message to the value in the "hop-count" field of the received message incremented by 1.

If the Relay Agent finds that the source IPv6 address in the IPv6 header of the IPv6 packet carrying the received message is a globally scoped IPv6 unicast address (i.e., IPv6 Global Unicast or Unique-Local address), it sets the "link-address" field of the new RELAY-FORWARD message to 0. Otherwise, the Relay Agent sets the message's "link-address" field to a globally scoped IPv6 unicast address (i.e., IPv6 Global Unicast or Unique-Local address) assigned to the interface on which the message was received, or includes an Interface-Id Option to identify the interface on which the message was received.

5.5.12.1.3   Relay Agent Behavior with DHCPv6 Prefix Delegation

A Relay Agent forwards DHCPv6 messages containing DHCPv6 Prefix Delegation Options just as it would relay IPv6 addresses as described in the two subsections above. According to **[RFC8415]**, if a Server and a Client communicate through a Relay Agent for the assignment of delegated IPv6 prefixes, the Server may need to run a specified protocol or be provided with other out-of-band communication capabilities to configure routing information for delegated IPv6 prefixes on any IPv6 router (through which the Client may forward IPv6 packets).

5.5.12.2   Relaying a RELAY-REPLY Message

When a Relay Agent receives a RELAY-REPLY message, it processes any Options included in this message in addition to the Relay Message Option (Option Code 9). The Relay Agent examines the Relay Message Option, extracts the message carried in it (another RELAY-REPLY message in this case), and then relays this message to the IPv6 address contained in the "peer-address" field of the received RELAY-REPLY message. The Relay Agent must not modify the relayed (encapsulated) message in the received RELAY-REPLY message.

Note that, for a received RELAY-FORWARD message, the Relay Agent relays this message verbatim to the next Relay Agent or directly to the target Server (encapsulated in a new RELAY-FORWARD message). For a RELAY-REPLY message (from another Relay Agent or from a Server), the Relay Agent extracts the contents of the Relay Message Option and relays it to another Relay Agent or directly to the target Client whose IPv6 address is in the "peer-address" field of the received RELAY-REPLY message. The process of relaying a RELAY-REPLY message involves decapsulating the contents of the Relay Message Option in the received RELAY-REPLY message (which might be another RELAY-REPLY message or a DHCPv6 message for a Client) and forwarding it to the next node (another Relay Agent or the target Client).

If the Relay Agent finds that the received RELAY-REPLY message includes an Interface-Id Option, it relays the embedded DHCPv6 message sent by the Server to the Client on the link identified by the included Interface-Id Option. Otherwise, if the Relay Agent sees that the "link-address" field of the received RELAY-REPLY message is not set to 0, it relays the encapsulated message on the link identified by the IPv6 address in the "link-address" field of the received message. The Relay Agent must process a received RELAY-REPLY message as defined above, regardless of the type of message encapsulated in the Relay Message Option.

5.5.12.3   Creation of RELAY-REPLY Messages

A DHCPv6 Server uses a RELAY-REPLY message for the following purposes:

- Return a response (contained in a RELAY-REPLY message) to a Client if the original DHCPv6 message from the Client was relayed to the Server in a RELAY-FORWARD message.
- Send a RECONFIGURE message (contained in a RELAY-REPLY message) to a Client if the Server does not have an IPv6 address that it can use to send the DHCPv6 message directly to the Client.

When the Server sends a response DHCPv6 message to a Client, that response must be relayed through the same Relay Agents that handled the original Client DHCPv6 message. To ensure the same Relay Agents handle the response message, the Server creates a RELAY-REPLY message that includes a Relay Message Option (Option Code 9) containing the response message, allowing the next Relay Agent on the return path to the Client to process the Option. The next Relay Agent on the return path processes the received RELAY-REPLY message containing another Relay Message Option, which may also contain another RELAY-REPLY message and Relay Message Option to be processed by the following Relay Agent, and so on; each Relay Agent extracts the message in the received Relay Message Option to pass it on.

The Server records the IPv6 addresses in the "peer-address" fields of the received RELAY-FORWARD message and its encapsulated RELAY-FORWARD messages, so that it can constructs the appropriate RELAY-REPLY messages (with several levels of encapsulation) containing the response DHCPv6 message from the Server. Figure 5.7 shows an example of how the RELAY-REPLY message is used.

When the Server sends a RECONFIGURE message to a Client through a Relay Agent, it constructs a RELAY-REPLY message that includes a Relay Message Option containing the RECONFIGURE message to be processed by the next Relay Agent on the return path to the Client. The Server creates the

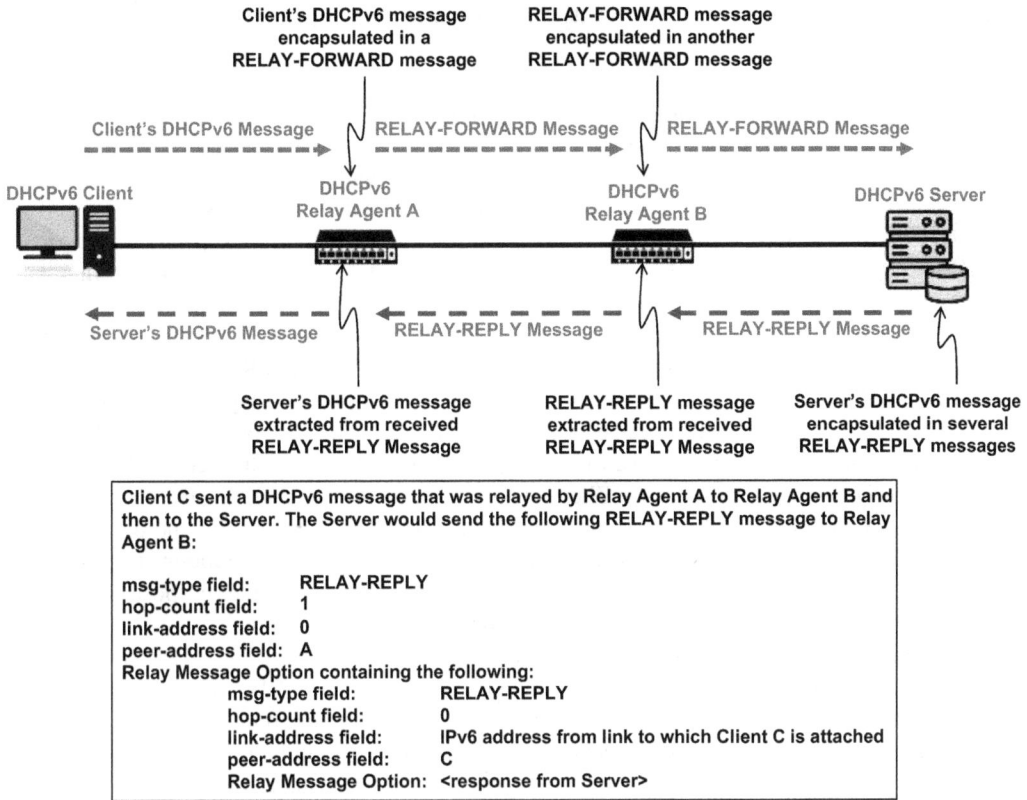

Client's DHCPv6 message encapsulated in a RELAY-FORWARD message

RELAY-FORWARD message encapsulated in another RELAY-FORWARD message

Client's DHCPv6 Message → RELAY-FORWARD Message → RELAY-FORWARD Message →

DHCPv6 Client | DHCPv6 Relay Agent A | DHCPv6 Relay Agent B | DHCPv6 Server

← Server's DHCPv6 Message ← RELAY-REPLY Message ← RELAY-REPLY Message

Server's DHCPv6 message extracted from received RELAY-REPLY Message

RELAY-REPLY message extracted from received RELAY-REPLY Message

Server's DHCPv6 message encapsulated in several RELAY-REPLY messages

Client C sent a DHCPv6 message that was relayed by Relay Agent A to Relay Agent B and then to the Server. The Server would send the following RELAY-REPLY message to Relay Agent B:

msg-type field: RELAY-REPLY
hop-count field: 1
link-address field: 0
peer-address field: A
Relay Message Option containing the following:
      msg-type field: RELAY-REPLY
      hop-count field: 0
      link-address field: IPv6 address from link to which Client C is attached
      peer-address field: C
      Relay Message Option: <response from Server>

FIGURE 5.7   Example use of the RELAY-REPLY message.

RELAY-REPLY message and sets the "peer-address" field of the message to the Client's IPv6 address, and sets the message's "link-address" field as required by the Relay Agent to allow the RECONFIGURE message to be relayed to the Client. The Server may use prior interactions with the Client or some external mechanism to obtain the Client's IPv6 addresses and those of the next Relay Agent.

5.5.12.4   Interaction between Relay Agents and Servers

As discussed above, each time a Relay Agent relays a DHCPv6 message to a Server, it adds a new encapsulation level around the message; each Relay Agent encapsulates a received RELAY-FORWARD message in a new RELAY-FORWARD message. The Relay Agent is also allowed to insert additional DHCPv6 Options when adding an encapsulation level but must not change anything in the DHCPv6 message being relayed and encapsulated. If multiple Relay Agents exist between a Client and a Server, the DHCPv6 message undergoes multiple encapsulations as it is relayed to the Server. Although these encapsulations make the processing of DHCPv6 messages slightly more complex at each Relay Agent and the Server, the major advantage is that they provide a clear indication to the Server about the particular Options inserted by each Relay Agent.

The DHCPv6 response message from the Server, relayed back to the Client, is expected to travel through the same Relay Agents but in reverse order. When the Server's DHCPv6 response message (encapsulated in several levels of RELAY-REPLY messages) is relayed back toward the Client, each Relay Agent removes one encapsulation level. The last Relay Agent next to the Client receives the final RELAY-REPLY message and removes the last encapsulation level, leaving only the Server's original DHCPv6 response message, which is then sent to the Client. The last Relay Agent decapsulates the Server's DHCPv6 response message from the last (innermost) RELAY-REPLY message and sends it to the Client.

The following explains why Relay Agents can add one or more Options in certain cases:

1. Relay Agents may be configured (by a server administrator) with network infrastructure information and to provide additional information about a Client. The server administrator may configure DHCPv6 Options that the Server can use to determine its IPv6 address/ prefix allocation policy. This source of information is usually more trusted than information from the Client, as it comes from the administrator and cannot easily be spoofed.
2. A Relay Agent may need some information to send a RELAY-REPLY message back to the Client. Relay Agents are expected to operate in a stateless manner and not retain any state after processing a DHCPv6 message. A Relay Agent may include the Interface-Id Option (Option Code 18) in the RELAY-FORWARD message to identify the interface on which a DHCPv6 message from a Client was received. When the Relay Agent receives a RELAY-REPLY message containing an Interface-Id Option, it relays the encapsulated DHCPv6 Server response message to the Client through the interface identified by the Option. The Relay Agent uses the interface identified by the included Interface-Id Option to send the response back to the Client. The Relay Agent may include other Options in a RELAY-FORWARD message and request the Server to echo one or more of those Options back in the response message. The Relay Agent can use these Options (which the Client will never see) to send the response back to the Client or for other purposes (see the DHCPv6 Relay Agent Echo Request Option in **[RFC4994]** for details).
3. In some cases, a Relay Agent is the best device to provide values for certain DHCPv6 Options. A Relay Agent may insert an Option into the RELAY-FORWARD message being relayed to the Server and request the Server to return that Option to the Client. The Client then receives that Option and processes it accordingly. It should be noted that the Server is ultimately the authority (depending on its configuration) to decide whether to return that Option to the Client (see the Relay-Supplied DHCP Options in **[RFC6422]** for details).

A Server may be configured, for various reasons, to retain the Relay Agent's information after completing the processing of a DHCPv6 message from a Client. One case is when the bulk leasequery mechanism is used to request all the IPv6 addresses and/or IPv6 prefixes that were assigned through a specific Relay Agent. Another is when the reconfigure mechanism is used, and a Server chooses not to send a RECONFIGURE message directly to the Client but instead through Relay Agents to the Client (a behavior that is not covered in **[RFC8415]**).

5.5.13 DHCPv6 Client Refreshing Configuration Information

Whenever a DHCPv6 Client detects that it may have moved to a new link, the IPv6 prefixes/ addresses previously assigned to the interfaces on the old link may no longer be appropriate for the new link. The following are examples of instances when a Client may have moved to a new link:

- The Client moves from one access point to another (e.g., changes a Wi-Fi access points).
- The Client reconnects to a link on which it previously obtained Leases.
- The Client is rebooting (and has a stable and persistent DHCPv6 state).
- The Client wakes up from sleep mode.

Upon detecting a move to a new link, if a DHCPv6 Server previously provided only IPv6 addresses to the Client and not delegated IPv6 prefixes, the Client should initiate a DHCPv6 message exchange using the CONFIRM and REPLY messages. The Client sends a CONFIRM message to the Server that includes any IAs (along with their IPv6 addresses) assigned to the Client interface that may have moved to a new link. Any Servers that receive the CONFIRM message will respond with a

REPLY message indicating whether those IPv6 addresses are appropriate for the new link to which the Client is attached.

If the DHCPv6 Server assigned any valid delegated IPv6 prefixes to the Client, the Client must initiate a DHCPv6 message exchange using REBIND and REPLY messages, except the Client should use retransmission parameters as specified in **[RFC8415]** for the CONFIRM message. The Client includes in the REBIND message sent to the Server the IA_NA, IA_TA, and IA_PD Options along with their associated Leases.

If the DHCPv6 Client has only used INFORMATION-REQUEST/REPLY message exchanges to obtain network information from the Server, it must initiate a DHCPv6 message exchange using INFORMATION-REQUEST and REPLY messages.

If the above-mentioned conditions are not applicable, a Client should initiate a RENEW/REPLY message exchange (as if the T1 interval carried in IA_NA and IA_PD Options has expired) or initiate an INFORMATION-REQUEST/REPLY message exchange if the Client detects that the IPv6 prefixes available on the link have significantly changed (due to the addition of new IPv6 prefixes or deprecation of existing IPv6 prefixes), as this may indicate a change in configuration information. However, the Client must rate-limit such DHCPv6 message transmissions to avoid flooding the Server with requests.

5.6 SUMMARY OF DHCPv6 CLIENT AND SERVER MESSAGE EXCHANGES

As discussed earlier, a DHCPv6 Client may use a four-message exchange process to obtain IPv6 addresses/prefixes and other configuration information from a Server. This section outlines the main operational steps in this DHCPv6 mode. The following steps summarize the DHCPv6 four-message exchange process:

1. **DHCP Server Discovery Phase:** The DHCPv6 Client searches for a Server on the link by multicasting a SOLICIT message to the link-scope IPv6 All_DHCP_Relay_Agents_and_ Servers multicast address (FF02::1:2).
2. **DHCPv6 Server Advertisement Phase**: Each DHCPv6 Server that receives the SOLICIT message selects an unassigned IPv6 address/prefix from a locally configured DHCPv6 address/prefix pool or an external source. The Server then responds by transmitting an ADVERTISE message to the Client, containing the selected IPv6 address/prefix and other configuration information.
3. **DHCPv6 Server Selection and Information Request Phase**: If the Client receives ADVERTISE messages from multiple DHCPv6 Servers, it selects the preferred Server according to the configured DHCPv6 policy. If the ADVERTISE message contains the Server Unicast Option (Option Code 12) and the Client supports this Option, the Client unicasts a REQUEST message to the Server. Otherwise, the Client multicasts the REQUEST message with the appropriate DHCPv6 Options, instructing the selected Server to provide the desired configuration information.
4. **DHCPv6 Information Delivery Phase**: The selected DHCP Server receives the REQUEST message and sends a REPLY message containing the requested IPv6 address/ prefix and other configuration information.

The DHCPv6 Client receives the REPLY message from the Server and uses the IPv6 address/prefix and other configuration information contained in the message for the required local parameter configurations. The Server's REPLY message to the Client includes the Preferred Lifetime, Valid Lifetime, Lease renewal time, and rebind time for the assigned IPv6 address/prefix. The default values of the Lease renewal time (T1) and rebind time (T2) are typically 50% and 80% of the Preferred Lifetime, respectively. Figure 5.8 shows the DHCPv6 four-message exchange process with some possible DHCPv6 Options.

DHCPv6 Client   DHCPv6 Server

SOLICIT
• Destination Address: FF02::1:2
• Options:Client Identifier Option,
         Option Request Option {IA_NA, DNS_SERVERS, DOMAIN_LIST}

ADVERTISE
Options: Server Identifier Option, Client Identifier Option,
         DNS_SERVERS, IA_NA {IAID, IA Prefix Option}

REQUEST
Options: Server Identifier Option, Client Identifier Option,
         Option Request Option {IA_NA, DNS_SERVERS, DOMAIN_LIST}

REPLY
Options: Server Identifier Option, Client Identifier Option,
         DNS_SERVERS = 2001:DB8:200::1
         IA_NA: IAID = -----
                IA Prefix Option: Preferred Lifetime = ------
                        Valid Lifetime = ------
                        Prefix = 2001:DB8:EF01:1::1/64

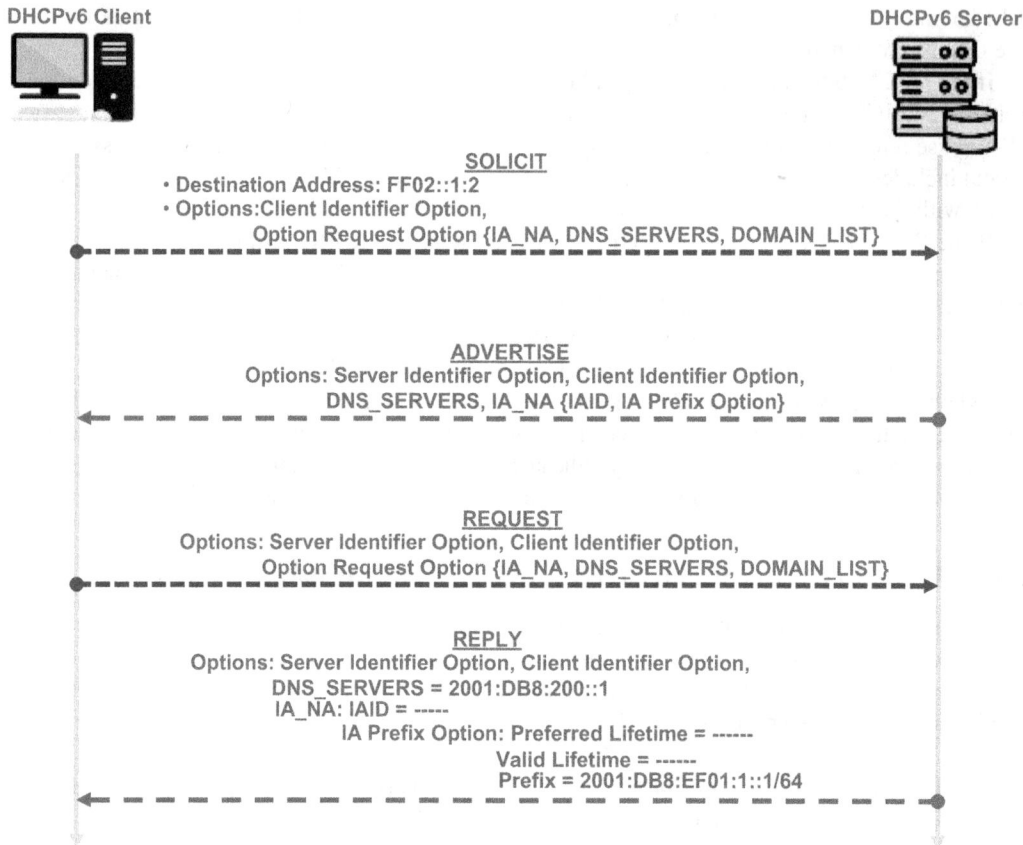

FIGURE 5.8   DHCPv6 four-message exchange process and possible DHCPv6 Options.

5.6.1   IPv6 Address and Prefix Renewal and Rebinding

When the Valid Lifetime of an IPv6 address/prefix assigned by a DHCPv6 Server expires, the DHCPv6 Client can no longer use the IPv6 address/prefix. To continue using the IPv6 address/prefix, the Client must send a RENEW message to the Server to renew the Lease time of the IPv6 address/prefix. T1 is the time interval after which the Client is expected to contact the Server that assigned the IPv6 address/prefix to renew (extend) the Lifetime of the IPv6 address/prefix.

As shown in Figure 5.9, at T1 (with the recommended value of 50% of the Preferred Lifetime), the Client transmits a RENEW message to the Server, which responds by sending a REPLY message to inform the Client about the outcome of the Lease renewal. If the Server indicates to the Client that it can receive DHCPv6 messages via unicast transmission (by sending a Server Unicast Option to the Client), the Client can unicast the RENEW message to the Server. Otherwise, the Client will need to multicast the RENEW message to the Server.

If, for some reason, the Client does not receive a response (REPLY message) from the Server after sending the RENEW message at T1, the Client will multicast a REBIND message to the IPv6 All_DHCP_Relay_Agents_and_Servers multicast address (FF02::1:2) at T2, hoping to reach all DHCPv6 Servers (see Figure 5.10). Typically, the recommended value of T2 is 80% of the Preferred Lifetime. A DHCPv6 Server, upon receiving the REBIND message, will respond by sending a REPLY message, informing the Client about the outcome of the Lease renewal. If the Client does not receive a response (REPLY message) from any available DHCPv6 Server before the Valid Lifetime of the Lease expires, it will stop using the assigned IPv6 address/prefix.

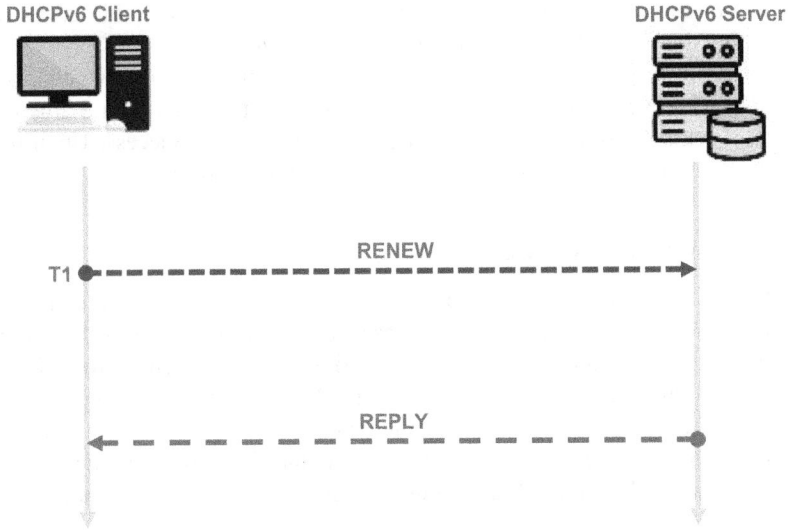

FIGURE 5.9   Using the RENEW message for IPv6 address/prefix Lease renewal.

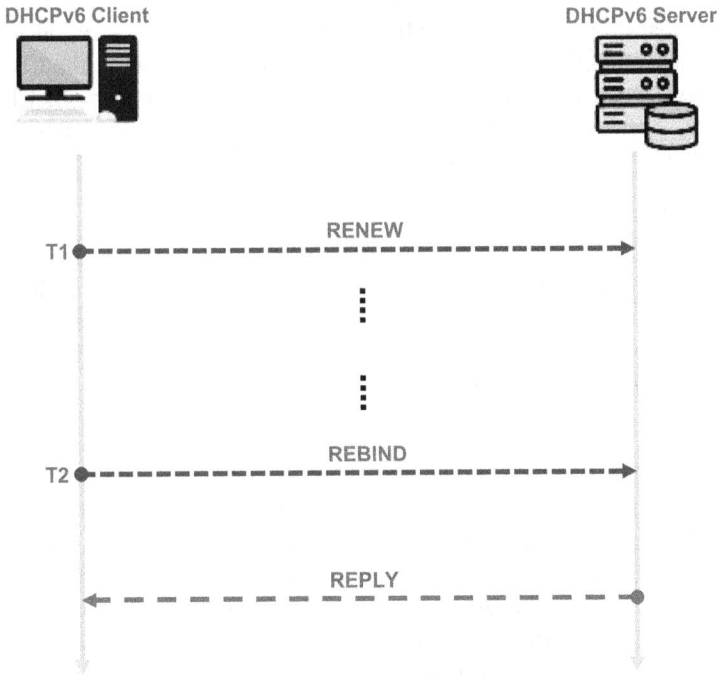

FIGURE 5.10   Using the REBIND message for IPv6 address/prefix Lease renewal.

5.6.2   CONFIRMING ASSIGNED IPV6 ADDRESSES AND PREFIXES

A DHCPv6 Client may need to check whether an assigned IPv6 address/prefix is still available for use when it detects that the link to which it is connected has changed. When the Client detects such a link change (e.g., the network cable detaches and reattaches, or an actual link change occurs), it can send a CONFIRM message to the Server to check whether the assigned IPv6 address/prefix is still valid for use on the current (presumably changed) link. The Client multicasts the CONFIRM message containing the IPv6 address/prefix to the Server for validation.

If the Server receives the CONFIRM message and determines that the IPv6 address/prefix can still be used, the Server sends a REPLY message to the Client containing a Status Code Option (Option Code 13) with the status of the IPv6 address/prefix set to Success. Upon receiving the REPLY message, the Client can continue to use the IPv6 address/prefix.

5.6.3   Detecting IPv6 Address Conflicts

If a DHCPv6 Client detects that an assigned IPv6 address is creating an address conflict on the link, it sends a DECLINE message to decline the address and notify the Server of the address conflict. The DECLINE message contains the conflicting IPv6 address assigned by the DHCPv6 Server. A conflicting IPv6 address cannot be used as the source IPv6 address of the DECLINE message.

If the DHCPv6 Client and Server have negotiated the use of unicast transmission, the Client can unicast the DECLINE message to the Server. Otherwise, the Client must multicast the DECLINE message. Upon receiving the DECLINE message, the Server marks the IPv6 address contained in it as a conflicting IPv6 address.

5.6.4   Releasing an Assigned IPv6 Address/Prefix

To free up an assigned IPv6 address/prefix, a DHCPv6 Client sends a RELEASE message to the Server containing that IPv6 address/prefix. If the Client and Server support unicast transmission, the Client can unicast the RELEASE message to the Server. Otherwise, the Client must multicast the RELEASE message. Upon receiving the RELEASE message from the Client, the Server releases the assigned IPv6 address/prefix and responds by sending a REPLY message to the Client.

5.7   DHCPv6 OPERATIONAL MODELS

In this section, we discuss the most common DHCPv6 operational models. These operational models are not mutually exclusive, meaning an IPv6 node may use them together in some cases. For example, an IPv6 node may start IPv6 address and parameter configuration in the Stateful DHCPv6 mode to obtain an IPv6 address and, after some time, use the Stateless DHCPv6 mode to request additional configuration parameters.

5.7.1   Stateless DHCPv6

IPv6 nodes (DHCP Clients) use Stateless DHCPv6 [RFC3736] when they autoconfigure IPv6 Global Unicast addresses but consult a DHCPv6 Server for one or more other configuration parameters, such as a list of DNS recursive Name Servers or DNS domain search lists [RFC3646]. In this case, IPv6 nodes are not able to use DHCPv6 to obtain all IPv6 address Leases in addition to other configuration parameters. An IPv6 node uses Stateless DHCPv6 when it initially powers up or at any time its local software requires expired or missing configuration information that can only be obtained from a DHCPv6 Server.

Stateless DHCPv6 is the simplest and most basic DHCPv6 operational model. This DHCPv6 mode requires a Client (and a Server) to use only two DHCPv6 messages: INFORMATION-REQUEST and REPLY (see Figure 5.4). In this mode of operation, DHCPv6 Servers and Relay Agents typically also support the use of the REPLY-FORWARD and RELAY-REPLY messages to handle DHCPv6 operations when Clients and Servers do not reside on the same link.

The following are the main features of SLAAC with Stateless DHCPv6:

- IPv6 routers attached to a link send ICMPv6 Router Advertisement messages to IPv6 hosts on the link, allowing them to autoconfigure their IPv6 addresses and default gateway(s).

- Each IPv6 router (which may be acting as a requesting router or DHCPv6 Client) on the link can initiate DHCPv6 Prefix Delegation with a DHCPv6 Server on the network by including an IA_PD Option along with a Client Identifier Option in its SOLICIT messages.
- The router (Client) may automatically configure IPv6 unicast addresses on its interfaces attached to the link using the Server's delegated IPv6 prefix information.
- The router may be configured to optionally set the M (Managed address configuration) or O (Other Configuration) Flags in Router Advertisement messages that it sends.
    - The router may also be configured to set the M Flag to 1 in Router Advertisement messages to notify hosts on the link that they can use Stateful DHCPv6 to obtain IPv6 addresses.
    - The router may be configured to set the O Flag to 1 in Router Advertisement messages to notify hosts on the link that they can use Stateless DHCPv6 to obtain non-IPv6 address configuration information, such as DNS information and NTP information, from a Server.
- To use DHCPv6 Prefix Delegation, a DHCPv6 Server on the network must be configured with the IA_PD or IA_NA address delegation pools. IPv6 addresses and prefixes to be allocated to Clients are stored in these delegation pools.

5.7.1.1   The IPv6 SLAAC Process

After autoconfiguring an IPv6 Link-Local address on an interface, an IPv6 host performs IPv6 router discovery to obtain globally unique IPv6 prefixes for configuring an IPv6 Global Unicast address on the interface. The IPv6 host uses the IPv6 Link-Local address for communication on the local link (on-link communication) and the IPv6 Global Unicast address for communication with IPv6 nodes outside the local link (off-link communication).

The SLAAC processes can be summarized as follows (see also **Chapter 4**):

1. **Phase 1 – Creating an IPv6 address for local connectivity:**
   - **IPv6 Link-Local Address Generation**: As soon as an IPv6 host enables IPv6 on an interface, it auto-generates an IPv6 Link-Local address (as a "bootstrapping" address) for that interface. The host creates this address by appending the interface ID to the link-local IPv6 prefix (FE80::/10). An IPv6 Link-Local address can also be manually configured on the interface (see details in **Chapter 3**).
   - **IPv6 Duplicate Address Detection**: Before assigning the generated IPv6 Link-Local address to the interface, the host first verifies the uniqueness of the address on the attached link. The host performs IPv6 Duplicate Address Detection by transmitting an ICMPv6 Neighbor Solicitation message destined for the newly generated IPv6 address. If the host receives a Neighbor Advertisement message with this IPv6 address, it becomes aware that the address is a duplicate, and the process stops, requiring network administrator intervention to configure the IPv6 address (see details in **Chapter 4**).
   - **IPv6 Link-Local Address Assignment**: If the host determines that the newly generated IPv6 address is unique, it assigns it to the interface.
        At this point, the IPv6 host has an IPv6 address for on-link communication. Note that Phase 1 (autoconfiguring a "bootstrapping" address) is not considered part of SLAAC but is a requirement for all IPv6 operations. Only IPv6 hosts perform Phase 2; IPv6 Global Unicast addresses on router interfaces must be configured through other means.
2. **Phase 2 – Creating an IPv6 address for global connectivity:**
   - **IPv6 Router Advertisement and Router Discovery**: The IPv6 host may receive periodic (unsolicited) Router Advertisement messages or send a Router Solicitation message to prompt all on-link routers to send Router Advertisement messages. When an IPv6 router is configured to provide stateless autoconfiguration information to attached hosts, the transmitted Router Advertisement messages contain IPv6 prefixes for use by the attached hosts (see details in **Chapter 4**).

- **IPv6 Global Unicast Address Generation**: Once the IPv6 host receives a Router Advertisement message with an IPv6 prefix from a router, it generates an IPv6 Global Unicast address for the receiving interface by appending the interface ID (typically in the modified EUI-64 format) to the provided IPv6 prefix as **described in Chapter 3**.
- **IPv6 Duplicate Address Detection**: The host performs IPv6 Duplicate Address Detection again to determine the uniqueness of the newly created IPv6 Global Unicast address.
- **IPv6 Global Unicast Address Assignment**: If the IPv6 address is found to be unique, the host assigns it to the interface.

Phase 2 ensures the IPv6 host has an IPv6 address for global communication with no manual address configuration and minimal intervention from external devices like IPv6 address servers.

5.7.1.2 Stateless DHCPv6 Configuration Process

After an IPv6 host on a link has autoconfigured an IPv6 Global Unicast address on an interface (using SLAAC), it uses Stateless DHCPv6 to obtain other configuration parameters from a DHCPv6 Server. The host (DHCPv6 Client) performs Stateless DHCPv6 if it receives an ICMPv6 Router Advertisement message with the M Flag set to 0 and the O Flag set to 1.

The host performs Stateless DHCPv6 as follows (see also Figure 5.11):

- The DHCPv6 Client sends an INFORMATION-REQUEST message to the Server with the message's destination IPv6 address set to the IPv6 All_DHCP_Relay_Agents_and_ Servers multicast address (FF02::1:2). The message contains the Option Request Option (Option Code 6) specifying the requested configuration parameters.
- The DHCPv6 Server responds by returning a REPLY message to the Client containing the requested configuration parameters.
- The Client receives the REPLY message and checks whether the received configuration parameters match those requested in the INFORMATION-REQUEST message. If the received information is acceptable, the Client uses those parameters for the required

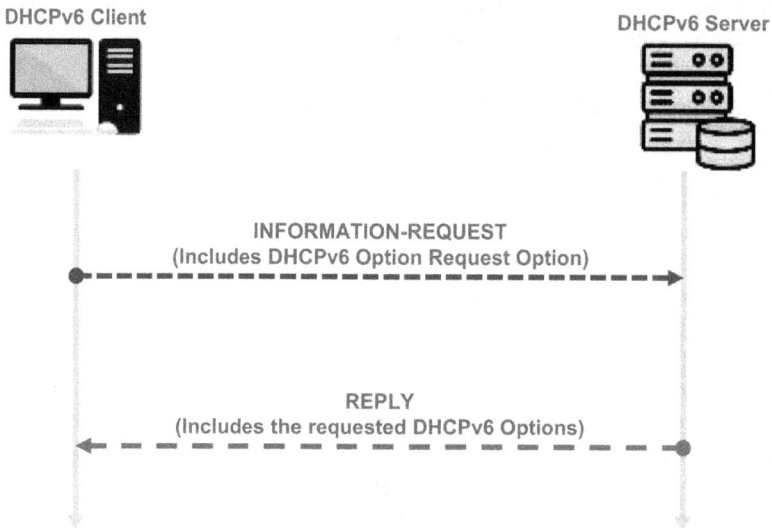

DHCPv6 Client

DHCPv6 Server

INFORMATION-REQUEST
(Includes DHCPv6 Option Request Option)

REPLY
(Includes the requested DHCPv6 Options)

FIGURE 5.11   Stateless DHCPv6 operation.

configuration. Otherwise, the Client ignores the configuration parameters. If the Client receives replies from multiple DHCPv6 Servers with configuration parameters matching those requested in the INFORMATION-REQUEST message, the Client uses the configuration parameters from the first REPLY message received.

Note that a SOLICIT, REQUEST, RENEW, REBIND, or INFORMATION-REQUEST message sent by the Client must include an Option Request Option to inform the Server about the DHCPv6 Options the Client wishes to receive. Table 5.4 in Reference **[RFC8415]** lists the DHCPv6 Option codes that can and cannot be included in the Option Request Option.

5.7.2 DHCPv6 for Non-Temporary Address Assignment

The Stateful DHCPv6 operational model is most suitable for situations where the use of IPv6 SLAAC alone is insufficient or impractical due to any of the following reasons: network policy constraints; IPv6 nodes on a link require additional information due to dynamic updates to the DNS Server; or DHCPv6 Clients have specific addressing and configuration requirements.

To perform non-temporary IPv6 address assignment, the DHCPv6 Server is configured with IPv6 prefixes from which it allocates IPv6 addresses to Clients. The Server is also supplied with any related network topology information that guides the allocation of specific IPv6 prefixes to each link in the network (i.e., which IPv6 prefixes go to which link). A DHCPv6 Client sends a request to the Server for a non-temporary IPv6 address assignment. The Server then selects the appropriate IPv6 address or addresses for the link on which the Client is connected and returns that information to the Client.

For each IPv6 address that the Server assigns to the Client, it associates Preferred and Valid Lifetimes with that address. This association constitutes an agreement between the Server and Client regarding the length of time the Client is allowed to use the allocated IPv6 address. A Client can request the Server to extend the Lifetimes of an allocated IPv6 address. The Client is also required to cease using an IPv6 address if its Valid Lifetime expires. Typically, when requesting IPv6 addresses from the Server, Clients will also request other configuration parameters at the same time, such as DNS Name Server addresses and DNS domain search lists. Clients may also request more than one IPv6 address or set of IPv6 addresses from the DHCPv6 Server.

5.7.3 DHCPv6 for Prefix Delegation

Another Stateful DHCPv6 mode of operation is the DHCPv6 prefix delegation method **[RFC3633]** **[RFC8415]**, which is used for delegating IPv6 prefixes from a DHCPv6 Server (delegating router) to DHCP Clients (requesting routers). This mechanism is suitable for environments in which the delegating router (DHCPv6 Server) does not have knowledge of the topology of the networks attached to the requesting router (DHCP Client) and does not require any information other than the requesting router's identity to allow the delegating router to select an appropriate IPv6 prefix for delegation.

5.7.3.1 Typical Use Case of DHCPv6 Prefix Delegation

An ISP may use this mechanism to delegate an IPv6 prefix to a subscriber. The subscriber receives the delegated IPv6 prefix and may create subnet prefixes to be assigned to the links within the subscriber's network. The following references provide example use cases of the DHCPv6 prefix delegation mechanism: **[RFC7084] [RFC7368] [RFC3769]**. It is important to note that the DHCPv6 prefix delegation mechanism does not necessarily require the DHCPv6 Client to be a router (requesting router) nor the DHCPv6 Server to be a router (delegating router). Figure 5.12 shows the Stateful DHCPv6 message exchange between a Server (configured for DHCPv6 Prefix Delegation) and a Client.

To perform DHCPv6 prefix delegation, the delegating router must first be provisioned with IPv6 prefixes to be delegated to requesting routers. The delegating router can obtain IPv6 prefixes for delegation through the following means:

- **Manual Configuration of IPv6 Prefixes with Static Binding on the Delegating Router**: The DUID of a Client and the associated IPv6 prefixes are statically or manually configured on the delegating router.
- **Using an IPv6 Prefix Pool on the Delegating Router**: The delegating router dynamically allocates IPv6 prefixes from a local IPv6 prefix pool.
- **Delegating Router Consults an External Source for IPv6 Prefix Information**: The delegating router receives IPv6 prefix requests from Clients and consults an external data source, such as a RADIUS Server, for the required information.
- **Delegating Router Runs a Local DHCPv6 Server**: The delegating router operates a local DHCPv6 Server that handles all IPv6 prefix requests from Clients.

As shown in Figure 5.12, a Client sends a request to the Server to obtain delegated IPv6 prefix(es). The Server selects appropriate IPv6 prefix(es) for delegation and sends that information to the Client. Upon receiving the delegated IPv6 prefixes, the Client is responsible for assigning IPv6 addresses and/or subnets from the delegated IPv6 prefix(es) to its downstream interfaces. For example, the Client may assign several IPv6 subnet prefixes from a delegated IPv6 prefix to some of its interfaces and start transmitting ICMPv6 Router Advertisement messages for those IPv6 prefixes on the attached links.

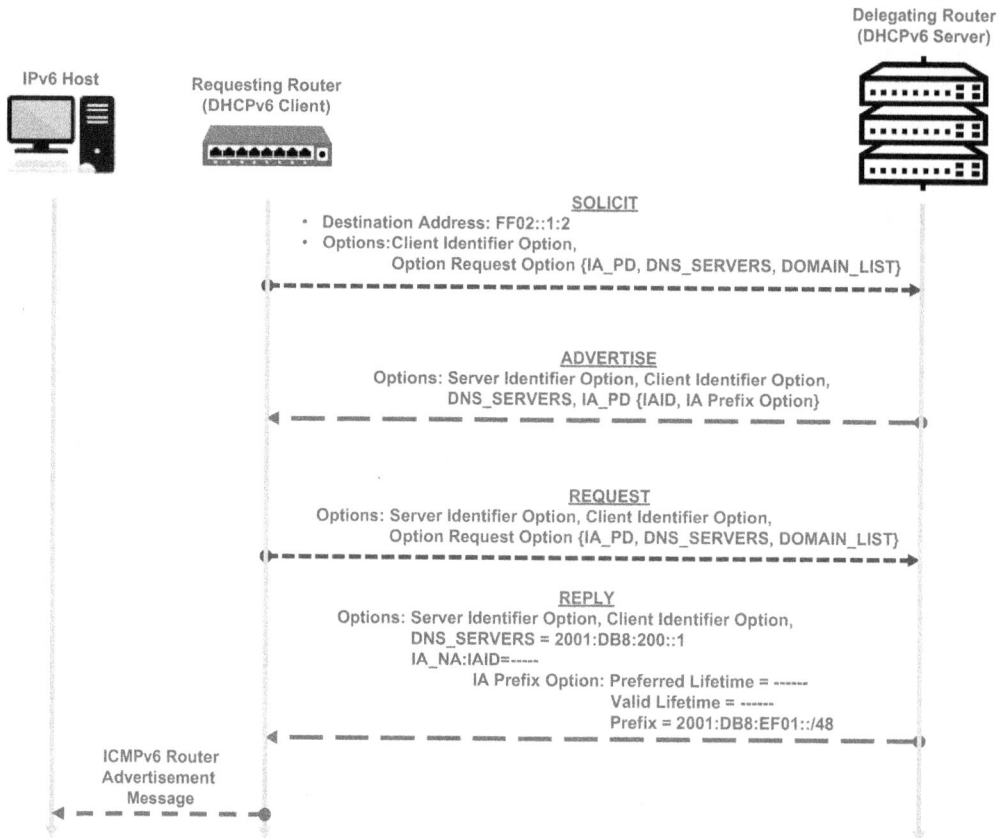

FIGURE 5.12 DHCPv6 prefix delegation message exchange.

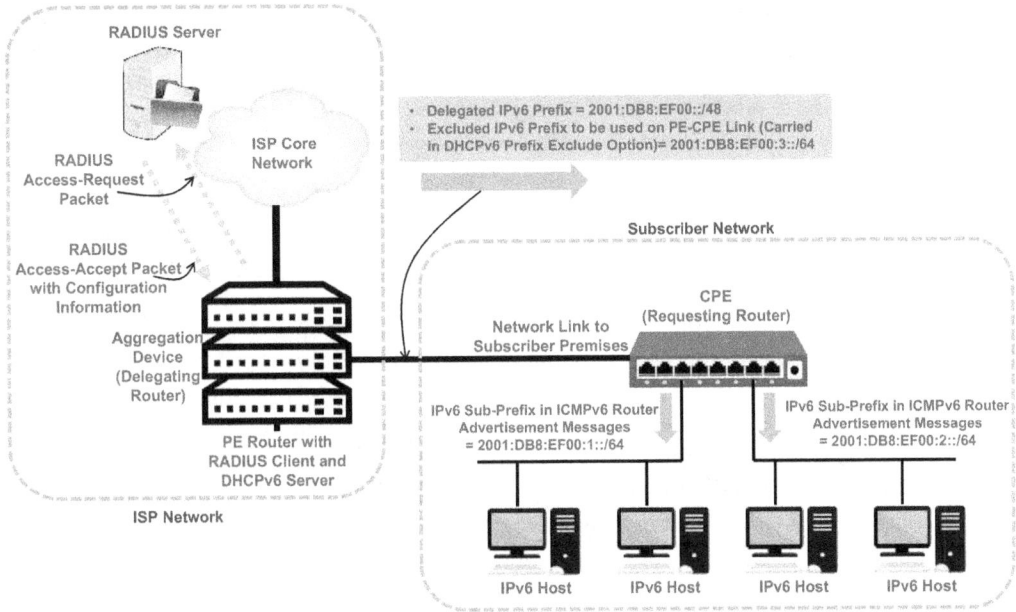

FIGURE 5.13   Example DHCPv6 prefix delegation network.

When the Server delegates an IPv6 prefix, it assigns Preferred and Valid Lifetimes for the prefix. These Lifetimes constitute an agreement between the Server and Client regarding the length of time the Client is allowed to use the delegated IPv6 prefix. A Client can request the Server to extend the Lifetimes of a delegated IPv6 prefix and is required to stop using the delegated prefix if its Valid Lifetime expires.

5.7.3.2   DHCPv6 Prefix Delegation in a Service Provider Network

Figure 5.13 shows an example network architecture that uses DHCPv6 prefix delegation. In this architecture, the DHCPv6 Server (delegating router) is provisioned with a set of IPv6 prefixes that it assigns to each customer when connecting to the ISP network. The DHCPv6 Server initiates the DHCPv6 prefix delegation process when the Client (requesting router) sends a request through DHCPv6 for configuration information. The Server receives the DHCPv6 messages from the Client (residing in the ISP aggregation device). Upon receiving the Client's request, the Server selects an available IPv6 prefix or prefixes to be delegated to the Client and uses DHCPv6 to return the delegated IPv6 prefix or prefixes to the Client.

The Client (subscriber) receives the delegated IPv6 prefix, creates appropriate subnet prefixes, and assigns them to links in the subscriber's network. In Figure 5.13, the Client may subnet a single delegated /48 IPv6 prefix into /64 IPv6 subnet prefixes and assign a /64 IPv6 subnet prefix to each of the attached links in the subscriber network. The DHCPv6 Server may use the DHCPv6 Prefix Delegation Options (i.e., the IA for Prefix Delegation Option with Option Code 25) **[RFC3633]** **[RFC8415]** along with other DHCPv6 Options to send configuration information to the Client.

The DHCP Client (requesting router) may, in turn, provide DHCPv6 services to IPv6 nodes residing on the links attached to it (i.e., to IPv6 devices on its internal network). For example, the ISP's DHCPv6 Server (delegating router) may supply the addresses of DNS and NTP Servers to the Client (requesting router), and then the DHCPv6 Server within the requesting router will pass that configuration information to the IPv6 hosts on the subscriber network.

When using a delegated IPv6 prefix to configure IPv6 addresses on its own interfaces or on other IPv6 nodes on attached links, the Client (requesting router) must ensure that the Preferred and Valid

Lifetimes of those IPv6 addresses are not greater than the remaining Preferred and Valid Lifetimes, respectively, for the delegated IPv6 prefix at any time. In particular, if the Client derived a delegated IPv6 prefix, or an IPv6 prefix from the IPv6 prefix delegated to it, and the Client in turn advertises those derived prefixes to other hosts for SLAAC **[RFC4862]**, the Client must not set the advertised Preferred and Valid Lifetimes greater than the corresponding remaining Lifetimes of the original delegated IPv6 prefix.

5.7.3.3   The DHCPv6 Prefix Delegation Process

The DHCPv6 prefix delegation process (shown in Figure 5.13) can be described as follows:

1. The CPE generates an IPv6 Link-Local address on the interface leading to the PE by appending the interface ID to the IPv6 Link-Local prefix (FE80::/10). This IPv6 Link-Local address is used for communication with the PE (the IPv6 prefix delegating router).
2. The CPE transmits a DHCPv6 SOLICIT message that includes an IA_PD Option to the PE.
3. The PE selects an IPv6 prefix for the CPE using information obtained from a local IPv6 prefix pool or from an external source (e.g., a RADIUS Server).
4. The PE sends an ADVERTISE message to the CPE. This message includes the delegated IPv6 prefix, an IA_PD Option (Option Code 25), and an IA_PD Prefix Option (Option Code 26). The value in the "prefix-length" field of the IA_PD Prefix Option may be 48. The Server can also add other configuration information in the ADVERTISE message, such as a maximum Lease time.
5. The CPE transmits a REQUEST message to the PE to request the IPv6 prefix that was advertised in the ADVERTISE message.
6. The PE uses a REPLY message to return the delegated IPv6 prefix to the CPE. This REPLY message also contains the delegated IPv6 prefix, an IA_PD Option, and an IA_PD Prefix Option. The Server may set the value in the "prefix-length" field of the IA_PD Prefix Option to 48. The Server can also add other configuration information in the REPLY message, such as a maximum Lease time.
7. The CPE receives the REPLY message and uses the delegated IPv6 prefix to allocate IPv6 Global Unicast addresses to devices on its attached links. The CPE may use ICMPv6 Router Advertisement messages, DHCPv6, or a combination of these two methods to allocate IPv6 addresses to devices on its attached links.

In an IPv6 network where the CPE is under the direct control of the service provider, the CPE can use a sub-prefix from the delegated IPv6 prefix to create an IPv6 address on its loopback interface and use this IPv6 address for communicating with the PE. This IPv6 loopback address can be used to manage the CPE and also as the source IPv6 address of packets when the CPE communicates with the PE.

5.7.3.3.1   *Configuring a Black Hole Route on the Requesting Router*

In Figure 5.13, the CPE may transmit ICMPv6 Router Advertisement messages on its downstream links, advertising IPv6 sub-prefixes (generated from the delegated prefix) to attached hosts. Note that a single link connects the CPE to the PE. This means the CPE can simply configure a default route in its IPv6 routing table, pointing to the PE. The default route points to the IPv6 address of the PE's downlink interface as the next-hop. The CPE also configures a */48 route* (called a *black hole route*) toward its *Null0 interface* for the delegated IPv6 prefix to ensure that it has (i.e., owns) routing information for the entire delegated IPv6 prefix address block (see discussion on Null0 interface and black hole route on page 100 of **[CISCPOPOC]**).

Without this black hole route, the CPE (requesting router) will forward IPv6 packets along the default route to the PE for parts of the delegated /48 prefix that the CPE has not yet configured on its links. The PE (delegating router) also has a routing entry for the delegated /48 prefix toward the CPE in its IPv6 routing table, which means that without the black hole route, there could be a routing loop on the PE-CPE link. The delegating router can insert the delegated IPv6 prefix assigned to the CPE as a static route with the next-hop being the IPv6 Link-Layer address of the CPE's uplink. Additionally, the delegating router records and maintains state for all the IPv6 prefixes delegated to its requesting routers in a *binding database*.

5.7.3.4 IPv6 Prefix Exclusion during DHCPv6 Prefix Delegation: Using the DHCPv6 Prefix Exclude Option

When strictly following the DHCPv6 prefix delegation mechanism defined in **[RFC3633]**, a requesting router (the CPE in Figure 5.13) cannot use an IPv6 sub-prefix derived from a delegated IPv6 prefix (assigned by the delegating router (the PE)) on the link connecting the two routers. This limitation means the delegating router has to assign two routes (i.e., two IPv6 prefixes) to the requesting router. One route (IPv6 prefix) is the delegated IPv6 prefix itself, which the requesting router (CPE) uses for the customer links behind it. The other route (IPv6 prefix) is for the link connecting the delegating router and the requesting router.

To overcome this limitation, **[RFC6603]** defined the DHCPv6 Prefix Exclude Option (Option Code 67), which allows one specific IPv6 prefix to be excluded from a delegated IPv6 prefix set when using the DHCPv6 prefix delegation mechanism. The requesting router uses the excluded IPv6 prefix (from the delegated IPv6 prefix) on the link between itself and the delegating router. This excluded IPv6 prefix is intended for use in the Layer 2 domain between the requesting router and the delegating router.

When excluding an IPv6 prefix during DHCPv6 prefix delegation, the requesting router includes the Option Request Option (Option Code 6) with the Prefix Exclude Option in a SOLICIT, REQUEST, RENEW, or REBIND message to inform the delegating router of its desire to support DHCPv6 prefix delegation with IPv6 prefix exclusion. When the delegating router receives any of these messages and finds the Prefix Exclude Option in an Option Request Option, it determines the specific IPv6 prefix to be excluded. The length of the excluded IPv6 prefix must be longer than that of the delegated IPv6 prefix (since it is a sub-prefix). The delegating router then adds the excluded IPv6 prefix in an IA Prefix Option (Option Code 26) to be returned to the requesting router. Any DHCPv6 Relay Agent on the path to the delegating router (Server) forwards the Prefix Exclude Option to the Server and also relays the excluded IPv6 prefix (assigned by the Server) back to the requesting router (Client).

Typically, the server administrator configures the IPv6 prefix length to be excluded from a delegated IPv6 prefix set pool on the delegating router (Server). The requesting router uses this prefix on the link leading to the delegating router. The length of the excluded IPv6 prefix is larger than that of the delegated IPv6 prefix length. For example, given the delegated IPv6 prefix 2001:DB8:EF00::/48, the server administrator may configure the excluded IPv6 prefix to be 2001:DB8:EF00:3::/64 for the delegated prefix. The excluded IPv6 prefix shares the same Preferred and Valid Lifetime as the delegated IPv6 prefix.

The server administrator may configure a Server to support the inclusion of the Prefix Exclude Option in the RECONFIGURE messages sent to Clients. Thus, in the case where the Server (delegating router) wants a Client (requesting router) to have the choice of requesting that an IPv6 prefix be excluded after reconfiguration, the Server sends a RECONFIGURE message with the Prefix Exclude Option added in an Option Request Option.

5.7.4 DHCPv6 for Customer Edge Routers

This DHCPv6 operational model combines the DHCPv6 for Non-temporary Address Assignment model and the DHCPv6 prefix delegation mechanism. In general, this model assumes that non-temporary IPv6 addresses and delegated IPv6 prefixes will be assigned when the DHCPv6 Client initiates a single set of transactions (i.e., a single set of DHCPv6 message exchanges) with the Server, or their Lifetimes can be extended through a single set of transactions. Reference **[RFC7084]** describes the DHCPv6 requirements and network architecture for customer edge routers.

A network provider may use DHCPv6 Prefix Delegation to automate IPv6 prefix assignment in its networks. This allows the network provider to centrally control IPv6 addressing. A network deploying DHCPv6 Prefix Delegation often uses Relay Relays between the CPE devices and the PE devices. Once a Server in the network delegates IPv6 prefixes to its customers, the customers can in turn assign IPv6 prefixes from the delegated IPv6 prefixes to their internal links.

Network providers use a combination of the following DHCPv6 features (**already discussed above and in Chapter 4**) to manage customer addressing, subnetting, and updates to link addressing:

- A network provider may use DHCPv6 Prefix Delegation to automate IPv6 prefix assignment in its networks. This allows the network provider to centrally control IPv6 addressing. A network deploying DHCPv6 Prefix Delegation often uses Relay Relays between the CPE devices and the PE devices. Once a Server in the network delegates IPv6 prefixes to its customers, the customers can in turn assign IPv6 prefixes from the delegated IPv6 prefixes to their internal links.
- Nodes can use Stateful DHCPv6 to obtain all IPv6 addressing information, as well as other configuration information. A DHCPv6 Server centrally manages all IPv6 address and prefix assignments, and DHCPv6 Clients obtain IPv6 addresses and/or prefix information from the Server. DHCPv6 Clients can obtain configuration information such as DNS and NTP Server addresses.

5.7.5 DHCPv6 FOR IPv6 TEMPORARY ADDRESSES

The concept of configuring IPv6 Temporary Addresses on IPv6 host interfaces was introduced to address privacy concerns associated with using IPv6 SLAAC and interface IDs based on the modified EUI-64 interface addressing mechanism (see **[RFC8981]**), **see the discussion in Chapter 4**. This DHCPv6 operational model allows DHCPv6 to assign IPv6 Temporary Addresses when the Client is using IPv6 Stateful DHCPv6 address assignment.

The use of Temporary Address assignment is similar to non-temporary address assignment. However, a Client is generally expected to use either of these two address types for only a short period and is not anticipated to request an extension of their Lifetimes, although a Client may request an extension from the Server.

5.7.6 MULTIPLE IPv6 ADDRESSES AND PREFIXES

This DHCPv6 operational model allows a Client to request and receive multiple IPv6 addresses. In a typical DHCPv6 operation, a Client transmits only one instance of an IA_NA Option to the Server, and the Server responds by assigning no more than one IPv6 address from each IPv6 prefix (assigned to the Client's link) to the Client. Specifically, the Server can be configured to allocate IPv6 addresses from multiple IPv6 prefixes assigned to a given link. This IPv6 address assignment method is useful in scenarios such as when a network address renumbering process is in progress. Typically, when DHCPv6 is deployed, the Server will assign only one IPv6 address for each IA_NA Option.

A DHCPv6 Client can explicitly request the Server to grant multiple IPv6 addresses by transmitting multiple IA_NA Options (and/or IA_TA Options). The Client can transmit multiple IA_NA (and/or IA_TA) Options in its initial transmissions to the Server. Alternatively, the DHCPv6 Client may choose to send an additional REQUEST message to the Server carrying new IA_NA (and/or IA_TA) Options, or the Client can include these additional Options in a RENEW message.

For IPv6 prefix delegation, this DHCPv6 mode allows a DHCPv6 Client to request the Server to delegate new IPv6 prefixes by sending additional IA_PD Options to the Server. However, a network operator would typically prefer to allow the DHCPv6 Server to delegate a single, larger IPv6 prefix to the Client. Most DHCPv6 deployments would permit the Client, in its initial transmissions, to request the Server to grant a larger IPv6 prefix rather than having the Client request additional

IPv6 prefixes at a later time. The DHCPv6 policy used by the Server for granting additional IPv6 addresses and prefixes is specific to the network operator.

5.8 UNDERSTANDING THE MAIN DIFFERENCES BETWEEN DHCPv6 AND DHCPv4

DHCPv4 and DHCPv6, like IPv4 and IPv6, have their similarities and differences. Table 5.4 presents the main differences between DHCPv6 [**RFC8415**] and DHCPv4 [**RFC2131**]. The main differences are primarily in the following areas:

- Message types, formats, and addresses used by DHCP Clients, Servers, and Relay Agents
- The way Clients and Servers are identified
- The UDP ports used for sending and receiving DHCP messages
- The data structures used for requesting, assigning, and managing IP addresses/prefixes, and the message exchange processes used
- The role of the IP router in host configuration

TABLE 5.4
Main Differences between DHCPv6 and DHCPv4

Feature	DHCPv6	DHCPv4
Destination IP addresses	The destination IPv6 address of a DHCPv6 message is usually a multicast address. The Client and Server may use an IPv6 unicast (Link-Local) address as the destination address when unicast delivery is negotiated.	The destination IPv4 address of a Client's DHCPv4 message is usually a broadcast address. A Server attempts to deliver DHCPOFFER, DHCPACK, and DHCPNAK messages directly to the Client using unicast delivery (using the "yiaddr" address). The Server uses broadcast delivery when unicast is not possible.
Source IP addresses	The source IPv6 address of a DHCPv6 message is set to the IPv6 Link-Local address of the sending interface.	DHCPv4 messages that are broadcast by a Client prior to obtaining its IPv4 address must have the source IPv4 address field set to 0. A Server uses its configured IPv4 as the source IPv4 address. After IPv4 address assignment, a Client may use its IPv4 unicast address as the source address.
UDP port number	DHCPv6 Clients receive DHCPv6 messages on UDP port 546. DHCPv6 Servers and Relay Agents receive DHCPv6 messages on UDP port 547.	DHCPv4 messages from a Client to a Server are sent to UDP port 67, and DHCPv4 messages from a Server to a Client are sent to UDP port 68.
DHCP Unique Identifier (DUID)	Each Client or Server has a DUID. A Server and a Client use their DUIDs to identify each other. The Client DUID is carried in the Client Identifier Option, while the Server DUID is carried in the Server Identifier Option.	The "server identifier" Option is used both to identify a Server in a DHCPv4 message and as a destination IPv4 address from Clients to Servers. The "client identifier" Option is used to pass an explicit Client identifier to a Server.
Identity Association (IA)	The Client uses an IAID to identify an IA, which is a construct through which a Server and a Client can identify, group, and manage a set of related IPv6 addresses/prefixes.	The Client chooses a Transaction ID (xid), a random number, which the Client and Server use to associate messages and responses between the Client and Server.
Four-message exchange	Uses the SARR messages: SOLICIT (S), ADVERTISE (A), REQUEST (R), and REPLY (R).	Uses the DORA messages: DHCPDISCOVER (D), DHCPOFFER (O), DHCPREQUEST (R), and DHCPACK (A).
Two-message exchange	Uses INFORMATION-REQUEST and REPLY messages, or SOLICIT (with DHCPv6 Rapid Commit Option) and REPLY messages.	Not supported.

The IP addresses on IPv4 nodes can either be statically configured or dynamically configured through DHCPv4. IPv6 nodes support several methods of assigning and configuring IPv6 addresses on interfaces. The IPv6 address of IPv6 nodes can also be statically configured or dynamically configured using two dynamic IPv6 address configuration methods: SLAAC (with or without Stateless DHCPv6) or Stateful DHCPv6. Both DHCPv4 and DHCPv6 have the same functional components: Client, Server, and Relay Agent. Both protocols also share the concept of a Server leasing IP addresses/prefixes to Clients.

The following elaborates on the DHCPv4 discussion in Table 5.4:

- DHCPv4 Clients send their DHCPDISCOVER and DHCPREQUEST messages as broadcasts. All other nodes on the local network segment receive the DHCPv4 message and process it to determine if they need to respond. A DHCPv4 Relay Agent will receive these unsolicited DHCPv4 broadcasts and forward them to the DHCPv4 Server.
- In both DHCPv4 and DHCPv6, a host (Client) faces the "chicken or the egg" dilemma, as it needs a source IP address to send an IP packet to a DHCP Server to obtain a unicast IP address for normal IP operation. The host requires a source IP address for its initial DHCP communication with a Server.
  - DHCPv4 Clients solve the "chicken or the egg" problem by using 0.0.0.0 as their initial source IPv4 address when sending DHCPDISCOVER and DHCPREQUEST messages. DHCPv6 Clients, on the other hand, use the IPv6 Link-Local address of the sending interface as the source address for all DHCPv6 messages. A Stateful DHCPv6 Client does not receive its IPv6 Global Unicast address until the full DHCPv6 four-way message exchange is completed.
  - DHCPv4 Clients rely on broadcasts to send DHCPDISCOVER and DHCPREQUEST messages to the Server or Relay Agent. A DHCPv4 Server or Relay Agent may use an IPv4 unicast address to respond to the Client. The DHCPv4 Client receives its allocated IPv4 address in the DHCPOFFER message, with the message's destination set to the allocated IPv4 address. DHCPv6 Clients primarily use well-known multicast addresses to contact Servers and Relay Agents but can also use a Server's IPv6 unicast address.
- A DHCPv4 Client uses its Link-Layer (MAC) address to identify itself. A DHCPv4 Server notes the Client's MAC address and associates the IPv4 address Lease with it. DHCPv6 uses a DUID to identify a Client. Servers are also identified by their DUIDs.

Both DHCPv4 and DHCPv6 support static assignment/reservation of IP addresses. DHCPv4 can create a fixed IPv4 address binding based on the Client's MAC address. DHCPv6 uses the Client's DUID for static binding to an IPv6 address/prefix.

Both DHCPv4 and DHCPv6 use Options, but there are some differences in how they handle them. DHCPv4 and DHCPv6 Clients and Servers use Options to send additional configuration information during IP address/prefix assignments. Some DHCPv6 Options are functionally equivalent to DHCPv4 Options.

IPv6 nodes on a link, use ICMPv6 Router Advertisement messages for IPv6 router discovery. Each IPv6 router sends these messages to the link-local IPv6 All-Nodes multicast address (FF02::1). An IPv6 router sends the Router Advertisement messages with the "Managed Address Configuration" (M) Flag set to "1" to indicate to Clients on a link to use Stateful DHCPv6 for IPv6 address/prefix assignment, as well as to obtain other configuration parameters. IPv4 does not have an equivalent IPv6 router discovery function (as described in **Chapter 4**). An IPv4 Client obtains its default gateway router through DHCPv4. A DHCPv4 Client that starts up has to broadcast a DHCPDISCOVER message to initiate the IPv4 address and default gateway assignment process.

For high-availability DHCP Server services (in case a DHCP Server fails), DHCPv4 supports the "DHC Load Balancing Algorithm" **[RFC3074]**, while DHCPv6 supports the "DHCPv6 Failover Protocol" **[RFC8156]**. In **[RFC8156]**, typically, two DHCPv6 Servers are deployed, one as the active primary Server and the other as the passive secondary Server (hot standby). The two DHCPv6

Servers are configured in an active–passive mode (or hot standby configuration), where, during normal DHCPv6 operation, one Server is active (and actively responds to DHCPv6 requests from Clients), while the second is passive (and receives requests from DHCPv6 clients but responds only to requests specifically directed to it). The secondary Server is passive but maintains a copy of the DHCPv6 binding database from the active Server and is ready to take over processing all incoming Client requests if the primary Server fails.

5.8.1 COMPARISON BETWEEN DHCPv6 AND DHCPv4 MESSAGES (SARR VERSUS DORA MESSAGES)

Table 5.5 shows the basic DHCPv6 messages and their corresponding DHCPv4 message counterparts (see DHCPv4 in [RFC2131]). The basic DHCPv6 messages and message exchange process (SOLICIT (S), ADVERTISE (A), REQUEST (R), and REPLY (R)) are sometimes referred to as the "SARR" process or exchange, while their DHCPv4 message counterparts and message exchange process (DHCPDISCOVER (D), DHCPOFFER (O), DHCPREQUEST (R), and DHCPACK (A)) are referred to as the "DORA" process. Table 5.6 describes the different messages used by DHCPv4.

TABLE 5.5
Basic DHCPv6 Messages and Their Corresponding DHCPv4 Messages (SARR versus DORA Messages)

DHCPv6 Messages	Description	Equivalent DHCPv4 Messages
SOLICIT (S)	Sent by a DHCPv6 Client to locate DHCPv6 Servers.	DHCPDISCOVER (D)
ADVERTISE (A)	Sent by a DHCPv6 Server to a DHCPv6 Client in response to a SOLICIT message to confirm that DHCPv6 services are available to the DHCPv6 Client.	DHCPOFFER (O)
REQUEST (R)	Sent by a DHCPv6 Client to a DHCPv6 Server to request configuration information (IPv6 addresses and other parameters).	DHCPREQUEST (R)
REPLY (R)	Sent by a DHCPv6 Server to a DHCPv6 Client with the requested configuration information.	DHCPACK (A)

TABLE 5.6
DHCPv4 Messages

DHCPv4 Messages	Description
DHCPDISCOVER	Sent by a DHCPv4 Client as a broadcast to locate available DHCPv4 Servers.
DHCPOFFER	Sent by a Server to a Client in response to a DHCPDISCOVER message with an offer of configuration parameters.
DHCPREQUEST	Sent by a Client to Servers either (a) requesting parameters offered by one Server, and implicitly declining offers from all others, (b) confirming the correctness of a previously allocated address after, e.g., system reboot, or (c) extending the Lease on a particular IPv4 address.
DHCPACK	Sent by a Server to a Client with configuration parameters, including committed IPv4 address.
DHCPNAK	Sent by a Server to a Client indicating that the Client's notion of the IPv4 address is incorrect (e.g., the Client has moved to a new subnet), or the Client's Lease has expired.
DHCPDECLINE	Sent by a Client to a Server indicating that an IPv4 address is already in use.
DHCPRELEASE	Sent by a Client to a Server relinquishing an IPv4 address and canceling the remaining Lease.
DHCPINFORM	Sent by a Client to a Server, requesting only local configuration parameters; the Client already has an externally configured IPv4 address.

5.8.2   ROLE OF IP ROUTERS IN HOST CONFIGURATION: IPv4 ROUTERS VERSUS IPv6 ROUTERS

A Stateful DHCPv6 Server is designed to maintain IPv6 addresses and "other information" that can be provided to IPv6 hosts. This Server also tracks the state of each assigned IPv6 address (while resolving duplicate address conflicts) and the IPv6 addresses still available in the address pool. Additionally, the Server logs and monitors the expiration times of all assigned IPv6 addresses.

However, the main difference between DHCPv6 **[RFC8415]** *and DHCPv4* **[RFC2131]** *is as follows: In IPv4, the DHCPv4 Server typically provides default gateway addresses to IPv4 hosts, whereas in IPv6, only IPv6 routers provide the default gateway address dynamically through the Router Advertisement messages they send.*

Recall that a Stateless DHCPv6 Server does not allocate IPv6 addresses to IPv6 Clients at all. IPv6 nodes can only obtain "other information," such as a DNS Server list and a domain name, from a Stateless DHCPv6 Server. When used in conjunction with SLAAC, IPv6 nodes can autoconfigure IPv6 Global Unicast addresses and then obtain other information from the Stateless DHCPv6 Server. This Server is "stateless" because it does not assign IPv6 addresses/prefixes nor keep track of the addresses/prefixes that have been assigned to IPv6 hosts or the addresses/prefixes that are still available for assignment.

In IPv4, routers do not participate in addressing IPv4 hosts. However, in IPv6, routers on a link can actively and dynamically participate in addressing IPv6 hosts on that link. In both Stateless and Stateful DHCPv6, an IPv6 router sends Router Advertisement messages to advertise its presence on a link. These Router Advertisement messages allow an attached IPv6 router to play the following important role in IPv6 host configuration:

- **An IPv6 Host on a Link Sets Its Default Gateway Based on Received Router Advertisement Messages**: If only one IPv6 router is attached to the link, the IPv6 host uses the source address of the Router Advertisement messages as its default gateway address. If multiple IPv6 routers are attached to the link, the Pref (Router Preference) Flag bits in the Router Advertisement messages may be set to Low, Medium, or High, allowing the IPv6 host to set its default gateway to the source address of the Router Advertisement messages with the highest preference value (see details in **Chapter 4**).
- **Router Advertisement Messages Contain Information That Indicate to IPv6 Hosts on a Link How to Proceed with Address Configuration**: Three flags in the Router Advertisement messages define how IPv6 hosts on a link can dynamically configure addresses:
  - **M Flag**: If set to 1, indicates to IPv6 hosts that they can obtain a Global Unicast address, as well as, DNS and a domain name from a Stateful DHCPv6 Server. In this case, IPv6 hosts do not use auto-addressing through SLAAC on the interface, and *both the A Flag and the O Flag are set to 0.*
  - **O Flag**: If set to 1, indicates to IPv6 hosts that they can obtain a DNS Server list and domain name information from a Stateless DHCPv6 Server, but IPv6 addressing information is not provided. Setting this flag to 1 means SLAAC is used for auto-addressing, and both the A Flag and the O Flag are set to 1.
  - **A Flag**: If set to 1, indicates to IPv6 hosts that they can auto-generate an IPv6 Global Unicast address using SLAAC. Setting this flag to 0 means IPv6 hosts on the link cannot use autoconfiguration (SLAAC) for IPv6 addresses.

5.9   DHCPv6 AUTHENTICATION

Reference **[RFC8415]** describes two security mechanisms for the authentication of DHCPv6 messages:

- Using IPSec for the authentication (and encryption) of DHCPv6 message exchanges between Servers and Relay Agents.
- Protection against the misconfiguration of a Client caused by a malicious DHCPv6 Server sending a RECONFIGURE message.

Reference [RFC8213] describes in detail how IPSec is used by Relay Agents and Servers when exchanging DHCPv6 messages.

DHCPv6 participants use the Authentication Option (Option Code 11) for the authentication of DHCPv6 messages. The Authentication Option carries authentication information that is used to reliably identify the originator of a DHCPv6 message and to ensure that the contents of the DHCPv6 message have not been tampered with. The Authentication Option is defined so that DHCPv6 can use multiple authentication protocols. The Reconfiguration Key Authentication Protocol (RKAP) defined in [RFC8415] is one such protocol. No DHCPv6 message is allowed to include more than one Authentication Option.

The Authentication Option has the following important fields [RFC8415]:

- A 1-byte "protocol" field contains a value that identifies the specific authentication protocol used to generate the authentication information included in the Option.
- A 1-byte "algorithm" field contains a value that identifies the specific algorithm used in the authentication protocol specified in the "protocol" field. For example, the algorithm may be a hash algorithm used to generate a Message Authentication Code to be included in the Option.
- A 1-byte "replay detection method (RDM)" field specifies the replay detection method used in the Option.
- An 8-byte "replay detection" field contains the replay detection information obtained from the RDM.
- A variable-length "authentication information" field contains the authentication information obtained from the authentication protocol and algorithm specified in the Option.

5.9.1 REPLAY DETECTION

The type of replay detection used in the Authentication Option is placed in the "RDM" field of the Option. If the value in the "RDM" field is set to 0x00, the sender of the Authentication Option must set the "replay detection" field to a value obtained from a strictly monotonically increasing 64-bit unsigned integer function (modulo 2^{64}). The goal of this technique is to reduce the chances of replay attacks. Reference [RFC8415] requires this method to be supported by all authentication protocols used in the Authentication Option. One possible strictly monotonically increasing 64-bit unsigned integer function is a 64-bit value in the NTP timestamp format [RFC5905].

When a Client receives a DHCPv6 message from a Server with the "RDM" field set to 0x00, the Client compares the Authentication Option's "replay detection" field with the value in the previous Option sent by the same Server (identified by the Server Identifier Option in the message). The Client only accepts the DHCPv6 message if the received "RDM" field value is greater. The Client then records this value as the new value if the "RDM" field value is accepted. If this is the first Authentication Option sent by a Server to be processed by the Client, the Client records the value in the Option's "replay detection" field and skips the replay detection check.

Servers that support the DHCPv6 reconfigure mechanism must retain the value in the "replay detection" field of the received Authentication Option between restarts. Failure to retain the "replay detection" field value may cause Clients to reject RECONFIGURE messages sent by the Server, effectively rendering the reconfigure mechanism useless.

5.9.2 RECONFIGURATION KEY AUTHENTICATION PROTOCOL (RKAP)

A malicious DHCPv6 Server may send a RECONFIGURE message that can misconfigure a Client. RKAP provides protection against attacks such as a malicious DHCPv6 Server using a RECONFIGURE message to mount a denial-of-service or man-in-the-middle attack on a Client.

Using RKAP, a DHCPv6 Server, in the initial exchange of DHCPv6 messages with a Client, sends a Reconfigure Key to the Client. The Client receives the Reconfigure Key and records it for authenticating subsequent RECONFIGURE messages sent by the Server. The Server then computes a Hashed Message Authentication Code (HMAC) from the Reconfigure Key and includes the HMAC in subsequent RECONFIGURE messages sent to the Client.

The Server sends the Reconfigure Key and the HMAC in subsequent RECONFIGURE messages to the Client as data in the "authentication information" field of an Authentication Option. The Server initiates the use of RKAP only if the Server and Client have negotiated to use RECONFIGURE messages. Reference **[RFC8415]** describes the format of the authentication information for RKAP.

The fields in an Authentication Option for RKAP are set as follows: "protocol" field=3, "algorithm" field=1, "RDM" field=0. The "authentication information" field for RKAP has a 1-byte "Type" field and a 16-byte "Value" field. The "Type" field is set to 1 to indicate a Reconfigure Key value in the "authentication information" field (used in the REPLY message), and set to 2 to indicate an HMAC-MD5 digest of the DHCPv6 message (used in the RECONFIGURE message).

It is important to note that RKAP can be compromised when an attacker intercepts the initial DHCPv6 message in which the Server sends the Reconfigure Key value to the Client "in plain text". Security mechanisms such as those described in **[RFC7610]** and **[RFC7513]** can be used to mitigate many of these attacks by rogue DHCPv6 Servers.

5.9.3 DHCPv6 Server Considerations for RKAP

When initiating a REQUEST/REPLY, SOLICIT/REPLY, or INFORMATION-REQUEST/REPLY message exchange with a Client, the Server selects a Reconfigure Key for the Client. The Server stores the Reconfigure Key and places a copy of that Key in an Authentication Option in the REPLY message sent to the Client. The 128-bit long Reconfigure Key chosen by the Server must be a cryptographically strong random or pseudorandom number that is hard to predict.

The Server selects a replay detection value according to the selected RDM to authenticate a RECONFIGURE message and uses the Reconfigure Key to compute an HMAC-MD5 over the RECONFIGURE message sent to the Client. The Server sets the HMAC-MD5 field in the Authentication Option to 0 while computing the HMAC-MD5. The HMAC-MD5 is computed over the entire RECONFIGURE message, including the Authentication Option. The Server then places the computed HMAC-MD5 in the "authentication information" field of an Authentication Option included in the RECONFIGURE message sent to the Client.

5.9.4 DHCPv6 Client Considerations for RKAP

The Client receives the initial REPLY message from the Server and extracts the Reconfigure Key from the included Authentication Option. The Client records the Reconfigure Key for authenticating subsequent RECONFIGURE messages sent by the Server.

When authenticating a RECONFIGURE message, the Client sets the HMAC-MD5 field in the Authentication Option to 0 and uses the Reconfigure Key received from the Server to compute an HMAC-MD5 over the received RECONFIGURE message. If the Client finds that the computed HMAC-MD5 matches the value in the received Authentication Option, it accepts the Server's RECONFIGURE message.

5.10 WHAT IS DHCPv6 SNOOPING?

DHCPv6 Snooping (typically implemented on a Layer 2 switch) ensures that DHCPv6 Clients receive IPv6 addresses/prefixes only from authorized DHCPv6 Servers on a network for security purposes (see Figure 5.14). The DHCPv6 Snooping switch examines packets passing through it, records the IPv6-to-MAC address bindings of DHCPv6 Clients (as DHCPv6 Snooping address entries in a local database), and also records the IPv6 prefix-to-port bindings of the DHCPv6 Clients (referred to as DHCPv6 Snooping prefix entries in the database). The DHCPv6 Snooping switch reads DHCPv6 messages exchanged between Clients and Servers to create and update DHCPv6 Snooping database entries, which include Ethernet MAC addresses of Clients, the IPv6 addresses/prefixes obtained by the Clients, the switch ports that connect to Clients, and VLANs to which the switch ports belong.

A DHCPv6 Snooping switch designates switch ports as trusted and untrusted to ensure that only DHCPv6 messages (IPv6 addresses/prefixes) from authorized DHCPv6 Servers reach Clients:

- **Trusted Port**: This is a switch port on a DHCPv6 Snooping switch that can correctly forward DHCPv6 messages from authorized DHCPv6 Servers to Clients. The trusted port forwards DHCPv6 response messages from the DHCPv6 Server to the Client.
- **Untrusted Port**: This switch port discards DHCPv6 messages received from unauthorized DHCPv6 Servers to prevent Clients from obtaining malicious or unauthorized DHCPv6 information.

The network administrator configures the DHCPv6 Snooping switch ports leading to the authorized DHCPv6 Server as trusted ports and configures all other switch ports as untrusted. Trusted ports and ports connected to Clients must be configured to be in the same VLAN or IPv6 subnet (i.e., they must be in the same Layer 2 broadcast domain). DHCPv6 Snooping is used between a DHCPv6 Client and a Server or between a Client and a DHCPv6 Relay Agent. DHCPv6 Snooping is not used between a DHCPv6 Server and a Relay Agent.

A DHCPv6 Snooping switch reads REPLY messages received from trusted ports and REQUEST messages from Clients to create DHCPv6 Snooping database entries. An entry in the DHCPv6 Snooping database can be an IPv6 address or a prefix. A DHCPv6 address entry in the database

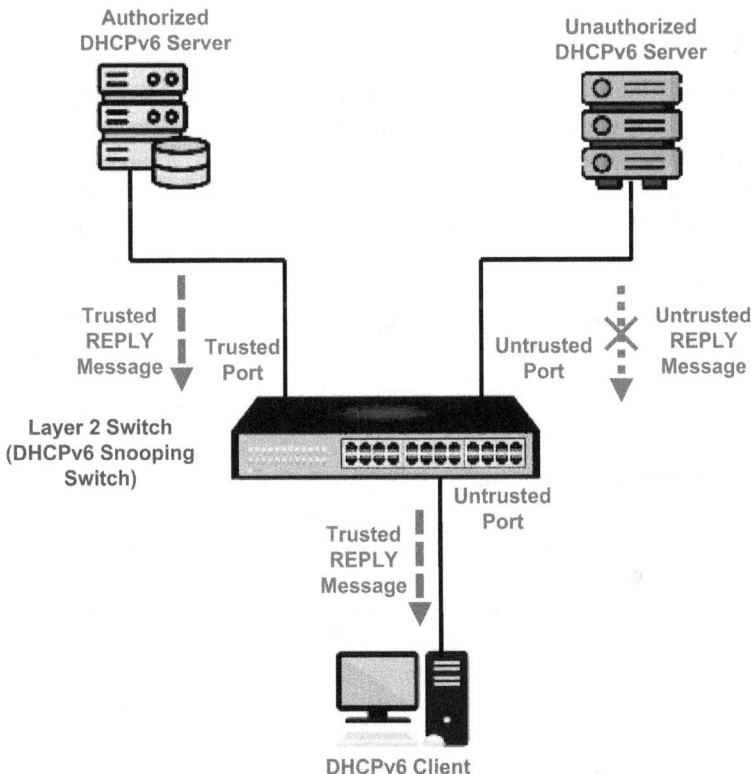

FIGURE 5.14　Trusted and untrusted ports in DHCPv6 Snooping.

includes the DHCPv6 Client's MAC and IP addresses, the switch port to which the Client is connected, and the Client's VLAN. A DHCPv6 prefix entry in the database includes the IPv6 prefix and Lease information assigned to the Client, the switch port to which the Client is connected, and the Client's VLAN.

A DHCPv6 Snooping switch may also be configured to check DHCPv6 RENEW, DECLINE, and RELEASE messages to protect the DHCPv6 Server against DHCPv6 Client spoofing attacks [H3CDHCPv6]. An attacker may send forged RENEW messages to a DHCPv6 Server to renew leases assigned to legitimate Clients that no longer need the IPv6 addresses/prefixes. The victim DHCPv6 Server, upon receiving such forged DHCPv6 messages, will be prevented from releasing the assigned IPv6 addresses/prefixes. An attacker may also send forged DECLINE or RELEASE messages to a DHCPv6 Server to terminate leases that have been assigned to legitimate Clients that still need the IPv6 addresses/prefixes.

When this capability is enabled on a DHCPv6 Snooping switch, the switch checks every received RENEW, DECLINE, or RELEASE message against the entries in the DHCPv6 Snooping database [H3CDHCPv6]:

- If any criterion in an entry in the database is matched, the DHCPv6 Snooping switch compares the entry with the information in the received DHCPv6 message.
  - If both pieces of information are consistent, the DHCPv6 Snooping switch considers the DHCPv6 message valid and forwards it to the DHCPv6 Server.
  - If they differ, the DHCPv6 Snooping switch considers the DHCPv6 message forged and discards it.
- If no matching entry exists in the database, the DHCPv6 Snooping switch forwards the DHCPv6 message to the DHCPv6 Server.

5.11   DNS EXTENSIONS FOR IPv6

DNS represents a distributed database that stores easily memorable domain name-to-IP address mapping information and mechanisms for mapping domain names to IP addresses, allowing users to locate and identify networked devices and services based solely on the name of a device or service (or vice versa). DNS is defined in several IETF standards, but the base documents for IPv4 are [RFC1034] and [RFC1035], while those for IPv6 are [RFC3596] and [RFC4472]. **Chapter 2 of [AWEYARCAP22]** provides an overview of the main components of DNS for IPv4 and how it works. This section discusses the extensions made to DNS for IPv6 operations.

We begin the discussion by presenting some key DNS terminology. The distributed Name Servers in DNS store name records as *Resource Records*. Some essential records include the following:

- **Start of Authority (SOA)**: Indicates the beginning of a DNS zone, typically, the first record for a domain in a particular Name Server.
- **Name Server (NS) Record**: Stores the DNS Server that is authoritative for a DNS entry or particular domain. This is the Name Server that contains the actual DNS records for the domain. A domain will often store multiple NS Records for the Name Servers designated as primary and backup for that domain.
- **Canonical Name (CNAME) Record**: Holds an alias (or another name) for the name being queried and does NOT contain an IP address. The alias allows the DNS resolver to continue the DNS lookup process by retrying the name resolution using the new name.
- **Address (A) Record**: Holds the 32-bit IPv4 address of a specific domain. It is the most fundamental of all DNS record types.
- **Pointer (PTR) Record**: Provides a domain name for a given IP address in a reverse DNS lookup. The PTR Record provides the exact opposite of the A Record – the PTR address points to the domain name associated with a given IP address.

- **Mail Exchange (MX) Record**: Holds information that maps a domain name to a list of mail servers, directing or routing mail to a mail server (or list of message transfer agents) for that domain (in accordance with the Simple Mail Transfer Protocol (SMTP), which is a standard protocol for email). An MX Record always points to a Server's A Record (for IPv4) or AAAA Record (for IPv6).
- **Service (SRV) Record**: Specifies a host and a port (within the specified host's IP address) for locating specific services such as VoIP and instant messaging. Most other DNS records only specify either a Server or an IP address (without port information), but an SRV Record specifies both the host's IP address and the appropriate port for the service. Some IP protocols require the information provided by SRV Records to function. An SRV Record always points to an A Record (for IPv4) or an AAAA Record (for IPv6).

IP hosts, when performing name-to-IP address mapping (using Resolvers), send DNS queries to Name Servers for the necessary Resource Records. Reference **[RFC3596]** defines the changes made to DNS to support IPv6; these changes were intended to be compatible with existing DNS implementations and applications. The following aspects of the DNS process have been updated to extend the DNS functionality to IPv6:

- Define a record type to store the 128-bit IPv6 address corresponding to a domain name.
- Define the IPv6 equivalent to the IPv4 PTR in-addr.arpa.com domain, supporting reverse DNS lookups when given an IPv6 address.
- Define changes to the DNS query messages for IPv6 and the method for transporting queries between the Resolver and the Name Server.

5.11.1 UPDATED DNS RESOURCE RECORDS AND DOMAIN INFORMATION FOR IPv6

Reference **[RFC3596]** defines the following changes:

- **AAAA Record (Quad-A Record)**: Holds the 128-bit IPv6 address of a domain name (equivalent to the A Record for IPv4). The IANA assigned the value of 28 (decimal) to this record type.
- **AAAA Data Format**: This is the format for encoding IPv6 addresses. A 128-bit IPv6 address is encoded in network byte order (high-order byte first) in the data portion of an AAAA Resource Record.
- **AAAA Query**: This is a DNS query sent for a specified domain name, and the DNS Server returns a response with the answer section containing all associated AAAA Resource Records. This query type does not trigger additional section processing.
- **Textual Format of AAAA Records**: A textual representation of an IPv6 address is placed in the data portion of the AAAA Resource Record in a master database file.
- **The ip6.arpa Domain**: This is a specific domain rooted at ip6.arpa, used for IPv6 DNS reverse lookups. This domain maps an IPv6 address to a domain name and is used for reverse DNS lookups when given an IPv6 address. A PTR record in the ip6.arpa zone contains a domain name corresponding to a particular IPv6 address.
- **Modifications to Existing DNS Query Types for IPv6**: All existing DNS query types that require DNS Servers to perform type A record additional section processing (such as for NS, SRV, and MX record types) are redefined to perform both IPv4 type A and IPv6 type AAAA additional section processing. These modifications to DNS to accommodate IPv6 require a Name Server when processing any of the above DNS queries, to add any relevant IPv4 addresses and any relevant IPv6 addresses available locally to the additional section of a DNS response.

TABLE 5.7

IPv4 versus IPv6 DNS Resource Records

	IPv4	IPv6
Name-to-IP address mapping	**A Record**: www.aweya.com A 172.30.40.156	**AAAA Record**: www.aweya.com AAAA 2001:DB8:B:C:D:E:F:1
IP address-to-name mapping	**PTR Record**: 156.40.30.172.in-addr.arpa PTR www.aweya.com	**PTR Record**: 1.0.0.0.F.0.0.0.E.0.0.0.D.0.0.0.C.0.0.0.B.0.0.0.8.B.D.0.1.0.0. 2.ip6.arp PTR www.aweya.com

Table 5.7 compares the IPv4 and IPv6 DNS Resource Records. All DNS query messages, whether using IPv4 or IPv6, can be transported over UDP or TCP.

To support IPv6 addresses, DNS Servers need to be set up with AAAA records (for DNS lookups) and PTR records (for reverse DNS lookups). A user may want to determine the IPv6 address associated with the domain name www.aweya.com. In this case, the user sends a DNS query to a DNS Server to search its AAAA records for the IPv6 address associated with the domain name www.aweya.com.

Conversely, the user may wish to determine the domain name associated with a specific IPv6 address. A reverse DNS lookup involves mapping a given IPv6 address to its associated domain name, allowing name identification of an IP node associated with a particular IPv6 address. In this case, a reverse DNS lookup is required, and the user sends a DNS query with an IPv6 address to a DNS Server to query the ip6.arpa zone to determine the corresponding domain name:

- If an AAAA record exists associating www.aweya.com with the IPv6 address 2001:DB8:B:C:D:E:F:1, then the DNS query for this domain name will return this IPv6 address to the user.
- A DNS query for a reverse DNS lookup for the IPv6 address 2001:DB8:B:C:D:E:F:1 will be performed using the ip6.arpa domain. The DNS Server will look for the PTR record, 1.0.0.0.F.0.0.0.E.0.0.0.D.0.0.0.C.0.0.0.B.0.0.0.8.B.D.0.1.0.0.2.ip6.arp PTR www.aweya.com, and then return the domain name www.aweya.com to the user.

REVIEW QUESTIONS

5.1. Explain the difference between Stateless DHCPv6 and Stateful DHCPv6.

5.2. Why are Options used in DHCPv6?

5.3. What is the purpose of the DHCPv6 Unique Identifier (DUID)?

5.4. What is a DHCPv6 Identity Association (IA)?

5.5. What is DHCPv6 Prefix Delegation?

5.6. What types of IPv6 address pools are used by a DHCPv6 Server?

5.7. What is the purpose of each message type in the DHCPv6 four-message exchange process using SOLICIT, ADVERTISE, REQUEST, and REPLY messages?

5.8. What is the purpose of each message type in the DHCPv6 two-message exchange using INFORMATION-REQUEST and REPLY messages?

5.9. What is the purpose of each message type in the DHCPv6 two-message exchange using a SOLICIT message (with the DHCPv6 Rapid Commit Option) and a REPLY message? Why is the DHCPv6 Rapid Commit Option included in the SOLICIT message?

5.10. What is the purpose of the DHCPv6 RECONFIGURE message?

5.11. What would cause a DHCPv6 participant to send a CONFIRM message?

5.12. What would cause a DHCPv6 participant to send a RENEW message?

5.13. What would cause a DHCPv6 participant to send a REBIND message?

5.14. What would cause a DHCPv6 participant to send a RELEASE message?

5.15. What is the purpose of the DHCPv6 RELAY-FORWARD message?

5.16. What is the purpose of the DHCPv6 RELAY-REPLY message?

5.17. When is a DHCPv6 Client allowed to unicast DHCPv6 messages to a Server?

5.18. What is the purpose of the DHCPv6 Prefix Exclude Option during DHCPv6 Prefix Delegation?

5.19. What DHCPv4 messages correspond to the DHCPv6 messages SOLICIT, ADVERTISE, REQUEST, and REPLY?

5.20. Explain briefly what DHCPv6 Snooping is.

REFERENCES

[ALLIEDDHCPv6]. Allied Telesis, "DHCP for IPv6 (DHCPv6): Feature Overview and Configuration Guide", Technical Guide, C613-22062-00 REV B.

[AWEYARCAP22]. J. Aweya, *Designing Switch/Routers: Architectures and Applications*, CRC Press, Taylor & Francis Group, ISBN 9781032317700, October 2022.

[CISCODHCPv6]. Cisco Systems, IP Addressing Configuration Guide, Cisco IOS XE 17.x, Chapter "IPv6 Access Services: DHCPv6 Prefix Delegation", November 15, 2022.

[CISCPOPOC]. Ciprian Popoviciu, Eric Levy-Abegnoli, and Patrick Grossette, *Deploying IPv6 Networks*, Cisco Press, 2006.

[H3CDHCPv6]. H3C, Layer 3-IP Services Configuration Guide, Chapter "DHCPv6 Configuration".

[RFC1034]. P. Mockapetris, "Domain Names – Concepts and Facilities", *IETF RFC 1034*, November 1987.

[RFC1035]. P. Mockapetris, "Domain Names – Implementation and Specification", *IETF RFC 1034*, November 1987.

[RFC2131]. R. Droms, "Dynamic Host Configuration Protocol", *IETF RFC 2131*, March 1997.

[RFC2865]. C. Rigney, S. Willens, A. Rubens, and W. Simpson, "Remote Authentication Dial in User Service (RADIUS)", *IETF RFC 2865*, June 2000.

[RFC3074]. B. Volz, S. Gonczi, T. Lemon, and R. Stevens, "DHC Load Balancing Algorithm", *IETF RFC 3074*, February 2001.

[RFC3162]. B. Aboba, G. Zorn, and D. Mitton, "RADIUS and IPv6", *IETF RFC 3162*, August 2001.

[RFC3596]. S. Thomson, C. Huitema, V. Ksinant, and M. Souissi, "DNS Extensions to Support IP Version 6", *IETF RFC 3596*, October 2003.

[RFC3633]. O. Troan and R. Droms, "IPv6 Prefix Options for Dynamic Host Configuration Protocol (DHCP) Version 6", *IETF RFC 3633*, December 2003.

[RFC3646]. R. Droms, Ed., "DNS Configuration options for Dynamic Host Configuration Protocol for IPv6 (DHCPv6)", *IETF RFC 3646*, December 2003.

[RFC3736]. R. Droms, "Stateless Dynamic Host Configuration Protocol (DHCP) Service for IPv6", *IETF RFC 3736*, April 2004.

[RFC3769]. S. Miyakawa and R. Droms, "Requirements for IPv6 Prefix Delegation", *IETF RFC 3769*, June 2004.

[RFC4291]. R. Hinden and S. Deering, "IP Version 6 Addressing Architecture", *IETF RFC 4291*, February 2006.

[RFC4472]. A. Durand, J. Ihren, and P. Savola, "Operational Considerations and Issues with IPv6 DNS", *IETF RFC 4472*, April 2006.

[RFC4818]. J. Salowey and R Droms, "RADIUS Delegated-IPv6-Prefix Attribute", *IETF RFC 4818*, April 2007.

[RFC4861]. T. Narten, E. Nordmark, W. Simpson, and H. Soliman, "Neighbor Discovery for IP Version 6 (IPv6)", *IETF RFC 4861*, September 2007.

[RFC4862]. S. Thomson, T. Narten, and T. Jinmei, "IPv6 Stateless Address Autoconfiguration", *IETF RFC 4862*, September 2007.

[RFC4994]. S. Zeng, B. Volz, K. Kinnear, and J. Brzozowski, "DHCPv6 Relay Agent Echo Request Option", *IETF RFC 4994*, September 2007.

[RFC5905]. D. Mills, J. Martin, Ed., J. Burbank, and W. Kasch, "Network Time Protocol Version 4: Protocol and Algorithms Specification", *IETF RFC 5905*, June 2010.

[RFC5908].   R. Gayraud and B. Lourdelet, "Network Time Protocol (NTP) Server Option for DHCPv6", *IETF RFC 5908*, June 2010.

[RFC6221].   D. Miles, Ed., S. Ooghe, W. Dec, S. Krishnan, and A. Kavanagh, "Lightweight DHCPv6 Relay Agent", *IETF RFC 6221*, May 2011.

[RFC6355].   T. Narten and J. Johnson, "Definition of the UUID-Based DHCPv6 Unique Identifier (DUID-UUID)", *IETF RFC 6355*, August 2011.

[RFC6422].   T. Lemon and Q. Wu, "Relay-Supplied DHCP Options", *IETF RFC 6422*, December 2011.

[RFC6603].   J. Korhonen, Ed., T. Savolainen, S. Krishnan, and O. Troan, "Prefix Exclude Option for DHCPv6-based Prefix Delegation", *IETF RFC 6603*, May 2012.

[RFC6879].   S. Jiang, B. Liu, and B. Carpenter, "IPv6 Enterprise Network Renumbering Scenarios, Considerations, and Methods", *IETF RFC 6879*, February 2013.

[RFC6911].   W. Dec, Ed., B. Sarikaya, G. Zorn, Ed., D. Miles, and B. Lourdelet, "RADIUS Attributes for IPv6 Access Networks", *IETF RFC 6911*, April 2013.

[RFC7084].   H. Singh, W. Beebee, C. Donley, and B. Stark, "Basic Requirements for IPv6 Customer Edge Routers", *IETF RFC 7084*, November 2013.

[RFC7283].   Y. Cui, Q. Sun, and T. Lemon, "Handling Unknown DHCPv6 Messages", *IETF RFC 7283*, July 2014.

[RFC7368].   T. Chown, Ed., J. Arkko, A. Brandt, O. Troan, and J. Weil, "IPv6 Home Networking Architecture Principles", *IETF RFC 7368*, October 2014.

[RFC7513].   J. Bi, J. Wu, G. Yao, and F. Baker, "Source Address Validation Improvement (SAVI) Solution for DHCP", *IETF RFC 7513*, May 2015.

[RFC7610].   F. Gont, W. Liu, G. Van de Velde, "DHCPv6-Shield: Protecting against Rogue DHCPv6 Servers", *IETF RFC 7610*, August 2015.

[RFC8156].   T. Mrugalski and K. Kinnear, "DHCPv6 Failover Protocol", *IETF RFC 8156*, June 2017.

[RFC8213].   B. Volz and Y. Pal, "Security of Messages Exchanged between Servers and Relay Agents", *IETF RFC 8213*, August 2017.

[RFC8415].   T. Mrugalski, M. Siodelski, B. Volz, A. Yourtchenko, M. Richardson, S. Jiang, T. Lemon, and T. Winters, "Dynamic Host Configuration Protocol for IPv6 (DHCPv6)", *IETF RFC 8415*, November 2018.

[RFC8981].   F. Gont, S. Krishnan, T. Narten, and R. Draves, "Temporary Address Extensions for Stateless Address Autoconfiguration in IPv6", *IETF RFC 8981*, February 2021.

6 Mobile IP
Mobility Mechanisms for IPv4 and IPv6

6.1 INTRODUCTION

Mobile IP is an IETF standard (defined in **[RFC5944]** for Mobile IPv4 and in **[RFC6275]** for Mobile IPv6) that specifies mobility mechanisms allowing a Mobile IP node to move from its *Home Network* to another network (a *Foreign Network*), while retaining the permanent IP address originally assigned to it by the Home Network, and maintaining connectivity with the Home Network while on the Foreign Network. The Home Network assigns the permanent routable unicast IP address to the Mobile Node (called the *Home IP Address*); it is the network to which the Mobile Node originally belongs. A Foreign Network is the current network being visited by the Mobile Node while away from its Home Network. Mobile IP provides location-independent routing of IP packets between the Mobile Node's Home Network and its current location (a Foreign Network) on the Internet.

Prior to Mobile IP, if a Mobile Node moved to a new network while keeping its assigned Home IP Address (an address that did not reflect its new point of attachment), routing protocols could not route IP packets to the Mobile Node correctly at its new location. In such cases, the Mobile Node had to be reconfigured with a different IP address that represented the new location before IP packets could be routed to it correctly. Without an appropriate mechanism, if the Mobile Node moved without changing its IP address to reflect the new location, it would lose IP packet routing and connectivity to its Home Network if the Home IP Address was still used.

Given that assigning a different IP address to the Mobile Node every time it moves is cumbersome, Mobile IP allows a Mobile Node to move to a Foreign Network and still maintain connectivity with its Home Network using two IP addresses: its Home IP Address and a temporary IP address assigned by the Foreign Network. By using both IP addresses and the Mobile IP functions, the Mobile Node can maintain seamless connectivity with its Home Network while visiting a Foreign Network.

With Mobile IP, each Mobile Node uses two IP addresses: a permanent Home IP Address (regardless of its current location on the Internet) and a *Care-of IP Address* (which identifies its current location outside its Home Network). The Mobile Node is associated with a Care-of IP Address while visiting a Foreign Network (away from its Home Network), which is an IP address linked to the network the Mobile Node is currently visiting. The Care-of IP Address of the Mobile Node changes with each Foreign Network (i.e., at each new point of attachment). As will be discussed later, Mobile IP involves creating an IP tunnel to a *Home Agent* on the Mobile Node's Home Network, with the Home IP Address associated with the endpoint of the tunnel at the Mobile Node's Home Agent. Mobile IP specifies various mechanisms for a Mobile Node on a Foreign Network to register with its Home Agent, allowing the Home Agent to route IP packets through the tunnel to the Mobile Node at its current location.

A Mobile Node is essentially a device that changes its point of attachment from its Home Network to another network (in the wider Internet) while still maintaining all existing communications with the Home Network using its Home IP Address. With Mobile IP, an IP node can roam freely on the wider Internet or on an organization's network while still retaining its originally assigned IP address (the Home IP Address). This allows the Mobile Node to maintain communication activities even when its point of attachment changes. While on a Foreign Network, the Mobile Node continues to use its permanent Home IP Address (assigned by the Home Network) as the source IP address of all IP packets it sends. Note that without Mobile IP, a device cannot simply move to a new IP network and connect to it using the IP address assigned to it by the previous IP network.

With Mobile IP, a Mobile Node can move to different networks (wireless and wireline) while using its Home IP Address to maintain connections and access applications/services permitted by its Home Network. A Mobile Node can roam across network boundaries while maintaining applications such as remote login, file transfers, remote printing, and others. Essentially, Mobile IP allows a Mobile Node to maintain uninterrupted communication with its Home Network. Additionally, a Mobile Node can still access certain network services using its Home IP Address, since many applications require devices to use software licenses and grant access privileges only when the device is using the IP addresses recognized by those applications (which are usually the Home IP Addresses). By handling mobility at the Network Layer (IPv4 and IPv6), Mobile IP makes the underlying network infrastructure transparent to all upper-layer protocols, as the IPv4/IPv6 layer is the only common layer for applications in the TCP/IP protocol suite.

6.2   MOBILE IPv4

Other than the Mobile Node itself, Mobile IPv4 **[RFC5944]** defined the following functional entities (Figure 6.1):

- **Home Agent**: This is a node (IP router or server) on a Mobile Node's Home Network that intercepts IP packets destined for the Mobile Node and delivers them through the Care-of IP Address on a Foreign Network to the Mobile Node. The Home Agent tunnels IP packets for delivery to the Mobile Node when it is away from its Home Network. The Home Agent stores information about Mobile Nodes and their associated Care-of IP Addresses and permanent Home IP Addresses for the Home Network. It also maintains a location directory for the Home Network's Mobile Nodes (i.e., current information about the locations of Mobile Nodes).
- **Foreign Agent**: This is a node (IP router or server) on a Foreign Network that stores information about visiting Mobile Nodes and advertises Care-of IP Addresses to be used by registered visiting Mobile Nodes. The Foreign Agent is a Mobility Agent that provides mobility services to visiting Mobile Nodes. It provides routing services to the registered visiting Mobile Node and also de-tunnels and delivers IP packets that were tunneled by the Mobile Node's Home Agent. The Foreign Agent may serve as a default router for a registered visiting Mobile Node and receive IP packets sent by the Mobile Node.

The Home Agent, usually a router, serves as an anchor point on the Home Network for communication with the Mobile Node roaming on another network. The Home Agent tunnels IP packets sent by a device on the Internet, called a Correspondent Node, to the Mobile Node visiting a Foreign Network. Depending on the type of Care-of IP Address used by the Mobile Node, a tunnel may be established between the Home Agent and the Foreign Agent, which functions as a point of attachment for the Mobile Node on the Foreign Network (delivering IP packets from the Home Agent to the Mobile Node) or may be established directly between the Home Agent and the Mobile Node.

6.2.1   CARE-OF IP ADDRESSES

A permanent routable unicast Home IP Address always identifies a Mobile Node, regardless of its location on the Internet (i.e., regardless of its point of attachment). The Home Link is the link (subnet/ VLAN) in the Home Network on which the *Home IP Subnet Prefix* of a Mobile Node is defined. External IP packets destined for the Home IP Address of a Mobile Node are sent to its Home Link through standard IP routing mechanisms. Particularly in the case of Mobile IPv6, a Mobile Node can have multiple Home IP Addresses, for instance, when the Home Link has multiple Home IPv6 Prefixes.

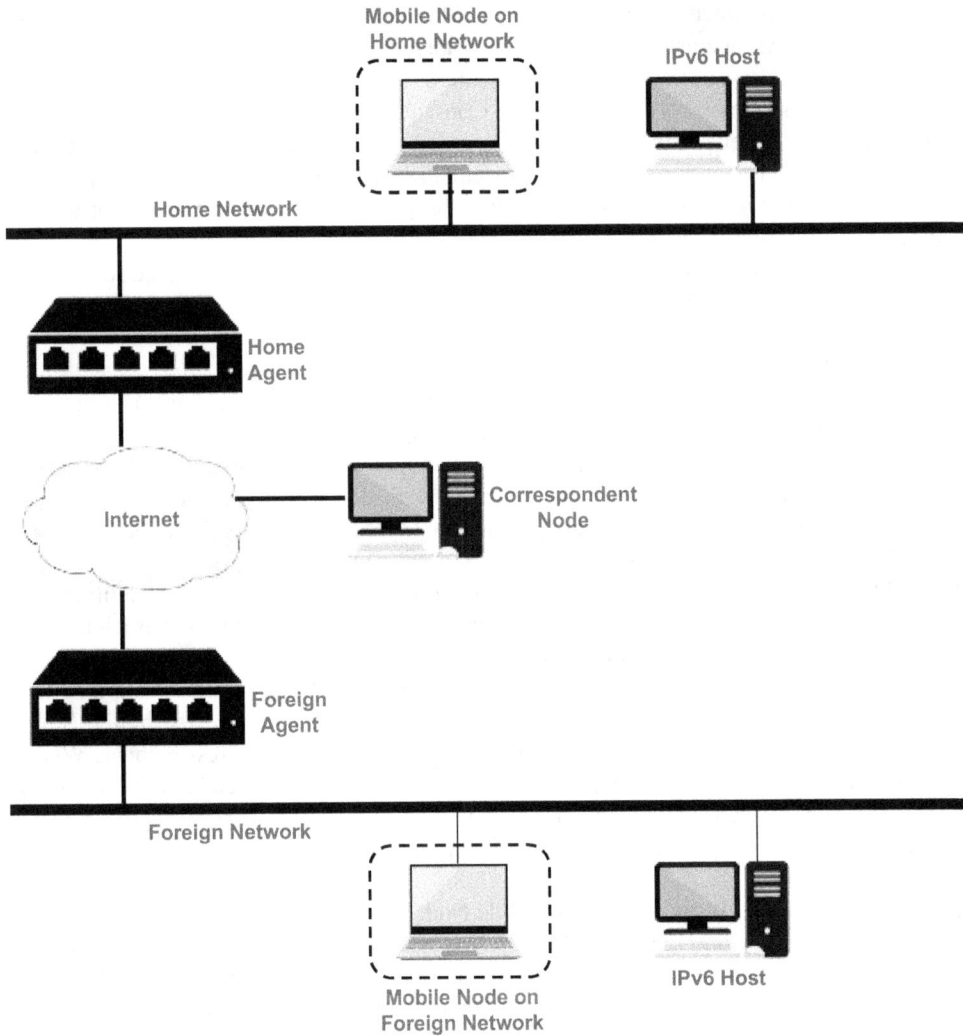

FIGURE 6.1   Mobile IPv4 functional entities.

When the Mobile Node moves away from its Home Network, a routable unicast Care-of IP Address (usually an IPv6 Global Unicast address) is assigned to the Mobile Node. The Care-of IP Address provides information about the Mobile Node's current point of attachment on a Foreign Network. The Care-of IP Address is a termination point of a tunnel at a Foreign Network for IP packets forwarded to the Mobile Node while it is away from its Home Network. The Foreign IP Subnet Prefix is any IP subnet prefix other than the Home IP Subnet Prefix of a Mobile Node. A Foreign Link is any link other than the Home Link of a Mobile Node. The IP subnet prefix of the Care-of IP Address is a Foreign IP Subnet Prefix.

Mobile IP defines a registration mechanism for registering the Care-of IP Address of a Mobile Node with its Home Agent. The Care-of IP Address may be allocated to a Mobile Node by a Foreign Agent or acquired by the Mobile Node from a DHCP Server. In the latter case, the Mobile Node acquires an IP address that is referred to as a *Co-located Care-of IP Address*. Among the multiple Care-of IP Addresses that may be assigned to a Mobile Node at any given time (e.g., each with a different IP subnet prefix), the address registered with the Home Agent of the Mobile Node and associated with a given Home IP Address is called the *Primary Care-of IP Address*.

The Home Agent redirects IP packets from the Mobile Node's Home Network to its Care-of IP Address. The Home Agent creates a new IP header for a redirected IP packet that contains the Mobile Node's Care-of IP Address as the destination IP address. Creating this new IP header results in a new IP packet that encapsulates the original IP packet. Consequently, the Mobile Node's Home IP Address has no effect on how the encapsulated IP packet is routed until it arrives at the Care-of IP Address on the Foreign Network. The encapsulation of the original IP packet as the payload of another IP packet is called *tunneling (IP-in-IP encapsulation)* [RFC2003]. After the IP packet arrives at the Mobile Node's Care-of IP Address, it is decapsulated and delivered to the Mobile Node.

Mobile IP provides the following alternative methods for a Mobile Node to acquire a Care-of IP Address at a Foreign Network:

- **Foreign Agent Care-of IP Address**: A Foreign Agent uses *Agent Advertisement* messages to provide this type of IP address to a Mobile Node. This routable unicast Care-of IP Address is normally the IP address of the Foreign Agent that sends the Agent Advertisement messages. In this case, the Foreign Agent is the endpoint of the IP tunnel. When IP packets are received through this tunnel, the Foreign Agent decapsulates them and delivers the inner IP packet to the Mobile Node. This addressing mode allows multiple Mobile Nodes to share the same Care-of IP Address (i.e., share the same Foreign Agent).
- **Co-located Care-of IP Address**: A Mobile Node obtains this local routable unicast IP address type through external means, usually through DHCP, and it serves as a temporary IP address. The Mobile Node then associates the acquired IP address with its own network interface. In some cases, the Mobile Node may also use this IP address as a long-term address. However, this Co-located Care-of IP Address can only be used by the Mobile Node while visiting the Foreign Network (subnet) to which the address belongs. When a Mobile Node uses a Co-located Care-of IP Address, it serves as the endpoint of the IP tunnel. In this case, the Mobile Node directly receives tunneled IP packets sent to it and performs IP packet decapsulation on them before processing the data in the inner IP packet.

A Co-located Care-of IP Address allows a Mobile Node to function on a Foreign Network without using a Foreign Agent. Consequently, a Mobile Node can move to a Foreign Network and use a Co-located Care-of IP Address, even if the network has not deployed a Foreign Agent. However, for a Mobile Node to use a Co-located Care-of IP Address, it must be located on the IP subnet identified by the network prefix of that IP address. Otherwise, IP packets destined for that Care-of IP Address cannot be delivered.

The Home Agent maintains an association between a Mobile Node's Home IP Address and its Care-of IP Address, which indicates the Mobile Node's current location on the Foreign Network. A Mobile Node is usually configured with its Home IP Address but may use another identifier, such as a Network Access Identifier (NAI), when visiting a Foreign Network.

When on a Foreign Network, tunneling allows the Mobile Node's Home IP Address to be hidden from intervening routers between its Home Network and its current location. The Care-of IP Address (Foreign Agent Care-of IP or Co-located Care-of IP Address) is simply the terminating point of the tunnel. The Care-of IP Address must be a routable IP address to which IP packets destined for the Mobile Node can be delivered via conventional IP routing. At the Care-of IP Address, the original IP packet is decapsulated from the tunneled IP packet and delivered to the Mobile Node.

6.2.2 AGENT DISCOVERY

The *Agent Discovery* process involves a Mobile Node discovering its Foreign and Home Agents. A Mobile Node uses the Agent Discovery process to determine the following information:

- Whether the node is on the Home Network or a Foreign Network
- When the node has moved from one Foreign Network to another

- The Care-of IP Address allocated by a Foreign Agent on the local network
- The mobility services provided by the Mobility Agent, along with flags and additional extensions advertised in the Agent Advertisement messages. A Mobility Agent can be either a Foreign Agent or a Home Agent.

A Mobile Node is responsible for determining whether it has moved to a Foreign Network or is currently connected to its Home Network. Home Agents and Foreign Agents periodically advertise their presence on their local networks. A Mobile Node informs its Home Agent about its current location using a special registration process. The Mobile Node always listens for messages sent by Mobility Agents (Home Agents and Foreign Agents) that advertise their presence.

Mobile IPv4 extends the ICMPv4 Router Discovery mechanism (defined in **[RFC1256]**) for *Mobile Agent Discovery*. Mobile IPv4 uses (but extends) the existing messages defined for ICMPv4 Router Discovery for mobility information exchange: the Router Advertisement message (ICMPv4 Type 9 message) and the Router Solicitation message (ICMPv4 Type 10 message). Mobile IP also defines a number of extensions (in TLV format) to allow optional information to be included in the Mobile IPv4 messages. Just like other ICMPv4 messages, the Mobile Agent Discovery messages are carried directly in IPv4 packets. The end of the list of extensions in each of these ICMPv4 messages is indicated by the value in the IPv4 header's Total Length field.

A Mobile Node uses the following advertisements to determine when it has moved to another IP subnet and to register with a Mobility Agent (Table 6.1). These messages are simply ICMPv4 Router Discovery messages extended for use in Mobile IPv4 Agent Discovery:

- **Agent Advertisement Message**: Mobility Agents (Foreign Agents and Home Agents) advertise their presence and services on their local networks by sending Agent Advertisement messages. An Agent Advertisement message is an ICMPv4 Router Advertisement that is extended to carry Mobility Agent advertisement information. A Foreign Agent must always transmit Agent Advertisement messages. *The Agent Advertisement messages allow a Mobile Node to determine whether it is on the Home Network or a Foreign Network.* Using Agent Advertisement messages, the Mobile Node determines whether its current point of attachment is on the Home Network or a Foreign Network.
- **Agent Solicitation Message**: Optionally, a newly arrived Mobile Node can send an Agent Solicitation message on the local network to request the sending of an Agent Advertisement message in order to discover if any prospective Foreign Agents are present. In the absence of Agent Advertisement messages, a Mobile Node can transmit Agent Solicitation messages. Sending an Agent Solicitation message allows the Mobile Node to connect to any Foreign Agent available on the local network. The ability to send Agent Solicitation messages is a requirement for every Mobile Node.

Mobility entities may protect these messages using the IPSec **[RFC4301]**.

When a Mobile Node determines that it has moved to a new location, it uses the (new) local Foreign Agent to send a *Registration message* to its Home Agent. The Mobile Node uses the same registration process when it moves from one Foreign Network to another. Additionally, when the Mobile Node detects that it has moved back to its Home Network, it stops using the mobility services. The Mobile Node also deregisters with its Home Agent when it returns to the Home Network. The Mobile Node exchanges *Registration Request* and *Registration Reply* messages with its Home Agent in order to accomplish the deregistration process.

6.2.3 Mobile IPv4 Registration

The *registration* process involves a Mobile Node registering its current location with the Foreign Agent and Home Agent. A Mobile Node detects when it has moved from one IP network to another through the receipt of Agent Advertisement messages. When the Mobile Node receives an Agent

TABLE 6.1

Mobile IPv4 Agent Discovery Messages and Extensions

Agent Discovery Messages		
Message Name	**ICMPv4 Message Type Value**	**Description**
Agent Advertisement	9	This message type is simply an ICMPv4 Router Advertisement message **[RFC1256]** that has been extended to include a Mobility Agent Advertisement Extension and, optionally, a Prefix-Lengths Extension and a One-Byte Padding Extension. A Mobility Agent transmits an Agent Advertisement message to advertise its services on a link. Mobile Nodes use these advertisements to determine their current point of attachment in the Internet.
Agent Solicitation	10	This message type is identical to an ICMPv4 Router Solicitation message, except that its IP Time-to-Live (TTL) MUST be set to 1.
Message Extensions		
Extension Name	**Extension Type Value**	**Description**
Mobility Agent Advertisement Extension	16	This extension follows the ICMPv4 Router Advertisement message fields **[RFC1256]** and is used to indicate that an ICMPv4 Router Advertisement message is also an Agent Advertisement being sent by a Mobility Agent.
Prefix-Lengths Extension	19	This extension MAY follow the Mobility Agent Advertisement Extension and is used to indicate the number of bits of the IPv4 network prefix that applies to each router IPv4 address listed in the ICMPv4 Router Advertisement portion of the Agent Advertisement.
One-Byte Padding Extension	0	Some IP protocol implementations insist on padding ICMP messages to an even number of bytes. If the ICMP length of an Agent Advertisement is an odd number, this extension MAY be included in order to make the ICMP length an even number. An Agent Advertisement SHOULD NOT include more than one One-byte Padding Extension, and if present, this extension SHOULD be the last extension in the Agent Advertisement message

Advertisement message indicating a move to a new network, it may register through the local network's Foreign Agent. Depending on the Mobile Node's method of attachment to the Foreign Network, it may register either directly with the Home Agent or through a Foreign Agent that relays the registration to the Home Agent.

The Mobile IP Registration process allows a Mobile Node to communicate its current location along with the necessary reachability information (Care-of IP Address) to its Home Agent. Through the registration process, a Mobile Node is able to perform the following tasks:

- Request IP packets to be forwarded to it when visiting a Foreign Network
- Inform the Home Agent about its current Care-of IP Address
- Renew its registration when it is about to expire
- Deregister when the Mobile Node moves back to the Home Network
- Request a Reverse Tunnel to be set up **[RFC3024]**

The Mobile Node, Foreign Agent, and Home Agent exchange information through Registration messages (see Table 6.2). *Registration messages are carried directly in UDP datagrams using the well-known UDP port number 434.* The sender adds a nonzero UDP checksum in the UDP header, and the recipient must verify the UDP datagram using this checksum. When on a Foreign Network, a Mobile Node registers with its Home Agent using a *Registration Request* message. Through this message, the Home Agent can create or modify the Mobile Node's *Mobility Binding* (e.g., with a

TABLE 6.2
Mobile IPv4 Registration Messages and Extensions

Registration Messages		
Message Name	Message Type Value	Description
Registration Request	1	A Mobile Node uses this message type to register with its Home Agent so that the Home Agent can create or modify a Mobility Binding for the Mobile Node (e.g., with a new Lifetime). The Registration Request message may be relayed to the Home Agent by the Foreign Agent through which the Mobile Node is registering, or it may be sent directly to the Home Agent in the case where the Mobile Node is registering a Co-located Care-of IP Address. The UDP ports of Registration Request messages are as follows: Source Port is variable, and Destination Port is 434.
Registration Reply	3	A Mobility Agent typically returns a Registration Reply message to a Mobile Node that has sent a Registration Request message. If the Mobile Node is requesting service through a Foreign Agent, that Foreign Agent will typically receive the Registration Reply from the Home Agent and subsequently relay it to the Mobile Node. Registration Reply messages contain the necessary codes to inform the Mobile Node about the status of its Registration Request, along with the Lifetime granted by the Home Agent, which MAY be smaller than the original Registration Request. The UDP ports of Registration Reply messages are as follows: Source Port is copied from the UDP Destination Port of the corresponding Registration Request message, and Destination Port is copied from the source port of the corresponding Registration Request message.
Message Extensions		
Extension Name	Extension Type Value	Description
Mobile-Home Authentication Extension	32	This Extension type is always an authorization-enabling extension for Registration messages. At least one authorization-enabling extension MUST be present in all Registration Request messages and also in all Registration Reply messages generated by the Home Agent.
Mobile-Foreign Authentication Extension	33	This Extension MAY be included in Registration Request and Reply messages in cases where a Mobility Security Association exists between the Mobile Node and the Foreign Agent.
Foreign-Home Authentication Extension	34	This Extension MAY be included in Registration Request and Reply messages in cases where a Mobility Security Association exists between the Foreign Agent and the Home Agent, as long as the Registration Request message is not for a deregistration (i.e., the Mobile Node requested a nonzero Lifetime and the Home Address is different from the Care-of Address). The Foreign-Home Authentication extension MUST NOT be applied to deregistration messages.

new Lifetime). A Mobility Binding is an association of a Mobile Node's Home IP Address with its assigned Care-of IP Address, along with the remaining Lifetime of that association. A Foreign Agent can pass on the Mobile Node's Registration Request to its Home Agent. However, if a Co-located Care-of IP Address is being registered by the Mobile Node, it can send the Registration Request message directly to its Home Agent. The Mobile Node must send the Registration Request message to the Foreign Agent if that Foreign Agent advertises the Registration messages.

A Mobile Node that has sent a Registration Request message receives a *Registration Reply* message from the Mobility Agent. If the Mobile Node sends a Registration Request message requesting service from the local Foreign Agent, that Foreign Agent relays the request and receives a Registration Reply message from the Home Agent. The Foreign Agent then relays the Registration Reply message to the Mobile Node. The Registration Reply message contains information indicating to the Mobile Node and the Foreign Agent the status of the Registration Request message.

The Lifetime granted by the Home Agent is also included in the Registration Reply message. The Lifetime value granted may be smaller than what was originally requested. The Registration Reply message may also include information about dynamic Home IP Address assignment.

The registration process creates or modifies a Mobile Node's Mobility Binding at its Home Agent. Registration includes associating the Mobile Node's Home IP Address with its Care-of IP Address for the specified Lifetime. The registration process also allows the Mobile Node to perform the following functions:

- Register with two or more Foreign Agents
- Deregister specific Care-of IP Addresses previously assigned to the Mobile Node while retaining other Mobility Bindings
- Discover the IP address of a Home Agent on the Home Network if the Mobile Node was not configured with this IP address

The following registration processes have been defined for a Mobile Node in Mobile IPv4:

- When a Mobile Node registers a Foreign Agent Care-of IP Address with the Home Agent, it informs the Home Agent that it is reachable through that Foreign Agent.
- When a Mobile Node receives an Agent Advertisement message that requires it to register through a Foreign Agent, it can still attempt to request (via, for example, a DHCP Server) a Co-located Care-of IP Address. The Mobile Node may also register with the advertising Foreign Agent or any other Foreign Agent on that IP subnet.
- When a Mobile Node uses a Co-located Care-of IP Address, it registers directly with its Home Agent (a Foreign Agent is not involved).
- When a Mobile Node moves back to its Home Network, it deregisters with the Home Agent.

The above registration processes involve the use of Registration Request and Registration Reply messages for information exchange.

6.2.3.1 Mobile Node Registration Process

The following steps describe the registration process when a Mobile Node registers through a Foreign Agent:

1. After discovering a Foreign Agent, the Mobile Node begins the registration process by adding a Registration Request message to its Pending List and then transmitting the request to the prospective Foreign Agent, if applicable.
   - Note that the Mobile Node sends the Registration Request message either to the Foreign Agent to be relayed to its Home Agent or directly to the Home Agent if it is using a Co-located Care-of IP Address. In the latter case, the Mobile Node is not required to register through the Foreign Agent.
2. The Foreign Agent checks the validity of the Mobile Node's Registration Request message, and if valid, processes and then relays the request to the Home Agent with the Care-of IP Address.
   - The validity checks at the Foreign Agent include checking if the requested Lifetime does not exceed what the Foreign Agent can support and if the requested tunnel encapsulation methods and the Reverse Tunnel are supported [RFC3024].
   - The Foreign Agent adds the visiting Mobile Node's Home IP Address to its *Pending List* before relaying a valid Registration Request message to the Home Agent.
   - If the request is not valid, the Foreign Agent sends a Registration Reply message to the Mobile Node with the appropriate error code.

3. The Home Agent receives and checks the validity of the Registration Request message, and if valid, processes it and then sends a Registration Reply to the Foreign Agent, granting or denying the request.
   - The validity checks at the Home Agent include authenticating the Mobile Node. For a valid Registration Request message, the Home Agent creates a Mobility Binding (which is an association of the Mobile Node's Home IP Address with its Care-of IP Address), a *Forward Tunnel* to the Care-of IP Address, and a routing entry for forwarding IP packets through the tunnel to the Mobile Node's Home IP Address.
   - The Registration Reply message is sent to the Foreign Agent to be forwarded to the Mobile Node (if the Registration Request message was received through a Foreign Agent) or directly to the Mobile Node.
   - If the Registration Request message is not valid, the Home Agent rejects the request and sends a Registration Reply message to the Mobile Node with the appropriate error code.
4. The Foreign Agent receives the Registration Reply message and checks its validity. If valid, the Foreign Agent creates an entry in its *Visitor List* for the Mobile Node, establishes a *Reverse Tunnel* to the Home Agent **[RFC3024]**, and creates a routing entry for forwarding IP packets destined for the Mobile Node's Home IP Address. The Foreign Agent then relays the Registration Reply message to the visiting Mobile Node.
   - The Registration Reply message check at the Foreign Agent includes ensuring that an associated Registration Request exists for the Mobile Node in the Foreign Agent's Pending List.
5. The Mobile Node receives the Registration Reply message and checks its validity, which includes ensuring that an associated Registration Request exists in its Pending List as well as confirming that the Home Agent has been properly authenticated.
   - The Mobile Node discards the Registration Reply message if it is not valid.
   - If the Registration Reply message is valid and indicates that the registration is accepted, the Mobile Node knows that the Mobility Agents are aware of its visit to the Foreign Network. Subsequently, the Mobile Node sends all IP packets to the Foreign Agent.
   - If the Mobile Node is using a Co-located Care-of IP Address, it creates a Reverse Tunnel to the Home Agent.

A Registration Reply message generally falls under one of the following three categories: the Registration is accepted, the Registration is denied by the Foreign Agent, or the Registration is denied by the Home Agent. After a successful Mobile IP Registration, a routing mechanism is set up for transporting IP packets between the Home Agent and the roaming Mobile Node. The Mobile Node may reregister by sending a Registration Request message to the Mobility Agents before its registration Lifetime expires. During reregistration, the Home Agent updates its Mobility Binding while the Foreign Agent updates its Visitor List entry.

A Mobile Node using a Co-located Care-of IP Address registers directly with its Home Agent. The Registration process requires only the following steps:

- The Mobile Node transmits a Registration Request message to its Home Agent.
- The Home Agent processes the request and sends a Registration Reply message back directly to the Mobile Node, granting or denying the request.

In addition, either the Foreign Agent or the Home Agent may initiate the establishment of a Reverse Tunnel **[RFC3024]**. If *Reverse Tunneling* is supported by the Foreign Agent, the Mobile Node can request a Reverse Tunnel during the registration process. The Mobile Node requests a Reverse Tunnel by setting the 1-bit T (Reverse Tunnel) Flag in the Registration Request message **[RFC5944]**.

6.2.4 FOREIGN AGENT CONSIDERATIONS

The role of the Foreign Agent in the Mobile IP Registration process is mostly passive. The Foreign Agent maintains a *Visitor List* that includes all registered Mobile Nodes. It relays Registration Request messages from Mobile Nodes to their corresponding Home Agents. When the Foreign Agent provides a Care-of IP Address to the Mobile Node, it receives tunneled (encapsulated) IP packets and decapsulates them for delivery to the Mobile Node. The Foreign Agent also transmits periodic Agent Advertisement messages to announce its presence to visiting Mobile Nodes.

A Foreign Agent advertises during the registration process if it supports Reverse Tunnels. The Mobile Node requests a Reverse Tunnel if both the Home and Foreign Agents support the establishment of Reverse Tunnels. In this case, the Foreign Agent tunnels all IP packets sent by the Mobile Node to the Home Agent. The Home Agent then decapsulates the tunneled IP packets and sends the original IP packets to the Correspondent Node. The Home Agent also tunnels all IP packets destined for the Mobile Node to the Foreign Agent for delivery to the Mobile Node. A Correspondent Node is a peer node on the Internet that communicates with the Mobile Node.

When multiple Mobile Nodes have the same (private) IP address, the Foreign Agent can only distinguish between them when they visit different interfaces on the Foreign Agent. In the Forward Tunnel, the Foreign Agent examines the incoming tunnel interface to differentiate between multiple Mobile Nodes that share the same private IP addresses. In this case, each incoming tunnel interface on the Foreign Agent corresponds to a unique Home Agent IP address.

6.2.5 HOME AGENT CONSIDERATIONS

The Home Agent plays an active role during the Mobile Node registration process. The Registration Request message from the Mobile Node is sent directly to the Home Agent if the Mobile Node is registering a Co-located Care-of IP Address. If the Mobile Node is using a Care-of IP Address provided by the Foreign Agent, the Registration Request is relayed by the Foreign Agent to the Home Agent. In either case, the Home Agent receives the Registration Request message and updates its Mobility Binding record for the Mobile Node. The Home Agent then returns a suitable Registration Reply message after processing each Registration Request message. Additionally, the Home Agent forwards IP packets to the Mobile Node at its point of attachment in the Foreign Network.

6.2.5.1 Mobile IPv4 Dynamic Home Agent Address Resolution

In some situations, the Mobile Node may not know the IP address of the Home Agent when registering from a Foreign Network. If the Home Agent's IP address is unknown, the Mobile Node can use the *Dynamic Home Agent Address Resolution* process **[RFC5944]** to discover the IP address. In this case, the Home Agent field of the Registration Request message is set to the *subnet-directed broadcast IP address* of the Mobile Node's Home Network to prompt the Home Agent to respond with a Registration Reply message (see **Appendix B** for a discussion on the difference between IPv4 directed broadcasts and limited broadcasts).

Each Home Agent that receives a Registration Request message with the Home Agent field set to a broadcast (destination) address will reject the Mobile Node's Registration Request message by returning a Registration Reply message that indicates rejection. This allows the Mobile Node to see the Home Agent's unicast IP address indicated in the Registration Reply message (indicating rejection) and to use this IP address in future registration attempts.

6.2.6 ROUTING IPv4 PACKETS TO AND FROM THE MOBILE NODE

This section describes how a Mobile Node, Home Agent, and Foreign Agent interact to route IP packets to a Mobile Node connected to a Foreign Network. A Home Agent and a Foreign Agent can use one of the following defined encapsulation methods to exchange IP packets over a tunnel: IP-in-IP

Encapsulation **[RFC2003]**, Minimal Encapsulation **[RFC2004]**, and Generic Routing Encapsulation (GRE) **[RFC2784]**. The same encapsulation method must be supported by both the Foreign Agent and Home Agent, or by the Mobile Node and Home Agent, when a Co-located Care-of IP Address is used by the Mobile Node. However, support for IP-in-IP Encapsulation is required by all Mobile IP entities (the default tunnel mode).

6.2.6.1   Routing Unicast IP Packets

A Mobile Node follows these rules to choose a default router when it registers on a Foreign Network:

- The process is straightforward when a Mobile Node registers and uses a Foreign Agent Care-of IP Address. The Mobile Node receives Agent Advertisement messages on the local network and selects its default router from the router IP addresses advertised in the message's ICMPv4 Router Advertisement portion. The Mobile Node may also use the source IP address of the Agent Advertisement message as the IP address of a default router.
- The Mobile Node may use a Co-located Care-of IP Address to register directly with its Home Agent. In this case, the Mobile Node selects its default router from the IP routers advertised in any received ICMPv4 Router Advertisement message on the local network. The IP network prefix of the selected default router must match the IP network prefix of the Mobile Node's Co-located Care-of IP Address (which it obtained through external means). The Co-located Care-of IP Address may match the source IP address of an Agent Advertisement message by considering only the IP network prefix of the address and the message. In this case, the Mobile Node may also use that source IP address as the IP address of a default router.
- After the Mobile Node is registered, a Foreign Agent that supports Reverse Tunneling routes the Mobile Node's unicast IP packets through the Reverse Tunnel to the Home Agent. If the Mobile Node is registered with a Foreign Agent that supports Reverse Tunnels, it must use that Foreign Agent as its default router.

6.2.6.2   Routing Broadcast IPv4 Packets

When a Home Agent receives a broadcast or multicast IP packet, it forwards that IP packet only to Mobile Nodes that have specifically requested to receive such IP packets. *A Mobile Node visiting a Foreign Network sets the B-bit (indicating "broadcast IP packets") in its Registration Request message to request its Home Agent to forward broadcast IP packets to it on the visited network* **[RFC5944]**. The D-bit (discussed below) is set to indicate that the Mobile Node is using a Co-located Care-of IP Address and is able to decapsulate tunneled IP packets sent to this IP address.

The method the Home Agent uses to forward broadcast and multicast IP packets to Mobile Nodes depends primarily on two factors: whether the Mobile Node is using a Foreign Agent Care-of IP Address or its own Co-located Care-of IP Address:

- **Method 1**: D-bit is set, indicating the Mobile Node is using a Co-located Care-of IP Address. In this case, the Home Agent tunnels broadcast IP packets directly to the Mobile Node at this IP address (using *single encapsulation*). The source IP address and destination address in the outer IP header (i.e., the tunnel header) are the Home Agent's IP address and the Co-located Care-of IP Address, respectively. The payload of the tunneled packet is the broadcast IP packet. The Mobile Node receives the tunneled packet (with the outer IP header) and decapsulates the broadcast IP packet on its own. The broadcast IP packets are sent through the *Bidirectional Tunnel* established between the Mobile Node and the Home Agent.
- **Method 2**: The D-bit is not set, indicating that the Mobile Node is using a Foreign Agent Care-of IP Address. In this case, a broadcast IP packet must be double encapsulated by the Home Agent; broadcast IP packets are sent to the Mobile Node using *double* encapsulation. The Home Agent first encapsulates the broadcast IP packet in a unicast IP packet

addressed to the Mobile Node's Home IP Address, and then tunnels the resulting IP packet (which contains the unicast IP packet with the broadcast IP packet inside it) to the Foreign Agent Care-of IP Address. The Home Agent performs this extra level of encapsulation so that the Foreign Agent can determine which Mobile Node should receive the broadcast IP packet after it is decapsulated. The Foreign Agent receives the tunneled unicast IP packet (with the encapsulated broadcast packet), extracts, and delivers the unicast IP packet to the Mobile Node as it would any other IP packet. In the unicast IP packet, the IP header's destination IP address identifies the Mobile Node to which the IP packet is to be delivered. However, it is important to note that a unicast destination address is not present in the IP header of broadcast or multicast IP packets. The outer IP header identifies the Mobile Node's Foreign Agent Care-of IP Address and serves as the usual tunnel header. In this double encapsulation method, the Home Agent places a broadcast IP packet in a unicast IP packet, and then places this unicast IP packet inside another IP packet (having the outer IP header) to be sent to the Foreign Agent.

In the above methods, the Mobile Node must decapsulate the received tunneled packet (in the first case) or the unicast IP packet (in the second case) in order to recover the original broadcast IP packet.

6.2.6.3   Routing Multicast IPv4 Packets

For a Mobile Node to receive multicast IP traffic while visiting a Foreign Network, it must join a multicast group using one of the following methods:

- **Method 1**: The Mobile Node may join a multicast group through a local multicast router on the Foreign Network. If the Mobile Node is using a Co-located Care-of IP Address, it can use this address as the source IP address of any IGMP Membership Report messages it sends to join a multicast group (otherwise, it may use its Home IP Address). An IP multicast router must be present on the Foreign Network being visited to handle these and other multicast messages.
- **Method 2**: The Mobile Node may join a multicast group via a Bidirectional Tunnel established to its Home Agent to receive IP multicast. In this case, the Mobile Node joins a multicast group on its Home Subnet by sending IGMP Membership Report messages through a Reverse Tunnel to the Home Agent. However, the Mobile Node's Home Agent must be configured to support multicast routing (it must be a multicast router). The Home Agent then forwards multicast IP packets through the Forward Tunnel to the Mobile Node on the Foreign Network. A Bidirectional Tunnel to the Mobile Node's Home Agent must first be established. The Mobile Node uses its Home IP Address as the source address (in the inner IP header) of IP packets sent through the tunnel to the Home Agent.
  - **Method 2a**: The D-bit is set in its Registration Request message, indicating that the Mobile Node is using a Co-located Care-of IP Address. In this case, the Home Agent uses this IP address to tunnel IP multicast packets directly to the Mobile Node. The Home Agent uses *single encapsulation* to send multicast packets directly to the Mobile Node. *A Mobile Node visiting a Foreign Network sets the D-bit (indicating "decapsulation by Mobile Node") in its Registration Request message if it is able to decapsulate IP packets sent to its Co-located Care-of IP Address on the visited network* **[RFC5944]**.
  - **Method 2b**: The D-bit is not set, meaning the Mobile Node is using a Foreign Agent Care-of IP Address. In this case, the Home Agent uses *double encapsulation* to send the multicast packet to the Mobile Node. The Home Agent first encapsulates each IP multicast packet in a unicast IP packet addressed to the Mobile Node's Home IP Address, and then tunnels the resulting IP packet (containing the unicast IP packet

with the IP multicast packet inside) to the Mobile Node's Foreign Agent Care-of IP Address. The Foreign Agent receives the tunneled unicast IP packet (with the encapsulated multicast packet), extracts it, and delivers the unicast IP packet to the Mobile Node.

- To use Methods 2a and 2b, the Mobile Node must be capable of decapsulating IP packets sent to its Home IP Address to receive the IP encapsulated multicast packets.

A Mobile Node visiting a Foreign Network may also wish to send IP packets to a multicast group. The Mobile Node may use one of the following two methods to accomplish this:

- **Method 1**: Send the IP multicast traffic directly on the visited Foreign Network. However, because multicast routing protocols (and routers) use the source IP address to forward IP multicast packets to receivers, a Mobile Node cannot use its Home IP Address to send multicast packets directly on the visited Foreign Network. Instead, the Mobile Node has to use a Co-located Care-of IP Address as the source IP address of multicast packets when sending them directly on the Foreign Network.
- **Method 2**: Send the IP multicast traffic via a Reverse Tunnel to its Home Agent. In this case, the Mobile Node uses its Home IP Address when tunneling IP multicast packets to its Home Agent. The Mobile Node must use its Home IP Address as the source IP address in both the (inner) IP header of the multicast packet and the (outer) IP header of the encapsulating IP packet. When using this second option, the Home Agent must be a multicast router.

It is important to note that IP multicast routing uses the source IP address of multicast packets to direct them toward receivers (a process called Multicast Reverse Path Forwarding (MRPF)). A multicast distribution tree is created from the multicast source (the root of the tree) to all receivers, with each receiver representing a leaf of the tree **[AWEBKMULT]**. A Mobile Node sending a multicast IP packet on a link must use a valid source IP address for that link. This means a Mobile Node must use a Co-located Care-of IP Address as the source IP address when sending multicast IP packets directly on the visited Foreign Network.

6.2.6.4 Summarizing How Mobile IPv4 Works
The following describes how an IP packet is transferred from one point to another in a Mobile IP network:

1. An IP host (a Correspondent Node) somewhere on the Internet sends an IP packet to a Mobile Node using its Home IP Address (this involves the normal IP routing process).
2. If the Mobile Node is on its Home Network, the IP packet is delivered to the Mobile Node through the normal IP routing process. A gateway (router) attached to the Home Network (also called the Home Link) receives the IP packet and delivers it to the Mobile Node. Otherwise, the Home Agent receives the packet from the Correspondent Node by listening for and intercepting the packet as it is transmitted on the Home Link. The Home Agent uses a Proxy ARP (Address Resolution Protocol) mechanism to intercept the IP packet (see Proxy ARP discussion in **Appendix E**).
3. The Home Agent intercepts the IP packet because it notices (through a Mobility Binding entry) that the Mobile Node has moved to a Foreign Network. The Home Agent then forwards the IP packet through a Forward Tunnel to the Mobile Node on the Foreign Network. The Home Agent uses IP-in-IP encapsulation (the default method) for forwarding the IP packet so that the Mobile Node's Foreign Agent Care-of IP Address or Co-located Care-of IP Address appears in the outer IP header. We assume that the Mobile Node is using a Foreign Agent Care-of IP Address on the Foreign Network.

4. The Foreign Agent decapsulates the tunneled IP packet and delivers it to the Mobile Node on the Foreign Network.
5. IP packets from the Mobile Node, when on its Home Network, are forwarded to the Correspondent Node using normal IP routing procedures. If the Mobile Node is on a Foreign Network, the IP packets are sent to the Foreign Agent, which then forwards them through a Reverse Tunnel to the Home Agent, which in turn forwards the packets to the Correspondent Node using normal IP routing procedures.

Discussion: In situations where IP routers in the network use ingress filtering (i.e., Unicast Reverse Path Forwarding (URPF) checks using the source IP address of an IP packet [AWEBKMULT]), the source IP address must be topologically correct for the IP subnet from which the IP packet originated; otherwise, the routers would not be able to forward the packet to its destination. Routers use URPF checks to guard against spoofed IP packets originating from malicious sources; packets that fail URPF checks are discarded, resulting in routing failures. If the routers between the Mobile Node and the Correspondent Node use URPF checks, the Foreign Agent needs to use Reverse Tunneling [RFC3024] to send the Mobile Node's IP packets to the Home Agent, so they can be sent to the Correspondent Node (Figure 6.2). The Reverse Tunnel is set up between the Foreign Agent and the Home Agent when the Mobile Node is using a Foreign Agent Care-of IP Address. The Foreign Agent uses Reverse Tunneling to deliver all IP packets that the Mobile Node sends to its Home Agent. The Home Agent then forwards IP packets addressed to the Correspondent Node through the path that the IP packet would have taken had the Mobile Node sent that packet from its Home Network. This Reverse Tunneling ensures that the source IP address is correct for all IP routers that the IP packet must traverse from the Foreign Agent to the Home Agent.

6.2.6.5   Reverse Tunneling in Mobile IPv4

All IP packets exchanged between a Correspondent Node and a Mobile Node use the Mobile Node's Home IP Address. The Correspondent Node sends IP packets to the Mobile Node using the Mobile Node's permanent Home IP Address as the destination IP address, and the Correspondent Node's IP address as the source IP address. Because the Home IP Address logically belongs to the Mobile Node's Home Network and Home Agent, normal IP routing is used to forward these IP packets to the Home Agent.

Instead of the Home Agent forwarding the Correspondent Node's IP packets to the Mobile Node's Home IP Address, which belongs to the same network as the Home Agent, the Home Agent redirects these IP packets toward the Foreign Agent through an IP tunnel. The Home Agent does this by encapsulating the Correspondent Node's IP packets with a new IP header containing the Mobile Node's Care-of IP Address (Figure 6.2). The Foreign Agent receives the IP packets, decapsulates them, and forwards them to the Mobile Node.

The Home IP Address is always used even when the Mobile Node has moved to a Foreign Network. The Care-of IP Address (which is not visible to the Correspondent Node) is used only for communication with the Mobility Agents (Home Agent and Foreign Agent). The Mobile Node sends IP packets with the source IP address always set to its Home IP Address. This effectively helps the Mobile Node maintain the appearance that it is always on its Home Network. Even while the Mobile Node is visiting Foreign Networks, maintaining the Home IP Address makes its movements transparent to all Correspondent Nodes.

IP packets destined for a Mobile Node on a Foreign Network (via its Home IP Address) are routed to its Home Network. The Home Agent intercepts these IP packets and tunnels them to the Mobile Node via its Care-of IP Address. The primary functions of tunneling are the encapsulation of IP packets to be sent to the tunnel endpoint and decapsulation when the IP packet reaches the tunnel endpoint. Tunneling IP packets to a Mobile Node while visiting a Foreign Network removes the limitations of using the Home IP Address on networks to which the address does not belong, as well as allows routers that perform URPF checks to forward the Mobile Node's packets without considering (checking) the Home IP Address.

When transmitting IP packets in Mobile IPv6, a Mobile Node on a Foreign Network has the option of sending these packets directly to the Correspondent Node. The Mobile Node does not send the IP packets through the Home Agent, using its permanent Home IP Address as the source IP address of the IP packets. The process of direct transmission to the Correspondent Node is known as *Triangular Routing* or *Route Optimization* in Mobile IPv6 [**RFC6275**]. If necessary, the Foreign Agent can use Reverse Tunneling to send the Mobile Node's IP packets to the Home Agent, which will then forward them to the Correspondent Node. Reverse Tunneling is needed in networks where IP routers perform URPF checks using the source IP address of received IP packets (the source IP address being the Mobile Node's Home IP Address). Mobile IPv6 specifies Reverse Tunneling as the default behavior, with Route Optimization as the optional behavior.

In many cases, routing within the Internet is independent of the source IP address of the IP packet (no URPF checks are done). However, intermediate routers may perform URPF checks to ensure a topologically correct source IP address. If any intermediate router on the path to the Home Agent performs URPF checks, a Mobile Node on a Foreign Network (or its Foreign Agent) needs to establish a Reverse Tunnel to the Home Agent. Setting up a Reverse Tunnel from the Mobile Node's Foreign Agent Care-of IP Address to the Home Agent ensures a topologically correct source IP address for the Mobile Node's IP packets. Mobility Agents (Foreign Agents and Home Agents) advertise their ability to support Reverse Tunnels (Figure 6.2) by setting appropriate Flag bits in the Mobility Agent Advertisement Extension of the Agent Advertisement messages they send:

- **M-bit = 1**: Mobility Agent can receive IP packets using IP Minimal Encapsulation [**RFC2004**]
- **G-bit = 1**: Mobility Agent can receive IP packets using Generic Routing Encapsulation [**RFC2784**]
- **T-bit = 1**: Foreign Agent supports Reverse Tunneling [**RFC3024**]
- **U-bit = 1**: Mobility Agent supports UDP Tunneling [**RFC3519**]

Note that IP-in-IP Encapsulation [**RFC2003**] is the default encapsulation for Mobility Agents. These settings allow a Mobile Node to request a Reverse Tunnel between the Foreign Agent and the Home Agent when it registers its location. A Reverse Tunnel starts at the Mobile Node's Foreign Agent Care-of IP Address or Co-located Care-of IP Address and terminates at its Home Agent.

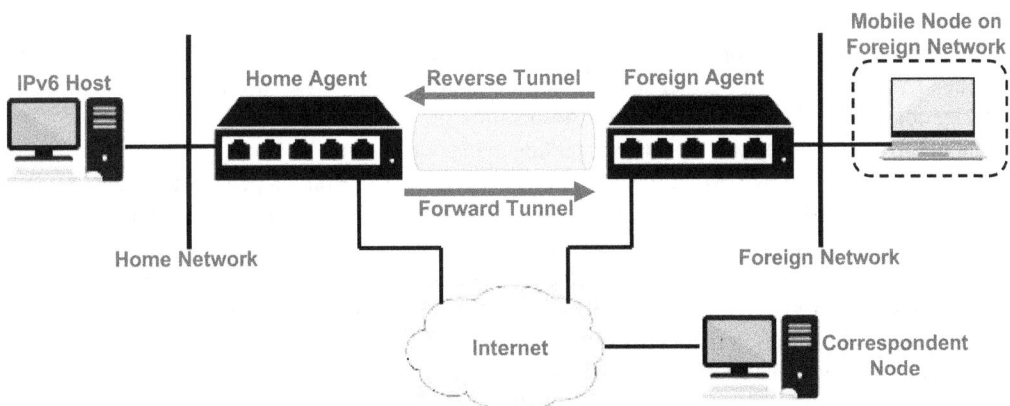

FIGURE 6.2 Mobile IPv4 with Reverse Tunneling.

6.2.6.6   Using Private IPv4 Addresses

Enterprises employ private IP addresses when internal nodes do not need to be visible to external networks, when the details of their connectivity need to be hidden from external networks, or when the nodes do not require direct connectivity to the Internet. Private IP addresses are not routable on the wider Internet, only within the networks in which they are used. A Mobile Node may be assigned a private IP address that is not globally routable on the Internet. In this case, the Mobile Node requires a Reverse Tunnel to communicate with its Home Agent.

With a private IP address, a Mobile Node can only communicate with a Correspondent Node by having its IP packets Reverse-Tunneled to the Home Agent. The Home Agent then decapsulates and delivers the IP packets to the Correspondent Node in the same way they would normally be delivered when the Mobile Node is on the Home Network.

6.2.6.7   Tunnel MTU Discovery

A Home Agent may use Tunnel MTU Discovery to determine the MTU of a tunnel **[RFC4459]** so that tunneled packets can be appropriately sized for transmission. This is a form of the Path MTU Discovery mechanism discussed in **Chapter 2**, but in this case, it is used to discover the MTU of a tunnel so that an encapsulating node (Foreign Agent or Home Agent) can avoid IP packet fragmentation when packets are being routed on the forwarding path between a Correspondent Node and a Mobile Node.

For IP packets destined for a Mobile Node, the Home Agent maintains an association of the MTU of the tunnel and the Mobile Node's Foreign Agent Care-of IP Address or Co-located Care-of IP Address, and also informs the Correspondent Node of the required tunnel MTU. Discovering the tunnel MTU improves the efficiency of routing over the tunnel by avoiding IP packet fragmentation and the associated packet reassembly at the tunnel endpoints. This ensures that IP packets sent will reach the Mobile Node without fragmentation.

6.2.7   SECURITY CONSIDERATIONS

In today's networks, Mobile Nodes primarily use wireless links to connect to networks. However, it is well-known that wireless links have several security vulnerabilities, including passive eavesdropping, active replay attacks, and other active attacks. Mobile IP acknowledges these vulnerabilities and employs various authentication mechanisms to protect Mobile IP Registration messages from such attacks. Mobile IP utilizes a robust authentication scheme to safeguard Registration messages.

A Home Agent, Foreign Agent, and Mobile Node must support a Mobility Security Association for exchanging mobility messages, indexed by a Security Parameter Index (SPI) and an IP address. A Mobility Security Association is a collection of security contexts shared between two nodes, which may be applied to the mobility messages they exchange. Each security context specifies an authentication algorithm and mode, a shared secret key (or appropriate public/private key pair) used to compute the Authenticator value, and the replay protection methods to be implemented. An SPI is an index that identifies a particular security context shared between two nodes among the available security contexts in the Mobility Security Association.

Table 6.2 describes the authorization-enabling extensions in Mobile IPv4 that allow Registration Request messages sent by a Mobile Node to be accepted by the Home Agent. A Home Agent uses the information in these authentication extensions to verify (using cryptographic techniques) the identity of the message originator.

The Registration message exchanges between a Mobile Node and its Home Agent must include the Mobile-Home Authentication Extension (MHAE), which contains an Authenticator value. The integrity of the Registration message exchanges between the Mobile Node and the Home Agent is protected using a pre-shared secret 128-bit key and the following algorithms:

- The default authentication algorithm used in Mobile IPv4 is HMAC-Message Digest Algorithm 5 (HMAC-MD5) **[RFC2104]**, which requires a key size of 128 bits or greater and manual key distribution. The Foreign Agent must also use HMAC-MD5 for authentication with key sizes of 128 bits or greater. In this case, the sender computes an Authenticator value over a Registration message using HMAC-MD5 and places this value in the MHAE. The receiver then computes an Authenticator value over the message and compares it with the value in the MHAE to verify the message's authenticity. The computed Authenticator value (a 128-bit "message digest") protects the Registration Request or Registration Reply message (i.e., the UDP payload and not the UDP header), along with the Extension and the Type, Length, and SPI of the Extension.

- The keyed MD5 in "prefix+suffix" mode **[RFC1321]** may also be used, although it is considered vulnerable to security attacks by the cryptographic community. This operational mode requires that the 128-bit key precedes and follows the Mobile Registration data to be hashed. In this case, the sender computes the Authenticator value for the appended MHAE using keyed MD5 in "prefix+suffix" mode.

Optionally, the messages exchanged between a Mobile Node and a Foreign Agent may be protected by appending the Mobile-Foreign Authentication Extension, while the messages exchanged between a Foreign Agent and a Home Agent may be protected by appending the Foreign-Home Authentication Extension. Several authentication algorithms, algorithm modes, key sizes, and key distribution methods can be used in Mobile IP.

The different authentication methods used in Mobile IP are designed to prevent Registration messages from being altered. Mobile IP also supports a replay protection mechanism that alerts Mobile IP entities when they receive duplicates of previously sent Registration messages. In the absence of such a replay protection method, a Mobile Node and its Home Agent may become unsynchronized if different versions of a Registration message are received by either mobile entity.

For example, a Home Agent might receive a duplicate Registration Request message for deregistration while the Mobile Node is registered through a Foreign Agent. Mobile IPv4 employs a method known as timestamps (mandatory) or Nonces (optional) to ensure replay protection **[RFC5944]**. A Nonce is a randomly selected value (different from previously selected values) that is inserted into a message to protect against replays. Home Agents and Mobile Nodes exchange Nonces and timestamps carried within their Mobile IP Registration messages.

The authentication mechanism ensures that Nonces and timestamps have not been altered by other parties. Consequently, if a Home Agent or Mobile Node receives a duplicate Mobile IP Registration message, the duplicate message can be detected and discarded. The use of tunnels in Mobile IP can present significant security vulnerabilities, especially if Registration messages are not authenticated. Additionally, when ARP messages sent on a network segment (the Home Link) are not authenticated, malicious entities can potentially use ARP to intercept a Mobile Node's traffic while it is visiting a Foreign Network.

6.2.7.1 Using IPSec with Mobile IPv4

Generally, the Mobility Agents (Home Agents and Foreign Agents) are fixed entities in the network. This makes it convenient for them to use IPSec authentication or encryption to protect both Mobile IP Registration messages, and the traffic carried on the Forward and Reverse Tunnels. However, it should be noted that, the use of IPSec works completely and independently of Mobile IP, and only depends on the Mobility Agent's ability to perform IPSec functions. Mobile Nodes can also protect their Registration messages using IPSec authentication.

In general, if a Mobile Node registers through a Foreign Agent, it cannot use IPSec encryption. This is because, by using IPSec encryption, the Foreign Agent cannot check the information carried in the Registration message. While the Mobile Node can use IPSec encryption when a Foreign Agent is not needed, the issue of a Co-located Care-of IP Address in the Foreign Network presents certain challenges because the Co-located Care-of IP Address can only be used while the Mobile Node is visiting the particular Foreign Network (subnet) to which the address belongs.

IPSec encryption is an IP-level (Network Layer) security mechanism that encrypts the entire Registration message when used. Consequently, encryption makes it difficult for the Home Agent to know the Co-located Care-of IP Address of a Mobile Node without prior configuration information or Registration messages.

6.2.8 USING ARP, PROXY ARP, AND GRATUITOUS ARP IN MOBILE IPv4

A Home Agent intercepts IP packets destined for a Mobile Node's Home Address and tunnels them to the Mobile Node's Foreign Agent Care-of IP Address or Co-located Care-of IP Address. The tunneled IP packets received at the tunnel endpoint (either at the Foreign Agent or at the Mobile Node itself) are decapsulated and delivered to the Mobile Node. When on its Home Network, IP packets originated by the Mobile Node are generally delivered via standard IP routing mechanisms to their destinations, not necessarily going through the Home Agent.

The Home Agent uses Proxy ARP and Gratuitous ARP mechanisms to learn and intercept IP packets on the Home Network that are destined for the Home IP Address of any registered Mobile Nodes. As discussed in **Appendix D**, Gratuitous ARP is an ARP message sent by a node on a network segment to prompt other nodes on that segment to update an entry in their local ARP Caches. In addition to the standard use of IPv4 ARP for discovering the Link-Layer (Medium Access Control (MAC)) address of a target node given its IP address, the following subsections describe the specific use of ARP on the Home Network of a Mobile Node.

6.2.8.1 Mobile Node Is Registered on a Foreign Network

After a Mobile Node has moved to a Foreign Network and registered, its Home Agent uses Proxy ARP to send an ARP Reply when it receives an ARP Request seeking the Mobile Node's Link-Layer (MAC) address. Upon receiving an ARP Request, the Home Agent first examines the Target IP Address indicated in the ARP Request to see if any Mobile Node in its registered Mobility Bindings has this IP address as its Home IP Address. If the registered Mobility Bindings have a matching entry, the Home Agent transmits an ARP Reply on behalf of the Mobile Node. The ARP Reply indicates that the Home Agent's own interface Link-Layer address is associated with the Mobile Node's Home IP Address.

Additionally, while the Mobile Node has a Mobility Binding registered on the Foreign Network, its Home Agent sends Gratuitous ARP messages to update the ARP Caches of nodes on the Home Network. Sending these ARP messages causes the nodes on the Home Network to associate the Home Agent's Link-Layer address with the Mobile Node's Home IP Address. When the Home Agent is registering a Mobility Binding for a Mobile Node for which no previous Mobility Binding exists (indicating that the Mobile Node was assumed to be on the Home Network), the Home Agent must broadcast a Gratuitous ARP message on behalf of the Mobile Node on the network segment associated with the Mobile Node's Home Address. The Gratuitous ARP messages should be retransmitted a small number of times, as broadcasts on the local network segment (such as Ethernet) are typically not guaranteed to reach all nodes.

While the Mobile Node is visiting a Foreign Network, it must not transmit any broadcast ARP Request or ARP Reply messages. Additionally, the Mobile Node must not reply to ARP Requests in which the Target IP Address is set to its own Home IP Address unless the ARP Request is a unicast ARP Request sent by a Foreign Agent with which the Mobile Node is attempting to register or by a Foreign Agent with which the Mobile Node has an unexpired Registration. In the latter case, the Mobile Node must send a unicast ARP Reply message in response to the Foreign Agent's unicast ARP Request.

Note that if the Mobile Node is using a Co-located Care-of IP Address on the Foreign Network and receives an ARP Request in which the Target IP Address is set to this Co-located Care-of IP Address, then the Mobile Node should send an ARP Reply in response to this ARP Request. It should also be noted that when the Mobile Node is transmitting a Registration Request message on the Foreign Network, it may discover a Foreign Agent's Link-Layer address by simply examining and storing the Link-Layer address associated with the Agent Advertisement message received from that Foreign Agent, as this prevents the need to broadcast an ARP Request message.

The following summarizes the operations performed by a Mobile Node when it leaves its Home Network:

- The Mobile Node decides to register on a Foreign Network, possibly because it has received an Agent Advertisement from a Foreign Agent and has not recently received one from its Home Agent.
- Before the Mobile Node transmits the Registration Request message, it disables its capability to respond to any future ARP Requests it may subsequently receive seeking the Link-Layer address associated with its Home IP Address, except when necessary to communicate with Foreign Agents on the visited Foreign Network.
- The Mobile Node proceeds to transmit its Registration Request message.
- Upon receiving and accepting the Mobile Node's Registration Request message, the Home Agent sends a Gratuitous ARP message on the Home Link on behalf of the Mobile Node and begins using Proxy ARP to reply to ARP Requests that it receives seeking the Link-Layer address of the Mobile Node. In the Gratuitous ARP message, the Home Agent sets the ARP Sender Hardware Address to its own Link-Layer address. If, on the other hand, the Home Agent rejects the Registration Request, it does not process any related ARP messages (neither Gratuitous nor Proxy ARP messages).

6.2.8.2   Mobile Node Returns to Its Home Network

When a Mobile Node moves back to its Home Network, both the Mobile Node and its Home Agent send Gratuitous ARP messages to prompt all local nodes on the Home Network to update their ARP Caches and once again associate the Link-Layer address of the Mobile Node with its Home IP Address. Before the Mobile Node transmits the (de)Registration Request message to its Home Agent, it must first send the Gratuitous ARP message as a local broadcast on its Home Link. The Mobile Node should retransmit the Gratuitous ARP message a few times to increase its chances of reaching all local nodes, but these retransmissions should occur in parallel with the transmission and processing of the (de)Registration Request message.

Upon receiving and accepting the Mobile Node's (de)Registration Request message, the Home Agent must also transmit a Gratuitous ARP message on the Mobile Node's Home Link. The purpose of transmitting this Gratuitous ARP is to prompt local nodes on the Home Link to associate the Mobile Node's Home IP Address with its Link-Layer address. The Mobile Node and Home Agent both send a Gratuitous ARP message because, in cases where the Home Network also supports wireless network interfaces, the transmission range of the Home Agent may differ from that of the Mobile Node. The Home Agent must send the ARP message as a local broadcast on the Mobile Node's Home Link, and this message should be retransmitted a few times to improve the chances of reaching all local nodes. However, the Home Agent should make these retransmissions in parallel with the transmission and processing of the Mobile Node's (de)Registration Reply message.

The following summarizes the operations performed by a Mobile Node when it returns to its Home Network:

- The Mobile Node receives an Agent Advertisement message from its Home Agent and decides to register at home.
- Before the Mobile Node transmits the Registration Request message, it re-enables its capability to respond to any future ARP Requests it may subsequently receive seeking its Link-Layer address.
- The Mobile Node transmits a Gratuitous ARP message on the local link announcing its presence. In this Gratuitous ARP message, the Mobile Node sets the ARP Sender Hardware Address to its own Link-Layer address.

- The Mobile Node proceeds to transmit its Registration Request message.
- Upon receiving and accepting the Mobile Node's Registration Request message, the Home Agent stops using Proxy ARP to reply to ARP Requests that it receives seeking the Link-Layer address of the Mobile Node and then transmits a Gratuitous ARP message on behalf of the Mobile Node. In this Gratuitous ARP message, the Home Agent sets the ARP Sender Hardware Address to the Mobile Node's Link-Layer address. If, on the other hand, the Home Agent rejects the Registration Request, it must not make any changes to the way it performs ARP processing (neither Gratuitous nor Proxy ARP) for the Mobile Node. In this case, the Home Agent should operate as if the Mobile Node is still on a Foreign Network and continue to perform Proxy ARP on behalf of the Mobile Node.

6.3   MOBILE IPv6

Mobile IPv6 [RFC6275] defines mobility mechanisms for IPv6, allowing IPv6 users to visit Foreign Networks with different Link-Layer technologies (e.g., Ethernet and WiFi). It enables a node to maintain the same permanent Home IPv6 Address while roaming on other networks. Just like Mobile IPv4, a Mobile Node can access applications on its Home Network while using its permanent Home IPv6 Address on Foreign Networks. A Mobile Node is able to maintain Transport Layer and upper-layer connectivity with its Home Network when changing locations. For example, a Mobile Node may move from a foreign Ethernet network segment to a foreign wireless LAN while its Home IPv6 Address remains unchanged. A Mobile Node can communicate with other nodes on other networks using its Home IPv6 Address even after changing its foreign Link-Layer point of attachment.

6.3.1   CHANGES IN IPv6 AND MOBILE IPv4 FOR MOBILE IPv6

The following changes were made to IPv6 and Mobile IPv4 to obtain Mobile IPv6 [RFC6275]:

- A new IPv6 extension header called the Mobility Header (with an IPv6 Next Header value of 135 in the immediately preceding header) was defined for the following Mobile IPv6 signaling messages (Table 6.3):
  - Binding Refresh Request Message (Type=0)
  - Home Test Init Message (Type=1)
  - Care-of Test Init Message (Type=2)
  - Home Test Message (Type=3)
  - Care-of Test Message (Type=4)
  - Binding Update Message (Type=5)
  - Binding Acknowledgement Message (Type=6)
  - Binding Error Message (Type=7)

  The Mobility Header is an IPv6 extension header used by Home Agents, Mobile Nodes, and Correspondent Nodes in all the messages they exchange related to the creation and management of Mobility Bindings. The Mobility Header messages must not be sent with a Type 2 Routing header, except for Binding Acknowledgement messages, and must not be used with the Home Address Option (Option Type 201), except for Binding Update messages.
- A set of IPv6 Mobility Options were defined to be included in the above mobility messages (Table 6.4). A mobility message is a Mobile IPv6 message that contains a Mobility Header. The IPv6 Mobility Options include the following:
  - Binding Refresh Advice Option (Type=2)
  - Alternate Care-of Address Option (Type=3)
  - Nonce Indices Option (Type=4)
  - Binding Authorization Data Option (Type=5)

- A new Home Address Option (Option Type=201) was defined to be carried in the IPv6 Destination Options extension header (IPv6 header value=60); see discussion in **Chapter 2**.
  - Note that the IPv6 Destination Options extension header (described in **Chapter 2**) carries optional information that needs to be examined only by the IPv6 node indicated in the Destination IPv6 Address field in the IPv6 header, not by intermediate routers.
- A new Type 2 Routing header (Routing Type=2) was defined for the Mobile IPv6 Route Optimization method and may be present in a packet as an IPv6 header extension; see discussion in **Chapter 2**.
  - As discussed in **Chapter 2**, the IPv6 Routing Header may be included in an IPv6 packet as an extension to the IPv6 header, indicating to downstream IPv6 nodes that the IPv6 payload must be delivered to a destination IPv6 address using a method different from standard IPv6 Routing.
- New ICMPv6 messages were defined for discovering the set of Home Agents on a network and obtaining the IPv6 prefix of the Home Link (Table 6.5):
  - ICMPv6 Home Agent Address Discovery Request message (ICMPv6 Type=144)
  - ICMPv6 Home Agent Address Discovery Reply message (ICMPv6 Type=145)
  - ICMPv6 Mobile Prefix Solicitation message (ICMPv6 Type=146)
  - ICMPv6 Mobile Prefix Advertisement message (ICMPv6 Type=147)
- Modifications to the IPv6 Neighbor Discovery protocol (described in **Chapter 4**) were made to include Mobile IPv6 attributes (Table 6.6). This resulted in the following modified IPv6 Neighbor Discovery messages and new options:
  - Modified Router Advertisement message (ICMPv6 Type=134)
  - Modified Prefix Information Option (Option Type=3)
  - New Advertisement Interval Option (Type=7)
  - New Home Agent Information Option (Type=8)
- Changes were made regarding how ICMPv6 Router Advertisements are sent.
- Changes were made to eliminate the use of Foreign Agents in Mobile IPv6; Mobile IPv6 no longer requires Foreign Agents. It operates on a Foreign Network without needing special support from the local router.
- Mobile IPv6 supports Route Optimization as a fundamental feature.
- Mobile IPv6 supports the IPv6 Neighbor Unreachability Detection feature to ensure symmetric reachability between a Mobile Node and its default router at its current point of attachment to a Foreign Network.
- By using the ICMPv6 Neighbor Discovery protocol (a Network Layer protocol) instead of the Link-Layer protocol ARP (used in Mobile IPv4), Mobile IPv6 is decoupled from any particular Link-Layer technology, thereby improving the versatility and robustness of Mobile IPv6.

6.3.2 BASIC MOBILE IPV6 OPERATION

Just as in Mobile IPv4, each Mobile Node in Mobile IPv6 is identified by two IPv6 addresses: its Home IPv6 Address and a Care-of IPv6 Address (we will drop the "v6" from now on in our discussion). The Home IP Address is a permanent IP address associated with the Home Network of the Mobile Node, identifying it regardless of its location on the Internet. While the Mobile Node is on its Home Network, IP packets sent to its Home IP Address are routed to the Home Link of the Mobile Node through conventional Internet routing mechanisms.

The Care-of IP Address provides information about the Mobile Node's current location on a Foreign Network and changes at each new point of attachment. When a Mobile Node visits a Foreign Network, it *must acquire* a Care-of IP Address, which the Mobile Node uses while visiting that network. *The Mobile Node may use the well-known methods of the IPv6 Neighbor Discovery protocol to obtain its Care-of IP Address. The Care-of IP Address may be acquired through*

TABLE 6.3

IPv6 Mobility Header (MH) Message Types

Message Name	MH Message Type Value	Description
Binding Refresh Request	0	A Correspondent Node sends this message type to request a Mobile Node to update (reestablish) its Mobility Binding with the Correspondent Node. This message is typically used when the cached Binding is in active use but the Binding's Lifetime is close to expiration. The Correspondent Node may use, for instance, recent traffic and open Transport Layer connections as an indication of active use.
Home Test Init	1	A Mobile Node sends this message type to initiate the Return Routability Procedure and to request a Home Keygen Token from a Correspondent Node. The Return Routability Procedure authorizes registrations through the use of a cryptographic token exchange. A Keygen Token is a number supplied by a Correspondent Node in the Return Routability Procedure to enable the Mobile Node to compute the necessary Binding Management Key for authorizing a Binding Update. A Binding Management Key (Kbm) is a key used for authorizing a Binding Cache Management message (e.g., Binding Update or Binding Acknowledgement).
Care-of Test Init	2	A Mobile Node sends this message type to initiate the Return Routability Procedure and to request a Care-of Keygen Token from a Correspondent Node. A Care-of Keygen Token is a Keygen Token sent by the Correspondent Node in the Care-of Test message.
Home Test	3	A Correspondent Node sends this message type in response to a Home Test Init message sent by a Mobile Node.
Care-of Test	4	A Correspondent Node sends this message type in response to a Care-of Test Init message sent by a Mobile Node.
Binding Update	5	This message type is sent by a Mobile Node to notify a Correspondent Node or the Home Agent of the Mobile Node of its current Binding (Care-of Address and Home Address). The Binding Update sent to the Mobile Node's Home Agent to register its primary Care-of Address is marked as a "Home Registration."
Binding Acknowledgement	6	This message type is sent by a Correspondent Node or a Home Agent to acknowledge receipt of a Binding Update from a Mobile Node if an acknowledgement was requested in the Binding Update (e.g., the Binding Update was sent to a Home Agent) or an error occurred.
Binding Error	7	This message type is sent by the Correspondent Node to signal an error related to mobility, such as an inappropriate attempt to use the Home Address Destination Option without an existing Binding. This message is also used by the Home Agent to signal an error to the Mobile Node if it receives an unrecognized Mobility Header Message Type from the Mobile Node.

stateless, stateful, or manual configuration methods available for IPv6 addressing (as discussed in **Chapters 4 and 5**). *The method through which the Care-of IP Address is acquired is irrelevant to how Mobile IPv6 works.* As long as the Mobile Node is on the corresponding Foreign Network, IP packets sent to the Care-of IP Address will be routed directly to the Mobile Node.

The main issue is for a Mobile Node to acquire a Care-of IP Address on a Foreign Network, and once that is done, the Mobile Node can register this address with its Home Network, allowing communication between the two to start. Using the Care-of IP Address, the Mobile Node and its Home Agent can communicate directly (via an established Bidirectional Tunnel) without using a Foreign Agent. This is why Mobile IPv6 does not support the concept of a Foreign Agent, unlike Mobile IPv4. The association or mapping between the Home IP Address and Care-of IP Address of a Mobile Node is referred to as a *Mobility Binding* (or simply, Binding) for the Mobile Node.

TABLE 6.4

IPv6 Mobility Message Options

Option Name	Option Type Value	Description
Pad1	0	This Option is used to insert one byte of padding in the Mobility Options area of a Mobility Header. If more than one byte of padding is required, the PadN Option should be used rather than multiple Pad1 Options.
PadN	1	This Option is used to insert two or more bytes of padding in the Mobility Options area of a mobility message.
Binding Refresh Advice	2	The Refresh Interval in this Option indicates the remaining time until the Mobile Node SHOULD send a new home registration to the Home Agent. This Option is only valid in a Binding Acknowledgement message and only on the Binding Acknowledgement messages sent by a Mobile Node's Home Agent in a reply to a Home Registration.
Alternate Care-of Address	3	Normally, a Binding Update specifies the desired Care-of Address in the Source IP Address field of the IPv6 header. However, this is not possible in some cases, such as when the Mobile Node wishes to indicate a Care-of Address that it cannot use as a topologically correct source IP address or when the security mechanism used does not protect the IPv6 header. The Alternate Care-of Address Option is provided for these situations. This Option is valid only in Binding Update messages. The Alternate Care-of Address field of this option contains an IP address to be used as the Care-of Address for the Binding, rather than using the address in the Source IP Address field of the packet as the Care-of Address.
Nonce Indices	4	This Option is valid only in the Binding Update message sent to a Correspondent Node and only when present together with a Binding Authorization Data Option. When the Correspondent Node authorizes the Binding Update, it needs to produce Home and Care-of Keygen Tokens from its stored random Nonce values. The Home Nonce Index field in this Option indicates to the Correspondent Node which Nonce value to use when producing the Home Keygen Token. The Care-of Nonce Index field in this Option is ignored in requests to delete a Binding. Otherwise, it indicates to the Correspondent Node which Nonce value to use when producing the Care-of Keygen Token.
Binding Authorization Data	5	This Option is valid in Binding Update and Binding Acknowledgement messages. The Authenticator field in this Option contains a cryptographic value that can be used to determine if the message in question comes from the right authority.

The Home Network must have at least one Home Agent configured on it, and every Mobile Node that belongs to the Home Network must be configured to know the IP address of its Home Agent. While visiting a Foreign Network, the Mobile Node registers its primary Care-of IP Address with a specific router (Home Agent) on its Home Link. This Binding Registration is performed by the Mobile Node sending a Binding Update message to the Home Agent. The Home Agent receives the Binding Update and creates an association between the Mobile Node's Home IP Address and the Care-of IP Address assigned to it. The Home Agent then returns a Binding Acknowledgement message to the Mobile Node.

Registration in Mobile IPv6 is the process during which a Mobile Node sends a Binding Update message to its Home Agent or a Correspondent Node, causing the recipient to register a Mobility Binding for the Mobile Node. Note that Home Registration is a registration between a Mobile Node and its Home Agent and involves the use of IPSec for the security protection of registration messages.

A Home Agent maintains a *Binding Cache* that contains the association between the Home IP Address and the Care-of IP Address for each Mobile Node it serves. The Home Agent intercepts any IP packet on the Home Link destined for a Home IP Address (possibly from a Correspondent

TABLE 6.5

ICMPv6 Messages for Mobile IPv6

Message Name	ICMPv6 Message Type Value	Description
Home Agent Address Discovery Request	144	A Mobile Node sends this message type to initiate the Dynamic Home Agent Address Discovery mechanism. The Mobile Node sends this message to the Mobile IPv6 Home-Agents Anycast IP Address for its own home subnet prefix.
Home Agent Address Discovery Reply	145	A Home Agent sends this message type to respond to a Mobile Node that uses the Dynamic Home Agent Address Discovery mechanism. The Home Agent Addresses field in this message contains a list of IPv6 addresses of Home Agents on the Home Link of the Mobile Node.
Mobile Prefix Solicitation	146	A Mobile Node sends this message type to its Home Agent while it is away from home. The purpose of this message is to solicit an ICMPv6 Mobile Prefix Advertisement message from the Home Agent, which will allow the Mobile Node to gather prefix information about its Home Network. This information can be used to configure and update Home Address(es) according to changes in IPv6 prefix information supplied by the Home Agent.
Mobile Prefix Advertisement	147	A Home Agent sends this message type to a Mobile Node to distribute IPv6 prefix information about the Home Link while the Mobile Node is traveling away from the Home Network. This message will be sent in response to an ICMPv6 Mobile Prefix Solicitation message, or as an unsolicited Advertisement.

TABLE 6.6

Modified and New IPv6 Neighbor Discovery Messages for Mobile IPv6

Message/Option Name	ICMPv6 Message/ Option Type Value	Description
Modified Router Advertisement message	134	Mobile IPv6 modified the format of the ICMPv6 Router Advertisement message by the addition of a single flag bit to indicate that the router sending the Router Advertisement message is serving as a Home Agent on this link.
Modified Prefix Information Option	3	Mobile IPv6 requires knowledge of a router's IPv6 global address in building a Home Agents List as part of the Dynamic Home Agent Address Discovery mechanism. However, the IPv6 Neighbor Discovery protocol only advertises a router's Link-Local address by requiring this address to be used as the Source IP Address of each Router Advertisement message. Mobile IPv6 extended the IPv6 Neighbor Discovery protocol to allow a router to advertise its IPv6 global address by the addition of a single flag bit in the IPv6 Prefix Information Option for use in Router Advertisement messages.
New Advertisement Interval Option	7	Mobile IPv6 defined this new Option to be used in Router Advertisement messages to advertise the interval at which the sending router sends unsolicited multicast Router Advertisement messages.
New Home Agent Information Option	8	Mobile IPv6 defined this new Option to be used in Router Advertisement messages sent by a Home Agent to advertise information specific to this router's functionality as a Home Agent.

Node on the Internet), encapsulates it, and tunnels the packet to the registered Care-of IP Address of the Mobile Node on a Foreign Network. The Mobile Node on the visited Foreign Network will then send a Binding Update to the Correspondent Node, informing it of its assigned Care-of IP Address. The Correspondent Node, upon receiving the Binding Update, creates an entry in its Binding Cache so that it can send subsequent IP packets directly to the Mobile Node at its Care-of IP Address (on the Foreign Network) without going through the Home Agent.

Mobility IPv6 provides the following basic functions at the Home Agent, a stationary Correspondent Node, and a router on a Foreign Network being visited by the Mobile Node.

- **Home Agent:**
  - Maintains a Binding Cache entry for each Mobile Node it serves.
  - Intercepts IP packets on the Home Link addressed to a Mobile Node's Home IP Address while the Mobile Node is visiting a Foreign Network.
  - Encapsulates the intercepted IP packets and tunnels them to the Mobile Node's Care-of IP Address indicated in the Home Agent's Binding Cache.
  - Returns a Binding Acknowledgment message in response to a received Binding Update message from the Mobile Node when the Acknowledge (A) bit is set.
  - Runs IPv6 Duplicate Address Detection on the Care-of IP Address of the Mobile Node to ensure the IPv6 address is unique.
  - Supports Dynamic Home Agent Address Discovery to assist Mobile Nodes visiting Foreign Networks in discovering the IP addresses of Home Agents.
  - Supports the reception of ICMPv6 Mobile Prefix Solicitation messages (ICMPv6 Type 146) and the sending of ICMPv6 Mobile Prefix Advertisement messages (ICMPv6 Type 147).
- **Stationary Correspondent Node:**
- Receives an IPv6 packet and processes the IPv6 Home Address Option (Option Type 201) carried in the IPv6 Destination Options extension header.
- Processes an IPv6 mobility message with a Binding Update (if its Acknowledge (A) bit is set) and returns a Binding Acknowledgment message.
- Receives Binding Updates and enters the Bindings indicated in them into a Binding Cache.
- Sends IPv6 packets to a Mobile Node using an IPv6 Routing header when there is an entry in the Binding Cache containing the Mobile Node's current Care-of IP Address.
- **An IPv6 router on a Foreign Network being visited by a Mobile Node:**
- Sends an Advertisement Interval Option (Option Type 7) in its ICMPv6 Router Advertisement messages (ICMPv6 Type 134) to aid in the detection of Mobile Node movements.
- Supports the sending of unsolicited multicast ICMPv6 Router Advertisement messages at a faster rate (configurable via the *MinRtrAdvInterval* variable in **[RFC4861]**).
- Sends a Home Agent Information Option (Option Type 8) (Home Agent preference and Lifetime) in its ICMPv6 Router Advertisement messages to aid Mobile Nodes select their Home Agents.

6.3.3 CONCEPTUAL DATA STRUCTURES

Mobile IPv6 introduces the following conceptual data structures:

- **Binding Cache**: This cache contains Mobility Bindings (i.e., Home Address and Care-of Address of Mobile Nodes) and is maintained by Home Agents and Correspondent Nodes. It contains both "Home Registration" entries and "Correspondent Registration" entries.
- **Binding Update List**: This list is maintained by a Mobile Node and contains both Correspondent and Home Registrations. It has an entry for every Mobility Binding that the Mobile Node has or is trying to establish with the Home Agent or a Correspondent Node. The Mobile Node deletes a Binding from the list as the Lifetime of the Binding expires.

- **Home Agents List**: A Home Agent stores in this list the other Home Agents on the same Home Link. The Home Agent uses this list to inform Mobile Nodes about the available Home Agents on the link during Dynamic Home Agent Address Discovery.

6.3.4   MOBILE NODE AND CORRESPONDENT NODE COMMUNICATIONS

A Correspondent Node is any node (either a stationary node or a Mobile Node) communicating with a Mobile Node. Mobile IPv6 allows a Mobile Node to provide information about its current location to a Correspondent Node. This is accomplished through the Correspondent Registration process, during which the Mobile Node and Correspondent Node perform a *Return Routability Procedure* (Test) to authorize the establishment of a Mobility Binding.

Mobile IPv6 provides two possible modes for a Mobile Node and a Correspondent Node to communicate with each other: *Bidirectional Tunneling* and *Route Optimization* (see Figure 6.3). Figure 6.3).

6.3.4.1   Bidirectional Tunneling

Bidirectional Tunneling does not require a Correspondent Node to support Mobile IPv6, and this mode can be used even if the Mobile Node has not registered its current Mobility Binding with the Correspondent Node. In this mode, IPv6 packets sent by the Correspondent Node are routed to the Mobile Node's Home Agent and then tunneled to the Mobile Node. IPv6 packets sent by the Mobile Node to the Correspondent Node are first tunneled (i.e., Reverse-Tunneled) from the Mobile Node to the Home Agent, and then routed through standard IP routing mechanisms from the Home Network to the Correspondent Node.

In this mode, the Home Agent uses IPv6 Proxy Neighbor Discovery on the Home Link to intercept any IPv6 packets sent to the Home IP Address (or Home IP Addresses) of the Mobile Node.

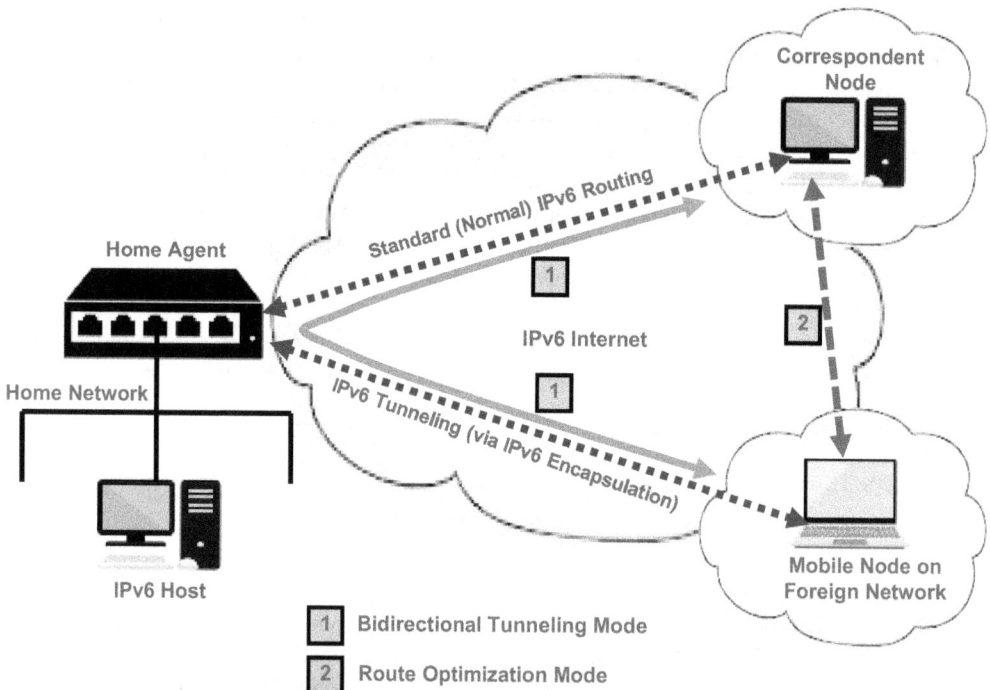

FIGURE 6.3   Mobile IPv6 Bidirectional Tunneling versus Route Optimization mode.

Each intercepted IPv6 packet is tunneled to the Mobile Node's primary Care-of IP Address. The Home Agent performs IPv6 packet tunneling using IPv6 encapsulation.

6.3.4.2 Route Optimization in Mobile IPv6

With *Route Optimization*, a Correspondent Node also supports the conceptual data structure known as the Binding Cache. The Binding Cache maintains bindings for the Home IP Address and the current Care-of IP Address of a Mobile Node. Each time the Home Agent receives an IP packet destined for a Mobile Node that is currently visiting a Foreign Network, it sends a Binding Update to the Correspondent Node to update the information in its Binding Cache. After this update, the Correspondent Node can tunnel IP packets directly to the Mobile Node on the Foreign Network.

The Route Optimization mode requires the Mobile Node to register its current Mobility Binding (i.e., Home IP Address and Care-of IP Address) with the Correspondent Node. Then, IPv6 packets sent by the Correspondent Node are routed directly to the Mobile Node's Care-of IP Address. Before sending an IPv6 packet to any destination, the Correspondent Node first checks its Binding Cache for an entry matching the packet's destination IPv6 address. If an entry exists in the Binding Cache for this destination IPv6 address, the Correspondent Node uses the new Type 2 IPv6 Routing Header defined for Mobile IPv6 **[RFC6275]** to route the IPv6 packet to the Mobile Node's Care-of IP Address indicated in the matching entry.

Routing the Correspondent Node's IPv6 packets directly to the Mobile Node's Care-of IP Address allows the IPv6 Routing mechanisms to use the shortest communications path to the Mobile Node. It also reduces the processing load on the Mobile Node's Home Agent and Home Link, potentially eliminating network congestion. Furthermore, the effects of any temporary failures at the Home Agent or links on the path to or from the Home Agent will be reduced.

When the Correspondent Node sends IPv6 packets directly to the Mobile Node, it sets the Destination IPv6 Address field in the IPv6 header to the Mobile Node's Care-of IP Address. The Correspondent Node also adds the new Type 2 IPv6 Routing Header to the IPv6 packet to carry the Mobile Node's Home IP Address. Similarly, when the Mobile Node sends IPv6 packets to the Correspondent Node, it sets the Source IPv6 Address field in the packet's IPv6 header to its current Care-of IP Address. The Mobile Node adds the new IPv6 Home Address Option (Option Type 201) in an IPv6 Destination Options extension header (IPv6 header value 60) to carry the Mobile Node's Home IP Address. Including the Home IP Address in these IPv6 packets makes the use of the Care-of IP Address transparent at the Transport Layer and above (i.e., above the Network (IP) Layer).

6.3.5 Mobile IPv6 Security

The Mobile IPv6 security features include the protection of the Binding Updates that a Mobile Node sends to both the Home Agent and the Correspondent Node, the protection of Mobile Prefix Discovery messages (i.e., ICMPv6 Mobile Prefix Solicitation and Mobile Prefix Advertisement messages), and the protection of the mechanisms used for the transportation of Mobile IPv6 data packets (such as the Mobile IPv6 Home Address Option and Type 2 Routing header).

The Binding Updates that a Mobile Node sends to a Correspondent Node or the Home Agent can be protected through the use of IPSec extension headers or the Mobility IPv6 Binding Authorization Data Option (Option Type 5). The Binding Authorization Data Option type involves using a Binding Management Key (Kbm), which the mobility nodes involved have established via the Return Routability Procedure. Protection of the Mobile Prefix Discovery messages is achieved through the use of IPSec extension headers.

6.3.5.1 Sending Binding Updates to a Home Agent

Mobile IPv6 entities can leverage IPSec (the IPv6 Authentication (AH) and Encapsulating Security Payload (ESP) extension headers described in **Chapter 2**) to protect the integrity and authenticity of Binding Update and Binding Acknowledgement messages. A Mobile Node and its Home Agent must use IPSec with ESP and a non-NULL payload authentication algorithm to protect the Binding Update and Binding Acknowledgement messages they exchange (i.e., for data origin authentication, data integrity, and optionally, anti-replay protection).

A Mobile Node and its Home Agent create appropriate security policy database entries to protect the messages they exchange with each other using IPSec. The Mobile Node's Home IP Address is used in Binding Update messages as the source IP address and in Binding Acknowledgement messages as the destination IP address. The Home IP Address is also used in the Mobile IPv6 Home Address Option and the Type 2 Routing header.

Mobile IPv6 supports manual configuration of security associations where the shared secrets used (distributed off-line to the Mobile Nodes) must be random and unique for each Mobile Node. Mobile IPv6 also supports automatic key management using the Internet Key Exchange Protocol version 2 (IKEv2) **[RFC4877] [RFC 5996]**.

6.3.5.2   Sending Binding Updates to a Correspondent Node

The Binding Update messages that a Mobile Node sends to a Correspondent Node do not require the configuration of security associations or the presence of authentication mechanisms between the Mobile Node and the Correspondent Node. Instead, Mobile IPv6 uses the Return Routability Procedure as the method for ensuring that the correct Mobile Node is sending the message. However, this method does not provide protection against attackers who are acting on the path between the Mobile Node's Home Network and the Correspondent Node. It should be noted that attackers on this part of the path can perform the same attacks even when Mobile IPv6 is not used. Even with its limitations, the main advantage of the Return Routability Procedure is that potential attacks are limited to the path between the Home Network and the Correspondent Node, and it guards against forged Binding Update messages from other parts of the path.

A Mobile Node uses a keyed-hash algorithm to protect the integrity and authenticity of the Binding Update messages sent to the Correspondent Node. The Mobile Node uses the Binding Management Key, Kbm, to key the hash algorithm. The data exchanged during the Return Routability Procedure is used to establish this key (Kbm). Node Keys, Nonces, Cookies, Tokens, and certain cryptographic functions in Mobile IPv6 are used to accomplish the data exchange.

A Binding Management Key (Kbm) is a key that a mobility node (Mobile Node, Home Agent, or Correspondent Node) uses for authorizing a Binding Cache Management message (e.g., a Binding Update or Binding Acknowledgement). The Return Routability Procedure specifies a mechanism for creating a Binding Management Key **[RFC6275]**.

6.3.5.2.1   *Node Keys*

Mobile IPv6 requires each Correspondent Node to maintain a secret key called the Node Key, Kcn, which is a random number of 20 bytes in length. The Correspondent Node uses this key to produce the Keygen Tokens sent to a Mobile Node. It also uses the Node Key to verify that the Keygen Tokens used by the Mobile Node to authorize a Binding Update indeed belong to it. The Node Key must not be shared with any other mobile entity. A fresh Node Key may be generated by the Correspondent Node at any time to avoid the need for secure persistent key storage.

6.3.5.2.2   *Nonces*

A Nonce is a random number (recommended length of 64 bits) used internally by a Correspondent Node when creating the Keygen Tokens for the Return Routability Procedure. Nonces are kept secret within the Correspondent Node and are not specific to any particular Mobile Node. A Correspondent Node uses a Nonce Index to indicate which Nonce has been used when creating the Keygen Token values, without revealing the Nonce itself.

A Correspondent Node generates Nonces at regular intervals using a random number generator with good randomness properties. It may use the same Node Key (Kcn) and Nonce for all the Mobile Nodes it is communicating with. The Correspondent Node also identifies each generated

Nonce by a Nonce Index. Each new Nonce generated is associated with a new Nonce Index. Nonce Indices are not used in the authentication process but allow the Correspondent Node to efficiently determine the particular Nonce value that it used in generating a Keygen Token.

6.3.5.2.3 Cookies and Tokens

A Cookie is a random number used by a Mobile Node during the Return Routability Procedure to prevent spoofing of messages by a fake or fraudulent Correspondent Node. The Return Routability Address Test Procedure uses Cookies as opaque values in Test Init messages, and Keygen Tokens as opaque values in Test messages. The following additional relevant terminology is defined:

- A Home Init Cookie is a 64-bit cookie included in the Home Test Init message that a Mobile Node sends to the Correspondent Node, which the Correspondent Node returns in the Home Test message.
- A Care-of Init Cookie is a 64-bit cookie included in the Care-of Test Init message that a Mobile Node sends to the Correspondent Node, which the Correspondent Node returns in the Care-of Test message.
- A Keygen Token is a number generated by a Correspondent Node and transmitted to a Mobile Node during the Return Routability Procedure to be used by the Mobile Node to compute the Binding Management Key needed for authorizing a Binding Update.
- A Home Keygen Token is a 64-bit Keygen Token included in the Home Test message that the Correspondent Node sends to a Mobile Node via the Home Agent.
- A Care-of Keygen Token is a 64-bit Keygen Token included in the Care-of Test message that the Correspondent Node sends to a Mobile Node via the Home Agent.

In every Home or Care-of Test Init message sent to the Correspondent Node, the Mobile Node sets the Home Init or Care-of Init Cookie to a newly generated random number. The Mobile Node uses these Cookies to verify that the Home Test or Care-of Test message it receives from the Correspondent Node matches the Home Test Init or Care-of Test Init message it sent, respectively. These Cookies also ensure that entities not involved in the message exchange cannot spoof the responses.

The Correspondent Node creates the Home and Care-of Keygen Tokens based on its currently active secret key, the Node Key (Kcn), and Nonces, in addition to the Home IP Address or Care-of IP Address, respectively. The Keygen Token produced by the Correspondent Node is valid as long as both the Node Key (Kcn) and the Nonce used to create it are valid.

6.3.5.2.4 Cryptographic Functions

Mobile IPv6 [**RFC6275**] specifies the SHA-1 algorithm [**FIPSPUB1801**] as the default function for computing hash values. This function is considered to offer sufficient protection for Mobile IPv6 control messages. The HMAC_SHA1 algorithm [**FIPSPUB1801**] [**RFC2104**] is then used to compute the Message Authentication Codes. The notation HMAC_SHA1(K, m) denotes a Message Authentication Code computed on message m using key K.

6.3.5.2.5 Return Routability Procedure

The Return Routability Procedure is a mechanism by which a Correspondent Node can determine with a reasonable level of assurance that the Mobile Node with which it wishes to communicate is indeed addressable at its declared Care-of IP Address as well as at its Home IP Address. The Correspondent Node needs this assurance to accept Binding Updates from the Mobile Node. The Mobile Node can then instruct the Correspondent Node to send data traffic directly to its declared Care-of IP Address.

The Return Routability Procedure involves the Correspondent Node testing whether packets addressed to the two declared Mobile Node IP addresses are routed to the Mobile Node. The Correspondent Node considers the Mobile Node to have passed the test only if it can supply proof that it has received certain pieces of information (the Keygen Tokens) that the Correspondent Node sent to the declared IP addresses. The Mobile Node combines these pieces of information into a Binding Management Key (Kbm).

The following four messages are used to perform the Return Routability Procedure to ensure the authorization of Binding Updates (Figure 6.4): Home Test Init, Home Test, Care-of Test Init, and Care-of Test. The Mobile Node sends the Home and Care-of Test Init messages simultaneously.

The Return Routability Procedure is summarized as follows [RFC6275]:

1. The Mobile Node sends a Home Test Init message on the Reverse Tunnel through the Home Agent to the Correspondent Node to acquire the Home Keygen Token. The contents of this message are as follows: Source IP Address=Home IP Address; Destination IP Address=Correspondent Node IP Address; Parameter=Home Init Cookie (the Correspondent Node must return this parameter value later).

2. The Mobile Node sends a Care-of Test Init message directly (not via the Home Agent) to the Correspondent Node to acquire the Care-of Keygen Token. The contents of this message are as follows: Source IP Address=Care-of IP Address; Destination IP Address=Correspondent Node IP Address; Parameter=Care-of Init Cookie (the Correspondent Node must return this parameter value later).

3. The Correspondent Node sends a Home Test message (via the Home Agent) in response to the Home Test Init message. The Home Agent tunnels this message to the Mobile Node. The contents of the message are as follows: Source IP Address=Correspondent Node IP Address; Destination IP Address=Home IP Address; Parameters={Home Init Cookie, Home Keygen Token, Home Nonce Index}. The algorithm for generating the Home Keygen Token is given in [RFC6275].

   • The Correspondent Node returns the Home Init Cookie to the Mobile Node in the Home Test message to assure that the message comes from a node on the path between the Home Agent and the Correspondent Node.

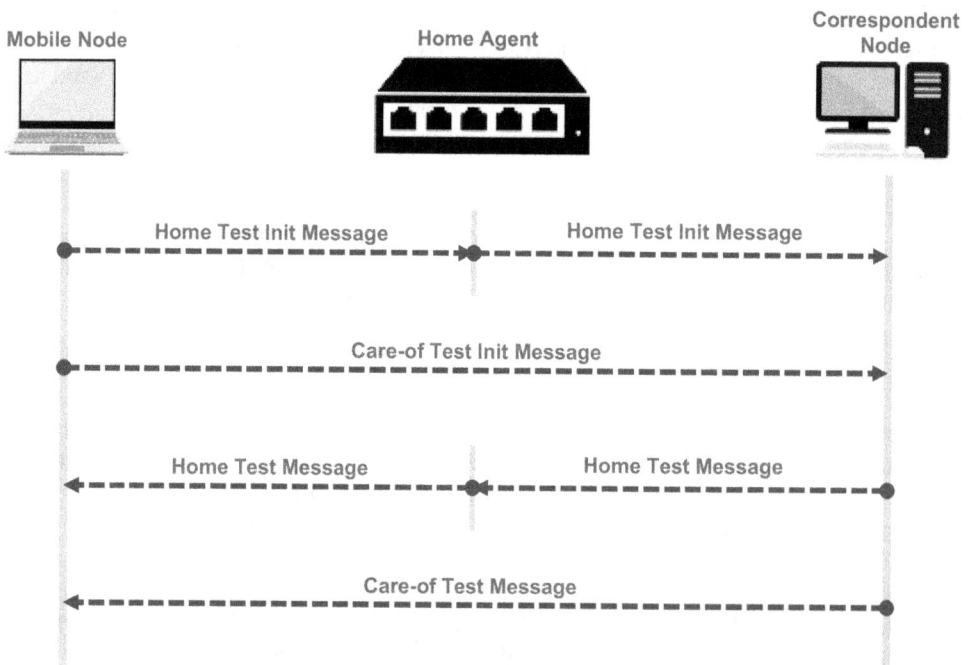

FIGURE 6.4 Return Routability Procedure.

- The Correspondent Node sends the Home Nonce Index to the Mobile Node to allow the Correspondent Node to efficiently find the Nonce value used in generating the Home Keygen Token.

4. The Correspondent Node sends a Care-of Test message (not via the Home Agent) to the Mobile Node in response to a Care-of Test Init message. The contents of this message are as follows: Source IP Address=Correspondent Node IP Address; Destination IP Address=Care-of IP Address; Parameters={Care-of Init Cookie, Care-of Keygen Token, Care-of Nonce Index}. The algorithm for generating the Care-of Keygen Token is given in **[RFC6275]**.
    - The Correspondent Node returns the Care-of Init Cookie in the Care-of Test Init message to assure that the message comes from a node on the path to the Correspondent Node. The Correspondent Node provides the Care-of Nonce Index so that the Nonce used for the Care-of Keygen Token can be identified.

The Return Routability Procedure is complete when the Mobile Node has received both the Home and Care-of Test messages. The completion of this procedure allows the Mobile Node to possess the data it needs to send a Binding Update to the Correspondent Node. The Mobile Node hashes the Home Keygen Token and the Care-of Keygen Token together to form a 20-byte Binding Management Key (Kbm). The algorithm for generating the Binding Management Key (Kbm) is given in **[RFC6275]**. Until the Correspondent Node receives the Binding Update from the Mobile Node, it does not create any state specific to the Mobile Node.

6.3.5.2.6   Authorizing Binding Management Messages

After creating the Binding Management Key (Kbm), the Mobile Node is now ready to send a verifiable Binding Update message to the Correspondent Node. The following steps summarize this registration process (Figure 6.5):

1. The Mobile Node generates a Binding Management Key (Kbm) from the Home Keygen Token and the Care-of Keygen Token. The contents of the Binding Update message include the following: Source IP Address=Care-of IP address; Destination IP Address=Correspondent Node IP Address; Parameters={Home IP Address (within the Mobile IPv6 Home Address Option if different from the Source IP Address), Sequence Number (within the Binding Update message header), Home Nonce Index (within the Nonce Indices Option), Care-of Nonce Index (within the Mobile IPv6 Nonce Indices Option), Output of the "First Function" in **[RFC6275]**}.
    - The Binding Update message contains a Mobile IPv6 Nonce Indices Option, indicating which Home Nonce and Care-of Nonce the Correspondent Node should use to recompute the Binding Management Key (Kbm).
    - The Mobile Node computes the Message Authentication Code using the Correspondent Node's IP address as the destination IP address and the Binding Update message itself as the Mobility Header Data.
    - Once the Message Authentication Code has been verified by the Correspondent Node, it creates an entry in the Binding Cache for the Mobile Node.
2. The Correspondent Node may, in some cases, send a Binding Acknowledgement message to acknowledge a Binding Update message. The contents of this message are as follows: Source IP Address=Correspondent Node IP Address; Destination IP Address=Care-of IP Address; Parameters={Sequence Number (within the Binding Update message header), Output of the "First Function" in **[RFC6275]**}.
    - The Binding Acknowledgement message contains the same Sequence Number as the Binding Update message.
    - The Correspondent Node computes the Message Authentication Code using its IP address as the destination IP address and the Binding Update message itself as the Mobility Header Data.

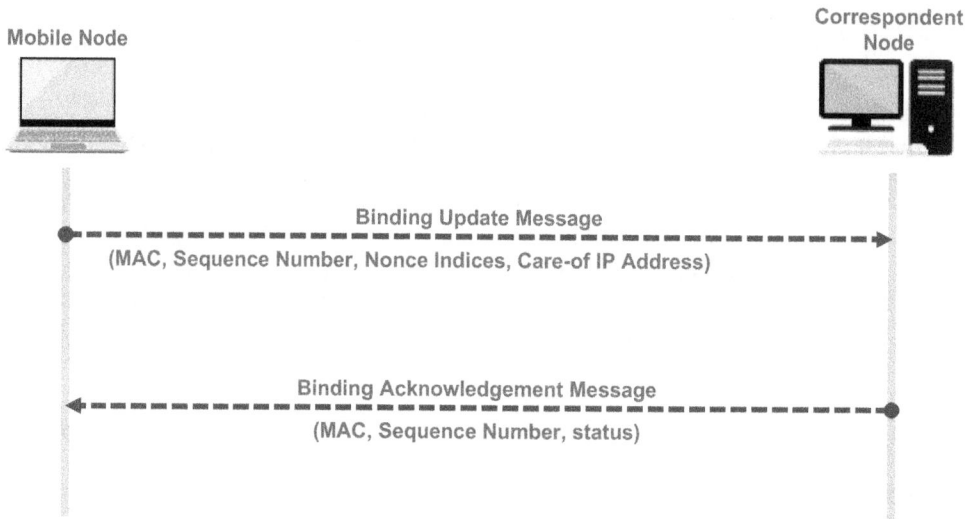

FIGURE 6.5   Authorizing Binding Management messages.

6.3.5.2.7   Updating Node Keys and Nonces

A Correspondent Node generates Nonces at regular intervals but keeps each Nonce (identified by a Nonce Index) usable for at least MAX_TOKEN_LIFETIME seconds after the Nonce has been first used to create a Return Routability Procedure message response. The Correspondent Node should update the secret Node Key (Kcn) simultaneously with each Nonce update to allow the Nonce Indices to identify both the Nonce and the Node Key. Therefore, the Correspondent Node must remember old Node Key (Kcn) values for as long as it retains old Nonce values.

6.3.5.2.8   Preventing Replay Attacks

Through the use of the Sequence Number and a Message Authentication Code, the Return Routability Procedure also protects the participating entities against replay attacks on Binding Updates. However, the Correspondent Node must exercise care when removing the Mobility Bindings it maintains. The Correspondent Node must retain Mobility Bindings and their associated Sequence Number information for at least as long as the Nonces it uses to authorize the Binding remain valid.

6.3.6   Home Agent Packet Processing and Role of IPv6 Proxy Neighbor Discovery in Mobile IPv6

The Home Agent of a Mobile Node intercepts IPv6 packets on the Home Link that are addressed to the Mobile Node and tunnels them to the Mobile Node. We assume that the Mobile Node has sent a Binding Update message from a Foreign Network to register its Mobility Binding.

6.3.6.1   Intercepting IPv6 Packets for a Mobile Node

The Home Agent starts by multicasting an ICMPv6 Neighbor Advertisement message onto the Home Link on behalf of the Mobile Node visiting a Foreign Network. Using the Mobile Node's Home IP Address specified in the Binding Update, the Home Agent sends a Neighbor Advertisement message addressed to the IPv6 All-Nodes multicast address (FF01::1) on the Home Link, advertising its own Link-Layer address as associated with the Mobile Node's Home IP Address. If the Binding Update message sent by the Mobile Node has the Link-Layer Address Compatibility (L) Flag set, the Home Agent will use the Mobile Node's IPv6 Link-Local address in the Target Address field of the Neighbor Advertisement message instead of the Mobile Node's Home IP Address.

The Home Agent identifies a Mobile Node through the source IPv6 address of the inner IPv6 header in the tunneled packet received from the Mobile Node. Typically, the Home Agent identifies the Mobile Node through its routable unicast Home IP Address, but identification can also be done through the Mobile Node's IPv6 Link-Local address. The Home Agent recognizes the latter type of address if the Link-Local Address Compatibility (L) bit is set in the Mobile Node's Binding Update message. The Link-Local Address Compatibility (L) bit is set when the Home IP Address reported by the Mobile Node has the same interface ID as the Mobile Node's IPv6 Link-Local address.

The Home Agent sets all fields in each Neighbor Advertisement message in the same way the Mobile Node would if it were sending this Neighbor Advertisement while on the Home Link, with the following exceptions:

- Sets the Target Address field in the Neighbor Advertisement message to the IPv6 address specified by the Mobile Node.
- Includes the Target Link-Layer Address Option in the Neighbor Advertisement message, specifying the Home Agent's own Link-Layer address.
- Sets the Router (R) bit in the Neighbor Advertisement message to zero.
- MUST NOT set the Solicited (S) Flag in the Neighbor Advertisement message, since it was not solicited by any Neighbor Solicitation message.
- Sets the Override (O) Flag in the Neighbor Advertisement message, indicating that the advertisement should override any existing Neighbor Cache entry at any neighboring node that receives it.
- Sets the Source Address field in the IPv6 header to the Home Agent's IPv6 address on the interface that is used to send the advertisement.

The Home Agent may retransmit a Neighbor Advertisement message up to MAX_NEIGHBOR_ADVERTISEMENT times to increase its chances of reaching all nodes on the Home Link. Nodes on the Home Link that receive the Neighbor Advertisement message will update their Neighbor Cache, associating the Mobile Node's IP address with the Link-Layer address of the Home Agent. This causes any node on the Home Link to transmit any future packets destined for the Mobile Node to the advertising Home Agent.

The Home Agent uses the IPv6 Proxy Neighbor Discovery mechanism to intercept unicast IPv6 packets on the Home Link addressed to the Mobile Node. The Home Agent acts as a proxy for the Mobile Node and replies to any ICMPv6 Neighbor Solicitation messages it receives that seek the Mobile Node's Link-Layer address. The Home Agent receives Neighbor Solicitation messages and checks if the Target Address specified in the message matches the IPv6 address of any Mobile Node with a Home Registration entry in the Binding Cache.

If the Home Agent determines that a matching entry exists in the Binding Cache, it replies to the Neighbor Solicitation message with a Neighbor Advertisement message, providing its own Link-Layer address as the Link-Layer address associated with the specified Target Address. In addition, the Home Agent sets the Router (R) bit in the Neighbor Advertisement message to zero (indicating that the sender is NOT a router). By acting as a proxy for off-link Mobile Nodes, other nodes on the Home Link can resolve a Mobile Node's IPv6 address, and the Home Agent can defend these addresses on the Home Link through IPv6 Duplicate Address Detection.

6.3.6.2 Processing Intercepted IPv6 Packets

A Home Agent (running IPv6 Proxy Neighbor Discovery) intercepts IPv6 packets on the Home Link addressed to the Mobile Node's Home IP Address and tunnels them to the Mobile Node using IPv6 encapsulation [RFC2473]. When encapsulating an intercepted IPv6 packet for tunneling to the Mobile Node, the Home Agent sets the Source IPv6 Address field in the new outer (tunnel) IPv6 header to the Home Agent's own IPv6 address and sets the Destination IPv6 Address field in the outer IPv6 header to the primary Care-of IP Address of the Mobile Node. Upon receiving the tunneled IPv6 packet, the Mobile Node decapsulates it and processes the original (i.e., encapsulated) IPv6 packet.

The Home Agent does not tunnel unicast or multicast packets addressed to the Mobile Node's IPv6 Link-Local address to the Mobile Node. Instead, the Home Agent discards these packets and returns an ICMPv6 Type 1 Destination Unreachable message indicating "No Route to Destination" (Code 3) to the packet's Source IPv6 Address. Before tunneling an IPv6 packet to the Mobile Node, the Home Agent performs any required IPSec processing on the packet as indicated by the security policy database.

6.3.6.3   IPv6 Multicast Membership Control

A Home Agent tunnels multicast packets addressed with a global scope to the Mobile Node only if the Mobile Node has successfully subscribed to that multicast group. Additionally, the Home Agent intercepts and tunnels multicast-addressed packets on the Home Link only if it supports handling multicast group membership control messages from the Mobile Node.

To forward multicast data packets from the Home Link to the Mobile Node, the Home Agent must be capable of receiving tunneled multicast group membership control information (i.e., Listener Report messages specified in Multicast Listener Discovery (MLD) **[RFC2710] [RFC3810]**) from the Mobile Node to determine which multicast groups the Mobile Node has subscribed to.

The Mobile Node sends multicast group membership control messages to the Home Agent through the Reverse Tunnel. These control messages are sent whenever the Mobile Node wants to receive packets for a multicast group, or in response to an MLD Query message sent by the Home Agent. The Mobile Node also sends multicast group control messages to the Home Agent to stop the transmission of multicast packets when it is no longer interested in receiving traffic for a particular multicast group.

To obtain the current multicast group membership of a Mobile Node (while visiting a Foreign Network), periodic MLD Query messages are transmitted by the Home Agent through the tunnel to the Mobile Node. These periodic MLD messages ensure that the Home Agent has accurate knowledge of the multicast groups in which the Mobile Node is interested, in case the Mobile Node's MLD group membership messages are lost.

All the MLD messages (with Link-Local addresses as the source address) are addressed to a link-scope multicast address, have an IPv6 Hop Limit of 1, and are exchanged directly between the Home Agent and the Mobile Node (over the tunnel). When exchanging the MLD messages, the Mobile Node and the Home Agent encapsulate these messages within the same outer (tunnel) IPv6 header used for other IPv6 packets sent between them.

6.3.6.4   Stateful IPv6 Address Autoconfiguration

A Home Agent may support Stateful DHCPv6 to enable address autoconfiguration on Mobile Nodes. If a Home Agent does not provide this support, it must not set the M and O bits on the ICMPv6 Mobile Prefix Advertisement messages it sends to Mobile Nodes. Any Mobile Node that sends DHCPv6 messages to a Home Agent that does not support DHCPv6 services will not receive a response. The 1-bit M (Managed Address Configuration) Flag, when set, indicates to IPv6 hosts to use an administered (stateful) protocol such as DHCPv6 for address autoconfiguration, as well as for any IPv6 addresses autoconfigured using IPv6 Stateless Address Autoconfiguration (SLAAC). The 1-bit O (Other Stateful Configuration) Flag, when set, indicates to IPv6 hosts to use an administered (stateful) protocol such as DHCPv6 for the autoconfiguration of other (non-address-related) information; the host has already autoconfigured an IPv6 address and only needs other configuration parameters.

If the Home Agent supports DHCPv6, it sends packets with IPv6 Link-Local addresses as source addresses either to a link-scope IPv6 multicast address or to an IPv6 Link-Local address. Mobile Nodes wishing to locate a DHCPv6 service may send standard DHCPv6 messages to the Home Agent over the Reverse Tunnel. Since the Home Agent cannot forward these link-scope packets onto the Home Network, it must implement either a DHCPv6 Relay Agent or a local DHCPv6 server function. The Home Agent must note the Reverse Tunnel or IPSec Security Association of DHCPv6 link-scope messages sent by each Mobile Node so that it can send back DHCPv6 responses to the appropriate Mobile Node. Additionally, the Home Agent sends DHCPv6 messages to the Mobile Node using a Link-Local address as the destination address, tunneling them within the same outer (tunnel) IPv6 header used for other IPv6 packets.

6.3.6.5   Handling Reverse-Tunneled IPv6 Packets

Unless a Mobile Node and a Correspondent Node have established a Mobility Binding, traffic sent by the Mobile Node to the Correspondent Node goes through a Reverse Tunnel. The Home Agent supports Reverse Tunneling as follows:

- The Mobile Node uses IPv6 encapsulation to tunnel traffic to the Home Agent's IPv6 address.
- Depending on the security policies configured on the Home Agent, it may discard IPv6 packets sent on the Reverse Tunnel unless the packets are accompanied by a valid IPv6 ESP header. By supporting authenticated Reverse Tunneling, the Home Agent can protect the Home Network and Correspondent Nodes from malicious entities impersonating a Mobile Node.
- When the Home Agent receives a tunneled IPv6 packet from the Mobile Node and decapsulates it, it must verify that the Source IP Address field in the tunnel IPv6 header contains the Mobile Node's primary Care-of IP Address. Failure to do this may allow any node on the Internet to send traffic through the Home Agent, bypassing ingress traffic filtering. This simple check places a burden on an attacker, forcing them to know the current location of the real Mobile Node and to circumvent ingress filtering. The Home Agent does not require this check if the IPv6 packets sent on the Reverse Tunnel are protected by ESP in Tunnel Mode.

6.3.7   DYNAMIC HOME AGENT ADDRESS DISCOVERY

Mobile IPv6 allows a Home Network to support multiple Home Agents, with limited reconfiguration of the Home Network. In such cases, a Mobile Node visiting Foreign Networks may not have a priori knowledge of the IPv6 address of its own Home Agent, and even its Home IPv6 Subnet Prefixes may change over time. The Mobile Node, while away from home, uses the optional *Dynamic Home Agent Address Discovery mechanism* to dynamically discover the IPv6 address of a Home Agent on its Home Link.

The Mobile Node can also use the *Mobile Prefix Discovery mechanism* to learn new information about the Home IPv6 Subnet Prefixes. The Dynamic Home Agent Address Discovery mechanism targets Mobile IPv6 deployments where security is not needed. A Home Agent maintains a Home Agents List that contains information about all the other active Home Agents on the Home Link, and also responds to queries sent by the Mobile Node.

It is recommended for the Mobile Node and the Home Agent to use an IPSec security association to protect the integrity and authenticity of the Mobile IPv6 Mobile Prefix Solicitation messages (ICMPv6 Type 146 messages) and the Mobile Prefix Advertisement messages (ICMPv6 Type 147 messages) they exchange. To provide data origin authentication, data integrity, and optionally, anti-replay protection, both the Mobile Node and the Home Agent use the ESP header in Transport Mode with a non-NULL payload authentication algorithm on the IPv6 packets they exchange.

6.3.7.1   Receiving ICMPv6 Router Advertisement Messages

Each Home Agent maintains a Home Agents List that contains information about all other Home Agents on the Home Link and uses this list in the Dynamic Home Agent Address Discovery mechanism. The Home Agent learns information about the presence of other Home Agents on the Home Link through the receipt of periodic (unsolicited) multicast Router Advertisement messages. This is similar to using IPv6 Neighbor Discovery to learn information for the Default Router List maintained by each IPv6 host on a link **[RFC4861]**. Each (other) Home Agent on the Home Link sends Router Advertisement messages with the Home Agent (H) bit set in them.

Upon receiving a valid ICMPv6 Router Advertisement message, the Home Agent performs the following operations in addition to any operations already required by the IPv6 Neighbor Discovery protocol:

- If the Home Agent (H) bit in the Router Advertisement message is not set, the Home Agent deletes the entry associated with the sending node in the current Home Agents List (if one exists) and skips all the remaining steps.
- Otherwise, the Home Agent extracts the Source IPv6 Address from the IPv6 header of the ICMPv6 Router Advertisement message. This IPv6 address is the IPv6 Link-Local address of the Home Agent on the Home Link that sent this Advertisement message.
- The Home Agent determines the Preference value for the sending Home Agent. If the Router Advertisement message contains a Mobile IPv6 Home Agent Information Option (Option Type 8), then the Home Agent takes the Preference value from the Home Agent Preference field in this Option; otherwise, the Home Agent uses the default Preference value of 0.
- The Home Agent determines the Lifetime for the sending Home Agent. If the Router Advertisement message contains a Mobile IPv6 Home Agent Information Option (Option Type 8), then the Home Agent takes the Lifetime value from the Home Agent Lifetime field in this Option; otherwise, the Home Agent uses the Lifetime value specified in the Router Lifetime field in the Router Advertisement message.
- If the IPv6 Link-Local address of the sending Home Agent is already present in the receiving Home Agent's Home Agents List and the received Home Agent Lifetime value is zero, then the receiving Home Agent will immediately delete this entry in its Home Agents List.
- Otherwise, if the IPv6 Link-Local address of the sending Home Agent is already present in the receiving Home Agent's Home Agents List, the receiving Home Agent resets the sender's Lifetime and Preference values to the values determined above.
- If the IPv6 Link-Local address of the sending Home Agent is not already present in the receiving Home Agent's Home Agents List and the Lifetime for the sending Home Agent is nonzero, the receiving Home Agent creates a new entry in its list and initializes the sender's Lifetime and Preference values to the values determined above.
- If the Home Agents List entry for the IPv6 Link-Local address of the sending Home Agent was not deleted as described above, the receiving Home Agent determines any IPv6 Global Unicast address(es) of the sending Home Agent based on each Prefix Information Option (Option Type 3) contained in the Router Advertisement message in which the Router Address (R) bit is set. The receiving Home Agent adds all such IPv6 Global Unicast addresses to the list of IPv6 Global Unicast addresses in its Home Agents List entry.

The Home Agent maintains an entry for each valid Home Agent IPv6 address in its Home Agents List until the Lifetime of that entry expires, after which the Home Agent deletes the entry.

A Mobile Node initiates the Dynamic Home Agent Address Discovery process by sending an ICMPv6 Home Agent Address Discovery Request message (ICMP Type 144 message) to the *Mobile IPv6 Home-Agents Anycast address* (i.e., the IPv6 Reserved Subnet Anycast address for Mobile IPv6 described in **Chapter 3**) **[RFC2526]** to discover its Home IPv6 Subnet Prefix (see Figure 6.6). Upon receiving a Home Agent Address Discovery Request message that is addressed to this IPv6 Subnet Anycast address, the Home Agent returns an ICMPv6 Home Agent Address Discovery Reply message (ICMP Type 145 message) to the Mobile Node with the Source IPv6 Address of the IPv6 packet carrying the Reply message, set to one of the Home Agent's IPv6 Global Unicast addresses. The Home Agent constructs the IPv6 addresses placed in the Home Agent Addresses field of the ICMPv6 Home Agent Address Discovery Reply message as follows:

- The Home Agent enters in the Home Agent Addresses field of the Reply message all the IPv6 Global Unicast addresses for each Home Agent currently listed in its own Home Agents List. The addresses are entered in the order of decreasing Preference values

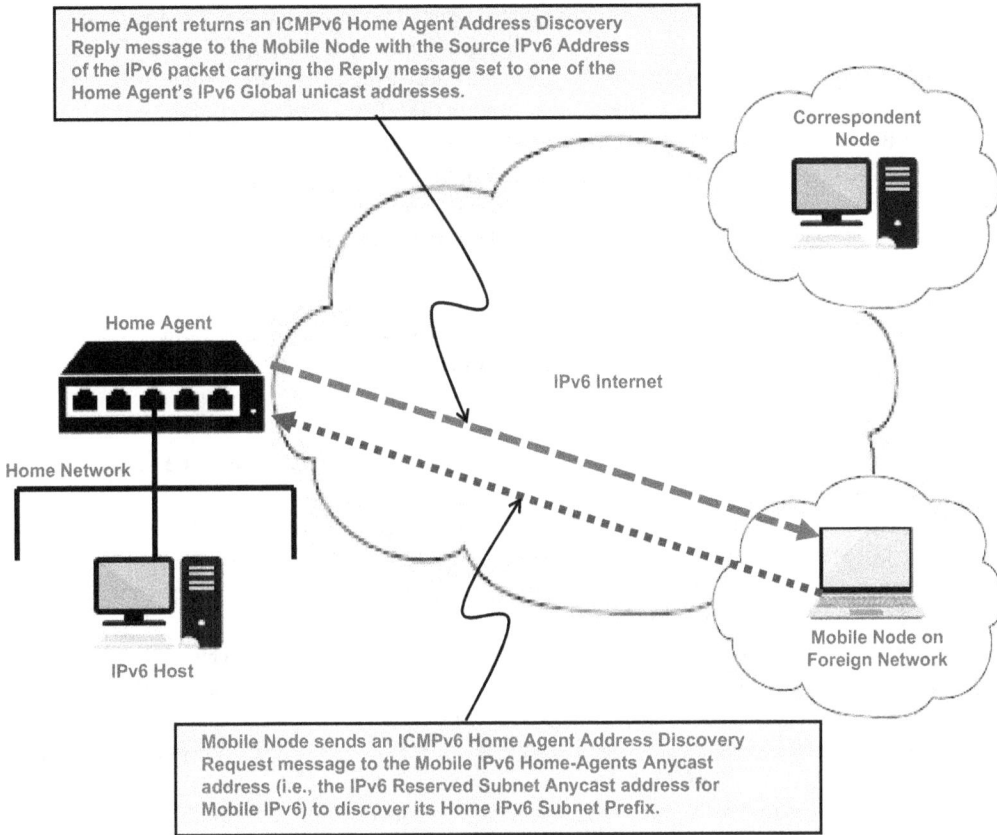

FIGURE 6.6   Mobile IPv6 Dynamic Home Agent Address Discovery.

indicated in the Home Agent Information Option, or based on the default Preference of 0 if no Preference value is advertised. Otherwise, the Preference value configured on the Home Agent itself may be used.

- If multiple Home Agents have equal Preference values, the Home Agent lists the IPv6 addresses in the Home Agent Addresses field of the Reply message in a randomized order.
- If more than one IPv6 Global Unicast address is associated with a Home Agent, the replying Home Agent lists these IPv6 addresses in a randomized order.
- The Home Agent should enter the Home Agent IPv6 addresses such that the Reply message would fit within the minimum IPv6 MTU **[RFC8200]** to avoid packet fragmentation (or rejection by an intermediate router and the sending of an ICMPv6 Packet Too Big message). The Home Agent Addresses selected are those with the highest Preference values.

6.3.8   Sending IPv6 Prefix Information to a Mobile Node

Mobile IPv6 supports a mechanism that enables the propagation of relevant IPv6 prefix information to a Mobile Node when it is visiting a Foreign Network, allowing the Mobile Node to use this information in Home IP Address configuration and network renumbering. In this mechanism, a Mobile Node on a Foreign Network receives ICMPv6 Mobile Prefix Advertisement messages (ICMPv6 Type 147 messages) which include the Prefix Information Options (Option Type 3) for the IPv6 prefixes configured on the Home Subnet interface(s) of the Home Agent.

If multiple Home Agents exist on a Home Link, differences in the advertisements (information) that those different Home Agents send can lead to a Mobile Node not being able to use a particular

Home IP Address when changing to another Home Agent. Therefore, to ensure that a Mobile Node receives the same information from different Home Agents, it is preferable to configure all the Home Agents on the same Home Link with the same addressing information for advertisement.

To support this mechanism, a Home Agent monitors the IPv6 prefixes it advertises by itself in addition to those advertised by other Home Agents on the Home Link. The Neighbor Discovery protocol **[RFC4861]** allows two routers to advertise different sets of IPv6 prefixes on the same link. Home Agents are able to detect the differences in the advertisements for a given Home IP Address. A Mobile Node communicates only with one Home Agent at any given time, and it needs to know the full set of IPv6 prefixes assigned to the Home Link.

6.3.8.1   Scheduling IPv6 Prefix Deliveries on a Home Agent

A Home Agent uses the following process to determine when to send IPv6 prefix information to a Mobile Node that is visiting another network:

- If a Mobile Node sends an ICMPv6 Mobile Prefix Solicitation message, the Home Agent replies with a Mobile Prefix Advertisement message right away.
- If the Home Agent has not sent a Mobile Prefix Advertisement message to the Mobile Node in the last *MaxMobPfxAdvInterval* seconds, then it ensures that an Advertisement message transmission is scheduled, but the actual transmission time is randomized by a small delay equal to RAND_ADV_DELAY.
- If the Home Agent has added an IPv6 prefix matching the Mobile Node's Home Registration on the Home Subnet interface, or if the Mobile Node's information changes in any way that does not deprecate the IPv6 address of the Mobile Node, the Home Agent ensures that an Advertisement message transmission is scheduled, but the actual transmission time is randomized by RAND_ADV_DELAY.
- If a Home Registration expires, the Home Agent cancels any scheduled Advertisement message to the Mobile Node.

The Home Agent sends the list of IPv6 prefixes in its entirety in the above cases to the Mobile Node. Furthermore, the Home Agent periodically retransmits unsolicited Mobile Prefix Advertisement messages to the Mobile Node until it acknowledges receipt by sending a Mobile Prefix Solicitation message.

If the Mobility Bindings of the Mobile Node expire before the Home Agent receives a matching Binding Update, then the Home Agent does not attempt any more retransmissions, even if it has not retransmitted all PREFIX_ADV_RETRIES messages. In the meantime, if the Mobile Node sends another Binding Update while still away from the Home Network, then the Home Agent begins transmitting unsolicited Mobile Prefix Advertisement messages again.

6.3.8.2   Sending ICMPv6 Mobile Prefix Advertisements to a Mobile Agent

A Home Agent constructs a packet as follows when sending an ICMPv6 Mobile Prefix Advertisement message to a Mobile Node:

- The Home Agent sets the Source IPv6 Address field in the packet's IPv6 header to the Home Agent's IPv6 address to which the Mobile Node addressed its current Home Registration, or the Home Agent's default IPv6 Global Unicast address if no Mobility Binding exists.
- If the Home Agent sends the Mobile Prefix Advertisement as a solicited message, it must be addressed to the source IPv6 address used in the Mobile Prefix Solicitation message. If the transmission was triggered by IPv6 prefix changes or renumbering, the destination of the Advertisement message will be the Mobile Node's Home IP Address in the Mobility Binding that triggered this.
- The Home Agent includes a Type 2 Routing header with the Mobile Node's Home IP Address.

- The Home Agent must support and use IPSec headers.
- The Home Agent must send the IPv6 packet containing the Mobile Prefix Advertisement message as it would any other unicast IPv6 packet that it originates.
- The Home Agent sets the Managed Address Configuration (M) Flag in the Mobile Prefix Advertisement message if the corresponding flag has been set in any of the ICMPv6 Router Advertisement messages from which the IPv6 prefix information was learned (including the messages sent by this Home Agent).
- The Home Agent sets the Other Stateful Configuration (O) Flag in the Mobile Prefix Advertisement message if the corresponding flag was set in any of the ICMPv6 Router Advertisement messages from which the IPv6 prefix information was learned (including the messages sent by this Home Agent).

The Lifetime value that the Home Agent returns in a Binding Acknowledgement message to the Mobile Node must not be greater than the remaining Valid Lifetime value for the IPv6 subnet prefix associated with the Mobile Node's Home IP Address. The goal of limiting the Lifetime of the Binding is to prohibit the use of the Home IP Address of a Mobile Node after it becomes invalid.

6.3.9   MOBILE NODE OPERATION

Each Mobile Node, when away from home, maintains a Binding Update List that contains information and the Lifetime of the Bindings that have not yet expired and for which the Mobile Node sent a Binding Update. The Mobile Node uses the Binding Update List to determine whether it sent a particular packet directly to the Correspondent Node or tunneled it through the Home Agent.

6.3.9.1   Conceptual Data Structures on the Mobile Node

The Binding Update List contains all the Bindings a Mobile Node sent to either its Home Agent or Correspondent Nodes. This list also contains the Binding Updates that are waiting for the completion of the Return Routability Procedure before the Mobile Node transmits them out. However, when the Mobile Node has sent multiple Binding Updates to the same destination IPv6 address, only the most recent Binding Update sent to that destination is entered in the Binding Update List (i.e., the Binding Update with the greatest Sequence Number value).

Each entry in the Binding Update List conceptually contains the following fields:

- The IPv6 address of the node to which the Mobile Node sent a Binding Update.
- The Home IP Address for which the Mobile Node sent that Binding Update.
- The Care-of IP Address included in the Binding Update sent. Knowing this address allows the Mobile Node to determine if it has sent a Binding Update when providing a new Care-of IP Address to this destination after changing its Care-of IP Address.
- The initial Lifetime field value the Mobile Node included in that Binding Update.
- The remaining Lifetime of the corresponding Binding. The Mobile Node initializes the Lifetime using the Lifetime value sent in the Binding Update and decrements it until the value reaches zero, at which point the Mobile Node deletes this entry from the Binding Update List.
- The maximum Sequence Number field value (16-bit field) sent in previous Binding Updates to this destination. The Mobile Node performs all comparisons between Sequence Number values using modulo 2^{16}.
- The last time the Mobile Node sent the Binding Update to this destination. The Mobile Node needs this time to implement rate limiting when sending Binding Update messages.
- The state of any retransmissions made by the Mobile Node related to this Binding Update. This state includes the time remaining until the Mobile Node attempts the next retransmission of the Binding Update and the current state of the exponential back-off mechanism used for Binding Update retransmissions.

- A Flag specifying whether or not the Mobile Node should send future Binding Updates to this destination. The Mobile Node sets this Flag in the Binding Update List entry when it receives an ICMPv6 Type 4 Parameter Problem message indicating "Unrecognized Next Header Type Encountered" (Code 1) in response to a Return Routability Procedure message or Binding Update sent to that destination.

The Binding Update List also contains the following conceptual data, which the Mobile Node uses when running the Return Routability Procedure. This data is relevant to the Mobile Node only when sending Binding Updates to Correspondent Nodes:

- The last time at which the Mobile Node sent a Home Test Init or Care-of Test Init message to this destination. The Mobile Node needs this time to implement rate limiting of messages in the Return Routability Procedure.
- The state of any retransmissions made by the Mobile Node related to the Return Routability Procedure. This state includes the time remaining until the Mobile Node attempts the next retransmission and the current state of the exponential back-off mechanism used for retransmissions.
- The Cookie values the Mobile Node included in the Home Test Init and Care-of Test Init messages.
- The Home and Care-of Keygen Tokens that the Mobile Node received from the Correspondent Node.
- The Home and Care-of Nonce Indices that the Mobile Node received from the Correspondent Node.
- The time at which the Mobile Node received each of the Tokens and Nonces from the Correspondent Node. The Mobile Node needs this information to implement the reuse of Tokens and Nonces (if necessary) while moving.

6.3.9.2   IPv6 Packet Processing on a Mobile Node
While a Mobile Node is visiting a Foreign Network, it continues to use its Home IP Address in addition to its single or multiple Care-of IP Addresses.

6.3.9.2.1   Sending IPv6 Packets While the Mobile Node Is Away from Home
When a Mobile Node is sending an IPv6 packet while away from home, it chooses an IPv6 address (from a number of addresses) as the source IPv6 address of the packet as follows:

- Upper-layer protocols over IP generally use the Mobile Node's Home IP Address as the source IP address for most packets. For Transport Layer connections established while the Mobile Node is at home, the Mobile Node uses its Home IP Address to send packets. Similarly, for packets sent over Transport Layer connections established while the Mobile Node was at home and that may still be used after moving to a Foreign Network, the Mobile Node uses its Home IP Address. If a Mobility Binding exists, the Mobile Node sends the IPv6 packets directly to the Correspondent Node. If a Binding does not exist, the Mobile Node sends IPv6 packets using Reverse Tunneling.
- The Mobile Node may decide to use one of its Care-of IP Addresses as the source IP address of an IPv6 packet, a mode not requiring the inclusion of a Home Address Option (Option Type 201) in the packet. Packets sent using the Mobile Node's Care-of IP Address as the source IP address generally have a lower overhead than those using the Mobile Node's Home IP Address, since no extra options are needed. These IPv6 packets can be routed directly between their source and destination using standard routing mechanisms, without relying on Mobile IPv6.

- While away from its Home Link, the Mobile Node must not use the Home Address Option in IPv6 packets when communicating with nodes on its Home Link. Similarly, the Mobile Node must not include the Home Address Option in IPv6 Neighbor Discovery packets.

Special Mobile IPv6 processing is required for IPv6 packets sent by the Mobile Node using its Home IP Address as the source IP address while it is away from home. This special processing is done in the following two ways: Route Optimization and Reverse Tunneling.

6.3.9.2.1.1   Route Optimization   This mode of delivering IPv6 packets between a Mobile Node and a Correspondent Node does not require packets to go through the Home Network, enabling faster and more reliable communication. The Mobile Node first ensures that an entry exists in its Binding Cache for its Home IP Address, allowing a Correspondent Node to process IPv6 packets sent by the Mobile Node. The Mobile Node checks the entry to ensure it fulfills the following conditions:

- The IPv6 packet being sent has the Source IP Address field set to the Home IP Address indicated in the Binding Update List entry.
- The IPv6 packet being sent has the Destination IP Address field set to the IP address of the Correspondent Node indicated in the Binding Update List entry.
- One of the Mobile Node's current Care-of IP Addresses is indicated as the Care-of IP Address in the Binding Update List entry.
- The Binding Update List entry indicates that a Mobility Binding has been successfully created.
- The Mobility Binding has a remaining Lifetime greater than zero.

When the above conditions are satisfied, the Mobile Node concludes that the Correspondent Node has a suitable entry in its Binding Cache.

The Mobile Node supplies its Home IP Address using a Home Address Option in an IPv6 packet sent to the Correspondent Node, and sets the Source IP Address field in the packet's IPv6 header to the Care-of IP Address that the Mobile Node has registered for communication with the Correspondent Node. The Correspondent Node receives the Home Address Option and then uses the IP address indicated in it for the function traditionally performed by the Source IP Address field in the IPv6 header of a packet; the Correspondent Node can use this address as the destination for IPv6 packets it sends to the Mobile Node. The Home IP Address of the Mobile Node is then supplied to upper-layer protocols and applications on the Correspondent Node.

Specifically, the Mobile Node performs the following operations when sending the IPv6 packet:

- It uses the Mobile Node's Home IP Address as the Source IP Address of the IPv6 packet in the same way as it would if it were at home. This process includes calculating the upper-layer checksums using the Home IP Address.
- Add a Home Address Option to the IPv6 Destination Option extension header of the IPv6 packet, with the Home Address field of the Option copied from the original value in the Source IP Address field of the packet.
- Change the Source IP Address field in the IPv6 header of the packet to one of the Mobile Node's Care-of IP Addresses.

By using the Care-of IP Address as the Source IP Address in the departing packet's IPv6 header, and entering the Home IP Address of the Mobile Node in the Home Address Option, the departing IPv6 packet will be able to safely pass through any router that implements URPF checks using the source IP address of packets (also known as ingress filtering).

6.3.9.2.2   Reverse Tunneling

This mode of communication involves the Mobile Node tunneling IPv6 packets to the Correspondent Node via the Home Agent. While this mode is not as efficient as the Route Optimization method, it is necessary if the Correspondent Node does not yet have a Mobility Binding for the Mobile Node. The Mobile Node uses this mechanism for IPv6 packets that are sent with the Mobile Node's Home IP Address as the Source IP Address in the IPv6 header, or with multicast control protocol messages (MLD messages).

In this case, the Mobile Node performs the following specific operations when sending an IPv6 packet:

- The Mobile Node tunnels the IPv6 packet to the Home Agent using IPv6 encapsulation **[RFC2473]**.
- The Source IP Address in the tunnel (outer) IPv6 header of the encapsulating IPv6 packet is the primary Care-of IP Address registered with the Home Agent.
- The Destination IP Address in the tunnel (outer) IPv6 header of the encapsulating IPv6 packet is the Home Agent's IPv6 address.

The Home Agent receives the encapsulating IPv6 packet, decapsulates it, and forwards the original (encapsulated) IPv6 packet to the Correspondent Node.

6.3.9.2.3   Interaction with Outbound IPSec Processing

This section describes the outbound Mobile IPv6 and outbound IPSec processing when a Mobile Node sends IPv6 packets while away from its Home Network:

- A higher-layer protocol and application (e.g., TCP) creates an IPv6 packet as if the Mobile Node was on its Home Link and Mobile IPv6 is not being used.
- The outgoing interface for the packet is determined. Different interfaces may be used depending on the selected mode of communication: Reverse Tunneling or Route Optimization.
- As part of outbound IPv6 packet processing, the Mobile Node compares the packet against the local IPSec security policy database to determine the required processing for the packet **[RFC4301]**.
- If the packet requires IPSec processing, the Mobile Node either maps the packet to an existing Security Association (or SA bundle) or creates a new SA (or SA bundle) for the packet, according to the defined IPSec procedures.
- Since the Mobile Node is visiting a Foreign Network, it uses either Reverse Tunneling or Route Optimization to send IPv6 packets to the Correspondent Node.
  - If the Mobile Node is using Reverse Tunneling, it constructs the packet in the normal manner and then tunnels it through the Home Agent to the Correspondent Node.
  - If the Mobile Node is using Route Optimization, it includes a Home Address Option in the packet and replaces the Source IP Address in the packet's IPv6 header with the Care-of IP Address used for communication with the Correspondent Node, as described above. The IPv6 Destination Option extension header, which the Mobile Node inserts the Home Address Option into, must appear in the IPv6 packet after the IPv6 Routing header (if present) and before the IPSec (Authentication Header (AH) or ESP) header, so that the destination node can process the Home Address Option before the IPSec header.
  - Finally, once the Mobile Node has fully assembled the IPv6 packet, it performs the necessary IPSec authentication (and encryption, if required) processing on the packet, initializing the Authentication Data in the IPSec header.

- The processing of the AH described in **[RFC4302]** is extended as follows. The Mobile Node calculates the AH authentication data as if the following conditions were true:
  - The source IPv6 address in the packet's IPv6 header contains the Home IP Address of the Mobile Node, and
  - The Home Address field of the Home Address Option contains the Mobile Node's new Care-of IP Address.

6.3.9.2.4 *Receiving IPv6 Packets While the Mobile Node Is Away from Home*

While a Mobile Node is away from home, it will receive IPv6 packets addressed to its Home IP Address through one of the following two methods:

- IPv6 packets sent by a Correspondent Node to a Mobile Node that do not have a corresponding entry in the Binding Cache will be sent to the Mobile Node's Home IP Address. These packets are captured by the Home Agent and tunneled to the Mobile Node.
- IPv6 packets sent by a Correspondent Node to a Mobile Node that has an entry in the Binding Cache and where the entry contains the Mobile Node's current Care-of IP Address will be sent using a Type 2 Routing header. The Correspondent Node addresses the packet to the Mobile Node's Care-of IP Address, with the final hop indicated in the Routing header and directing the packet to the Home IP Address of the Mobile Node. The processing of this last hop information in the Routing header is done entirely internally to the Mobile Node, since both the Home IP Address and the Care-of IP Address are IP addresses within the Mobile Node.

If the Mobile Node receives IPv6 packets by the first method, it must check that the source IPv6 address of the tunneled packet is the Home Agent's IPv6 address. The Mobile Node may also transmit a Binding Update message to the node that originated the IPv6 packet.

If the Mobile Node receives IPv6 packets by the second method, it will use the following rules to enable the packet to be processed normally by the Mobile Node's upper-layer protocols as if the IPv6 packet had been addressed to the Mobile Node's Home IP Address.

- An IPv6 node that receives a packet destined for its own IP address (i.e., one of its IPv6 addresses indicated in the destination IPv6 address field) examines the IPv6 Next Header field values in the chain of IPv6 header and extension headers and processes them accordingly. When the node encounters a Type 2 Routing header while processing these headers, it performs the following checks, and if any of them fails, the node silently discards the IPv6 packet.
  - Checks that the Length field value in the Type 2 Routing header is equal to 2.
  - Checks that the value in the Segments Left field in the Routing header is 1. However, an implementation may choose to process the Routing header so that the Segments Left field value becomes 0 after the node has processed the Routing header, but before the rest of the packet is processed.
  - Checks that the IPv6 address in the Home Address field of the Routing header is one of the node's Home IP Addresses if the value in the Segments Left field is 1. The address in the Home Address field must be a routable unicast IPv6 address.

After performing the above checks, the node swaps the destination IPv6 address field of the IPv6 packet with the Home Address field in the Type 2 Routing header, decrements the Segments Left field value by one, and resubmits the IPv6 packet to the IPv6 processing module for the processing of the IPv6 Next Header. Since the IPSec headers (AH and ESP) follow the Routing header, any IPSec processing will require the node to process the IPv6 packet with the Home IP Address in the destination IPv6 address field and the Segments Left field value set to zero.

6.3.9.2.5   Routing IPv6 Multicast Packets to a Mobile Node That Is on a Foreign Network

This section describes the behavior of a Mobile Node when it is away from its Home Link. A Mobile Node on its Home Link operates in the same manner as any other (non-mobile) node. Thus, when on the Home Link, the Mobile Node functions similarly to other multicast traffic senders and receivers.

To receive IPv6 packets sent to a multicast group, a Mobile Node must first join that multicast group. A Mobile Node may join a multicast group through an IPv6 multicast router on the local Foreign Link being visited. In this case, the Mobile Node joins the multicast group using its assigned Care-of IP address and not with the Home Address Option, which it uses when sending MLDv1 or MLDv2 Multicast Listener Report messages (requesting to join a group **[RFC2710] [RFC3810]**).

Alternatively, the Mobile Node may join a multicast group through a Bidirectional Tunnel established to its Home Agent. In this case, the Mobile Node tunnels IPv6 packets containing its multicast group membership control packets (MLDv1 or MLDv2 Multicast Listener Report messages) to the Home Agent. The Home Agent can then tunnel multicast packets back to the Mobile Node. The Mobile Node does not tunnel multicast group membership control packets until the following occurs:

- The Home Agent has created a Mobility Binding for the Mobile Node.
- The Home Agent has sent at least one multicast group membership control message (Multicast Listener Query messages (General Query or Multicast-Address-Specific Query) **[RFC2710] [RFC3810]**) via the tunnel to the Mobile Node.

The following two options are available to a Mobile Node that wishes to send packets to a multicast group:

- **Send Multicast Packets Directly on the Foreign Link Being Visited**: In this case, the multicast application on the Mobile Node uses the Care-of IP Address as a source IP address for multicast traffic, similar to what it would do using a stationary IP address. The Mobile Node does not use the Home Address Option in such multicast traffic.
- **Send Multicast Packets via a Reverse Tunnel to Its Home Agent**: Given that multicast routing in general forwards a multicast packet using the Source IP Address in the IPv6 header of the packet, a Mobile Node that tunnels a multicast packet to its Home Agent must use its Home IP Address as the Source IPv6 Address of the encapsulated (i.e., original/inner) multicast packet.

Note that the option of sending multicast traffic directly from the Foreign Link is only applicable while the Mobile Node is connected to that Foreign Link. This is because the multicast distribution tree on which the traffic is sent is associated with that specific source location (a source-rooted or source-specific tree), and any change of location or source IP address will invalidate the source-rooted tree and its branches to the multicast group members.

6.3.9.3   Home Agent and IPv6 Prefix Management

In some cases, a Mobile Node may wish to send a Binding Update to its Home Agent to register its newly assigned primary Care-of IP Address, but the Mobile Node may not know the IP address of the Home Agent to use. For example, a new node on the Home Link may have been configured to act as the Home Agent while the Mobile Node is away from home. In this case, the Mobile Node must find a way to discover the IP address of the active Home Agent on its Home Link.

6.3.9.3.1   Dynamic Home Agent Address Discovery by a Mobile Node

To discover the IPv6 address of a Home Agent on its Home Link, the Mobile Node sends an ICMPv6 Home Agent Address Discovery Request message (ICMPv6 Type 144 message) to the Mobile IPv6 Home Agent Anycast address **[RFC2526]** associated with its IPv6 Home Subnet Prefix. The Home

Agent receives this Request message and returns an ICMPv6 Home Agent Address Discovery Reply message (ICMPv6 Type 145 message) to the Mobile Node. The Reply message contains the IPv6 addresses of the Home Agents (in the message's Home Agent Addresses field) operating on the Home Link.

Upon receiving this Reply message, the Mobile Node may then send a Binding Update message for a Home Registration to any of the unicast IPv6 addresses listed in the Home Agent Addresses field of the Reply message. The Mobile Node attempts Home Registration with each of these IP addresses, one at a time (in the order they appear in the Reply message), until one accepts the registration. The Mobile Node sends a Binding Update to one of these IP addresses and waits for a corresponding Binding Acknowledgement message before moving on to the next IPv6 address if no response is received. The Mobile Node waits for a period of at least *InitialBindackTimeoutFirstReg* seconds before transmitting a Binding Update message to the next IPv6 address.

If the Mobile Node sends a Home Agent Address Discovery Request message to the IPv6 Home Agent's Anycast address and does not receive a corresponding Reply message within a time period of INITIAL_DHAAD_TIMEOUT seconds, it may retransmit the same Request message to the same Home Agent's Anycast address. The Mobile Node may repeat this retransmission up to a maximum of DHAAD_RETRIES attempts but delays each retransmission by twice the time delay used for the previous retransmission.

6.3.9.3.2 *Sending of ICMPv6 Mobile Prefix Solicitations by a Mobile Node*

If a Mobile Node is assigned a Home IP Address that is about to become invalid, the Mobile Node sends an ICMPv6 Mobile Prefix Solicitation message to its Home Agent to acquire fresh IPv6 Routing prefix information. Obtaining the new IPv6 prefix information also enables the Mobile Node to participate in any possible IPv6 address renumbering operations that may be affecting the Home Network.

The Mobile Node must use the Home Address Option (included in an IPv6 Destination Option extension header (Next Header value of 60)) to carry its Home IP Address. IPSec (which the Mobile Node must support) must be used to protect the Solicitation message. The 16-bit Identifier field in the ICMPv6 Mobile Prefix Solicitation message header must be set to a random value.

The Binding Updates that the Mobile Node sends to other nodes must have a Lifetime value that does not exceed the remaining Lifetime associated with its primary Care-of IP Address Home Registration. Any Binding Updates that the Mobile Node sends should have Lifetime values constrained to be within the remaining Valid Lifetime for the IPv6 prefix associated with its Home IP Address. When the Lifetime for a changed IPv6 prefix decreases, there is a chance that Mobility Bindings cached by Correspondent Nodes in their Binding Update List may be stored beyond the newly reduced Lifetime. In such cases, the Mobile Node must transmit a Binding Update to all Correspondent Nodes. These limits placed on the Lifetime of a Binding are intended to prevent the Home IP Address of a Mobile Node from being used after it becomes invalid.

6.3.9.3.3 *Receiving ICMPv6 Mobile Prefix Advertisements at a Mobile Node*

This section describes the mechanisms a Home Agent uses to provide boot time configuration and renumbering information to a Mobile Node about its Home IPv6 subnet while the Mobile Node is visiting a Foreign Network. The Home Agent transmits an ICMPv6 Mobile Prefix Advertisement message (ICMP Type 147 message) to the Mobile Node on the Foreign Network, providing it with important IPv6 Prefix Information Option (Option Type 3) data that describes changes in the IPv6 prefixes in use on its Home Link.

The ICMPv6 Mobile Prefix Solicitation message (ICMPv6 Type 146 message) **[RFC6275]** is similar to the ICMPv6 Router Solicitation message (ICMPv6 Type 133 message) used in the IPv6 Neighbor Discovery protocol **[RFC4861]**, except the ICMPv6 Type 146 message is routed from the Mobile Node on the Foreign Network to the Home Agent on the Home Network using standard IPv6 unicast routing methods.

Upon receiving a Mobile Prefix Advertisement message, the Mobile Node validates it according to the following test:

- Checks that the Source IP Address of the IPv6 packet carrying the ICMPv6 Mobile Prefix Advertisement message matches the IPv6 address of the Home Agent to which the Mobile Node last sent a Home Registration Binding Update to register its primary Care-of IP Address. If no such registrations exist for the Mobile Node, it checks that the IPv6 address matches the Mobile Node's stored Home Agent IPv6 address, if one exists. If the Mobile Node has not yet discovered the IPv6 address of its Home Agent, it accepts the Mobile Prefix Advertisement message.
- Checks that the IPv6 packet has a Type 2 Routing header and is protected by an IPSec header.
- If the ICMPv6 Identifier value in this Mobile Prefix Advertisement message matches the 16-bit ICMPv6 Identifier in the Mobile Prefix Solicitation message that the Mobile Node recently sent, and no other Mobile Prefix Advertisement message has been received for this value, then the Mobile Node considers this Advertisement message to be solicited and processes it further. Otherwise, it considers the Advertisement message to be unsolicited and discards it. In this case, the Mobile Node sends an ICMPv6 Mobile Prefix Solicitation message.

The Mobile Node silently discards any received Mobile Prefix Advertisement message that does not meet these criteria.

For any Mobile Prefix Advertisement message that the Mobile Node accepts, it processes the Managed Address Configuration (M), Other Stateful Configuration (O), and the Prefix Information Options in the message as if they were received in an ICMPv6 Router Advertisement message **[RFC4861]** on the Mobile Node's Home Link.

6.3.9.4 Mobile Node Movement Considerations

The primary goal of Mobile Node movement detection is to identify IP-level movements and handovers. This section describes a generic method that harnesses the IPv6 Neighbor Discovery mechanisms [RFC4861], including the IPv6 Router Discovery and Neighbor Unreachability Detection functions, for Mobile Node movement detection.

6.3.9.4.1 Mobile Node Movement Detection

With generic movement detection, a Mobile Node uses the IPv6 Neighbor Unreachability Detection function **[RFC4861]** to detect when the default router it is using on a Foreign Network is no longer bidirectionally reachable (see the discussion in **Chapter 4**). When this occurs, the Mobile Node must discover a new active default router (usually on a new Foreign Link). However, the Mobile Node performs this detection only when it has IPv6 packets to send and does not receive frequent ICMPv6 Router Advertisement messages or any indication from the Link-Layer, which can cause the Mobile Node to become unaware that an IP-level handover has occurred. Therefore, it is recommended that the Mobile Node supplement this detection method with additional information available to it (e.g., from lower-layer protocols).

When the Mobile Node detects an IP-level handover, it performs IPv6 Duplicate Address Detection [RFC4861] on the local link using its IPv6 Link-Local address, selects a new active default router using the information obtained from the IPv6 Router Discovery function [RFC4861], and then performs IPv6 Prefix Discovery with that new default router on the link to create new Care-of IP Address(es). The Mobile Node then sends a Binding Update to register the newly created primary Care-of IP Address with its Home Agent. After updating its Home Registration with the Home Agent, the Mobile Node sends Binding Updates to update associated Mobility Bindings on Correspondent Nodes with which it is communicating via Route Optimization.

A Mobile Node typically considers the following events as indications that an IP-level handover may have occurred. Upon noticing such events, the Mobile Node uses the IPv6 Router Discovery function to discover the IPv6 routers and prefixes on the new link.

- If the Mobile Node receives ICMPv6 Router Advertisement messages that include the Advertisement Interval Option (Option Type 7), it may use the value in the 32-bit Advertisement Interval field to gauge the frequency at which future Advertisement messages from that router should be expected. The value in this field specifies the minimum rate (i.e., the maximum time spacing between successive Advertisement messages) that the Mobile Node should anticipate. If this duration elapses and the Mobile Node has not received any Advertisement message from the router, it can conclude that at least one Advertisement message sent by the router has been lost. The Mobile Node can then apply a well-defined policy (provided by the network administrator) to determine how many lost Advertisement messages from the current default router constitute an IP-level handover indication.
- The IPv6 Neighbor Unreachability Detection function run by the Mobile Node may indicate that the default router is no longer reachable.

6.3.9.4.2   Home Link Detection on a Mobile Node

When a Mobile Node detects that it has moved to a new link using the Movement Detection Algorithm or during bootstrapping, it performs the following operations to determine if it is on the Home Link:

- The Mobile Node generates a new primary Care-of IP Address using standard IPv6 mechanisms (either Stateless or Stateful DHCPv6 address autoconfiguration) and configures it on the interface to the link. It also keeps track of all the on-link IPv6 prefix(es) received in the ICMPv6 Router Advertisement messages along with their prefix lengths.
- If the Mobile Node's Home IPv6 Prefix has not been statically configured, it uses a bootstrapping procedure **[RFC5026]** to determine the Home IPv6 Prefix.
- Using its Home IPv6 Prefix, the Mobile Node checks whether this prefix matches one of the IPv6 prefixes received in the ICMPv6 Router Advertisement messages. If a match exists, the Mobile Node concludes that it is connected to the Home Link.

6.3.9.4.3   Using Multiple Care-of IP Addresses on a Mobile Node

Mobile IPv6 allows a Mobile Node to use more than one Care-of IP Address on a Foreign Network, particularly when the Mobile Node is roaming over overlapping wireless cells. This makes it effectively reachable through multiple wireless links simultaneously, possibly using different on-link IPv6 subnet prefixes. In such cases, the Mobile Node must ensure that the primary Care-of IP Address used always has an IPv6 prefix that is advertised by the current default router. After selecting a new primary Care-of IP Address, the Mobile Node must transmit a Binding Update message containing that Care-of IP Address to the Home Agent, with the Home Registration (H) and Acknowledge (A) bits set.

To facilitate smooth handovers while moving from one cell to another, it is beneficial for the Mobile Node to retain the previous primary Care-of IP Address as a (non-primary) Care-of IP Address, while still accepting IPv6 packets at this old address, even after registering the new primary Care-of IP Address with the Home Agent. This is logical, as the Mobile Node could only receive IPv6 packets sent to the previous primary Care-of IP Address if it is still connected to that link. If the previous primary Care-of IP Address was allocated through Stateful IPv6 Address Autoconfiguration, it is preferable for the Mobile Node not to release the address immediately upon switching to the new primary Care-of IP Address.

As soon as the Mobile Node determines that it is no longer reachable through a given link, it is recommended that the Mobile Node invalidate all Care-of IP Addresses associated with the

IPv6 address prefixes assigned by the default routers on the unreachable link, if they are not part of (i.e., different from) the current set of IPv6 address prefixes advertised by the (possibly new) current default router.

6.3.9.4.4 Mobile Node Returning to the Home Link

A Mobile Node uses the Movement Detection Algorithm [**RFC6275**] to determine if it has returned to its Home Link. Through this algorithm, the Mobile Node detects that its Home IPv6 Subnet Prefix matches its on-link address again. To send and receive IPv6 packets using its Home IP Address on the Home Link (with no Care-of IP Addresses used in this case), the Mobile Node sends a Binding Update to its Home Agent, instructing it to stop intercepting or tunneling IPv6 packets on its behalf. Until the Home Agent receives this deregistration Binding Update, the Mobile Node must not attempt to send or receive packets using its Home IP Address, even while on the Home Link. Unless deregistration occurs, the Home Agent will continue to intercept all IPv6 packets addressed to the Home IP Address of the Mobile Node and tunnel them to the previously registered Care-of IP Address.

In registering its return to the Home Link (Home Registration), the Mobile Node must set the Acknowledge (A) and Home Registration (H) bits in the Binding Update sent to the Home Agent. The Mobile Node must also set the Lifetime field to zero and specify its own Home IP Address as the Care-of IP Address for the binding. In this case, the source IP address in the Binding Update message is the Mobile Node's Home IP Address.

When sending this Binding Update message to the Home Agent, the Mobile Node must exercise caution in how it uses ICMPv6 Neighbor Solicitation messages (if needed) to discover the Link-Layer address of the Home Agent. This is because the Home Agent will currently be configured to intercept IPv6 packets addressed to the Home IP Address of the Mobile Node using the IPv6 Proxy Neighbor Discovery mechanism. Specifically, the Mobile Node will be unable to use its Home IP Address as the source IP address of the Neighbor Solicitation messages until the Home Agent stops guarding against the use of the Home IP Address.

It will typically not be necessary for the Mobile Node to send Neighbor Solicitation messages seeking the Home Agent's address, since the Mobile Node has already discovered the Link-Layer address of the Home Agent from a Source Link-Layer Address Option included in an ICMPv6 Router Advertisement message. However, if the Home Link has multiple Home Agents, it may still be necessary for the Mobile Node to send a Neighbor Solicitation message. In this special case, upon returning home, the Mobile Node must multicast the Neighbor Solicitation message and set the source IP address of this message to the IPv6 Unspecified address (::). The Target Address field of this message must be set to the Mobile Node's Home IP Address, and the destination IP address must be set to the IPv6 Solicited-Node multicast address (derived from the Mobile Node's Home IP Address). The Home Agent will respond by sending a multicast ICMPv6 Neighbor Advertisement message back to the Mobile Node with the Solicited (S) Flag set to zero. The Mobile Node should record the information contained in the Source Link-Layer Address Option included in the Neighbor Advertisement message and set the state of the entry in the Neighbor Cache associated with the Home Agent to REACHABLE.

The Mobile Node then sends the Binding Update message to the Link-Layer address of the Home Agent, instructing it to stop serving as the Mobile Node's Home Agent. After processing this Binding Update message, the Home Agent will stop defending the use of the Mobile Node's Home IP Address for Duplicate Address Detection and will cease responding to ICMPv6 Neighbor Solicitation messages related to the Mobile Node's Home IP Address. This allows the Mobile Node to be the only node on the Home Link to receive IPv6 packets sent to the Mobile Node's Home IP Address.

In addition, when the Mobile Node returns to its Home Link prior to the expiration of a current Mobility Binding for its Home IP Address and configures its Home IP Address on the network interface connected to the Home Link, it must not perform Duplicate Address Detection on this Home IP Address (see Chapter 4), to avoid conflicts or confusion since the Home Agent may still be using the same Home IP Address for similar operations on the Home Link at the same time. This rule also applies to the Mobile Node's IPv6 Link-Local address if the Link Local Address Compatibility (L) bit in the Binding Update message **[RFC6275]** was set when the Mobility Binding was created. If the Mobile Node returns to its Home Link after the Mobility Bindings for all of its Care-of IP Addresses have expired, then the Mobile Node should perform Duplicate Address Detection immediately.

A Mobile Node must be prepared to reply to ICMPv6 Neighbor Solicitation messages for its Home IP Address after it sends the Binding Update message to the Home Agent. The Mobile Node sends each reply as a unicast Neighbor Advertisement message to the Link-Layer address of the Neighbor Solicitation message sender. It is necessary for the Mobile Node to reply to Neighbor Solicitation messages since the Home Agent may need to perform IPv6 Neighbor Discovery when sending the Binding Acknowledgement message to the Mobile Node, and the Mobile Node may not be able to distinguish ICMPv6 Neighbor Solicitation messages originating from the Home Agent from other Neighbor Solicitation messages. It is important to note that a race condition occurs when both the Mobile Node and the Home Agent respond to the same Neighbor Solicitation messages sent by other nodes on the Home Link. However, this condition will only be temporary until the Home Agent accepts the Binding Update message.

Upon receiving the Binding Acknowledgement message from the Home Agent after sending the Binding Update message, the Mobile Node must send a multicast ICMPv6 Neighbor Advertisement message (to the IPv6 All-Nodes multicast address) onto the Home Link to advertise the Link-Layer address associated with its own Home IP Address. The Mobile Node must set the Target Address field in this Neighbor Advertisement message to its own Home IP Address, and this message must include a Target Link-Layer Address Option specifying the Mobile Node's Link-Layer address.

The Mobile Node must send a multicast Neighbor Advertisement message for each of its Home IP Addresses associated with the current on-link IPv6 prefixes, including its IPv6 Link-Local address. The Mobile Node MUST NOT set the Solicited (S) Flag in these Neighbor Advertisement messages, since they were not solicited by any Neighbor Solicitation message. However, the Mobile Node MUST set the Override (O) Flag in these Neighbor Advertisement messages to indicate that these Advertisements SHOULD override any existing entries in the Neighbor Cache of any node that receives them.

Given that multicast transmissions on the local link (typically based on Ethernet technologies) are generally not guaranteed to be reliable, the Mobile Node may have to retransmit these Neighbor Advertisement messages up to MAX_NEIGHBOR_ADVERTISEMENT times to increase their chances of reaching their intended target nodes. This means that, even if some nodes on the Home Link do not receive any of these messages, they will eventually be able to recover the information through the IPv6 Neighbor Unreachability Detection mechanism. Note that the IPv6 tunnel previously created by the Home Agent to the Mobile Node while visiting the Foreign Network typically stops operating at the same time that the Home Agent deletes the Mobile Node's Mobility Binding.

6.3.9.5 Performing the Return Routability Procedure at a Mobile Node

This section describes the rules that a Mobile Node must follow when initiating and performing the Return Routability Procedure.

6.3.9.5.1 *Sending Home Test Init and Care-of Test Init Messages*

A Mobile Node, when initiating a Return Routability Procedure, must transmit (in parallel or, more precisely, back-to-back) a Home Test Init and a Care-of Test Init message. However, if one or both Home or Care-of Keygen Tokens and associated Nonce Indices were recently received for the desired IPv6 addresses, the Mobile Node may reuse them. This means the Mobile Node may, in some cases, complete the Return Routability Procedure using only one message pair.

The Mobile Node may even complete the procedure without using any messages at all if it has a recent Home Keygen Token and has previously visited the same Foreign Network associated with the Care-of IP Address, which also means it has a recent Care-of Keygen Token. If the Mobile Node intends to send a Binding Update message to its Home Agent with the Lifetime field set to zero and the Care-of IP Address set to its Home IP Address, for example, when returning to its Home Link, sending a Home Test Init message is sufficient. In this case, the need for the Mobile Node to generate the Binding Management Key depends exclusively on the Home Keygen Token.

The creation of the Home Test Init and Care-of Test Init messages is briefly described in a section above. The Mobile Node must record in its Binding Update List the following fields when a Home Test Init or Care-of Test Init message is sent:

- The IPv6 address of the node to which the Mobile Node sent the message.
- The Home IP Address of the Mobile Node, which can be taken from the Source IP Address field of the IPv6 packet carrying the Home Test Init message. Note that when the Mobile Node sends a Care-of Test Init message directly to the Correspondent Node, the Source IP Address is the Mobile Node's Care-of IP Address, and the Destination IP Address is the Correspondent Node's IP address.
- The time at which the Mobile Node sent each of these messages.
- The Home Init Cookie used in the Home Test Init message and the Care-of Init Cookie used in the Care-of Test Init message.

Note that the information associated with a single Care-of Test Init message may be sufficient even when the Mobile Node supports multiple Home IP Addresses. In this case, the Mobile Node may record the same information in multiple entries in the Binding Update List.

6.3.9.5.2   Receiving Home Test and Care-of Test Messages

A Mobile Node validates a packet according to the following tests upon receiving an IPv6 packet carrying a Home Test message:

- The Source IP Address of the IPv6 packet belongs to a Correspondent Node for which the Mobile Node has an entry in the Binding Update List indicating that the Return Routability Procedure is in progress. Note that the Binding Update List may have multiple such entries.
- The Binding Update List indicates that the Mobile Node has not yet received a Home Keygen Token.
- The Destination IP Address field of the IPv6 packet contains the Mobile Node's Home IP Address, and the IPv6 packet has been received on an IPv6 tunnel from the Home Agent.
- The Home Init Cookie field in the Home Test message matches the value stored in the Binding Update List.

The Mobile Node silently ignores any Home Test message that does not satisfy all of these tests; otherwise, it records the Home Nonce Index and Home Keygen Token in the Binding Update List. The Mobile Node continues waiting for the Care-of Test message if the Binding Update List entry does not contain a Care-of Keygen Token.

A Mobile Node validates a packet according to the following tests upon receiving an IPv6 packet carrying a Care-of Test message:

- The Source Address of the IPv6 packet belongs to a Correspondent Node for which the Mobile Node has an entry in the Binding Update List indicating that the Return Routability Procedure is in progress. Note that the Binding Update List may have multiple such entries.
- The Binding Update List indicates that the Mobile Node has not yet received a Care-of Keygen Token.
- The Destination IP Address field of the IPv6 packet contains the Mobile Node's current Care-of IP Address.
- The Care-of Init Cookie field in the Care-of Test message matches the value stored in the Binding Update List.

The Mobile Node silently ignores any Care-of Test message that does not satisfy all of these tests; otherwise, it records the Care-of Nonce Index and Care-of Keygen Token in the Binding Update List. The Mobile Node continues waiting for the Home Test message if the entry in the Binding Update List does not have a Home Keygen Token.

If the Mobile Node has performed the above actions after receiving either the Home Test or the Care-of Test message, and the entry in the Binding Update List contains both the Home and the Care-of Keygen Tokens, the Return Routability Procedure is considered complete. The Mobile Node then proceeds to send a Binding Update message.

6.3.9.6   Processing Mobility Bindings on the Mobile Node

This section describes how a Mobile Node processes Mobility Bindings, including sending Binding Updates to the Home Agent, registering with the Correspondent Node, receiving Binding Acknowledgments, receiving Binding Refresh Requests, and handling retransmissions and rate limiting.

6.3.9.6.1   Sending Binding Updates to the Home Agent

For a Mobile Node to change its primary Care-of IP Address, it must register the new Care-of IP Address with its Home Agent to designate this address as its primary Care-of IP Address. Additionally, if the Mobile Node wishes to extend the services of the Home Agent beyond the current registration period, it sends a new Binding Update message to the Home Agent well before the expiration of this period, even if the request does not involve changing the Mobile Node's primary Care-of IP Address. However, if the Home Agent returns a Binding Acknowledgement message to the Mobile Node for the current registration with the 8-bit Status field set to 1 (Code 1, meaning "Accepted but Prefix Discovery Necessary" [RFC6275]), the Mobile Node should not attempt to register again with the Home Agent until it has confirmed the validity of its Home IPv6 Prefixes through the ICMPv6 Mobile Prefix Discovery mechanism [RFC6275]. This procedure is typically necessary each time a Mobile Node receives this Status value (1), as information it learned previously may have changed.

To register a Care-of IP Address or extend the lifetime of an existing registration, the Mobile Node sends an IPv6 packet containing a Binding Update message to its Home Agent, with the IPv6 packet constructed as follows:

- The Home Registration (H) bit in the Binding Update message must be set to 1.
- The Acknowledge (A) bit in the Binding Update must be set.
- The IPv6 packet must contain a Home Address Option (Option Type 201), providing the Mobile Node's Home IP Address for the Mobility Binding.
- The Care-of IP address for the Binding is used as the Source IP Address in the IPv6 header of the packet, unless an Alternate Care-of Address Option (Mobility Option Type 3) is included in the Binding Update message. The Mobile Node must include this Mobility Option (Type 3) in all Home Registrations, as the IPv6 ESP protocol cannot protect Care-of IP Addresses in the packet's IPv6 header. Mobile IPv6 implementations that are aware they are using IPSec AH to protect a particular message might avoid including this Mobility Option.
- If the IPv6 Link-Local address of the Mobile Node has the same interface ID as the Home IP Address for which the Mobile Node is supplying a new Care-of IP Address, then the Mobile Node should set the Binding Update message's Link-Local Address Compatibility (L) bit.
- If the Mobile Node generated the interface ID of the Home IP Address based on a randomly generated value as described in [RFC8981], then the IPv6 Link-Local address is unlikely to have a compatible interface ID. In this case, the Mobile Node must clear (set to zero) the Binding Update message's Link-Local Address Compatibility (L) bit.
- If the Mobile Node and the Home Agent have dynamically established their IPSec security associations, and the Mobile Node's endpoint in the key management protocol can be

updated to the new Care-of IP Address every time the Mobile Node moves, the Mobile Node should set the Binding Update message's Key Management Mobility Capability (K) bit. Otherwise, the Mobile Node must clear (i.e., not set) the bit.

- The value specified in the Binding Update message's 16-bit Lifetime field must be nonzero and should be less than or equal to the remaining Valid Lifetime of the Home IP Address and the Care-of IP Address specified for the Mobility Binding.

The purpose of the Acknowledge (A) bit in the Binding Update message is to request that the Home Agent respond with a Binding Acknowledgement message upon receiving this Binding Update message. The Mobile Node should retransmit this Binding Update message to the Home Agent until it receives a Binding Acknowledgement message. Once the Mobile Node reaches a retransmission timeout period of MAX_BINDACK_TIMEOUT, it should restart the process of sending the Binding Update message, but instead, try the next Home Agent indicated by the Dynamic Home Agent Address Discovery mechanism. If only one Home Agent exists, the Mobile Node should continue to periodically retransmit the Binding Update message at this rate until the Home Agent acknowledges it or until the Mobile Node decides to register a different primary Care-of IP Address.

The Mobile Node uses the Binding Update message to request a Home Agent to serve as the Home Agent for the Mobile Node's Home IP Address. Until the Lifetime (as indicated in the Lifetime field) of this registration expires, the Home Agent serves as the Home Agent for this Home IP Address. Each Binding Update message is authenticated as coming from the correct Mobile Node. The Mobile Node must include its Home IP Address (either in the Home Address Option or in the Source IP Address field of the IPv6 header) in Binding Update messages sent to the Home Agent. This is necessary to ensure IPSec policies are applied to the correct Home IP Address. When the Mobile Node sends a Binding Update message to its Home Agent, it must also create or update the corresponding Binding Update List entry.

A Mobile Node stores the last Sequence Number value sent to the Home Agent in a Binding Update message within the message's 16-bit Sequence Number field. If the correct Sequence Number value is not known to the Mobile Node, it may start at any value. If the Home Agent rejects the Sequence Number value sent, it sends back a Binding Acknowledgement message with a Status field code value of 135 (indicating "Sequence Number Out of Window"), along with the last accepted Sequence Number in the Sequence Number field of the Binding Acknowledgement message. The Mobile Node stores this information and derives the next Sequence Number value from it for the next Binding Update message it sends.

In the case where the Mobile Node has additional Home IP Addresses, it sends an additional IPv6 packet containing a Binding Update message to its Home Agent to register the Care-of IP Address associated with each of the other Home IP Addresses.

The Home Agent will only perform IPv6 Duplicate Address Detection for the Mobile Node's Home IP Address when the Mobile Node has provided a valid Mobility Binding between its Home IP Address and a Care-of IP Address. If some time elapses during which the Home Agent has no Mobility Binding for the Mobile Node, it is possible that another node has autoconfigured the Home IP Address of the Mobile Node. Therefore, the Mobile Node must treat the creation of a new Mobility Binding with the Home Agent using an existing Home IP Address the same as the creation of a new Mobility Binding with the Home Agent using a new Home IP Address.

In the unlikely event that the Home IP Address of the Mobile Node is autoconfigured as the IPv6 address of another node on the Home Network, the Home Agent will reply to a subsequent Binding Update message from the Mobile Node by sending a Binding Acknowledgement message containing a Status field code value of 134 (indicating "Duplicate Address Detection Failed"). In this case, the Mobile Node, upon receiving such a status code, MUST NOT attempt to reuse the same Home IP Address. The Mobile Node should continue to register the Care-of IP Addresses associated with its other Home IP Addresses, if any exist. Reference **[RFC5026]** allows Mobile Nodes to acquire new Home IP Addresses to replace the address for which a status code 134 was received.

6.3.9.6.2 *Correspondent Node Registration*

When a Mobile Node, after communicating with the Home Agent, receives an indication that its Home IP Address is valid, it can initiate a Correspondent Registration to allow the Correspondent Node to cache the current Care-of IP Address of the Mobile Node. This starts with the Mobile Node performing the Return Routability Procedure, followed by a Correspondent Registration. This section describes when the Mobile Node initiates the Correspondent Registration and the rules it follows while performing the Registration.

After sending a Binding Update message to the Home Agent to register a new primary Care-of IP Address, the Mobile Node initiates a Correspondent Registration for each node that is already present in its Binding Update List. The Mobile Node carries out these procedures to either update or delete Mobility Binding information in the Correspondent Node. For nodes that are not in the Binding Update List, the Mobile Node may initiate a Correspondent Registration at any convenient time after sending the Binding Update message to the Home Agent.

A Mobile Node may also initiate the Correspondent Registration in response to receiving an IPv6 packet that satisfies all of the following criteria:

* The IPv6 packet was tunneled to the Mobile Node using IPv6 encapsulation.
* The Destination IP Address in the outer (tunnel) IPv6 header matches any of the Mobile Node's Care-of IP Addresses.
* The Destination IP Address in the inner (original) IPv6 header matches one of the Mobile Node's Home IP Addresses.
* The Source IP Address in the outer (tunnel) IPv6 header differs from the Source IP Address in the inner (original) IPv6 header.
* The IPv6 packet does not contain a Home Test Init, Home Test, Care-of Test Init, or Care-of Test message.

If a Mobile Node has multiple Home IP Addresses, selecting the appropriate Home IP Address for the Correspondent Registration becomes an important consideration. The Home IP Address chosen must be used as the Destination IP Address of the received original (inner) IPv6 packet.

The Mobile Node determines the peer IP address to be used in the procedure as follows:

* If a Home Address Option (Option Type 201) is present in the inner (original) IPv6 packet, the Mobile Node uses the IP address from this Option.
* Otherwise, the Mobile Node uses the Source IP Address in the inner (original) IPv6 header of the packet.

Note that the Mobile Node checks the validity of the original IPv6 packet before attempting to initiate the Correspondent Registration. A Mobile Node may also choose to keep its network (topologically) location private from certain Correspondent Nodes and refrain from initiating the Correspondent Registration for those nodes.

After the Mobile Node has successfully completed the Return Routability Procedure and received a successful Binding Acknowledgement message from the Home Agent, it may send a Binding Update message to the Correspondent Node.

For any Binding Update message that the Mobile Node sends, it sets the Care-of IP Address (to be entered either in the Source IP Address field of the packet's IPv6 header or in the Care-of IP Address field of the Alternate Care-of Address Option (Mobility Option Type 3) of the Binding Update message) to one of the Care-of IP Addresses currently used by the Mobile Node, or to the Mobile Node's Home IP Address. The Mobile Node may use a different Care-of IP Address when sending Binding Update messages to different Correspondent Nodes. A Mobile Node may also transmit a Binding Update message to a Correspondent Node, instructing it to delete any existing Mobility Binding in its Binding Cache for the Mobile Node. Even in this case, the completion of a successful Return Routability Procedure is required first.

If the Mobile Node has not set the Care-of IP Address to its Home IP Address, the Mobile Node's Binding Update message will request that the Correspondent Node create or update an entry for the Mobile Node in the Correspondent Node's Binding Cache. The Correspondent Node does this to record the Mobile Node's Care-of IP Address for use in sending future IPv6 packets to the Mobile Node. In this case, the value specified in the Lifetime field of the Binding Update message should be less than or equal to the remaining Lifetime of the Home Registration and the Care-of IP Address specified for the Mobility Binding. The Care-of IP Address that the Mobile Node specifies in the Binding Update message may differ from the Mobile Node's primary Care-of IP Address.

If the Mobile Node sends a Binding Update message to the Correspondent Node, requesting the deletion of any existing entry in the Binding Cache for the Mobile Node, it sets the Care-of IP Address to its Home IP Address and the Lifetime field to zero. In this case, Binding Management Key generation is done exclusively using the Home Keygen Token. This situation requires setting the Care-of Nonce Index to zero. The Binding Update creation rules require the Mobile Node to set the Care-of IP Address to the Home IP Address if it is at home, or to the current Care-of IP Address if it is away from home. If the Mobile Node wishes to ensure that its new Care-of IP Address has been entered into the Binding Cache of a Correspondent Node, it needs to request an acknowledgment by setting the Binding Update message's Acknowledge (A) bit.

The Mobile Node creates a Binding Update message as follows:

- The Mobile Node's current Care-of IP Address is sent either in the Source IP Address field of the IPv6 header or in the Alternate Care-of Address Option.
- The Destination IP Address field of the IPv6 header contains the Correspondent Node's IPv6 address.
- The IPv6 Mobility Header is constructed, including the Binding Authorization Data and, possibly, the Nonce Indices Option (Mobility Option Type 4).
- The Mobile Node's Home IP Address is added to the packet in a Home Address Option (Option Type 201), unless the Source IP Address is the Home IP Address.

Each Binding Update message has a Sequence Number that is greater than the Sequence Number value sent in the previous Binding Update message to the same destination IP address (if any). The Sequence Numbers are compared modulo 2^{16}. However, **[RFC6275]** places no requirement on the Sequence Number value being strictly incremented by 1 with each new Binding Update message sent or received, as long as the value stays within the window.

A Mobile Node stores the last Sequence Number value sent to a destination in a Binding Update message in its Binding Update List entry for that destination. If there is no Binding Update List entry for that destination, the Sequence Number starts at a random value. The Mobile Node does not use the same Sequence Number in two different Binding Update messages to the same Correspondent Node, even if the Binding Update messages indicate different Care-of IP Addresses.

A Mobile Node is responsible for completing the Correspondent Registration, in addition to any necessary retransmissions (subject to the rate limitation discussed below).

6.3.9.6.3 *Receiving Binding Acknowledgments at a Mobile Node*

Upon receiving an IPv6 packet containing a Binding Acknowledgement message, a Mobile Node validates the packet according to the following tests:

- The IPv6 packet satisfies the authentication requirements for Binding Acknowledgement messages. Specifically, if the Mobile Node sent the Binding Update message to the Home Agent, the underlying IPSec protection is used. If the Mobile Node sent the Binding Update message to a Correspondent Node, the Binding Authorization Data Option (Mobility Option Type 5) must be present in the Binding Acknowledgement message and contain a valid value.

- The Binding Authorization Data Option, if present in the Binding Acknowledgement message, must be the last option and must not have trailing padding.
- The Sequence Number field value matches the Sequence Number that the Mobile Node sent to this destination IP address in an outstanding Binding Update message, and the Status field value is not 135 (indicating "Sequence Number Out of Window").

The Mobile Node silently ignores any Binding Acknowledgement message that does not satisfy all of these tests.

When a Mobile Node receives an IPv6 packet containing a valid Binding Acknowledgement message, it must examine the Status field as follows:

- If the Status field indicates that the Binding Update message was accepted by the Home Agent (i.e., the value in the Status field is less than 128 [RFC6275]), then the Mobile Node must update the corresponding entry in its Binding Update List to reflect that the Binding Update message has been acknowledged. The Mobile Node must then cease retransmitting the Binding Update message. Additionally, if the Lifetime field value in the Binding Acknowledgement message is less than the Lifetime value sent in the Binding Update message being acknowledged, the Mobile Node must determine the new remaining Lifetime value as described in [RFC6275]. The Mobile Node should transmit a new Binding Update message well before the expiration of this period to extend the Lifetime.
- If the Binding Acknowledgement message successfully passes authentication and the value in the Status field is 135 (indicating "Sequence Number Out of Window"), then the Mobile Node must update its Binding Sequence Number to match the Sequence Number indicated in the Binding Acknowledgement message. However, if the value in the Status field is 135 but the Binding Acknowledgement message fails authentication, then the Mobile Node must silently ignore the message.
- If the value in the Status field is 1 (indicating "Accepted but Prefix Discovery Necessary"), the Mobile Node should send an ICMPv6 Mobile Prefix Solicitation message (ICMPv6 Message Type 146) to its Home Agent to update its information regarding the available IPv6 prefixes.
- If the value in the Status field indicates that the Binding Update message was rejected by the Home Agent (i.e., the Status field value is greater than or equal to 128), then the Mobile Node can take the necessary steps to address the cause of the error and retransmit the Binding Update message (with a new Sequence Number value), but subject to the rate limiting restriction as described below. If no remedy is found for the cause of the error, then the Mobile Node should record in its Binding Update List that future Binding Update messages should not be sent to this destination.

The treatment of the Binding Refresh Advice Option (Mobility Option Type 2), when included in the Binding Acknowledgement message, depends on who sent the acknowledgement. The Mobile Node must ignore this Option if the acknowledgement came from a Correspondent Node. If it was sent by the Home Agent, the Mobile Node uses the value in the 16-bit Refresh Interval field in the Option as a suggestion for when the Mobile Node should attempt to refresh its Home Registration at the indicated small interval.

6.3.9.6.4 *Receiving Binding Refresh Requests at a Mobile Node*

A Correspondent Node sends a Binding Refresh Request message (Mobility Header Message Type 0) to request that a Mobile Node update its Mobility Binding. When a Mobile Node receives an IPv6 packet containing a Binding Refresh Request message, it processes the message as follows:

- If the Mobile Node has an entry in its Binding Update List for the sender of the Binding Refresh Request message and wishes to retain its Binding Cache entry at the Correspondent Node, it should initiate a Return Routability Procedure.

- If the Mobile Node prefers to have its Binding Cache entry at the Correspondent Node removed, it can either ignore the Binding Refresh Request message and wait for the Mobility Binding to time out, or it can delete its Mobility Binding from the Correspondent Node at any time by sending an explicit Binding Update message with a zero Lifetime and the Care-of IP Address set to the Home IP Address.
- If the Mobile Node is uncertain whether it needs the Binding Cache entry, the decision it makes is implementation-dependent, such as being based on available resources.

Note that a Mobile Node should take measures not to respond to Binding Refresh Request messages for IP addresses not in the Binding Update List to avoid being subjected to denial-of-service attacks.

If the Mobile Node has successfully completed the Return Routability Procedure, it should send a Binding Update message as described above. The Mobile Node should set the Lifetime field in this Binding Update message to a new Lifetime value, extending any current Lifetime remaining from a previous Binding Update message sent to this destination (as indicated in any existing Binding Update List entry for this destination). The Lifetime value should again be less than or equal to the remaining Lifetime of the Home Registration and the Care-of IP Address specified for the Mobility Binding. When the Mobile Node sends this Binding Update message, it must update its Binding Update List in the same manner as it would for any other Binding Update message it sends.

6.3.9.6.5   Retransmissions and Rate Limiting of Mobility Messages

A Mobile Node is responsible for message retransmissions and rate limiting when performing the Return Routability Procedure, registrations, and solicited IPv6 Prefix Discovery. When a Mobile Node sends an ICMPv6 Mobile Prefix Solicitation, Home Test Init, Care-of Test Init, or Binding Update for which it expects a response, it must determine a value for the initial retransmission timer as follows:

- If the Mobile Node is transmitting an ICMPv6 Mobile Prefix Solicitation message, it should use an initial retransmission interval of INITIAL_SOLICIT_TIMER.
- If the Mobile Node is transmitting a Binding Update message and does not have an existing Mobility Binding at the Home Agent, it should use *InitialBindackTimeoutFirstReg* **[RFC6275]** as the value for the initial retransmission timer. This long retransmission interval allows the Home Agent to complete the IPv6 Duplicate Address Detection procedure mandated in this case.
- Otherwise, the Mobile Node should use the INITIAL_BINDACK_TIMEOUT value specified in **[RFC6275]** for the initial retransmission timer.

If the Mobile Node does not receive a valid response matching the message sent within the selected initial retransmission interval, the message should be retransmitted until a response is received. The Mobile Node must use an exponential back-off process for message retransmissions, in which the timeout period is doubled after each retransmission, until either the Mobile Node receives a response or the timeout period reaches the value MAX_BINDACK_TIMEOUT. The Mobile Node may elect to continue transmitting these messages at this slower rate indefinitely.

The Mobile Node should start a separate exponential back-off process for retransmissions of different message types, different Home IP Addresses, and different Care-of IP Addresses. Additionally, the Mobile Node should apply an overall rate limitation for messages transmitted to a particular Correspondent Node. Applying this overall rate limitation ensures that the Correspondent Node has sufficient time to respond when Mobility Bindings for multiple Home IP Addresses are registered. The Mobile Node must not transmit Mobility Header messages of a particular type more than MAX_UPDATE_RATE times within a second to a specific Correspondent Node.

The Binding Update messages retransmitted by the Mobile Node must use a Sequence Number value greater than that used for the previous transmission of this Binding Update message. The Mobile Node must use new Cookie values for retransmitted Home Test Init and Care-of Test Init messages.

REVIEW QUESTIONS

6.1. What is the role of the Home Agent and Foreign Agent in Mobile IPv4?

6.2. What is the difference between a Foreign Agent Care-of IP Address and a Co-located Care-of IP Address in Mobile IPv4?

6.3. What messages are used in Agent Discovery in Mobile IPv4?

6.4. What messages are used in Mobile Node registration in Mobile IPv4?

6.5. What is a Correspondent Node in Mobile IP?

6.6. What is the role of IPv4 Proxy ARP in Mobile IPv4?

6.7. Describe briefly the Dynamic Home Agent Address Resolution process in Mobile IPv4.

6.8. What is a Mobility Binding and a Binding Cache in Mobile IP?

6.9. Explain briefly how a Home Agent in Mobile IPv4 exchanges unicast IP packets with a Mobile Node using a Foreign Agent Care-of IP Address on a Foreign Network.

6.10. Explain briefly how a Home Agent in Mobile IPv4 exchanges unicast IP packets with a Mobile Node using a Co-located Care-of IP Address on a Foreign Network.

6.11. What is the role of IPv6 Proxy Neighbor Discovery in Mobile IPv6?

6.12. Why does Mobile IPv6 not support Foreign Agents?

6.13. What is the difference between Bidirectional Tunneling and Route Optimization in Mobile IPv6?

6.14. Describe briefly the Dynamic Home Agent Address Resolution process in Mobile IPv6.

6.15. What messages are used in Mobile Node registration in Mobile IPv6?

6.16. What is the Return Routability Procedure in Mobile IPv6?

6.17. What is the purpose of the Binding Update List in Mobile IPv6?

6.18. What is the purpose of the Home Agent List in Mobile IPv6?

REFERENCES

[AWEBKMULT]. J. Aweya, *IP Multicast Routing Protocols: Concepts and Designs*, CRC Press, Taylor & Francis Group, ISBN 9781032701929, May 2024.

[FIPSPUB1801]. National Institute of Standards and Technology, "Secure Hash Standard", *FIPS PUB 180–1*, April 1995.

[RFC1256]. S. Deering, Ed., "ICMP Router Discovery Messages", *IETF RFC 1256*, September 1991.

[RFC1321]. R. Rivest, "The MD5 Message-Digest Algorithm", *IETF RFC 1321*, April 1992.

[RFC2003]. C. Perkins, "IP Encapsulation within IP", *IETF RFC 2003*, October 1996.

[RFC2004]. C. Perkins, "Minimal Encapsulation within IP", *IETF RFC 2004*, October 1996.

[RFC2104]. H. Krawczyk, M. Bellare, and R. Canetti, "HMAC: Keyed-Hashing for Message Authentication", *IETF RFC 2104*, February 1997.

[RFC2473]. A. Conta and S. Deering, "Generic Packet Tunneling in IPv6 Specification", *IETF RFC 2473*, December 1998.

[RFC2526]. D. Johnson and S. Deering, "Reserved IPv6 Subnet Anycast Addresses", *IETF RFC 2526*, March 1999.

[RFC2710]. S. Deering, W. Fenner, and B. Haberman, "Multicast Listener Discovery (MLD) for IPv6", *IETF RFC 2710*, October 1999.

[RFC2784]. D. Farinacci, T. Li, S. Hanks, D. Meyer, and P. Traina, "Generic Routing Encapsulation (GRE)", *IETF RFC 2784*, March 2000.

[RFC3024]. G. Montenegro, Ed., "Reverse Tunneling for Mobile IP, Revised", *IETF RFC 3024*, January 2001.

[RFC3519]. H. Levkowetz and S. Vaarala, "Mobile IP Traversal of Network Address Translation (NAT) Devices", *IETF RFC 3519*, April 2003.

[RFC3810]. R. Vida and L. Costa, "Multicast Listener Discovery Version 2 (MLDv2) for IPv6", *IETF RFC 3810*, June 2004.

[RFC4301]. S. Kent and K. Seo, "Security Architecture for the Internet Protocol", *IETF RFC 4301*, December 2005.

[RFC4302]. S. Kent, "IP Authentication Header", *IETF RFC 4302*, December 2005.

[RFC4459].   P. Savola, "MTU and Fragmentation Issues with In-the-Network Tunneling", *IETF RFC 4459*, April 2006.

[RFC4861].   T. Narten, E. Nordmark, W. Simpson, and H. Soliman, "Neighbor Discovery for IP Version 6 (IPv6)", *IETF RFC 4861*, September 2007.

[RFC4877].   V. Devarapalli and F. Dupont, "Mobile IPv6 Operation with IKEv2 and the Revised IPsec Architecture", *IETF RFC 4877*, April 2007.

[RFC5026].   G. Giaretta, J. Kempf, and V. Devarapalli, "Mobile IPv6 Bootstrapping in Split Scenario", *IETF RFC 5026*, October 2007.

[RFC5944].   C. Perkins, Ed., "IP Mobility Support for IPv4, Revised", *IETF RFC 5944*, November 2010.

[[RFC 5996].   C. Kaufman, Hoffman, P., Nir, Y., and P. Eronen, "Internet Key Exchange Protocol Version 2 (IKEv2)", *IETF RFC 5996*, September 2010.

RFC6275].   C. Perkins, Ed., D. Johnson, and J. Arkko, "Mobility Support in IPv6", *IETF RFC 6275*, July 2011.

[RFC8200].   S. Deering and R. Hinden, "Internet Protocol, Version 6 (IPv6) Specification", *IETF RFC 8200*, July 2017.

[RFC8981].   F. Gont, S. Krishnan, T. Narten, and R. Draves, "Temporary Address Extensions for Stateless Address Autoconfiguration in IPv6", *IETF RFC 8981*, February 2021.

Appendix A
Ethernet Frame Format

A.1 INTRODUCTION

Ethernet refers to a family of wired networking technologies based on the Institute of Electrical and Electronics Engineers (IEEE) 802.3 standards **[IEEE802.3.2022]**. The set of IEEE 802.3 specifications covers the application of Ethernet in a number of areas that include, but are not limited to, Local Area Networks (LANs), Metro Area Networks (MANs), Wide Area Networks (WANs), and backplanes of devices (Backplane Ethernet). The various specifications define the Physical Layer, Medium Access Control (MAC) sublayer, and Logical Link Control (LLC) sublayer of the different Ethernet varieties used in these application areas. In the seven-layer Open Systems Interconnection (OSI) network reference model, the MAC and LLC sublayers belong to the OSI Data Link layer.

The LLC sublayer, defined as an interface between the (upper) Network Layer (IPv4, IPv6) and the (lower) MAC sublayer, provides several capabilities, including multiplexing of upper-layer Protocol Data Units (PDUs), allowing multiple network protocols (e.g., IPv4, IPv6) to coexist within a network node and to be transported over the same MAC sublayer and Physical Layer of the node. The LLC also supports a flow control mechanism for throttling data flow to avoid network congestion and data loss, as well as automatic repeat request (ARQ), which is a mechanism for error management.

The MAC sublayer supports various features, including Ethernet frame delimiting, fields for end-node addressing, encapsulation and transparent transfer of upper-layer data (LLC PDUs), error protection using a Frame Check Sequence (FCS), and access control to the Physical Layer (i.e., the transmission medium). An Ethernet frame (also called the Ethernet MAC frame, or simply the MAC frame) is the standardized data structure, with well-defined fields, created at the MAC sublayer for encapsulating upper-layer data (PDUs) and possibly control data introduced by the MAC sublayer itself.

Layer 2 (Ethernet) switches forward Ethernet frames and primarily process the fields in the Ethernet frame header and trailer. Switch/routers (or integrated switching and routing devices) forward Ethernet frames within an IP subnet/Virtual LAN (VLAN) and forward IP packets between attached IP subnets/VLANs. Switch/routers can process the header fields of Ethernet frames and IP packets. Routers move IP packets between IP subnets/VLANs and mainly process IP header fields; a router only processes the Ethernet frame header and trailer information for frame integrity checks to avoid forwarding IP packets that have been corrupted. Thus, to understand the operation of Ethernet switches, switch/routers, and routers, it is essential to understand the Ethernet frame format.

A.2 ETHERNET FRAME FORMAT

By defining the Ethernet frame format at the MAC sublayer, the IEEE 802.3 standard ensured that this base format is applicable to all Ethernet device implementations, regardless of the wired transmission medium type (copper or optical fiber). The IEEE also defined other optional fields (like the single IEEE 802.1Q tag and the double IEEE 802.1ad tags) that can be used to extend Ethernet's basic capabilities. The basic IEEE 802.1Q tagged Ethernet frame starts with a Preamble field followed by six additional fields, as shown in Figure A.1.

A.2.1 PREAMBLE FIELD

A 56-bit (7 bytes[1] or octets) Preamble field precedes every Ethernet frame. The Preamble consists of a pattern of alternating 1s and 0s placed at the beginning of an Ethernet frame to indicate to a receiving device that an Ethernet frame is being transmitted. This pattern also serves as a reference signal for the frame-reception mechanism in the Physical Layer of the receiving device, allowing it to synchronize its bit-level timing (clock) to the incoming bit stream. The Preamble provides a recognizable pattern that the receiver's Physical Layer can detect to achieve steady-state synchronization with the incoming bit stream before the Ethernet frame's actual Start-of-Frame Delimiter (SFD) field is received.

A.2.2 START-OF-FRAME DELIMITER (SFD) FIELD

The 1-byte SFD field indicates the end of the 57-bit Preamble and the beginning of the Ethernet frame. The 8-bit SFD consists of a pattern of 6 alternating 1s and 0s, ending with two consecutive 1 bits ("11"). The SFD signals to the receiver that the actual Ethernet frame information follows, and that the bit immediately after the SFD is the leftmost bit in the leftmost byte of the destination MAC address of the Ethernet frame. The SFD, with the binary value of 10101011, is transmitted starting with the least-significant bit. It is important to note that bytes (or octets) in the fields of an Ethernet frame are transmitted starting with the least-significant bit (see the discussion on bit-ordering and byte-ordering below). The main purpose of the SFD is to allow the receiver to identify the beginning of the Ethernet frame and synchronize with the frame's byte boundaries; it serves somewhat like a frame synchronization mechanism.

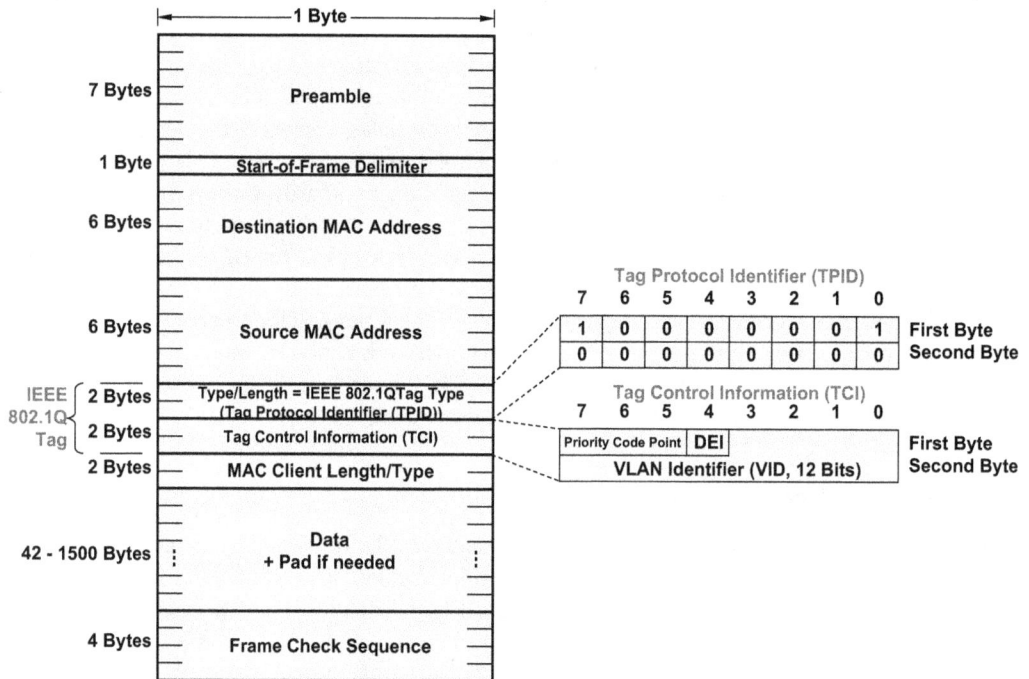

FIGURE A.1 VLAN-tagged Ethernet frame format.

---

[1] The terms "octet" and "byte" both represent groups of eight contiguous bits, and for purposes of this book, the terms are interchangeable.

A.2.3 Destination Address (DA) Field

The 6-byte (48-bit) DA field identifies the Ethernet device(s) to which the Ethernet frame is destined. The leftmost bit in the DA field (see Figure A.2) indicates whether the MAC address is an individual address, meaning it is sent to a single endpoint (bit set to 0), or a group address, meaning it is sent to multiple endpoints (bit set to 1). The second bit from the left indicates whether the DA is globally administered (bit set to 0) or locally administered (bit set to 1). The remaining 46 bits of the DA field are assigned a unique value that identifies a single MAC endpoint, a defined group of MAC endpoints, or all MAC endpoints on the network segment. *An endpoint can be a physical or logical attachment point of a device on a* network.

Individual MAC addresses are simply unicast MAC addresses that are often single MAC addresses uniquely assigned by the MAC device manufacturer from a block of addresses allocated by the IEEE. Group addresses (also referred to as multicast MAC addresses) identify endpoints belonging to a particular group interested in the information contained in the Ethernet frame and are generally generated by mapping an IP multicast address to a corresponding MAC address. Ethernet frames sent to a multicast MAC address are received by all MAC endpoints on a network that have been configured to receive frames sent to that MAC address.

A special group MAC address (the all 1s or broadcast address) indicates that an Ethernet frame is to be sent to all MAC endpoints on a network segment. Ethernet frames sent to the broadcast address (containing all ones) are received by all endpoints on an IP subnet or VLAN. The broadcast MAC address in hexadecimal format is FF:FF:FF:FF:FF:FF. A broadcast frame is flooded in an IP subnet/VLAN and is forwarded to and accepted by all other nodes on the network segment.

A.2.4 Source Addresses (SA) Field

The 6-byte (48-bit) SA field identifies the MAC endpoint that sent an Ethernet frame. The SA is always an individual MAC address, and the leftmost bit in the SA field is always 0. The SA must never be a group address or broadcast address; only the DA can have such addresses. A single physical endpoint on a device may have multiple logical endpoints configured on it, each with its own (logical) MAC address.

A.2.5 Type/Length Field

This is a 2-byte field that contains either the Ethernet frame type identifier (ID) for indicating the upper-layer protocol (over the MAC sublayer) encapsulated in the payload of the frame or the number of MAC-client data bytes contained in the data field of the frame (if the Ethernet frame is created/assembled using an optional format) (see Figure A.1). *The Type is often called the EtherType and is primarily used in today's networks; the Length, in practical terms, is now deprecated.* The Type/Length field is used in the following ways:

- If the value in the Type/Length field is less than or equal to 1,500 (0x05DC), the Data field of the Ethernet frame contains LLC data, and the number of LLC data bytes carried in this field is equal to the Type/Length field value.
- If the value in the Type/Length field is greater than 1,536 (0x0600), the Ethernet frame is a Type frame (i.e., an Ethernet frame that contains EtherType values), and the Type/Length field value identifies the particular upper-layer protocol data carried.
- Type/Length field values between 1,500 and 1,536, exclusive, are undefined.

The EtherType value identifies the upper-layer protocol encapsulated in the Data field of the Ethernet frame. For example, an EtherType value of 0x0800 indicates that the frame contains an IPv4 packet. An EtherType of 0x0806 indicates an ARP frame, 0x8100 indicates an IEEE 802.1Q frame, and 0x86DD indicates an IPv6 packet.

Although both EtherType and Length frame formats are formally approved by the IEEE 802.3 standard, the EtherType frame format or encapsulation is the more commonly used one in today's networks.

A.2.6   DATA FIELD

The Data field carries the actual data from upper-layer protocols, which is a sequence of N bytes, where N is less than or equal to 1,500. If the data included in the Data field is less than 46 bytes, the sender must compensate for the shortfall by adding redundant data (using padding or filler data of 0s) to bring the Data field length to 46 bytes.

When an Ethernet frame carries EtherType data as payload, in the absence of a payload length indicator in this Ethernet frame format, information in the upper-layer protocol is used to determine the length of data in the frame's Data field. The value in the 16-bit Payload Length field of an IPv6 packet specifies the number of actual/true data bytes carried in the payload field of an IPv6 packet (see **Chapter 2**). For IPv4 packets, the values in the 4-bit Internet Header Length and the 16-bit Total Length fields are used to determine the length of data in a packet's payload field (see **Appendix B**).

A.2.6.1   Ethernet Frame Size Issues

An Ethernet frame has a minimum size of 64 bytes, which consists of a 14-byte Ethernet frame header, a 4-byte trailer (FCS), and a 46-byte payload. An untagged Ethernet frame has a maximum size of 1,518 bytes (which includes 18 bytes for the frame header and trailer) and a maximum payload size of 1,500 bytes. If the upper-layer data results in an Ethernet frame size of less than the minimum 64 bytes, the MAC sublayer adds padding bytes to ensure that the frame meets the minimum Ethernet frame size of 64 bytes.

The MAC sublayer attaches a 7-byte Preamble, a 1-byte SFD, and a 12-byte Interframe Gap (IFG) to every frame, although the IFG is not considered part of the Ethernet frame. When all of these are added to a 64-byte frame, this totals $64 + 7 + 1 + 12 = 84$ bytes on the Ethernet link. It is not possible to create a valid Ethernet frame smaller than this on the transmission medium.

If an upper-layer protocol is to send a 1,500-byte packet in a tagged Ethernet frame (i.e., an IEEE 802.1Q tagged frame), the maximum Ethernet frame size becomes 1,522 bytes due to the extra 4 bytes used in the tagged Ethernet frame (see the appropriate discussion below). The size of an untagged Ethernet frame varies from 64 to 1,518 bytes, with a payload ranging from 46 to 1,500 bytes. The minimum tagged Ethernet IEEE 802.1Q frame size remains unchanged at 64 bytes, but an Ethernet bridge may extend the minimum frame size from 64 to 68 bytes when transmitting a frame, allowing other switches to remove the IEEE 802.1Q tag without having to add padding to a frame (if its size happens to fall below the 64-byte Ethernet minimum frame size). In this case, when the Ethernet bridge receives a 64-byte frame with an IEEE 802.1Q tag, it will extend it to a 68-byte frame so that any other bridge that removes the tag will not have to add padding to the frame since it will still be a valid size. A *runt frame* refers to an Ethernet frame that is less than the minimum of 64 bytes.

A.2.7   FRAME CHECK SEQUENCE (FCS)

The 4-byte FCS field that ends each Ethernet frame contains a 32-bit cyclic redundancy check (CRC) value generated by the sending MAC device. The polynomial used for CRC generation is

$$G(x) = x^{32} + x^{26} + x^{23} + x^{22} + x^{16} + x^{12} + x^{11} + x^{10} + x^8 + x^7 + x^5 + x^4 + x^2 + x + 1$$

The sending node generates the FCS over the DA, SA, Type/Length, and Data plus Pad fields for each transmitted frame. The receiving MAC device recalculates the FCS to check for damaged or corrupted frames. The receiver compares the FCS value in the received frame with the new FCS value it computes as the frame is being received to determine if the frame is worth processing further. The FCS provides error detection over the entire frame (the DA, SA, Length/Type, Data+Pad, and the FCS fields); error detection extends to cover the FCS field itself. The sender transmits the FCS field such that the first bit corresponds to the coefficient of the x^{32} term (Most Significant Bit (MSB) first) and the last bit to the coefficient of the x^0 term. Unlike the byte and bit order in other fields of the Ethernet frame, the FCS is treated as a special single 32-bit field rather than as one consisting of four individual octets.

A.2.8   INTERFRAME GAP (IFG)

The IFG, also called the Interpacket Gap (not shown in Figure A.1), represents the idle time between Ethernet frames. After the sending MAC device has transmitted a frame (for 100 Mb/s Ethernet), the sender is required to maintain a minimum of 96 bits (12 bytes) of idle line state before transmitting the next frame. After the transmission of each Ethernet frame for 100 Mb/s Ethernet, the sender must wait for a period of 0.96 microseconds, and 0.096 microseconds for Gigabit Ethernet. For the now rarely used 10 Mb/s Ethernet, this corresponds to 9.6 microseconds, about the time it takes to transmit 12 bytes.

The purpose of the IFG is to allow the transmitted signal containing an Ethernet frame enough time to propagate through the receiver's electronics at the destination MAC device before the next frame is sent. Specifically, the pause provided by the IFG gives the receiver sufficient time to perform clock recovery on the incoming bit stream, decode, and accept the data in the Ethernet frame before the next frame arrives. It is important to note that just as each frame requires some processing time at the transmitter, the receiver also requires time to process each frame. The IFG can be viewed as a special guard band or interval between Ethernet frames. While MAC devices must pause for the IFG duration between Ethernet frame transmissions, receivers do not necessarily perceive the IFG or idle/silent period. The IFG is generally too small to be noticeably significant to end applications.

A.3   ETHERNET MAC ADDRESS FORMAT

Each Ethernet interface on a network has a 48-bit MAC address in the format shown in Figure A.2. This address is programmed into the MAC of the network interface, which is why it is called a MAC address. Every network interface card (NIC) or module available commercially is assigned a unique MAC address by the manufacturer, as explained below. This prevents any two NICs manufactured from having the same MAC address.

A.3.1   ORGANIZATIONAL UNIQUE IDENTIFIER (OUI) AND NIC-SPECIFIC IDENTIFIER

The OUI is the basic mechanism the IEEE uses to administer MAC addresses globally. It occupies bytes 0 to 2 of the 6-byte Ethernet MAC address. In the OUI field, bits 0 and 1 of byte 0 are used as the Individual/Group (I/G) bit and the Universal/Local (U/L) bit, respectively, as described below. The IEEE assigns one or more OUIs to each manufacturer of Ethernet network interfaces. Using OUIs allows the IEEE to keep track of fewer (often only one) OUIs per manufacturer instead of individual MAC addresses.

Each manufacturer is responsible for assigning a unique organization-specific identifier for each network interface module manufactured using the IEEE-assigned OUI. The NIC-Specific Identifier is the part of the 48-bit MAC address assigned to the network interface module by the manufacturer. It occupies bytes 3–5 of the MAC address. The organization (manufacturer) is responsible for tracking the NIC-Specific Identifiers it assigns to manufactured network interface modules. The 24-bit NIC-Specific Identifier field allows a manufacturer to create 16 million network interface modules with unique MAC addresses before needing another OUI.

A.3.2   INDIVIDUAL/GROUP (I/G) ADDRESS BIT

The first bit of byte 0 (i.e., bit 0) in the 48-bit Ethernet MAC address (Figure A.2) indicates whether the address is an *individual* (I) or *group* (G) address. This first bit is commonly referred to as the I/G bit or flag. *Individual MAC addresses* are assigned to only one interface in an Ethernet network. MAC addresses with the I/G (i.e., first) bit set to 0 are unicast MAC addresses and are always unique to a single interface on the network.

When the I/G bit is set to 1, the MAC address is a *group address* and is typically referred to as a *multicast MAC address*. A group address is one that can be assigned to one or more network interfaces on an Ethernet LAN. Ethernet frames sent to a group address are received and processed by all network interfaces on the Ethernet LAN configured with that group address. Multicast MAC addresses enable Ethernet frames to be sent to a subset of network interfaces on an Ethernet LAN.

- If the I/G bit is set to 1, then bits 1 through 47 of the MAC address are treated as the multicast address.
- If bits 1 through 47 are all 1s, then the MAC address is the well-known Ethernet broadcast MAC address (FF.FF.FF.FF.FF.FF).

Multicast MAC addresses are similar to broadcast MAC addresses, except that multicast frames can be received by none, one, some, or all nodes on the LAN. A multicast MAC address has the I/G bit set to 1, and at least one of the other bits is a 0. If all the other bits are 1s, then we get a broadcast address. A network node can choose to listen for and copy frames carrying only certain multicast addresses. A node can listen for the multicast frames of interest and copy only those frames. The MAC of the network interface is responsible for filtering and copying multicast frames. Note that a broadcast or multicast MAC address can only be carried in the destination MAC address field of an Ethernet frame and not in the source MAC address field. The source MAC address of a frame can only be a unicast MAC address.

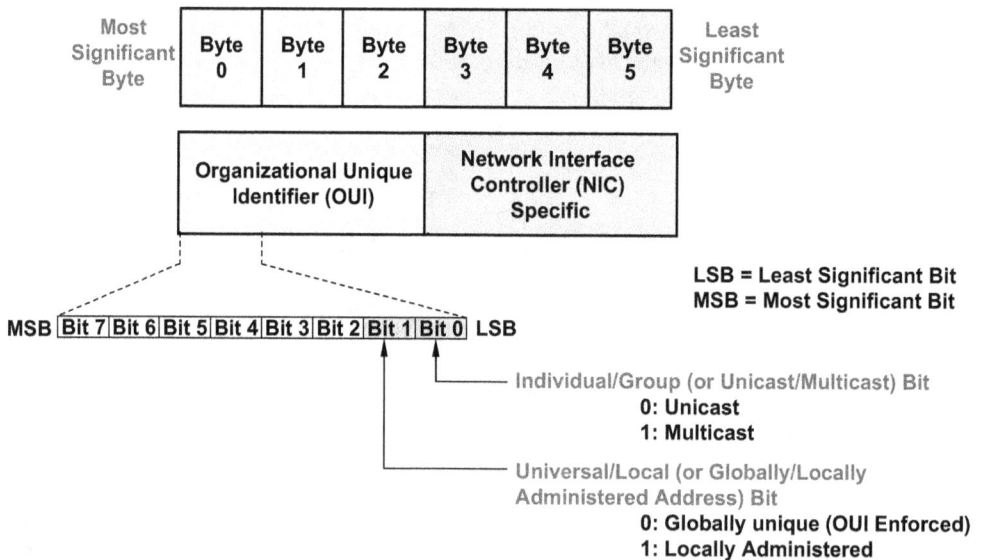

FIGURE A.2   MAC address format.

A.3.3 Universal/Local (U/L) Address Bit

The second bit of byte 0 (i.e., bit 1) in the 48-bit Ethernet MAC address (Figure A.2) is used to indicate whether the MAC address is globally or locally administered. An Ethernet MAC address is a *globally* or *universally administered MAC address* if the U/L bit is set to 0. If both the I/G and the U/L bits are 0, then the MAC address is unique to a single network interface. The MAC address is universally unique because it is assigned to the network interface by the manufacturer using a combination of the IEEE-assigned OUI and the organization's NIC-Specific Identifier.

An Ethernet MAC address with the U/L bit set to 1 is a *locally administered MAC address*. Setting this bit to 1 means that someone other than the NIC manufacturer has configured the MAC address. For example, the network administrator of an organization may set the MAC address on a network interface to a value that has only local significance by setting the U/L bit to 1 and then choosing bits 2 through 47 as a locally chosen value. In this case, the organization would have to keep track of the locally administered MAC addresses to ensure that there are no duplicate addresses. However, since all NICs are delivered with universally administered addresses, locally administered addresses are rarely used.

A.4 VLANS – A MECHANISM FOR LIMITING BROADCAST TRAFFIC

An instance where bridges (or Layer 2 switches) perform very poorly is when broadcast frames are sent on an Ethernet LAN. A broadcast frame uses a fairly primitive technique to force all nodes on a LAN or VLAN to read the broadcast frame. This frame uses the reserved destination MAC address (FF.FF.FF.FF.FF.FF), which does not actually belong to any individual node on the LAN. Since this destination MAC address belongs to no particular port or node, its location can never be learned, so bridges have no choice but to flood broadcast frames. Under some conditions, large amounts of broadcast frames may be sent on the network, reaching almost all corners of the LAN and resulting in a condition called a *broadcast storm*. Furthermore, the broadcast MAC address causes frames from any connected segment (not separated by routers) to be flooded onto all other segments in the same broadcast domain, regardless of IP address or other logical address assignment.

Broadcast storms are the primary reason networks moved from simple bridges to switches with VLAN capabilities **[IEEE802.1D04] [IEEE802.1Q05]** and routers **[RFC791]**. A bridging loop in an Ethernet LAN can cause bridges to forward broadcast and multicast frames endlessly. VLANs, like IP subnets, divide large broadcast domains in a network into smaller, more manageable or controlled broadcast segments. Furthermore, VLANs allow a network administrator to create logical connectivity of nodes that is separate from the physical network connectivity—something akin to a software patch panel. A network designer can create (i.e., overlay) multiple logical broadcast domains (VLANs) over a single physical Ethernet network. Recall that a broadcast domain is essentially a group of nodes in a bridged (i.e., Layer 2) network that receive each other's broadcast frames. Thus, using the concept of VLANs, a single broadcast domain can be divided into one or more broadcast segments (VLANs).

Whenever hosts in one VLAN need to communicate with hosts in another VLAN, the traffic must be routed between them (i.e., via a router). This is known as *inter-VLAN routing*. Routers are used in an internetwork of VLANs to filter broadcast traffic, manage inter-VLAN traffic flow, enhance security (using various security mechanisms typically present on routers), and summarize IP addresses. During inter-VLAN routing, the traditional traffic filtering and security functions of a router can be employed for various traffic control and management purposes.

A switch running the still widely used transparent bridging algorithm **[IEEE802.1D04]** floods unknown and broadcast frames on all the ports that are in the same VLAN as the received frame. The flooding of unknown and broadcast frames presents a potential problem in a VLAN. If the LAN switches running this algorithm happen to be misconfigured into a physical loop in the network, flooded frames (such as broadcasts) will be forwarded continuously and endlessly from switch to switch, creating endless forwarding loops. Depending on the topology of the LAN segment where the switches are located, the number of frames may multiply exponentially in volume as a result of the flooding algorithm, which can cause serious network problems or even network collapse.

There is a benefit, however, to having physical loops in a LAN, as the links creating the loops can actually be used to provide redundancy in the network (as long as forwarding loops are not created). The only requirement here is to logically block some switch ports, thereby creating a logical tree (i.e., loop-free) topology (i.e., a Spanning Tree) in the LAN, even though it contains physical loops. If one link fails, the LAN topology is logically rearranged, allowing the other link(s) to still provide alternative paths for the traffic to reach its destination. To derive benefits from this sort of redundancy without creating problems like broadcast storms (in the network due to the need to flood unknown and broadcast frames), the Spanning Tree Protocol (STP) was created and standardized in the IEEE 802.1D specification [IEEE802.1D04]. Newer, more efficient versions of STP are the Rapid Spanning Tree Protocol (RSTP), standardized in IEEE 802.1w, and the Multiple Spanning Tree Protocol (MSTP), standardized in IEEE 802.1s.

The purpose of STP and its newer variants (RSTP and MSTP) is to identify and temporarily block the ports creating loops in a network segment or VLAN to prevent the flooding problem described above. We use STP to represent all of these loop prevention mechanisms. The switches run STP, which supports loop prevention mechanisms. Part of these mechanisms involves electing a root bridge or switch. STP (and its variants) creates a logical loop-free topology of the LAN, called a Spanning Tree, from the root bridge. The other switches in the LAN segment measure their distance from the root switch, and if there is more than one path to get to the root switch, it can be safely assumed that there is a loop. The switches use STP to determine which ports should be blocked to break any loop when creating a Spanning Tree for the LAN.

STP is dynamic and responds to network topology changes, creating a new Spanning Tree as changes occur. If a link in the segment fails, ports that were originally blocking may be changed to forwarding mode. The Spanning Tree Algorithm and Protocol [IEEE802.1D04] are responsible for monitoring, evaluating, and configuring (or reconfiguring) the Ethernet LAN topology to ensure that there is only one active network path at any given time between any pair of end stations.

The bridges in the LAN use Bridge PDUs to communicate with each other to discover the topology of the LAN and to detect switching loops. If the bridges discover loops, they cooperate with each other to place selected bridge ports in the *Discarding* (or *blocking*) mode to prevent the loops while still maintaining a Spanning Tree that reaches all nodes. The Spanning Tree Algorithm and Protocol [IEEE802.1D04] allows a bridged network to be intentionally built with physical switching loops to provide redundant backup paths between LAN segments. Once the bridges have computed and built the Spanning Tree, they monitor the network to ensure that all the links are functioning as intended (*Discarding*, *Learning*, or *Forwarding*).

A.4.1   IEEE 801.1Q

The IEEE 802.1Q standard defines procedures for supporting VLANs on an Ethernet network [IEEE802.1Q05]. The standard establishes a VLAN tagging system for Ethernet frames and the accompanying procedures to be used by bridges and switches in handling tagged Ethernet frames. It also defines a mechanism for implementing a QoS prioritization scheme for Ethernet networks commonly known as IEEE 802.1p.

In addition, IEEE 802.1Q defines the Generic Attribute Registration Protocol (GARP), now replaced by the Multiple Registration Protocol (MRP). MRP (added as the amendment IEEE 802.1ak to the IEEE 802.1Q standard) is a generic registration framework. Like GARP, MRP allows bridges, switches, or other similar devices to register and de-register attribute values, such as VLAN identifiers (VLAN IDs) and multicast group membership across an Ethernet LAN.

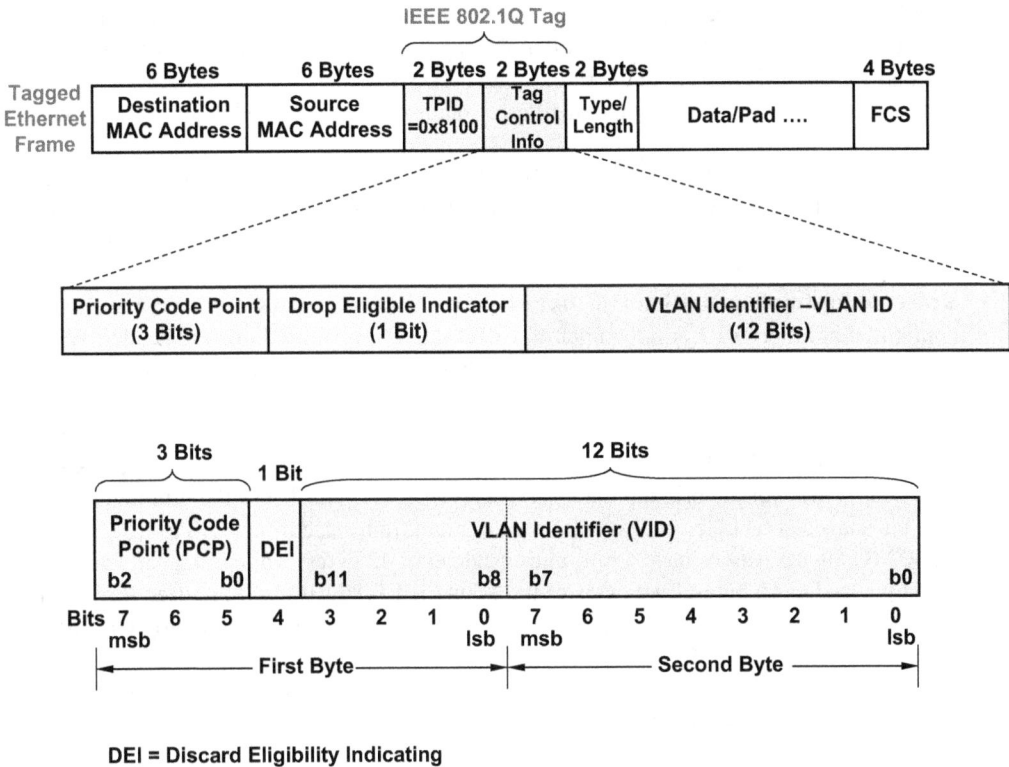

FIGURE A.3 VLAN Tag TCI (TAG Control Information field) format.

IEEE 802.1Q specifies a tag that is placed at a defined spot in an Ethernet MAC frame (Figures A.3 and A.4). The 4-byte tag field is inserted between the source MAC address and the Type/Length fields of the original (untagged) Ethernet frame. The IEEE 802.1Q tag consists of the following parts:

- **Tag Protocol Identifier (TPID)**: The 2-byte TPID field is set to a value of 0x8100 (hexadecimal) to identify a frame as an IEEE 802.1Q-tagged frame. As illustrated in Figures A.3 and A.4, the TPID field is located in the same position as the EtherType/Length field in untagged Ethernet frames, which allows tagged frames to be distinguished from untagged frames.
- **Tag Control Information (TCI)**: The TCI field consists of a Priority Code Point (PCP) (also called User Priority), Drop Eligible Indicator (DEI) (previously called Canonical Format Indicator), and VLAN ID, as shown in Figure A.3.
  - *Priority Code Point (PCP)*: The 3-bit PCP (or User Priority) field specifies the IEEE 802.1p priority or class-of-service (CoS) associated with the frame (i.e., it indicates the frame's priority level). These values are used by network devices to prioritize different classes of traffic on a network (e.g., voice, video, data, etc.).
  - *Drop Eligible Indicator (DEI)*: The 1-bit DEI field may be used separately or with the PCP to indicate whether a frame is eligible to be dropped by a network device in the presence of congestion.
  - *VLAN Identifier (VLAN ID)*: The 12-bit VLAN ID field specifies the VLAN to which the Ethernet frame belongs.

In the 12-bit VLAN ID field (Figure A.3 and A.4), the hexadecimal values of 0x000 and 0xFFF are reserved. All other values may be used as VLAN IDs, allowing for up to 4,094 VLANs.

- **The Null VID (0x000):** The reserved value 0x000 indicates that the Ethernet frame does not belong to any VLAN. It signifies that the tag header contains only priority information; no VLAN ID is present in the frame. This VID value must not be configured as a Port VID, a member of a VID set, or in any filtering database entry, or used in any management operation.
- **The Default VID (x001):** On bridges, VLAN 1 (the default VLAN ID) is often reserved for a management VLAN, but this is vendor-specific. The default VID value is used for classifying frames on the ingress port of a bridge. The Port VID value of a port can be changed by management.
- **Reserved for Implementation Use (0xFFF):** This VID value is reserved and must not be configured as a Port VID or a member of a VID set, or transmitted in a tag header. When used, this VID value indicates a wildcard match for the VID in management operations or filtering database entries.

As illustrated in Figure A.4, IEEE 802.1Q adds a 4-byte field between the source MAC address and the EtherType/Length fields of the original untagged Ethernet frame. This keeps the minimum Ethernet frame size unchanged at 64 bytes but extends the maximum frame size from 1,518 to 1,522 bytes.

IEEE 802.1Q tagged frames have a minimum payload of 42 bytes, while untagged frames have a minimum payload of 46 bytes. Two bytes of the 4-byte IEEE 802.1Q field are used for the TPID, while the other two bytes are used for the TCI. The TCI field is further divided into PCP, DEI, and VID. Inserting the IEEE 802.1Q tag into an Ethernet frame modifies its contents, thus requiring recalculation of the 4-byte FCS field in the Ethernet frame trailer; any node that adds or removes an IEEE 802.1Q tag must recalculate the FCS for the Ethernet frame.

The Maximum Transmit Unit (MTU) is the size (in bytes) of the largest PDU that a protocol layer can pass to another entity. As discussed earlier, the standard Ethernet frame MTU is 1,500 bytes (Figure A.4). This does not include the Ethernet header and trailer fields (which take up 18 bytes), meaning the total Ethernet frame size is actually 1,518 bytes, while the Ethernet frame size refers to the entire Ethernet frame, including the header and the trailer.

"*Baby giant*" frames refer to Ethernet frames with a size of up to 1,600 bytes, and "*jumbo*" frames refer to Ethernet frames with a size of up to 9,216 bytes **[CISCBABY]**. Changing the maximum Ethernet frame size from 1,518 to 1,522 bytes to accommodate the 4-byte VLAN tag may be

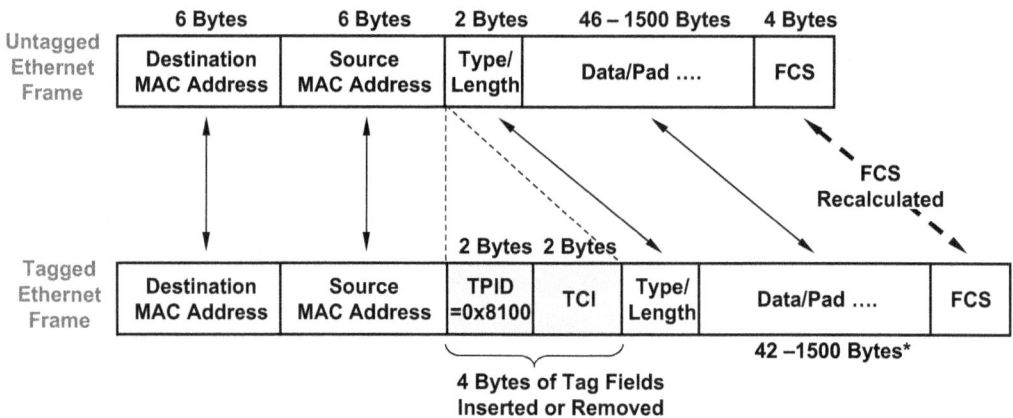

FIGURE A.4 Mapping between untagged and tagged Ethernet frame formats.

problematic for some network devices that do not understand IEEE 802.1Q tagged frames. Some network devices that do not support the larger frame size (i.e., tagged frames) will process the tagged frame successfully but may report them as "baby giant" anomalies **[CISCBABY]**.

A network can be constructed to have segments that are VLAN-aware (i.e., IEEE 802.1Q conformant), where frames include VLAN tags, and segments that are VLAN-unaware (i.e., only IEEE 802.1D conformant), where frames do not contain VLAN tags. When a frame enters the VLAN-aware segment of the network, a tag is added (see Figure A.4) to represent the VLAN membership of the frame (and a new FCS must be calculated for the frame). Each frame must be distinguishable as belonging to exactly one VLAN.

As noted above, the VLAN ID field in the IEEE 802.1Q tag is 12 bits long, meaning up to 4,096 VLANs can be supported. While this number is adequate for most smaller networks, many networking scenarios require double-tagging (IEEE 802.1ad, also known as provider bridging, Stacked VLANs, or simply QinQ or Q-in-Q) to scale up a network, especially in service provider networks. Double-tagging can be useful for large networks and Internet Service Providers, allowing them to support a larger number of VLANs, in addition to other important benefits.

Benefits of using double-tagging include enabling the service provider to implement more granular service differentiation for different customers on the provider network (without using complex traffic management mechanisms and routing protocols between the provider network and customers) and delivering different services (e.g., voice, video, Internet access) to different subscribing customers on the same provider network while maintaining clear segregation between the services (e.g., a specific customer is identified by the inner tag, while the service being provided to the customer is identified by the outer tag). A double-tagged frame has a theoretical limitation of $4,096 \times 4,096 = 16,777,216$.

A.5   IEEE 802.1P/Q

IEEE 802.1p specifies a CoS mechanism for prioritizing VLAN-tagged Ethernet frames. This is done using the 3-bit PCP field (or User Priority field) within VLAN-tagged Ethernet frames as defined by IEEE 802.1Q **[IEEE802.1Q05]** (see Figure A.3). IEEE 802.1p (which is only a technique and not a standard or amendment published by the IEEE) specifies an Ethernet frame priority value from 0 to 7 to differentiate Ethernet traffic.

The 3-bit PCP field in the IEEE 802.1Q header of tagged Ethernet frames provides eight different classes of service. IEEE 802.1p was incorporated into the IEEE 802.1Q standard to allow Ethernet devices to specify the CoS (in the VLAN tag) associated with Ethernet frames as they pass through Ethernet switches. As shown in Figures A.3 and A.4, the IEEE 802.1Q tag is placed between the 6-byte source MAC address field and the 2-byte Type/Length field.

The IEEE 802.1Q tag is recognizable by VLAN-tag-aware Ethernet switches and does not require the switch to parse any fields beyond the Ethernet frame header. Essentially, as stated above, IEEE 802.1p defines 8 priority levels (0–7) and serves only as a mechanism for tagging Ethernet frames with a priority value at Layer 2, without defining how tagged frames should be treated in a network. The treatment of traffic assigned any particular IEEE 802.1p priority value is not defined and is left to user/vendor implementation. However, some broad recommendations have been made by the IEEE on how users/vendors can implement these traffic classes, as shown in Table A.1.

Ethernet switches may support the creation of VLANs based on port groupings on a single switch or based on IEEE 802.1Q tags for VLANs that may extend across multiple switches. With IEEE 802.1Q, a tag header is added to the Ethernet frame immediately after the destination and source MAC address fields. The source device (end-user or network access device) may set the CoS value of a frame, and this value may be reset (to another value) by intermediate network devices (depending on network policy and conditions) as a frame traverses the network to its destination.

Since the VLAN ID field in the IEEE 802.1Q tag is 12 bits long, up to 4,096 VLANs can be created. While this number is likely adequate for most smaller networks (such as many enterprise

TABLE A.1
IEEE 802.1p Priority Values and Associated Traffic Types

Priority Code Point (PCP)	Priority	Binary	Traffic Type
1	0 (Lowest priority)	001	Background
0	1 (Default priority)	000	Best effort
2	2	010	Excellent effort
3	3	011	Critical applications
4	4	100	Video
5	5	101	Voice
6	6	110	Internetwork control
7	7 (Highest priority)	111	Network control

networks), some high-end switches also support VLAN stacking (or double-tagging defined in IEEE 802.1ad), where a second VLAN tag is added to the frame, expanding the number of possible VLANs to over 16 million. Note that each tag in a frame with double-tagging has a 3-bit PCP field, and their use is dependent on the network operator.

A.6   ETHERNET BIT AND BYTE-ORDERING

The leading byte in the 48-bit Ethernet MAC address is structured as shown in Figure A.5. Figure A.6 shows the Ethernet frame format and the byte and bit transmission ordering used (bit-ordering within a field is Little-Endian). Endianness refers to the order in which a network protocol sends and receives bits and bytes of an integer field of protocol data. A Big-Endian system transmits the most significant byte (or bit) first, while a Little-Endian system transmits the least-significant byte (or bit) first. Figure A.7 shows the Little-Endian and Big-Endian bit-ordering of protocol data.

Lower layer protocols such as Ethernet (and the now deprecated protocols Token Ring, FDDI, and ATM) define the bit/byte-ordering of data, which in turn determines how data transmission and reception should occur. Some of these lower layer protocols implement the bit/byte order in a manner that is the reverse of that of the supported upper-layer protocol. For Ethernet, the transmission byte order is Big-Endian, meaning the source transmits the leftmost or most significant byte first.

However, the bit order within a field of an Ethernet frame is Little-Endian, i.e., the source transmits the bit corresponding to the 2^0 numerical position or Least-Significant Bit (LSB) of the byte first, and transmits the bit corresponding to the 2^7 numerical position or MSB of the byte last. The byte- and bit-ordering in the Ethernet frame is shown in Figure A.6. The source transmits the bytes in each field in Big-Endian, meaning "left byte first," but transmits the bits within each byte in the reverse order, "LSB first" (Little-Endian).

Layer 2 protocols such as Ethernet (IEEE 802.3) and the deprecated Token Bus (IEEE 802.4) transmit bytes over the transmission medium starting with the most significant byte (left to right), but with the LSB in each byte transmitted first (Figure A.6). By convention, when presenting the binary fields of the Ethernet frame, the LSB is shown as the leftmost bit and the MSB as the rightmost. This is also the standard notation (also called *canonical format*) for presenting MAC addresses; that is, addresses are written using the transmission bit order with the LSB transmitted first. The I/G bit is the LSB of Byte 0 and is transmitted first in that field.

For example, let us consider a MAC address in canonical form 12-34-56-78-9A-BC in hexadecimal digits. This address in binary form is 00010010-00110100-01010110-01111000-10011010-1011 1100. This address would be transmitted over the transmission medium as 01001000-00101100-01 101010-00011110-01011001-00111101 in the standard transmission order (LSB first). On the other hand, the deprecated Layer 2 protocols, Token Ring (IEEE 802.5) and Distributed Queue Dual Bus (IEEE 802.6), send bytes over the transmission medium with the MSB first.

Transmission Byte Order (Left to Right) –Big Endian Byte Order

Most   Least
Significant   Significant
Byte   Byte

| Byte 0 | Byte 1 | Byte 2 | Byte 3 | Byte 4 | Byte 5 |

7   0 7   0 7   0 7   0 7   0 7   0

u g

MSB   LSB

Individual/Group (or Unicast/Multicast) Bit
0: Unicast
1: Multicast

Transmission
Bit Order
(Little Endian
Within a Byte)

Universal/Local (or Globally/Locally Administered Address) Bit
0: Globally unique (OUI enforced)
1: Locally administered

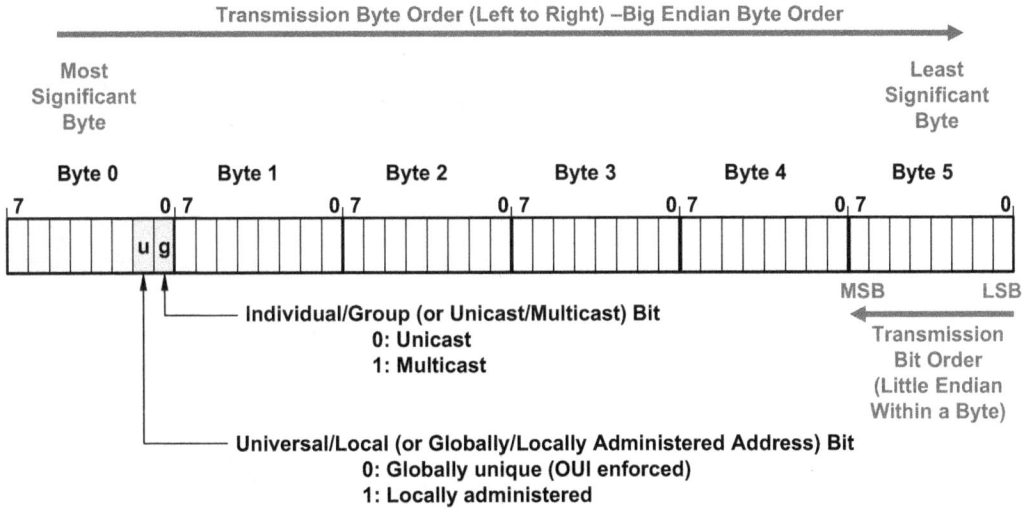

FIGURE A.5   Leading byte in the 48-bit Ethernet MAC address format.

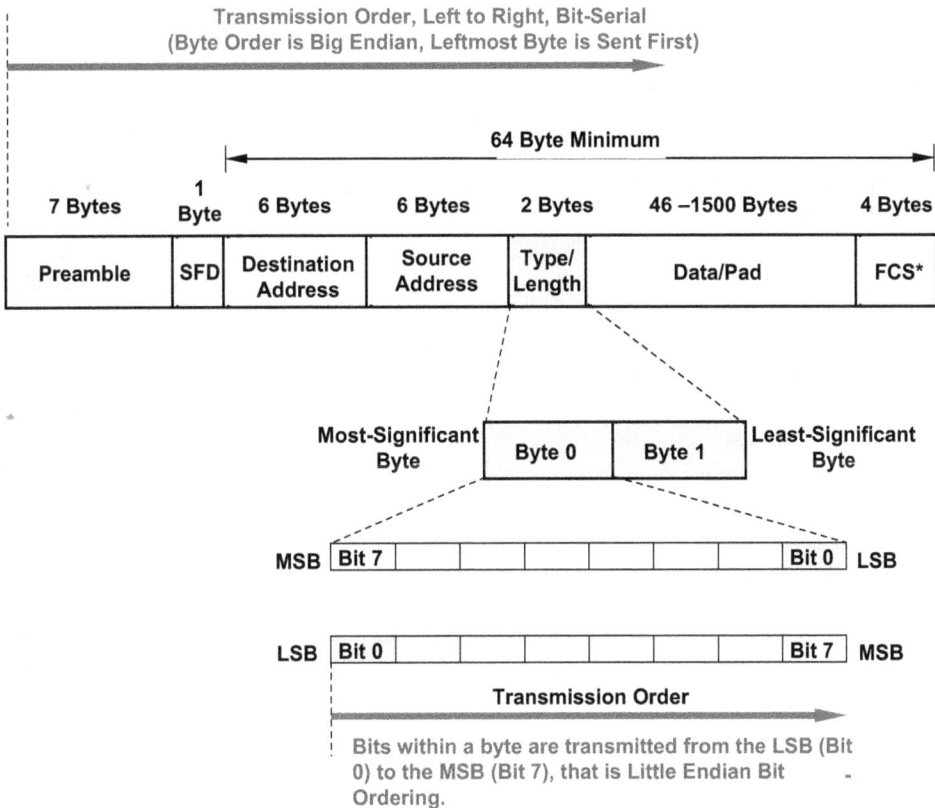

Transmission Order, Left to Right, Bit-Serial
(Byte Order is Big Endian, Leftmost Byte is Sent First)

64 Byte Minimum

7 Bytes	1 Byte	6 Bytes	6 Bytes	2 Bytes	46 –1500 Bytes	4 Bytes
Preamble	SFD	Destination Address	Source Address	Type/ Length	Data/Pad	FCS*

Most-Significant | Byte 0 | Byte 1 | Least-Significant
Byte   Byte

MSB | Bit 7 | | | | | | Bit 0 | LSB

LSB | Bit 0 | | | | | | Bit 7 | MSB

Transmission Order

Bits within a byte are transmitted from the LSB (Bit
0) to the MSB (Bit 7), that is Little Endian Bit
Ordering.

*Note: The byte and bit order shown is typical for
all fields except the FCS which is formatted with the
high order bits to the right.

FIGURE A.6   Ethernet frame format and transmission order – Little-Endian bit-ordering.

Little Endian Bit-Ordering

Bit Transmission Order within Byte

◄— — — — — — — —|

MSB 7 6 5 4 3 2 1 0 LSB

	Byte 0	
	Byte 1	
	Byte 2	
	Byte 3	
	Byte 4	
	Byte 5	
	⋮	
	Byte N	

Transmission Order within MAC Frame (Byte-by-Byte)

Big Endian Bit-Ordering

Bit Transmission Order within Byte

|— — — — — — — —►

MSB 7 6 5 4 3 2 1 0 LSB

	Byte 0	
	Byte 1	
	Byte 2	
	Byte 3	
	Byte 4	
	Byte 5	
	⋮	
	Byte N	

Transmission Order within MAC Frame (Byte-by-Byte)

LSB = Least-Significant Bit
MSB = Most-Significant Bit

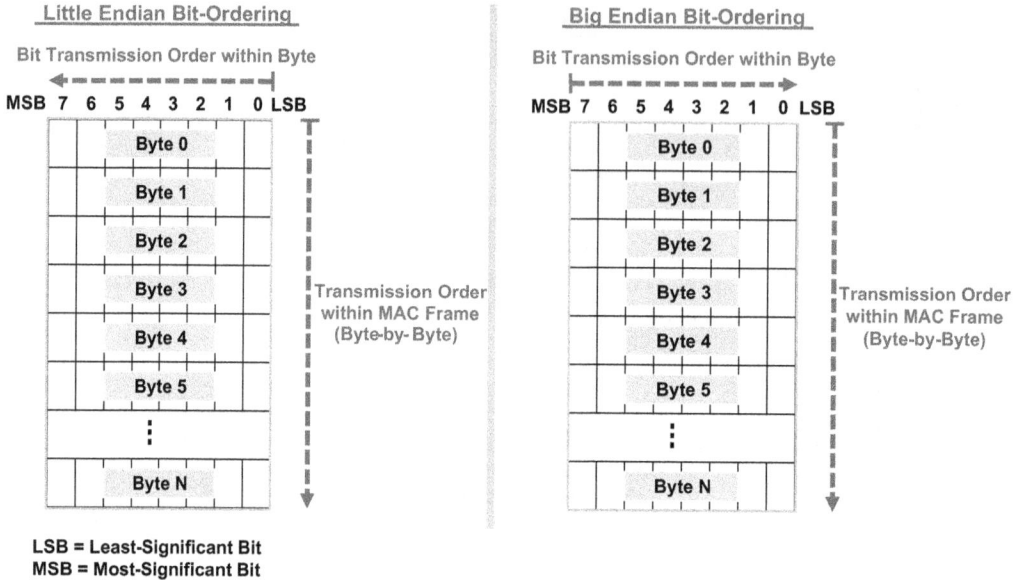

FIGURE A.7   Bit-ordering.

It is important to note one exception in Ethernet data transmission as shown in Figure A.6. *The FCS of the Ethernet frame has the same byte-ordering as other fields, but a different bit-ordering is used.* The source transmits the FCS with the high-order bit (MSB) of the sequence first. Data in all other fields of the Ethernet frame is transmitted with the most significant byte first, and within each byte, the LSB is transmitted first. The byte and bit orders are the same for all fields of the Ethernet frame, except the FCS, which is treated as a special (single) 32-bit field rather than as 4 individual bytes; the entire 4 FCS bytes are treated as a single 32-bit block used in the CRC computation.

As discussed above, the 48-bit MAC address (universal or local) is normally expressed as a string of 6 bytes, usually in hexadecimal digits. The bytes (in hexadecimal digits) are written from left to right, in the order they are transmitted on the transmission medium, separated by hyphens (-) or colons (:). IPv4 addresses, by convention, are written using dotted-decimal notation, while IPv6 addresses are written using colon-hexadecimal notation. Typically, each byte of the MAC address is expressed as two hexadecimal digits, or two bytes as four hexadecimal digits. The bits within the byte are transmitted on the transmission medium from left to right.

In the binary representation, the first bit transmitted of each byte on the transmission medium is the LSB of that byte. The I/G bit in the MAC address is the LSB, and the leftmost bit of the binary representation (the I/G bit) of a MAC address distinguishes individual from group MAC addresses. The U/L address bit is the next bit following the I/G address bit; the U/L bit indicates whether the MAC address has been universally or locally assigned.

A.7   LEGAL AND ILLEGAL UNTAGGED ETHERNET FRAMES

The minimum and maximum sizes of the Ethernet frame (in bytes) are determined as follows:

$$\text{Full Minimum Frame Size} = \text{Header}(14) + \text{FCS}(4) + \text{Data\_Min}(46) = 64$$

$$\text{Full Maximum Frame Size} = \text{Header}(14) + \text{FCS}(4) + \text{Data\_Max}(1{,}500) = 1{,}518$$

The 7-byte Preamble, 1-byte SFD, and IFG are not included in the frame size calculations as they are not considered part of the Ethernet frame. The untagged Ethernet header consists of three fields: a 6-byte Destination Address, a 6-byte Source Address, and a 2-byte Type/Length field.

A.7.1 ILLEGAL ETHERNET FRAMES

An Ethernet device that receives frames deemed illegal will drop them. It is then the responsibility of the higher-layer protocols, such as TCP, to notify the sending device that a frame was dropped. The following are considered illegal Ethernet frames.

A.7.1.1 Runt Frames

The minimum size of an Ethernet frame is 64 bytes, which consists of an 18-byte Ethernet frame header and FCS plus 46 bytes of payload data. An Ethernet device considers an Ethernet frame smaller than 64 bytes to be illegal and will drop that frame. This type of illegal frame is sometimes called a "runt." The most common causes of runt frames are collisions (seen in the now deprecated half-duplex Ethernet technologies), buffer underruns, malfunctioning NIC s, or software bugs on a device. In half-duplex Ethernet networks, runt frames result from collisions when multiple devices contend for the transmission medium. Ethernet devices are required to discard all runt frames.

Padding Ethernet frames smaller than the minimum size required with redundant data prevents runts from occurring. If an upper-layer protocol has data to send that is less than 46 bytes, the MAC sublayer adds a sufficient number of padding bytes (consisting of all 0s), also known as null padding characters, to the data to meet the minimum Ethernet frame size requirement.

A.7.1.2 Giant Frames

The untagged Ethernet frame has a maximum size of 1,518 bytes. An Ethernet frame larger than the maximum frame size is sometimes called a "giant." Oversized Ethernet frames may be due to a malfunction in the Physical Layer of an Ethernet device. Similar to runt frames, Ethernet devices are required to discard all giant frames.

Some implementations of Ethernet (mostly, higher speed Ethernet versions) support larger frames, known as *jumbo frames*. This type of frame is not covered in this Appendix.

A.7.1.3 Misaligned Frames

An Ethernet frame must contain an integer number of bytes (64–1,518 for untagged Ethernet frames). Ethernet devices consider frames that do not contain an integer number of bytes to be illegal. However, an Ethernet device has no way of knowing which bits in a received frame are legal. The receiver can only compute the FCS of the frame and check if an integer number of bytes is received in a frame. Ethernet devices are required to discard all illegal frames.

A.8 IPv4 MULTICAST ADDRESSES AND MULTICAST SUPPORT AT LAYER 2

This section describes the formats of IPv4 multicast and Ethernet multicast MAC addresses. We also discuss how IPv4 multicast addresses are mapped to corresponding Ethernet MAC addresses when transmitting multicast traffic to hosts on an IP subnet or VLAN. The MAC address ambiguities that may result from IPv4-to-MAC address mapping are also addressed here.

A.8.1 IPv4 MULTICAST ADDRESSES

An *IP multicast address* is a logical identifier for a specific stream of packets sent from a multicast traffic source to an arbitrary group of hosts that have expressed interest in the traffic (i.e., by sending Internet Group Management Protocol (IGMP) Membership Report messages) [AWEMULT24]. The group of recipients of the traffic sent by the multicast source is often referred to as a *multicast group.* Note that the IP multicast address logically identifies both the multicast traffic itself and the group of receivers (i.e., the multicast group). An IP unicast address uniquely identifies only a single endpoint in the network, usually a host interface; each interface on a host has a unique IP unicast address. A multicast source may send traffic before hosts join the multicast group or may send traffic when one or more hosts subscribe to the traffic. A host may leave a multicast group by sending an IGMP Leave Group message or may silently leave without sending such a message.

The now obsolete IPv4 classful addressing scheme reserved the Class D address range for IPv4 multicast addressing. The Class D address space has the binary prefix of 1110 in the first 4 bits of the first byte of the IPv4 address, as shown in Figure A.8. With the elimination of IPv4 classful addressing (Class A, B, and C) and the adoption of Variable Length Subnet Mask (VLSM) and Classless Inter-Domain Routing (CIDR), it is no longer appropriate to refer to IPv4 multicast addresses as Class D addresses, but rather as IPv4 addresses with the binary prefix 1110 (i.e., simply as IPv4 multicast addresses).

IPv4 multicast addresses, defined with the binary prefix 1110, span the address range 224.0.0.0– 239.255.255.255 in the dotted-decimal IPv4 address notation, but still adhering to the old Class D address boundaries. IPv4 multicast addresses have a prefix length of /32 (in CIDR notation), and the IPv4 multicast address range from 232.0.0.0 to 232.255.255.255 can be expressed as 232.0.0.0/8 or 232/8. The reserved address 224.0.0.0 is called the base address and cannot be assigned to any multicast group. The multicast address block of 224.0.0.1–224.0.0.255 is reserved for local IPv4 subnet use. IPv4 addresses in this range are assigned for various uses on a subnet, such as for routing protocols and local discovery mechanisms.

The multicast address range of 239.0.0.0–239.255.255.255 is reserved for IPv4 *administratively scoped addresses* (also called *limited scope addresses*) [AWEMULT24]. Multicast packets addressed to administratively scoped multicast addresses do not cross multicast administrative boundaries that have been explicitly configured. These administratively scoped multicast addresses are locally assigned for use within the configured boundary and do not need to be unique across administrative boundaries.

A.8.2 Mapping IPv4 Multicast Addresses to Ethernet Multicast MAC Addresses

On Layer 2 networks such as those based on Ethernet, IPv4 packets with multicast addresses are carried in Ethernet frames with corresponding MAC multicast addresses. The MAC multicast addresses enable the switches on the Ethernet LAN to forward the encapsulated IPv4 multicast packets to all possible receivers of the multicast group. When an Ethernet LAN has receivers of a multicast group, the last-hop router attached to that LAN is responsible for encapsulating the IPv4 multicast packets in Ethernet frames and mapping the IPv4 multicast address to a corresponding Ethernet MAC multicast address. The LAN switches use the mapped MAC multicast address to direct the encapsulated IPv4 packets to all host receivers on the LAN.

Each host receiver that is a member of the multicast group will listen at Layer 2 for Ethernet multicast frames carrying the mapped MAC multicast address. For IPv4 packets to reach the host

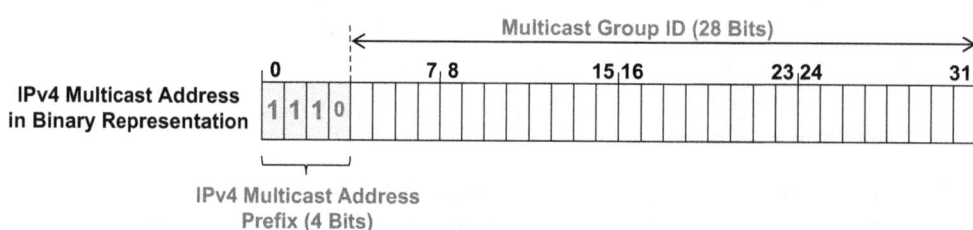

FIGURE A.8 IPv4 multicast address format.

receivers on the LAN, the IPv4 multicast addresses must be mapped to a corresponding MAC multicast address as described in this section. Note that network devices operating at Layer 2 use the Layer 2 (Ethernet) destination addresses for forwarding packets, while those operating at Layer 3 use the Layer 3 (IP) destination addresses for forwarding packets.

Note that (for obvious reasons) using Layer 2 broadcast to forward encapsulated IPv4 multicast packets is highly inefficient and undesirable for sending multicast packets to receivers on the Layer 2 network. The IPv4 multicast address to MAC address mapping method described here provides a simple yet efficient way to send multicast packets over an Ethernet LAN.

This section describes how IPv4 multicast addresses are mapped to corresponding Ethernet MAC addresses. The Ethernet address OUI 01:00:5E (consisting of 24 bits), which is owned by the Internet Assigned Numbers Authority, is used for mapping IPv4 multicast addresses to Ethernet frames. IPv4 multicast packets are mapped to the Ethernet MAC address range 01:00:5E:00:00:00 through 01:00:5E:7F:FF:FF. As shown in Figures A.9 and A.10, the use of this OUI leaves 23 bits of the available MAC address space for mapping the IPv4 multicast group identifier (ID). The first byte (0x01) of the MAC address includes the I/G bit.

All IPv4 multicast addresses have the first 4 bits set to the IPv4 multicast prefix 1110, leaving the low-order 28 bits as meaningful address information. When mapping IPv4 multicast addresses to Ethernet multicast MAC addresses, each MAC address begins with the 24-bit prefix 01:00:5E. This means only half of the 48-bit Ethernet MAC address is available for mapping the IPv4 multicast address.

The steps for converting an IPv4 address to a corresponding 48-bit Ethernet MAC address can be summarized as follows:

1. Ignore the first (higher-order) 9 bits of the IPv4 address and copy the remaining 23 bits.
   - **Note**: All IPv4 multicast addresses have the same 4-bit prefix (1110), meaning there are, in reality, only 4 bits in the first or higher-order byte, not 8 bits. The last bits of the IPv4 address must not be dropped because these are almost guaranteed to be host bits, depending on the IPv4 subnet mask used. However, the high-order bits of the IPv4 address (i.e., the leftmost bits) are almost always network address bits.

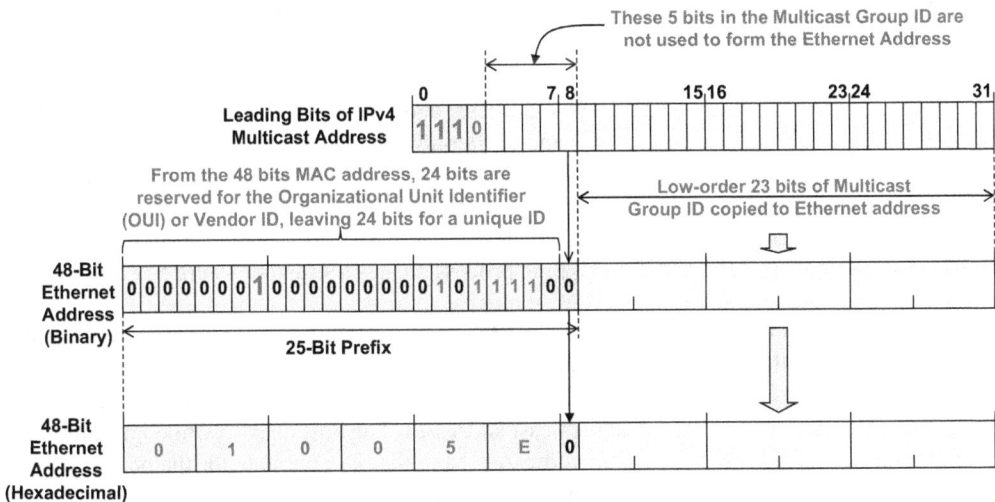

For IPv4, the high-order 4 bits of the Layer 3 IP address is fixed to "1110", to indicate the "Class D" multicast address space between "224.0.0.0" and "239.255.255.255". The special OUI multicast MAC addresses start with "01:00:5E", allowing for a range from "01:00:5E:00:00:00" to "01:00:5E:7F:FF:FF".

FIGURE A.9   Mapping of IPv4 multicast address to 48-bit Ethernet MAC address.

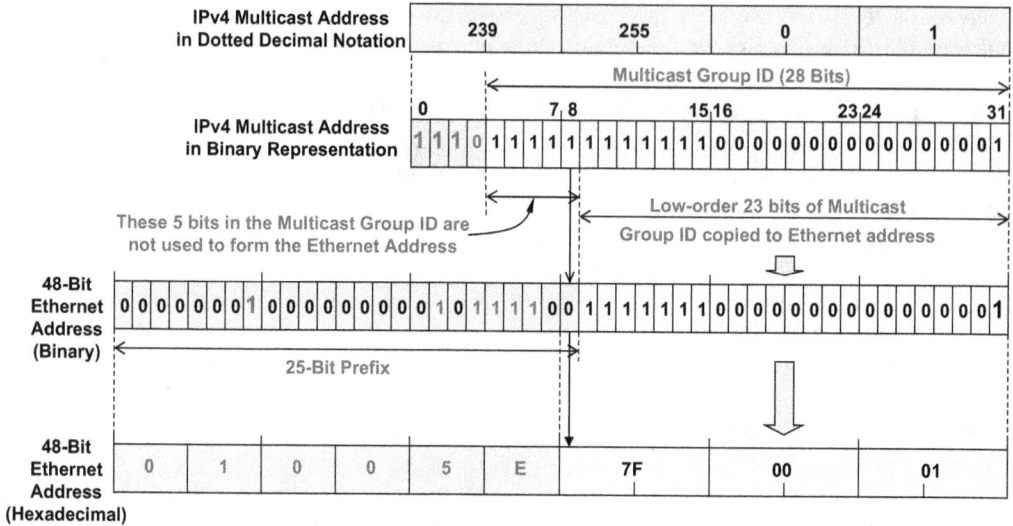

FIGURE A.10 Example mapping of IPv4 multicast address to 48-bit Ethernet MAC address.

2. Add a 0 as the first bit of the copied 23 bits of the IPv4 address (making 24 bits)
   - **Note**: The first bit of the remaining 24 MAC address bits (after the prefix 01:00:5E) is reserved. Setting this bit to 0 indicates an Internet multicast address, so the 5 bits following the IPv4 address prefix 1110 are dropped.
3. Discard the last (lower-order) 24 bits of the Ethernet MAC address.
4. Copy the 24 bits generated from the IPv4 address above and use them as the last 24 bits of the Ethernet MAC address.
   - **Note**: The 23 remaining bits of the IPv4 multicast address are mapped one-to-one into the last 23 bits of the MAC multicast address.
5. The Ethernet MAC address now has the 24-bit prefix 01:00:5E, followed by a 0, and then the copied lower-order 23 bits of the IPv4 address.

Given that the next 5 bits following the IPv4 multicast address prefix 1110 are not used in forming the MAC address as shown in Figures A.9 and A.10, only the low-order 23 bits of the IP multicast address are placed in the MAC address. This means that only 23 bits of the MAC address are available for mapping the IPv4 multicast address. Effectively, 28 bits of the IPv4 multicast address map into only 23 bits of the MAC address, which can create address ambiguities in some cases, as described below. Note that the address mapping process creates a situation where 32 (2^5) IPv4 multicast addresses could map to the same MAC multicast address.

Once a host determines the MAC multicast address for an IPv4 multicast group, its operating system instructs the NIC to join or leave the multicast group as needed. Once a multicast group is joined, the host accepts Ethernet multicast frames carrying the mapped MAC multicast address, as well as Ethernet frames sent to the host's unicast addresses. The host does so while ignoring (filtering) frames sent to other multicast group addresses. Note that it is possible for the host to join and receive multicast frames from more than one multicast group simultaneously.

A.8.3 ETHERNET MULTICAST MAC ADDRESS AMBIGUITIES

Given that the lower 23 bits of the available 28-bit IPv4 multicast group address are mapped into the 23 bits of the available MAC address space, there is bound to be some ambiguity when mapping multicast addresses and delivering multicast packets, as shown in Figure A.11. Mapping the

28-bit IPv4 multicast group address space to the available 23-bit Ethernet MAC address space means that 5 bits of the IPv4 address are lost in the mapping process. These 5 bits result in 2^5 (or 32) address ambiguities as shown in Figure A.11. All of these IPv4 multicast addresses map to the same Ethernet multicast MAC address. This also means that an Ethernet multicast MAC address can represent 32 potential IPv4 multicast addresses, resulting in a 32:1 IPv4 multicast address-to-Ethernet multicast MAC address ambiguity.

This MAC multicast address ambiguity can cause problems when transmitting IPv4 multicast traffic. For example, if any two hosts on the same IPv4 subnet or VLAN join different multicast groups with IPv4 multicast addresses that differ only in the first 5 bits, Ethernet multicast frames for both multicast groups will be delivered to both hosts, requiring the hosts' interface cards to filter and discard all unwanted packets. Note that if an Ethernet switch is not able to interpret the multicast addresses in received packets, it will flood such packets to all hosts on the LAN. In this case, the hosts' interface cards will have to filter all packets sent to multicast groups for which they have not joined.

If Host A joins the IPv4 multicast group 225.129.1.1, it will program its Ethernet interface card with the multicast MAC address 01:00:5E:01:01:01 to receive traffic sent to this group. However, this Ethernet multicast MAC address may also be used by 31 other IPv4 multicast groups. This means that if any of these 31 IPv4 multicast groups is active on the local IPv4 subnet or VLAN of Host A, the Ethernet interface card of Host A will receive each multicast packet sent to any of these addresses. The Ethernet interface card will need to examine the IPv4 multicast address of each packet to determine if it is destined for the group 225.129.1.1, a process that can significantly degrade the processing resources and performance of Host A. Continuous filtering of unwanted

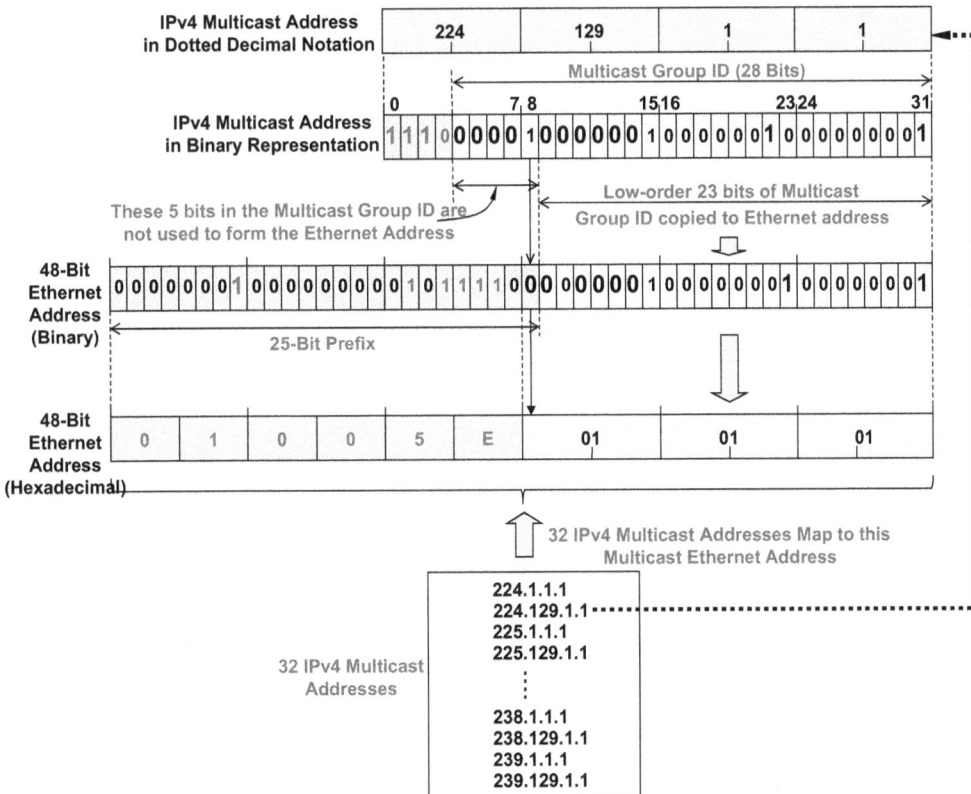

FIGURE A.11   MAC address ambiguities resulting from IPv4 to MAC address mapping.

multicast traffic can further degrade Host A's *performance. Additionally, this multicast MAC address ambiguity complicates the ability to manage the flooding of multicast traffic in an IPv4 subnet or VLAN based solely on Ethernet multicast MAC addresses, since each can correspond to 32 different IPv4 multicast* addresses.

REFERENCES

[AWEMULT24].   J. Aweya, *IP Multicast Routing Protocols: Concepts and Designs*, CRC Press, Taylor & Francis Group, ISBN 9781032701929, May 2024.

[CISCBABY].   Cisco Systems, "Understanding Baby Giant/Jumbo Frames Support on Catalyst 4000/4500 with Supervisor III/IV", *Document ID: 29805*, March 24, 2005.

[IEEE802.3.2022].   "IEEE Standard for Ethernet", *IEEE 802.3-2022*.

[IEEE802.1D04].   "IEEE Standard for Local and Metropolitan Area Networks: Media Access Control (MAC) Bridges", June 2004.

[IEEE802.1Q05].   "IEEE Standard for Local and Metropolitan Area Networks: Virtual Bridged Local Area Networks", *IEEE Std 802.1Q-2005*, May 2006.

[RFC791].   "Internet Protocol", *IETF RFC 791*, September 1981.

Appendix B
IPv4 Packet Format and Addressing

B.1   INTRODUCTION

IETF standard **[RFC791]** defined IPv4 as the fourth version of the Internet Protocol (IP) in the development of Network Layer protocols for global-scale internetworking, the Internet. Although there were other competing Network Layer protocols such as IPX (Internetwork Packet Exchange), IPv4 became the only protocol to be widely deployed and continues to drive the majority of today's networks (enterprise, service provider, and the Internet), with some transitioning to IPv6. **Chapter 1** discusses the limitations of IPv4 and outlines the reasons that spurred the development of IPv6. This **Appendix** is included in this book to provide the most important features of IPv4, allowing readers to better appreciate the improvements provided by IPv6.

A number of protocols work directly over IPv4 just as they do in IPv6. IPv4 sends and receives data segments, called Protocol Data Units (PDUs), directly from Transport Layer protocols such as TCP (protocol number 6), UDP (protocol number 17), and SCTP (protocol number 132). Other upper-layer protocols such as ICMP (protocol number 1), IGMP (protocol number 2), and OSPF (protocol number 89) also work directly over IPv4. The IPv4 layer receives PDUs from its upper-layer protocols and adds its own header information to create an IPv4 packet (Figure B.1).

The PDUs received from the upper-layer protocols constitute the payload of IPv4 packets. The IPv4 header contains all the information needed to route a packet from its source, through an IPv4 network, to the destination. A packet's destination may be a unicast address (pointing to a single network interface on the Internet) or a multicast destination (pointing to multiple interfaces on the Internet, possibly geographically dispersed). As illustrated in Figure B.1, each IPv4 packet created is encapsulated in a Link-Layer frame (e.g., an Ethernet frame as discussed in **Appendix A**) to be transmitted on the underlying network (Ethernet).

B.2   IPv4 HEADER

The source node adds an IPv4 packet header to every IPv4 packet created. The header consists of 13 mandatory fields plus one optional field. The IPv4 header without options is normally 20 bytes in length, but when options are included (of variable length), the header can extend up to 60 bytes. The Options field is located after the Destination Address field (Figure B.2). The IPv4 header fields are structured with the most significant byte written first (using the Big-Endian byte order), and within each byte, the most significant bit is written first. For example, the IPv4 header Version field occupies the four most significant bits of the first byte of the header. The IPv4 header fields are described in the following sections.

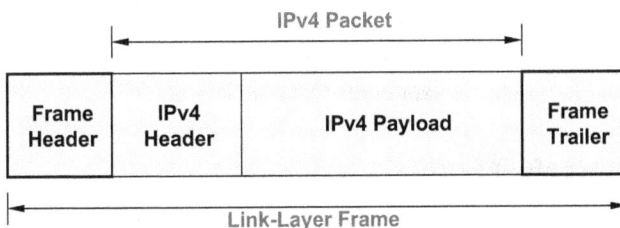

FIGURE B.1   IPv4 packet in a Link-Layer frame.

DOI: 10.1201/9781003710646-8

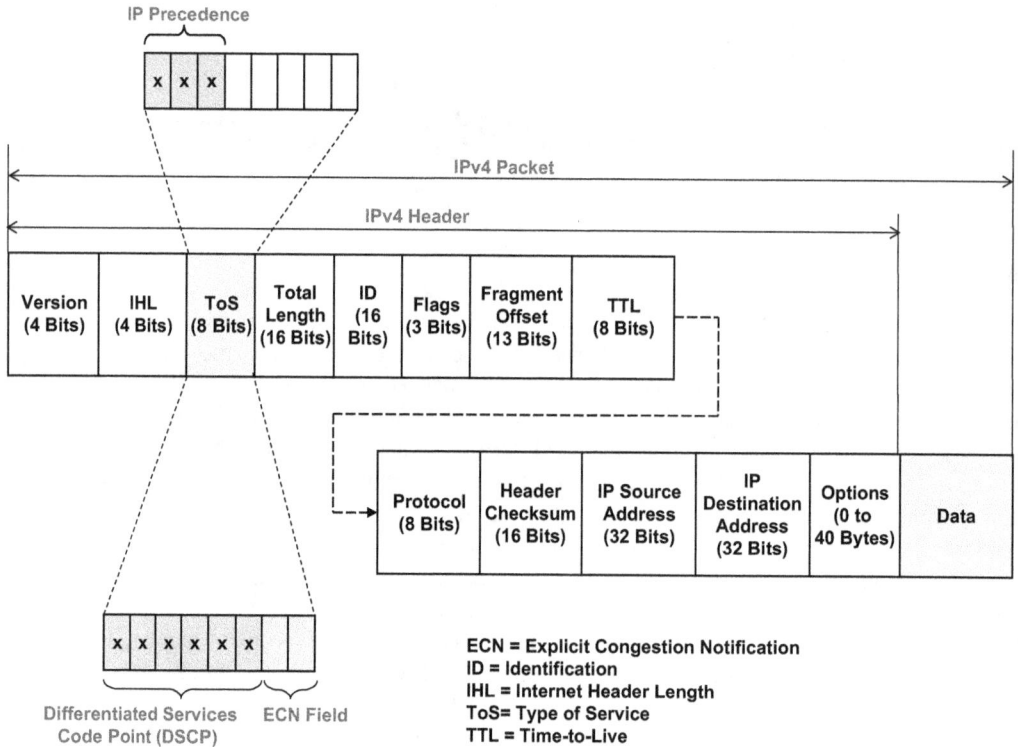

FIGURE B.2 IP Precedence and DSCP in the ToS byte.

B.2.1 VERSION FIELD

The 4-bit Version field specifies the IP version (number) associated with the packet, which also indicates the format of the IP packet header. The IP header contains all the Network Layer information associated with the IP version used. This field carries a value of 4 for the version number discussed here, meaning, IPv4. The Version field in IPv6 packets contains the value 6.

B.2.2 INTERNET HEADER LENGTH (IHL) FIELD

The 4-bit IHL field indicates the length of the entire IPv4 header (including the length of the data in the Options field, when present). The value in this field indicates the length of the IPv4 packet header in 32-bit (4 byte) words. The source determines the IHL in bits (or bytes) and then converts this into an integer by dividing by 32 (or 4) to be entered into the IHL field (Figure B.2). The minimum IHL field value for a valid IPv4 header is 5 (words), because the minimum IPv4 header is 20 bytes ($5 \times 32 = 160$ bits), when no Options are included in the IPv4 header. The maximum IHL field value is 15, because the maximum IPv4 header is 60 bytes (15×32 bits $= 480$ bits), which happens when Options are included in the IPv4 header. A value of 15 in the IHL field means the header can carry a maximum of 40 bytes of data in the Options field.

B.2.3 TYPE-OF-SERVICE (ToS) FIELD

The 8-bit ToS field has taken various meanings over the years since IPv4 was developed. It was originally defined as a mechanism for labeling IPv4 packets with priority values that indicate the kind of service the packets would require (low-latency, high-throughput, or high-reliability service) as they are routed to their destinations. Based on its ToS value, a packet is handled at each routing device according to the policies associated with the ToS value that will deliver the desired service. The most recent redefinition of the IPv4 ToS field (which corresponds to the Traffic Class field in IPv6 packets, as discussed in **Chapter 2**), splits the 8 bits into a 6-bit Differentiated Services Code Point (DSCP) field and a 2-bit Explicit Congestion Notification (ECN) field. These fields are described below.

B.2.3.1   DSCP Field

The 6-bit DSCP field is defined in **[RFC2474]** and occupies the six most significant bits of the older ToS field, as shown in Figure B.2. The remaining two bits of the ToS field are redefined as the ECN field (discussed below). The old ToS field, as updated in **[RFC1349]**, defined a mechanism for specifying the service to be given to a packet (through the setting of the packet's ToS field bits) according to several criteria: IP Precedence, minimizing delay, maximizing throughput, maximizing reliability, minimizing monetary cost, and normal service. These settings were intended for use by networks to define how packets should be handled as they are transported to their destinations. The goal was to allow routers to use the ToS field values to prioritize packets so that the required services, such as low latency or high throughput, can be delivered.

However, the ToS field, as defined in **[RFC1349]**, was difficult to implement in real-life networks due to a lack of clarity on how networks should interpret the ToS field settings and implement different services based on the criteria of minimizing delay, maximizing throughput, maximizing reliability, minimizing monetary cost, and normal service, as specified in **[RFC1349]**. Network operators struggled to understand what these services actually meant in practical terms and how they could be implemented; different operators interpreted and implemented the ToS settings and services differently, if they implemented them at all. Other than the use of the 3-bit IP Precedence bits by a few router vendors (which provided a simple traffic classification and prioritization mechanism), the ToS field was essentially ignored by network operators.

However, the rapid growth of real-time traffic on IP networks (such as voice and video) reignited interest in the ToS field. The DSCP field and associated IETF standards were defined to provide a simple yet practical mechanism for prioritizing and delivering differentiated services on IP networks while avoiding the ambiguities and lack of clarity in **[RFC1349]**. The DSCP and ECN fields have replaced the original ToS field. The DSCP field and related mechanisms were defined to allow networks to classify end-user traffic and provide differentiated service based on end-user needs, thereby improving the end-user experience while still effectively utilizing overall network resources.

The IETF Differentiated Services standard introduced the concept of Per-Hop Behaviors (PHBs), with each PHB defining how packets belonging to a particular behavior aggregate (i.e., packets considered to have the same forwarding characteristics) should be handled at an individual network node **[RFC3140]**. The source node does not indicate PHBs directly in the IP packet headers; instead, it writes DSCP values in the IP header to be used in implementing the PHBs on each network node. The 6-bit DSCP field allows for 64 (2^6) possible DSCP values, but in reality, there is no limit on the number of PHBs that can be implemented on a node.

A network operator can implement locally defined mechanisms for mapping DSCP values to PHBs in any given network domain. The IETF has defined standardized PHBs with recommended DSCP mappings, but network operators may choose to implement suitable alternative mappings. The DSCP field and its applications are discussed in greater detail in the **IETF Differentiated Services (DiffServ)** section below. The 8-bit Traffic Class field in the IPv6 header (see **Chapter 2**) also supports the DSCP and ECN fields, allowing the same service differentiation functions to be supported on IPv6 networks.

B.2.3.2   ECN Field

The 2-bit ECN field, defined in **[RFC3168]**, allows an IP packet to carry information about the state of congestion along the path taken by the packet from its source to its destination. ECN is an optional feature and is only used (effectively) when the underlying network supports congestion detection and packet marking capabilities, allowing for the signaling/notification of network congestion state on an end-to-end basis.

ECN can only be used when the data source and the intermediate network support ECN processing capabilities. A network that uses ECN does not drop packets (i.e., the intermediate network nodes do not drop packets), but instead marks the ECN fields on the packets with congestion notification information, allowing the data sources to react appropriately to reduce or eliminate the congestion.

B.2.4 TOTAL LENGTH FIELD

The 16-bit Total Length field contains a value that indicates the total length (in bytes) of the entire IPv4 packet. The length of the entire IPv4 packet includes the IPv4 header (possibly with Options) and the IPv4 payload, which is data from upper-layer protocols. The minimum theoretical length of an IPv4 packet is 20 bytes, in which case the packet has 20 bytes of IPv4 header and 0 bytes of payload data. However, according to **[RFC791]**, the minimum recommended IPv4 packet length is 576 bytes, and all network links are expected to handle packets of this minimum size. Note that IPv6 mandates a minimum packet length of 1,280 bytes (see **Chapter 2**).

In Ethernet networks, the standard Ethernet frame payload has a maximum size of 1,500 bytes, which means an IPv4 packet can have this maximum size (see **Appendix A**). Note that when IPv4 routers perform packet fragmentation, an IPv4 packet fragment is considered a complete IPv4 packet in itself by downstream nodes (since it has its own IPv4 header after packet fragmentation). Since this field is 16 bits long, the theoretical maximum IPv4 packet length is 65,535 bytes (i.e., $2^{16}-1$ bytes); however, creating packets of this size is impractical for most nodes.

B.2.5 IDENTIFICATION FIELD

The 16-bit Identification field value identifies the fragments of an IPv4 packet that has undergone fragmentation from those of another (different) IPv4 packet. When a router performs fragmentation on an IPv4 packet on its way to a destination, it assigns the same (unique) identification number to all fragments of that packet to enable the destination to identify and reassemble the fragments into the original IP packet they belong to. The router (source) creating the fragments sets the value in the Identification field to a value that must be unique for that source-destination pair, and this value must be unique for the time the IPv4 packet will be alive/active on the network.

B.2.6 FLAGS FIELD

The 3-bit Flags field is used by a router performing fragmentation on a received IPv4 packet to convey information to a destination that helps in the correct reassembly of the packet fragments. For various reasons (dictated by the outgoing link characteristics on which an IPv4 packet is to be forwarded), a router may determine that an IPv4 packet is too large to be transmitted on the link, but the "flags" in the packet may indicate whether the packet can be fragmented or not. A fragment is part of a received IPv4 packet but has its own IPv4 header. The most significant bit of the 3-bit Flags field is always set to 0. The 3-bit Flags field is defined as follows (from high- to low-order bit):

- **1-Bit R (Reserved) Flag**: Set to 0.
- **1-Bit Don't Fragment (DF) Flag**: This indicates if fragmentation can be performed on the IPv4 packet (0=Fragment if necessary; 1=Do not fragment).
- **1-Bit More Fragments (MF) Flag**: This indicates if another fragment follows this current fragment of a packet (0=This is the last fragment; 1=More fragments follow this fragment).

When a source (originator) is sending a single complete IPv4 packet on a network to its destination, the source clears the packet's MF bit to 0 and the Fragment Offset field to 0 before transmitting the packet.

B.2.7 FRAGMENT OFFSET FIELD

The 13-bit Fragment Offset field contains a value that indicates the exact position (offset) of the fragment in the original (unfragmented) IPv4 packet. The offset is expressed in units of eight-byte blocks (64 bits) and indicates the offset of a particular fragment from the beginning of the original unfragmented IPv4 packet. The destination uses this information to properly reassemble the fragments to obtain the original IPv4 packet.

B.2.8 TIME TO LIVE (TTL) FIELD

The 8-bit TTL field value is used to track the lifetime of an IPv4 packet as it travels from the source node through a network to its destination. Each router that receives an IPv4 packet decrements the TTL value by 1, and when this value reaches 0, the packet is discarded. The purpose of the TTL value is to set an upper limit on the number of routers a packet can visit to avoid packets traveling (circulating) in loops in a network.

Every packet is sent with the TTL field set to an initial value that represents the maximum number of routers (hops) the packet is allowed to traverse, which often reflects the maximum diameter of the network. Typically, the source node sets the initial TTL value to a preconfigured integer, indicating the number of hops that packets from that source can cross. At each router, the TTL value is decremented by one; however, when the value reaches 0 and the packet is for local delivery (within the router), the packet is delivered instead of being discarded.

B.2.9 PROTOCOL FIELD

The 8-bit Protocol field contains a value specifying the upper-layer protocol at the source node that provided the payload of the IPv4 packet. The destination node uses this value to determine the upper-layer protocol to which the packet's payload should be sent, i.e., the client protocol. For example, ICMP has the protocol number of 1, IGMP is 2, TCP is 6, UDP is 17, and SCTP is 132. IPv6 uses the same protocol numbers (see **Chapter 2**).

B.2.10 HEADER CHECKSUM FIELD

The 16-bit header Checksum field carries a checksum value that the source node computes over the entire IPv4 header only. Any node on the packet's path, including the destination, uses this value to check if the IPv4 packet has been received free of errors. The source computes the 16-bit checksum as the 16-bit one's complement of the one's complement sum of all 16-bit words in the IPv4 header, including all Options, if present.

When a node receives an IPv4 packet, it computes the checksum of the received IPv4 header and compares this value to the value in the packet's Checksum field. Note that the receiving node zeros the Checksum field before computing the new checksum. If the two checksum values do not match, the node discards the packet. When a router modifies any part of a packet's IPv4 header (e.g., the TTL), a recomputation of the IPv4 Checksum field value is required. Note that routers decrement the TTL field values of packets by 1 before forwarding them. Both UDP and TCP have their own Checksum fields used for error verification at the receiving nodes. This means that errors in the payload of an IPv4 packet are handled by upper-layer protocols.

B.2.11 Source Address Field

This 32-bit Source Address field contains the IPv4 address of the sender (or source) of the IPv4 packet. The source address, which identifies the sender, is always a unicast address and never a multicast address. It uniquely identifies an interface on the IPv4 network. Each interface on an IPv4 node uses a unique source address when sending IPv4 packets. The source IPv4 address may be changed in transit by a Network Address Translation (NAT) device when the sender is on a network that uses private IPv4 addresses.

B.2.12 Destination Address Field

The 32-bit Destination Address field contains the IPv4 address of a single receiver (during unicast transmission) or a group of receivers (using an IPv4 multicast group address during multicast transmission of the IPv4 packet). In unicast transmission, the destination address may also be changed in transit by a NAT device. IPv4 multicast addresses are discussed in a section below.

B.2.13 Options Field

The variable-length Options field (0–40 bytes in length) contains optional information if the value in the IHL field is greater than 5 (but not greater than 15). The Options field may provide information for purposes such as security, record route, time stamp, etc. When used, the Options field increases the IPv4 header length from 20 bytes to a maximum of 60 bytes. This means the value in the IHL field becomes greater than 5 if the IPv4 header includes Options. The maximum size of the Options field is obtained as follows: $(15-5) \times 32$ bits $= 320$ bits $= 40$ bytes.

B.2.14 Data Field

The variable-length Data field contains information provided by an upper-layer protocol, specifically the client protocol. The value in the Protocol field of the IPv4 header indicates the upper-layer protocol that supplies information for the Data field, the packet's payload (Figure B.2). Since the IPv4 header has a minimum size of 20 bytes, the maximum payload (data in the Data field) is limited to 65,515 bytes (i.e., $65535 - 20$ bytes). If the IPv4 packet carries the maximum number of IPv4 Options, then the maximum payload becomes 65,495 bytes ($65,535 - 40$ bytes).

The source node typically creates the IPv4 header, followed by either a Transport Layer (UDP, TCP, or SCTP) header, an ICMP header, or an IGMP header, which is usually followed by the specific upper-layer protocol data. The number of bytes in the data field (payload) of the upper-layer protocol is determined by the IPv4 header Total Length field value minus the IHL field value (20–60 bytes) minus the length of the upper-layer protocol header (Transport Layer, ICMP, or IGMP header).

A source node may send an IPv4 packet containing a UDP datagram with a 20-byte IPv4 packet header, an 8-byte UDP header, and 500 bytes of payload, resulting in an IPv4 packet with a Total Length field value of 528 bytes. The source may add variable-length padding data as a redundant filler to ensure that the data in the IPv4 packet aligns with a 32-bit boundary. Note that the source does not include the payload (data portion) of the IPv4 packet in the IPv4 header checksum computation.

B.3 IPv4 ADDRESSING

As discussed in **Appendix A**, a MAC address is an identifier assigned to a physical or virtual/logical interface on an Ethernet device or on devices using now obsolete technologies like Token Ring and FDDI. Typically, a unique MAC address is permanently programmed on a network interface adapter to uniquely identify the interface in a network. MAC addresses are Data Link-Layer addresses, while IP addresses are Network Layer addresses.

The IP address of an interface on a network device may change as the device moves from one IP subnet/VLAN to another, switches between WiFi networks, or when the device powers up and is assigned an IP address by a Dynamic Host Configuration Protocol (DHCP) server. However, the MAC address may remain the same because it is associated with the Data Link-Layer interface of the device. As discussed in **Appendix A**, each network adapter manufactured is assigned a unique MAC address by the manufacturer.

The 32-bit Source Address field of a packet (which contains the IPv4 address identifying the packet's source) may be modified by a NAT device. Additionally, the source IP address of a packet can be all 0s in certain cases (called the unspecified IPv4 address), for example, as the default address or as a placeholder when the IPv4 address of an interface is not yet known or is not applicable in that particular use case. The packet's source IPv4 address can never be a multicast address; only the destination IPv4 address can be a multicast address (which identifies a group of receivers interested in traffic from that multicast address). The 32-bit Destination Address field of a packet (which contains the IPv4 address of the packet's receiver) may also be modified by a NAT device. The destination IPv4 address can be a unicast or multicast IPv4 address, but it can never be all 0s (the unspecified IPv4 address).

To make IPv4 addresses more convenient and easier to read and use, 32-bit IPv4 addresses are often written in dotted-decimal notation (IPv6 addresses are written in colon-hexadecimal notation). Using dotted-decimal notation involves splitting the 4-byte IPv4 address into 4 groups, with each group consisting of a 1-byte word. Each 1-byte group is then expressed as a decimal value (ranging from 0 to 255) and separated from adjacent groups by a period (.).

The dotted-decimal notation allows 32-bit IPv4 addresses to be conveniently expressed in decimal form, making them easier to work with (imagine working with IP addresses in binary form). Within each 1-byte group of an IPv4 address, the rightmost bit represents 2^0 (or 1), while the left-most bit (i.e., the first or highest-order bit in the byte) is 2^7 (or 128), meaning, a 1-byte group can take a value from 00000000 binary (or 0 decimal) to 11111111 binary (or 255 decimal).

The following are examples of IPv4 addresses expressed in both binary and dotted-decimal formats:

```
00001010.00011010.00100101.00110000 → 10.26.37.48
01111111.00001011.00010110.00100001 → 127.11.22.33
10101100.00010000.01011000.01100011 → 172.16.88.99
10111110.00101101.00111000.01000011 → 190.45.56.67
```

IPv4 addresses, in general, are structured in two primary parts: a network prefix and a host identifier. This results in an IPv4 address having two groups of bits corresponding to these parts. The first group (the network prefix) contains the most significant bits and constitutes the network address (or IPv4 prefix or network block). The IPv4 prefix identifies a whole network or subnet.

The host identifier consists of the remaining least-significant bits of the IPv4 address. This part identifies a particular physical or logical interface associated with a node on a network identified by an IPv4 prefix. The IPv4 prefixes (identifying networks or subnets) form the basis of traffic routing between IPv4 networks and subnets. The variable-length IPv4 prefixes also form the basis of IPv4 address allocation policies in today's networks.

The concept of supernetting (also called prefix aggregation, route aggregation, or route summarization) **[RFC1519]** allows several IPv4 prefixes that share a common pattern in the higher-order bits to be summarized into a single representative super IPv4 prefix (see Classless Inter-Domain Routing (CIDR) below). This super IPv4 prefix can then be advertised by routing protocols instead of advertising all the individual (smaller) IPv4 prefixes that make up the super IPv4 prefix.

All IPv4 (host) interfaces within a single network or subnet share the same IPv4 prefix. Furthermore, each individual interface (host) within an IPv4 prefix (network/subnet) is assigned a unique identifier. The host identifier uniquely identifies a particular physical or logical interface within an IPv4 prefix, which is also unique in the network. Note that an IPv4 prefix may be globally unique (i.e., a globally routable prefix) or unique only within a particular network (i.e., a private IPv4 prefix that is only routable within that network, not globally (see private IPv4 addresses below)).

As discussed below, the IPv4 address assigned to an interface may be globally or locally unique. Globally unique IPv4 addresses are allocated to interfaces that need to be accessible to other IPv4 nodes outside their local networks (e.g., web servers, video servers, email servers). Interfaces that are accessible only within their local network are allocated locally unique IPv4 addresses, also known as private IPv4 addresses. The IPv4 addresses used on the IPv4 Internet are globally unique.

The Internet Assigned Numbers Authority (IANA) is the central numbering authority responsible for assigning IPv4 and IPv6 prefixes and Autonomous System Numbers, as well as performing other related functions such as managing the root zone in the Domain Name System (DNS). The IANA is responsible for ensuring that IP prefixes allocated to the Regional Internet Registries (RIRs) representing different regions in the world are globally unique. The IANA has also reserved a large IPv4 address space for use as private addresses within networks that are not accessible outside those networks.

The IANA allocates (blocks of) IPv4/IPv6 prefixes to the RIRs, which then assign parts of their allocated prefixes to their customers (Local Internet Registries (LIRs), Internet Service Providers (ISPs), organizations) who carry out the actual allocation to end users. An LIR receives IPv4/IPv6 prefix allocation from an RIR and then assigns parts of the prefixes to their customers; most LIRs also operate as ISPs.

Since the development of IPv4, address allocation has undergone a number of historical changes that resulted in different allocation strategies. The process began with the original Advanced Research Projects Agency Network (ARPANET) address allocation scheme, progressed to the IPv4 Classful addressing scheme, then to addressing with Variable-Length Subnet Mask (VLSM), and finally to CIDR.

B.3.1 ORIGINAL **ARPANET** ADDRESSING SCHEME

In the ARPANET addressing scheme, the 32-bit IPv4 address is structured into two parts: a fixed-size network identifier and a fixed-size host identifier. The fixed-size network identifier (or network number field) consists of the most significant (or highest-order) bytes of the 4-byte IPv4 address. The host identifier (or local address) comprises the remaining 3 bytes of the IPv4 address (these 3 bytes are also called the *rest field*). The well-defined network identifier field (the most significant bits of an address) specifies the particular network to which a host belongs, while the host identifier (the rest field) uniquely identifies a host connected to that network. A network with a 1-byte network identifier allows for the creation of a maximum of 256 unique networks.

This addressing scheme was adequate for the ARPANET (the first distributed wide-area packet network) because only a few distributed IPv4 networks existed at that time. However, with the wide and rapid proliferation of IPv4 networking, along with the deployment of local area networks (LANs), subnets, and large individual IP networks (academic, enterprise, and ISPs), it became apparent that the ARPANET addressing scheme was inefficient and not scalable for future IPv4 network growth.

B.3.2 IPv4 CLASSFUL ADDRESSING (DEPRECATED)

In the IPv4 Classful addressing scheme, the high-order bytes of the 4-byte (32-bit) IPv4 addresses are structured into different non-overlapping address blocks, each associated with a unique address space called an IPv4 address class. The IPv4 Classful addressing scheme was developed to address the limitations of the original ARPANET addressing scheme and to provide flexibility in how addresses are allocated to networks with different sizes and addressing needs. This IPv4 addressing scheme defined five address classes: Class A, B, C, D, and E [RFC791]. Each IPv4 address class is encoded in the first four bits of the 32-bit IPv4 address space. Additionally, each class defines either a network size—specifically, the number of potential hosts that would require unique unicast IPv4 addresses (corresponding to Class A, B, and C addresses)—or multicast addresses (corresponding to Class D addresses).

The Class A, B, and C addresses are defined with a different number of bits that correspond to the network identifier for that address class. Each address class has a network identifier that falls on a byte boundary. The remaining bits in an address class (the host identifier) are used to identify a particular host within a network using that address class. The IPv4 Classful addressing scheme resulted in each address class having a different maximum number of host identifiers/addresses that can be allocated to potential hosts.

Class D was defined mainly for IPv6 multicast addressing, while Class E was reserved for experimental purposes or future networking use. Using the IPv4 Classful addressing scheme, a network node processing IPv4 packets, would examine the first few bits of the packet's IPv4 address to determine the class of the address and where the actual network identifier starts and ends.

The different classes of the IPv4 Classful addressing scheme are presented in Table B.1. This table shows that each IPv4 address class reserves or specifies a different number of bits for the network identifier (now commonly called the IPv4 prefix) and for the host identifier:

- Class A addresses use only the first (higher-order) byte of the 4-byte IPv4 address space for the network prefix (IPv4 prefix) and the remaining 3 bytes for the individual host identifiers.
- Class B addresses use the first 2 bytes of the 4-byte IPv4 address space for the network prefix and the remaining 2 bytes for the host identifiers.
- Class C addresses use the first 3 bytes of the 4-byte IPv4 address space to specify the network prefix, while the last byte is used for host identifiers.

The first three IPv4 address classes (Class A, B, and C) are expressed in binary format as follows, with an h representing each bit in the host identifier:

Class A: 0NNNNNNN hhhhhhhh hhhhhhhh hhhhhhhh
Class B: 10NNNNNN NNNNNNNN hhhhhhhh hhhhhhhh
Class C: 110NNNNN NNNNNNNN NNNNNNNN hhhhhhhh

TABLE B.1
Classful Addressing

Class	Leading Bits (Class Identifier)	Size of Network Identifier Field (Bits)	Size of Host Identifier Field (Bits)	Number of Networks (or Prefixes)	Addresses per Network	Start Address	End Address
Class A	0	8	24	$128 (= 2^7)$	$16,777,216$ $(= 2^{24})$	0.0.0.0	127.255.255.255
Class B	10	16	16	$16,384 (= 2^{14})$	$65,536 (= 2^{16})$	128.0.0.0	191.255.255.255
Class C	110	24	8	$2,097,152$ $(= 2^{21})$	$256 (= 2^8)$	192.0.0.0	223.255.255.255
Class D (multicast)	1110	Not defined	Not defined	Not defined	Not defined	224.0.0.0	239.255.255.255
Class E (reserved)	1111	Not defined	Not defined	Not defined	Not defined	240.0.0.0	255.255.255.255

Each bit (h) in the host identifier portion of an IPv4 address can have a value of 0 or 1. For illustrative purposes, let us assume that only 3 bits are reserved for specifying the host identifier. The possible host identifiers then are:

    000; 001; 010; 011; 100; 101; 110; 111

The host identifier uniquely identifies a particular host in the network using the IPv4 Classful address. If H is the number of host identifier bits, then for each IPv4 address class, the maximum number of host identifiers supported by that address class (or IPv4 prefix) is 2^H:

    Class A: Maximum number of host identifiers = 2^{24} (= 16,777,216), H = 24
    Class B: Maximum number of host identifiers = 2^{16} (= 65,536), H = 16
    Class C: Maximum number of host identifiers = 2^8 (= 256), H = 8

However, in each address class, the maximum number of usable IPv4 addresses for individual hosts is $2^H - 2$. The subtraction of 2 accounts for the pre-defined IPv4 address of all 0s used in the IPv4 Unspecified address and the IPv4 address of all 1s used in the IPv4 broadcast address. The mask in an IPv4 Classful address identifies where an IPv4 prefix starts and ends and is implicitly derived (inferred) from the IPv4 address itself (i.e., from the leading address bits as shown in Table B.1).

In common network practice, the host identifier with all 0s is reserved for referring to all hosts on a particular network (the entire network or subnet). The host identifier with all 1s is used as a broadcast address in the given network or subnet. These reserved IPv4 addresses reduce the number of identifiers/addresses available for hosts on a network or subnet by 2. The /31 IPv4 prefix (255.255.255.254) is rarely used, typically only on point-to-point links ([**RFC3021**]). A point-to-point link supports only two hosts (the endpoints), making the specification of IPv4 network-wide and broadcast addresses unnecessary for such links.

B.3.3 IPv4 Variable-Length Subnet Masks (VLSM)

Network designers often segment large networks into smaller networks/subnets to address the physical, architectural, and management challenges associated with operating large networks. Let us assume IPv4 Subnet Delta has three hosts connected to it, and Subnet Gamma also has three other hosts connected to it. These six hosts and two subnets (Delta and Gamma) can be combined to form a larger network than the individual subnets. If we assume that the combined (larger) network is assigned the IPv4 prefix (a Class B address) 192.14.0.0, then each of the 6 hosts will be assigned an IPv4 address that belongs to this IPv4 prefix.

In addition to all 6 hosts sharing the same IPv4 prefix (i.e., 192.14) for the combined network, the hosts on each IPv4 subnet will share the same IPv4 subnet prefix (192.14.*Delta*.0 and 192.14.*Gamma*.0). All hosts on the same IPv4 subnet must have the same IPv4 subnet prefix. Let us assume that IPv4 Subnet Delta is allocated the IPv4 subnet prefix 192.14.125.0, while Subnet Gamma is assigned the IPv4 subnet prefix 192.14.18.0.

The IPv4 prefix of Subnet Gamma, 192.14.18.0, can be expressed in binary form as follows:

    11000000.00001110.00010010.xxxxxxxx

For this subnet using a Class B IPv4 prefix, the first 24 bits in the 32-bit IPv4 address are used to identify the subnet itself, leaving the last 8 bits for host identification. The IPv4 prefix of Subnet Gamma is usually expressed in CIDR notation as 192.14.18.0/24 (or simply 192.14.18/24). The /24 in this notation represents the subnet mask (also written as 255.255.255.0).

In the past, IPv4 subnets were created based on the IPv4 address classes defined in Table B.1. An IPv4 subnet could have a network identifier (IPv4 prefix) with either 8 bits (Class A; /8), 16 bits (Class B; /16), or 24 bits (Class C; /24), corresponding to a maximum of 2^{24}, 2^{16}, or 2^8 hosts, respectively. In this addressing scheme, if an entire Class B prefix (/16 subnet) is allocated to a network that requires only 600 IPv4 addresses, then 64,936 ($2^{16} - 600 = 64,936$) addresses will be wasted.

The concept of VLSMs was introduced to allow IPv4 address spaces (i.e., prefixes) to be allocated more efficiently without the address space wastage seen in the IPv4 Classful addressing scheme **[RFC950] [RFC1878]**. VLSM allows network operators to allocate IPv4 prefixes and addresses more efficiently, tailored closely to the needs and size of each network/subnet (see Table B.2). VLSM allows network operators to allocate IPv4 prefixes and addresses more efficiently, closely tailored to the needs and size of each network/subnet (see Table B.2). VLSM was developed to enable the creation of IPv4 network identifiers (prefixes) more conveniently and efficiently, without being constrained by the byte-based address boundary limitations of the IPv4 Classful addressing scheme, particularly the address wastage (unused address space) that occurs due to the need for IPv4 prefixes to align with class (byte) boundaries. VLSM provides greater flexibility in designing IPv4 networks and subnets of varying sizes without unnecessary address space wastage. VLSM was the basis for the CIDR addressing scheme, which allows multiple networks sharing a common prefix to be created and advertised by routing protocols (discussed below).

Let us consider another example where a (larger) network with the IPv4 prefix 192.14.18/24 is divided into two smaller IPv4 subnets, one supporting 19 hosts and the other 47 hosts. To accommodate 19 hosts, the first IPv4 subnet must have an address space that has 2^5 (32) host identifiers. Assigning 5 bits from the 32-bit address space to the host identifier will result in 27 bits left for the subnet identifier (subnet prefix). The IPv4 address of the first subnet (with 19 hosts) then becomes 192.14.18.128/27, which can be expressed in binary form as:

11000000.00001110.00010010.**100**xxxxx

To obtain the "128" in the above address, the "**100**xxxxx" is converted to "**100**00000", which equals the decimal value of 128. The IPv4 subnet mask of /27 covers the first 27 most significant bits of the IPv4 address. For the IPv4 second subnet with 47 hosts, the network must have 26 (64) host identifiers. Assigning 6 bits from the 32-bit address space to the host identifier will leave 26 bits for the subnet identifier. The IPv4 address of this second subnet is, therefore, 192.14.18.64/26, which in binary form is:

11000000.00001110.00010010.**01**xxxxxx

To obtain the "64" in the above address, "**01**xxxxxx" is converted to "**01**000000", which equals the decimal value of 64.

The IPv4 prefixes of the two subnets are as follows:

11000000.00001110.00010010.**100**xxxxx → 192.14.18.128/27
11000000.00001110.00010010.**01**xxxxxx → 192.14.18.64/26

Thus, using a larger /24 IPv4 prefix, which encompasses the two (/27 and /26) subnet prefixes, the network operator can assign address bits within the /24 prefix to create the two smaller IPv4 subnets. Using VLSMs allows for more efficient use of the allocated IPv4 address space. Table B.2 shows how VLSMs can be applied to a 32-bit IPv4 address space (w.x.y.z) to create networks of different sizes (different IPv4 prefix lengths with corresponding numbers of possible IPv4 addresses).

B.3.4   IPv4 CLASSLESS INTER-DOMAIN ROUTING (CIDR)

As the Internet expanded to handle more users and various types of services, many organizations requested larger IPv4 address blocks from the IANA than what a Class C (/24) prefix could provide. The IANA, therefore, allocated Class B (/16) address blocks to these organizations, which in many

TABLE B.2
Using VLSMs

IPv4 Address Format	Network Mask	Number of IPv4 Addresses	
		Decimal	2^H
w.x.y.z/32	255.255.255.255	1	2^0
w.x.y.z/31	255.255.255.254	2	2^1
w.x.y.z/30	255.255.255.252	4	2^2
w.x.y.z/29	255.255.255.248	8	2^3
w.x.y.z/28	255.255.255.240	16	2^4
w.x.y.z/27	255.255.255.224	32	2^5
w.x.y.z/26	255.255.255.192	64	2^6
w.x.y.z/25	255.255.255.128	128	2^7
w.x.y.0/24	255.255.255.0	256	2^8
w.x.y.0/23	255.255.254.0	512	2^9
w.x.y.0/22	255.255.252.0	1,024	2^{10}
w.x.y.0/21	255.255.248.0	2,048	2^{11}
w.x.y.0/20	255.255.240.0	4,096	2^{12}
w.x.y.0/19	255.255.224.0	8,192	2^{13}
w.x.y.0/18	255.255.192.0	16,384	2^{14}
w.x.y.0/17	255.255.128.0	32,768	2^{15}
w.x.0.0/16	255.255.0.0	65,536	2^{16}
w.x.0.0/15	255.254.0.0	131,072	2^{17}
w.x.0.0/14	255.252.0.0	262,144	2^{18}
w.x.0.0/13	255.248.0.0	524,288	2^{19}
w.x.0.0/12	255.240.0.0	1,048,576	2^{20}
w.x.0.0/11	255.224.0.0	2,097,152	2^{21}
w.x.0.0/10	255.192.0.0	4,194,304	2^{22}
w.x.0.0/9	255.128.0.0	8,388,608	2^{23}
w.0.0.0/8	255.0.0.0	16,777,216	2^{24}
w.0.0.0/7	254.0.0.0	33,554,432	2^{25}
w.0.0.0/6	252.0.0.0	67,108,864	2^{26}
w.0.0.0/5	248.0.0.0	134,217,728	2^{27}
w.0.0.0/4	240.0.0.0	268,435,456	2^{28}
w.0.0.0/3	224.0.0.0	536,870,912	2^{29}
w.0.0.0/2	192.0.0.0	1,073,741,824	2^{30}
w.0.0.0/1	128.0.0.0	2,147,483,648	2^{31}
0.0.0.0/0	0.0.0.0	4,294,967,296	2^{32}

cases were much larger than the organizations truly required. Additionally, due to the rapid growth of enterprise and service provider networks, as well as the Internet as a whole, the pool of unassigned Class B prefixes ($2^{14} = 16,384$) was rapidly depleted.

Furthermore, during the early stages of the Internet's development, the IANA allocated address spaces to some organizations that were far larger than they actually needed. These factors, among others, contributed greatly to inefficiencies in IPv4 address allocation and use, as well as created inefficient routing in networks due to poorly defined address allocation for many networks. Given that Class B addresses were depleting at a rapid rate, the IANA resorted to distributing a large number of Class C addresses. However, allocating a large number of smaller Class C addresses (which were used to create networks that, in many cases, were geographically dispersed) resulted in very large IPv4 routing tables on Internet routers. These Class C addresses were mostly used on smaller networks that were geographically dispersed, making it difficult to perform route summarization or aggregation.

CIDR (which relies on VLSM) was developed to address the limitations of the IPv4 Classful addressing scheme, which offered no opportunities for route summarization or aggregation **[RFC1517] [RFC1518] [RFC1519] [RFC4632]**. The IPv4 Classful addressing scheme, coupled with how routing of IPv4 packets is performed on networks, made it difficult to scale networks designed with the smaller IPv4 address classes. The CIDR scheme was developed to provide flexibility in network design, allowing a designer to (re)partition any address space (without being constrained by address class boundaries) to create networks with larger or smaller prefixes according to network size and needs. Apart from replacing the inefficient IPv4 Classful addressing scheme, CIDR, along with VLSM, slowed down the rapid depletion of IPv4 addresses and the growth of routing table sizes on Internet routers.

As discussed above, the network addresses (prefixes) in IPv4 Classful addressing are placed in a field of one to three bytes in length, resulting in the Class A, B, or C addresses shown in Table B.1. IPv4 address allocations were therefore based on the byte boundaries of the 4-byte IPv4 address space. A full IPv4 address for a network interface was created by concatenating a 1-, 2-, or 3-byte network prefix and a corresponding 3-, 2-, or 1-byte host identifier. This addressing scheme provided Class C addresses as the smallest address allocation space for interfaces with a maximum of 256 host identifiers. This address space was often too small for most organizations. The larger Class B addresses support 65,536 individual host identifiers, which were also often too large for even large networks or organizations at that time.

As enterprise and service provider networks were extended to handle more users and services, it became increasingly apparent that IPv4 networks needed more flexible and efficient addressing methods. Using CIDR and VLSM, the address space (prefix) allocated to an organization can be subnetted on any arbitrary bit boundary of the address instead of on a 1-byte boundary. CIDR ushered in a period of efficient IPv4 address usage (despite the IPv4 address depletion rate), allowing a network designer to partition a larger IPv4 prefix into various-sized IPv4 subnet prefixes, facilitating the efficient creation and sizing of networks to meet the requirements of the organization.

The CIDR notation (now the industry-accepted method of representing both IPv4 and IPv6 addresses) provides a simple yet effective method for specifying IP addresses and their associated prefixes for various purposes, such as advertising routing information in networks. Using CIDR notation, a network address or IP prefix is written with a suffix indicating the number of bits in the prefix, that is, the higher-order bits that identify a particular network. Examples of IPv4 and IPv6 prefixes are 192.168.22.0/20 and 2001:db8:abcd:ef44::0/64, respectively.

- The CIDR notation is derived from the IP prefix and its length in the IP address (which is equivalent to the number of consecutive leading 1 bits in the prefix).
- An IP address or prefix can be expressed (in dotted-decimal for IPv4 or colon-hexadecimal for IPv6) as the address/prefix digits followed by a separator character, the slash ('/') character, and the prefix length expressed as a decimal number. The CIDR notation is constructed by concatenating the prefix, a slash character, and the number of leading bits in the prefix expressed as a decimal number (e.g., 10.25.0.0/10).
- The IP address constructed using CIDR notation may represent the address of a single, distinct interface in a network or the routing/network prefix of an entire network or subnet. The maximum size of the network/subnet (i.e., the number of distinct host/interface identifiers that can be supported by the prefix) is derived from the decimal equivalent of the remaining lower-order bits after the network prefix digits. An IP address followed by a slash (/) and a decimal number (e.g., 127.125.0.3/10) indicates a block of addresses (host/ interface identifiers) that are using a prefix with a length equal to the decimal number indicated in the address. The following are important features of CIDR notation:
    - The IPv4 address 192.168.125.28/24 represents the IPv4 address 192.168.125.28 and its associated network/routing prefix 192.168.125.0. The prefix can also be obtained by applying the IPv4 subnet mask 255.255.255.0 (which has 24 leading 1-bits) to the IPv4 address 192.168.125.28.

- The IPv4 address block 192.168.125.0/20 represents 4096 individual IPv4 addresses from 192.168.112.0 to 192.168.127.255 (using a $32-20=12$ bits of the host identifier space, 2^{12}). This is equivalent to the IPv4 address in binary notation:
  11000000.10101000.0111**0000**.**00000000** $\rightarrow$ 192.168.112.0
  to
  11000000.10101000.0111**1111**.**11111111** $\rightarrow$ 192.168.127.255
- CIDR notation provides a more compact representation of IPv4 and IPv6 addresses and prefixes than dot-decimal and colon-hexadecimal notations, by expressing both the address prefix and the prefix length together. For example, 192.168.125.0/24 is written in a longer dot-decimal form as 192.168.125.0/255.255.255.0.
- The number of host/interface identifiers in a network/subnet (defined by the network prefix (or mask)) can be calculated as $2^{IP\_Address\_Size - Prefix\_Length}$, where "IP_Address_Size" is 32 for IPv4 (and 128 for IPv6). For example, in IPv4, a prefix length of /18 gives: $2^{32-18} = 2^{14} = 16{,}384$ distinct host/interface identifiers.

The introduction of CIDR allowed the allocation of address blocks to organizations while considering their actual short-term and projected long-term addressing needs. Additionally, the CIDR prefix-based method of representing IP addresses and their associated route aggregation properties allows blocks of addresses with similar characteristics to be grouped into single entries for routing advertisements and the routing table. Route aggregation or summarization enables routing to be done more efficiently on internetworks, particularly the Internet. These address groups (commonly called CIDR blocks) share a common shorter prefix that can be advertised or entered into the routing table in place of the individual address groups.

The most compelling feature of CIDR is its ability to aggregate multiple contiguous network prefixes (a process often called route aggregation, route summarization, or prefix aggregation) for the creation of supernetworks (or supernets) in networks. A supernet, when created, has a subnet mask (network prefix) that is smaller than the individual subnet masks (prefixes) used in creating the supernet. Routers advertise supernet prefixes as aggregates, thereby reducing the number of entries in routing tables. The following are the notable advantages of CIDR and route aggregation:

- Using CIDR for supernetting allows the aggregation of multiple routes leading to different smaller networks.
- Route aggregation results in smaller routing table sizes, particularly on core routers, as well as reduces the memory storage requirements for the routing tables on the routing devices.
- Smaller routing tables allow for faster destination address lookups and packet forwarding in routing devices, leading to quicker and simplified routing decisions.
- Smaller routing tables (and the fewer number of smaller networks that are visible to outside networks) reduce the routing advertisements made to neighboring routers.
- Supernetting allows a network (the supernet) to hide internal topology changes from outside routers. This helps improve the stability of the entire internetwork by limiting the propagation of routing information updates outside the supernet after a network link fails internally.
- If a router advertises only an aggregate/summarized route (to a supernet) to peer routers, it does not need to advertise any changes in the individual smaller subnets that comprise the supernet (summarized route). Route aggregation can significantly reduce unnecessary routing information updates following a topology change within the supernet. This increases the network convergence speed and allows the overall network to be more stable.

The IANA manages the CIDR address blocks with assistance from the RIRs. The IANA allocates large, short-prefix CIDR address blocks to the RIRs, which are responsible for distributing those address blocks to their customers. The RIRs (responsible for address management and allocation in each geographic area, such as North America, Europe, and Africa) divide their allocated short-prefix CIDR address blocks and allocate the sub-blocks to the LIRs. Similarly, the LIRs receive address sub-blocks from the RIRs and subdivide them for allocation to their customers. The end-user networks receive appropriately sized address prefixes from the LIRs according to their network needs.

B.3.5   Reserved IPv4 Addresses

The IANA reserved certain blocks of IPv4 prefixes for use as special addresses. The addresses described in this section are examples of the reserved IPv4 addresses.

B.3.5.1   IPv4 Private Addresses

IPv4 private addresses were defined for use within the confines of a particular network without making these addresses visible and routable outside that network **[RFC1918]**. Private addresses within a home, office, campus, company, or enterprise network are only visible within these networks and not outside. A network uses private addresses when it does not require or is not obliged to use globally routable IPv4 addresses. The IANA and RIRs do not delegate or manage IPv4 private addresses because they have no global significance. These addresses are not allocated to any specific organization, and an organization can use them as needed as long as their limitations are adhered to. IPv4 packets carrying these addresses cannot be transmitted on the public IPv4 Internet. Nodes on a network that uses IPv4 private addresses need a NAT mechanism to communicate with nodes outside the network.

The IANA reserved the following three blocks of the IPv4 address space for private networks:

- **Class A Private** Address–10.0.0.0/8 **(255.0.0.0) Addresses**: 10.0.0.0–10.255.255.255; $2^{24} = 16,777,216$ host identifiers
- **Class B Private** Address–172.16.0.0/12 **(255.240.0.0) Addresses**: 172.16.0.0–172.31.255.255; $2^{20} = 1,048,576$ host identifiers
- **Class C Private** Address–192.168.0.0/16 **(255.255.0.0) Addresses**: 192.168.0.0–192.168.255.255; $2^{16} = 65,536$ host identifiers

It can be seen from Table B.1 that only parts of the "172" address range of Class B and the "192" address range of Class C blocks are designated for private use. The remaining IPv4 addresses in Classes B and C are public and routable on the global IPv4 Internet.

IPv4 packets with private addresses are not routable on the IPv4 Internet, meaning routers outside a private network are required to drop such packets. To communicate with outside networks, packets with IPv4 private addresses must be translated to public (routable) IPv4 addresses using a NAT device or a Web Proxy Server (which is placed between a user on a private network and the Internet to act as an intermediary mechanism for handling Web requests and replies on behalf of the user).

The IANA created the range of private addresses (within the Classes A, B, and C blocks) as one of several mechanisms for managing the assignment of the already-limited IPv4 public routable address pool. By encouraging homes, offices, campuses, organizations, and similar environments to use private addresses, the demand for globally routable IPv4 addresses decreased significantly. The widespread use of private addresses also helped delay the depletion of routable IPv4 addresses.

B.3.5.2   IPv4 Loopback Addresses

The IPv4 address range 127.0.0.0–127.255.255.255 (127.0.0.0/8) was reserved by the IANA for use as an IPv4 host's self-address, also called the loopback address **[RFC6890]**. The loopback address is sometimes called the localhost address. The host's operating system implements and manages the loopback (localhost) address as it normally does with most networking functions on a host. IPv4 packets carrying a loopback address as the source IPv4 address are never transmitted outside the host itself. A host uses a loopback address to enable local server and client processes on the host itself to communicate with each other.

When a process on a host generates an IPv4 packet with the destination address set to the IPv4 loopback address, the operating system loops the packet back to the process without involving the host's network interface adapter. A process sends data to a loopback address, and the operating system forwards the data to a virtual network interface within the operating system, which then turns it around. Network designers and administrators primarily use the loopback address for testing how a client–server process on the same host works after implementation.

B.3.5.3   IPv4 Broadcast Address

The IANA reserved certain addresses for use as IPv4 broadcast addresses, which are special IPv4 addresses that allow a node to send an IPv4 packet to all nodes on the same IPv4 network or subnet (limited broadcast), or to all nodes on a particular remote network (directed broadcast). The destination address of an IPv4 packet may be set to the special IPv4 broadcast address, 255.255.255.255 (a limited broadcast), to send the packet to all nodes on the local network. This broadcast address confines the packet to the local network because it is never forwarded across a router, unlike an IPv6 packet sent as a directed broadcast, which can cross a router.

A node on another (remote) network may send an IPv4 packet with the destination address set to the specific IPv4 subnet broadcast address, 192.30.40.255 (the host identifier portion of the IPv4 address is 255 in decimal, or all "1"s in binary), to send the packet to all nodes on the network 192.30.40.0/24. This type of IPv4 broadcast is called a directed broadcast because the IPv4 packet can cross an IPv4 router to the target IPv4 subnet, 192.30.40.0/24 (whose IPv4 broadcast address is 192.30.40.255).

Protocols such as DHCPv4 (see **Chapter 5**) and the now-deprecated RIPv1 (Routing Information Protocol version 1) use IPv4 broadcasts as part of their operations. DHCPv4 clients send DHCPDISCOVER messages as broadcasts on their networks/subnets by setting the destination address of the IPv4 packets carrying the DHCPv4 messages to 255.255.255.255 (limited broadcast) or to the specific IPv4 broadcast address of the target subnet (directed broadcast). Address Resolution Protocol (ARP, discussed in **Appendix C**), on the other hand, uses Layer 2 broadcasts (using the MAC address FF-FF-FF-FF-FF-FF in hexadecimal) on a network segment (subnet or VLAN) to resolve IPv4 addresses to their corresponding MAC addresses.

IPv4 packets sent to the address 255.255.255.255 are never forwarded by routing devices to other networks but remain in the local broadcast domains (IPv4 subnet or VLAN) from which they originated. Note that IPv6 does not support broadcast addresses; instead, it uses a number of well-known IPv6 multicast addresses to implement the broadcast functionality (see **Chapters 3 and 4**).

B.3.5.4   IPv4 Multicast Addresses

As shown in Table B.1, IPv4 multicast addresses are identified by the four highest-order address bits of 1110. This definition of IPv4 multicast addresses originates from the IPv4 Classful addressing scheme, where multicast addresses are designated as Class D addresses. An IPv4 multicast address starts with 224.x.x.x, and the multicast address range is from 224.0.0.0 to 239.255.255.255. The IPv4 multicast address range in CIDR notation is 224.0.0.0/4. IPv4 address assignments from the multicast address range are specified in **[RFC5771]**. Note that the source address of an IPv4 packet must never be an IPv4 multicast address; only IPv4 unicast addresses can be used as source addresses.

B.3.5.5   IPv4 Link-Local Addresses

Reference **[RFC6890]** defines IPv4 Link-Local addresses as the addresses in the range 169.254.0.0–169.254.255.255 (IPv4 address block 169.254.0.0/16). Link-Local addresses are not routable and are only used (and valid) on a single link, such as a point-to-point connection (between two interfaces) or on a single local network segment (IPv4 subnet/VLAN) connected to a host interface. IPv4

Link-Local addresses are not guaranteed to be unique beyond the link (network segment) on which they are configured. Such addresses are only used to communicate with nodes on the same network segment; therefore, routers do not forward packets carrying Link-Local addresses. IPv4 packets meant to traverse a router must not carry Link-Local addresses in their source or destination address fields. IPv6 Link-Local addresses are described in **Chapter 3**.

Link-Local addresses on network interfaces may be configured manually by a network administrator or automatically through mechanisms and procedures supported by a node's operating system **[RFC3927]**. In cases where a host is unable to obtain an IPv4 address from a DHCPv4 Server for an interface and the interface has not been manually configured with any IPv4 address, the host can autoconfigure the interface with an IPv4 address from the range of reserved IPv4 Link-Local addresses. In the absence of a DHCPv4 Server, the host may randomly select an IPv4 address from the range of reserved IPv4 Link-Local addresses for the interface and then use Gratuitous ARP (as discussed in **Appendix D**) to ensure that no other host has assigned the same IPv4 address to an interface on the same network segment. Gratuitous ARP for IPv4 is equivalent to the IPv6 Duplicate Address Detection feature discussed in **Chapter 4**.

Once the hosts on the same single network segment have configured their interfaces with Link-Local addresses, they can communicate directly with each other (not across a router). Only hosts connected to the same physical or logical network link or segment (a point-to-point link or broadcast network segment like an Ethernet LAN) can use IPv4 Link-Local addresses to communicate with each other.

B.4 IPv4 ADDRESS DEPLETION ISSUES

The pervasiveness and rapid growth of IPv4 networks and the Internet drastically increased the number of users who need globally unique IPv4 addresses to communicate with others on the Internet. It became apparent that enterprises and service providers could not continue to allocate globally unique IPv4 addresses to their end users. This is because enterprises and service providers could not obtain new globally unique IPv4 addresses for expanding their networks due to the limited availability of such addresses. In spite of these hurdles, service providers knew they still had to continue serving existing customers and accepting new ones to remain competitive and profitable.

A service provider can accept new customers requesting globally unique IPv4 addresses only if its allocated IPv4 address space can accommodate them. The 32-bit (4-byte) IPv4 address field provides a total IPv4 address space of 4,294,967,296 (2^{32}) addresses. At the start of the Internet, the 32-bit IPv4 address space was seen as large enough for future addressing needs, and there was little concern about IPv4 address depletion.

However, the rapid growth of the Internet, along with the number of wired and wireless devices (such as laptops and smartphones), created an increased demand for unique IPv4 addresses, a situation that was not foreseen at the start of the Internet. As unique IPv4 addresses were assigned to an increasing number of new users, the number of unassigned unique IPv4 addresses decreased. Furthermore, the rising use of mobile devices raised great concerns that the globally unique IPv4 address space might eventually be depleted sooner than initially thought. To address these concerns, the networking industry adopted various practices (in addition to CIDR and VLSM) to combat the rapid depletion of the available globally unique IPv4 addresses.

B.4.1 PRIVATE IPV4 ADDRESSES

We have already discussed IPv4 private addresses above. The IANA designated several blocks of IPv4 addresses for private use within private networks (on interfaces that are not visible to the outside world). The use of IPv4 private addresses has significantly reduced the demand for globally unique IPv4 addresses. Using private addresses with NAT (discussed next) has become widespread practice (from residential to enterprise and service provider networks), further helping to decrease the demand for public IPv4 addresses.

B.4.2 NETWORK ADDRESS TRANSLATION

NAT is a mechanism that allows multiple hosts on a network with IPv4 private addresses to communicate with hosts in the outside world using public IPv4 addresses, utilizing one or a few public (routable) IPv4 addresses. Most devices on private networks (e.g., residential, campus, or enterprise networks) are assigned IPv4 private addresses, which are not routable on the Internet. IPv4 routers do not forward packets with private IP addresses; such packets are dropped. Thus, to communicate with hosts that have public IPv4 addresses, hosts on private networks must go through a NAT device, which translates between private and public addresses. When a host on a private network sends an IPv4 packet, the NAT device replaces the packet's IPv4 private address with the public IPv4 address of the NAT device and vice versa.

B.4.3 DYNAMIC HOST CONFIGURATION PROTOCOL FOR IPv4 (DHCPv4)

DHCPv4 is a protocol through which a host interface can obtain an IPv4 address from a pre-defined IPv4 address pool maintained by a DHCPv4 Server. The DHCPv4 Server may also provide additional information, such as the default gateway (router) for a host, an IPv4 subnet mask, the IPv4 address of a DNS Server (for name-to-IPv4 address resolutions), and the lease time for the assigned IPv4 address, among other details. Networks use DHCPv4 services to manage the assignment of IPv4 addresses automatically and more efficiently. DHCPv6 is described in **Chapter 5**.

B.4.4 PROXY SERVER

Hosts, typically on a private network, may access the Internet via a Proxy Server that acts as an intermediary for the hosts. A Proxy Server is assigned a public IPv4 address on its Internet-facing interface. All the hosts on the network send Web requests to the Proxy Server, which then forwards the requests to the appropriate Web Servers on the Internet. The Proxy Server acts on behalf of the hosts to send the Web requests to the Servers (located on the Internet) and relays responses from the Servers to the hosts. All requests and responses go through the Proxy Server transparently, without the hosts being aware of its presence. Using Proxy Servers on private networks has been an effective method for controlling Internet access and facilitating the implementation of web-based access policies.

B.4.5 UNUSED PUBLIC IPv4 ADDRESSES

Upon recognizing the rapid depletion of IPv4 addresses, the IANA and the RIRs embarked on a policy of reclaiming unused IPv4 addresses to be reassigned to new users. By encouraging many organizations to implement renumbering of their networks using IPv4 best practices based on VLSM/CIDR, the RIRs were able to reclaim large blocks of unused IPv4 address space that had been allocated to organizations during the early stages of the Internet. Additionally, the RIRs exercised tighter management and control over the allocation of IPv4 address blocks to the LIRs.

B.4.6 TRANSITION TO IPv6

The various limitations of IPv4 discovered since its inception, including the rapid depletion of the IPv4 address space, spurred the development of IPv6 in the 1990s. IPv6 has been in various stages of commercial deployment since 2006 and is experiencing rapid adoption due to the huge number of devices that now need globally unique addresses. The IPv6 address space was redesigned with the main goal of addressing the drawbacks of the IPv4 address space. IPv6 provides many improvements over IPv4 (as discussed in **Chapter 1**), including enhanced addressing, flow labeling, security, node configuration and maintenance, and the elimination of Network Layer broadcast addresses as seen in IPv4. IPv6 defines a 128-bit address field, large enough to accommodate a very large number of devices that require unique IP addresses.

A vast majority of devices on the Internet still use IPv4, and it is anticipated that the transition to total IPv6 use is still well into the future. This means IPv4 and IPv6 will coexist for many years to come, and this coexistence must be made transparent to users of either protocol. For this reason, a number of mechanisms were developed **[RFC2893] [RFC7059]** to allow IPv4 and IPv6 to coexist until networks eventually move to only IPv6:

- NAT mechanism
- Dual IPv4/IPv6 Stack
- Tunneling (6to4, 4to6, etc.)

It is envisioned that the best long-term solution to the IPv4 address depletion problem is the transition to IPv6. However, the networking industry is still debating the long-term use of IPv4. As discussed in Chapters 1–6, IPv6 provides many more features than just a much larger address space. The IPv6 addressing architecture allows the creation of hierarchical networks with more efficient route aggregation and offers large IPv6 prefix allocations to organizations, avoiding the use of NAT devices. Migration to IPv6 is still in progress, and complete migration is not expected for the foreseeable future.

Enterprises and service providers have to make tough decisions about IPv4 and IPv6. They must choose between expanding their networks using IPv6 and continuing to serve existing and new customers using IPv4. The technologies and solutions discussed above were developed to enable enterprises and service providers to implement mixed IPv4 and IPv6 solutions while they build IPv6 networks to accommodate new services and users.

B.5   UNDERSTANDING IPv4 OPTIONS

The value in the IHL field indicates the length of the entire IPv4 packet header in 32-bit (4-byte) words. If the value is greater than 5, then the packet carries Options that must be processed by the current router. The variable-length Options field (of up to 40 bytes) consists of the following sub-fields:

- **1-Bit C (Copy) Flag**: This indicates if the Options in the IPv4 header are to be copied into all fragments when the router performs packet fragmentation (0=Do not copy; 1=Copy).
- **2-Bit Class Field**: This indicates the class to which the IPv4 Options belongs (0=Control; 1=Reserved; 2=Debugging and measurement; 3=Reserved).
- **5-Bit Option Field**: This indicates the type of Options carried in the IPv4 header. Types of IPv4 Options: 0=End of Options list; 1=No operation; 2=Security; 3=Loose Source Route; 4=Timestamp; 7=Record Route; 9=Strict Source Route; 18=Traceroute.

The source node creating an IPv4 packet with Options must include a value in the IHL field to account for all the 32-bit Options words in the Options field (plus any padding needed to ensure that the IPv4 header contains an integer number of 32-bit words). The IPv4 Options field was not widely used in practice for several reasons:

- Most routers did not implement mechanisms for processing IPv4 Options, leading to a lack of widespread support.
- There were concerns that allowing routers to process IPv4 Options would introduce unnecessary processing that could slow down IPv4 packet forwarding. Note that early implementations of routers were primarily software-based, and processor and memory technologies were not as advanced as today's technologies.

- There were risks of malicious actors exploiting the Options field for network security attacks. In particular, security concerns discouraged the use of the Loose Source Route, Record Route, and Strict Source Route Options.

B.6 FRAGMENTATION AND REASSEMBLY OF IPv4 PACKETS

IPv4 allows routers to fragment packets (into multiple smaller packets) if an interface cannot handle packets larger than the interface's maximum transmission unit (MTU). Fragments of a packet must be reassembled at the destination node using information in the IPv4 header, as discussed above; each fragment is sent as a separate IPv4 packet with its own header. Because of the complexity of the IPv4 fragmentation process, IPv6 simplified it by moving fragmentation to the packet's source; only the source node performs fragmentation.

Given that different links on a network can have different MTUs, MTU mismatches can occur on routers. When the MTU of the outgoing interface of a router is smaller than the MTU of the inbound interface, an MTU mismatch occurs. This mismatch can cause a router to fragment an incoming packet or simply discard it. It is possible for an upstream router to fragment an IPv4 packet, and for the fragments themselves (carried in whole IPv4 packets with their own headers) to be fragmented again at a downstream router.

The 16-bit Identification field in the IPv4 header identifies the original IPv4 packet to which a fragment belongs (serving as an ID for all fragments of a packet). The destination node uses this information to reassemble all fragments with the same ID into the original IPv4 packet. The router performing the fragmentation assigns a unique Identification value (fragment ID) to each fragment of the original packet.

In IPv4, any node along the forwarding path of an IPv4 packet can fragment packets (including the packet's source). Usually, only the destination endpoint reassembles fragments with the Identification value into the original IPv4 packet. However, it is possible for an intermediary network device (such as a firewall, Proxy Server, or border router at the edge of a network) to reassemble fragments into the original packets to enforce security filtering rules. In IPv6, only the source node can perform packet fragmentation, and an IPv6 Fragment extension header is included in the IPv6 header, containing the information needed by the destination node to reassemble fragments into the original IPv6 packets.

The highest-order (first) bit of the 3-bit Flags field in the IPv4 header is reserved, and all nodes originating a packet must set this bit to zero. The second bit, the DF Flag, is set to 1 by a packet's source to indicate to any downstream router that the packet must not be fragmented. If a router receives an IPv4 packet with the DF bit set and the outgoing interface cannot handle a packet of that size, the router must drop that packet and send an ICMP Destination Unreachable message to the packet's source.

In IPv4, the source node mainly uses the DF Flag when it wants to send packets to another node but does not want those packets to be fragmented; instead, it only wants to determine if any interface on the forwarding path cannot forward the packet. The DF Flag is used in the Path MTU Discovery mechanism [RFC1191], a feature on host operating systems, or by diagnostic tools such as Ping [RFC792] [RFC1122] and Traceroute (IPv4 Option 18) [RFC792]. The third bit of the Flags field, the MF Flag, is set by the packet's source (a router performing fragmentation on an IPv4 packet) to indicate to the receiver that there are more fragments of the packet following the particular fragment carrying the set MF bit. IPv4 packets that have not undergone fragmentation always have their MF Flag set to 0. Except for the last fragment of an IPv4 packet (which has MF set to 0), all other fragments of the packet have their MF Flag set to 1.

The destination node uses the 13-bit Fragment Offset field when reassembling fragments of a packet. The offset value in a particular fragment is measured in 8-byte blocks and represents the offset from the start of the original IPv4 packet. The first fragment of an IPv4 packet (which constitutes the start of the packet) has an offset of 0. The last fragment of a packet carries a nonzero Offset field value, allowing it to be easily differentiated from an IPv4 packet that has not been fragmented.

The following explains how the Fragment Offset field is used in practice:

- The 13-bit Fragment Offset field provides a maximum offset value of 8,191 (= $2^{13}-1$).
- This means the maximum offset value for a fragment of an IPv4 packet is $(2^{13}-1)\times 8 = 65,528$ bytes.
- The 16-bit Total Length field of the IPv4 header means the maximum length of an IPv4 packet is 65,535 bytes (i.e., $2^{16}-1$), including any IPv4 header Options.
- The maximum IPv4 payload (i.e., of an IPv4 packet without Options) is limited to $65,535-20$ bytes $= 65,515$ bytes.
- Dividing the IPv4 payload data of 65,515 bytes by 8-byte (the unit of the offset) results in a maximum of 8,189 offset units.
- This means the maximum fragment offset of 8,191 (offset units) is greater than the maximum payload length of an IPv4 packet, which equals 8,189 offset units.

The above analysis shows that the Fragment Offset field in reality is limited to maximum of 8,189 actual offset units (not 8,191 (i.e., $2^{13}-1$) as indicated by the 13-bit Fragment Offset field). An IPv4 fragment carrying a Fragment Offset value of 8,189 (i.e., in the last fragment), could have a maximum payload of only 3 bytes:

- Maximum IPv4 packet length of 65,535 bytes $-$ minimum IPv4 header length of 20 bytes $-$ (8,189 offset units $\times$ 8 bytes per offset unit) $=$ maximum of 3 bytes.

Each router that receives an IPv4 packet, performs an IPv4 routing table lookup using the packet's destination IPv4 address to determine the packet's outgoing interface and the interface's MTU. If the packet size is larger than the interface's MTU and the DF bit is set to 0, the router is allowed to fragment the packet. Upon detecting an MTU mismatch, the router may decide to divide the packet into fragments if it is configured to perform packet fragmentation.

The maximum size of a fragment that can be sent over an interface is the MTU of the interface minus the IPv4 header size. The minimum IPv4 header size is 20 bytes (IPv4 packet without Options), and the maximum is 60 bytes (IPv4 packet with Options). The router constructs each fragment into an IPv4 packet with its own IPv4 header as follows:

- Sets the Total Length field of the new IPv4 packet to the size of the fragment plus the IPv4 header size.
- Sets the MF Flag of the new packet to 1 (this is done for all fragment packets except the last one, which is set to 0).
- Appropriately sets the Fragment Offset field in the new packet (measured in 8-byte units) as described above.
- Recalculates the Checksum field value in the IPv4 header of the new IPv4 packet (see discussion below).

Let us consider an interface with an MTU of L bytes and IPv4 packets with a basic IPv4 header size of 20 bytes. In this case, the router creates fragments with the fragment offsets being multiples of $(L-20)/8$. If the MTU of the interface is 1,500 bytes and the minimum IPv4 header size is 20 bytes, then the fragment offsets to be written in the Fragment Offset field of each new fragment packet would be multiples of $(1,500-20)/8 = 185$, that is, 0, 185, 370, 555, 740, ...

The receiver identifies an arriving IPv4 packet as a fragment by checking if at least one of the following conditions is true for the packet:

- The MF Flag is set to 1 (which is true for all fragments of a packet except the last one).
- The Fragment Offset field is nonzero (which is true for all fragments of a packet except the first one).

The receiver uses the value in the Identification field (fragment ID) to identify fragments that belong to the same original IPv4 packet so that reassembly can be performed. Using both the Fragment Offset field values and the MF Flag, the receiver reassembles the fragments (with the same Identification field value) into the original IPv4 packet.

To perform reassembly, the receiver typically places the fragments in a reassembly buffer, with each newly arriving fragment appropriately positioned in the reassembly buffer at its corresponding Fragment Offset field value (×8 bytes) from the beginning of the buffer. Upon receiving the last fragment of a packet (with the MF Flag set to 0), the receiver computes the total length of the payload data of the original IPv4 packet by multiplying the offset value in the last fragment by 8 and adding the size of the payload data in the last fragment. After receiving all fragments of a packet, the receiver sequences them in the correct order using their offset values. The reassembled original IPv4 packet is then passed on to the upper-layer protocol (indicated by the value in the packet's 8-bit Protocol field) for further processing.

If a source transmits a 2,500-byte IPv4 packet, which is fragmented by a downstream router into fragments of 1,020 bytes, three fragments will be created as follows:

- Fragment # 1; MF Flag = 1; Total Length = 1,020; Data Size = 1,000; Offset = 0
- Fragment # 2; MF Flag = 1; Total Length = 1,020; Data Size = 1,000; Offset = 125
- Fragment # 3; MF Flag = 0; Total Length = 520; Data Size = 500; Offset = 250

The "Data Size" values in the above fragmentation process include the length of any upper-layer protocol headers, such as ICMP, IGMP, or Transport Layer headers.

B.7   ENCAPSULATING IPv4 PACKETS IN ETHERNET FRAMES

The maximum theoretical length of IPv4 packets is 65,535 bytes, which is much larger than the maximum length of untagged Ethernet frames (1,518 bytes, with a payload of 1,500 bytes). This means an IPv4 packet (which becomes the payload of an Ethernet frame) larger than 1,500 bytes must be segmented and carried in several Ethernet frames. For example, we can calculate the number of Ethernet frames required to transport an IPv4 packet with a maximum size of 65,535 bytes as $65,535 \div 1,500 = 43.69$.

This means it takes 44 Ethernet frames to transport one maximum-size IPv4 packet across an Ethernet interface. However, this example is only for illustrative purposes because, in practice, IPv4 packets are not created with the maximum size. Large IPv4 packets are always segmented/fragmented before being encapsulated in Ethernet frames. This is because IPv4 applications send packets in data blocks not greater than the maximum Ethernet frame payload size.

B.8   IMPLEMENTING TRAFFIC CLASSES IN IPv4 AND IPv6

The traffic classification methods discussed in this section apply to both IPv4 and IPv6. As discussed in **Chapter 2**, the IPv6 header has an 8-bit Traffic Class field that indicates the class or priority of an IPv6 packet. This field is also structured to include the traffic prioritization fields defined for the IPv4 header, harmonizing the traffic classes and prioritization methods in both protocols.

It is more practical to classify IP-based traffic into distinct traffic classes and manage these classes rather than classify each individual application or user on the network. This concept of using traffic classes makes the problem of quality-of-service (QoS) much more manageable. Both the IEEE and IETF have defined mechanisms for supporting the differentiation of traffic based on Layer 2, Layer 3, and higher protocol layer data into eight distinct classes within a network domain.

Some important classification mechanisms are described below. However, for any QoS services to be applied to the traffic in today's networks, which are primarily based on Ethernet and IP, there must be a way to tag or prioritize an IP packet or an Ethernet frame. The CoS fields discussed below are used to achieve this.

B.8.1 PRACTICAL ASPECTS OF THE IPv4 ToS

The 8-bit ToS field was originally defined as part of the IPv4 packet header **[RFC791]**. Figure B.2 shows the location of the ToS field in the IPv4 header. Similar to the IEEE 802.1Q tag in Ethernet frames, the IPv4 header was designed to include a field that specifies a priority value for an IPv4 packet. The ToS is now an obsolete IP header mechanism for providing packet prioritization and has been replaced with a 6-bit DSCP field **[RFC2474]** and a 2-bit ECN field **[RFC3168]**; the original 8-bit ToS field has been superseded by these two fields. ECN provides an optional end-to-end mechanism for signaling network congestion to network devices without dropping packets. The optional ECN feature (the two least-significant bits) may be used between two ECN-enabled nodes when the underlying network infrastructure supports this capability.

Prior to being deprecated, the ToS field was defined to have a 3-bit Precedence subfield, a 3-bit ToS subfield, and 2 unused bits. In practice, only the upper 3-bit IP Precedence subfield was ever utilized. Similar to IEEE 802.1p, a higher IP Precedence field value indicates a higher priority for the IP packet. The three most significant bits of the ToS field (i.e., the IP Precedence subfield) yields eight priority values (Figure B.2), providing for eight levels of IP Precedence or priority levels. The newly defined DSCP field offers a method for assigning priority values to IPv4 and IPv6 packets. The 6-bit DSCP field (which corresponds to the 6 most significant bits of the ToS field) yields 64 different priority values (Figure B.2). It should be noted that the upper 3 bits of the DSCP field were defined to provide values that maintain compatibility with the 3-bit IP Precedence values.

IP Precedence was the only industry-accepted packet prioritization mechanism for traffic prioritization in IPv4 routers. Its prioritization features are somewhat similar to IEEE 802.1p, but are implemented at Layer 3 by routers and Layer 3 switches, rather than by Layer 2 switches. IP Precedence uses priority values 0–7, much like IEEE 802.1p, but within the IP packet header (as opposed to the IEEE 802.1Q tag, which is implemented at Layer 2). In fact, IP Precedence is the only part of the ToS that was ever truly implemented in some routing platforms, particularly Cisco routers. Table B.3 lists the eight different IP Precedence values defined in **[RFC791]**.

In the networking industry, the ToS is sometimes mistakenly referred to as IP Precedence. In addition to the 3 bits used for IP Precedence, there were additional definitions for the other bits in the ToS field. One of the other bits in the ToS byte, when set, would indicate that the packet should receive low delay, high throughput, and other benefits. These older semantics of ToS, aside from IP Precedence, are mostly ignored and were never deployed.

Also, the actual deployment of IP Precedence in the Internet and private networks was not carried out as originally intended in the IETF standards, but was frequently left to the needs of specific network service providers or router vendors. Generally, a Precedence value of 0 indicates that a packet should receive only best-effort service. The other values, however, had different meanings for different providers or vendors; usage mostly depended on the service provider or router vendor and the methods employed for QoS control in a network.

TABLE B.3
IP Precedence Values and Associated Traffic Types

Precedence Value	Binary	Precedence Name	Recommended Use
0 (Lowest priority)	000	Routine or Best Effort	Default marking value
1	001	Priority	Data applications
2	010	Immediate	
3	011	Flash	Call signaling
4	100	Flash Override	Video conferencing and streaming video
5	101	Critical	Voice
6	110	Internetwork Control	Network control traffic (such as routing, which is
7 (Highest priority)	111	Network Control	typically precedence 6)

B.8.2   IETF Differentiated Services (DiffServ)

DiffServ is a more recent QoS architecture defined by the IETF **[RFC2474] [RFC2475] [RFC3260]**. DiffServ specifies a simple and scalable coarse-grained, class-based mechanism for traffic forwarding in IP (IPv4 and IPv6) networks. It defines a mechanism for classifying and marking packets as belonging to a specific CoS. It includes the concept of marking IP packets with priority values that enable routers to classify the marked packets into traffic classes, each associated with certain forwarding behaviors in the network. Using DiffServ-based classification, each packet is placed into a limited number of traffic classes (or queues), in contrast to the fine-grained, flow-based architecture (Integrated Services (IntServ) architecture **[RFC1633]**), where network traffic is differentiated based on the requirements of an individual flow. DiffServ allows each router on the network to differentiate traffic based on a limited range of packet markings and traffic classes. Each traffic class can be managed differently, allowing routers to provide preferential treatment for higher-priority traffic on the network.

A *DiffServ domain* consists of a group of routers that implement a common, administratively defined set of policies based on DiffServ traffic markings. Traffic entering a DiffServ domain is subjected to a well-defined set of classification and conditioning policies. Traffic may be classified based on various parameters, such as source IP address, destination IP address, Transport Layer protocol type (TCP or UDP), source port number, and destination port number. A traffic classifier in a domain may honor the DiffServ markings in arriving packets or may choose to override or ignore those markings. Additionally, traffic in each class may be conditioned by subjecting it to traffic policing and shaping. Typically, all traffic classification and policing, as well as other traffic conditioning, are performed at the boundaries between DiffServ domains.

As discussed above, packet marking is performed using bits in the IPv4 header field formally designated as the ToS field, now redefined as the DSCP field (Figure B.2). The term DSCP is commonly used to describe the value with which an IPv4/v6 packet is marked. The DSCP contains 6 bits and is written into the left-most (most significant) 6 bits of the previous ToS byte of the IPv4 header (see Figure B.2) **[RFC2474] [RFC2475]**. The ECN occupies the least-significant 2 bits.

The three most significant bits of the DSCP field are defined to provide values that are backward compatible with the old IP Precedence, while the remaining bits do not maintain backward compatibility with the semantics of the other bits in the old IP header ToS byte. For backward compatibility, the eight values obtained from the upper 3 bits of the DSCP field correspond to the eight old IP Precedence values, which were defined to mean the same as the old IP Precedence values. Since the IP Precedence is now represented by the three most significant bits (rather than the least-significant bits) of the 6 bits of the DSCP field, the eight values are not identified as 0–7. Instead, the DSCP value corresponding to IP Precedence value n is redefined as $n \times 8$, for $n = 0$–7. IP Precedence values 0, 1, and 7, correspond to DSCP values 0, 8, and 56, respectively. DSCP value 40 (decimal) corresponds to IP Precedence value 5. Although the DSCP field supports backward compatibility with IP Precedence marking, it provides a richer set of traffic classifications and behaviors.

The eight special values of the DSCP field that are used for backward compatibility with IP Precedence are called the *Class Selector* (CS) codepoints. IP routers that are DiffServ-aware implement PHBs **[RFC3140]**, which define how traffic should be treated based on its class, that is, the packet-forwarding properties associated with traffic classes. Different PHBs may be defined in a network to provide, for example, low-loss or low-latency traffic delivery.

DiffServ allows a network to support (in theory) up to 64 ($= 2^6$) different traffic classes using the full range of markings in the DSCP field. Most networks use the following commonly-defined PHBs.

B.8.2.1   Default PHB

This is typically used to forward best-effort traffic. Any traffic that does not meet the requirements of any of the other DiffServ-defined classes is placed in the Default PHB **[RFC2474]**. The recommended DSCP for the Default PHB is 000000 (in binary).

B.8.2.2 Expedited Forwarding (EF) PHB

This is dedicated to low-loss, low-latency, and low-jitter (i.e., low PDV) traffic such as real-time streaming voice and video **[RFC3246]**. Traffic that conforms to the EF PHB is admitted into a DiffServ network using a Call Admission Control (CAC) procedure. EF traffic may also be subjected to traffic policing and other mechanisms to ensure that delay and PDV requirements are not violated. EF traffic is typically transferred using strict priority queuing relative to all other traffic classes. The recommended DSCP for the EF PHB is 101110 (i.e., 46 in decimal or 2E in hexadecimal).

B.8.2.3 Voice Admit PHB

This PHB is defined in **[RFC5865]** and has identical characteristics to the EF PHB. Both PHBs allow traffic to be admitted by a network using a CAC procedure. However, traffic conforming to the Voice Admit PHB is admitted by a CAC procedure that also involves authentication, authorization, and capacity admission control, or the traffic is subjected to very coarse capacity admission control (refer to **[RFC5865]** for a description of authentication, authorization, and capacity admission control). The recommended DSCP value for the Voice Admit PHB is 101100 (44 in decimal or 2C in hexadecimal).

B.8.2.4 Assured Forwarding (AF) PHB

This PHB provides assurance of traffic delivery under certain prescribed conditions **[RFC2597]** **[RFC3260]**. AF PHB ensures traffic delivery as long as the traffic does not exceed some pre-defined rate. Traffic that exceeds the pre-agreed rate has a higher probability of being dropped if network congestion occurs. Four separate AF classes are defined for the AF PHB group, with Class 4 having the highest priority. Packets within each AF class are assigned a drop precedence (i.e., high drop precedence, medium drop precedence, or low drop precedence).

A higher drop precedence means relatively more packet dropping. Also, three sub-classes exist within each class x (i.e., AFx1, AFx2, and AFx3), with each sub-class defining a relative drop precedence that determines which packets should be dropped first if a class queue is full. For example, within class 2, traffic assigned to the AF23 sub-class (i.e., high drop precedence in class 2) will be discarded before traffic in the AF22 sub-class (i.e., medium drop precedence in class 2), which in turn will be discarded before traffic in the AF21 sub-class (i.e., low drop precedence in class 2).

The combination of classes and drop precedence yields 12 separate DSCP encodings from AF11 through AF43 (see Table B.4). During periods of congestion affecting AF classes, traffic in the higher AF class is given priority. AF PHB generally does not use strict priority queuing; instead, more balanced queue scheduling algorithms such as weighted fair queuing are used. When congestion occurs within an AF class, packets with higher drop precedence (AF sub-classes with higher drop precedence) are dropped first.

To prevent problems associated with queues using tail drop, AF PH often uses more sophisticated packet drop algorithms such as *random early detection*, as discussed below. AF PHB, in general, uses mechanisms that ensure some measure of priority and proportional fairness between traffic in different AF traffic classes.

B.8.2.5 Class Selector PHBs

This maintains backward compatibility with the IP Precedence field in the old IP header ToS field, allowing interoperability with network devices that still use the IP Precedence field. The CS codepoints are of the form "xxx000," (binary), where the first three bits (xxx) are the IP Precedence bits **[RFC4594]**. Each IP Precedence value can be mapped into a corresponding DiffServ class.

For example, a packet with a DSCP value of 111000 or 56 (equivalent to an IP Precedence of 7) is provided preferential treatment over a packet with a DSCP value of 101000 or 40 (equivalent to an IP Precedence of 5). The different CS PHBs and their corresponding binary and decimal values are given in Table B.5. If a DiffServ-aware router receives a packet from a non-DiffServ-aware router that uses IP Precedence markings, the DiffServ router can still interpret the encoding as a CS codepoint.

B.8.2.6 Some Implementation Issues

Simply put, DiffServ provides a framework that allows for classification and differentiated treatment in networks. The standard traffic classes described in the IETF standards serve to simplify and streamline interoperability between different vendors' equipment and various networks. It should be noted, however, that the details of how individual routers handle the DSCP field and packet markings are operator-specific. Unless two network operators coordinate and interoperate their DSCP markings, it is difficult to predict end-to-end CoS behavior. A network operator may choose to implement classification and differentiated traffic forwarding within the local network in any manner they find suitable, as long as there are no issues regarding interworking and interoperability with other network providers.

DiffServ defines the concept of a Bandwidth Broker, which is an agent equipped with knowledge of the priorities and policies used by a network operator, allocating bandwidth according to those policies [RFC2638]. To facilitate end-to-end resource allocation across separate DiffServ domains, the Bandwidth Broker managing a particular DiffServ domain must communicate with adjacent Bandwidth Broker peers to enable end-to-end services based on bilateral DiffServ interworking agreements.

Table B.6 provides a summary of the DiffServ classifications for various types of traffic recommended in IETF RFC 4594 [RFC4594]. The intent of the recommendation is to establish a level of consistency among service providers regarding DiffServ traffic classifications and PHBs. DiffServ has become the most commonly used mechanism for implementing QoS in enterprise and service provider networks.

TABLE B.4
Assured Forwarding (AF) Behavior Group

	Class 1	Class 2	Class 3	Class 4
Low drop	AF11 (DSCP 10)	AF21 (DSCP 18)	AF31 (DSCP 26)	AF41 (DSCP 34)
Medium drop	AF12 (DSCP 12)	AF22 (DSCP 20)	AF32 (DSCP 28)	AF42 (DSCP 36)
High drop	AF13 (DSCP 14)	AF23 (DSCP 22)	AF33 (DSCP 30)	AF43 (DSCP 38)

TABLE B.5
Class Selector Values

DSCP	Binary	Decimal ($n \times 8$)	Corresponding IP Precedence (n)
CS0 (Default)	000 000	0	0
CS1	001 000	8	1
CS2	010 000	16	2
CS3	011 000	24	3
CS4	100 000	32	4
CS5	101 000	40	5
CS6	110 000	48	6
CS7	111 000	56	7

TABLE B.6
Recommended DiffServ Markings in RFC 4594

Service Class	DCSP	DSCP Value	Examples
Network control	CS6	48	Routing updates
IP telephony	EF	46	VoIP bearer, VCoIP audio
Signaling	CS5	40	VoIP, VCoIP signaling
Video conferencing	AF41, AF42, AF43	34, 36, 38	VCoIP payload
Real-time interactive	CS4	32	Gaming
Streaming video	AF31, AF32, AF33	26, 28, 30	Internet video
Broadcast video	CS3	24	IP TV
Low-latency data	AF21, AF22, AF23	18, 20, 22	ERP, CRM
OAM	CS2	6	OAM
High-throughput data	AF11, AF12, AF13	10, 12, 14	Bulk data, FTP
Standard	DF (CS0)	0	Other data apps
Low-priority data	CS1	8	Applications with no assured bandwidth

In a DiffServ domain, complex functions such as packet classification, packet marking, and policing are typically carried out at the edge of the network by edge DiffServ-aware routers. Generally, no classification and rate-limiting functions, such as policing, are required in core routers, keeping functionality on these devices simple. Core routers simply apply various DiffServ PHBs to packets based on their markings. The treatment of packets according to the configured PHB is achieved in routers using a combination of queuing and scheduling policies. Core routers are relieved of the complexities associated with enforcing policies or agreements and collecting data for billing purposes. Traffic crossing DiffServ domains may be subjected to the more complex functions of packet (re)classification and rate limiting.

REFERENCES

[RFC791]   IETF RFC 791, "Internet Protocol", *IETF RFC 791*, September 1981.
[RFC792]   J. Postel, "Internet Control Message Protocol", *IETF RFC 792*, September 1981.
[RFC950]   J. Mogul and J. Postel, "Internet Standard Subnetting Procedure", *IETF RFC 950*, August 1985.
[RFC1122]   R. Braden, Ed., "Requirements for Internet Hosts - Communication Layers", *IETF RFC 1122*, October 1989.
[RFC1191]   J. Mogul and S. Deering, "Path MTU Discovery", *IETF RFC 1191*, November 1990.
[RFC1349]   P. Almquist, "Type of Service in the Internet Protocol Suite", *IETF RFC 1349*, July 1992.
[RFC1517]   R. Hinden, Ed., "Applicability Statement for the Implementation of Classless Inter-Domain Routing (CIDR)", *IETF RFC 1517*, September 1993.
[RFC1518]   Y. Rekhter and T. Li, "An Architecture for IP Address Allocation with CIDR", *IETF RFC 1518*, September 1993.
[RFC1519]   V. Fuller, T. Li, J. Yu, and K. Varadhan, "Classless Inter-Domain Routing (CIDR): An Address Assignment and Aggregation Strategy", *IETF RFC 1519*, September 1993.
[RFC1633]   R. Braden, D. Clark, and S. Shenker, "Integrated Services in the Internet Architecture: An Overview", *IETF RFC 1633*, June 1994.
[RFC1878]   T. Pummill and B. Manning, "Variable Length Subnet Table for IPv4", *IETF RFC 1878*, December 1995.
[RFC1918]   Y. Rekhter, B. Moskowitz, D. Karrenberg, G. J. de Groot, and E. Lear, "Address Allocation for Private Internets", *IETF RFC 1918*, February 1996.
[RFC2474]   K. Nichols, S. Blake, F. Baker, and D. Black, "Definition of the Differentiated Services Field (DS Field) in the IPv4 and IPv6 Headers", *IETF RFC 2474*, December 1998.
[RFC2475], S. Blake, D. Black, M. Carlson, E. Davies, Z. Wang, and W. Weiss, "An Architecture for Differentiated Services", *IETF RFC 2475*, December 1998.
[RFC2638]   K. Nichols, V. Jacobson, and L. Zhang, "A Two-bit Differentiated Services Architecture for the Internet", *IETF RFC 2638*, July 1999.

[RFC2597]   J. Heinanen, F. Baker, W. Weiss, and J. Wroclawski, "Assured Forwarding PHB Group", *IETF RFC 2597*, June 1999.

[RFC2893]   R. Gilligan and E. Nordmark, "Transition Mechanisms for IPv6 Hosts and Routers", *IETF RFC 2893*, August 2000.

[RFC3021]   A. Retana, R. White, V. Fuller, and D. McPherson, "Using 31-Bit Prefixes on IPv4 Point-to-Point Links", *IETF RFC 3021*, December 2000.

[RFC3140]   D. Black, S. Brim, B. Carpenter, and F. Le Faucheur, "Per Hop Behavior Identification Codes", *IETF RFC 3140*, June 2001.

[RFC3168]   K. Ramakrishnan, S. Floyd, and D. Black, "The Addition of Explicit Congestion Notification (ECN) to IP", *IETF RFC 3168*, September 2001.

[RFC3246]   B. Davie, A. Charny, J.C.R. Bennett, K. Benson, J.Y. Le Boudec, W. Courtney, S. Davari, V. Firoiu, and D. Stiliadis, "An Expedited Forwarding PHB (Per-Hop Behavior)", *IETF RFC 3246*, March 2002.

[RFC3260]   D. Grossman, "New Terminology and Clarifications for Diffserv", *IETF RFC 3260*, April 2002.

[RFC3927]   S. Cheshire, B. Aboba, and E. Guttman, "Dynamic Configuration of IPv4 Link-Local Addresses", *IETF RFC 3927*, May 2005.

[RFC4594]   J. Babiarz and F. Baker, "Configuration Guidelines for DiffServ Service Classes", *IETF RFC 4594*, August 2006.

[RFC4632]   V. Fuller and T. Li, "Classless Inter-Domain Routing (CIDR): The Internet Address Assignment and Aggregation Plan", *IETF RFC 4632*, August 2006.

[RFC5771]   M. Cotton, L. Vegoda, and D. Meyer, "IANA Guidelines for IPv4 Multicast Address Assignments", *IETF RFC 5771*, March 2010.

[RFC5865]   F. Baker, J. Polk, and M. Dolly, "A Differentiated Services Code Point (DSCP) for Capacity-Admitted Traffic", *IETF RFC 5865*, May 2010.

[RFC6890]   M. Cotton, L. Vegoda, R. Bonica, Ed., and B. Haberman, "Special-Purpose IP Address Registries", *IETF RFC 6890*, April 2013.

[RFC7059]   S. Steffann, I. van Beijnum, and R. van Rein, "A Comparison of IPv6-over-IPv4 Tunnel Mechanisms", *IETF RFC 7059*, November 2013.

Appendix C
Address Resolution Protocol (ARP) for IPv4

C.1 INTRODUCTION

IPv4 ARP **[RFC826]** provides a mechanism for discovering the Media Access Control (MAC) address associated with an IPv4 address. ARP enables an IPv4 host to obtain the MAC address associated with a specified IPv4 address on the local network, allowing the host to send IPv4 packets to the owner of that IPv4 address (i.e., the target node). The source host broadcasts an ARP Request containing the target's IPv4 address, and the target replies with its MAC address in an ARP Reply. The source node can then encapsulate any IPv4 packets destined for the target node in Ethernet frames with the destination MAC address being the target node's provided MAC address.

C.2 HOW ARP WORKS

ARP is a request–response protocol in which ARP messages are directly encapsulated in Ethernet frames and transmitted within the boundaries of a single subnet or VLAN; such messages are never routed. The Proxy ARP and Gratuitous ARP features discussed in **Appendices D and E** are special use cases of ARP. Given that ARP works directly over Ethernet (the Link-Layer), the Ethernet EtherType of 0x0806 (in hexadecimal) is used to identify an Ethernet frame containing an ARP message. Note that the EtherType of 0x0800 indicates that an Ethernet frame contains an IPv4 packet. The EtherType for IPv6 is 0x86DD.

However, it should be noted that ARP **[RFC826]** is only meant for resolving IPv4 addresses to corresponding MAC addresses; the Sender and Target Protocol Address fields in all ARP messages are 4 bytes (32 bits) long. The IPv6 counterpart of ARP is the Neighbor Discovery Protocol **[RFC4861]** described in **Chapter 4**. Figure C.1 shows the structure of the Ethernet frame with an ARP message. The payload of the Ethernet frame contains ARP information consisting of four addresses: the hardware (MAC) and protocol (IP) addresses of the message sender and receiver.

The ARP message header specifies the Operation Code (OpCode) for the ARP message type; ARP Request has a value of 1, and ARP Reply has a value of 2. The ARP message payload (for Ethernet operations) consists of four addresses: the MAC and IPv4 addresses of the sender and receiver. In Figure C.2, four IPv4 hosts are connected to the same network segment with no intervening gateway or router. Host 1 has an IPv4 packet that it needs to send to IPv4 address the 172.16.10.33, which happens to be the IPv4 address of Host 3. However, Host 1 needs the MAC address associated with 172.16.10.33 so that it can encapsulate the IPv4 packet destined for Host 3 on the local network.

Host 1 broadcasts an Ethernet frame containing an ARP Request message on the local network segment (172.16.10/24) addressed to the well-known Ethernet broadcast MAC address FF-FF-FF-FF-FF-FF, requesting a response from any local IPv4 node with the IPv4 address 172.16.10.33. The ARP Request message contains the following information:

- Sender MAC Address = 00-AA-00-11-11-11 (Host 1's MAC address)
- Sender IPv4 Address = 172.16.10.11 (Host 1's IPv4 address)
- Target MAC Address = 00-00-00-00-00-00 (Unknown/Unspecified MAC address)
- Target IPv4 Address = 172.16.10.33 (Host 3's IPv4 address)

DOI: 10.1201/9781003710646-9

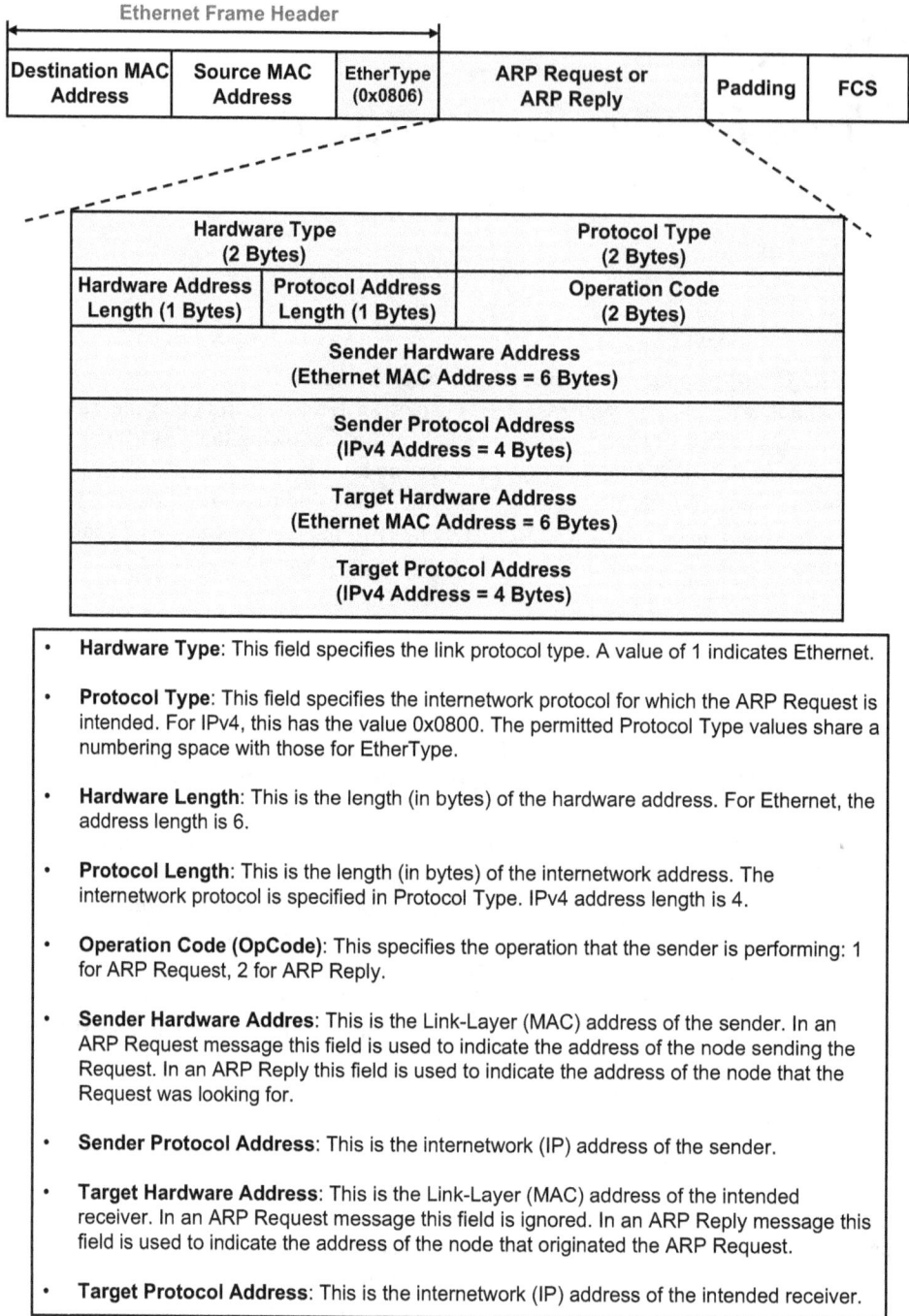

- **Hardware Type**: This field specifies the link protocol type. A value of 1 indicates Ethernet.

- **Protocol Type**: This field specifies the internetwork protocol for which the ARP Request is intended. For IPv4, this has the value 0x0800. The permitted Protocol Type values share a numbering space with those for EtherType.

- **Hardware Length**: This is the length (in bytes) of the hardware address. For Ethernet, the address length is 6.

- **Protocol Length**: This is the length (in bytes) of the internetwork address. The internetwork protocol is specified in Protocol Type. IPv4 address length is 4.

- **Operation Code (OpCode)**: This specifies the operation that the sender is performing: 1 for ARP Request, 2 for ARP Reply.

- **Sender Hardware Addres**: This is the Link-Layer (MAC) address of the sender. In an ARP Request message this field is used to indicate the address of the node sending the Request. In an ARP Reply this field is used to indicate the address of the node that the Request was looking for.

- **Sender Protocol Address**: This is the internetwork (IP) address of the sender.

- **Target Hardware Address**: This is the Link-Layer (MAC) address of the intended receiver. In an ARP Request message this field is ignored. In an ARP Reply message this field is used to indicate the address of the node that originated the ARP Request.

- **Target Protocol Address**: This is the internetwork (IP) address of the intended receiver.

FIGURE C.1 Ethernet frame with ARP message.

All IPv4 nodes on that network segment receive the message, but only Host 3 replies since it is the owner of the requested IPv4 address. Host 3 responds with an ARP Reply message containing its MAC address (00-AA-00-33-33-33), which Host 1 receives. The ARP Reply message contains the following information:

- Sender MAC Address=00-AA-00-33-33-33 (Host 3's MAC address)
- Sender IPv4 Address=172.16.10.33 (Host 3's IPv4 address)

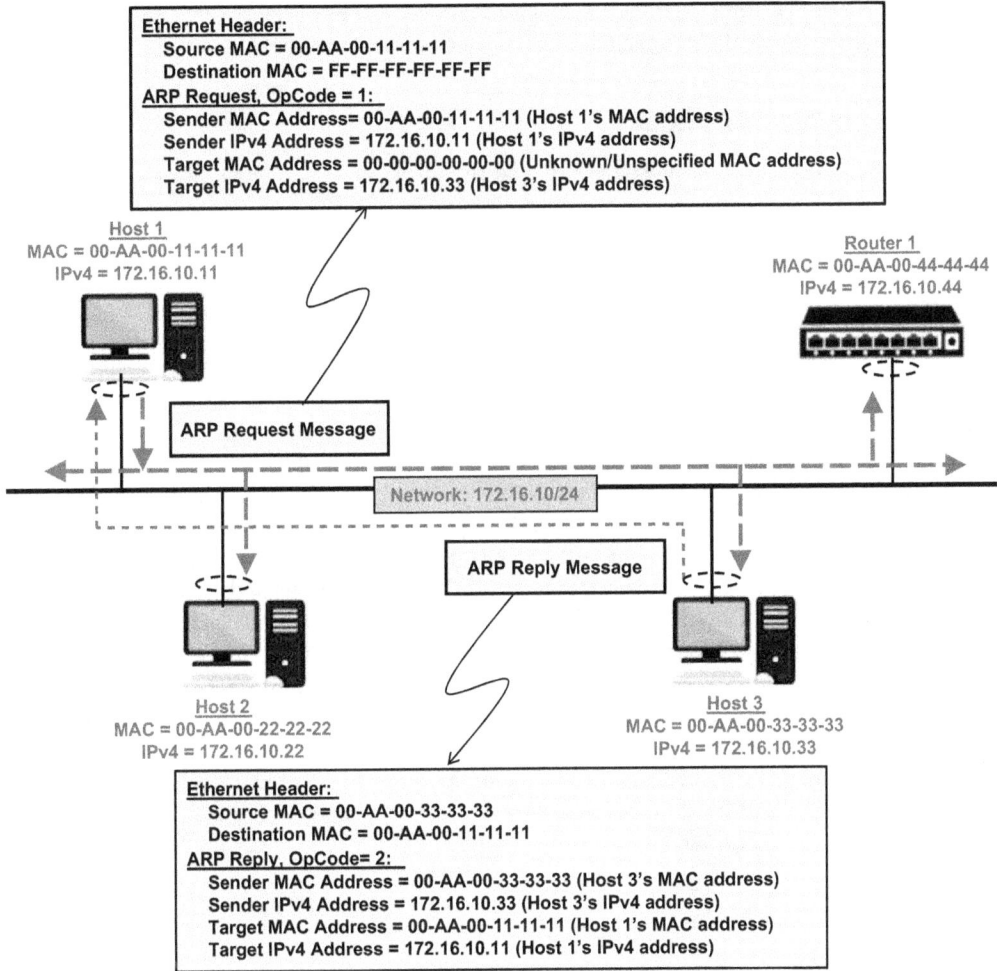

FIGURE C.2   Address Resolution in IPv4.

- Target MAC Address=00-AA-00-11-11-11 (Host 1's MAC address)
- Target IPv4 Address=172.16.10.11 (Host 1's IPv4 address)

An ARP Reply is always unicast to the node that sent the original ARP Request. Host 1 is now able to send IPv4 packets encapsulated in Ethernet frames on the link and addressed to Host 3's MAC address.

Typically, an IPv4 node maintains an ARP Cache that associates IPv4 and MAC addresses. In Figure C.2, Host 1 first looks up its local ARP Cache for a matching entry, so it does not have to broadcast an ARP Request if an entry exists. Additionally, when Host 3 receives Host 1's ARP Request, it caches the IPv4 and MAC address mapping (in its local ARP Cache), so that when it needs to send an IPv4 packet to Host 1 later, it does not have to send an ARP Request to find Host 1's MAC address. Additionally, when Host 1 receives the ARP Reply from Host 3, it caches the IPv4 and MAC address mapping for future IPv4 packets to be sent to Host 3's IPv4 address.

All IPv4 host operating systems have ARP Caches, allowing a host to first check the Cache to see if an IPv4-to-MAC address mapping entry has already been created for a target node. An ARP Cache has limited size, meaning that older unutilized entries have to be purged regularly to free up space for newer entries. Typically, address mapping entries tend to stay in the Cache for only a few minutes and must be purged regularly to make space. Stale entries (i.e., unutilized address mappings) are deleted during the ARP Cache purging process. For purging stale entries, each entry in the ARP Cache is typically assigned an Aging Time or ARP Timeout.

C.3   WHAT IS AN ARP PROBE?

An ARP Probe in IPv4 is an ARP Request that an IPv4 host sends with the following information:

- Sender MAC Address=MAC address of the sending host
- Sender IPv4 Address=all 0s
- Target MAC Address=all 0s
- Target IPv4 Address=IPv4 address being probed.

If any other IPv4 host on the network segment receives this ARP Request and sees that the IPv4 address (in the Target IPv4 Address field of the ARP Request) is its own address, it will respond with an ARP Reply about the received ARP Probe, informing the Probe's sender of the IPv4 address conflict; the ARP Reply is sent to the Sender MAC Address of the probing host.

If, on the other hand, no host on the network segment replies to indicate that the Target IPv4 Address in the ARP Probe is its own, and after several such Probes have been sent (separated by small random delays), then the sender of the ARP Probe can conclude that the Target IPv4 Address has no conflict. Since the original ARP Probe message contains neither a valid Sender MAC Address/Sender IPv4 Address pair (only a Sender MAC Address) nor a valid Target MAC Address/Target IPv4 Address pair (only a Target IPv4 Address), this eliminates the risk of any host on the network segment using the ARP Probe information to update its ARP Cache with potentially invalid information. It is best practice for an IPv4 node to first check if the Target IPv4 Address is already in use before using that address (whether configured manually or through DHCP) in outgoing IPv4 packets. The host must first ensure IPv4 address uniqueness by broadcasting ARP Probe messages on the network.

REFERENCES

[RFC826].   D. C. Plummer, "An Ethernet Address Resolution Protocol", *IETF RFC 826*, November 1982.
[RFC4861]. T. Narten, E. Nordmark, W. Simpson, and H. Soliman, "Neighbor Discovery for IP version 6 (IPv6)", IETF RFC 4861, September 2007.

Appendix D
Gratuitous ARP for IPv4

D.1   INTRODUCTION

ARP for IPv4 **[RFC826]**, as discussed in **Appendix C**, involves resolving an IPv4 address to its corresponding MAC address. ARP is a protocol that allows IPv4 nodes to map the IPv4 addresses of other nodes on the same network segment (IP subnet or Virtual LAN) to their respective MAC addresses. In practice, each IPv4 node maintains a mapping table (called the ARP Cache or table), which indicates the MAC address of a node and its corresponding IPv4 address.

Gratuitous ARP is a mechanism for an IPv4 node on a network segment to announce or update its IPv4-to-MAC address mapping. IPv4 nodes also use Gratuitous ARP **[RFC5227]** to detect duplicate IPv4 addresses on a network segment. The Gratuitous ARP mechanism is the IPv4 equivalent of the IPv6 Duplicate Address Detection function of the Neighbor Discovery protocol described in **Chapter 4** (specified in **[RFC4861]**).

D.2   GRATUITOUS ARP MECHANISM

A Gratuitous ARP message is a special type of ARP message. Specifically, a Gratuitous ARP message is an ARP message in which the sending host includes its own ARP mapping (MAC address and corresponding IPv4 address) and broadcasts the message on the local network segment without any other node requesting it. Gratuitous ARP serves as an address announcement protocol. IPv4 hosts on the network may use the address information announced to update their IPv4-to-MAC address mapping in the ARP Cache when the sender's IPv4 address or MAC address changes.

A Gratuitous ARP message could be sent as a Gratuitous ARP Request or Gratuitous ARP Reply:

- **Gratuitous ARP Request**: This is an ARP Request message whose source and destination IPv4 addresses are both set to the IPv4 address of the host issuing the message, and the destination MAC address of the Ethernet frame is the broadcast MAC address FF:FF:FF:FF:FF:FF. *In this message, the Sender IPv4 Address is the same as the Target IPv4 Address, but the Target MAC Address is set to zero.* Ordinarily, no ARP Reply message will be sent in response to the ARP Request.
- **Gratuitous ARP Reply**: This is a message for which no corresponding ARP Request was issued; a node can send an unsolicited Gratuitous ARP Reply message on its own. A Gratuitous ARP Reply is not prompted by the receipt of an ARP Request. *In this message, the Sender IPv4 Address is set equal to the Target IPv4 Address, and the Sender MAC Address is also set equal to the Target MAC Address.*

Both Gratuitous ARP Request and ARP Reply messages are acceptable ways of address announcements, but the ARP Request method is usually preferred. An IPv4 host may be configured to use either of these two types of announcing addresses. Gratuitous ARP announcements are not intended to solicit an ARP Reply; instead, hosts may use the addressing information contained in them to update their ARP Cache entries. The Operation Code (OpCode) in the Gratuitous ARP announcement may indicate if the message is either an ARP Request or ARP Reply (see **Figure C.1 in Appendix C**).

Many operating systems allow a host to issue a Gratuitous ARP announcement during startup. This helps the starting host resolve addressing problems that would otherwise occur if, for example, the network card on the host was recently changed (creating a change in the IPv4 address-to-MAC address mapping), and other hosts on the network are still using the old address mapping in their ARP Caches.

An IPv4 node sends a Gratuitous ARP Request as a broadcast looking for its own IPv4 address. If an IPv4 node sends an ARP Request for its own IPv4 address and receives no ARP Reply, it concludes that the IPv4 address is not being used by any other node. However, if an ARP Reply is received, the requesting node concludes that the IPv4 address is already being used by another node on the network segment (this is equivalent to the IPv6 Duplicate Address Detection mechanism discussed in **Chapter 4**).

A Gratuitous ARP Reply is an ARP Reply message sent to the broadcast MAC address, with the Target IPv4 Address field in the message set to the same address in the Sender IPv4 Address field. When an IPv4 node receives a Gratuitous ARP Reply, it can insert an entry for that reply in its ARP Cache. *In both Gratuitous ARP Request and Reply messages, the Sender IPv4 Address and the Target IPv4 Address fields are both set to the IPv4 address of the issuing node.*

An IPv4 node sends Gratuitous ARP (Request or Reply) messages for the following purposes:

- **Duplicate IPv4 Address Detection**: This is to determine whether the sender's IPv4 address is already being used by another IPv4 node. If the IPv4 address is already in use, the sender of the Gratuitous ARP message will be informed through an ARP Reply about the address conflict.
- **Update ARP Cache Mapping When the MAC Address of an Interface Changes**: This is to inform other IPv4 nodes on the local network segment about a change in its MAC address so that they can update their ARP Cache entries. This might happen (although rarely) if the MAC address on an IPv6 node is manually modified (network adapter change) but the host retains the same IPv4 address. The host now has a new MAC address; therefore, the ARP Cache mapping on all the nodes on the network segment, which are communicating with this host, must be updated.

D.3 GRATUITOUS ARP USE CASES

IPv4 Gratuitous ARP has a number of use cases, including the following:

1. **Configuring an IPv4 Node to Learn Gratuitous ARP Messages**: If an IPv4 node is configured to learn Gratuitous ARP messages, upon receiving one, it adds the sender's IPv4 and MAC addresses contained in the message to its ARP Cache if no corresponding ARP entry exists. If a corresponding ARP entry exists, the node updates the ARP Cache entry. If this feature is disabled, the address information in the Gratuitous ARP messages that the IPv4 node receives may be used to update existing ARP Cache entries only, but not to create new ARP entries. An IPv4 node can use Gratuitous ARP to announce its presence on a network segment.
2. **Configuring an IPv4 Node to Send Periodic Gratuitous ARP Messages**: Sending periodic Gratuitous ARP messages enables downstream nodes to update their corresponding ARP Cache entries or MAC entries more quickly. A network administrator can use this feature for the following purposes:
   - **Prevent Gateway Spoofing**: When an attacker transmits forged Gratuitous ARP messages to IPv6 hosts on a network segment, traffic sent by genuine hosts on the network segment to the gateway would instead be sent to the attacker. This can lead to the hosts being unable to access external networks. To prevent such gateway spoofing attacks, the gateway can be configured to transmit Gratuitous ARP messages at

specific intervals containing its primary IPv4 address and any manually configured secondary IPv4 addresses. This allows each IPv4 host on the segment to learn the correct gateway address information.

- **Prevent ARP Cache Entries from Aging Out**: During periods of heavy network traffic or when a host's CPU usage is high, the host may discard or not process received ARP messages in time. Eventually, the dynamic ARP Cache entries maintained by the host will age out, and traffic between the host and the corresponding IPv4 nodes on the network segment will be interrupted until the host recreates the ARP Cache entries. To avoid this problem, the gateway can be configured to transmit periodic Gratuitous ARP messages. These messages sent by the gateway contain its primary IPv4 address or one of its manually configured secondary IPv4 addresses. This allows the receiving hosts to update ARP Cache entries on time and thus ensure continuous traffic flow.

REFERENCES

[RFC826].   D. C. Plummer, "An Ethernet Address Resolution Protocol", *IETF RFC 826*, November 1982.
[RFC4861].   T. Narten, E. Nordmark, W. Simpson, and H. Soliman, "Neighbor Discovery for IP Version 6 (IPv6)", *IETF RFC 4861*, September 2007.
[RFC5227].   S. Cheshire, "IPv4 Address Conflict Detection", *IETF RFC 5227*, July 2008.

Appendix E
Proxy ARP for IPv4

E.1 INTRODUCTION

Proxy ARP in IPv4 is the process by which an IPv4 node, usually a router, answers ARP queries (ARP Requests) received on a network segment (subnet/VLAN) on behalf of another node not on that network segment. The Proxy ARP device answers ARP queries for the MAC address corresponding to a target IPv4 address that is not on that network **[RFC1027]**. The Proxy is aware of the actual location of the queried IPv4 address and node, and offers its own MAC address in place of the target node's IPv4 address. IPv4 traffic directed to the queried IPv4 address is then typically forwarded by the Proxy ARP device to the intended IPv4 destination through one of its other interfaces or via a tunnel. The IPv6 Proxy Neighbor Discovery functionality described in **Chapter 4** is the IPv6 equivalent of Proxy ARP for IPv4 (see also **[RFC4389]**).

Proxy ARP allows IPv4 hosts on an IPv4 subnet/VLAN to reach hosts on remote subnets/VLANs without the need for configuring IPv4 routing or a default gateway. One use case of Proxy ARP is when the Home Agent in Mobile IP receives IPv4 packets on a network segment on behalf of a Mobile Node that is visiting a Foreign Network and tunnels the packets to the actual Home IPv4 Address of that Mobile Node (using the Care-of IPv4 Address assigned to the Mobile Node by the Foreign Network). The Care-of IPv4 Address forms the outer IPv4 address of the tunneled IPv4 packet whose IPv4 header contains the Mobile Node's Home IPv4 Address. Mobile IP is discussed in detail in **Chapter 6**.

E.2 HOW IPv4 PROXY ARP WORKS

Each IPv4 host on an Ethernet LAN uses ARP to map IPv4 addresses to their corresponding Ethernet MAC addresses (see **Appendix C**). Each host maintains an ARP Cache that contains the mapping of MAC addresses to IP addresses. A host consults this mapping in its ARP Cache when forwarding IPv6 packets to other hosts. If a host finds that the ARP Cache does not contain a MAC address entry for a destination IPv4 address, it broadcasts an ARP Request for that host's MAC address and stores the response in the ARP Cache.

Note that ARP broadcasts are not propagated across IP routers and between hosts on different network segments. This means a host will not receive a response to its ARP Request if the destination is on a different subnet/VLAN or on an isolated segment in the same VLAN (see **Appendix F**). A Proxy ARP device allows the hosts to transparently communicate with each other through it. The most common use case is to deploy Proxy ARP to enable IPv4 hosts on one subnet/VLAN to reach remote subnets/VLANs without configuring IPv4 routing or a default gateway.

In Figure E.1, Host 1 (172.16.10.11/16) on IPv4 Subnet 172.16.10/24 needs to send IPv4 packets to Host 4 (172.16.20.44/24) on Subnet 172.16.20/24. *Note that Host 1 is configured with a /16 IPv4 subnet mask.* Because Host 1 has the same IPv4 subnet prefix (/16), it believes that it is directly connected to all of IPv4 network 172.16.0.0/16. When Host 1 needs to communicate with any IPv4 host it sees as directly connected to its subnet, it sends an ARP Request to that target host. Therefore, Host 1 sends an ARP Request broadcast to Host 4, requesting its MAC address and believing that Host 4 is directly connected. The ARP Request contains the following information:

- Sender MAC Address=00-AA-00-11-11-11 (Host 1's MAC address)
- Sender IPv4 Address=172.16.10.11 (Host 1's IPv4 address)

DOI: 10.1201/9781003710646-11

- Target MAC Address=00-00-00-00-00-00 (Unknown/Unspecified MAC address)
- Target IPv4 Address=172.16.20.44 (Host 4's IPv4 address)

Host 1 encapsulates the ARP Request in an Ethernet frame with the MAC address of Host 1 as the source MAC address, and the destination MAC address set to the broadcast address (FFFF.FFFF. FFFF). Since the ARP Request is an Ethernet broadcast frame, it reaches all nodes in IPv4 subnet 172.16.10/24, which includes Port 1 of Router 1, but does not reach Host 4. The Ethernet broadcast frame does not reach Host 4 because routers, by default, do not forward broadcasts.

Since Router 1 is aware that the target IPv4 address (172.16.20.44) is on another subnet (172.16.20/24) and can reach Host 4, it replies with its own MAC address to Host 1 in a Proxy ARP Reply message:

- Sender MAC Address=00-AA-00--66-66-66 (MAC address of Port 1 of Router 1)
- Sender IPv4 Address=172.16.20.44 (Host 4's IPv4 address)
- Target MAC Address=00-AA-00-11-11-11 (Host 1's MAC address)
- Target IPv4 Address=172.16.10.11 (Host 1's IPv4 address)

The Proxy ARP Reply that Router 1 sends to Host 1 is encapsulated in an Ethernet frame with MAC address of Port 1 of Router 1 as the source MAC address, and the MAC address of Host 1 as the destination MAC address. The ARP Reply messages are always unicast to the node that sent the original ARP Request. Upon receiving this ARP Reply, Host 1 updates its ARP Cache as follows:

- IPv4 Address=172.16.20.44 (Host 4's IPv4 address)
- MAC Address=00-AA-00--66-66-66 (MAC address of Port 1 of Router 1)

From now on, Host 1 forwards all IPv4 packets addressed to 172.16.20.44 (Host 4) to the Port 1 MAC address 00-AA-00--66-66-66 (of Router 1). Since Router 1 knows how to reach Host 4, it forwards the IPv4 packet to Host 4. Also, the ARP Caches of all IPv4 hosts on IPv4 subnet 172.16.10/24 are populated with the MAC address of Port 1 of Router 1 for communication with all hosts on IPv4 subnet 172.16.20/24. Host 1 and all hosts on its subnet see Port 1 of Router 1 as the owner of Host 4's IPv4 address (172.16.20.44). Hence, all IPv4 packets destined for Host 4's subnet

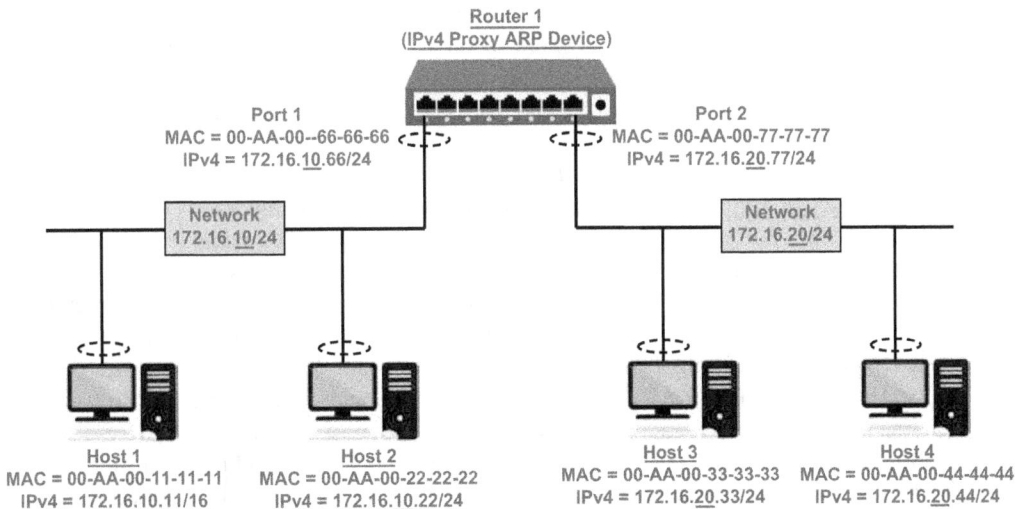

FIGURE E.1   IPv4 Proxy ARP use case.

(172.16.20/24) are sent to Router 1 to be forwarded to IPv4 hosts on that subnet. Router 1 acts as a relay for communication between hosts on the two IPv4 subnets.

The ARP Cache of Host 1 is as follows:

IPv4 Address	MAC Address
172.16.20.44	00-AA-00--66-66-66
172.16.20.33	00-AA-00--66-66-66
172.16.10.66	00-AA-00--66-66-66
172.16.10.22	00-AA-00--22-22-22

E.3   ADVANTAGES AND DISADVANTAGES OF IPv4 PROXY ARP

The main advantage of IPv4 Proxy ARP is that it can be configured on a single IPv4 router on a network segment without disturbing the IPv4 routing tables of the other routers on the network. However, Proxy ARP must be used only on network segments where IPv4 hosts do not have any routing intelligence (i.e., no routing protocols running) or are not configured with an IPv4 default gateway.

The main advantages of Proxy ARP include the following:

- Enables an IPv4 node to respond to ARP queries for MAC addresses by offering its own MAC address.
- Enables an IPv4 node to act as a Proxy ARP device, allowing IPv4 hosts to transparently communicate with each other through the Proxy.
- Enables IPv4 hosts on one IPv4 subnet/VLAN to communicate with remote subnets/ VLANs without having to configure routing or a default gateway.

The disadvantages of Proxy ARP include the following:

- Proxy ARP can undermine network security; an IPv4 host can claim to be another host in order to intercept IPv4 packets sent to that host. The network is vulnerable to ARP spoofing (also known as ARP Cache poisoning) attacks, where malicious devices can impersonate IPv4 hosts and a Proxy ARP device. A malicious device impersonating a Proxy ARP device can intercept or modify IPv4 traffic between hosts by sending out fake ARP messages on a target LAN. Particularly, because ARP does not have mechanisms for authenticating ARP Reply messages on a network segment, ARP Reply messages can be created by IPv4 hosts other than the target host with the required MAC address.
- It increases the amount of ARP traffic on a network segment due to many ARP Requests and Reply messages.
- IPv4 hosts need to maintain larger ARP Caches (because the Proxy ARP device interfaces have to be included) in order to handle IP-to-MAC address mappings.
- Proxy ARP does not generalize to all IPv4 network topologies; for example, it cannot be used where more than one IPv4 router connects two physical networks.
- Proxy ARP can be vulnerable to Denial-of-Service (DoS) attacks because the Proxy ARP device has the ability to receive IPv4 packets destined for other IPv4 hosts on other network segments (by offering its own MAC address in response to ARP Requests for other hosts). However, the Proxy ARP device may not have enough processing power to handle genuine ARP packets as well as IPv4 packets from other hosts in the face of a DoS attack and forward those genuine packets to their final destinations, thus blackholing the received IPv4 packets. Attackers can use DoS attacks to overwhelm the Proxy ARP device.
- Scalability in address resolution using Proxy ARP can be an issue since ARP queries routed in this manner can tax or overwhelm the Proxy ARP device.

- Reliability in address resolution can also be an issue since no fallback mechanism is present when the Proxy ARP functionality does not work.
- Proxy ARP can hide IPv6 host misconfigurations on a network segment, such as a missing or incorrect default gateway.
- Proxy ARP may introduce inconsistencies and confusion about the understanding of the topology of a network; it may make the IPv4 addressing scheme unclear and may conceal the actual locations and identities of IPv4 hosts.

Being a system that answers ARP Requests on behalf of another IPv4, a Proxy ARP device is vulnerable to ARP spoofing attacks. In ARP spoofing, the spoofer sends ARP Replies upon receiving an ARP Request for another host's MAC address, with the aim of intercepting traffic bound for that host. A malicious user may use ARP spoofing to perform DoS or a man-in-the-middle attack on other users on a network. It is not hard these days to find freely available amateur software that can both detect and perform ARP spoofing attacks, although ARP itself was not designed to provide any mechanisms for protecting against such attacks.

REFERENCES

[RFC1027]. S. Carl-Mitchell and J. S. Quarterman, "Using ARP to Implement Transparent Subnet Gateways", *IETF RFC 1027*, October 1987.

[RFC4389]. D. Thaler, M. Talwar, and C. Patel, "Neighbor Discovery Proxies (ND Proxy)", *IETF RFC 4389*, April 2006.

Appendix F
Private VLANs and Port Isolation

F.1 INTRODUCTION

In general, Port Isolation is a method used to restrict specific ports on the same Layer 2 switch from communicating with one another. Devices connected to Layer 2 switch ports that have Port Isolation enabled are unable to communicate with each other. These switch ports can still communicate with non-isolated switch ports. Isolated Ports can only communicate with each other through a special port called the Promiscuous Port. A Private VLAN (using the concept of Port Isolation) is a method that allows certain switch ports in a VLAN to be restricted to only communicate with other switch ports on a given Uplink (called the Promiscuous Port). These restricted switch ports are also sometimes called Private Ports in the context of the Private VLAN. The different types of restricted or Private Ports are described in a section below.

Simply put, a Private VLAN is a mechanism for limiting communication within a single VLAN, which is itself a restricted Layer 2 broadcast domain. In a Private VLAN, traffic flow is restricted to member switch ports (Private Ports), and these ports can communicate only with specified ports or with a specified Uplink Port within the same VLAN. This is achieved by applying special Layer 2 forwarding constraints (filters and access control lists (ACLs)) on the restricted ports.

The traditional VLAN is configured to create a restricted Layer 2 broadcast domain, where switch ports operate to limit Layer 2 broadcast traffic to only that domain. However, in scenarios where hosts belonging to the same VLAN are restricted from communicating with one another, Port Isolation (within a Private VLAN) becomes a useful tool. A Private VLAN is typically configured to have many Private Ports and a single Uplink. The Uplink is typically, a single switch port (or a logical port (Link Aggregation Group) based on IEEE 802.3ad Link Aggregation technology, now IEEE 802.1AX) connected to an IP router, server, firewall, gateway to a service provider network or to a centralized resource.

The concept of Private VLANs was introduced primarily to address the limitation on the number of VLANs (using the single VLAN tagging scheme) that can be created on a network, a limit that can quickly be exceeded when a large number of VLANs need to be deployed on a network. Particularly, when there is a need to create multiple segregated Layer 2 domains/regions within a given VLAN (given the scalability limitations of the single-tag VLAN technology), Private VLANs provide an effective solution.

The 12-bit VLAN ID field in a single-tag Ethernet frame allows a network to support only a theoretical maximum of 4,094 VLANs (noting that VLAN numbers 0 and 4,095 are reserved). If a network administrator assigns one VLAN per user using the single-tag Ethernet VLAN technology, then the network can only support a maximum of 4,094 users. Additionally, assigning a separate VLAN per user potentially leads to wastage of IP addresses since each VLAN is usually associated (in practice) with a separate IP subnet. The use of Private VLANs offers a granular and flexible approach for Layer 2 network segregation when the available IP address space is limited.

Table F.1 presents the main differences between traditional VLANs and Private VLANs. The main features of Private VLANs are the following:

- Switches in a Private VLAN will not forward Layer 2 traffic (unicast, multicast, or broadcast) between switch ports that are configured as protected. Data traffic exchanged between the protected ports must be routed via a Layer 3 device.

DOI: 10.1201/9781003710646-12

- Control traffic, such as IP routing protocol updates, is not subject to restriction (it is exempt) and will be forwarded between protected ports.
- Traffic forwarding behavior between a protected switch port and a nonprotected switch port is conducted normally according to the default Layer 2 forwarding behavior.

F.2   PRIVATE VLAN USE CASES

Private VLANs allow a network administrator to implement a higher level of network isolation and access control in a Layer 2 network domain without using advanced Layer 3 and upper-layer isolation and security techniques, making them suitable for many networking environments. A Private VLAN provides Layer 2 isolation between switch ports within a single VLAN by dividing the VLAN into multiple discrete broadcast subdomains. The benefits of Private VLANs can be summarized as follows:

- **Simplified Network Configuration**: Private VLANs allow a network administrator to simplify network configuration and reduce the number of VLANs needed without resorting to complex network segregation techniques. Compared to traditional VLANs, the use of Private VLANs provides a simple, yet efficient method of creating smaller Layer 2 subdomains with greater isolation and control features within a single VLAN, eliminating the need for configuring numerous VLANs to meet the different isolation requirements of users.
- **IP Address Conservation**: The use of Private VLANs allows a network to conserve the available pool of IP addresses. Since Secondary VLANs share the same IP subnet as the Parent/Primary VLAN in which they are created, a network will require fewer IP addresses to meet the needs of multiple devices, thereby conserving IP address usage.
- **Security**: A network administrator can configure a Private VLAN on a network to restrict communication between hosts and reduce potential attack surfaces. By assigning hosts to Secondary VLANs or Isolated Ports, direct communication between hosts can be limited, thereby increasing network security. An organization may configure a dedicated Private VLAN to separate a part of the network that contains high-value or sensitive information from the rest of the organization's network.
- **Flexibility**: A Private VLAN allows multiple Secondary VLANs to be created within a single VLAN, with different communication permissions and access conditions assigned

TABLE F.1
Traditional VLANs versus Private VLANs

	Traditional VLAN	**Private VLAN**
Protocol layer	VLAN is a broadcast domain and operates at Layer 2. Inter-VLAN communication is done at Layer 3.	Private VLAN is a subdomain within a VLAN. It is an intra-VLAN segmentation method that operates at Layer 2. Inter-Private Port communication is done at Layer 3.
Criteria for network segmentation	A network can be segmented into multiple VLANs, each belonging to a different IP subnet.	Different Private VLANs within a larger VLAN belong to the same IP subnet (the IP subnet of the larger VLAN).
Network span	A VLAN can span multiple switches.	Private VLAN can span multiple switches.
Application	Has general Layer 2 application space.	Private VLANs are only necessary for specific requirements, where certain switch ports within a single VLAN are restricted and not allowed to communicate with each other.

to each Secondary VLAN. Through this, network administrators can configure granular access control and fine-grained isolation and security features for different hosts or host groups according their requirements, providing greater flexibility in network control.

The remainder of this section discusses some typical use cases of Private VLANs.

F.2.1 Network Segregation

This use case of Private VLANs is to simplify IP address assignment in a network using mainly Layer 2 techniques. A Layer 2 network can be configured into a segregated Layer 2 network without the need for changing the current IP addressing of hosts in the network. Hosts can be assigned to various Secondary VLANs without changing their IP addresses. The network administrator does not need to use new IP subnet prefixes because a Private VLAN allows all of its Secondary VLANs to share the same IP subnet prefix. The use of Isolated VLANs allows an endless number of segregated Layer 2 domains to be created within the same VLAN.

In this use case, switch ports are configured to be isolated from each other at Layer 2 (e.g., using appropriate port filters and ACLs, mainly for security or performance reasons), while allowing all those isolated switch ports to still belong to the same IP subnet/VLAN. In such cases, IP hosts on different protected ports can communicate directly with one another only through the Uplink connection using a Proxy ARP-based solution (see Appendix E) or MAC-Forced Forwarding.

MAC-Forced Forwarding, defined in **[RFC4562]**, is a technique for controlling or restricting host-to-host communication and unwanted broadcast traffic on a common IP subnet/VLAN. This is done by configuring network devices (switches) to direct all network traffic coming from hosts on the same IP subnet/VLAN but at different locations to an upstream gateway device, which is responsible for redirecting the traffic to external destinations or back to hosts on the common IP subnet/VLAN. This is an alternative method for providing security at Layer 2 (particularly for hosts on a common IP subnet/VLAN) since no traffic is allowed to pass directly between the hosts.

F.2.2 Secure Hosting

The use cases under this category are numerous, and the following are common examples:

- An important use case of Private VLANs for network segregation is hosting in hotel operations or Ethernet to the home/residential networks, where each room/apartment is assigned an isolated device port for Internet access. For example, in hotel hosting operations, Private VLANs allow easy segregation between customers on a single Layer 2 network. A hotel might deploy VLANs and then divide different guest rooms within each VLAN using Port Isolation techniques to prevent guest rooms from exchanging traffic directly with each other. The network administrator does not need to create a separate IP subnet for each customer (which requires assigning IP prefixes from the allocated IP prefix range to each subnet). Using an isolated VLAN, an endless number of customers can be accommodated on the Layer 2 network without experiencing the deleterious effects of broadcast traffic.
- Similarly, Port Isolation can be used to restrict traffic on Ethernet-based Digital Subscriber Line Access Multiplexers (DSLAMs). In these scenarios, allowing direct Layer 2 communication between customer nodes increases the potential for equipment malfunction or damage due to misconfiguration in the network, as well as exposing the local network to various security attacks, such as ARP spoofing.
- An organization may also use Private VLANs to separate different types of users (e.g., corporate versus guest) within the same Layer 2 network. By limiting the spread of Layer 2 broadcasts and multicasts through the use of Private VLANs, sensitive corporate data can be isolated from guests, reducing the network attack surface. The use of Private VLANs to

prevent direct communication between corporate and guest devices provides an additional layer of security within the same VLAN.

- A multi-tenant data center may deploy Private VLANs to separate and isolate customer servers on a larger VLAN while maintaining shared access to Internet services or firewalls. An ISP may deploy a server farm (data center) and Private VLANs to provide web hosting for different customers, where locating all customer servers within a single data center facilitates management. Using Private VLANs in the data center for isolating customer servers helps to eliminate security concerns compared to placing all customer servers on the same VLAN, because Layer 2 broadcasts would reach all customer servers in a VLAN without customer server isolation. This approach of deploying Private VLANs on single-tag VLANs balances tenant isolation needs with the cost-effectiveness of shared multi-tenant data center resources.
- Similar to hotels, conference centers may use Private VLANs to separate guest traffic from the center's internal network services. Each guest is given Internet access while their devices remain isolated from the center's production network, protecting privacy. Additionally, in a conference center hosting several different conferences, rather than creating separate VLANs for each conference, solitary VLANs can be created for each conference based on Private VLANs.
- Factories, offices, and smart homes may use Private VLANs to segregate and contain their IoT devices. This method of containment prevents compromised IoT devices from accessing critical and sensitive data (usually carried on industrial systems and enterprise networks). Furthermore, critical systems like servers that are hosting personal and financial records can be placed on their own Private VLANs within the shared physical network, restricting unauthorized communication and access while minimizing the risk of breaches during cyberattacks.
- The simple approach of using Private VLANs is particularly useful in public or shared spaces like hotels, apartment complexes, and multi-tenant environments. A service provider may provide Layer 2 Ethernet access to rental communities, assorted homes, and businesses. Deploying a single VLAN per end-user presents many network management difficulties and is also not scalable, leading to potential IP address space wastage. Using Private VLANs provides a simple, yet more efficient and secure solution. For example, in apartment complexes, a service provider may deploy a combination of VLANs and Private VLANs as a simple mechanism that allows multiple residences to share the same physical network infrastructure. Port Isolation (on Private VLANs) can be used to create barriers between individual residences, effectively preventing any unauthorized access to a residence's private devices like computers, printers, storage devices, IoT devices, etc.

The above use cases show how a network operator can deploy VLANs and Private VLANs as a simple and quick method for restricting communication between certain devices on a Layer 2 network, without changing IP subnet addressing and configurations. Traditional VLANs and Port Isolation are complementary tools that allow a network administrator to provide robust network segmentation, with simplified yet effective security that can be tailored for specific networking needs. Private VLANs can be implemented on existing VLAN infrastructure, providing a simple and more cost-effective solution that meets many use cases while avoiding the need for more complex Layer 3 and higher security solutions.

F.3 PRIVATE VLAN IMPLEMENTATION

To implement a Private VLAN, a VLAN (i.e., the original/parent or Primary VLAN) is divided into sub-VLANs (i.e., Secondary VLANs), while maintaining the Primary VLAN's existing IP subnet and routing configuration. A regular VLAN is a single Layer 2 (broadcast) domain, and a Private

VLAN is created by partitioning that single broadcast domain (Primary VLAN) into multiple smaller broadcast subdomains (Secondary VLANs). The Primary VLAN forwards Ethernet frames downstream to all of its Secondary VLANs. A Private VLAN can be configured on a single Layer 2 switch or can span multiple Layer 2 switches. We discuss below one approach for implementing a Private VLAN **[CISCPRNST08] [RFC5517]**.

F.3.1 Types of Secondary VLANs

A Primary VLAN moves traffic from a Promiscuous Port to Community, Isolated, and other Promiscuous Ports within it (i.e., the Primary VLAN). A Secondary VLAN can be one of the following types: Isolated VLAN or Community VLAN. Each sub-VLAN type has well-defined, port-related characteristics:

- **Isolated VLAN**: An Isolated VLAN transfers traffic from Isolated Ports to a Promiscuous Port in the Primary VLAN. Any switch port that is associated with an Isolated VLAN *can* communicate with the Promiscuous Port in the Primary VLAN, but *not* with any other Secondary VLAN. *Additionally, hosts on different Isolated Ports associated with the same Isolated VLAN cannot communicate directly with each other.*
  - **Key Feature**: Hosts belonging to different Isolated Ports on the same Isolated VLAN can only communicate through the Promiscuous Port associated with that VLAN. They *cannot* communicate directly at Layer 2 with other hosts belonging to other Isolated or Community VLANs. For hosts on an Isolated Port to communicate with different hosts within other switch ports on the Private VLAN, the traffic must go through the Promiscuous Port.
- **Community VLAN**: A Community VLAN transfers traffic between Community Ports within it and also to Promiscuous Ports. Switch ports that are associated with a single Community VLAN *can* communicate with each other and *with* the Promiscuous Port in the Primary VLAN, but *not* with ports in other Secondary VLANs (i.e., other Isolated and Community VLANs). A Private VLAN may have multiple distinct Community VLANs.
  - **Key Feature**: Hosts belonging to the same Community VLANs can communicate directly with each other and also with the Promiscuous Port associated with that Private VLAN. Hosts residing in different Community VLANs *cannot* communicate with each other at Layer 2. Traffic from a Community VLAN to another Secondary VLAN (Isolated or Community VLANs) must go through the Promiscuous Port.

F.3.2 Types of Ports in a Private VLAN

A Private VLAN supports two main types of ports: Promiscuous Port and Host Port (see Figure F.1). Each switch port type has its own unique set of rules that regulate the port's ability to communicate with other switch ports within the same Private VLAN.

- **Promiscuous Port**: This switch port type belongs to the Primary VLAN and can communicate with all other switch ports within the Primary VLAN (i.e., any Secondary VLAN). Specifically, a Promiscuous Port can communicate with all switch ports, including the Community and Isolated Ports within the Private VLAN. This port type is allowed to send and receive traffic from any other switch port on the Primary VLAN. The purpose of the Promiscuous Port is to forward traffic between switch ports in Community or Isolated VLANs.

  A single Private VLAN may support *multiple* Promiscuous Ports **[RFC5517]**, and those ports serve all the Community and Isolated VLANs in the Private VLAN. *A Promiscuous Port can use ACLs to identify which traffic to pass between these sub-VLAN types.*

A Promiscuous Port usually connects to an IP router (for inter-Secondary VLAN communications and routing to external networks), firewall, servers, backup servers, network management devices, administrative workstations, or other common gateways and trusted devices.

- **Host Ports**: A Host Port (belonging to a Secondary VLAN) can be further categorized into two types: Isolated Port and Community Port:
  - **Isolated Port**: This switch port type belongs to a Secondary VLAN and can only forward and receive traffic from Promiscuous Ports in the Primary VLAN, but *cannot* communicate with any other Isolated Port, even those in the same Isolated VLAN. Isolated Ports mainly connect to regular hosts that require isolation within the same Isolated VLAN. An Isolated Port has complete Layer 2 separation from other Isolated and Community Ports within the same Private VLAN, but not from the Promiscuous Ports. This isolation includes broadcasts, except those coming from the Promiscuous Port. *An Isolated Port can forward traffic only to the Promiscuous Ports and no others.*
  - **Community Port**: This switch port type belongs to a Secondary VLAN and communicates with Promiscuous Ports and switch ports on the same Community VLAN. *A Community Port has complete Layer 2 isolation from all other switch ports in other Community or Isolated VLANs within the Private VLAN.* Broadcast traffic propagates only between Community Ports associated with a particular Community VLAN and the Promiscuous Port. Community Ports connect to regular hosts that reside on a particular Community VLAN.

In a Primary VLAN, downstream traffic from Promiscuous Ports can be transmitted to all Ports within the Primary VLAN's Secondary VLANs. Switch ports within an Isolated VLAN can communicate only with a single Promiscuous Port (the Uplink Port). A single Private VLAN can have only one Isolated VLAN for practical implementation reasons. Only one Isolated VLAN can be used to connect all Isolated Ports to the Promiscuous Port. However, a Private VLAN may have multiple Isolated VLANs, for example, in cases where these sub-VLANs need to use distinct paths for security reasons, although there are challenges in implementing these multiple Isolated VLANs in practice. Even in this case, the switch ports within each sub-VLAN remain isolated from each other.

F.3.3 Layer 2 Trunk Ports in Private VLANs

Note that a Private VLAN comprises the following three elements: the Private VLAN itself, the Secondary VLANs (Isolated and Community VLANs), and the Promiscuous Port. In a Private VLAN, traffic associated with an Isolated or Community Port can enter or leave a switch through a Trunk Port, because Trunk Ports are designed to carry VLAN traffic exchanged between Isolated, Community, and Promiscuous Ports. A Private VLAN can be extended across multiple Layer 2 devices within a VLAN. This is done by trunking (via the Trunk Port) the Primary VLAN traffic along with its Isolated and Community VLANs to other Layer 2 devices that support that Private VLAN.

Trunk Ports facilitate Layer 2 communication between different network devices using tagged Ethernet frames. With Layer 2 protocols such as IEEE 802.1Q, Ethernet frames can be tagged (with corresponding VLAN IDs) by one switch and then forwarded over a Trunk Port to another device that supports those VLAN IDs. Switch ports receive the tagged Ethernet frames and use their VLAN IDs to process and forward the frames to their intended destination VLANs. An Access Port on a Layer 2 switch is usually configured with only one VLAN and is designated to carry Layer 2 traffic for that VLAN alone. A Trunk Port, on the other hand, can be configured to carry Layer 2 (tagged) traffic for two or more VLANs simultaneously.

F.3.4   ETHERNET MAC ADDRESS LEARNING AND FORWARDING IN PRIVATE VLANS

In a Private VLAN, the Ethernet MAC address learning and forwarding procedures remain unchanged, similar to those in normal VLANs. Additionally, the flooding procedure for unknown, broadcast, and multicast Ethernet frames within the boundaries of the Primary and Secondary VLANs remains unchanged. A switch in a Private VLAN will forward all Ethernet frames received from a Private Port to the Uplink Port, regardless of the frame's destination MAC address or VLAN ID. The switch forwards Ethernet frames received from an Uplink Port in the normal way (i.e., to the switch port associated with the frame's destination MAC address, or to all switch ports in the VLAN for frames with unknown or broadcast destination MAC addresses). This forwarding behavior results in the switch blocking direct peer-to-peer traffic between peer Private Ports on the switch, requiring any such peer-to-peer traffic to go through the Uplink. While Private VLANs provide traffic isolation between peer Private Ports at Layer 2, communication at the IP layer (via a router) can occur, but the network must be appropriately configured to allow that.

Through the deployment of Primary VLANs and Secondary VLANs (with Isolated and Community Ports) within a larger VLAN, a network administrator can provide enhanced access control and device isolation, addressing the specific security requirements of the network while improving network security and reliability.

F.4   PRIVATE VLANS ARCHITECTURE AND VLAN PAIRINGS

A port in a VLAN (a "VLAN port") can be a physical or logical interface on a network device (switch, switch/router, or router) that provides connectivity to facilitate communication within that VLAN. These ports pass traffic to specific VLANs in a network, ensuring the desired flow of data in the network while providing efficient network segmentation and traffic isolation. The VLAN port type plays a central role in determining how the various devices and switches within a VLAN interact to handle traffic in a VLAN. There are three main types of VLAN ports (Access, Trunk, and Hybrid), each with specific functions and serving a unique purpose depending on the network configuration (and applications). Each port type plays a unique role in how the VLAN manages data flow and achieves traffic segmentation.

- **Access Port**: This port type is the most basic of the VLAN port types. It connects end-user devices (e.g., computers, servers, printers, IP phones) to a single VLAN. This port type takes incoming Ethernet frames and strips their VLAN tags, allowing non-VLAN-aware devices to process the (untagged) frames. Any device connected to an Access Port belongs only to the particular VLAN assigned to that port. This simplifies device management in the VLAN and provides improved security (compared to security a flat Layer 2 network) by allowing easy segregation of traffic between different user groups on different Access Ports.
- **Trunk Port**: This port type handles traffic from multiple VLANs at the same time. A Trunk Port uses a protocol such as IEEE 802.1Q to tag Ethernet frames according to the VLAN they belong to. The tagging process associates a VLAN ID with each Ethernet frame so that its VLAN can easily be identified. This allows Ethernet frames from different VLANs to be carried seamlessly and simultaneously over a single physical link, an important feature for inter-switch communication and efficient utilization of network bandwidth.

  Trunk ports are particularly crucial in large networks where switches must process Ethernet frames across multiple VLANs. A Trunk Port tags Ethernet frames with VLAN IDs so that they can be identified as they traverse the network. A Trunk Port can handle both tagged and untagged Ethernet frames depending on configuration. Trunk Ports are mainly used for communication between VLAN-enabled switches (e.g., switch-to-switch, switch-to-router) and may also be used for carrying traffic from various VLANs in a network to routers for forwarding to other networks (as well as during inter-VLAN communications). Trunk Ports provide an efficient way to consolidate connections between devices in the network and to manage multi-VLAN traffic, a feature that is essential for complex VLAN setups.

- **Hybrid Port**: This port type handles both tagged and untagged traffic. A Hybrid Port supports multiple VLANs with selective Ethernet frame tagging. Hybrid Ports offer flexibility in VLAN design by supporting the capabilities of Access and Trunk Ports. It can handle untagged Ethernet frames like an Access Port and allows customizable Ethernet frame tagging for different VLAN traffic. Being capable of handling both tagged and untagged Ethernet frames makes Hybrid Ports ideal for network environments that require mixed configurations or dynamic VLAN setups.

    Hybrid Ports manage VLAN and non-VLAN traffic efficiently and are ideal for multi-purpose networks with varying requirements. By combining the strengths of Access and Trunk Ports, Hybrid Ports can effectively manage diverse traffic types across different users. Hybrid Ports are particularly useful in network environments where devices need to communicate across multiple VLANs, and the network has mixed access and trunking configurations, such as networks that connect devices that may not support VLAN tagging.

Access Ports are generally sufficient for simple VLAN designs. Trunk Ports tend to be more suitable for multi-VLAN communication, while Hybrid Ports are typically used in dynamic environments that require adaptability. Table F.2 presents the main differences between Access, Trunk, and Hybrid Ports. The types of VLAN ports used depend on the size, complexity, and requirements of the network; each port type is designed for a specific task in the network. Generally, Trunk Ports are limited to inter-switch links or critical devices (routers, gateways, servers) to reduce network complexity.

Figure F.1 describes the basic model of a Private VLAN based on the switch port types described above. An Inter-Switch Link (ISL) Port, also called a Trunk Port, is simply a regular port that connects two switches or a switch and a router (and carries two or more VLANs). Table F.3 summarizes

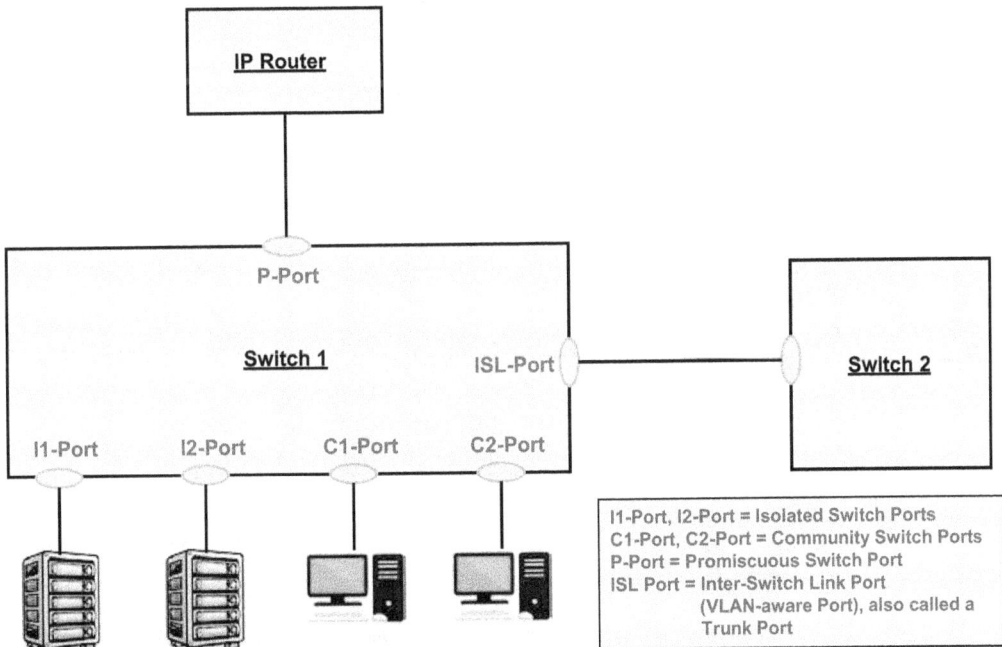

FIGURE F.1   Switch ports in a Private VLAN.

the communication privileges between the different switch port types in a Private VLAN. It should be noted that Community, Isolated, and Promiscuous Ports in a Private VLAN can be either *Access*, *Trunk*, or *Hybrid* Ports, just like in regular VLANs.

Private VLANs are subdomains created within the same VLAN domain; however, a subdomain within a VLAN cannot simply be identified using only one IEEE 802.1Q VLAN ID tag. Instead, [RFC5517] proposes the pairing of VLAN IDs as a mechanism for identifying and implementing Private VLANs. Specifically, subdomains can be represented by pairs of VLAN numbers, <Vp, Vs>, where Vp is the Primary VLAN ID and Vs is the Secondary VLAN ID (Figure F.2). The identifier Vs can be either Vi (indicating an Isolated VLAN) or Vc (indicating a Community VLAN).

A Private VLAN domain is created by defining at least one pair of VLAN IDs: a single Primary VLAN ID (Vp) and one or more Secondary VLAN IDs (Vs). Each Secondary VLAN in the Primary VLAN (Vp) then is assigned a VLAN ID: Isolated VLAN (Vi) or Community VLAN (Vc). The Primary VLAN ID (Vp) is a unique and common VLAN ID for the whole Private VLAN domain and of all its Secondary VLANs, each having the VLAN ID pair (<Vp, Vs>).

It is important to note that the VLAN pairing scheme requires that all Layer 2 traffic transported within a specific Primary VLAN and its Secondary VLANs must be tagged according to the IEEE 802.1Q standard with at most a single standard IEEE 802.1Q VLAN ID tag. The VLAN pairing

TABLE F.2
Comparison of VLAN Port Types

Feature	Access Port	Trunk Port	Hybrid Port
Traffic handling	Single VLAN	Multiple VLANs	Tagged plus Untagged
Primary use case	Connecting End Devices	Switch-to-switch or switch-to-router links	Mixed environments that require flexibility
VLAN tagging	Strips incoming tags	Preserves all tags	Selective tagging (can handle both tagged and untagged frames)
Flexibility	Low	Moderate	High
Security	Higher security; limited to a single VLAN	Potential security concerns if misconfigured	Moderate security
Configuration complexity	Simple to configure	More complex to configure (requires VLAN tagging)	Moderate complexity
Management	Easier to manage	Requires careful management to maintain security and prevent unauthorized access	Presents management difficulties if not properly configured, which can lead to security breaches

TABLE F.3
Communication Privileges between the Different Private VLAN Port Types

	I-Port	P-Port	C1-Port	C2-Port	ISL Port
I-Port	Deny	Permit	Deny	Deny	Permit/Deny[a]
P-Port	Permit	Permit	Permit	Permit	Permit
C1-Port	Deny	Permit	Permit	Deny	Permit
C2-Port	Deny	Permit	Deny	Permit	Permit
ISL Port	Permit/Deny[a]	Permit	Permit	Permit	Permit

[a] Traffic from an ISL Port to an Isolated Port will be denied if the ISL Port is in an Isolated VLAN; and Traffic from an ISL Port to an Isolated Port will be permitted if the ISL Port is in the Primary VLAN.

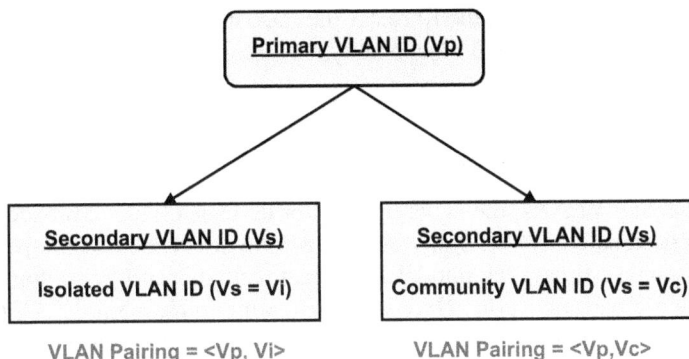

FIGURE F.2 VLAN numbers and pairings.

scheme does not require special double-tagging due to the 1:1 correspondence between a Secondary VLAN and its associated unique Primary VLAN ID (Vp). *This means Ethernet frames within a particular (unique) Primary VLAN (Vp) are tagged with the VLAN ID of the Secondary VLAN to which they belong (Vi or Vc); the frames carry only a single VLAN ID corresponding to their Secondary VLAN type.*

However, the switch ports in a Private VLAN domain derive their special characteristics and behaviors from the VLAN pairing(s) configured on them: <Vp, Vi> for Isolated Ports or <Vp, Vc> for Community Ports. The filtering behaviors at the switch ports within the Primary VLAN (Vp) are based on the single Secondary VLAN IDs carried in the frames (Vi or Vc). Switch ports (Community, Isolated, and Promiscuous Ports) in a Private VLAN (Vp) use the Secondary VLAN ID (Vi or Vc) carried in the frames and their configured local VLAN pairing <Vp, Vs> information to implement their filtering and isolation behaviors. Note that Private VLAN traffic could also be trunked. Only the Secondary VLAN IDs (Vi or Vc) are used to tag frames, and the Trunk Port carries these tagged frames, just like in regular VLANs.

It is possible for Community, Isolated, and Primary VLANs to span multiple switches in a Layer 2 network, just like regular VLANs. ISL (or Trunk) Ports need not be aware of the Secondary VLAN IDs and will carry frames tagged with these special VLAN IDs just like they do with any other frames. However, it is important to ensure that traffic from an Isolated Port on one Layer 2 switch does not reach another Isolated or Community Port on a different Layer 2 switch, even after traversing the ISL or Trunk Link. By using the Secondary VLAN IDs to embed the isolation information for a Private VLAN and transporting this information along with tagged Ethernet frames, it is possible to maintain consistent isolation behavior throughout the network. This mechanism restricts Layer 2 communication between two Isolated Ports on the same Layer 2 switch, and also restricts Layer 2 communication between two Isolated Ports on different Layer 2 switches.

In a Private VLAN, all devices share a common IP address space that is part of a single IP subnet associated with the Primary VLAN. An end device can be assigned an IP address manually or through a DHCP server connected to a Promiscuous Port of the Primary VLAN. IP addresses are assigned from a larger IP prefix (address pool) shared by all devices in the Private VLAN domain. Layer 3 devices are not directly aware of the existence of individual devices in a Private VLAN; all of these end devices appear as part of the Primary VLAN.

In Figure F.1, the isolation behavior between devices on I1-Port and I2-Port of Switch 1 operates only at the Layer 2-level. These devices can still communicate at the Layer 3 level via the IP router connected to the Promiscuous Port (P-Port) of Switch 1. Since devices on I1-Port and I2-Port of Switch 1 are part of the same IP subnet, the IP router assumes that hosts on these ports should be able to communicate directly with each other. However, this is prevented by the specific behaviors of Isolated Ports in Private VLANs. Thus, to enable the devices on I1-Port and I2-Port of Switch

1 to communicate via the IP router, the IP router interface must support Proxy ARP (for IPv4) or Proxy Neighbor Discovery (for IPv6) functionality (as discussed below). The Private VLAN concept applies to both IPv4 and IPv6 subnets.

F.5   INTER-VLAN COMMUNICATION

In a network deploying VLANs, the network operator divides a Layer 2 broadcast domain into smaller domains designated as VLANs, with each VLAN associated with a particular IP subnet. Segregating a physical network into VLANs creates smaller broadcast domains, helping to restrict and contain broadcast traffic. *Only hosts belonging to the same VLAN (IP subnet) can communicate directly with each other, while hosts belonging to different VLANs can only communicate through an IP router (i.e., inter-VLAN communication occurs at Layer 3).* Inter-VLAN communication (routing) works just like Inter-IP subnet communication since both IP subnets and VLANs use non-overlapping or distinct IP address spaces; they are assigned distinct IP prefixes.

The following methods can be used to accomplish inter-VLAN communication [**AWEYFCDM22**]:

- The VLANs are connected to separate physical Layer 3 (routed) ports of an external router, which performs routing to the desired outgoing VLAN attached to its corresponding physical port.
- The VLANs are connected through a single physical port (each on a separate logical interface) to a *one-armed router* (also called a *router-on-a-stick*) that performs routing to the desired outgoing VLAN on its corresponding logical interface. In this case, the router uses VLAN tagging techniques to distinguish VLANs and direct outgoing packets to their respective VLANs; each logical interface is associated with a VLAN ID.
- The VLANs are connected to a switch/router (an integrated Layer 2/Layer 3 device) that performs routing to the desired outgoing VLAN through a *Switch Virtual Interface (SVI)* or *Routed VLAN Interface (RVI)* associated with each VLAN (see SVI in [**AWEYFCDM22**] and RVI discussion below). Each SVI or RVI is associated with a unique VLAN ID or IP subnet prefix.

The concept of SVIs and RVIs can also be used for communication in a network with Private VLANs and Secondary VLANs.

F.6   LAYER 3 AND PROXY ARP ASSISTED COMMUNICATION IN A NETWORK WITH PRIVATE VLANS

Private VLANs further split a Primary VLAN (segregated Layer 2 broadcast domain) into multiple Layer 2 broadcast subdomains (creating VLANs within a VLAN). Typically, a VLAN corresponds to a single IP subnet. Using a Private VLAN, an IP subnet prefix is allocated to the Primary VLAN, and all hosts in its Secondary VLANs belong to the same IP subnet prefix. The IP addresses assigned to hosts within the Secondary VLANs are based on the IP subnet prefix associated with the Primary VLAN. In addition, a host's IP subnet masking information reflects that of the IP subnet associated with the Primary VLAN. However, each Secondary VLAN of the Primary VLAN constitutes a separate broadcast domain.

The Private VLAN concept allows a network administrator to split a large Layer 2 broadcast domain into smaller subdomains (Parent/Primary VLANs) and then further divide a subdomain (Primary VLAN) into one or more Secondary VLANs. A subdomain consists of a Primary VLAN and one or more Secondary VLANs (Community VLANs and Isolated VLANs); all the Secondary VLANs share the same Primary VLAN. As discussed earlier, Private VLANs allow a network administrator to perform network segmentation at a finer level than what can be done with traditional VLANs, allowing more granular network traffic control.

F.6.1 Using a Network Device with Proxy ARP for Enabling Communication between Secondary VLANs

Hosts on different VLANs are not allowed to communicate directly with each other, as discussed above. Inter-VLAN communication requires the presence of a Layer 3 device to forward packets between the VLANs. The same concept of communicating through a Layer 3 device applies to the Secondary VLANs of a Private VLAN. Given that Private VLANs (subdomains) are segregated at Layer 2, they need a Layer 3 forwarding entity to enable hosts on different Secondary VLANs to communicate with each other. A regular VLAN usually corresponds to a single distinct IP subnet in the network.

When a Private VLAN is split into separate Secondary VLANs, hosts on these different Secondary VLANs still belong to the same IP subnet, that of the Primary VLAN. Hosts on the different Private VLANs still need to use a Layer 3 device to communicate with each other as hosts on different VLANs would [RFC5517]. This Layer 3 device must support local IPv4 Proxy ARP (or IPv6 Proxy Neighbor Discovery) functionality to enable the device to participate in ARP Replies and Requests to identify the IP-to-MAC address mappings on the attached Secondary VLANs, since they belong to the same IP subnet. IPv4 Proxy ARP is discussed in **Appendix E,** and IPv6 Proxy Neighbor Discovery in **Chapter 4**.

A situation where a Layer 3 device with Proxy ARP (or Proxy Neighbor Discovery) may be used for communication between Secondary VLANs in a Private VLAN is when hosts on restricted ports are allowed to access certain network resources (like data and media servers, email servers, printers, and media gateways) on other restricted ports in the Private VLAN. Such resources may be placed in their own restricted zones/ports but can be accessed via ARP Proxy devices available to certain restricted zones or ports. Reference [JUNESUG24] describes various Juniper Network's approaches for implementing Private VLANs and how hosts in different Secondary VLANs of the same Private VLAN can communicate with each other.

F.6.2 Using ACLs on the Promiscuous Port for Filtering Communication between Secondary VLANs

It is noted above that a Promiscuous Port in a Private VLAN can use ACLs to identify which traffic to permit or deny between the Secondary VLAN types (Community VLANs and Isolated VLANs, which by default should not be able to communicate with each other). VLAN or Port ACLs may also be configured on the Layer 2 switches in the Private VLAN to deny/permit access to certain shared network resources [CISCPRNST08]. Using VLAN or Port ACLs, if some hosts are allowed to communicate with other hosts (in the same Private VLAN at Layer 2), then the network administrator configures appropriate VLAN or Port ACLs on the switches to deny or permit certain peer communications.

Port ACLs are configured on Layer 2 interfaces of a switch to filter only inbound traffic (i.e., traffic entering a port from the switch). The switch examines a Port ACL on a given interface and permits or denies incoming packets based on the packet-matching criteria defined in the Port ACL. Port ACLs can also be applied to a Trunk Port, allowing the ACLs to filter traffic on the VLANs carried on the Trunk Port.

A VLAN ACL (also called a VLAN Map) can be used to filter packets of all types that are Layer 2 forwarded (bridged) within a VLAN or Layer 3 forwarded (routed) to or from a VLAN. A VLAN ACL does not consider the direction of traffic flow (inbound or outbound) when filtering traffic. A switch checks all packets entering the VLAN (bridged or routed) against the VLAN ACL. The direction of traffic can be considered when filtering by combining VLAN ACLs and Private VLAN features.

F.6.3 Understanding RVIs

Instead of using the Promiscuous Port connected to an IP router to route Layer 3 traffic between Community and Isolated VLANs, an RVI can be configured on the switch for that purpose, as illustrated in Figure F.3. An RVI, also called an Integrated Routing and Bridging Interface, is a logical (virtual) interface that allows Layer 3 (routing) and Layer 2 (bridging) between different VLANs (traditional VLANs and Private VLANs) as needed [**JUNESUG24**]. An RVI is a special type of Layer 3 virtual interface.

An RVI allows routing and bridging on the same interface. With an RVI, traffic that should remain in the VLAN (the bridge group), that is, the traffic to be bridged, will be Layer 2 forwarded among the switch ports/interfaces within that VLAN, while traffic that needs to go out of the VLAN to another network (the routed traffic) will be Layer 3 forwarded (routed) internally by the RVI to the appropriate outbound routed interface and VLAN. In this case, each VLAN interface is assigned an IPv4 address. Integrated Routing and Bridging (IRB) *or RVI functions like a switch/router that processes Layer 2 packets during intra-VLAN/IP subnet communications and processes Layer 3 packets during inter-VLAN/IP subnet communications* [**AWEYFCDM22**].

An RVI is conceptually similar to an SVI, which is a logical interface that allows traffic to be Layer 3 forwarded (routed) between different VLANs by providing a default gateway for the VLANs (**see also the SVI discussion in Chapter 4**). To use the RVI routing technique in a Private VLAN, an RVI is configured for each Secondary VLAN on a switch in the Private VLAN. When IP packets are received from a Secondary VLAN on its RVI, they are mapped to and routed by the switch through outbound RVIs to their corresponding Secondary VLANs or to external destinations in the network. Only one RVI or SVI can be associated with any given VLAN when regular VLANs are used (or a Secondary VLAN when a Private VLAN is deployed).

An RVI enables a switch to identify packets that need to be sent to local addresses within a particular VLAN (or Secondary VLAN) so that they are Layer 2 forwarded (bridged) whenever possible and Layer 3 forwarded (routed) only when needed. Whenever packets are Layer 2 forwarded instead of Layer 3 forwarded, the more complex processing involved in Layer 3 (IP) forwarding is avoided. Layer 2 forwarding involves fewer address lookup and forwarding operations.

F.6.3.1   How RVI Works

An RVI is needed when traffic must be routed between VLANs (or Secondary VLANs of a Private VLAN), Layer 3 IP connectivity is required to a switch, or when individual VLANs (or Secondary VLANs) need to be monitored for various purposes such as traffic monitoring, proofing, or billing [**JUNESUG24**].

Using RVIs on a Private VLAN, one RVI must first be configured for each Secondary VLAN in the Private VLAN. Each RVI handles Layer 3 forwarding for its entire Secondary VLAN, regardless of whether it includes one or more Layer 2 switches. After configuring an RVI, it receives Layer 3 traffic from its Secondary VLAN to be mapped and routed to other Secondary VLAN RVIs. *When the RVIs are set up, Proxy ARP must also be enabled on the switch so that the RVIs can handle ARP Requests received on their associated Secondary VLANs* [**JUNESUG24**].

An RVI is associated with a logical unit number and a corresponding IP address [**JUNESUG24**]. Only one RVI is configured for each VLAN (or Secondary VLAN). For example, if the network has two VLANs (VLAN 10 and VLAN 20) with corresponding IP subnet prefixes, one RVI must be configured with a logical unit and IP address in IP subnet 10 (VLAN 10), and another RVI must be configured with a different logical unit and IP address in IP subnet 20 (VLAN 20), as illustrated in Figure F.3. Logical units with IP addresses must be created for each of the IP subnets associated with the VLANs (or Secondary VLANs) between which traffic must be routed.

Switch 3 in Figure F.3 automatically creates (internally) direct routes to both IP subnet 10 and IP subnet 20 and uses these routes to forward traffic between VLAN 10 and VLAN 20. Packets arriving on a Layer 2 interface that are destined for the MAC address of Switch 3 are classified as Layer 3 traffic, while those that are not destined for Switch 3's MAC address are classified as Layer 2 traffic (see **Chapter 5** of [**AWEYFCDM22**] for a detailed discussion on Layer 2 versus Layer 3 forwarding on a single switch/router or integrated Layer 2/Layer 3 forwarding device).

Packets addressed to the MAC address of Switch 3 are sent to the RVI associated with the sending VLAN (or Secondary VLAN). Packets from Switch 3's routing engine are sent out the RVI associated with the VLAN (or Secondary VLAN) of the packet's destination IP address. Switch 3

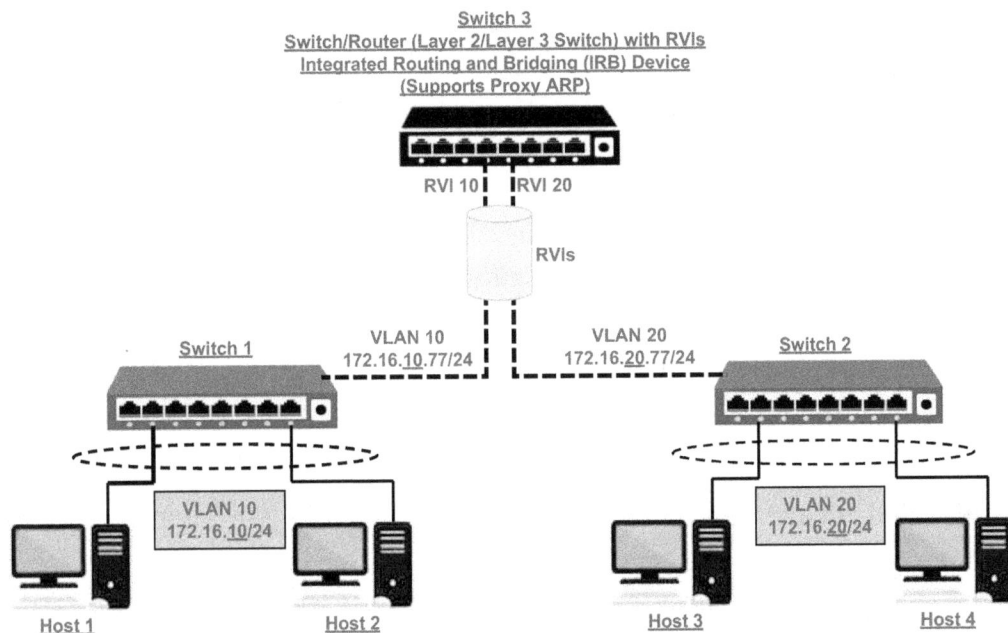

FIGURE F.3 RVI on a switch/router providing routing between two VLANs.

detects both MAC addresses and IP addresses on each RVI, then routes IP packets to other RVIs or switches them on the same VLAN (or Secondary VLAN).

An RVI may be set up to detect IPv4, IPv6 unicast, and multicast virtual routing and forwarding (VRF) traffic **[JUNESUG24]**. A VRF is often used with Layer 3 sub-interfaces, allowing a single physical interface to receive traffic that can be differentiated and associated with multiple virtual routers.

F.6.3.2 Configuring RVI in a VLAN

The basic steps in configuring an RVI are as follows **[JUNESUG24]**:

- Configure the VLANs (or Secondary VLANs).
- Create an RVI for each VLAN (or Secondary VLAN).
- Assign an IP address to each VLAN (or Secondary VLAN).
- Bind the VLANs (or Secondary VLANs) to their corresponding RVIs. There must be a one-to-one mapping between a VLAN (or Secondary VLAN) and an RVI; only one RVI can be mapped to a VLAN (or Secondary VLAN).

REFERENCES

[AWEYFCDM22].   J. Aweya, *Designing Switch/Routers: Fundamental Concepts and Design Methods*, CRC Press, Taylor & Francis Group, ISBN 9781032317694, October 2022.

[CISCPRNST08].   Y. Bhaiji, *Network Security Technologies and Solutions (CCIE Professional Development Series)*, Chapter "Security Features on Switches", Cisco Press, March 20, 2008.

[JUNESUG24].   J. Networks, *Ethernet Switching User Guide*, January 2025.

[RFC4562].   T. Melsen and S. Blake, "MAC-Forced Forwarding: A Method for Subscriber Separation on an Ethernet Access Network", *IETF RFC 4562*, June 2006.

[RFC5517].   S. HomChaudhuri and M. Foschiano, "Cisco Systems' Private VLANs: Scalable Security in a Multi-Client Environment", *IETF RFC 5517*, February 2010.

Index

A

Address Resolution Protocol (ARP), 1, 7, 21, 106, 107, 127, 129, 425
  ARP Cache, 127, 168, 235, 237, 336, 427, 431, 432
  ARP Probe, 428
  ARP Reply, 236, 237, 336, 425, 427
  ARP Request, 7, 106, 235, 237, 336, 337, 425, 427, 432, 448
  ARP spoofing, 435
  Gratuitous ARP, 127, 160, 336, 337, 429
    Gratuitous ARP Reply, 429
    Gratuitous ARP Request, 429
  Proxy ARP, 127, 331, 336–338, 432, 447, 448
administrative distance, 13, 15, 19, 223, 231, 232

B

bit and byte ordering
  Big-Endian, 247, 388, 397
  Little-Endian, 388
  network byte order, *See* Big-Endian
bridges. *See* switches

C

Classless Inter-Domain Routing (CIDR), 1, 18, 22, 79, 391, 407, 409
  CIDR notation, 2, 84, 406, 407, 409, 410, 412
  CIDR prefix blocks, 79
communication modes
  anycast, 87
  broadcast, 87
  multicast, 87
  one-to-any, 87
  one-to-one, 86
  one-to-many, 87, 103
  one-to-nearest (or one-to-closest) interface communication, 87
  unicast, 86

D

Differentiated Services, 399, 420, 422
  Bandwidth Broker, 422
  DiffServ domain, 420, 422
  Per-Hop Behaviors (PHBs), 399, 420
    Assured Forwarding (AF) PHB, 421
    Class Selector (CS), 420, 421
    Default PHB, 420
    Expedited Forwarding (EF) PHB, 421
    Voice Admit PHB, 421
DNS (Domain Name System), 78
  DNS for IPv6, 314
    AAAA data format, 315
    AAAA Query, 315
    AAAA Record (Quad-A Record), 315
    ip6.arpa domain, 315

fully qualified domain name (FQDN), 152
root nameservers, 78
root zone, 78
unqualified host name, 152
Resource Records, 314
  Address (A) Record, 314
  Canonical Name (CNAME) Record, 314
  Mail Exchange (MX) Record, 315
  Name Server (NS) Record, 314
  Pointer (PTR) Record, 314
  Service (SRV) Record, 315
  Start of Authority (SOA), 314
Dynamic Host Configuration Protocol for IPv4 (DHCPv4), 1, 7, 191, 307, 310, 403, 404, 414
  DHCPACK, 309
  DHCPDECLINE, 309
  DHCPDISCOVER, 309
  DHCPINFORM, 309
  DHCPNAK, 309
  DHCPOFFER, 309
  DHCPRELEASE, 309
  DHCPREQUEST, 309
Dynamic Host Configuration Protocol for IPv6 (DHCPv6), 1, 94–96, 182, 191, 244
  automatic binding table, 254, 261
  Binding, 246
  binding database, 261
  database agent, 261
  DHCP domain, 246
  DHCPv6 address pools, 253, 255
    local DHCPv6 address pool, 254
    local DHCPv6 prefix delegation pool, 254
  DHCPv6 configuration pools, 253
  DHCPv6 Client, 244
  DHCPv6 four-message exchange, 267
  DHCPv6 Relay Agent, 244, 270, 289–293
  DHCPv6 Server, 244
  DHCPv6 Snooping, 312, 314
    trusted port, 312
    untrusted port, 312
  DHCPv6 two-message exchange, 267, 268
  DUID (DHCP Unique Identifier), 246, 252
  IA (Identity Association), 246
  IAID (IA Identifier), 246
  IA_NA (IA for Non-temporary Addresses), 246
  IA_PD (IA for Prefix Delegation), 246
  IA_TA (IA for Temporary Addresses), 246
  IPv6 All_DHCP_Relay_Agents_and_Servers Multicast Address (FF02::1:2), 249, 265, 270
  IPv6 All_DHCP_Servers Multicast Address (FF05::1:3), 249
  IPv6 address assignment, 255
    dynamic IPv6 address assignment, 256
    static binding, 255
    static IPv6 address assignment, 255
  IPv6 prefix assignment, 256
    dynamic IPv6 prefix assignment, 256

Dynamic Host Configuration Protocol for (*cont.*)
    static binding, 256
    static IPv6 prefix assignment, 256
  Lease, 245
  Prefix Delegation mechanism, 182, 245, 253, 301,
        304, 305
    delegating router, 245, 263
    requesting router, 245, 263
  messages
    ADVERTISE, 210, 213, 248, 282–284, 309
    CONFIRM, 248, 274, 275, 286, 297
    DECLINE, 248, 281, 282, 286, 298
    INFORMATION-REQUEST, 210, 248, 279, 280,
        287, 288
    REBIND, 248, 277, 278, 288, 296
    RECONFIGURE, 248, 269, 287–289, 305, 310
    RELAY-FORWARD, 248, 289–293, 298
    RELAY-REPLY, 248, 288, 289, 291–293, 298
    RELEASE, 248, 280, 281, 286, 298
    RENEW, 248, 275–277, 288, 296
    REPLY, 210, 248, 277, 279–282, 284–286,
        298, 309
    REQUEST, 214, 248, 272, 273, 309
    SOLICIT, 210, 213, 248, 270, 271, 309
  non-temporary address, 245, 258
  Options, 244, 247, 250
    Authentication Option, 250, 311
    Client Identifier Option, 250, 252
    Container Option, 246
    Elapsed Time Option, 250
    Encapsulated Option, 246
    IA (Identity Association) Option, 246
    IA Address Option, 250
    IA Prefix Option, 251
    IA_NA (IA for Non-temporary Addresses)
        Option, 250
    IA_PD (IA for Prefix Delegation) Option, 251
    IA_TA (IA for Temporary Addresses) Option, 250
    INF_MAX_RT Option, 251, 252
    Information Refresh Time Option, 251, 287
    Interface-ID Option, 251
    Option Request Option, 250, 287
    Preference Option, 250, 267
    Prefix Exclude Option, 183, 184, 186, 305
    Rapid Commit Option, 251, 268, 269, 284
    Reconfigure Accept Option, 251, 269
    Reconfigure Message Option, 251, 287
    Relay Message Option, 250, 270, 292
    Server Identifier Option, 250, 252
    Server Unicast Option, 250, 269
    Singleton Option, 246
    SOL_MAX_RT Option, 251, 252
    Status Code Option, 250, 270
    Top-Level Option, 246
    User Class Option, 251
    Vendor Class Option, 251
    Vendor-specific Information Option, 251
  Reconfiguration Key Authentication Protocol (RKAP),
        311, 312
  replay detection method (RDM), 311
  server discovery, 265
  Stateful DHCPv6, 94, 95, 191, 200, 206, 212, 214, 244,
        301, 352
  Stateless DHCPv6, 191, 208, 209, 211, 244,
        298, 300, 306
  T1, 246, 262
  T2, 246, 263
  temporary addresses, 245, 258, 306
  Transaction ID, 246

E

Ethernet frame, 377
  baby giant, 386, 387
  broadcast frame, 383
  double IEEE 802.1ad tags, 377, 388
  giant frames, 391
  IEEE 802.1p, 384, 387, 419
  IEEE 802.1Q frame, 379, 384
  illegal frames, 391
  jumbo, 386, 391
  QoS prioritization, 384
  runt frame, 380, 391
  single IEEE 802.1Q tag, 377, 385,
        386, 419
  tagged Ethernet frame, 67, 380
  untagged Ethernet frame, 67, 385, 386, 418
  VLAN tagging, 384, 387, 444
Ethernet frame fields
  Data, 380
  Destination Address, 379
  Drop Eligible Indicator (DEI), 385
  EtherType, 26, 34, 129
  Frame Check Sequence (FCS), 3, 380
  Interframe Gap, 67, 381
  Preamble, 67, 378
  Priority Code Point (PCP), 385, 387
  Source Address, 379
  Start of Frame Delimiter (SFD), 67, 378
  Tag Control Information (TCI), 385
  Tag Protocol Identifier (TPID), 385
  Type/Length, 379
  VLAN ID (VID), 384, 385, 387, 436
    Default VID, 386
    Null VID, 386
Ethernet MAC address, 379, 380
  broadcast MAC address, 235, 379, 382, 383
  Globally/Locally address bit, *See* U/L address bit
  group (multicast) address, 111, 382
  IEEE-administered company ID, 100, 381
  IEEE-administered manufacturer ID, *See* company ID
  individual (unicast) address, 111, 382
  Individual/Group (I/G) address bit, 111, 381,
        382, 390
  locally administered address, 110, 383
  manufacturer-selected extension ID, 110
  manufacturer-selected board ID, *See* extension ID
  Media Access Control (MAC) address, 7
  multicast MAC addresses, 379, 382
  NIC-Specific Identifier, *See* company ID
  Organizational Unique Identifier (OUI), 381, 393
  unicast MAC addresses, 379
  Unicast/Multicast bit, *See* I/G address bit
  Universal/Local (U/L) address bit, 110, 112–114, 118,
        119, 381, 383, 390
  universally administered address, 110, 383

H

hubs, 20

I

IEEE 802.1AX Link Aggregation, 203
    Link Aggregation Group (LAG), 204
IEEE 802.3ad. *See* IEEE 802.1AX
IEEE 802.3 specification, 377
    Logical Link Control (LLC) sublayer, 377
    Medium Access Control (MAC) sublayer, 377
    Physical Layer, 377
Internet Assigned Numbers Authority (IANA), 77
    Local Internet Registries (LIRs), 79, 404, 411
    Regional Internet Registries (RIRs), 78, 404, 410
        African Network Information Centre (AFRINIC), 78
        American Registry for Internet Numbers (ARIN), 78, 93
        Asia Pacific Network Information Centre (APNIC), 78
        Latin America and Caribbean Network Information Centre (LACNIC), 78
        Réseaux IP Européens Network Coordination Centre (RIPE NCC), 78
Internet Control Message Protocol for IPv4 (ICMPv4), 5
    Address Mask Request/Reply, 127
    Destination Unreachable, 71, 73, 416
    Redirect, 5, 127
    Router Discovery, 5, 7, 127
    Router Advertisement message (ICMPv4 Type 9 message), 323
    Router Solicitation message (ICMPv4 Type 10 message), 323
Internet Control Message Protocol for IPv6 (ICMPv6), 4, 103
    Destination Unreachable (Message Type 1), 5, 6, 19, 74, 352
    Echo Reply (Message Type 129), 6
    Echo Request (Message Type 128), 6
    Packet Too Big (Message Type 2), 6, 34, 50, 68, 69, 74
    Parameter Problem (Message Type 4), 6, 37, 39, 49, 50, 64
    Time Exceeded (Message Type 3), 6, 32, 63, 64, 73
Internet Group Management Protocol (IGMP), 5, 7
    IGMPv2, 5
    IGMPv3, 5
Internet Service Providers (ISPs), 79
IP network
    link, 7, 125
    prefix aggregation, 403, 410
    route aggregation, 403, 410
    route summarization, 403, 410
    subnet, 7, 21, 125
    supernetting, 403
IP packet fragmentation, 1, 3
IP routers, 7, 21
    forwarding information base (FIB), *See* forwarding table
    forwarding table, 18, 22, 234
    longest prefix matching (LPM), 18, 71, 224, 234
    routing information base (RIB), *See* routing table
IP routing 7
    Autonomous System, 8, 12

Autonomous System Number (ASN), 9, 78
Bellman–Ford algorithm, 10
distance-vector routing protocols (DVRPs), 10
equal-cost multipath (ECMP) routing, 14, 19, 90, 203
Enhanced Interior Gateway Routing Protocol (EIGRP), 10, 14, 90
Exterior (or External) Gateway Protocol (EGP), 9
Interior (or Internal) Gateway Protocol (IGP), 8
Intermediate System-to-Intermediate System (IS-IS)
    link-state packets (LSPs), 11
    link-state Protocol Data Units, 11
    IS-IS for IPv6, 8, 11, 14
link-state routing protocols (LSRPs), 11
    Dijkstra algorithm, 11
    link-state database (LSDB), 11
    LSDB (also known as the Topology Table), 11
    neighbor discovery process, 12
    Neighbor Table (or Adjacency Database), 12
    shortest path first (SPF) algorithm, 11, 12
Multiprotocol Extensions for BGP (MBGP), 8
OSPF
    link-state advertisements (LSAs), 11
    OSPF for IPv4 (OSPFv2), 11
    OSPF for IPv6 (OSPF version 3 (OSPFv3)), 8, 11
path-vector routing protocol (PVRP), 12
    BGP, 12
    BGP Next-Hop attribute, 13
    BGP Origin attribute, 13
    BGP Path attributes, 13
    BGP UPDATE message, 13
    Multiprotocol BGP (MBGP), 101
routing domain, 8
routing metric or cost, 223
routing policy, 9
routing protocols, 8
RIP for IPv4 (RIPv2), 10
RIP next generation (RIPng), 8, 10
static routes, 8
unequal-cost multipath routing, 14, 90, 203
IP routing table, 8, 12, 18, 19, 221
    administrative distance, 222
    default route, 18, 223
    destination IPv6 address or prefix, 17
    directly connected routes, 17, 221
    connected route, 226, 228
    dynamic routes, 222, 228
    exact matches, 18
    host routes, 18, 221
    lifetime, 223
    local route, 226
    loopback addresses, 221
    next-hop address, 17, 222
    next-hop interface, 17
    next-hop router, 234
    outgoing interface, 222
    remote network routes, 18
    routing metric or cost, 223
    static routes, 222, 228, 233
        directly attached static route, 229
        floating static route, 231
        fully specified static route, 230
        recursive static route, 229
        static default route, 233
    variable-length prefixes, 18

IP Security (IPSec), 2, 172, 310, 335, 336, 345, 360
IPv4 address
    administratively scoped addresses, 392
    broadcast address, 412
        directed broadcast, 412
        limited broadcast, 412
    Classful addressing, 404, 406, 407
    dotted-decimal notation, 4, 79, 403
    IPv4 multicast group identifier (ID), 393
    IPv4 multicast to Ethernet MAC address mapping, 392
    IPv4 prefix, 84
    limited scope addresses, 392
    Link-Local addresses, 412
    loopback addresses, 411
    MAC address ambiguities, 394, 396
    prefix length, 84
    private IP addresses, 89, 411, 413, 414
IPv4 Dead Gateway Detection, 127
IPv4 packet fields
    Data, 402
    Destination Address, 7, 29, 71, 402
    Differentiated Services Code Point (DSCP), 27, 29, 399, 419, 420
    Explicit Congestion Notification (ECN), 27, 29, 399, 419
    Flags, 29, 58, 400
        Do not Fragment (DF), 29, 58, 72, 400, 416, 417
        More Fragments (MF), 30, 58, 400, 417, 418
    Fragment Offset, 29, 58, 401, 416–418
    Header Checksum, 3, 7, 29, 30, 71, 73, 401, 417
    Identification, 29, 400, 416, 418
    Internet Header Length (IHL), 27, 29, 398
    IP Precedence field, 419, 420
    Options, 26, 29, 30, 34, 71, 402, 415
    Protocol, 29, 30, 401
    Source Address, 7, 29, 402
    Time-to-Live (TTL), 29, 30, 71, 401
    Total Length, 29, 400, 417
    Type of Service (ToS), 27, 398, 419
    Version, 29, 71, 398
IPv6 address
    anycast address, 87, 115, 120, 141
        Reserved Anycast Address, 118
        Reserved Subnet-Router Anycast addresses, 118, 119, 354
    broadcast address, 4, 7, 77, 87, 89
    colon-hexadecimal representation, 4, 79, 403
    double colon, 80, 83
    hextets, 4, 80
    interface identifier (ID), 90, 109, 112, 217
        64-bit random number generator, 217
        IEEE EUI-64 address, 95, 109–111, 113, 217, 218
        Randomized Interface Identifier, 218, 219
    IPv4/IPv6 Dual-Stack node, 100
    IPv6 prefix, 84, 221
    network scope, 87
        global scope, 88, 90
        link-scope, 87, 89
        unique-local scope, 89
    multicast address, 4, 87, 89, 105, 120
        All-Nodes multicast address (FF02::1), 7
        admin-local Scope, 104
        global scope, 105
        interface-local scope, 104, 120

        IPv6 multicast to Ethernet MAC address mapping, 115
        link-local scope, 104, 120
        node-local, 120
        organization-local scope, 105
        site-local scope, 104
        Solicited-Node multicast address, 105, 120, 127, 128, 137, 161
        Unicast-Prefix-Based multicast address, 107
    off-link address, 125
    on-link address, 87, 125, 223
    prefix length, 84, 85, 221
    stateful address configuration, 4
    stateless address configuration, 4
    temporary IPv6 addresses, 218, 219
    unicast address, 86, 87, 89, 120
        Global Unicast address, 2, 88, 89, 93, 116, 121, 205, 227
        IPv4-Compatible IPv6 address, 99
        IPv4-Mapped IPv6 addresses, 89
        Link-Local address, 4, 87, 89, 94, 96, 120, 121, 200, 227, 232
        Loopback address, 87, 89, 102, 120, 121
        Pseudorandom Global ID Generation, 98
        Subnet-Router Anycast address, 2, 117
        Unicast Address with EUI-64 Interface Identifier, 118–119
        Unicast Address with non-EUI-64 Interface Identifier, 119–120
        Unique-Local Unicast address, 89, 97
    Unspecified address, 87, 89, 102, 162, 203
    Zero Compression rule, 80, 82
IPv6 address states
    Deprecated Address, 194
    Invalid Address, 194
    Preferred Address, 194
    Preferred Lifetime, 194, 223, 263
    Tentative Address, 194
    Valid Address, 194, 263
    Valid Lifetime, 194, 223
IPv6 Dead Gateway Detection, 168
IPv6 extension headers, 7, 26, 34, 36, 37
    Authentication header, 65
    Destination Options header, 40, 47, 360
    Encapsulating Security Payload (ESP) header, 66
    Hop-by-Hop Options header, 37, 40, 46
    Fragment header, 57, 61
    No Next Header, 46
    Routing header, 48, 49, 116, 360
    Segment Routing Header (SRH), 52
IPv6 extension header options, 39
    Home Address Option, 45, 48
    Jumbo Payload Option, 44
    Option Data field, 40, 42
    Option Length field. 40, 42
    Option Type field, 40, 42
    Pad1 Option, 42, 43
    PadN Option, 43
    Router Alert Option, 44
IPv6 host data structures
    Default Gateway, 213
    Default Router List, 131, 153, 154, 168
    Destination Cache, 17, 152, 153, 165, 237
    Neighbor Cache, 117, 152, 153, 168, 170, 174, 199

neighbor discovery reachability states, 168
Prefix List, 152
IPv6 Neighbor Discovery, 4, 5, 106, 127, 339
  Address Autoconfiguration, 127
    Stateful Autoconfiguration, 192, 193
    Stateless Autoconfiguration, 192, 193
  Address Resolution, 5, 126, 127, 135, 154, 155, 168
    Duplicate Address Detection, 5, 94, 126, 127, 136,
      159, 161–163, 191, 198, 206, 209, 214, 217, 300
      binding table, 188
      Duplicate Address Detection Proxy, 188, 189
      local tracking database, 188
  messages
    Neighbor Advertisement message (ICMPv6
      Message Type 136), 6, 7, 117, 118, 137, 138,
      140, 141, 154, 155, 167, 172, 239, 350
    Neighbor Solicitation message (ICMPv6 Message
      Type 135), 6, 7, 107, 117, 118, 135, 154, 166,
      167, 172, 239
    Redirect message (ICMPv6 Message Type 137),
      6, 143
    Router Advertisement message (ICMPv6 Message
      Type 134), 6, 7, 96, 129, 155, 158, 208, 209,
      213, 214
    Router Solicitation message (ICMPv6 Message
      Type 133), 6, 7, 129, 155, 158, 212
  Neighbor Discovery Proxying, 127, 171, 172, 174,
    351, 447
    Proxy Address List, 174
    proxy interfaces, 135
  Neighbor Unreachability Detection, 5, 126, 127, 158,
    166–169, 202
    asymmetric reachability, 167
    symmetric reachability, 167
  Next-hop Determination, 127, 153
  Options, 146
    DNS Search List (DNSSL), 152, 191
    MTU, 148
    Prefix Information, 147, 197
    Recursive DNS Server, 151, 191
    Redirected Header, 147
    Route Information Option, 149
    Source Link-Layer Address, 147
    Target Link-Layer Address, 147
  Parameter Discovery, 126, 127
  Prefix Discovery, 126, 127, 133
  Proxy Neighbor Advertisements, 5, 142
  Router Discovery, 5, 127, 131, 157, 159
  Router Redirect, 5, 127, 163, 164
IPv6 Neighbor Discovery Snooping, 215, 216
  DHCPv6 Snooping table, 215, 216
  IPv6 binding table, 215
IPv6 packet
  IPv6 minimum link MTU, 67
  Jumbograms, 27, 45, 58
  Maximum Transmission Unit (MTU), 34
  packet fragmentation, 57
    fragmentable part, 60
    fragmentation process, 59
    Per-Fragment Headers, 59, 61, 63
    reassembly process, 62
    unfragmentable part, 60
    TCP and UDP "pseudo-header" for IPv6,
      69, 71

IPv6 packet fields
  Destination Address, 7, 28, 32, 74
  Differentiated Services Code Point (DSCP), 1
  Explicit Congestion Notification (ECN), 1
  Hop Limit, 28, 32, 73, 129, 146
  Flow Label, 3, 7, 14, 28, 31
  Next Header, 3, 26, 28, 32, 34, 37, 61, 74
  Payload Length, 28, 32
  Source Address, 7, 28, 32
  Traffic Class, 28, 31, 418
  Version, 28, 73
IPv6 source guard, 215
IPv6 Stateless Address Autoconfiguration (SLAAC), 93,
  95, 192, 209, 299

L

Layer 4+ switches. See Web/content switches
Link-Layer address, 7, 109

M

Mobile IP
  Care-of IP Address, 173, 319, 320, 325
  Correspondent Node, 320, 327, 332, 343, 345
  Dynamic Home Agent Address Resolution, 328, 353
  Foreign Network, 173, 174, 319
  Home Agent, 173, 174, 319, 320, 343
  Home IP Address, 173, 319
  Home IP Subnet Prefix, 320
  Home Link, 173
  Home Network, 319
  Mobile Node, 173, 174, 319
  Mobility Agent, 323
  Mobility Binding, 324, 327, 340
  Mobility Binding Cache, 173, 174, 341, 343
  multicast reverse path forwarding (MRPF), 331
  unicast reverse path forwarding (URPF), 332, 333
Mobile IPv4, 172, 319
  Agent Discovery, 322
    Agent Advertisement message (ICMPv4 Message
      Type 9), 322–324, 326
    Agent Solicitation message (ICMPv4 Message
      Type 10), 323, 324
    Mobility Agent Advertisement Extension
      (Extension Type 16), 324
    One-Byte Padding Extension (Extension
      Type 0), 324
    Prefix-Length Extension (Extension Type 19), 324
  Authenticator value, 334
  Co-located Care-of IP address, 321, 322, 327
  Foreign Agent, 320
  Foreign Agent Care-of IP address, 322
  Mobile IPv4 registration, 323, 326, 327
    Foreign-Home Authentication Extension
      (Extension Type 34), 325
    Mobile-Home Authentication Extension (Extension
      Type 32), 325, 334
    Mobile-Foreign Authentication Extension
      (Extension Type 33), 325
    Registration Reply message (Message Type 3), 323,
      325, 327
    Registration Request message (Message Type 1),
      323–327

Mobile IPv4 (*cont.*)
   Mobility Security Association, 334
   Pending List, 326
   Primary Care-of IP Address, 321
   Security Parameter Index (SPI), 334
   tunnelling, 320
      Bidirectional Tunnel, 329
      Generic Routing Encapsulation (GRE), 329
      IP-in-IP encapsulation, 322, 329, 333
      Minimal Encapsulation, 329
      Reverse Tunnel, 326–328, 332, 333
      Tunnel MTU Discovery, 333
   Visitor List, 327, 328
Mobile IPv6, 172, 319, 338
   Bidirectional Tunneling, 344
   Binding Management Key, 346, 348, 349
   Binding Update List, 343
   Cookie, 347
      Care-of Init Cookie, 347
      Home Init Cookie, 347
   Correspondent Registration, 371
   Home Agents List, 344
   ICMPv6 messages for Mobile IPv6, 342
      Home Agent Address Discovery Reply (ICMPv6 Message Type 145), 342, 363
      Home Agent Address Discovery Request (ICMPv6 Message Type 144), 342, 362
      Mobile Prefix Advertisement (ICMPv6 Message Type 147), 342, 355, 356, 363, 364
      Mobile Prefix Solicitation (ICMPv6 Message Type 146), 342, 363
   IPv6 Neighbor Discovery messages for Mobile IPv6, 342
      IPv6 Home Address Option (Option Type 201), 343, 358, 363, 371, 372
      Modified Router Advertisement message (ICMPv6 Message Type 201), 342
      Modified Prefix Information Option (Option Type 3), 342, 355, 363
      New Advertisement Interval Option (Option Type 7), 342, 365
      New Home Agent Information Option (Option Type 8), 342, 355
   Message Authentication Codes, 347, 349
   Mobile IPv6 Home-Agents Subnet Anycast address, 119, 354, 362
   Mobile Prefix Discovery mechanism, 353
   Mobility Header (MH) messages, 340
      Binding Acknowledgement (MH Message Type 6), 340, 345, 372
      Binding Error (MH Message Type 7), 340
      Binding Refresh Request (MH Message Type 0), 340, 373
      Binding Update (MH Message Type 5), 340, 345
      Care-of Test (MH Message Type 4), 340
      Care-of Test Init (MH Message Type 2), 340
      Home Test (MH Message Type 3), 340
      Home Test Init (MH Message Type 1), 340
   Mobility message options, 341
      Alternate Care-of Address (Option Type 3), 341, 371
      Binding Authorization Data (Option Type 5), 341, 372
      Binding Refresh Advice (Option Type 2), 341, 373
      Nonce Indices (Option Type 4), 341
      Pad1 (Option Type 0), 341
      PadN (Option Type 1), 341
   Node Key, 346, 350
   Nonce, 346, 350
   replay attacks, 350
   Return Routability Procedure, 344, 346–348, 373
   Reverse Tunneling, 360
   Route Optimization, 333, 344, 345, 359
   Tokens
      Care-of Keygen Token, 347
      Home Keygen Token, 347
      Keygen Token, 347
   Triangular Routing, 333
multicast communication
   multicast distribution trees, 103
   multicast group, 103, 391
   multicast group address, 103
   multicast group membership, 103
   multicast routing protocols, 103
Multicast Listener Discovery (MLD), 4, 103
   MLDv1, 5
      Multicast Listener Done (ICMPv6 Message Type 132), 5, 6
      Multicast Listener Query (ICMPv6 Message Type 130), 5, 6
      Multicast Listener Report (ICMPv6 Message Type 131), 5, 6
   MLDv2, 5
      Multicast Listener Report (ICMPv6 Message Type 143), 5, 6
   MLD Snooping, 156, 157
multilayer switch. *See* switch/router

N

Network Address Translation (NAT), 1, 183, 414
network functions virtualization (NFV), 92
Network reference models, 20
   layers, 20
   Open Systems Interconnection (OSI) reference model, 20, 377
   TCP/IP reference model, 20
Network Time Protocol (NTP), 244, 262

P

packet transmission methods. *See* packet communication methods
Path MTU Discovery, 34, 67, 127, 149
   path MTU, 57, 68
proxy server, 414

R

RADIUS, 254
   Delegated-IPv6-Prefix attribute, 260
   Framed-IPv6-Pool attribute, 260
   Framed-IPv6-Prefix attribute, 259, 260
   RADIUS Access-Request packet, 259, 260
   RADIUS IPv6-Delegated-Pool-Name attribute, 260
   RADIUS Delegated-IPv6-Prefix attribute, 259
   RADIUS Client, 254, 259

RADIUS Server, 254, 259–261
Repeaters. *See* hubs
Route Preference. *See* Administrative Distance

S

Segment Routing (SR), 52
    Binding SID, 52
    Network Configuration Protocol (NETCONF), 53
    Path Computation Element Communication Protocol
        (PCEP), 53
    Segments, 52
    Segment Identifier (SID), 52
    SR Controller, 53
    SR domain, 52
    SR Global Block (SRGB), 53
    SR Local Block (SRLB), 53
    SR over IPv6, 52
    SR Policy, 53
Spanning Tree, 384
    blocking, 384
    discarding, 384
    forwarding, 384
    learning, 384
    Multiple Spanning Tree Protocol (MSTP), 384
    Rapid Spanning Tree Protocol (RSTP), 384
    Spanning Tree Algorithm and Protocol, 384
    Spanning Tree Protocol (STP), 384
sub-interfaces, 91
switch/router, 22, 446
switches, 21
    broadcast storm, 383
    Filtering Database, 21
    Layer 2 forwarding table, 21
    MAC address table, 21
    switch ports, 441
        access port, 441, 442
        hybrid port, 443
        Inter-Switch Link (ISL) port, 443
        trunk port, 441–443
        uplink port, 436, 442

V

variable-length subnet mask (VLSM), 1, 18, 392, 407, 409
virtual interfaces, 91
virtual local area network (VLAN), 7, 21, 90, 175, 179,
        215, 383, 436, 446
    broadcast domain, 21, 22, 91, 175, 179, 436, 439, 446
    Host Ports, 441
        Community Ports, 441
        Isolated Ports, 436, 437
    Integrated Routing and Bridging (IRB), 175, 447, 448
    inter-VLAN communication, 91, 175, 383, 446, 447
        external router, 446
        Layer 3 (routed) ports, 446
        one-armed router, 446
        router-on-a-stick, 446
    Layer 2 isolation, 437
    MAC-Forced Forwarding, 438
    Port ACLs, 447
    Private Ports, 436
    Promiscuous Port, 436, 440, 441
    Routed VLAN Interface (RVI), 175, 446–448
    Switch Virtual Interface (SVI), 175, 446, 448
    Port Isolation, 179, 188, 436
    Parent (Primary) VLAN, 437, 439, 440, 446
        Primary VLAN ID, 444, 445
    Private VLANs, 175, 436, 438, 445, 446
    Secondary VLANs, 175, 437, 439, 441, 446
        Community VLAN, 440, 441
        Isolated VLANs, 438, 440, 441
        Secondary VLAN ID, 444
    VLAN ACL, 447
    VLAN Interface, 175
    VLAN pairing, 444
virtual machines (VMs), 92
virtual router (VR), 92
VXLAN (Virtual eXtensible Local Area Network), 215

W

Web/content switches, 23

For Product Safety Concerns and Information please contact our EU
representative GPSR@taylorandfrancis.com
Taylor & Francis Verlag GmbH, Kaufingerstraße 24, 80331 München, Germany

www.ingramcontent.com/pod-product-compliance
Lightning Source LLC
Chambersburg PA
CBHW080130220326
41598CB00032B/5011

* 9 7 8 1 0 4 1 1 9 2 1 3 8 *